D1689842

MOVERS AND SHAKERS

MOVERS AND SHAKERS

THE BRAINS AND
BRAVADO BEHIND BUSINESS

BLOOMSBURY

A BLOOMSBURY REFERENCE BOOK
Created from the Bloomsbury Business Database
www.ultimatebusinessresource.com

© Bloomsbury Publishing Plc 2003
Management Thinkers © Chartered Management Institute 2003

All rights reserved; no part of this publication may be reproduced, stored in a retrieval system, or transmitted by any means, electronic, mechanical, photocopying or otherwise, without the prior written permission of the Publisher.

No responsibility for loss caused to any individual or organisation acting or refraining from action as a result of the material in this publication can be accepted by Bloomsbury Publishing or the authors.

First published in 2003 by
Bloomsbury Publishing Plc
38 Soho Square
London W1D 3HB

British Library Cataloguing in Publication Data
A CIP record for this book is available from the British Library.

ISBN 0-7475-6242-3 (hardback)
ISBN 0-7475-6970-3 (paperback)

Design by Fiona Pike, Pike Design, Winchester
Typeset by RefineCatch Limited, Bungay, Suffolk
Printed in Great Britain by Clays Ltd, St Ives plc

All papers used by Bloomsbury Publishing are natural, recyclable products made from wood grown in sustainable, well-managed forests. The manufacturing processes conform to the environmental regulations of the country of origin.

CONTENTS

A NOTE TO THE USER — vii

FOREWORD BY ROBERT HELLER — viii

Management Thinkers

John Adair	1	Theodore Levitt	105
Igor Ansoff	5	Kurt Lewin	109
Chris Argyris	9	Niccolò Machiavelli	113
R. Meredith Belbin	13	Abraham Maslow	116
Warren Bennis	16	Elton Mayo	119
Kenneth Blanchard	20	Douglas McGregor	123
Dale Carnegie	24	Henry Mintzberg	127
Alfred Chandler	28	Ikujiro Nonaka	131
Stephen Covey	32	Kenichi Ohmae	135
Philip Crosby	37	Taiichi Ohno	139
W. Edwards Deming	41	Robert Owen	143
Peter Drucker	45	Richard Tanner Pascale	147
Henri Fayol	53	Tom Peters	151
Mary Parker Follett	57	Michael Porter	155
Henry Gantt	61	C.K. Prahalad	159
Ghoshal and Bartlett	64	Reg Revans	163
Frank and Lillian Gilbreth	68	Edgar Schein	167
Daniel Goleman	72	Peter Senge	171
Gary Hamel	76	Adam Smith	175
Charles Handy	80	Sun Tzu	179
Frederick Herzberg	84	Genichi Taguchi	183
Geert Hofstede	88	Frederick Winslow Taylor	187
Joseph Juran	92	Alvin Toffler	191
Rosabeth Moss Kanter	96	Victor Vroom	195
Kaplan and Norton	101	Max Weber	199

Business Giants

John Jacob Astor	205	Edwin Land	336
Phileas Taylor Barnum	208	Allen Lane	339
Jeff Bezos	212	Estée Lauder	343
William Boeing	216	Ralph Lauren	346
Warren Buffett	220	William Levitt	349
Leo Burnett	224	Henry Robinson Luce	353
Andrew Carnegie	227	Konosuke Matsushita	357
Willis Haviland Carrier	230	Louis Mayer	360
Steve Case	234	Cyrus Hall McCormick	363
John Chambers	237	Scott McNealy	367
Walter Chrysler	241	Charles Merrill	370
Jim Clark	244	J.P. Morgan	373
Christos Cotsakos	247	Akio Morita	376
Michael Dell	251	Rupert Murdoch	379
Walt Disney	254	David Ogilvy	382
James Buchanan Duke	257	Jorma Jaakko Ollila	386
William Crapo Durant	260	Pierre Omidyar	390
George Eastman	264	David Packard	394
Thomas Edison	267	Arthur Rock	397
Michael Eisner	270	John Rockefeller	401
Larry Ellison	274	Anita Roddick	404
Henry Ford	278	Julius Rosenwald	407
Bill Gates	281	David Sarnoff	410
Harold Geneen	285	Ricardo Semler	413
Lou Gerstner	288	Stan Shih	417
King Camp Gillette	291	Alfred Sloan Jr	421
Roberto Goizueta	294	Masayoshi Son	424
Andy Grove	297	Levi Strauss	428
William Randolph Hearst	300	Eiji Toyoda	431
Hugh Hefner	303	Ted Turner	434
Milton Snavely Hershey	306	Theodore Newton Vail	437
Soichiro Honda	309	Cornelius Vanderbilt	440
Howard Hughes	312	Samuel Walton	443
Lee Iacocca	315	Thomas Watson Sr	446
Steve Jobs	319	Jack Welch	449
Ingvar Kamprad	323	Oprah Winfrey	453
Herb Kelleher	327	Robert Woodruff	456
Phil Knight	330	Frank Woolworth	459
Ray Kroc	333	Index	462

A NOTE TO THE USER

Drawing on the lives and impact of over 100 of the world's leading management thinkers and leaders, **Movers and Shakers** offers concise and colourful overviews of the theories behind, and the practice of, successful international business.

The **management thinkers** section (pp. 1–202) contains over 45 summaries of the lives, careers, and impact of the most world's most influential management gurus and writers, ranging from Peter Drucker to Tom Peters, Sun Tzu to Machiavelli.

The profiles of the **business giants** (pp. 203–461) make up a highly selective gallery of some of the world's most effective leaders and entrepreneurs. As with any list, it is as much distinguished by whom it omits as who is included. Our aim has been to identify the key figures in a range of industries who by their efforts have transformed the way a business is conducted. Being nice is not one of the main criteria; being effective is.

For more information about BUSINESS: The Ultimate Resource™ and other related titles, please visit: **www.ultimatebusinessresource.com**

To register for free electronic monthly upgrades, please go to: **www.ultimatebusinessresource.com/register**, type in your e-mail address, and key in your password: **Roddick**

To develop your leadership skills and gain hands-on management support, visit the Chartered Management Institute's website at www.managers.org.uk.

As the champion of management, the Chartered Management Institute shapes and supports the managers of tomorrow. By sharing the latest insights and setting standards in management development, the Institute helps to deliver results in a dynamic world.

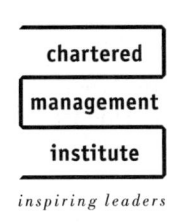

chartered management institute

inspiring leaders

FOREWORD
BY ROBERT HELLER

The rare individuals featured here have changed the world. The prime movers and shakers are the business people who created mighty companies, built great fortunes, innovated with new products, services, methods and markets. Their own philosophies, ideas, and methods have made massive contributions to the theory and practice of business management. But their careers run in parallel with the very important intellectual contribution of thinkers, writers, and teachers; men and women who both describe the evolution of management and prescribe the actions, strategic and tactical, which can achieve success for all managers, not just the heroes.

All managers truly can gain inspiration and guidance from both the business giants and the management thinkers. The giants have rarely added to management literature in person, although some have written business autobiographies, following the lead of Alfred P. Sloan, the creator of General Motors (GM). His account, rich in organisational lore, was a riposte to Peter Drucker's study of GM, *The Concept of the Corporation*, with which Drucker made his first indelible mark on management. Sloan took exception to Drucker's book, a fact which epitomises the uneasy relationship between gurus and champion achievers.

The best-selling management tomes move in their millions mostly to men and women who will never found empires, launch lasting innovations, or make breakthroughs in the arts and science of the manager. They may be highly efficient, and the writers and teachers may well add to their efficiency, but great originals in business are the same breed as supreme masters of science, painting, literature, war, politics, medicine—all human activity. They make their own rules, and seldom obey anybody else's, which is one of their most important qualities. The most successful of retailers, Sam Walton of Wal-Mart, expressed this perfectly in principles distributed to his staff (or 'associates'). The last rule was 'Break All the Rules'. Walton wanted people to act and think more like entrepreneurs than hired hands. The hired-hand executive not only lives in a forest of fixed rules, regulations, and manuals, but adds to the trees. The entrepreneur, though, usually works in a context where nothing is fixed. This is *terra incognita*, unknown land—and pioneering, too, is a dominant characteristic of the master of business.

Foreword

Time and again, the mover and shaker breaks new ground, 'gets in on the ground floor'. Whether it's John D. Rockefeller I exploiting brand new oil finds In Pennsylvania and Ohio, Louis Mayer seizing a 'once-in-a-lifetime' opportunity to break out from cinemas into studio films, or Jeff Bezos abandoning Wall Street to create Amazon.com, the first online sales empire, the pattern is the same. The future tycoon not only sees the opportunity, but seizes it with total disregard for the risks involved in being first. On the contrary, the tycoons see being first as *reducing* risk, because it means that competition either lags behind or doesn't exist at all.

The idea of real risk, like that of a gambler backing a horse, is abhorrent to the great entrepreneurs. They like to bet on what they see as dead certs, sure things. The fact that others fail to see the same certainties in no way bothers the movers and shakers. They *know* that they are right. This self-confidence, rarely found inside corporations, drives them forward with a total absorption that covers every aspect of the venture. Their enterprises, like their personalities, are typically egocentric—and eccentric. Their management innovations (another marked characteristic of the breed) stem not from books or consultants, but rather from personal taste, trial and error, and success.

This is one reason why management authorities tend to dwell, not on the entrepreneurial achievers, but on the big-time corporate managers and their corporations. The latter are also the most fertile ground for theories and systems designed to make management more organised and 'scientific'. Frederick Winslow Taylor, the father of 'scientific management', demonstrated its effectiveness at the Bethlehem Steel Works, a giant of its day, and indeed later days. A true mover and shaker, he changed the world.

Taylor's insistence on measurement and analysis echoes another common characteristic of tycoons; a passionate, driving insistence on improvement. Part of Rockefeller's irresistible advantage over other early oil barons lay in detailed changes and innovations that gave him enormously lower costs. The same passion led him to pursue technological possibilities that others ignored. In modern times, Sam Walton's gigantic expansion at Wal-Mart was accompanied and enabled by investment in the most effective computer systems in retail—and Walton, no whiz-kid, was a man of the pre-computer generation.

A direct line connects Taylor and a host of other efficiency experts to the quality gurus of the later twentieth century, such as like W. Edwards Deming and Joseph Juran from the United States and Genichi Taguchi from Japan. Total Quality Management is more than a productivity tool, though: it is a philosophy of work and its management. While TQM can claim world-changing impact—notably in the phenomenal rise of Japan to industrial leadership—its adoption as a way of corporate life has lagged. This has little to do with any defects or difficulties in TQM: rather, it testifies to the problematic nature of management.

No two companies and no two managers are the same, and, what's more, everything changes over time. Any general theory of management can therefore only be partially true, and its relevance will also be subject to flux. Every one of the students and teachers of management described in this volume has contributed

Foreword

influential insights, often profound, into every aspect of management, from motivation (Frederick Herzberg) to strategy (Michael Porter), from marketing (Theodore Levitt) to futurology (Alvin Toffler). Yet none, not even the far-seeing Peter Drucker, has the definitive, comprehensive answer to all the issues that concern managements. Those issues, as noted, change all the time, and that partly explains the notorious 'fad and fashion' nature of management theorising. Themes like Management by Objectives (of which Drucker is the intellectual father), Business Process Engineering, or TQM (to name but three) arrive, are warmly accepted, and then dwindle away. Yet each had (and has) much to teach practising managers, and each has 'shaken and made' during its peak influence and after.

In contrast, few business builders have influenced management practice outside their own empires and industries—even those who have written books. They include Lee Iaccoca, the ex-Ford saviour of Chrysler; Harold Geneen, onetime boss of the *ur*-conglomerate, ITT; Andy Grove, the driving force behind Intel and the microprocessor revolution; Jack Welch of GE; and Bill Gates of Microsoft. Such books have become more common, thanks to high sales, and the high prices consequently paid by publishers. Many managers, of course, have read these works (often ghost-written), but they are not templates for managerial success. Rather, they are spurs to encourage readers to search with equal alertness and vigour for the ground-floor opportunity into which they can pour their whole being.

That's another great difference between the paid executive and the fortune-building entrepreneurs. The latter don't pause to worry about 'life-work balance'. Their lives *are* their work. This subordination to the prime objective is basic, and the urge to succeed carries genius through all obstacles and setbacks – like the early bankruptcies survived by Henry Ford I. A man of narrow intellect, but broad vision, he was able to embrace new concepts as revolutionary as the assembly line and a highly paid work force, while unable to comprehend the social justice of organised labour.

Like many others—Bill Gates is a modern example—Ford is inseparable from the field in which he operated. It's as difficult to see Ford outside automobiles as to envisage Gates without PCs. Ford's vision of a Model T for every man is akin to Gates's vision of a PC on every desk—using, of course, Microsoft software. The mover and shaker not only sees in the tiny present the mass markets of the future, but instinctively seeks to monopolise them. The effort may fail, as Ford did in face of GM, and the Watson family's IBM did when confronted by the Gates-driven PC. But the urge remains.

The urge is for power rather than money. The power is not political, but economic: control of the market and domination of its sales. Of course, huge money flows from that power. But the heroes are rarely motivated by money alone. Their attitude is ambivalent. They understand instinctively what combination of revenues and costs ('business model', in modern parlance) will yield the greatest and fastest-growing rewards. They exploit that combination with ruthless zeal. But big money is the consequence of implementing the master plan—a strategy for the business, not the bank balance.

Foreword

As it happens, bankers and other financiers are thinly represented here: men like J.P. Morgan, anyway, made their mark more by industrial wheeling and dealing than money-lending. Even the supreme investor Warren Buffett counts as a major industrialist, running a sprawling conglomerate. He is, however, the most thoughtful creator of wealth, one of the few who has reasoned argument for all his actions, and who has given would-be followers clear recipes and prescripts. Yet few have followed in his footsteps, either as investors or as managers. For example, Buffett has consistently opposed high-priced mergers and sky-high pay packets: yet both have grown mountainously during his career. The leaders described here mostly share Buffett's preference for organic growth and for the 'inevitable' wealth (his adjective) created by neo-monopolistic customer franchises, such as those of Coca-Cola and Gillette—or Microsoft and Intel. The inevitability, however, is not what it was. It has to be worked for. Eastman Kodak's hold over photography, like that of Xerox over copiers, has been permanently broken by failure to meet competition from Japan.

The impact of great men like Konosuke Matsushita, Soichiro Honda, and Akio Morita also cracked the superiority complex of Western (mostly US) capitalism. There was, it appeared, a different and in some respects much improved model for management and wealth creation. The dictatorship of Western captains of industry, sometimes amounting to tyranny, was outperformed on everything from productivity to creativity by hero managers who ruled by consensus and collaboration rather than carrot and stick. The consequent shock waves from Japan have been felt by managers and gurus alike.

Ricardo Semler fits both definitions. His engineering company, Semco, is tiny in comparison to others featured here, but his ideas on empowering the entire workforce by combining democracy with effectiveness have been widely disseminated. They strike the same new chord as Tom Peters's call for managing with 'Wow!'. Gary Hamel's crusade for dynamic strategy is in the same vein, expressed by Rosabeth Moss Kanter as 'getting elephants to dance'.

The profound changes in capitalism over the past century, in other words, have led to real changes in business needs—and in the movers and shakers. Their new businesses are notably less stable, especially those dealing in the hardware and software of the IT revolution (another key force for change). IT giants dominate the late century tycoon list, along with another up-and-coming class, that of the hero CEO. These people have not created a business, but taken over historic assets (like Coca-Cola or General Electric) and transformed their profitability. The new leaders may still have vision, but tend not to deploy the imaginative capture of a latent future that makes their founder-predecessors such exciting subjects.

Would-be imitators need an early start (meaning their 30s, not necessarily the 20s of Michael Dell or IKEA's Ingvar Kamprad). They also require a Big Idea, not only in its ability to change the world, but in the potential size of its commercial impact. They seldom operate in partnership, as Bill Hewlett did so sensationally with Dave Packard, but they must surround themselves with excellence. Here trust is doubly important: Rockefeller attributed his triumphs to trusting men whom he had given

Foreword

reason to trust him. Tenacity, too, matters: big corporations often give up too early, while the great entrepreneur typically never gives up at all.

Genius, true, is helpful—and unbiddable. You don't, however, need genius to see and emulate the wisdom deployed by the first-named business pioneer in this book, John Jacob Astor. He provided excellent customer service, stayed close to markets, bought cheaply, and sold where the price was best. This type of simplicity is generally the hallmark of the supreme mover and shaker, and of the greatest teachers. It makes it easier for readers to learn their lessons and to apply the management wisdom of a world-changing mind. What if, at first, you don't succeed? Like the giants, try, try again. And when you do succeed, still imitate them—try even harder.

MANAGEMENT THINKERS

JOHN ADAIR

1934	Born.
1963–1969	Senior lecturer in military history and leadership training adviser, Royal Military Academy, Sandhurst.
1969–1973	Assistant director at Industrial Society; pioneered 'action-centred leadership'.
1979	Becomes the world's first professor in leadership studies, at the University of Surrey.

> **SUMMARY**
>
> John Adair, best known for his three-circle model of 'action-centred leadership', is widely regarded as Britain's foremost authority on leadership in organisations.
>
> Adair believes that leadership can be taught, and his works have been instrumental in overturning the 'great man' theories of leadership. He draws a distinction between leadership and management.
>
> Adair's ideas are practical and relevant to all managers. Many of his other ideas on the practical aspects of leadership were ahead of their time.

LIFE AND CAREER

John Adair's early career was varied and colourful, and undoubtedly formed the basis for his views on leadership. After joining the Scots Guards he became the only national serviceman to serve in the Arab Legion, where he was adjutant in a Bedouin regiment. Before going to university he qualified as a deckhand and worked on an Icelandic trawler. He also worked as an orderly in a hospital operating theatre. After studying at Cambridge University, he became a senior lecturer in military history and leadership training adviser at the Royal Military Academy, Sandhurst. He went on to become the director of studies at St George's House in Windsor Castle, and two years later was appointed assistant director of the Industrial Society, where he pioneered action-centred leadership.

In 1979, Adair became the world's first professor in leadership studies at the University of Surrey. He has been visiting professor in leadership studies at the University of Exeter, and acts as a consultant to many organisations around the world in business, government, education, health, and the voluntary sector.

For over three decades his overlapping, three-circle model of action-centred leadership has been integrated into company cultures and individual leadership styles, and is an established hallmark of management training for many organisations.

CONTRIBUTION
Action-centred leadership
This simple and practical model is based on three overlapping circles, representing the task, the team, and the individual. The model has endured well, probably because it is a fundamental description of the actions leaders must take in order to be effective:

- achieve the task
- build and maintain the team
- develop the individual

John Adair

Adair's concept asserts that the three needs of task, team, and individual are the building blocks of leadership, as people expect their leaders to help them achieve the common task, build the synergy of teamwork, and respond to individuals' needs.

- The task needs work groups or organisations to come into being because one person alone cannot accomplish it.
- The team needs constant promotion and retention of group cohesiveness to ensure that it succeeds. The team functions on the 'united we stand, divided we fall' principle.
- The individual's needs are the physical ones (such as salary) and the psychological ones of recognition, sense of purpose and achievement, status, and the need to give and receive from others in a work environment.

For Adair, the needs of the task, team, and individual overlap.

- Achieving the task builds the team, and satisfies the individuals.
- If the team needs are not met (if the team lacks cohesiveness), performance of the task is impaired and individual satisfaction is reduced.
- If individual needs are not met, the team will lack cohesiveness and performance of the task will be impaired.

He holds that leadership exists at three different levels:

- team leadership, of teams of between 5 and 20 people
- operational leadership, where a number of team leaders report to one main leader
- strategic leadership, of a whole business or organisation, with overall accountability for all levels of leadership

Regardless of the level at which leadership is being exercised, Adair's model remains the same: task, team, and individual needs must constantly be considered.

The strengths of the concept are that it is both timeless and independent of situation or organisational culture. It can also help a leader to identify where he or she may be losing touch with the real needs of the group or situation.

The functions of leadership

In order to fulfil the three aspects of leadership and achieve success, Adair believes that there are eight functions that must be performed by the leader.

- Defining the task: individuals and teams need to have the task distilled into a clear objective that is SMART (Specific, Measurable, Achievable, Realistic, and Time Constrained).
- Planning: planning requires a search for alternatives, best done with others in an open-minded, positive, and creative way. Contingencies should be planned for and plans should be tested.
- Briefing: team briefing is viewed as essential for creating the right atmosphere, promoting teamwork, and motivating each individual.
- Controlling: excellent leaders get maximum results with the minimum of resources. To achieve this, they need self-control, good control systems in place, and effective delegation and monitoring skills.
- Evaluating: leaders need to be good at assessing consequences, evaluating team performance, appraising and training individuals, and judging people.
- Motivating: Adair distinguishes eight principles for motivating others: be motivated yourself; select people who are highly motivated; treat each person as an individual; set

realistic and challenging targets; remember that progress motivates; create a motivating environment; provide fair rewards; and give recognition.
- Organising: good leaders have to be able to organise themselves, their team, and the organisation (including structures and processes). Leading change requires a clear purpose and effective order to achieve results.
- Setting an example: leaders need to set an example both to individuals and to the team as a whole. Since a bad example is noticed more than a good one, providing a positive pattern to follow must be worked at constantly.

These leadership functions need to be developed and honed constantly to improve the leader's ability.

Motivating people
In many ways, Adair's ideas in the area of motivating people are in line with those of the classic motivational theorists, such as Maslow, McGregor, and Herzberg.

The 50:50 rule
Just as the Pareto principle (or 80:20 rule) is the ratio of the vital few and the trivial many, the Adair 50:50 rule (from *Effective Motivation*) states that '50% of motivation comes from within a person and 50% from his or her environment, especially from the leadership encountered therein'.

Adair's view is that people are motivated by a number of complex factors. So, for example, he does not dismiss the 'carrot and stick' approach, but sees it rather as one stimulus-response factor among many that might influence a person's actions.

The strength of an individual's motivation is affected by what outcome the person expects from certain actions—and also what he or she would prefer that outcome to be (as demonstrated by Victor Vroom in the 1960s). Conditions in the working environment and the individual's own perceptions and fears are also factors that have an impact on strength of motivation.

Adair's eight rules for motivating people
Adair proposes that understanding what motivates individuals is fundamental to engaging their interest and focusing their efforts. The will that leads to action is governed by motives, and motives are inner needs or desires that can be conscious, semiconscious, or unconscious. In *The John Adair Handbook of Management and Leadership*, the point is made that 'motives can also be mixed, with several clustered around a primary motive'.

Adair emphasises the importance of a motivating environment and a motivated individual. Another crucial factor is the role of the leader, who must, he believes, be completely self-motivated. In *Effective Motivation*, eight basic rules are outlined to guide leaders in motivating people to act:

- be motivated yourself
- select people who are highly motivated
- treat each person as an individual
- set realistic and challenging targets
- remember that progress motivates
- create a motivating environment
- provide fair rewards
- give recognition

Developing a personal sense of time
Adair's view of time management accords closely with Peter Drucker's, in that he argues that it is essential to manage time in order to manage anything else. He was

one of the first management thinkers to emphasise the critical importance of time management and its central role in focusing action and helping leaders to achieve goals. Time management is not simply about being organised or efficient, or completing certain tasks, Adair states. It is about focusing on achievement: time management should be goal-driven and results-oriented.

Success in time management should be measured by the quantity of productive work achieved, and the quality of both the work and the person's private life. Ten principles of time management given in *How to Manage Your Time* are:

- develop a personal sense of time
- identify long-term goals
- make medium-term plans
- plan the day
- make the best use of your best time
- organise office work
- manage meetings
- delegate effectively
- make use of committed time
- manage your health

Of these 10 principles, developing a personal sense of time and increasing personal effectiveness are central to Adair, again highlighting his emphasis on individual characteristics.

CONTEXT AND CONCLUSIONS

Adair's ideas were very 'different' when they first appeared, and for many people their main value lay in the successful challenge they offered to the 'great man' theories that dominated then. These theories, because they insisted that leaders were born and not made, eliminated the possibility of training or developing people in leadership skills. So Adair's new ideas were welcomed and quickly became established.

Given the pace and scale of changes in the work environment during the last 20 years, however, it is perhaps not surprising that there has been something of a backlash against Adair, with critics claiming that his approach (developed in the 1960s) has itself now become outdated.

One criticism of action-centred leadership is that it takes little account of the flat structures that are advocated as the best organisational form. It is also judged to be too 'authoritarian'—applicable in a formal, military-type environment but less relevant to the modern workplace, where the leadership emphasis is on leading change, empowering, enabling, managing knowledge, and fostering innovation.

Another criticism levelled at Adair's approach in recent years is that his ideas are too simplistic, merely stating the obvious, common-sense view. For many people, however, it is exactly this simplicity and clarity about what a leader should do that is so valuable.

THE BEST SOURCES OF HELP
Books:
Adair, John. *Action-Centred Leadership*. London: McGraw-Hill, 1984.
Adair, John. *The Skills of Leadership*. Aldershot: Gower, 1984.
Adair, John. *Effective Motivation*. Guildford: Talbot Adair Press, 1987.
Adair, John. *The Action-Centred Leader*. London: Industrial Society, 1988.
Adair, John. *Effective Leadership*. London: Pan, 1988.
Adair, John. *Great Leaders*. Guildford: Talbot Adair Press, 1989.
Adair, John. *Understanding Motivation*. Guildford: Talbot Adair Press, 1990.
Adair, John. *How to Manage Your Time*. Guildford: Talbot Adair Press, 1990.

IGOR ANSOFF

1918	Born.
1936	Family emigrates to the United States.
1950	Joins the Rand Corporation.
1957	Publishes article 'Strategies for diversification' that presents the Ansoff Matrix.
1963	Appointed professor of industrial administration at the Carnegie Institute of Technology, Pittsburgh.
1965	*Corporate Strategy* published.
1983	Joins US International University as professor of strategic management.
2000	Retires from academic life.
2002	Dies.

SUMMARY

Igor Ansoff was the originator of the strategic management concept, and was responsible for establishing strategic planning as a management activity in its own right. His landmark book, *Corporate Strategy* (1965), was the first text to concentrate entirely on strategy and, although the ideas outlined are complex, it remains one of the classics of management literature.

LIFE AND CAREER

Igor Ansoff was born in Russia in 1918 and his family emigrated to the United States in 1936. His early academic focus was on mathematics, and he obtained a PhD in applied maths from Brown University, in Rhode Island. He joined the Rand Corporation in 1950, and moved on to the Lockheed Aircraft Corporation, where he eventually became vice-president, plans and programmes, and then vice-president and general manager of the industrial technology division.

In 1963 Ansoff was appointed professor of industrial administration at the Carnegie Institute of Technology in Pittsburgh. He went on to hold a number of positions in universities in both the United States and Europe. He retired from academia in 2000 and was named Distinguished Professor Emeritus at the United States International University.

CONTRIBUTION

Until the publication of *Corporate Strategy*, companies had little guidance on how to plan for, or make decisions about, the future. Traditional methods of planning were based on an extended budgeting system that used the annual budget, projecting it a few years into the future. By its very nature this system paid little or no attention to strategic issues. With the advent of greater competition, higher interest in acquisitions, mergers, and diversification, and greater turbulence in the business environment, however, strategic issues could no longer be ignored. Ansoff felt that, in developing strategy, it was essential to anticipate future environmental challenges to an organisation systematically and draw up appropriate strategic plans for responding to these challenges.

He explored these issues in *Corporate Strategy* and built up a systematic approach to strategy formulation and strategic decision-making through a framework of theories, techniques, and models.

Igor Ansoff

Strategy decisions

Ansoff identified four standard types of organisational decisions as related to strategy, policy, programmes, and standard operating procedures. The last three of these, he argued, are designed to resolve recurring problems or issues and, once formulated, do not require an original decision each time. This means that the decision process can easily be delegated. Strategy decisions are different, however, because they always apply to new situations and so need to be made anew every time.

Ansoff developed a new classification of decision-making, partly based on Alfred Chandler's work *Strategy and Structure* (Cambridge, Massachusetts: MIT Press, 1962). This distinguished decisions as: *strategic* (focused on the areas of products and markets); *administrative* (organisational and resource allocating), or *operating* (budgeting and directly managing). Ansoff's decision classification became known as Strategy-Structure-Systems, or the 3S model. (Sumantra Ghoshal has since proposed a 3Ps model—purpose, process, and people—to replace it.)

Components of strategy

Ansoff argued that within a company's activities there should be an element of core capability, an idea later adopted and expanded by Hamel and Prahalad. To establish a link between past and future corporate activities (the first time such an approach was undertaken), Ansoff identified four key strategy components:

- product-market scope—a clear idea of what business or products a company was responsible for (predating the exhortations of Peters and Waterman to 'stick to the knitting');
- growth vector—as explained in the section below on the Ansoff matrix, this offers a way of exploring how growth may be attempted;
- competitive advantage—those advantages an organisation possesses that will enable it to compete effectively—a concept later championed by Michael Porter;
- synergy—Ansoff explained synergy as '2+2=5', or how the whole is greater than the mere sum of the parts; it requires an examination of how opportunities fit the core capabilities of the organisation.

Ansoff Matrix

Variously known as the 'product-mission matrix' or the '2 x 2 growth vector component matrix', the Ansoff Matrix remains a popular tool for organisations that wish to understand the risk component of various growth strategies, including product versus market development, and diversification. The matrix was first published in a 1957 article called 'Strategies for diversification' and the example below illustrates what such a matrix may look like:

	Present	New
Present	1. Market penetration	2. Market expansion
New	3. Product expansion	4. Diversification

Of the four strategies given in the matrix, *market penetration* requires increasing existing product market share in existing markets; *market expansion* requires the identification of new customers for existing products; *product expansion* requires developing new products for existing customers; and *diversification* requires new products to be produced for new markets.

Ansoff's article focused particularly on diversification as a potentially high-growth but also high-risk strategy that necessitates careful prior planning and analysis before any decision is taken. In Ansoff's view it requires organisations to 'break with past patterns and traditions' as they enter on 'uncharted paths' where, generally, new skills, techniques, and resources will be required. His matrix offered a method of carefully analysing and evaluating the profit potential of diversification strategies.

Paralysis by analysis
It has sometimes been suggested that the application of the ideas in *Corporate Strategy* can lead to an over-emphasis on analysis. Ansoff himself recognised this possibility, however, and coined the now famous phrase 'paralysis by analysis' to describe the type of procrastination caused by excessive planning.

Turbulence
The issue of turbulence underlies all of Ansoff's work on strategy. One of his key aims in establishing a better framework for strategy formulation was to improve the existing planning processes of the stable, post-war economy of the United States, since he realised these would not be sufficient to cope with the pressures that rapid and discontinuous change would place on them.

By the 1980s change, and the pace of change, had become a key issue for management in most organisations. Ansoff recognised, however, that, if some organisations were faced with conditions of great turbulence, others still operated in relatively stable conditions. Consequently, although strategy formulation had to take environmental turbulence into account, one strategy could certainly not be made to fit every industry. These ideas are discussed in *Implanting Strategic Management*, where five levels of environmental turbulence are outlined as:

- repetitive—change is at a slow pace, and is predictable
- expanding—a stable marketplace, growing gradually
- changing—incremental growth, with customer requirements altering fairly quickly
- discontinuous—characterised by some predictable change and some more complex change
- surprising—change that cannot be predicted and that both develops, and develops from, new products or services

CONTEXT AND CONCLUSIONS
Although Ansoff's work is frequently referred to by strategists, it has not become as generally recognised as that of other theorists. The complexity of his work and its reliance on the disciplines of analysis and planning are perhaps among the reasons why Ansoff is not popularly viewed as belonging to the top echelons of management thinkers.

Other theorists were working on similar themes to Ansoff at similar times. In the 1960s Ansoff's notion of competence (which was later developed by Hamel and Prahalad) was not unique and, although Ansoff seems to have been the originator of his 2 x 2 growth vector component matrix, a similar matrix had been published earlier. It is likely that much work done during the 1980s and 1990s by other theorists on strategy formation under conditions of uncertainty or chaos owed something to Ansoff's theory of turbulence, though it is difficult to evaluate the extent of the debt.

A debate between Ansoff and Henry Mintzberg over their differing views of strategy has been reflected in print over many years, particularly in the *Harvard Business Review*. Ansoff has often been criticised by Mintzberg, who dislikes the idea of strategy being built from planning that is supported by analytical techniques. This criticism is based on the belief that Ansoff's reliance on planning suffers from three fallacies: that events can be predicted, that strategic thinking can be separated from operational management, and that hard data, analysis, and techniques can produce novel strategies.

Ansoff was one of the earliest writers on strategy as a management discipline, and laid strong foundations for several later writers to build upon, including Michael Porter, Gary Hamel, and C.K. Prahalad. He invented the modern approach to strategy, and his work pulled together various ideas and disparate strands of thought, giving a new coherence and discipline to the concept he described as strategic planning. During the 1970s and 1980s, this concept shaped more ideas about management as other writers took up ideas of Ansoff's such as core competence or 'sticking to the knitting'.

THE BEST SOURCES OF HELP
Books:
Ansoff, Igor. *Corporate Strategy*. New York: McGraw-Hill, 1965.
Ansoff, Igor, Roger P. DeClerck, and Robert L. Hayes. *From Strategic Planning to Strategic Management*. New York: John Wiley/Interscience, 1975.
Ansoff, Igor. *Strategic Management*. London: MacMillan, 1979.
Ansoff, Igor. *Implanting Strategic Management*. Englewood Cliffs, New Jersey: Prentice Hall, 1984.
Ansoff, Igor. *The New Corporate Strategy*. New York: Wiley, 1988. (Revised edition of *Corporate Strategy*)
Journal Articles:
Ansoff, Igor. 'Strategies for diversification.' *Harvard Business Review*, Sept./Oct., vol. 35 no. 5, 1957, pp. 113–124.
Ansoff, Igor. 'The firm of the future.' *Harvard Business Review*, Sept./Oct., vol. 43 no. 5, 1965, pp. 162–174.
Hussey, David. 'Igor Ansoff's continuing contribution to strategic management.' *Strategic Change*, vol. 8, no. 7, 1999, pp. 375–392.

CHRIS ARGYRIS

1923	Born.
1960	Publication of *Understanding Organizational Behavior.*
1968	Moves from Yale to Harvard Business School.
1971	Appointed James Bryant Conant Professor of Education and Organization Behavior, Harvard Business School.
1978	Publication of *Organizational Learning.*

> **SUMMARY**
> Chris Argyris's career may look more like that of a classical academic than that of a management guru, but a stuffy academic he is not. His passionate interest in management and organisational problems makes him one of the most respected management thinkers of our time. He is also as much at home in the factory and boardroom as in the lecture theatre.
> Argyris is first and foremost a behavioural scientist, and his career has been devoted to understanding how organisations behave and how managers learn.

LIFE AND CAREER

Chris Argyris was born in 1923 and at an early age developed an interest in how people learn. 'It sounds corny, but I love learning for its own sake,' is how he explains it. After service in the Second World War he returned home and, like so many young men at that time, felt a strong determination to help create a better world. He chose to direct his interest in education towards the needs of organisations and the individuals working in them. His great energy and formidable academic qualifications—a Baccalaureate in psychology, a Masters in economics, and a Doctorate in organisation behaviour—equipped him perfectly for the task, and by the early 1950s he was teaching and carrying out research at Yale University.

By the mid-1960s he was professor of industrial administration at Yale and in 1968 he moved to the Harvard Business School, where, in 1971, he became the James Bryant Conant Professor of Education and Organization Behavior.

His consulting work has been wide-ranging and highly influential. Clients have included IBM, DuPont and Shell, along with the US State Department, other US government bodies and several overseas governments.

CONTRIBUTION

A staunch supporter of job enrichment, Argyris has always challenged the extremes of Taylorism, especially the suggestion that one 'hires a hand', rather than a whole person. Underlying virtually all his thinking is a fundamental belief in people, and he tirelessly reminds us of the mutual benefit that comes when organisations assist and encourage individuals to develop their full potential. He believes that each person already has the 'psychological energy' that provides motivation. The challenge, he suggests, is not to find ways of artificially motivating people; it is to recognise and channel this innate energy.

T-groups

Chris Argyris was the main force behind the ground-breaking T-group experiments in the 1960s. 'T-group training' is a phrase used to describe a number of similar training methods, the purpose of which is to increase the trainee's skills in working with other people—and a considerable proportion of time on such a training course is spent in discussing the trainees' relationships with one another. Argyris was not alone in being elated by the success of T-groups, by their power to unfreeze the rigid, authoritarian behaviour of so many managers and to generate a feeling of liberation and excitement. However, as we now know, for most people these positive effects are short-lived. Once back in the turmoil of life in their organisation, mixing again with those who have not been trained, the resolution and ideas are quickly forgotten, and people revert to their old ways of doing things.

This rapid return to their original behaviour patterns by people who had been extremely enthusiastic about the 'new approach' generated by T-group training led Argyris to formulate an idea that has affected people's views about organisational behaviour for many years. The way people behave in organisations, he suggests, shows that there is a sharp difference between the beliefs they profess and the beliefs on which they appear to act.

'Espoused Theories' and 'Theories-in-use'

Argyris coined the term 'Espoused Theories' for things that people profess to believe, and the term 'Theories-in-use' for those that they appear to believe when faced with problems in the real world, concluding, after much research, that, no matter how genuinely we believe in some approach to a situation, at the first sign of threat, embarrassment, or loss of face, most of us fall back on a deep-rooted 'master programme' of behaviour. This behaviour, which is characterised by a powerful defensive attitude and a tendency to blame others while struggling to maintain control and save face, is surprisingly consistent across different cultures and classes.

Not only do people slip easily into defensive routines, but they also remain totally unaware that they are doing so. It is a reflex action, an automatic response to any threat or challenge. Argyris argues that the organisation can inhibit learning because it imposes—perhaps unconsciously—rules over the ways in which people relate to one another. He maintains that problem-solving and decision-making can be dominated by an almost unconscious drive to 'save face', 'protect others', or maintain the status quo. What concerns him most about this behaviour is that it blocks any opportunity people have to learn from experience and provides an all too effective strategy for avoiding change.

Single-loop and double-loop learning

Concern at people's failure to learn from experience has led Argyris to the theory for which he is best known: the concept of single- and double-loop learning. Developed in collaboration with Donald Schön and described in their book *Organizational Learning* published in 1978, the theory stresses the importance of human reasoning as a basis for decisions and action.

Their work also produced the idea of a 'learning organisation'. An organisation, Argyris and Schön suggest, differs from a mob by having procedures for making collective decisions, by delegating authority to individuals to act for the 'collectivity', and by setting out boundaries and rules. Norms and strategies are developed for all this activity, but in a healthy organisation these are constantly being tested and challenged as people interact and learn new ideas. When the constant learning of people within an organisation is reflected in the way the organisation itself changes and develops, then the organisation itself can reasonably be described as learning—hence the term 'learning organisation'.

The two types of learning—single-loop and double-loop—refer to the way people respond to changes in their environment. Single-loop learning occurs when a manager responds to a problem with a simple 'application of the rules'. For example, problem: budgets are being exceeded; solution: cut costs. Argyris uses a thermostat as an analogy for single-loop learning; the thermostat switches the heating on and off in response to temperature changes.

Double-loop learning goes beyond this simple feedback response and questions the assumptions on which the response is based. In the thermostat model, the double-loop approach would be to question the validity of the selected temperature. In the example involving exceeded budgets, the double-loop approach would be to check the appropriateness of the budget figure and the basis on which it was calculated. Speaking to a conference in 1982, Argyris described the theory thus:

'Learning can be defined as occurring under two conditions. First, learning occurs when an organisation achieves what it intended; that is, there is a match between its design for action and the actual outcome. Second, learning occurs when a mismatch between intention and outcome is identified and corrected; that is, a mismatch is turned into a match...Single-loop learning occurs when matches are created, or when mismatches are corrected by changing actions. Double-loop learning occurs when mismatches are corrected by examining and altering first the governing variables and then the actions.'

CONTEXT AND CONCLUSIONS

Argyris's work is rarely a comfort to managers. He raises profound questions about how we run organisations and frequently throws into doubt much of what is widely accepted to be 'good practice'. And when he does outline solutions they are never simple or easy. What he offers, and what makes his contribution to management thinking so important, is a profound and detailed exploration of the fundamental principles of organisation behaviour and human interaction in the workplace. He pulls no punches when showing us how hard we will have to work, and how much we will have to change if we are to achieve our full potential; but he is equally convincing when describing the rewards we will receive for our efforts.

Future

In recent years Argyris has been looking at leadership and, after considerable research, he claims the massive literature on this overworked subject has failed to produce anything practical. Such strong views have made his recent book on leadership, *Flawed Advice and the Management Trap*, compelling reading.

He is also taking a lively interest in IT, something he feels will play a key role in learning within organisations. He says, 'In the past the one-way, top-down approach gained strength from the fact that a lot of behaviour is not transparent. IT makes transactions transparent so that behaviour is no longer hidden. It creates fundamental truths where none previously existed.'

THE BEST SOURCES OF HELP
Books:
Argyris, Chris. *Personality and Organization: The Conflict between the System and the Individual.* New York: Harper & Row, 1957.
Argyris, Chris. *Understanding Organizational Behavior.* London: Tavistock, 1960.
Argyris, Chris. *Reasoning, Learning, and Action: Individual and Organization.* London: Jossey-Bass, 1982.
Argyris, Chris. *Overcoming Organizational Defenses: Facilitating Organizational Learning.* Boston: Allyn and Bacon, 1990
Argyris, Chris. *Knowledge for Action.* San Francisco: Jossey-Bass, 1993.
Argyris, Chris. *On Organizational Learning.* Cambridge, Massachusetts: Blackwell Business, 1994.
Argyris, Chris, and Donald Schön. *Organizational Learning II: Theory, Method, and Practice* (2nd edition). Reading, Massachusetts: Addison-Wesley, 1996.
Argyris, Chris. *Flawed Advice and the Management Trap.* New York: Oxford University Press USA, 1999.

Journal Articles:
Argyris, Chris. 'Teaching smart people how to learn.' *Harvard Business Review*, May/Jun. 1991, pp. 99–109.
Argyris, Chris. 'Education for leading learning.' *Organizational Dynamics*, Winter 1993, pp. 5–17.
Argyris, Chris. 'Good communication that blocks learning.' *Harvard Business Review*, Jul./Aug. 1994, pp. 77–85.

R. MEREDITH BELBIN

1926	Born.
1981	Publication of *Management Teams: Why They Succeed or Fail*.
1993	Publication of *The Coming Shape of Organization*.
1997	Publication of *Changing the Way We Work*.
2000	Publication of *Beyond the Team*.
2001	Publication of *Managing without Power*.
	Visiting professor of leadership at the University of Exeter.

> **SUMMARY**
>
> R. Meredith Belbin is acknowledged as the father of team-role theory. As a result of research carried out in the 1970s, he identified eight (later extended to nine) useful roles that are necessary for a successful team. His contribution has gained in significance because of the widespread adoption of teamworking in the late 1980s and 1990s.

LIFE AND CAREER

Belbin, who was born in 1926, is an academic who has also spent periods working in industry and who now has his own consultancy company. It was while working at the Industrial Training Research Unit in Cambridge that he was asked by Henley Management College to conduct some research into the operation of management teams. The college's approach to management education was based on group work, and it had been noticed that some teams of individually able executives performed poorly and others well. This impression was reinforced when a business game was introduced to one of the courses. Belbin discovered that it was the contribution of particular personality types, rather than the merits of the individuals themselves, that was important to the success and failure of such teams.

CONTRIBUTION

There has been a continuing interest in Belbin's work because teamworking is an increasingly important strategy for organisations. There are many reasons for this. Teamworking is variously seen as a means of:

- providing greater worker flexibility and co-operation
- helping to achieve cultural shifts within an organisation
- improving problem-solving and project management
- tapping the talents of everyone in the organisation

There are also different types of team involved in working together: for example, temporary teams, cross-functional teams, top management teams, and self-directed teams. Because of this interest in teams, the issue of team building, including team selection, group dynamics, and team performance, has become particularly vital. Although there are many models of team relationships, such as the Team Management Systems (TMS) developed by Margerison and McCann, Belbin's model is probably the best known.

Team role theory

It is important to remember that Belbin's findings relate to teams of managers rather than other types of team. They were first published in *Management Teams:*

Why They Succeed or Fail and later refined in *Team Roles at Work*. In Belbin's own words, a team role 'describes a pattern of behaviour characteristic of the way in which one team member interacts with another where his performance serves to facilitate the progress of the team as a whole'.

The essence of his theory is that, given knowledge of the abilities and characteristics of individual team members, success or failure can be predicted within certain limits. As a result, unsuccessful teams can be improved by analysing their shortcomings and making changes. But it is also important for individuals within the team to understand the roles that others play, when and how to let another team member take over, and how to compensate for shortcomings. Although each of the eight roles has to be filled for a team to work effectively, the eight roles are not needed in equal measure, nor are they needed at the same time. There can be fewer than eight people in a team, since people are capable of taking on back-up roles where there is less need for them to fulfil a primary team role.

The roles themselves are determined largely by the psychological make-up of the individuals who instinctively adopt them. Four principal factors are involved: intelligence; dominance; extroversion/introversion; and stability/anxiety. Each role demands a particular combination of the four. Any individual can be rated in terms of them. In the list of team role contributions, the ratings for each particular trait are shown.

The self-perception inventory and the *Interplace* system

Belbin devised a self-perception inventory, which has been through several revisions, as a quick and easy way for individual managers to work out what their own team roles should be. It was taken up by organisations and used to determine employees' team types, and it has been questioned whether it is psychometrically acceptable for this purpose. Academics were concerned that it was too subjective and recommended that feedback should come instead from a range of sources. Belbin answered this criticism by reiterating that the inventory was never designed for this purpose and by developing a computerised system called *Interplace* to cater for the wider needs of organisations.

Interplace is a more sophisticated approach to role analysis than the self-perception inventory because it incorporates feedback from other people, not just the individual concerned. The main inputs to the *Interplace* system use data from self-perception exercises, observer assignments, and job requirement evaluations. *Interplace* filters, scores, stores, converts, and interprets the data gathered. It offers advice based on the three inputs with respect to counselling, team role chemistry, career development, and the behaviours needed in certain jobs and team positions. The system works as a diagnostic and development tool for organisations.

Later theories

In the 1990s Belbin extended his work on teams to explore the link between teams and the organisational environment in which they operate. He suggested that an effective model for the new flatter organisation might be a spiral or helix in which individuals and teams move forward on the basis of excellence rather than of function.

He has also very recently devised a system for defining jobs which he calls

'Workset'. The aim of the concept is to define the boundaries and content of a job through an interactive communication process between the manager and the job holder. The system uses colour to denote different aspects of the job. There should be five key outcomes:

- the facilitation of empowerment
- the encouragement of greater job flexibility
- the promotion of teamworking
- the support of cultural change
- a continuous improvement process for jobs and job holders

It is too early to say what impact the Progression Helix theory or Workset system will have. They are undoubtedly a contribution, however, to management in today's delayered organisations and flexible working environments, with their associated need to involve and communicate with staff.

CONTEXT AND CONCLUSIONS

Although independent recent research has thrown doubt on the existence of eight separate team roles, Belbin's broad findings have not been questioned, nor has the popularity of his theories been disputed. There has been an enduring interest in team role categories on the part of practising managers in a wide variety of organisations. This is because:

- there is an increasing interest in teamworking
- Belbin made his ideas accessible to the lay person
- Belbin is recognised as the first to develop our understanding of the dynamics of teams

THE BEST SOURCES OF HELP
Books:
Key works by Belbin
Belbin, R. Meredith. *Management Teams: Why They Succeed or Fail*. London: Heinemann, 1981.
Belbin, R. Meredith. *Team Roles at Work*. Oxford: Butterworth-Heinemann, 1993.
Belbin, R. Meredith. *The Coming Shape of Organization*. Oxford: Butterworth-Heinemann, 1996.
Belbin, R. Meredith. *Changing the Way We Work*. Oxford: Heinemann, 1997.
Journal Articles:
Belbin, R. Meredith, Barrie Watson, and Cindy West. 'True colours.' *People Management*, 6 March 1997, pp. 36–38, 41.
Furnham, Adrian, Howard Steele, and David Pendleton. 'A psychometric assessment of the Belbin team role self-perception inventory.' *Journal of Occupational and Organizational Psychology*, vol. 66 no. 3, 1993, pp. 245–261. (This article includes Belbin's criticism of the research and the response of the authors.)
Senior, Barbara. 'An empirically-based assessment of Belbin's team roles.' *Human Resource Management Journal*, vol. 8 no. 3, 1998, pp. 54–60.
Website:
www.belbin.com contains a useful list of answers to frequently asked questions about team role theory, as well as an online team analysis and reports service. It also contains helpful information on Belbin's latest work on work roles.

WARREN BENNIS

1925	Born.
1959	Sets up department for organisational studies at MIT.
1967	Appointed Provost of State University of New York (SUNY).
1971	President of the University of Cincinnati.
1979	Professor of Management at the University of Southern California.
1985	Publication of *Leaders: The Strategies for Taking Charge*.
1989	Publication of *On Becoming a Leader*.
1997	Publication of *Organizing Genius*.

> **SUMMARY**
>
> Warren Bennis's career has been extremely wide-ranging. He has worked as an educator, writer, administrator, and consultant, besides authoring or co-authoring many books on different topics. He has carried out highly respected work in the areas of small group dynamics, change in social systems, T-groups, and sensitivity training, and during the 1960s became a recognised futurologist. Bennis wrote his first article on leadership in 1959, and he has become a widely accepted authority on the subject since 1985, when *Leaders* was published.

LIFE AND CAREER

Bennis was born in New York in 1925 and educated at Antioch College, Ohio, and the Massachusetts Institute of Technology (MIT). Later, he studied group dynamics, and during the 1950s was involved in the US National Training Laboratories teamworking experiments. His early field of work was organisational development. Bennis was a great admirer of Douglas McGregor and his 'Theory Y' approach to motivation. In fact, Bennis became very close to McGregor and was strongly influenced by him. His career path even followed McGregor's to some extent. First, he was an undergraduate student at Antioch College while McGregor was President there, and later, in 1959, he was recruited by McGregor to set up a new department for organisation studies at MIT. From the late 1960s, Bennis's career moved for a time from academic research and teaching to administration. He became Provost at the State University of New York (SUNY), Buffalo, in 1967, staying there until 1971, when he moved to take on the post of President of the University of Cincinnati.

As an administrative leader from 1967 to 1978, Bennis attempted to put McGregor's motivation theories into practice, and found them unworkable without some adaptation in the form of strengthened structure and direction.

During the 1960s, Bennis became known as a student of the future, and predicted (with co-author Philip Slater in a March 1964 article for the *Harvard Business Review* called 'Democracy is inevitable') the downfall of communism in the face of inevitable democracy. By the mid-1960s, he was predicting the demise of bureaucratic organisation. His 1968 book, *The Temporary Society*, explored new forms of organisation, advocating an 'adhocracy' of free-moving project teams as a necessity for the future, an idea taken up by Alvin Toffler and Henry Mintzberg.

In an adhocracy, responsibility and leadership are distributed to groups or task forces on the basis of the relevance of members' qualifications or abilities for the specific task or purpose of the group. For Bennis, adhocracy was an important concept as a counter to hierarchy, centralised control, and bureaucratic organisation.

CONTRIBUTION
In his early book on leadership, *The Unconscious Conspiracy* (1976), Bennis highlights how leaders can positively influence others to bring about change. His most distinctive ideas on the subject, however, partly grew out of the broad, general response to a landmark *Harvard Business Review* article of 1977 by Abraham Zaleznik (then Professor of Social Psychology of Management at Harvard).

The Zaleznik article was entitled 'Managers and leaders—are they different?' Bennis's research and writing were extreme in emphasising a complete, qualitative difference between management and leadership, and he drew up a list of sharp distinctions that ended with the now familiar aphorism: 'Managers do things right, leaders do the right thing.' While Bennis considers that managers can become leaders through learning and development, he is firm about the functional differences between the roles and the approaches involved, and the distinctions he draws echo throughout most of his writings on leadership.

The Leaders study
In 1979, on his return to research and teaching as Professor of Management at the University of Southern California, Bennis sought to unravel the lessons of his practical experience of leadership. He explored the subject through a 1985 serial study that was published as a book coauthored with Burt Nanus, called *Leaders: The Strategies for Taking Charge* (1985). While Bennis has written or co-written many other books relating to leadership, these largely expand on the ideas developed in *Leaders*.

Leaders aimed to identify common characteristics among 90 successful American leaders who had all, the authors considered, demonstrated 'mastery over present confusion' in their careers. The leaders ranged from an orchestra conductor to Ray Kroc, the founder of McDonalds, and included a baseball player and a tightrope walker, as well as the astronaut Neil Armstrong. It was Bennis's second book on leadership, selling over 300,000 copies, and is still considered an important text on the subject.

In *Leaders*, Bennis and Nanus identify four common factors amongst the subjects, and these form the core of their ideas about leadership.

- Attention through vision—all had an agenda, an intense vision and commitment that drew others in. The leaders also gave much attention to other people.
- Meaning through communication—all had an ability to communicate their vision and bring it to life for others, sometimes using drawings or models as well as metaphor and analogy.
- Trust through positioning—through establishing a position with a set of actions to implement their vision, and staying the course, the leaders established trust.
- The deployment of self through positive self-regard—the creative deployment of self is essential to leadership, involving an honest appreciation of oneself and one's own worth, and instilling confidence in others.

Positive self-regard is related to 'emotional wisdom', and five key skills in emotional wisdom are given as the abilities to:

- accept others as they are
- approach things in terms of only the present

- treat others, even familiar contacts, with courteous attention
- trust others, even where the risk seems high
- do without constant approval and recognition.

One quality common to these leaders that Bennis and Nanus particularly distinguished was their way of responding to failure as a learning experience. Karl Wallenda, the great tightrope aerialist, was taken as a main example. The authors illustrate his manner of putting his energies completely into his task, thinking of failure as a mistake from which he could learn, and viewing this experience (of learning based on failure) as a new beginning, rather than the end, for a project or idea.

'Transformative' leadership

The style of leadership discussed by Bennis and Nanus is termed 'transformative', in that it is said to have an empowering effect on others, enabling them to translate intentions into reality. A transformative leadership style is described as one that motivates through identification with the leader's vision, pulling rather than pushing others on.

Four elements of empowerment are distinguished as:

- significance—a feeling of making a difference
- competence—development and learning 'on the job'
- community—a sense of inter-reliance and involvement in a common cause
- enjoyment—capacity to have fun at work because it is enjoyable and involving

The four major characteristics of transformative leaders identified earlier are linked to strategic approaches through which a leader leads.

- The creation of a compelling vision: a leader must develop and communicate an image, or vision, of a credible and attractive future for the organisation.
- The translation of meaning into social architecture: social architecture is the intangible variable that translates the buzz and confusion of organisational life into meaning. While similar to culture, social architecture is more precise in meaning, in that it can be defined, assessed, and, to some extent, managed. Three styles of social architecture are distinguished as formalistic, collegial, and personalistic.
- The position of the organisation in the outside world: positioning of an organisation is described as the process by which it establishes a viable niche in its environment. It encompasses all that must be done to align the internal and external environments of the organisation.
- The development of organisational learning: good leaders are experts at learning within an organisational context, and their behaviour can help to direct and energise innovative learning within the organisation as a whole.

The end result of transformative leadership is, Bennis and Nanus consider, an empowering environment and accompanying culture, enabling employees to generate a sense of meaning in their work. Higher profits and wages, the authors suggest, inevitably accompany this sort of culture, if it is genuinely established.

At the end of the book, five myths about leadership are identified and contradicted.

- That leadership is a rare skill—it is not.
- That leaders are born—they are not.
- That leaders are charismatic—most are ordinary.

- That leadership can exist only at the 'top'—it is relevant at all levels.
- That leaders control, direct, and manipulate—they do not. Transformative leaders align the energies of others behind an attractive goal.

Later work

A later, prominent book by Bennis, *On Becoming a Leader* (1989), looks at learning to lead, developing leadership qualities, and how leadership can be taught. It uses 29 well-known Americans as case studies to illustrate leadership qualities. Its main message suggests that becoming a leader involves continual learning, development, and the reinvention of the self.

Bennis has since written or co-written many books and articles that expand on and develop his ideas on leadership. His more recent works focus on the important roles of followers and groups, as well as on leadership. In *Organizing Genius* (1997), a collaborative work with Patricia Ward Biederman, Bennis almost returns to his roots in group work. The book looks at the history of seven well-known groups in action, including Walt Disney's animation studios, President Clinton's 1992 election campaign, and Lockheed's 'skunk works'. Common features of these successful groups are highlighted, and the mutually interdependent relationship between great leaders and great groups is stressed.

CONTEXT AND CONCLUSIONS

The importance of Bennis's work in the field of leadership is indisputable, and his informal and easy-mannered style of writing and use of practical illustrations have made his books very approachable. The management writer Stuart Crainer emphasises Bennis's humane approach to leadership. Bennis views leadership as a skill that can be developed by ordinary people and that centres on enabling and empowering others rather than on control and direction. He is sometimes criticised as a romantic in his approach and has himself affirmed (in *The Director* of October 1988) that he is indeed a romantic, if that term accurately describes someone who believes in possibilities, and is optimistic.

THE BEST SOURCES OF HELP

Books:

Bennis, Warren. *The Unconscious Conspiracy: Why Leaders Can't Lead*. New York: AMACOM Press, 1976.

Bennis, Warren, and Burt Nanus. *Leaders: The Strategies for Taking Charge*. New York: Harper & Row, 1985.

Bennis, Warren. *On Becoming a Leader*. Reading, Massachusetts: Addison-Wesley, 1989.

Bennis, Warren. *Why Leaders Can't Lead: The Unconscious Conspiracy Continues*. San Francisco: Jossey-Bass, 1989.

Bennis, Warren. *An Invented Life: Reflections on Leadership and Change*. Reading, Massachusetts: Addison-Wesley, 1993.

Bennis, Warren, and Patricia Ward Biederman. *Organizing Genius: The Secrets of Creative Collaboration*. Reading, Massachusetts: Addison-Wesley, 1997.

Bennis, Warren. *Managing People Is Like Herding Cats*. London: Kogan Page, 1998.

Bennis, Warren, and Robert Thomas. *Geeks and Geezers*. Boston, Massachusetts: Harvard Business School Press, 2002.

KENNETH BLANCHARD

1939	Born.
1982	Publication of *The One Minute Manager*.
1984	Publication of *Putting the One Minute Manager to Work*.

> **SUMMARY**
>
> *The One Minute Manager* was first published in the United States in 1982. Lambasted as trite and shallow by academics, it has since sold over 7 million copies, been translated into over 25 languages, and is frequently found on managers' bookshelves. It launched a new genre of management publishing, providing the model for a host of imitations.

LIFE AND CAREER

Kenneth Blanchard graduated from Cornell University in Government and Philosophy and went on to complete his PhD in Administration and Management. In the early 1980s he was Professor of Leadership and Organizational Behavior at the University of Massachusetts, Amherst. He wrote and researched extensively in the fields of leadership, motivation, and the management of change, and his *Management of Organizational Behaviour: Utilizing Human Resources* (co-authored with Paul Hersey) is now in its 8th edition and has become a classic text. In the Introduction to *The One Minute Manager* (OMM), Blanchard and his co-author Spencer Johnson describe the book as an allegory, a simple compilation of what 'many wise people have taught us and what we have learned ourselves'.

CONTRIBUTION
One-minute management

The framework story of *The One Minute Manager* imagines a young manager going off in search of that holy grail of the aspiring newcomer—an effective manager on whom to model his own thinking and actions. The novice—a cross between *Le Petit Prince* and *Candide*—is caught between the two extremes of the scientific and human relations schools: some managers get good results (but at a price that few colleagues and subordinates seem willing to support), whilst others (whose people really like them) have results which leave much to be desired. Our hero, however, soon comes across a manager who gets excellent results as a result of—apparently—very little effort on his part—the One Minute Manager. The OMM has three simple secrets that bring about increases in productivity, profits, and satisfaction—one-minute goal-setting, one-minute praising, and one-minute reprimanding.

One-minute goal-setting

Although staff cannot know how well they are doing without clear goals, claims the OMM, many are not clear on priorities, and many are spoken to only when they make a mistake. The OMM requires managers to make it clear what tasks people are to do and what sort of behaviour or performance is expected of them, and to get staff to write down their most important goals on a single sheet of paper for continued clarification.

One-minute praising

The second secret—one-minute praising—is the key to improved performance and increased productivity. Instead of catching people out for doing something wrong, the opposite is recommended: 'the key to developing people is to catch them doing something right'. There are three steps in one-minute praising.

- Praise someone as close in time to the good behaviour as possible. If you can't find someone to praise every day, then you should wonder why.
- Be specific. Make it clear what it was that was performed well.
- Share feelings—tell them how you feel about what they did, not what you think about what they did.

One-minute reprimanding

The third secret of the One Minute Manager is the key to changing the attitude of the poor performer, and there are four aspects to it.

- Immediacy—when a reprimand is necessary, it is best to deliver it as soon as possible after the instance of poor performance that led to it.
- Be specific—don't tell people about your reactions or give vent to your feelings, tell them what they did wrong; admonish the action, not the person.
- Share feelings—once you have established what was wrong, share your feelings.
- Tell them how good they are—the last step in the reprimand. If you finish on negative feedback, they will reflect on your style of behaviour, not on their own performance.

The development of one-minute management

Putting the One Minute Manager to Work was a follow-up in 1984 by Blanchard and co-author Richard Lorber (an expert in performance improvement) to flesh out some of the basic ideas which had met initial success in *The One Minute Manager*. Subtitled *How to Turn the Three Secrets Into Skills*, the 1984 follow-up focuses on the 'ABCs' of management, 'effective reprimanding', and the 'PRICE' system.

The ABCs

- Activators—those things that a manager has to do before anyone else can be expected to achieve anything, such as goal-setting, laying down areas of accountability, issuing instructions, and setting performance standards.
- Behaviour—or performance—what a person says or does, such as filing, writing, selling, ordering, buying etc.
- Consequence—what a manager does after performance, such as sharing feelings, praising, reprimanding, supporting etc.

Effective reprimanding

A manager has to distinguish between a situation where an employee can't do something—which implies a need for training and signals a return to the activator of goal-setting—and one where an employee won't do something—which implies an attitude problem and a case for a reprimand. Reprimands do not teach skills, they can only change attitudes. Positive consequences on the other hand can influence future performance to the good, so it is important, as *The One Minute Manager* had already suggested, to end a reprimand with praise, making the employee think about his or her own behaviour, not that of the reprimander.

Kenneth Blanchard

The PRICE system
PRICE takes the three basic secrets of one-minute management and turns them into five distinct steps.

- **Pinpointing**—defining key performance areas in measurable terms – part of one-minute goal-setting.
- **Recording**—gathering data to measure actual performance and keep track of progress.
- **Involving**—sharing the information recorded with whomsoever is responsible.
- **Coaching**—providing constructive feedback on improving performance.
- **Evaluating**—part of coaching, also part of reprimanding or praising.

Later works
Leadership and the One Minute Manager stresses that there is no single, best method of leadership, but that there are in fact four styles: directing, delegating, coaching, and support. Whichever style is employed depends on the situation to be managed. 'Situational leadership is not something you do to people, but something you do with people.' Blanchard turns conventional leadership thinking on its head, using the analogy of turning the organisational pyramid upside down; instead of staff working for their boss, the boss should work for the staff.

The One Minute Manager Builds High-Performing Teams can be seen as a companion to *Leadership* and concentrates on integrating the simplicity of the one-minute techniques into understanding group dynamics and adjusting leadership style to meet developing circumstances.

The One Minute Manager Meets the Monkey deals with the problems of time management and overload. Paying tribute to Bill Oncken, Blanchard's coauthor who created the monkey analogy, Blanchard points the finger at the concept of the manager as the 'hero with all the answers', stressing that bosses are not there to try and tackle every problem themselves, rather to get others to come up with solutions. The monkey is the problem being passed from subordinate to superior, making the superior rapidly ineffective; the one-minute manager is not a collector of monkeys, rather a facilitator and coach helping others to solve their own problems.

CONTEXT AND CONCLUSIONS
So where does Blanchard sit in the Hall of Fame of management thinkers?

In the early years of the 21st century, much of what Blanchard et al. have to say in the One Minute Manager series no longer seems earth-shattering. Countless publications and endless seminars on leadership, change, delegation, and time management have, unsurprisingly, rendered a glance back to Blanchard an entertaining experience, yes, and a comforting one in its confirmation of what one has learned elsewhere, but—like the key message of a contemporaneous publication *In Search of Excellence* (Peters and Waterman, 1982)—one-minute management is no longer the inspiration it was.

When asked why *In Search of Excellence* did so well, critics and commentators argued that its timing was impeccable: it was published at a time when Western business concepts were being rubbished in favour of analyses of the Japanese business boom. If Peters and Waterman were largely about re-invigorating pride in successful American organisations, Blanchard's book was excellently timed for its impact on individual skills and techniques.

It is important to remember that before Blanchard, Peters, and the host of others following in their wake, management—as far as the hard-nosed manager was concerned—was a stuffy, dry subject reserved for lengthy academic treatises and exposés. Most books—not that there were many of them—focused on building the arguments of the human relations school and tackling the monstrous scientific/bureaucratic establishment so convincingly constructed by Taylor, Ford, and Weber. Books on management were not popular, not widely read, and certainly not best-sellers. It is often claimed that Peters and Waterman changed all that. But Ken Blanchard's contribution was also hugely influential. *The One Minute Manager* may have been panned by the academics, but it did more to make management digestible, readable, and accessible to a wide audience than any of its predecessors. By means of allegory, anecdotes, and allusions, it brought management to a level where many believed they could do it and do it well. Others have followed the story-telling format of OMM, *One Page Management* (Khadem) and *Zapp! The Lightning of Empowerment* (Byham) to name but two.

So what is the appeal of *The One Minute Manager*, rejected (like Maslow) by academia, but wholeheartedly adopted (as was Maslow) by practising managers around the world? Blanchard's book was, first and foremost, short and to the point. Moreover, it was written in readable, everyday language, offering practical, everyday solutions to practical, everyday problems. This was no dry, stuffy theory, but a collection of honest sensible techniques to try out straight away. This is where Blanchard scored a first.

Any author who sells over 7 million copies deserves a place in the Management Hall of Fame. For Blanchard, that place has to be broadly in the human relations school alongside the great popularisers of empowerment on the one hand and the self-help school, stretching from Samuel Smiles and Dale Carnegie to present-day figures like Stephen Covey and, latterly, with Tom Peters, on the other. Blanchard's message may not be original but few have spread the simple messages more effectively, or to such a wide audience.

THE BEST SOURCES OF HELP
Books:
Blanchard, Kenneth, and Spencer Johnson. *The One Minute Manager*. London: Willow Books, 1983.
Blanchard, Kenneth, and Robert Lorber. *Putting the One Minute Manager to Work*. London: Fontana, 1985.
Blanchard, Kenneth, Patricia Zigarmi, and Drea Zigarmi. *Leadership and the One Minute Manager*. London: Collins, 1986.
Blanchard, Kenneth, William Oncken, and Hal Burrows. *The One Minute Manager Meets the Monkey*. London: Collins, 1990.
Blanchard, Kenneth, Donald Carew, and Eunice Parisi-Carew. *The One Minute Manager Builds High-Performing Teams*. London: Fontana, 1993.
Blanchard, Kenneth, and Margret McBride. *The One Minute Apology*. London: HarperCollins, 2003.

DALE CARNEGIE

1888	Born.
1908	Graduates from State Teachers College, Warrensburg, Missouri.
1912	Teaches first public speaking class at YMCA in upper Manhattan.
1912–1920	Formalises course in public speaking.
1926	Publication of textbook *Public Speaking: A Practical Course for Businessmen*.
1936	Publication of *How to Win Friends and Influence People*.
1939	Introduces sales course.
1955	Dies.

> **SUMMARY**
>
> Dale Carnegie's main focus is on dealing with people successfully—making them like you, and making them do what you want without making them dislike you. His best-known work, *How to Win Friends and Influence People* (1936), puts forward the essential principles for doing this in the form of commonsense advice, such as that you should never criticise, complain about, or condemn another person, that you should give sincere appreciation to others, and that, in order to motivate people, you need to stimulate a specific desire in them.

LIFE AND CAREER

Dale Carnegie (1888–1955) came from a poor, farming background and had to struggle through college. Looking for a way to distinguish himself, he began to enter speaking contests and, despite a shaky start, was soon winning every contest he entered. On leaving college he worked for some time as a salesman, making his territory the most successful one in the company, before deciding to train and work as an actor. This was another false start, however. He gave up the stage to run his own business, and then eventually decided to write novels and support himself by teaching at night.

Carnegie's first courses on public speaking for businessmen at the YMCA schools in New York were run purely on a commission basis, as he was initially refused any pay. The courses did well, however, and their popularity made him a great success. They were so successful, in fact, that he was able to turn them into a series of popular books that extended beyond his initial sphere of public speaking into the realm of human relations in general. Providing simple rules on how to achieve success with people, illustrated from his own and others' experiences, and stories about historical figures such as Roosevelt and Lincoln, the books became runaway successes in their turn. Carnegie went on to found the Dale Carnegie Institute of Effective Speaking and Human Relations to spread his ideas yet further. In 1997, over 40 years after his death, *How to Win Friends and Influence People*, the book that made him internationally famous, was still on the bestseller list in Germany.

CONTRIBUTION

Carnegie believed that criticism was counterproductive and should never be used to try to change or motivate people. In his view, people who are criticised tend to respond by justifying themselves and condemning the critical person in return.

Great leaders such as Abraham Lincoln achieved their success partly because they never criticised others. Carnegie recommended instead the practice of self-control, understanding, and forgiveness. Most importantly, he advised that you should always try to see the other person's point of view.

In order to influence people and achieve your aims, Carnegie suggests, it is necessary to understand individual motivation. You need to ask yourself what will motivate a person to want to do a task for you, before you attempt to persuade them to do it. He considers most people to be interested only in their own desires, but suggests that, if they are given what they want, they can help the giver to achieve great success in business.

People may simply want to drive a better car or buy a bigger house. For most people, however, the desire to be important is a main, if not the main motivator. It can inspire them to do great things, such as become important leaders or make their fortune in business. It can also take morbid forms. Sometimes individuals become invalids to gain attention or become insane so that they can live in a dream world where their importance is exaggerated by imagination. In any event the urge to be important should not be ignored. Using very human, anecdotal evidence, Carnegie illustrates how nourishing a person's self-esteem can achieve far better results than criticism.

The rules

How to Win Friends and Influence People has 'in a nutshell' conclusions at the end of each section. In them Carnegie summarises the main messages each section offers in terms of behaviour. Some of these are paraphrased below.

Six ways to make people like you:
1. Show a genuine interest in other people.
2. Be happy and positive.
3. Remember that people love hearing the sound of their own name.
4. Listen to other people and develop good listening skills.
5. Talk about others' interests rather than your own.
6. Give others a sincere sense of their importance.

Twelve ways to win people to your way of thinking:
1. To get the best of a situation, avoid arguments.
2. Always listen to others' opinions and never tell anyone they are wrong.
3. Admit it if you are wrong.
4. Show friendliness.
5. Make statements that the other person can agree with.
6. Let the other person talk more than you.
7. Make the other person feel that an idea is their own.
8. See the other person's point of view.
9. Show empathy with others' ideas and desires.
10. Infuse some drama into your ideas.
11. Appeal to the better nature of others.
12. Finish with a challenge.

Nine ways to change people without arousing resentment:
1. Start with genuine praise and appreciation.
2. Draw attention to people's mistakes gradually.
3. Admit that you have made mistakes and then talk to other people about theirs.

4. Don't give direct orders but ask questions.
5. Never humiliate anyone, and let people keep their pride intact.
6. Use plenty of genuine praise and encouragement when there is the slightest improvement.
7. Give people a reputation to maintain.
8. Encourage people. Show them that their task is easy to accomplish.
9. Suggest what you want them to do and make them happy about it.

Becoming a good public speaker

Some of the advice given by Dale Carnegie at the start of his career, when he trained and wrote to help people to make speeches in public, is summarised below.

Preparation

From the beginning, Carnegie suggested, you should generate an enthusiasm within yourself for public speaking, whether you have a financial or a social goal in view. Prepare as much as possible for the speech and have it ready well in advance. Begin planning as soon as you can and look for a topic that you know a lot about. Always try to use your own ideas, but bring the topic of your talk into conversation, so that you can explore any interesting stories on the subject that others may be able to tell you. Think about your talk at every possible opportunity and research it thoroughly, using libraries and other sources and collecting more material than you will need.

Do not memorise the talk word for word, as you will then be more likely to forget it. It may also lose much of its effectiveness if it seems too studied. While having plenty of material prepared, you should not try to say too much in the talk itself. Your material needs to be structured simply, so that you can talk as if you were in ordinary conversation.

Most people are nervous about talking in public. If you try to act bravely and pretend that you feel more confident than you really do, you will often actually gain in confidence. Practice will help you to feel more certain of yourself, and it is a good idea to rehearse your speech as much as possible, maybe in front of the mirror, or with family and friends as an audience.

Delivery

Dress the part for your speech. Smile, and make sure you are clearly visible to your audience. Show respect and affection for the audience, and let the first sentence capture their attention. Examples of techniques to help you to achieve this are:

- start with a striking incident or example
- state an arresting fact
- ask for a show of hands
- use an exhibit
- do or say something to arouse suspense
- promise to tell the audience how they can get something they want

You should not, however, open a talk with either an apology or a funny story. Humorous stories often fail to work, and this is particularly likely to be the case when you are nervous.

Use statistics or the testimony of experts to support your main ideas, but know your audience and do not use technical terms if you are addressing a lay audience. Be eager to share your talk with your listeners, putting passion into your way of speaking and using your emotions without fear. Represent things visually when possible, turning a fact into a picture to help your audience to understand what you are talking about and using specific instances and concrete cases.

Stress important words and avoid any hackneyed expressions or clichés. Once your talk is launched, you may feel freer to be humorous when appropriate, but take care to target any fun at yourself rather than others.

Your talk should have some marked form of closure. Summarise what you have said, then use a finalising climax or close of some sort that is appropriate within the context, for example:

- make an appeal for action
- pay the audience a sincere compliment
- raise a final laugh
- use a fitting verse of poetry or a quotation

Carnegie's concluding advice
- Remember that many famous speakers were originally terrified of speaking in public and that a certain amount of stage fright is useful.
- Predetermine your mind to success and seize every opportunity to practise.
- Remember that as you increase your experience your fear will lessen, so seek opportunities to speak in public, and believe in yourself.

CONTEXT AND CONCLUSIONS
Carnegie claimed that his theories do really work and that he had seen them transform the lives of many people. Some management writers have, however, dismissed Carnegie's ideas as being simple wisdom dressed up in a commercial coating.

Certainly, Carnegie's ideas are based on common sense and are hardly revolutionary. All his self-help books are based on down-to-earth and simply illustrated basic principles. Despite this simplicity, Carnegie has expressed many general truths which people acknowledge and, whatever his critics may say, the books he wrote are still popular.

In fact, Carnegie created a highly successful business out of his ideas, and his books have sold millions. Even today, much money is still being made from his work, which suggests that people still find him very relevant. Certainly, it is possible to see Carnegie's influence in some of today's ideas about management, particularly in discussions on the treatment of customers, and in approaches to interpersonal skills development.

THE BEST SOURCES OF HELP
Books:
Carnegie, Dale. *How to Win Friends and Influence People*. London: Hutchinson Books, 1994.
Carnegie, Dale. *How to Enjoy Your Life and Your Job*. London: Vermilion, 1990.
Carnegie, Dale. *How to Stop Worrying and Start Living*. London: Vermilion, 1990.

ALFRED CHANDLER

1918	Born.
1952	Completes PhD at Harvard.
1962	Publication of *Strategy and Structure*.
1970	Appointed Isidor Strauss Professor of Business History, Harvard Business School.
1977	Publication of *The Visible Hand: The Managerial Revolution in American Business*

> **SUMMARY**
> The US academic Alfred Chandler Jr is the first historian in the modern era to both forge his own subject area and dominate it for almost half a century. When he stumbled on the genre after the Second World War, business history was just a virgin cousin of the emerging and wider-based topic called economic history, a largely theoretical discipline that deals with macrofiscal issues as they affect national and international economies.

LIFE AND CAREER

Chandler was born in 1918 and acquired his first interest in history from Wilbur Fiske Gordy's *Elementary History of the United States*, which his father gave him at the age of seven. He was educated at Phillips Exeter Academy, Harvard College, the University of North Carolina, where he received his MA, and Harvard University, where he completed his PhD in history in 1952. His wartime experience was with a unit responsible for analysing photographs of gunnery exercises by the Atlantic Fleet and bombing raids in the Pacific.

He acquired an interest in sociology and saw the value of explicit concepts, generalisations, and theories in analysing human behaviour, but it was when he came to choose his dissertation topic that his interest in business history was initially sparked. His great-aunt died suddenly, and Chandler and his family moved into her house, in which were stored the personal papers of his grandfather, Henry Varnum Poor. Poor, whose name survives as one half of the business information company Standard and Poor's Corporation, had been one of the people most knowledgeable about American railways, having edited the *American Railway Journal* for nearly 20 years. Using Poor's personal papers, together with the extensive backfiles of his newspapers and related publications in the Baker Library at Harvard, he produced a classic series of articles, his dissertation, and a book entitled *Henry Varnum Poor: Business Editor, Analyst, and Reformer*. This treatise, a seminal work on American railway companies during their formative years, enabled him to develop—through his genius at widespread comparative analysis—what became his characteristic way of extracting clear historical patterns that tended towards inductively derived theory.

Chandler's career as a working business historian was spent at the Massachusetts Institute of Technology, where he had the opportunity of working on the individual histories of Du Pont, General Motors, Standard Oil (now Exxon), and Sears, Roebuck & Co, a course of study that culminated in *Strategy and Structure*; at the Johns Hopkins University, where he wrote the biography of Pierre du Pont; and later at the Harvard Business School, where in 1970 he was appointed the Isidor Strauss Professor of Business History, the world's only endowed chair in the field at the time. Since then he has led a growing field of teachers and studies; about 200 American academics now work on the subject.

CONTRIBUTION

Until Chandler turned to business history as his principal interest, mainstream economic history predominated as the subject matter of business education. There was, admittedly, a detour, the result of imported Western European attitudes, when both popular journalism and academia started to take an interest in the corrupt practices of businessmen. The perception emerged that they were 'robber barons', a viewpoint that only started to change when Joseph Schumpeter's *The Theory of Economic Development*, which depicted the businessman as a force for positive advancement, was translated from German into English in 1934. Several notable academics started to re-evaluate the same robber barons as constructive, daring, and far-seeing 'industrial statesmen', who deserved credit for making the United States a predominant economic power, able to defend itself and its allies from the totalitarian assaults on freedom of the 20th century. Nevertheless, it was Chandler who made business history a linchpin of the curriculum.

His work has been pioneering in several other respects. It has been conducted in front of a largely unreceptive audience: the majority of management educators long resisted the concept of using the real example of corporate and business history as a teaching tool. With an attachment to the more empirical methodologies dominated by macroeconomics and quantitative analysis, they believed that business historians painted with too broad a brush on too wide a canvas and lacked a solid or explicitly stated methodology. They also accused the genre of being largely irrelevant given the perceived pace of change. Chandler's work has done much to change these attitudes, although it is instructive to note that business and management teachers—unlike educators in disciplines such as the military, politics, music, architecture, sociology, and so on—still widely resist both the concept and the development of history-based experiential learning in their own discipline. Chandler has also spent his life challenging economic thinking, in particular the static equilibrium theory. Although he used the results of quantitative research, he did not employ mathematical notation, remaining sceptical of highly theorised arithmetical manipulations that, he says, while elegantly logical, distort intelligible generalisations about the past.

In shifting the focus of business history, Chandler's work, which in fact specifically addresses the process of evolution and change, uses a systematic and analytical approach that has evolved from an intellectual outlook, which he labelled 'managerial enterprise'. As he explains it, this concept moves in two directions—forward from the past to the present and backward from the present to the past. Using the former perspective, for example, he examined why early 19th-century industry did not employ any managers, a phenomenon which changed decisively and for ever in the second half of the 19th century. Using the latter perspective, he questioned the 1950s moves by industry towards decentralisation of their functionally specialised and multi-departmentalised organisations. His answers—in a landmark book entitled *Strategy and Structure*, published in 1962—took business history into a new dimension by establishing a fresh framework and rationale for the subject. He introduced the feature of making comparisons within and between industries and over time, and enabled business history to acquire relevance in a wide range of related fields.

In *The Visible Hand*, another milestone book, Chandler used the concept of managerial enterprise to illustrate how Germany became the most powerful industrial nation in Europe before the Second World War, the United States became the most productive country in the world for 40 years until the 1960s, and Japan became its most successful competitor thereafter. For this book he won the Pulitzer Prize. These and other works—including, with Richard Tedlow, *The Coming of Managerial Capitalism*—are routinely used in at least 30 higher educational establishments in the United States and many more abroad.

Business history's role at the operational level, Chandler explains, is not about teaching specific management techniques. It has a more strategic function. Any meaningful analysis of an organisation today, he says, must be based on an accurate understanding of its past. 'Such data has to come from business history based on company records or from historically based case studies. Certainly a restructuring of enterprises to meet changing conditions requires an understanding of both why and how the existing organisation evolved and how and why competitive conditions changed. Managers facing such problems can get insights by observing the working out of such processes in other enterprises.' Companies such as McKinsey & Co and AT & T have applied *Strategy and Structure* to this end. The former, for example, has used it to teach its clients about the timing of strategic change and how to adjust their organisational structures, while the latter put it to use in one of its reorganisations.

At the wider education level, Chandler believes that business history can provide insights into the processes of businesses such as the development of competitive strategy, the restructuring of organisational forms, and the effectiveness of investment and monitoring techniques. His view is that the value of teaching business histories in universities is to make MBA students and those in more advanced management courses aware of recent as well as long-term changes in functional activities such as production, marketing, research and development, finance, labour relations, and the like; also in monitoring and coordinating the activities of the current operations of an enterprise as well as in locating resources for future production and distribution. 'Not only can the students learn something about the nature of the functions, but also the complexities of carrying out change,' he says.

CONTEXT AND CONCLUSIONS

For students and practitioners alike, Chandler's name may be remembered principally as the pioneer who placed strategy before structure in his seminal work published in 1962. Not only has he championed the systematic study of modern bureaucratic administration in an original way, he has also turned what is often dismissed as an artless medium into a valid and powerful educational tool. Using the conglomerate history of individual companies to arrive at a historical theory of big business instead of the mainstream—economic—discipline of the day, he revolutionised the fledgling discipline by refocusing attention away from individual entrepreneurs and seeking patterns in the rise of large-scale modern business. Almost uniquely, his work—which has given rise to the term 'Chandlerianism'—has had a profound effect on historians and business thinking all over the world, particularly in Japan and Germany. Some of his books have been translated into Chinese and Russian.

Following his lead, US business historians have moved to more thematic areas: for example, how companies formulate and implement policy, how industries evolve, the impact of administrative hierarchies on the modern economy, industrial evolution across national boundaries, the interaction of business with governmental institutions and regulatory bodies, and organised labour and the consumer.

History will no doubt endow him with the distinction of giving modern management educators a less theoretical way of teaching the business of business. In essence, he has skilfully recycled the tried and tested past to provide both practising and aspiring managers with an inheritance that has practical corporate application in today's highly competitive world. In truth, history is the only way individuals and companies can learn from experience. And learning from experience is the only way to increase productivity and competitiveness.

THE BEST SOURCES OF HELP
Books:
Chandler, Alfred. *Strategy and Structure*. Cambridge, Massachusetts: MIT Press, 1962.
Chandler, Alfred. *The Visible Hand: The Managerial Revolution in American Business*. Cambridge, Massachusetts: Harvard University Press, 1977.
Chandler, Alfred. *Managerial Hierarchies*. Cambridge, Massachusetts: Harvard University Press, 1980.
Chandler, Alfred, and Richard Tedlow. *The Coming of Managerial Capitalism*. Boston, Massachusetts: Irwin, 1985.
Chandler, Alfred. *Scale and Scope: The Dynamics of Industrialized Capitalism*. Cambridge, Massachusetts: Harvard University Press, 1994.
Chandler, Alfred. *Big Business and The Wealth of Nations*. Cambridge: Cambridge University Press, 1997.
Chandler, Alfred. *The Dynamic Firm*. Oxford: Oxford University Press, 1998.

REFERENCES: Both quotations are extracts from Chandler's private correspondence.

STEPHEN COVEY

1932	Born.
1985	Founds Covey Leadership Center.
1989	Publication of *The Seven Habits of Highly Effective People*.
1997	Covey Leadership Center merges with Franklin Quest.

> **SUMMARY**
>
> In *The Seven Habits of Highly Effective People*, Stephen Covey offers a holistic approach to life and work that has struck a significant chord with the perplexed manager working in turbulent times. The recurring themes in his various works are the transforming power of principles rooted in unchanging natural laws that govern human and organisational effectiveness; the necessity of adapting every aspect of one's life to accord with these principles; effective leadership; and empowerment.

LIFE AND CAREER

Stephen Covey is founder and chairman of the Covey Leadership Center—now part of Franklin Covey—and the Institute for Principle-Centered Leadership in Utah. Born in 1932, he received an MBA from Harvard Business School and a doctorate from Brigham Young University, where he was subsequently Professor of Organizational Behaviour and Business Management.

At the Covey Leadership Center, through his writing—chiefly *The Seven Habits of Highly Effective People* (which has sold over five million copies)—and through consultancy (he was invited to Camp David by President Clinton), his message has reached millions of individuals in business, government, and education.

CONTRIBUTION

The Seven Habits of Highly Effective People

The Seven Habits is addressed to readers not only in their capacity as managers, but also as members of a family, and as social, spiritual, sporting, and thinking individuals. It offers a 'life-transforming prescription', which calls for a rethink of many fundamental assumptions and attitudes (paradigms), and builds on the fundamental concept of interdependence. Covey traces a personal development outline from:

- dependence in childhood (many people never grow out of a dependency culture), through...
- independence in adolescence—self-assurance, a developing personality, and a positive mental attitude, to...
- interdependence—recognition that the optimum outcome results from everyone giving of their best, each aiming for a common goal, sharing the same mission and vision, but having the freedom to use their best judgment as to how to go about achieving that common goal.

Habit 1

Be proactive.

Covey distinguishes between proactive people—those who focus their efforts on things which they can do something about—and reactive people, who blame, accuse, behave like victims, pick on other people's weaknesses, and complain about external factors over which they have no control (for example, the weather).

Proactive people are responsible for their own lives. Covey breaks down the word *responsibility* into 'response' and 'ability'. Proactive people recognise their responsibility to make things happen. Those who allow their feelings to control their actions have abdicated responsibility and empowered their feelings. When proactive people make a mistake, they not only recognise it as such and acknowledge it, they also correct it if possible and, most importantly, learn from it.

Habit 2

Begin with the end in mind.

Leadership is about effectiveness—the vision of what is to be accomplished. It calls for direction (in every sense of the word), purpose, and sensitivity. Management, on the other hand, is about efficiency—how best to accomplish the vision. It depends on control, guidance, and rules.

To identify the end, and to formulate one's route or strategy to achieving that end, Covey maintains the need for a 'principle-centred' basis to all aspects of life. Most people adopt something as the basis (or pivotal point) of their life—spouse, family, money, church, pleasure, friends (and, in a perverse way, enemies), sport, etc. Of course all of these have some influence over the life of every individual. However, only by clearly establishing one's own principles, in the form of a personal mission, does one have a solid foundation.

Habit 3

Put first things first.

Covey's first major work, *First Things First*, sets out his views on time management. It argues that the important thing is not managing time, but managing oneself, focusing on results rather than on methods when prioritising within each compartment of work and life.

He breaks down life's activities into four quadrants:

Quadrant 1: Urgent and important—for example, crises, deadlines, unexpected opportunities.

Quadrant 2: Not urgent, but important—for example, planning, recreation, relationship-building, doing, learning.

Quadrant 3: Urgent, but not important—for example, interruptions, meetings.

Quadrant 4: Not urgent and not important—for example, trivia, time wasters, gossip.

Essentially all activity of effective people should focus on the second quadrant, apart from the genuinely unpredictable quadrant 1 events. However, effective planning and doing in Quadrant 2 should minimise the number of occasions on which crises occur.

The outcomes of a Quadrant 2 focus include: vision, perspective, balance, discipline, and control. On the other hand, the results of placing one's main focus on the other quadrants are:

Quadrant 1: stress, burn-out, inability to manage time (and thus loss of control of one's own life).

Quadrant 3: short-termism, loss of control, shallowness, feelings of being a victim of circumstances.
Quadrant 4: irresponsibility, dependency, unsuitability for employment.

Habit 3 is therefore about managing oneself effectively, by prioritising according to the principles adopted in Habit 2. This approach transcends the office diary or day-planner, embracing all roles in life—as manager, mentor, administrator, strategist, and also as parent, spouse, member of social groups, and as an individual with needs and aspirations.

Habits 1–3 are grouped under the banner 'Private Victory'. They are about the development of the personal attributes that provide the foundations for independence. Habits 4–6 are described by Covey as the 'Public Victory', as they are the basic paradigms of interdependence.

Habit 4

Think win/win.

Interdependence occurs when there is co-operation, not competition, in the workplace (or the home). Covey holds that competition belongs in the marketplace.

Covey points out that, from childhood, many people are conditioned to a win/lose mentality by school examinations, by parental approval being rationed to 'success', by external comparisons and league tables. This results in a 'scarcity mentality', a belief that there is only a finite cake to be shared: a 'scarcity mentality' is evident in people who have difficulty in sharing recognition or credit, power or profit. It restricts their ability to celebrate other people's success, and even brings about a perverse satisfaction at others' misfortune.

By contrast Covey advocates an 'abundance mentality' that:

- recognises unlimited possibilities for positive growth and development
- celebrates success, recognising that one person's success is not achieved at the expense, or to the exclusion, of others
- understands and seeks a win/win solution

Covey argues that, to be true to your ideals, it is sometimes necessary to walk away, if the other party is interested only in a win/lose outcome: Covey describes this as 'win/win or no deal'.

Habit 5

Seek first to understand, then to be understood.

'I just can't understand my son ... he won't listen to me.' The absurdity of this statement is highlighted by Covey in emphasising the importance of listening in order to understand. Clearly, the parent needs to stop and listen to the son if he or she truly wants to understand him.

However, most people want to make their point first, or are so busy looking for their opportunity to butt into the conversation that they fail to hear and understand the other party. Covey defines the different levels of listening as:

- hearing but ignoring
- pretending to listen ('Yes', 'Oh', 'I see...')
- selective listening (choosing to hear only what we want to hear)

- attentive listening, without evaluation (e.g., taking notes at a lecture)
- empathic listening (with intent to understand the other party)

True empathic listening requires a great deal of personal security, as one is vulnerable to being influenced, to having one's opinions changed. 'The more deeply you understand other people,' Covey says, 'the more you appreciate them, the more reverent you feel about them.'

Likewise, when you feel that someone is genuinely seeking to understand your point of view, you recognise and share their openness and willingness to negotiate and to reach a win/win situation.

Habit 6
Synergise.

The essence of synergy is where two parties, each with a different agenda, value each other's differences. Everything in nature is synergistic, with every creature and plant being interdependent with others.

We also have personal effectiveness where there is synergy at an individual level—where both sides of the brain are working in tandem on a problem or situation, the intuitive, creative, visual right side and the analytical, logical, verbal left side combining to achieve the optimum outcome.

Synergy is lacking in insecure people: they either clone others, or else try to stereotype them. Of such insecurity is born prejudice—racism, bigotry, nationalism, and any other form of prejudging others.

Habit 7
Sharpen the saw.

The seventh and final habit relates to renewal. Just as a motor car or any other sophisticated tool needs regular care and maintenance, so too do the human body and mind.

Covey uses the metaphor of a woodcutter who is labouring painfully to saw down a tree. The saw is obviously in need of sharpening, but when asked why he doesn't stop and sharpen the saw, the woodcutter replies, 'I can't stop—I'm too busy sawing down this tree.'

The warning is quite clear. Everyone can become so engrossed in the task in hand that the basic tools are neglected:

- the physical self—which requires exercise, a sensible and balanced diet, and management of stress
- the social/emotional self—which connects with others through service, empathy, and synergy, and which is the source of intrinsic security
- the spiritual self—which through meditation, reflection, prayer, and study helps to clarify and refine our own values and strengths, and our commitment to them
- the mental self—building on to our formal education through reading, visualising, planning, writing, and maintaining a coherent programme of continuing personal development

CONTEXT AND CONCLUSIONS
Commentators have both attacked and applauded Covey's approach for mixing the self-help message, which can be traced back to Samuel Smiles, with the positive self-drive of winning friends and influencing people (Dale Carnegie), current management theories, and religious fervour.

In times of change and confusion, however, when failure, redundancy, and unemployment dominate individual thinking and lead to stress, Covey's message offers the individual something to hang on to. *First Things First*, coauthored with Roger and Rebecca Merrill, has achieved twice the sales of *The Seven Habits* over the same period.

He is undoubtedly a philosopher for our times, highlighting the significance of changing industrial and human relations in this post-confrontational era, and recognising the potential of the untapped resources within each individual.

THE BEST SOURCES OF HELP
Books:
Covey, Stephen. *The Seven Habits of Highly Effective People*. London: Simon & Schuster, 1989.
Covey, Stephen. *Principle-centred Leadership*. London: Simon & Schuster, 1999.
Covey, Stephen, A. Roger Merrill, and Rebecca R. Merrill. *First Things First*. London: Simon & Schuster, 1996.

PHILIP CROSBY

1926	Born.
1952	After war service, begins his career working on an assembly line.
1961	Establishes 'zero concepts' while working for Martin-Marietta.
1965	Joins ITT.
1979	*Quality Is Free* published. Leaves ITT to found Philip Crosby Associates II, Inc.
1984	*Quality without Tears* published.
1988	*The Eternally Successful Organization* published.
1991	Launches Career IV Inc.
2001	Dies.

> **SUMMARY**
>
> Philip Crosby wrote the best-seller *Quality Is Free* at a time when the quality movement was a rising, innovative force in business and manufacturing. In the 1980s, his consultancy was advising 40% of the Fortune 500 companies on quality management.
>
> His popularity as a consultant can be partly attributed to his ability to talk about quality management ideas in terms that were easy to understand, and this ability was undoubtedly the result of over 40 years' hands-on management experience.

LIFE AND CAREER

Crosby was born in West Virginia in 1926. A graduate of Western Reserve University, he saw service in the Korean War, and started his working life on the assembly line in 1952, becoming quality manager for Martin-Marietta, where he developed the 'zero defects' concept. After working his way up, Crosby was corporate vice-president and director of quality at ITT for 14 years.

As a result of the interest shown in *Quality Is Free* (1979), he left ITT to set up Philip Crosby Associates II, Inc. and started to teach organisations quality principles and practice as laid down in his book. In 1985, his company was floated for $30 million. In 1991 he retired from Philip Crosby Associates to launch Career IV Inc., a consultancy advising on the development of senior executives. He died in August 2001.

CONTRIBUTION

Quality, Crosby emphasised, is neither intangible nor immeasurable. It is a strategic imperative, something that can be quantified and put to work to improve the bottom line. 'Acceptable' quality or defect levels produced by means of traditional quality control measures, for Crosby, represent evidence of failure rather than an assurance of success. The goal is to meet requirements on time, first time, and every time. The emphasis, therefore, should be on prevention, not inspection and cure.

Crosby's approach to quality was unambiguous. In his view, good, bad, high, and low quality are meaningless concepts in the abstract; the meaning of quality is 'conformance to requirements'. What that means is that a product should conform to the requirements that the company has itself established based on its customers' needs. He also believed that the prime responsibility for poor quality lies with management, not with the workers. Management sets the tone for the quality initiative from the top.

Nonconforming products are ones that management has failed to specify or control. The cost of nonconformance equals the cost of not doing it right first time, and not rooting out any defects in processes.

'Zero defects' does not mean that people never make mistakes, but that companies should not begin with 'allowances' or substandard targets with mistakes as an in-built expectation. Instead, work should be seen as a series of activities or processes, defined by clear requirements and carried out to produce identified outcomes. Systems that allow things to go wrong—and that result in those things having to be done again—can cost organisations between 20% and 35% of their revenues, in Crosby's estimation.

His seminal approach to quality was set out in *Quality Is Free*, and is often summarised as the 'Fourteen Steps'.

The Fourteen Steps

1. Management commitment: the need for quality improvement must be recognised and accepted by management, who then draw up a quality improvement programme with an emphasis on the need for defect prevention. Quality improvement equates to profit improvement. A quality policy is needed which states that 'each individual is expected to perform exactly like the requirement or cause the requirement to be officially changed to what we and the customer really need'.

2. The quality improvement team: representatives from each department or function should be brought together to form a quality improvement team. Its members should be people who have sufficient authority to commit the area they represent to action.

3. Quality measurement: the status of quality should be determined throughout the company. This means establishing and recording quality measures for each area of activity in order to show where improvement is possible and where corrective action is necessary. Crosby advocated delegation of this task to the people who actually do the job, thus setting the stage for defect prevention on the job, where it really counts.

4. The cost of quality evaluation: the cost of quality is not an absolute performance measurement, but an indication of where the action necessary to correct a defect will result in greater profitability.

5. Quality awareness: this involves making employees aware of the cost to the company of defects, through training and information, and the provision of visible evidence of the results of a concern for quality improvement. Crosby stressed that this sharing process is a key, or even *the* key, step in the progress of an organisation towards quality.

6. Corrective action: discussion of problems will result in the finding of solutions and will also bring to light other elements that are in need of improvement. People need to see that problems are regularly being resolved. Corrective action should then become a habit.

7. Establishing an ad hoc committee for the zero defects programme: zero defects is not a motivation programme: its purpose is to communicate and instil the notion that everyone should do things right first time.

8. Supervisor training: all managers should undergo formal training on the fourteen steps before they are implemented. Managers should understand each of the fourteen steps well enough to be able to explain them to their people.

9. Zero defects day: it is important that the commitment to zero defects as the performance standard of the company makes an impact, and that everyone gets the same message in the same way. Zero defects day, when supervisors explain the programme to their people, should make a lasting impression as a 'new attitude' day.

10. Goal setting: all supervisors ask their people to establish specific, measurable goals that they can strive for. Usually, these comprise 30-, 60-, and 90-day goals.

11. Error-cause removal: employees are asked to describe, on a simple, one-page form, any problems that prevent them from carrying out error-free work. Problems should be acknowledged and begin to be addressed within 24 hours by the function or unit to which the memorandum is directed. This constitutes a key step in building up trust, as it will make people begin to grow more confident that their problems will be attended to and dealt with.

12. Recognition: it is important to recognise those who meet their goals or perform outstanding acts with a prize or award, although this should not be in financial form. The act of recognition itself is what is important.

13. Quality councils: the quality professionals and team leaders should meet regularly to discuss improvements and upgrades to the quality programme.

14. Doing it over again: during the course of a typical programme lasting from 12 to 18 months, turnover and change will dissipate much of the educational process. It is important to set up a new team of representatives and begin the programme again, starting with zero defects day. This 'starting over again' helps quality to become ingrained in the organisation.

Putting quality to the test

Crosby often used stories to convey his message and also used audit techniques and questionnaires to clarify organisational and individual understanding.

Below we reproduce a quick 'true or false' questionnaire that features in *Quality Is Free*. (The answers are given at the end of this piece.)

1. Quality is a measure of goodness of the product that can be defined as fair, good, excellent.
2. The economics of quality require that management establish acceptable quality levels as performance standards.
3. The cost of quality is the expense of doing things wrong.
4. Inspection and test should report to manufacturing so manufacturing can have the proper tools to do the job.
5. Quality is the responsibility of the quality department.
6. Worker attitudes are the primary cause of defects.
7. I have trend charts that show me the rejection level at every key operation.
8. I have a list of the ten biggest quality problems.
9. Zero defects is a worker motivation programme.
10. The biggest problem today is that customers don't understand.

Later work

In his 1984 book, *Quality without Tears*, Crosby developed the idea of a 'quality vaccination serum', which would be made up of the following ingredients:

- integrity for the chief executive officer, all managers, and all employees
- systems for measuring conformance, and educating all employees and suppliers so that quality, corrective action, and defect prevention become routine
- communications that enable problems to be identified, progress to be conveyed, and achievement to be recognised
- operations organised in such a way that procedures, products, and systems are proven before they are implemented and are then continually examined
- policies that are clear, unambiguous, and establish the primacy of quality throughout the organisation

The Eternally Successful Organization (1988) presented a broader approach to improvements. In it Crosby identified five characteristics essential for an organisation to be successful:

- people routinely do things right first time
- change is anticipated and used to advantage
- growth is consistent and profitable
- new products and services appear when needed
- everyone is happy to work there

CONTEXT AND CONCLUSIONS

Throughout his work, Crosby's thinking was consistently characterised by four absolutes:

- the definition of quality is conformance to requirements
- the system of quality is prevention
- the performance standard is zero defects
- the measurement of quality is the price of nonconformance

The major contribution made by Crosby to management thinking is indicated by the fact that his phrases 'zero defects', 'getting it right first time', and 'conformance to requirements' have now entered not only the vocabulary of quality itself, but also the general vocabulary of management.

When Crosby's name is not mentioned in the very same sentence as the best-known quality thinker of them all, Deming, then it is almost certain to be mentioned in the next. Crosby's practical and easy-to-read books on quality became—and remain—bibles for many, demystifying a great deal of the jargon formerly associated with quality management. His timing was perfect for the quality movement, and his writing has marketed quality to a wide audience.

ANSWERS TO QUESTIONNAIRE

1. F; 2. F; 3. T; 4. F; 5. F; 6. F; 7. T; 8. F; 9. F; 10. F

THE BEST SOURCES OF HELP
Books:
Crosby, Philip. *Quality Is Free: The Art of Making Quality Certain*. New York: McGraw-Hill, 1979.

Crosby, Philip. *Quality without Tears: The Art of Hassle-free Management*. New York: McGraw-Hill, 1984.

Crosby, Philip. *The Eternally Successful Organization: The Art of Corporate Wellness*. New York: McGraw-Hill, 1988.

W. EDWARDS DEMING

1900	Born.
1928	Completes PhD at Yale.
1950	Begins teaching quality management in Japan.
1986	Publication of *Out of the Crisis*.
1987	Receives US National Medal of Technology.
1993	Founds W. Edwards Deming Institute.
1993	Dies.

> **SUMMARY**
>
> W. Edwards Deming is widely acknowledged as the leading management thinker in the field of quality. He is credited with being the most influential catalyst of Japan's post-war economic transformation, although it wasn't until much later that the value of his ideas and practices began to be recognised by the US manufacturing and service industries.

LIFE AND CAREER

Deming obtained a PhD in mathematical physics from Yale University in 1928 and concentrated on lecturing and writing on mathematics, physics, and statistics for the next ten years. It was only in the late 1930s that he became familiar with the work of Walter Shewhart, who was experimenting with the application of statistical techniques to manufacturing processes. Deming became interested in applying Shewhart's techniques to nonmanufacturing processes, particularly clerical, administrative, and management activities. After joining the US Census Bureau in 1939, he applied statistical process control to their techniques, which contributed to a six-fold improvement in productivity. Around this time he also started to run courses for engineers and designers on his—and Shewhart's—evolving methods of statistical process control.

Deming's expertise as a statistician was instrumental in his posting to Japan after the Second World War as an adviser to the Japanese census. At this time the United States was the leading economic power, with products much envied by the rest of the world; it saw no need for Deming's new ideas. The Japanese, on the other hand, recognised that their own goods were shoddy by international standards. Moreover, after the war, they could not afford the wastage of raw materials that post-production inspection processes brought about and were consequently looking for techniques to help them address these problems. While in Japan, Deming became involved with the Union of Japanese Scientists and Engineers (JUSE) and his career of lecturing to the Japanese on statistical methods and company-wide quality, a combination of techniques now known as Total Quality Management (TQM), had begun.

It was only in the late 1970s that the United States became aware of his achievements in Japan. The 1980s saw a spate of publications explaining his work and influence. In his American seminars during 1980, Deming talked of the need for the total transformation of Western-style management. In 1986 he published *Out of the Crisis*, which documented the thinking and practice that had led to the transformation of Japanese manufacturing industry. His ideas gained acceptance in the United Kingdom following the foundation of the British Deming Association in 1987. Deming died in 1993.

W. Edwards Deming

CONTRIBUTION

Deming's work and writing constitute not so much a technique as a philosophy of management, one that focuses on quality and continuous improvement, but that has also, justifiably, had a much wider influence.

Below we consider Deming's interest in variation and his approach to systematic problem-solving, which led on to his development of the 14 points that have gained widespread recognition and are central to the quality movement.

Variation and problem-solving

The key to Deming's ideas on quality lies in his recognition of the importance of variation. In *Out of the Crisis* he states that 'the central problem in management and in leadership...is failure to understand the information in variation'.

Deming was preoccupied with why things do not behave as predicted. All systems (be they the equipment, the process, or the people) have variation, but, he argued, it is essential for managers to be able to distinguish between special and common causes of variation. He developed a theory of variation: that special causes of variation are usually attributable to easily recognisable factors such as a change of procedure, change of shift or operator, and so on, but that common causes will remain when special causes have been eliminated and are normally inherent in the design, process, or system. These common causes often are recognised by workers, but only managers have the authority to change them to avoid repeated occurrence of the problem. Deming estimated that management was responsible for more than 85% of the causes of variation. This formed his central message to the Japanese.

Deming's 14 points for management

Deming created 14 points that provided a framework for developing knowledge in the workplace and guiding long-term business plans and aims. The points constitute not so much an action plan as a philosophical code for management. They have been extensively interpreted, both by commentators on quality control and by experts on other management disciplines.

- Create constancy of purpose towards the improvement of products and services, with the aim of becoming competitive, staying in business, and providing jobs.
- Adopt the new philosophy. Western management must awaken to the challenge, learn its responsibilities, and take on leadership for change.
- Cease dependence on mass inspection. Build quality into the product from the start.
- End the practice of awarding business on the basis of price tag alone. Instead, minimise total cost. Move towards a single supplier for any item, based on a long-term relationship of loyalty and trust.
- Improve constantly and forever the system of production and service to improve quality and reduce waste.
- Institute training and retraining.
- Institute leadership. The aim of supervision should be to lead and help people to do a better job.
- Drive out fear so that everyone can work effectively for the company.
- Break down barriers between departments. People in research, design, sales, and production must work as a team, to foresee and solve problems of production.

- Eliminate slogans, exhortations, and targets for the workforce, as they do not necessarily achieve their aims.
- Eliminate numerical quotas, in order to take account of quality and methods, rather than just numbers.
- Remove barriers to pride in workmanship.
- Institute a vigorous programme of education and retraining for both the management and the workforce.
- Take action to accomplish the transformation. Management and workforce must work together.

These principles are relevant to management in general, not simply to quality and process control. They contributed to Deming's status as a founder of the quality management movement, and attracted an audience much wider than the quality lobby.

CONTEXT AND CONCLUSIONS

Naturally enough, no one as universally acclaimed as Deming escapes without criticism. Some have criticised his approach as being good for improvement but uninspiring for creativity and innovation. Others say his approach is not effective in generating new products or penetrating new markets.

Others—particularly Juran, another quality guru—accuse him of over-reliance on statistical methods. Deming's American lectures in the 1980s, however, pointed time and time again to a mistaken preoccupation with the wrong type of statistics. He argued against figures that focused purely on productivity and control and argued for more evidence of quality, a message that Tom Peters adopted in the 1980s and 1990s.

Deming also stirred up wide interest with his rejection of management by objectives and performance appraisals. Similarly, his attitude toward integrating the workforce led TQM to be perceived as a caring philosophy. Paradoxically, however, his focus on cost-reduction has been pointed to as a cause of downsizing.

Although in the 1980s America paid tribute to Deming—not only for what he did in Japan, but also for his thinking and approach to quality management—few American companies use his methods today. One reason for this is perhaps that, by the 1980s, Deming was selling a system that worked, thereby implying that he had discovered the only way to achieve quality; thus he was no longer alert to changes in the problems. In Japan, in the beginning, he had listened to Japanese needs and requirements, showed them respect, and developed his thinking with them. In the United States of the 1980s, he appeared to try to dispense his philosophy rather than readapt it to a different culture.

In 1951, in early recognition of their debt to Deming, the JUSE awarded the Deming prize to Japanese organisations that excelled in company-wide quality. It was not until the 1980s that the United States recognised Deming's achievements in Japan and elevated him to guru status. In 1987 the British Deming Association was founded to disseminate his ideas in the United Kingdom. From the 1990s it seemed as if Deming's legacy was likely to have both a lasting and significant impact on management theory. Why is this?

The first reason must lie in the nature of his achievement. Deming has been universally acclaimed as one of the founding fathers of Total Quality Management, if not the founding father. The revolution in Japanese manufacturing management that led to the economic miracle of the 1970s and 1980s has been attributed largely to him.

Second, if the 14 points make less of an impact today than they did just after the Second World War in Japan, it is probably because many aspects of those points were adopted, assimilated, and integrated into management practice in the 1990s and have been continuously debated and taught in business schools around the world.

The third reason is more complex and lies in the scope of his legacy. Deming's 14 points add up to a code of management philosophy that spans the two major schools of managerial thought that have predominated since the early 20th century: scientific (hard) management on the one hand, and human relations (soft) management on the other. Deming succeeds—despite criticisms of his over-use of statistical techniques—in marrying them together. Over half of his 14 points focus on people as opposed to systems. Many management thinkers veer towards one school or the other. Deming, like Drucker, melds them together.

The originality and freshness of Deming is that he took his philosophy not from the world of management, but from the world of mathematics, and wedded it with a human relations approach that did not come from management theory, but from observation and from seeing what people needed from their working environment in order to contribute of their best.

THE BEST SOURCES OF HELP
Book:
Deming, W. Edwards. *Out of the Crisis: Quality, Productivity, and Competitive Position*. Cambridge: Cambridge University Press, 1986.

PETER DRUCKER

1909	Born.
1927	Commences study at University of Hamburg.
1931	Doctorate in public and international law, University of Frankfurt, Germany.
1933	Moves to London to work as an investment banker.
1937	Leaves for United States to become investment adviser and correspondent for *Financial News*.
1939	Publication of *The End of Economic Man*.
1940	Private consultant to business and on government policy; teacher at Sarah Lawrence College; Professor at Bennington College, Vermont.
1943	Spends 18 months interviewing senior management at General Motors, which results in the bestselling *The Concept of the Corporation*.
1950	Professor of Management at New York University Graduate School of Business.
1954	Publication of *The Practice of Management*.
1969	Publication of *The Age of Discontinuity*.
1971	Marie Rankin Clarke Professor of Management, Graduate School, Claremont.
1974	Publication of *Management: Tasks, Responsibilities, Practices*.
1975	Columnist for *Wall Street Journal*.
1990	Founding of The Peter F. Drucker Foundation for Non-Profit Management.
1999	Publication of *Management Challenges for the 21st Century*.

> **SUMMARY**
>
> Peter Drucker is accepted by both practising managers and writers throughout the world as *the* management guru. He himself prefers to be known as a writer. He does not claim to have invented management—but does concede that he discovered it as a way of life central to the well-being of society and the economy.
>
> He has shown interests as diverse as journalism, art appreciation, mountaineering, and reading. With more than 33 books published over seven decades Drucker is, by common consent, the founding father of modern management studies.

LIFE AND CAREER

Peter Ferdinand Drucker was born in Vienna in 1909 into a high-achieving, intellectual family and was surrounded in his early years by members of the pre-war Viennese cultural elite. He commenced his studies at the University of Hamburg, but transferred to the University of Frankfurt, where he obtained a doctorate in public and international law in 1931.

While still a student in Frankfurt he worked on the city's *General Anzeiger* newspaper and rose to the posts of foreign and financial editor. Recognised as a talented writer, he was offered a job in the Ministry of Information. Observing the Nazis' rise to power with abhorrence, he wrote a philosophical essay condemning Nazism; this was probably instrumental in hastening his departure to England in 1933. It was in 1937 that he left for the United States to become an investment adviser to British industry and correspondent for several British newspapers, including the *Financial Times*, then called the *Financial News*.

His first book, *The End of Economic Man*, appeared in 1939. In 1940 he set up as a private consultant to business and government policy-makers, specialising in the German economy and external politics. From 1940 to 1942 he was a teacher at Sarah

Lawrence College, and this was followed by the post of Professor of Philosophy, Politics, History, and Religion at Bennington College, Vermont.

It was in the early stages of this appointment that he was invited by the vice-president of General Motors (GM) to investigate what constitutes a modern organisation, and to examine what the managers running it actually do. Although Drucker was relatively inexperienced in business at the time, his analysis led to the publication, in 1946, of *The Concept of the Corporation*—published as *Big Business* in the United Kingdom—which had a mixed reception but nonetheless confirmed Drucker's future as a management writer.

The period 1950–1972 was a time of prolific writing, teaching, and consulting while he was Professor of Management at New York University Graduate School of Business. In 1971 he was appointed the Marie Rankin Clarke Professor of Social Science and Management at the Graduate School in Claremont, a school that was subsequently named after him. In 1994 he was appointed Godkin Lecturer at Harvard University.

Drucker holds decorations from the governments of Austria and Japan as well as 22 honorary doctorates from universities in Belgium, Japan, Spain, Switzerland, the United Kingdom, and the United States. He is also a Fellow of the American Association of Science, an Honorary Member of the National Academy of Public Administration, a Fellow of the American Academy of Arts and Sciences, and a Fellow of the American, British, Irish, and International Academies of Management. He lives in Claremont, 40 miles east of Los Angeles, and has four children and six grandchildren.

CONTRIBUTION

Drucker's management writings are phenomenal in their coverage and impressive in their clarity. With over 33 books to his credit, we can provide only a snapshot of his thinking here. His earlier works made a significant contribution to establishing what constitutes management practice; his later works tackle the complexities—and the management implications—of the post-industrial 1980s and beyond. It is that range and development that we have tried to represent in our comments on the books covered here.

The End of Economic Man — 1939

The End of Economic Man concentrates on the politics and economics of the 1930s in general and the rise of Nazism in particular; Drucker signalled a warning about the Holocaust and predicted that Hitler would forge an alliance with Stalin. This was his first book in English as sole author; J.B. Priestley said of it: 'At once the most penetrating and the most stimulating book I have read on the world crisis. At last there is a ray of light in the dark chaos.'

This was followed by *The Future of Industrial Man* (1942), which assumed Hitler's defeat and started to look ahead to peacetime, warning of the dangers of an approach to planning founded on the denial of freedom. It attracted the interest of critics, who argued that it mixed economics with social sciences; it was, in fact, the first book to argue that any organisation is both an economic and social organ. As such it laid the foundations for Drucker's interest in management in general and, as it turned out, General Motors in particular.

The Concept of the Corporation — 1946

When General Motors invited Drucker to write about the company, it was expected that the invitation would result in a glowing description of GM's success. What in fact emerged was something different, something that recognised success but also looked to the future.

General Motors provided Drucker with the opportunity to test in practice the theory he had propounded in *The Future of Industrial Man*, i.e. that an organisation was essentially a social system as well as an economic one. *The Concept of the Corporation* questioned whether what had worked in the past—a foolproof system of objective policies and procedures throughout every layer of the organisation—would continue to work in a future of global competition, changing social values, and automation, and with the drive for quality and the growth of the knowledge worker.

The assembly line, he argued, actually created inefficiency because activity took place at the pace of the slowest. Demotivation was rife because no one saw the end result, and initiative was stifled by the minutiae of checks, rules, and controls. The layers of bureaucracy slowed down decision-making, created adversarial labour relations, and did nothing to create a 'self-governing plant community' (the phrase Drucker used for an empowered workforce). Drucker reported the benefits of decentralised operations—an issue that critics were quick to praise and organisations quick to mimic—but suggested that the GM hierarchy of commands and controls would be slow to respond in a rapidly changing future.

The fundamental difference between Drucker and GM was that GM saw the workforce as a cost in the quest for profits, whereas Drucker saw people as a resource who would be better able to satisfy customers if they had more involvement in their jobs and gained some satisfaction from doing them. *The Concept of the Corporation*, consequently, was decades ahead of its time in terms of its espousal of empowerment and self-management. Although Alfred Sloan—the chief executive and powerhouse behind General Motors' success—had no time for Drucker's book, Drucker was, in the early 1950s, to advise Sloan on setting up a school of administration at MIT. His criticism of Sloan was implicit rather than explicit, saying he had vision rather than perspective, and implying that leadership had been sacrificed to the rulebook. Sloan was measured in his reply—after all, at the time, General Motors was the largest and arguably one of the most successful companies in the world. His response came in 1963 with the publication of *My Years with General Motors*, which sets out the scientific credo of GM's philosophy, yet talks little of people, transparently because they had little importance relative to the systems they were following.

Another effect of *The Concept of the Corporation* was the establishment of management as a discipline, bringing to the fore the notions of:

- the social and environmental responsibility of the organisation
- the relationship between the individual and the organisation
- the role of top management and the decision-making process
- the need for continual training and retraining of managers with the focus on their own responsibility for self-development
- the nature of labour relations
- the imperatives of community and customer relations

It is interesting that Japanese industry listened to these messages and US industry did not.

The Practice of Management — 1954

The Practice of Management was Drucker's second book on management, and it established him as a leader in his field. It set trends in management for decades, and reputations were built by adopting and expanding on the ideas that he set out in it. It is still regarded by many as the definitive management text.

Drucker states that there is only one valid purpose for the existence of a business: that is, to create a customer. It is not, he argues, the internal structure, controls, organisation, and procedures that keep a business afloat; rather, it is the customer—who pays, and decides what is important—who fills this role. He sets out eight areas in which objectives should be set and performance should be measured:

- market standing
- innovation
- productivity
- physical and financial resources
- profitability
- managers' performance and development
- workers' performance and attitude
- public responsibility

The Practice of Management is probably best remembered for setting out the principles of management by objectives and self control (Drucker's term, although he didn't coin it)—a management process that has become the accepted basis for management theory and practice.

The book also identified the seven tasks of the manager of tomorrow. He or she must:

- manage by objectives
- take risks and allow risk-taking decisions to take place at lower levels in the organisation
- be able to make strategic decisions
- be able to build an integrated team whose members are capable of managing and measuring their own performance and results in relation to overall objectives
- be able to communicate information quickly and clearly, and motivate employees so as to gain commitment and participation
- be able to see the business as a whole and to integrate his or her function within it
- be able to relate the product and industry to the total environment, to find out what is important and what needs to be taken into account. This perspective must embrace developments outside the company's particular market or country and the manager must begin to see economic, political, and social developments on a worldwide scale

Management: Tasks, Responsibilities, Practices — 1974

Much of the work in *The Practice of Management* is updated, expanded, and revised in *Management: Tasks, Responsibilities, Practices*, which establishes where management has come from, where it is now, and where it needs to go. It draws upon a wide range of international examples and sets out principles for managers and management. Effectively, it is a complete management handbook.

Moving on from his earlier work, Drucker defines the manager's work in terms of five basic operations. He or she:

- sets objectives
- organises
- motivates and communicates
- measures
- develops people, including him/herself

Top management's tasks are to:

- define the business mission
- set standards
- build and maintain the human organisation
- develop and maintain external relationships
- perform social and civic functions
- know how to get on with the task in hand if and when necessary

Management: Tasks, Responsibilities, Practice is regarded by many as Drucker's finest book. It is the only management book to have been selected by a Desert Island Discs castaway.

The Age of Discontinuity — 1969 (reissued 1992)

It is in *The Age of Discontinuity* that Drucker describes the very changes that he had signalled to General Motors 23 years earlier. He writes in the preface: 'This book does not project trends; it examines discontinuities. It does not forecast tomorrow; it looks at today. It does not ask: "What will tomorrow look like?" It asks instead: "What do we have to tackle today to make tomorrow?"'

The book deals with the forces changing society as new technology impacts on old industries, changing social values impact on consumer behaviour, and markets become international. Drucker advocates privatisation, pointing out the ineffectiveness of government in leading and stimulating change; he examines the role of organisations in society in an age of discontinuity and looks at different ways of managing the knowledge worker.

Managing in Turbulent Times — 1980

The issues raised in *The Age of Discontinuity* were revisited a decade later in *Managing in Turbulent Times*. Change, uncertainty, and turbulence are the underpinning themes as Drucker highlights the new realities of changing population demographics, global markets, and a 'bisexual' workforce.

Drucker issues challenges to junior, middle, and senior management.

- In the knowledge organisation, the 'supervisor' has to become an 'assistant', a 'resource', a 'teacher'.
- The very term 'middle management' is becoming meaningless [as some] will have to learn how to work with people over whom they have no direct line control, to work transnationally, and to create, maintain, and run systems—none of which is a traditionally middle management task.
- It is top management that faces the challenge of setting directions for the enterprise, of managing the fundamentals. It is top management that will have to restructure itself to

meet the challenges of the 'sea-change', the changes in population structure and population dynamics.
- It is top management that will have to concern itself with the turbulences of the environment, the emergence of the world economy, the emergence of the employee society, and the need for the enterprises in its care to take the lead in respect to political process, political concepts, and social policies.

Drucker said it first

Part of Drucker's success and longevity as a management expert was that he had a remarkable knack of spotting trends that were later picked up and made fashionable by others. Invariably, research will trace the origin back to something Drucker wrote ten years—sometimes 20 years—ago. It is interesting that Drucker noted that one of the key aspects of leadership is timing; he, in fact, upbraided himself for being ten years ahead with his forecasts.

The following section is adapted from work by Clutterbuck and Crainer, who summarised the work of James O'Toole, professor of management at the University of Southern California. O'Toole said that Drucker was the first to:

- define the role of top managers as the keepers of corporate culture
- advocate mentoring, career planning, and executive development as top management tasks
- say that success hinges on the vision expressed by the CEO
- show that structure follows strategy
- suggest a reduction of management layers between the top and the bottom
- argue that success comes from sticking to the basics
- state that the primary purpose of the organisation is to create a customer
- say that success boils down to sensitivity to the consumer and the marketing of innovative products
- suggest that quality is a measure of productivity
- describe the coming knowledge worker
- state that new approaches to management would be needed in the post-industrial age

It must be said, however, that Drucker also prophesied the continuing growth of the middle manager as he or she evolved into the knowledge worker of post-industrial society. It has not quite happened like that and the massive delayerings of the early 1990s suggest that Drucker may well have got it wrong...so far.

'Druckerisms'

On business:

A business is not defined by the company's name, statutes, or articles of incorporation. It is defined by the want the customer satisfies when he buys a product or service. (*Management: Tasks, Responsibilities, Practices*)

On leadership:

There is no substitute for leadership. But management cannot create leaders. It can only create the conditions under which potential leadership qualities become effective; or it can stifle potential leadership. (*The Practice of Management*)

On management:

The function which distinguishes the manager above all others is his educational one. The one contribution he is uniquely expected to make is to give others vision and ability to perform. It is vision and moral responsibility that, in the last analysis, define the manager. (*The Practice of Management*)

On decision-making:

[In] these specifically managerial decisions, the important and difficult job is never to find the right answer, it is hard to find the right question. For there are few things as useless—if not as dangerous—as the right answer to the wrong question. (*The Practice of Management*)

On the knowledge worker:

Increasingly, the knowledge workers of tomorrow will have to know and accept the values, the goals, and the policies of the organisation—to use current buzzwords, they must be willing—nay, eager—to buy into the company's mission. ('Drucker speaks his mind', *Management Review*)

[The knowledge worker]...may realise that he depends on the organisation for access to income and opportunity, and that without the investment the organisation has made—and a high investment at that—there would be no opportunity for him. But he also realises, and rightly so, that the organisation equally depends on him. (*The Age of Discontinuity*)

CONTEXT AND CONCLUSIONS

Critical of the business school system in general, Drucker always set himself apart from mainstream management education. He said of himself: 'I have always been a loner. I work best outside. That's where I'm most effective. I would be a very poor manager. Hopeless. And a company job would bore me to death. I enjoy being an outsider.'

An outsider maybe, but commentators point consistently to his gentlemanly old-world charm, his humility, and the fact that he has never criticised negatively, always politely and constructively.

Drucker's earlier works no longer strike the reader with the same force that they did in the 1950s, 1960s, and 1970s. But this is entirely to his credit. His thinking has become absorbed and adopted as the prevailing wisdom behind the philosophy and practice of modern management.

What does strike the modern reader, however, is the sheer force of his writing, his clear mastery of the subject matter, and the clarity of his expression. It is as well to remember that readable books on management were very few and far between when Drucker wrote *The Concept of the Corporation* and *The Practice of Management*. Texts for managers concentrated usually on technical and industrial engineering and were too complex to have either a wide readership or the impact or influence that Drucker has had.

'For many business leaders across the world...he remains the doyen of modern management theory, not so much because he can lay claim to being the founder of any particular concept such as business re-engineering, or total quality management, rather because he has demonstrated a rare ability to apply commonsense understanding to the analysis of management challenges and their solutions.' ('Interview with Peter Drucker', the *Financial Times*)

One of Drucker's achievements lies in the fact that he, a devotee of the human relations school, recognised the value of Taylor's scientific, work-study approach, and succeeded in striking a balance between the two approaches. Management by objectives, when carried out properly, is an effective marriage of both schools, which attaches significance to culture and to the fact that organisations are held together not just by a dictated vision, but by a shared vision of the future.

So, although Drucker awards the accolade of 'guru's guru' to F.W. Taylor, the world of management will always attribute it to Drucker himself. His ability to see management with a long historical perspective and in a broad social and political context is very rare in management writers. With his capacity for demystifying the apparent complexities of management for millions worldwide, he stands, as he said of himself, quite alone.

THE BEST SOURCES OF HELP
Books:
Drucker, Peter. *The Future of Industrial Man: A Conservative Approach.* London: Heinemann, 1943.
Drucker, Peter. *The Practice of Management.* London: Heinemann, 1955.
Drucker, Peter. *Managing for Results: Economic Tasks and Risk-taking Decisions.* London: Heinemann, 1964.
Drucker, Peter. *The Concept of the Corporation.* New York: New American Library, 1964.
Drucker, Peter. *The Effective Executive.* London: Heinemann, 1967.
Drucker, Peter. *The End of Economic Man.* New York: Harper & Row, 1969.
Drucker, Peter. *Technology, Management, and Society.* London: Heinemann, 1970.
Drucker, Peter. *Management: Tasks, Responsibilities, Practices.* New York: Harper & Row, 1973.
Drucker, Peter. *Managing in Turbulent Times.* London: Heinemann, 1980.
Drucker, Peter. *The Changing World of the Executive.* London: Heinemann, 1982.
Drucker, Peter. *Innovation and Entrepreneurship: Practice and Principles.* London: Heinemann, 1985.
Drucker, Peter. *The Frontiers of Management: Where Tomorrow's Decisions Are Being Made Today.* London: Heinemann, 1986.
Drucker, Peter. *Managing the Non-Profit Organization: Practices and Principles.* Oxford: Butterworth-Heinemann, 1990.
Drucker, Peter. *Managing for the Future: The 1990s and Beyond.* Oxford: Butterworth-Heinemann, 1992.
Drucker, Peter. *Managing in a Time of Great Change.* Oxford: Butterworth-Heinemann, 1995.
Journal Articles:
Donkin, Richard. 'Interview with Peter Drucker.' *Financial Times*, 14 June 1996, p. 13.
Johnson, Mike. 'Drucker speaks his mind.' *Management Review*, October 1995, pp. 10–14.

HENRI FAYOL

1841	Born.
1872	Appointed as director of a group of mines.
1918	Retires.
1925	Dies.
1950s	*General and Industrial Management* published; Fayol's reputation as 'the founding father of the administration school' established.

SUMMARY Henri Fayol remained comparatively unknown outside his native France for almost a quarter of a century after his death. However, in the 1950s, *General and Industrial Management* was published and he posthumously gained widespread recognition for his work on administrative management. Today Fayol is often described as the founding father of the administration school.

LIFE AND CAREER

Fayol spent his entire career in one company, the French mining and metallurgical combine Comentry-Fourchamboult-Decazeville. He began as a mining engineer, was appointed director of a group of mines in 1872, and became managing director in 1888—a post which he held until his retirement in 1918. He retained the honorary title until his death.

When Fayol began his career, the financial health of the mining combine was poor. By the time he retired, however, there had been a complete turnaround and the company was prospering. Fayol's success is often attributed to his development and championing of the 'functional principle'. This involved:

- preparing yearly and 10-yearly plans, and acting on them
- preparing organisation charts to demonstrate and encourage order
- recruiting and training carefully to ensure each employee was in the right place
- adhering to the principle of the chain of command
- arranging regular meetings with heads of departments and divisions to ensure coordination

CONTRIBUTION

Administration Industrielle et Générale—Prévoyance, Organisation, Commandement, Contrôle (General and Industrial Management—Planning, Organisation, Command and Control)

In his writing, Fayol attempted to construct a theory of management that could be used as a basis for formal management education and training. First, he divided all organisational activities into six functions:

- technical: engineering, production, manufacture, adaptation
- commercial: buying, selling, exchange
- financial: the search for optimum use of capital
- security: protection of assets and personnel
- accounting: stocktaking, balance sheets, costs, statistics
- managerial: planning, organising, commanding, coordinating, controlling

Although well understood in their own right, none of the first five functions takes account of drawing up a broad plan of where the business is going and how it will operate; organising people; coordinating all of the business efforts and activities, and monitoring to check that what is planned is actually carried out. Fayol's sixth function, therefore, acts as an umbrella to the previous five.

Fayol argued that to manage is to:

1. Plan: a good plan of action should be flexible, continuous, relevant, and accurate. Its function is to unify the organisation by focusing on the nature, priorities, and condition of the business; the longer-term predictions for the industry and economy; the intuitions of key thinkers; and strategic sector analyses from specialist staff.

For effective planning, managers should be skilled in the art of handling people, and possess considerable energy and a measure of moral courage. It is also important that they have some continuity of tenure; be competent in the specialised requirements of the business; have general business experience; and be able to generate creative ideas.

2. Organise: organising is as much about lines of responsibility and authority as it is about communication flow and the use of resources. Fayol lays down the following organisation duties for managers.

- Ensure the plan is judiciously prepared and strictly carried out.
- See that human and material structures are consistent with objectives, resources, and general operating policies.
- Set up a single guiding authority and establish lines of communication throughout the organisation.
- Harmonise activities and coordinate efforts.
- Formulate clear, distinct and precise decisions.
- Arrange for efficient personnel selection.
- Define duties clearly.
- Encourage a liking for initiative and responsibility.
- Offer fair recompense for services rendered.
- Make use of sanctions in cases of fault and error.
- Maintain discipline.
- Ensure that individual interests are subordinated to the general interest.
- Pay special attention to the authority of command.
- Supervise both material and human order.
- Have everything under control.
- Fight against excess regulation, red tape, and paperwork.

3. Coordinate: coordination involves determining the timing and sequencing of activities so that they mesh properly; allocating the appropriate resources, time, and priority; and adapting means to ends.

4. Command: managers who are in charge should:

- gain a thorough knowledge of their personnel
- eliminate the incompetent (this is not as final as it sounds! Fayol takes pains to point out that any decision to part with employees should be the result of careful thought; that the employees should have had fairly assigned work for which they were trained; that they should have been appraised fairly and objectively and provided with honest

feedback; that they should have been given every opportunity for additional training, offered guidance and—where possible—reassigned to alternative work. Fayol also mentions procedures involving written warnings and protection against bias and 'inequities'.)
- be well versed in the agreements between the business and its employees
- set a good example
- conduct periodic audits of the organisation
- bring together senior assistants to ensure unity of direction and focus of efforts
- not become engrossed in detail
- aim at making energy, initiative, loyalty, and unity prevail among employees

5. Control: controlling means checking that:

- everything occurs according to the plan adopted, the principles established, and the instructions issued
- appropriate corrective action is taken
- weaknesses, errors, and deviations from the plan have not slipped in
- the plan is kept up to date (it is not cast in stone but adapts to changing developments)

Fayol's principles of management

Fayol's five-point approach advises managers on their tasks, duties and activities. From his own experience, he established a number of general principles of management, which lend definition to this approach.

- division of work: specialisation allows the individual to build up expertise and therefore be more productive
- authority: the right to issue commands, along with the appropriate responsibility
- discipline: two-sided—employees obey orders only if managers play their part by providing good leadership
- unity of command: one man, one boss—with no other conflicting lines of command
- unity of direction: staff involved in the same activities should have the same objectives
- subordination of individual interest to the general interest: the good of the organisation must come first over any group, just as the interests of any agreed team should come first over the individual
- remuneration: should be fair and equitable, encouraging productivity by rewarding well-directed effort; it should not be subject to abuse
- centralisation: there is no formula to advocate centralisation or decentralisation; much depends on the optimum operating conditions of the business
- scalar chain: Fayol recognised that although hierarchies are essential, they do not always make for the swiftest communication; lateral communication therefore is also fundamental
- order: avoidance of duplication and waste through good organisation
- equity: a 'combination of kindliness and justice' in dealing with employees
- stability of tenure: the more successful the business, the more stable the management
- initiative: encouraging people to use their initiative is a source of strength for the organisation
- esprit de corps: management must foster and develop the morale of employees and encourage each person to use his or her abilities

CONTEXT AND CONCLUSIONS

It is hard to overestimate the influence Fayol has brought to bear on management thinking and management thinkers. Labelled 'the founding father of the administration school', he was the first author to look at the organisation from the 'top down'; to identify management as a process; to break that process down into logical subdivisions; and to lay out a series of principles to make best use of people—thereby establishing a syllabus for management education.

The fact that Fayol's influence has endured is expressed no better than in the influential classic management formula, POSDCORB, a notion directly derived from his writings. It directs that managers should Plan, Organise, Staff, Direct, Coordinate, Report, and Budget.

Looking more closely at the detail of Fayol's five management activities, it is obvious that the conflicts and concerns, responsibilities and duties, styles, and problems that he identified a century ago are still just as relevant today. How do we 'ensure that individual interests are subordinated to (harmonised with) the general interest'? How do we 'encourage a liking for initiative and responsibility'? And if the 'fight against an excess of regulation, red tape, and paperwork' was problematic enough for Fayol to regard as a management duty in his day, he would surely be disappointed at how little progress has been made.

Fayol's last two management activities, command and control, have been taken to describe the hierarchical structure and management style that large organisations adopted from the 1950s through to the 1980s. But again, if we look closely at what Fayol actually says—especially about command—it is not too distant from a description of an empowering, rather than a 'commanding', manager today.

Fayol's views have been criticised for weakness of analysis and assessment; for the overlap in his principles, elements, and duties; for confusing structure with process; and for an over-reliance on top-down bureaucracy. However, his principles of management do not differ greatly from the characteristics of formal organisations as set out by Max Weber. Fayol's influence as the first to describe management as a top-down process based on planning and the organisation of people will ensure his prominence amongst students and practising managers alike.

THE BEST SOURCES OF HELP
Books:
Brech, Edward. *The Principles and Practice of Management*. 3rd ed. London: Longman, 1975.
Crainer, Stuart. *Financial Times Handbook of Management*. London: Pitman, 1995.
Fayol, Henri, revised by Irwin Gray. *General and Industrial Management*. London: Pitman, 1984.
Pugh, Derek, and David Hickson. *Great Writers on Organisations*. 4th ed. Aldershot: Dartmouth, 1993.

MARY PARKER FOLLETT

1868	Born.
1888	Attends Society for Collegiate Instruction of Women, Harvard.
1896	Publication of *The House of Representatives*.
1890	Spends a year at Newnham College, Cambridge.
1918	Begins writing *The New State*.
1933	Gives inaugural series of lectures for Department of Business Administration (now Department of Industrial Relations) at the London School of Economics.
1933	Dies.

> **SUMMARY**
>
> Mary Parker Follett was one of the first people to apply psychological insight and social science findings to the study of industrial organisation.
>
> Her work focused on human relations within industrial groups. She viewed business as a pioneering field within which solutions to human relations problems were being tested out.
>
> After the Second World War her ideas were largely neglected, except in Japan. Yet her work foreshadowed current Western approaches emphasising involvement and cross-functional communications.

LIFE AND CAREER

Born in Massachusetts to a well-off Boston family, Follett was a brilliant scholar who graduated at the age of 12. She was educated at the Thayer Academy, Boston, and Radcliffe College, Massachusetts. At 20 she attended an annex of Harvard University called the Society for Collegiate Instruction of Women. In 1890, as a student of 22, she spent a year at Newnham College, Cambridge and went on to Paris as a postgraduate student. Pauline Graham describes Follett as a polymath, and records that she read law, economics, government, and philosophy at Harvard, and history and political science at Newnham. While at Cambridge, Follett gave a paper, which she later developed into her first book, *The House of Representatives*. This was taken seriously enough to be reviewed by Theodore Roosevelt in the *American Historical Review* of October 1896.

Follett's family life was difficult. Her father, to whom she was close, died when she was in her early teens. Her mother was an invalid with whom Follett did not get on very well. From an early age Follett ran the household and later she also ran the family housing business.

Eventually, Follett broke all family ties and went to share a home with her friend Isobella Briggs. Over the next 30 years, Isobella provided a stable domestic background, while her social connections were helpful to Follett's work. When Isobella died in 1926, Follett lost her home life as well as her closest friend. Later that year she met Dame Katherine Furse, an Englishwoman who was strongly involved with the Girl Guide movement. Follett later moved to England to share a house in Chelsea with Furse.

Follett the social worker

Follett was expected to become an academic, but instead she went into voluntary social work in Boston, where her energy and practicality (as well as her financial support on occasions) achieved much in terms of community-building initiatives. For over 30 years, she was immersed in this work, and proved to be an innovative, hands-on manager whose practical achievements included the original use of schools as out-of-hours centres for community education and recreation. This was Follett's own idea, and the resulting community centres became models for other cities throughout the United States.

Follett set up vocational placement centres in Boston schools, and represented the public on the Massachusetts Minimum Wage Board. From 1924 she began to give regular papers relating to industrial organisation, especially at conferences of the Bureau of Personnel Administration in New York. She became, in effect, an early management consultant, as businessmen began to seek her advice about their organisational and human relations problems.

In 1926 and 1928, Follett gave papers for the Rowntree Lecture Conference and to the National Institute of Industrial Psychology. In 1933, she gave an inaugural series of lectures for the newly founded Department of Business Administration (now the Department of Industrial Relations) at the London School of Economics (LSE). Later in 1933, Follett returned to America, where she died on the 18th December of that year, aged 65.

CONTRIBUTION
The New State was written during 1918, and argues for group-based democracy as a process of government. Through this book, Follett became widely recognised as a political philosopher. It was based on her social work experience rather than on business organisations, but the ideas it contains were later applied in the business context.

The New State presented an often visionary interpretation of what Follett viewed as the progress of social evolution, and the tone is occasionally infused with poetical, religious feeling. The text argues that democracy 'by numbers' should give way to a more valid process of group-based democracy. This form of democracy is described as a dynamic process through which individual conflicts and differences become integrated in the search for overall group agreement. Through it, people will grow and learn as they adapt to one another's views, while seeking a common, long-term good.

The group process works through the relating of individuals' different ideas to each other and to the common interests of the group as a whole. Appropriate action would, Follett held, become self-evident during the consultation process. This would eventually reveal a 'law of the situation', representing an objective that all could see would be the best course for the group as a whole to pursue. Conflict and disagreement were viewed as positive forces, and Follett considered social evolution to progress through the ever-continuous integration of diverse viewpoints and opinions in pursuit of the common good.

The New State envisages the basic group democratic process following right through to the international level, feeding up from neighbourhoods via municipal and state government into the League of Nations. Sometimes, Follett refers to an almost autonomous group spirit, which develops from the community between people.

The Creative Experience was also written during 1918, and again focused on democratic governance, using examples from business to illustrate ideas. *Dynamic*

Management—The Collected Papers of Mary Parker Follett and *Freedom and Co-ordination* were both published posthumously and edited by L. Urwick. *Freedom and Co-ordination* collects together six papers given by Follett at the LSE in 1933, and these represent the most developed and concise distillation of her thoughts on business organisation.

Follett's business writings extended her social ideas into the industrial sphere. Industrial managers, she saw, confronted the same difficulties as public administrators as regards control, power, participation, and conflict. Her later writings focused on management from a human perspective, using the new approach of psychology to deal with problems between individuals and within groups. She encouraged businessmen to look at how groups formed and how employee commitment and motivation could be encouraged. The participation of everyone involved in decisions affecting their activities is seen as fundamental, in that Follett viewed group power and management through co-operation as the obvious route to achievements that would benefit all.

Views on power, leadership, authority, and control

Follett envisaged management responsibility as being diffused throughout a business rather than wholly concentrated at the hierarchical apex. Degrees of authority and responsibility are seen as spread all along the line. For example, a truck driver can act with more authority than the business owner in terms of knowing most about the best order in which to make his drops. Leadership skills are required of many people rather than just one person, and final authority, while it does exist, should not be overemphasised. The chief executive's role lies in coordinating the scattered authorities and varied responsibilities that make up the organisation into group action and ideas, and also in foreseeing and meeting the next situation.

Follett's concept of leadership as the ability to develop and integrate group ideas, using 'power with' rather than 'power over' people, is very modern. She understood that the crude exercise of authority based on subordination is hurtful to people, and cannot be the basis of effective, motivational management control. Partnership and co-operation, she sought to persuade people, were of far more ultimate benefit to everyone than hierarchical control and competition.

Follett viewed the group process as a form of collective control, with the experience of all who perform a functional part in an activity feeding into decision-making. Control is thus realised through the coordination of all functions rather than imposed from the outside.

Follett's four fundamental principles of organisation

Follett identified four principles of coordination that she considered basic to effective management.

- Co-ordination consists in the 'reciprocal relating' of all the factors in a situation.
- Co-ordination should be by direct contact, operating by means of direct communication between all responsible people involved, whatever their hierarchical or departmental positions.
- Co-ordination should begin in the early stages. It should involve all the people directly concerned, right from the initial stages of designing a project or forming a policy.

- Co-ordination should be a continuing process, based on the recognition that there is no such thing as unity, but only the continuous process of unifying.

CONTEXT AND CONCLUSIONS
The context of evolutionary progress

Follett's thinking was ahead of her time, yet was founded on a conviction of social, evolutionary progress, which the course of subsequent history has shown to be flawed. She lived through momentous times, when social and technological change seemed to make a new order inevitable. The destruction caused by the First World War also seemed to dictate the clear need for a determined effort to create a social order that would not break down so disastrously. Simultaneously, the war created pressures in both England and America for labour participation in management, and led to a growth in internationalist ideas and to the birth of the League of Nations. Like other writers of the time, Follett made leaps of the imagination that grew out of the factual changes that were actually taking place. Her view was rational and progressive, and she could not know the degree to which some things would remain constant, undermining the apparently inevitable dynamic of social 'progress'.

Looking back on the whole of the 20th century, of which Follett saw only the beginning, we have only too full a knowledge of the Second World War and countless other conflicts, of the discrediting of Russian Communism, and of worsening ethnic divisions and continuing human barbarities. The progressive, internationalist vision seems to be, from our contemporary perspective, a fast-receding dream.

Yet, while Follett's optimistic expectations of radical social change were largely mistaken, she drew from it the imaginative vision to transform at least some of her convictions into ideas about ways of living and working that have contributed much to both social and management practice. In fact, it is almost disheartening to read Follett and realise that she clearly and strongly stated, so many years ago, ideas that are being proffered as 'new' today and that are still rarely practised in any sustained way.

THE BEST SOURCES OF HELP
Books:

Graham, Pauline, ed. *Mary Parker Follett: Prophet of Management—A Celebration of Writings from the 1920s*. Boston: Harvard Business School Press. 1995

Follett, Mary Parker. *The Speaker of the House of Representatives*. New York: Longmans, Green & Co., 1896.

Follett, Mary Parker. *The New State: Group Organization—the Solution for Popular Government*. New York: Longmans, Green & Co., 1920.

Follett, Mary Parker. *Creative Experience*. New York: Longmans, Green & Co., 1924.

HENRY GANTT

1861	Born.
1884	Qualifies as mechanical engineer.
1887–1893	Employment at Midvale Steel Company, Philadelphia.
1901	Introduction of task and bonus system.
1917	Contributes to war effort for Frankford Arsenal and for the Emergency Fleet Corporation. Creates Gantt chart.
1919	Dies.

> **SUMMARY**
> Henry Laurence Gantt's legacy to management is the Gantt chart. Accepted as a commonplace project management tool today, it was an innovation of worldwide importance in the 1920s. But the chart was not Gantt's only legacy; he was also a forerunner of the human relations school of management and an early spokesman for the social responsibility of business.

LIFE AND CAREER

Henry Gantt was born into a family of prosperous farmers in Maryland in 1861. His early years, however, were marked by some deprivation as the Civil War brought about changes to the family fortunes. He graduated from Johns Hopkins University and was a teacher before becoming a draughtsman in 1884 and qualifying as a mechanical engineer. From 1887 to 1893 he worked at the Midvale Steel Company in Philadelphia, where he became Assistant to the Chief Engineer (F.W. Taylor) and then Superintendent of the Casting Department.

Gantt and Taylor worked well in their early years together and Gantt followed Taylor to Simonds Rolling Company and on to Bethlehem Steel. From 1900 Gantt became well known in his own right as a successful consultant as he developed interests in broader, even conflicting, aspects of management.

In 1917 Gantt accepted a government commission to contribute to the war effort in the Frankford Arsenal and for the Emergency Fleet Corporation. He died in 1919.

CONTRIBUTION

Gantt is often seen as a disciple of Taylor and a promoter of the scientific school of management. In his early career, the influence of Taylor—and Gantt's aptitude for problem-solving—resulted in attempts to address the technical problems of scientific management. Like Taylor, Gantt believed that only the application of scientific analysis to every aspect of work could produce industrial efficiency, and that improvements in management came from eliminating chance and accidents.

Gantt made four individual and notable contributions.

The task and bonus system

Gantt's task and bonus wage system was introduced in 1901 as a variation on Taylor's differential piece-rate system. Under Gantt's system, the employee received a bonus in addition to his regular day rate if he accomplished the task for the day; he still received the day rate even if the task was not completed. Taylor's piece-rate system, by contrast, penalised employees for substandard performance. As a result of introducing Gantt's system, which enabled workers to earn a living while learning to increase their efficiency, production often more than doubled. This convinced Gantt that concern for the worker and employee morale was one of the most important factors in management and led him eventually to part company with Taylor on the fundamentals of scientific management.

The perspective of the worker

Gantt realised that his system offered little incentive to do more than just meet the standard. He subsequently modified it to pay according to time allowed, plus a percentage of that time if the task were completed within the specified time or less. Hence a worker could receive three hours' pay for doing a two-hour job in two hours or under. But here Gantt brought in an innovation, by paying the foreman a bonus if all the workers met the required standard. This constituted one of the earliest recorded attempts to reward the foreman for teaching workers to improve the way they worked. In *Work, Wages, and Profits* Gantt wrote:

'Whatever we do must be in accord with human nature. We cannot drive people; we must direct their development...the general policy of the past has been to drive; but the era of force must give way to that of knowledge, and the policy of the future will be to teach and lead, to the advantage of all concerned'.

Gantt was interested in an aspect of industrial education which he called the 'habits of industry'—habits of industriousness and co-operation that entailed carrying out work to the best of one's ability, and taking pride in the quality as well as the quantity of work performed.

From his experience as a teacher, Gantt hoped that his bonus system would help to convert the foreman from an overseer and driver of workers to a helper and teacher of subordinates.

The chart

Gantt's bar chart started as a humble but effective mechanism for recording the progress of workers towards the task standard. A daily record was kept for each worker—in black, if he met the standard, in red, if he didn't. This expanded into further charts on quantity of work per machine, quantity of work per worker, cost control, and other subjects.

It was whilst grappling with the problem of tracking all the various tasks and activities of government departments on the war effort in 1917, that Gantt realised he should be scheduling on the basis of time and not of quantities. His solution was a bar chart that showed how work was scheduled over time through to its completion. This enabled management to see, in graphic form, how well work was progressing and indicated when and where action would be necessary to keep on time.

Gantt charts have been applied to all kinds of projects to illustrate how scheduling may be best achieved. To illustrate the principle we might take the mini-project of redecorating an office. The operation would be broken down into the following steps:

- establishing the terms of reference and standards of quality, the cost, and the time
- informing all appropriate personnel and customers
- arranging alternative accommodation

- preparing the office
- redecorating

Each step would be allocated a specific amount of time that would be represented on the chart. The Gantt chart provided a graphic means of planning and controlling work and led to its modern variation—PERT (Programme Evaluation and Review Technique).

The social responsibility of business

After the death of Taylor in 1917, Gantt seemed to distance himself further from the core principles of scientific management and extended his management interests to the function of leadership and the role of the firm itself. As his thinking developed, he believed increasingly that management had obligations to the community at large, and that the profitable organisation had a duty towards the welfare of society.

In *Organizing for Work*, he argued that there was a conflict between profits and service, and that the businessman who says that profits are more important than the service he renders 'has forgotten that his business system had a foundation in service, and as far as the community is concerned has no reason for existence except the service it can render'. These concerns led him to assert that 'the business system must accept its social responsibility and devote itself primarily to service, or the community will ultimately make the attempt to take it over in order to operate it in its own interest'. Gantt was hugely influenced by the events in Russia in 1917 and, in fear that big business was sacrificing service to profit, he began to attack the profit system itself, calling for public service corporations to ensure service to the community.

CONTEXT AND CONCLUSIONS

Gantt was a prolific writer and speaker. He addressed the American Society of Mechanical Engineers on a number of occasions. One of his papers—'Training workmen in habits of industry and co-operation' (1908)—has been noted by several commentators as giving a unique insight into the human relations dimension of management at a time when scientific management was at its peak.

His approach to the foreman as teacher marks him as an early contributor to human behavioural thought in a line that stretches back to Owen and forward with Mayo to the present day. His approach to the duty of the firm towards society also singles him out as one of the earliest spokesmen on the social responsibility of business. But it is as the inventor of the Gantt chart that he will be remembered.

THE BEST SOURCES OF HELP
Books:

Duncan, W. Jack. *Great Ideas in Management*. San Francisco: Jossey-Bass, 1989.
Gantt, Henry. *Work, Wages, and Profits*. New York: Engineering Magazine Co, 1910.
Gantt, Henry. *Industrial Leadership*. New Haven, Connecticut: Yale University Press, 1916.
Gantt, Henry. *Organizing for Work*. London: Allen & Unwin, 1919.
George, Claude S. *The History of Management Thought*. 2nd ed. Englewood Cliffs, New Jersey: Prentice Hall, 1972.
Urwick, Lyndall. *The Golden Book of Management*. London: Newman Neame, 1956.
Wren, Daniel A. *The Evolution of Management Thought*. New York: John Wiley, 1987.

GHOSHAL AND BARTLETT

> **SUMMARY**
>
> Pioneering research with collaborator Christopher Bartlett into what makes large global organisations tick, and an enquiring mind committed to management as the wealth creator, have contributed to the emergence of Sumantra Ghoshal as one of the most respected management thinkers of his generation.
>
> Already a sought-after consultant, teacher, speaker, and prolific writer, his research will continue to play an important role during this era of globalisation in guiding companies through their transformation processes.

LIFE AND CAREER
Born in India in 1946, Sumantra Ghoshal took a degree in physics before spending 12 years (1969–81) at the Indian Oil Corporation. He demonstrated his appetite for understanding what makes organisations work by obtaining two doctorates, one from MIT, champion of the rigorous scientific method, the other from more pragmatic Harvard, whose approach is based on case studies, observation, and practice.

After lecturing at MIT and INSEAD, Ghoshal became professor of business policy at INSEAD in 1992, and professor of strategic leadership at the London Business School in 1994. He first came to international prominence with the publication in 1989 of *Managing Across Borders*, coauthored with Christopher Bartlett.

LIFE AND CAREER
Christopher Bartlett is Thomas D. Casserly Jr. Professor of Business Administration at Harvard Business School. Before joining the faculty of Harvard, he was a marketing manager with Alcoa in Australia, a management consultant in McKinsey and Company's London office, and general manager at Baxter Laboratories' subsidiary company in France.

His research interests have focused on the strategic and organisational challenges which managers face in running multinational corporations, and these interests have been reflected in his most successful books.

Managing Across Borders was cited by the *Financial Times* as one of the 50 most influential business books of the century.

CONTRIBUTION
Managing across borders
Ghoshal and Bartlett's thinking begins with two fundamental questions:

- What does strategy mean?
- Why do the time-honoured business models—exemplified by Alfred Sloan's General Motors—no longer work?

Their initial research involved asking over 250 managers in nine multinational companies how their companies were facing up to the complexities of international competition and the growing global marketplace. They identified a pervasive organisational inability to cope, survive, and succeed in the face of growing diversity and accelerating change.

They found three types of organisational model in operation:

- the multinational model, exemplified by Philips or Unilever—a decentralised federation of local firms held together by posting key people from the centre
- the global model, exemplified by Ford and Matsushita—benefiting from large-scale economies and conduits into new market opportunities
- a more widespread international model—focusing on technology and the transfer of knowledge to less advanced environments

They concluded that a fourth model was necessary—the transnational—which would combine all the elements of the other three and, in addition, exploit local know-how as the key weapon in identifying opportunities, and not operate overseas sites as outposts of the centre.

Efficiency versus economic progress

To understand why the old models no longer worked, Ghoshal examined Alfred Sloan's General Motors, the pioneer of the three Ss (Strategy—Structure—Systems), emulated by other companies for decades.

The three Ss were designed to make the management of complex organisations systematic and predictable. The top people in the organisation crafted the strategy, then designed the structure that enabled it to unfold and the systems that made it operational. The information systems they relied on dealt with facts and reduced the human element to a minimum. Employees on Ford's assembly lines, for example, were viewed as replaceable parts; ITT, under Harold Geneen, abolished the possibility of surprise by constantly establishing 'unshakeable facts'.

For years, this systematic approach worked. It started to break down only in the 1980s, when converging technologies, fluctuating markets, overnight competition, and technological innovation combined to make its control systems cumbersome, unresponsive, and ultimately a risk to the survival of the organisation itself. An article by Ghoshal, Christopher Bartlett, and Peter Moran in the *Sloan Management Review*, Spring 1999 ('A new manifesto for management', pp. 9–20) pointed out that criticisms of these systems for stifling initiative, creativity, and diversity were valid: 'They were designed for an organisation man who has turned out to be an evolutionary dead end.' (p. 11)

In the same article, the authors implicitly attacked Michael Porter's work. Porter had influenced strategic thinking for over a decade by arguing that organisations must beat the competition by gaining a stranglehold on value, that is, by either reducing competitors' value (perhaps through competitive incremental cost or quality improvements) or buying them out. Ghoshal wrote: 'Porter's theory is static in that it focuses strategic thinking on getting the largest possible share of a fixed economic pie.' (p. 12) For Ghoshal, companies exist not to appropriate value, but to create it—and they get themselves into a position to be able to create value by 'changing the smell of the place'.

Fontainebleau and Calcutta: the 'springtime theory'

Ghoshal developed his 'springtime theory' while teaching business policy at INSEAD in the forest of Fontainebleau, south of Paris. During a summer visit to his home city of Calcutta, he found the humidity oppressive and draining, and likened this to the stultifying atmosphere in control- and system-oriented corporate climates. Later, walking in the woods at Fontainebleau, he realised that the fresh, energising forest reminded him of the cultural atmosphere of more open and dynamic organisations. From this, he went on to propound his 'springtime theory', arguing that managers and approaches to management strongly affect cultures and can create or change the organisational context, 'the smell of the place'. But how?

The three Ps

Ghoshal considers that today's leading companies are built around the 'three Ps': Purpose, Process, and People. In an interview in *Management Skills and Development*, he claimed that, as shapers of purpose, senior managers need 'to create a shared ambition among their staff, instil organisational values, and provide personal meaning for the work their staff do'. Creating that shared ambition is an active management process that challenges poor performance, establishes a common goal, demonstrates managers' commitment and self-discipline, and provides 'meaning for everyone's efforts'. (p. 40)

In the same interview, Ghoshal also stresses the need for organisations to:

- start thinking outside the 'strategic planning' box and examining how they actually learn
- complement vertical information flows with horizontal personal relationships
- build a trust-based culture by spreading a message of genuine openness
- share all the information that has traditionally been a source of power

He says: 'You cannot have faith in people unless you take action to improve and develop them. The success of businesses depends now more than ever on the talent of people working for them.' (p. 39) In short, organisations need to forge a 'new moral contract' with their people.

The new moral contract

In the past, the contract between organisations and employees promised relative security in return for conformity. In the 1980s and 1990s, however, this changed: job security was undermined by downsizing and re-engineering, while managerial approaches such as total quality management and customer focus demanded more involvement and initiative from employees. The new contract Ghoshal proposes is based on developing employability, and providing challenging jobs rather than functional boxes. It should be viewed neither as altruism on the company's part nor as something imposed on employees. It is, rather, a new management philosophy that recognises that personal development both improves employees' performance and makes them more employable in their future working lives, and that market performance stems from the initiative, creativity, and skills of all employees, and not just the wisdom of senior management.

Such a contract involves a great leap for both organisations and employees. Employers must create a working environment with opportunities for personal and professional growth, within a management environment in which it is understood that talented, growing people mean talented, growing organisations. Employees must make greater commitment to continuous learning and development, and accept that, in a climate of constant change and uncertainty, the will to develop is the only hedge against a changing job market.

Companies as value creators

Ghoshal feels strongly that organisations must stop focusing on squeezing out every last cost saving, waste reduction, or improvement in quality or efficiency. That may seem like the ultimate goal of TQM and continuous improvement, but organisations with that sole aim are only good at improving existing activities. Their emphasis is wholly on conservation, which, as Ghoshal points out, Jack Welch of GE described as a 'ticket to the boneyard'.

The main message of Ghoshal and Bartlett's more recent book, *The Individualized Corporation* (1998), is that the key to competitive advantage in a turbulent economy is a company's ability to innovate its way out of relentless market pressures. As companies shift emphasis from acquiring value to creating it, managers should shift their focus away from obedience, control, and conformity to initiative, relationship building, and continuous challenge of the status quo. Instead of being cogs in a system, they should become facilitators and people developers, drawing creativity from others.

In an interview published in the *Professional Manager*, Ghoshal points out that the modern world has brought about an enormous improvement in the quality of our lives and that this improvement—this value—has been created by business. Politicians create the context; they do not, in Ghoshal's view, create value: this comes from companies and managers. From this perspective, management is the most important social profession today; the wealth of the nation depends on it: 'The quality of BT's management matters, perhaps matters more than a quarter per cent change in interest rates, because it creates value. If BT, ICI, or Marks and Spencer are poorly managed...the UK loses, because these institutions are the engines of the country's progress. The most important source of a nation's progress is the quality of its management.' ('Professor of the spring strategy', *Professional Manager*, May 2000, pp. 20–23)

CONTEXT AND CONCLUSIONS

In the 10 years or so since Ghoshal came to prominence, his focus has shifted from international strategy to the importance of putting people, creativity, and innovation at the top of the agenda and of emphasizing high-quality management as a social and moral value-creating force.

It will be interesting to see where the 'smell in the air' takes him next, especially in the light of a 1999 article in the *Financial Times* ('Guru with a teaching mission for his country', 12 April, p. 14) in which he describes his plans to open a new business school for India.

THE BEST SOURCES OF HELP
Books:
Bartlett, Christopher, and Sumantra Ghoshal. *Managing Across Borders*. 2nd ed. London: Hutchinson Business, 1989.
Bartlett, Christopher, and Sumantra Ghoshal. *The Individualized Corporation: A Fundamentally New Approach to Management*. London: Heinemann. 1998
Journal Articles:
Bartlett, Christopher, and Sumantra Ghoshal. 'Changing the role of top management: beyond strategy to purpose.' *Harvard Business Review*, Nov./Dec., 1994, pp. 79–88.
Bartlett, Christopher, and Sumantra Ghoshal. 'Changing the role of top management: beyond structure to processes.' *Harvard Business Review*, Jan./Feb., 1995, pp. 86–96.
Bartlett, Christopher, and Sumantra Ghoshal. 'Changing the role of top management: beyond systems to people.' *Harvard Business Review*, May/Jun., 1995, pp. 132–142.

FRANK AND LILLIAN GILBRETH

1868	Frank born.
1878	Lillian born.
1885	Frank develops theory of work simplification.
1895	Frank founds engineering consulting company, Gilbreth Inc.
1890s	Frank founds Society to Promote the Science of Management, in conjunction with F.W. Taylor.
1904	Frank and Lillian marry; go on to produce 12 children.
1912–1913	Lillian's book, *Psychology in the Workplace*, published in instalments by the Society of Industrial Engineers.
1915	Lillian awarded a PhD in applied management by Brown University.
1921	Lillian becomes first woman member of the Society of Industrial Engineers; later becomes first woman member of the American Society of Mechanical Engineers.
1924	Frank dies. Lillian presents a paper of his at the International Management Conference in Prague.
1925	Lillian continues the work of Gilbreth Inc., conducting seminars on motion study and accepting consulting jobs.
1972	Lillian dies, having been the first and, to date, only female recipient of the Gilbreth Medal, the Gantt Gold Medal, and the CIOS Gold Medal.
1995	Lillian included in the National Women's Hall of Fame in the United States.

> **SUMMARY**
>
> Management practitioners today largely ignore the Gilbreths, possibly because the principles pioneered by them are now unfashionable. Motion study entailed the detailed examination of the movements individual workers made in their work. However through Frank's concerns that the efficiency of employees should be balanced by economy of effort and minimisation of stress, and Lillian's interest in the psychology of management, they laid the foundations for the modern concepts of job simplification, meaningful work standards, and incentive wage plans.

LIFE AND CAREER

Frank Gilbreth (1868–1924) began his career as a bricklayer and, by the age of 27, had worked his way up through the profession to found his own engineering consulting company, Gilbreth Inc. He had a particular interest in the development of people to their fullest potential through training, work methods, and improving the working environment and tools, as well as through the creation of healthier working conditions. An adherent to the principles of scientific management, Frank was one of the first to find practical applications for it. Although he had disagreements with F.W. Taylor (mostly through Taylor's claiming Frank's work as his own, and then implying that it was nothing new), Frank was an advocate of Taylor's methods and founded the Society to Promote the Science of Management (renamed the Taylor Society after Taylor's death).

Frank and Lillian married in 1904, and were the parents of 12 children (one daughter died of diphtheria, aged five). Frank apparently informed Lillian that he wanted six sons and six daughters. In an interview with the *New York Post* in 1941, Lillian was quoted as having once asked him, 'How on earth could anybody have

12 children and continue a career?' To which Frank had replied, 'We teach management, so we'll have to practise it.'

Lillian Moller Gilbreth (1878–1972) was an inspirational woman. In what was very much a man's world at the time—particularly in the area of engineering consulting work, which she entered with Frank—Lillian achieved an astounding amount. When she completed a thesis on the psychology of management, the University of California refused to award her a doctorate unless she returned to campus for a year's residency. This was impractical, so the family moved to the East Coast, where Lillian undertook a PhD in applied management at Brown University, writing a new thesis, entitled 'Some aspects of eliminating waste in teaching'. Her PhD was finally awarded in 1915.

Lillian worked closely with Frank in Gilbreth Inc., as well as running their household and bringing up their children. Within a few days of Frank's death in 1924, she travelled to Europe to present a paper that he had intended to give at the International Management Conference in Prague. As Frank's widow, Lillian continued the work of Gilbreth Inc. by conducting seminars on motion study and accepting any consulting jobs that she was not barred from taking simply because she was female.

Often called 'the first lady of management', Lillian became the first woman member of both the Society of Industrial Engineers (1921) and the American Society of Mechanical Engineers. She was also the first and, to date, the only female recipient of the Gilbreth Medal, the Gantt Gold Medal, and the CIOS Gold Medal. In 1995, Lillian Gilbreth was included in the National Women's Hall of Fame in the United States.

CONTRIBUTION
Work simplification
Work simplification was based on respect for the dignity of people and work, and was developed by Frank Gilbreth from the age of 17, when he began work as a bricklayer. He documented the different ways that individuals laid bricks and from these observations determined the most efficient way to carry out this task. For Frank, efficiency was of benefit both to the employer through an increase in the number of bricks laid, and to the employee, through minimising the levels of exertion required, and so reducing tiredness and the risk of injury. Through his extensive analysis, Frank pioneered a new system of laying bricks that increased output per worker from 1,000 to 2,700 bricks per day.

Another application of Frank's efficiency studies can be seen in operating theatres in hospitals around the world today. Prior to the efficiency study he carried out, surgeons would find all the instruments they needed for operations for themselves, wasting precious minutes as the patient lay on the table. Frank introduced the procedure of a nurse assisting the surgeon by passing instruments into an open hand, as they were required.

Frank took his efficiency systems very seriously, even at home. In *Cheaper by the Dozen*, it is stated that he used two shaving brushes to lather his face in order to save 17 seconds on his shaving time. He abandoned attempts to shave with two razors however: while it saved 44 seconds in shaving time, he also had to spend an extra two minutes bandaging his cuts.

Neither were the Gilbreths' children exempt from their parents' efficiency methods. They were all given their own tasks and became individually responsible for duties such as buying the family's birthday presents, or being chairperson of the house budget committee.

Therbligs
In their study of hand movements, the Gilbreths found that terms such as 'move hand' were too general to allow detailed analysis. They split hand movements into 17 basic units of motion that could then, through various combinations, form the hand movements being monitored. These units were known collectively as 'therbligs'—Gilbreth spelled backwards, with the 'th' transposed.

Microchronometer
In the course of their motion study work, the Gilbreths used photographs to record and then analyse workers' movements. To aid in the clear analysis of their films, they developed the microchronometer—a clock that could record time to 1/2000 of a second—which was placed in the area being photographed. This device is still sometimes used today.

Process and flow charts
Around the time that the Gilbreths began working, Henry Gantt developed the ideas that grew into what came to be known as the Gantt chart—a system of recording the planning and controlling of work in progress. Frank and Lillian used a Gantt chart in their work and, in their turn, added process charts and flow diagrams. These new tools graphically demonstrated the constituent parts that need to be carried out to complete a task.

Psychology of management and personnel issues
The importance of employee welfare was reflected throughout the work of both the Gilbreths, ranging from Frank's concern over the minimisation of employee fatigue and stress to their mutual interest in incentives, promotion, and employee welfare. Although not the originator of the discipline of industrial psychology, Lillian's research for her doctoral thesis raised awareness of the importance of the human element in industry. Many publishers refused to publish a book by a woman on such a technical subject, but *Psychology in the Workplace* was eventually published in instalments by the Society of Industrial Engineers between 1912 and 1913. The Gilbreths' interest in industrial psychology continued throughout their lives and was demonstrated by Lillian's participation in various US government committees, on subjects ranging from unemployment and war production to problems related to ageing and disability.

CONTEXT AND CONCLUSIONS
The Gilbreths are largely unknown and uncelebrated in today's modern corporate world, which tends to minimise the importance of measurement minutiae and favours the space and thinking time needed for creativity and innovation. Earlier in the 20th century, however, management writers from the 1940s on, such as Lyndall Urwick and Edward Brech, had lionised the Gilbreths, along with Taylor and Fayol, as scientific management became the popular gospel.

As we move into the 21st century, any glory for original time and motion work is largely assigned to Taylor, and the work of the Gilbreths is often forgotten or ignored. As the human relations school of management gained in momentum, with the Hawthorne studies and the work of motivational theorists such as McGregor, Maslow, Likert, and Herzberg, people rather than processes slowly became the central pivot for many management thinkers.

The overwhelming influence of scientific management faded from the 1960s onwards. The work of the Gilbreths, however, combining the disciplines of both motion study and industrial psychology, deserves to be recognised for its lasting contribution to management thought, and to the ways in which we work today.

THE BEST SOURCES OF HELP
Books:
Gilbreth Jr, Frank, and Ernestine Gilbreth Carey. *Cheaper by the Dozen*. New ed. New York: Yearling, 2000.

Spriegel, William, and Clark E. Myers eds. *Writings of the Gilbreths* (A compendium of various books and papers by the Gilbreths including: *Field System, Concrete System, Bricklaying System, Primer of Scientific Management, Motion Study, Applied Motion Study, Motion Study for the Handicapped, Fatigue Study, Psychology of Management*). Homewood, Illinois: Richard Irwin, 1953.

Wren, Daniel. *Evolution of Management Thought*. 3rd ed. New York: John Wiley, 1987.

Yost, Edna. *Frank and Lillian Gilbreth: Partners for Life*. New York: American Society of Mechanical Engineers, 1949.

DANIEL GOLEMAN

1946	Born.
1984	Joins editorial staff of *New York Times*.
1995	Publication of *Emotional Intelligence*.
1997	Founds Consortium for Research on Emotional Intelligence at Rutgers University.
1998	Publication of *Working with Emotional Intelligence*.

> **SUMMARY**
>
> Daniel Goleman is usually credited with challenging the traditional view of the IQ (intelligence quotient) by drawing together research on how the brain works and developing this to promote and popularise the concept of emotional intelligence. In *Working with Emotional Intelligence* (1998), Goleman defined emotional intelligence as a capacity for recognising our own and others' feelings, for motivating ourselves, and for managing our emotions, both within ourselves and in our relationships.

LIFE AND CAREER

Goleman, born in 1946, gained his PhD in psychology from Harvard, where he also taught. His best-selling book, *Emotional Intelligence: Why It Matters More Than IQ*, was published in 1995, and in 1998 this was followed by *Working with Emotional Intelligence*. Goleman has frequently written for the *New York Times* on behavioural science, and currently acts as the chief executive of Emotional Intelligence Services in Sudbury, Massachusetts, which is affiliated with the Hay Group and offers courses in training and assessment for emotional intelligence. Goleman is also co-chairman of the Consortium for Research on Emotional Intelligence, based at Rutgers University.

Goleman's interest in EI arose from a realisation that a high IQ is not necessarily a prerequisite for having a successful life. In *Emotional Intelligence* he identifies many people who, while brilliant academically, were nevertheless failures socially or in corporate life. Conversely, he identifies others who were not well qualified or distinguished in academic terms, but were still highly successful in terms of their lives and business achievements. Goleman went on to relate business acumen to emotional intelligence. In *Working with Emotional Intelligence* he later identified 25 EI competencies, or surface behaviours, and discussed how high emotional intelligence can make all the difference between success and failure.

CONTRIBUTION

Emotional intelligence and the brain

In *Emotional Intelligence*, Goleman describes how the evolution of the brain has implications for our emotions and behavioural responses. He outlines how, during its evolution over millions of years, the brain has now come to comprise three main areas.

- The brain stem is situated at the base of the brain and at the top of the spinal cord. It controls bodily functions and instinctive survival responses, and is the most primitive part of the brain.
- The hippocampus evolved after the brainstem and is situated just above it. It includes the amygdala region, the importance of which was identified by Joseph LeDoux during the 1980s. Here, the brain stores emotional, survival-linked responses to visual and other inputs. The amygdala seems able to 'hijack' the brain in some circumstances, taking over people's reactions literally before they have had time to think, and provoking an

immediate response to a situation. Mammals or human beings who have had their amygdala removed show no signs of emotional feeling at all. The amygdala can catalyse the sort of impulsive actions that may sometimes overpower rational thought and the capacity for considered reactions.
- The neo-cortex is the large, well-developed, top region of the brain which comprises the centre for our thinking, memory, and reasoning functions.

Because of this course of evolution, our emotions and thinking intelligence—the two main functions of the brain regulating our behaviour—are situated in separate areas. Furthermore, our emotional centres receive 'input' before our thinking centres, and can react very quickly and very strongly in some situations. The results of this for human behaviour can be catastrophic in that, unless we are aware of the situation and practised in controlling our initial feelings, we may allow inappropriate emotional responses to pre-empt behaviour based on consideration of more appropriate options. Our emotions have a 'wisdom' of their own that we should learn to use more, particularly in terms of the intuitive sense they offer. Yet, when people confront stimuli that prompt, for example, extreme fear, anger, or frustration, their first impulse to active response comes from the amygdala. Unless intelligent control is exerted, the brain moves into survival mode, stimulating instinctive actions that, while possibly right for the situation, are not rationally considered, and may be very wrong.

Today, we usually have no need to fight or run away from dangers of the sort faced by prehistoric people. While some instinctive reactions may be wise in given circumstances, we need to be aware of how the primitive response in the brain's emotional centre precedes all rational evaluation and response. Emotional intelligence is largely about understanding this and making use of our EI, while also controlling our responses to take account of it.

Goleman's framework of emotional intelligence

Goleman developed a framework to explain emotional intelligence in terms of five elements he described as self-awareness, self-regulation, motivation, empathy, and social skills. Each of these elements has distinctive characteristics, as outlined below.

- *Self-awareness*: examining how your emotions affect your performance; using your values to guide decision-making; looking at your strengths and weaknesses and learning from your experiences (self-assessment); and being self-confident and certain about your capabilities, values, and goals.
- *Self-regulation*: controlling your temper; controlling your stress by being more positive and action-centred; retaining composure and the ability to think clearly under pressure; handling impulses well; and nurturing trustworthiness and self-restraint.
- *Motivation*: enjoying challenge and stimulation; seeking out achievement; commitment; ability to take the initiative; optimism; and being guided by personal preferences in choosing goals.
- *Empathy*: the ability to see other people's points of view; behaving openly and honestly; avoiding the tendency to stereotype others; and being culturally aware.
- *Social skills*: the use of influencing skills such as persuasion; good communication with others, including employees; listening skills; negotiation; co-operation; dispute resolution; ability to inspire and lead others; capacity to initiate and manage change; and ability to deal with others' emotions—particularly group emotions.

Daniel Goleman

Goleman claims that people who demonstrate these characteristics are more likely to be successful in senior management, citing research from various sources that suggests senior managers with a higher emotional intelligence rating perform better than those without. He gives several anecdotal case studies to illustrate ways in which emotional intelligence can make a real impact in the workplace.

The Emotional Competence Inventory

Goleman believes that emotional intelligence can be developed over a period of time and he developed an Emotional Competence Inventory (ECI), in association with the Hay Group, to use in assessing and developing EQ competencies at work. The ECI reduces the original five components of emotional intelligence to four:

1. Self-awareness
- being aware of your emotions and their significance
- having a realistic knowledge of your strengths and weaknesses
- having confidence in yourself and your capacities

2. Self-management
- controlling your emotions
- being honest and trustworthy
- being flexible and dedicated

3. Social competence
- being empathic, being able to perceive another's thoughts and points of view
- being aware of and sensing a group's dynamics and inter-relationships
- focusing on others' needs, particularly when they are customers

4. Social skills
- helping others to develop themselves
- effective leadership
- skill in influencing others
- excellent interpersonal communication skills
- change-management skills
- ability to resolve arguments and discord
- ability to nourish and build good relationships
- team-player skills

Leadership styles

Goleman, in association with Hay/McBer, has more recently been involved in researching leadership styles, as he reported in a 2000 *Harvard Business Review* article. On the basis of findings with 3,781 executive participants, the research suggests that leaders gain the best results by using a combination of six leadership styles, each of which has a central characteristic feature and uses different components of emotional intelligence.

- *Coercive leaders*—demand instant obedience. Coercive leaders are self-motivated, initiate change, and are driven to succeed.
- *Authoritative leaders*—energise people towards a goal. Authoritative leaders initiate change and are empathetic.

- *Affliliative leaders*—build relationships. Affiliative leaders are empathic and have good communication skills.
- *Democratic leaders*—actively encourage team involvement in decision-making. Democratic leaders are good at communication, listening, and negotiation.
- *Pacesetting leaders*—set high standards of performance. Pacesetting leaders use their initiative, and are self-motivated and driven to succeed.
- *Coaching leaders*—expand and develop people's skills. Coaching leaders have the ability to listen well, communicate effectively, and motivate others.

The research evidence suggests that the six leadership styles identified are each appropriate for different types of situations, and also that leadership styles have a direct influence on the working atmosphere of an organisation, which, in turn, influences financial results.

CONTEXT AND CONCLUSIONS

The conviction that success depends to a high degree on interpersonal skills is not new, and Goleman has often been criticised for taking others' ideas, to some extent, and repackaging them as a new concept. Goleman himself, however, freely discusses the origins of his ideas, and acknowledges fellow academics when he uses their work.

A critical article by Charles Woodruffe in 2001 reviewed Goleman's version of EI, and suggested that:

- Goleman contradicts himself in claiming that emotional intelligence is inherent and biologically based, yet is a skill that can be learned and developed
- the self-report measures of emotional intelligence used by Goleman have considerable limitations, particularly in terms of accuracy
- the EI behaviours or competencies put forward by Goleman, such as self-confidence and leadership, are not at all new, and are factors that have often been recognised as commonly associated with high achievement levels

Whatever truth there might be in these criticisms, Goleman has certainly promoted management thinking on the subject of EI. He has taken some quite complex ideas relating to human behaviour and biological evolution, and put these into a more simple and comprehensible format that, under the label of 'emotional intelligence', is easy to understand. As a result, many people have found his core proposition, that we can use intelligence to better manage our emotions and draw on our emotional intuition to guide our thinking, to be a helpful approach in both their lives and their work.

THE BEST SOURCES OF HELP
Books:
Goleman, Daniel. *Emotional Intelligence: Why It Can Matter More Than IQ.* London: Bloomsbury, 1995.
Goleman, Daniel. *Working with Emotional Intelligence.* London: Bloomsbury, 1998.
Journal Articles:
Goleman, Daniel. 'Leadership that gets results.' *Harvard Business Review*, vol. 78 no. 2, Mar./Apr. 2000, pp. 78–90.
Woodruffe, Charles. 'Promotional intelligence.' *People Management*, vol. 7, no. 1, 2000, pp. 26–29.

GARY HAMEL

1954	Born.
1980	Gains a PhD in international business from the University of Michigan, where he meets C.K. Prahalad.
1983	Starts teaching at the London Business School.
1990s	Comes to prominence through journal articles containing revolutionary views on strategy.
1994	Co-writes *Competing for the Future* with C.K. Prahalad.
1995	Sets up Strategos Inc with C.K. Prahalad; is currently chairman.
Present	Visiting professor in strategic and international management at London Business School; research fellow at Harvard Business School.

SUMMARY

Professor Gary Hamel (1954–) is one of the most respected contributors to the debate on strategy of the late 20th century. His fresh and often hard-hitting approach to organisational innovation has brought wide acknowledgment from academics and practitioners alike. His reputation developed from the early 1990s, when, with C.K. Prahalad, he began to communicate his revolutionary views on strategy, in the process creating the concepts of organisational core competencies, strategic intent, and strategic architecture.

LIFE AND CAREER

Hamel worked as a hospital administrator until 1978, when he began to study for a PhD in international business at the University of Michigan. While there, he met C.K. Prahalad, who later became his mentor, collaborator, and colleague in research, writing, and business. Hamel first came to prominence through journal articles in the early 1990s, and as the coauthor of the 1994 book *Competing for the Future*, written (like most of the articles) with Prahalad.

Now at the forefront of thinking on strategy, Hamel is visiting professor in strategic and international management at the London Business School, distinguished research fellow at Harvard Business School, and chairman of Strategos Inc., the strategy services company he set up with Prahalad in 1995.

CONTRIBUTION

Why a new approach to strategy?

At the beginning of the 1980s, Hamel argues, organisational development was no longer driven by strategic forces but by incrementalism. Companies were concerned with getting bigger and better through downsizing, delayering, re-engineering, and continuous quality improvement, and their goal became to mimic best practice. The result of all these incremental improvements was to squeeze cost efficiencies to the point where there was nothing left to gain.

At the same time, there were various new forces at work that were changing the nature of competition and the base of traditional industries that had enjoyed primacy in the past. These forces included:

- deregulation and privatisation, particularly in the airline, telecommunications, and financial services sectors
- blurring, fragmentation, and an increase in newcomers to the computer and telecommunications industries

- changing customer expectations, in terms of price, quality, and service
- continuous technological growth, particularly with the Internet
- shifting boundaries of control and authority, as workforces became more widely distributed, more empowered, and less layered
- changes in traditional loyalties, as people became simultaneously the most valuable, but also the most expendable, asset
- the lowered value of experience, as change undermined its relevance for the future

Strategic questions to address

Hamel argues that a compelling view of the future is necessary if one is not to be tied to the orthodoxies of the past, and highlights the number of companies that lost money because they stuck too long to the same game instead of trying to get ahead. Although no view of the future can be accurate or perfect, a view of some sort is essential. This can be developed through addressing questions about the possibility of unleashing the corporate imagination, turning technicians into dreamers, turning planners into strategists, and creating an organisation that really lives and makes its decisions in the future.

In a 1996 article Hamel states that, while we can all recognise a great strategy once it is proved to be successful in action, we find it difficult to generate a great strategy in the first place. He argues that strategy generation is not a purely analytical process, but is multi-faceted and involves risk, gut feelings, intuition, and emotion, as well as analysis. ('Competing in the new economy: managing out of bounds', with C.K. Prahalad, *Strategic Management Journal*, vol. 17, pp. 237–242.)

Strategy as core competence

The concept of corporate competencies was highlighted by Hamel and Prahalad in journal articles and in the book *Competing for the Future*. In the latter they argued that, for too long, organisational focus had been on returns from individual business units, as opposed to the conditions, processes, and competencies that enabled those returns. They define 'core competencies' as the collective learning in the organisation and, especially, the coordination of diverse production skills and integration of multiple streams of technologies.

Hamel and Prahalad ask organisations to look upon themselves as portfolios of core competencies by analysing what it is that they do better than others. Viewing the organisation as systems of activities and building blocks means asking:

- How does activity X significantly improve the end product for the customer?
- Does activity X offer access to a range of applications and markets?
- What would happen to our competitiveness if we lost our strength in activity X?
- How difficult is it for others to imitate activity X and compete with us?

In order to realise the potential that core competencies create, the organisation's people must have the imagination to visualise new markets and the ability to move into them, ahead of the competition. One of the keys to core competencies and effective competition is, therefore, the process through which an organisation releases corporate imagination. And one of the words that recurs increasingly through Hamel's writing is 'revolution'.

Gary Hamel

Strategy as revolution

In a seminal article, 'Strategy as revolution' (*Harvard Business Review*, Jul./Aug. 1996, pp. 69–82), Hamel sets out 10 principles that strategy generators should bear in mind.

- Strategic planning is not strategic: rather, it is a calendar-driven ritual involving plans and sub-plans, instead of something challenging and innovative that might lead to discovery.
- Strategy making should be subversive: great strategies come from challenging the status quo and doing something different. Anita Roddick, founder of the highly innovative Body Shop, is quoted as saying, 'I watch where the cosmetics industry is going and then walk in the opposite direction.'
- The bottleneck is at the top of the bottle: the most powerful defenders of strategic orthodoxy are senior management, and strategy making needs to be freed from the tyranny of their experience.
- Revolutionaries exist in every company: let everyone have their voice, so that new and young as well as tried and tested contributors are part of strategy making.
- Change is not the problem—engagement is: people will support change and welcome the responsibility for engendering it, if this gives them some control over their own future.
- Strategy making must be democratic: the capability for strategic thinking is not limited to senior people, and it is impossible to predict where a good, revolutionary idea may be lurking.
- Anyone can be a strategy activist: people who care about their organisation do not wait for permission to act.
- Perspective is worth 50 IQ points: subversive strategy means gaining a new perspective on the world, and looking at potential markets through new eyes.
- Top-down and bottom-up are not alternatives: if top-down can achieve unity of purpose among the few involved, bottom-up will bring diversity of perspective. Bring the two together.
- You can't see the end from the beginning: surprises do not appeal to everyone, but delving into discontinuities and identifying potential competencies will bring about unpredictable outcomes. These will probably not fit the orthodox strategic mould—but strategy making is about letting go.

So how do we begin to put these principles into a framework for creating strategy as a systemic capability?

Creating strategy

'Strategy innovation is the only way for newcomers to succeed in the face of enormous resource disadvantages, and the only way for incumbents to renew their lease on success.' ('Strategy innovation and the quest for value', *Sloan Management Review*, Winter 1998, pp. 7–14)

While some strategies result from analysis and others from inspiration and vision, many strategies also evolve and emerge. To achieve strategies that are neither too random nor too ordered or ritualistic, Hamel suggests we look to the roots of strategy creation, which he regards as a relatively simple phenomenon amid the complexity of organisational life. In 'Strategy, innovation and the quest for value' (cited above), Hamel turns his revolutionary principles into action points, and urges organisations to adopt a new stance through:

- new voices—top management relinquishing its hold on strategy and introducing newcomers; young people and people from different groups bring richness and diversity to strategy formulation
- new conversations—the same people discussing the same issues over and over again leads to sterility; new opportunities arise from juxtaposing formerly isolated people
- new passions—people will go for change when they can steer it and benefit from it
- new perspectives—search for new ways of looking at markets, customers, and organisational capabilities; think different, see different
- new experiments—small, low-risk experiments can accelerate the organisation's learning and will indicate what may work and what may not

CONTEXT AND CONCLUSIONS

While it is not possible to pigeonhole Hamel, we can place him roughly in the progressive (if sometimes ragged) line of strategic thinking stretching back to Chandler and Ansoff and including Porter and Mintzberg, as well as Hamel's collaborator and colleague, Prahalad. Hamel's curiosity and tendency to challenge the status quo make it difficult to predict where his future research interests may take him next. However it is likely that he will continue to move in tune with, if not ahead of, the rapidly changing business environment. For example, *Leading the Revolution* (2000), is about throwing away the old rule book, imagining a future that others have not seen, and then taking the initiative to act on it.

THE BEST SOURCES OF HELP
Books:
Hamel, Gary, and C.K. Prahalad. *Competing for the Future*. Boston: Harvard Business School Press, 1994.
Hamel, Gary, and Yves Doz. *Alliance Advantage: The Art of Creating Value Through Partnering*. Boston: Harvard Business School Press, 1998.
Hamel, Gary. *Strategic Flexibility: Managing in a Turbulent Environment*. Chichester: John Wiley, 1998.
Hamel, Gary. *Leading the Revolution*. Boston: Harvard Business School Press, 2000.
Journal Articles:
Hamel, Gary, and C.K. Prahalad. 'Strategy as stretch and leverage.' *Harvard Business Review*, Mar./Apr. 1993, pp. 75–84
Hamel, Gary, and C.K. Prahalad. 'The core competence of the corporation.' *Harvard Business Review*, May/Jun. 1990, pp. 79–91

CHARLES HANDY

1932	Born.
1967	Founder of Sloan Programme, London Business School.
1972	Professor, London Business School.
1974	Governor, London Business School.
1976	Publication of *Understanding Organizations*.
1977	Warden, St George's House, Windsor Castle.
1985	Publication of *Gods of Management*.
1989	Publication of *The Age of Unreason*.
1994	Publication of *The Empty Raincoat*.

> **SUMMARY**
>
> Charles Handy (1932–) is well known for his work on organisations. Culminating in the formation of a vision of the future of work and of the implications of change for the ways in which people manage their lives and careers, his observation of work in modern society has identified discontinuous change as the (paradoxically) continuing characteristic of working lives and organisations. He has forecast a future—so far, with a good deal of accuracy—where half of the United Kingdom's workforce will no longer be in permanent full-time jobs.

LIFE AND CAREER

Born in Ireland, Charles Handy is a self-employed writer, teacher, and broadcaster. He is a visiting professor at the London Business School and consultant to a wide range of organisations in government, business, and the voluntary and educational sectors.

After he graduated from Oxford, his working life began in the marketing and personnel divisions of Shell International and as an economist with Anglo-American Corporation. He then returned to academia at the Sloan School of Management of the Massachusetts Institute of Technology. In 1967 he was the founder and director of the Sloan Programme at the London Business School, where he also taught managerial psychology and development. Appointments as professor and governor of the School followed in 1972 and 1974 respectively. In 1977 he was appointed Warden of St George's House in Windsor Castle, a private conference and study centre with a strong focus on the discussion of business ethics. As a teacher he later concentrated on the application of behavioural science to management, the management of change, the structure of organisations, and on the theory and practice of individual learning in life.

He is a past chairman of the Royal Society of Arts; in 1994 he was Business Columnist of the Year. He has also been a regular contributor to Thought for the Day on the *Today* programme on BBC Radio 4.

CONTRIBUTION

Four of Handy's books in particular consider the structure of organisations in detail, and offer a perspective on the ways in which they work. These are: *Understanding Organizations* (1976), *Gods of Management* (1985), *The Age of Unreason* (1989), and *The Empty Raincoat* (1994).

Understanding Organizations
Handy's *Understanding Organizations*—described by publishers and commentators alike as 'a landmark study'—is equally valuable for the student of management and for the practising manager. Among the subjects with which it deals are motivation, roles and interactions, leadership, power and influence, the workings of groups, and the culture of organisations. They are dealt with both as 'concepts' and 'concepts in application'. A 'guide to further study' points the way for further examination of each concept.

Gods of Management
Handy identifies some established structures in organisations and suggests new forms that are emerging. He perceives that, currently, organisations embrace four basic 'cultures'.

- *Club Culture.* This is represented metaphorically by Zeus, the strong leader who has, likes, and uses power, and graphically by a spider's web. All lines of communication lead, formally or informally, to the leader. Such organisations display strength in the speed of their decision-making; their potential weakness lies in the calibre of the 'one-man bands' running them.
- *Role Culture.* This is personified as Apollo, the god of order and rules, represented by a Greek temple. Such organisations are based on the assumptions that people are rational, and that roles can be defined and discharged with clearly defined procedures. They display stability and certainty, and have great strength in situations marked by continuity; they often display weakness in adapting to, or generating, change.
- *Task Culture.* This is likened to Athena, the goddess of wisdom, and is found in organisations where management is concerned with solving a series of problems. The structure is represented by a net, resources being drawn from all parts of the organisation to meet the needs of current problems. Working parties, sub-committees, task forces, and study groups are formed on an ad hoc basis to deal with problems. This type of culture is seen to advantage when flexibility is required.
- *Existential Culture.* This is represented by Dionysus, the god of wine and song. Organisations characterised by a culture of this type are those that exist to serve the individual and in which individuals are not servants of the organisation. They consist of groups of professionals, for example, doctors or lawyers, with no 'boss'. Coordination may be provided by a committee of peers. Such structures are becoming more common as more conventional organisations increasingly contract out work to professionals and specialists whose services are used only as and when required.

The changing organisation
The link between this analysis of organisational structures and Handy's later work is, in part, provided by the development of 'contracting out'—one of a number of changes that he observes in the world of employment. Another major change is the basing of the quest for profit on intelligence and professional skills rather than on manual work and machines. Yet another is that the days of working for one employer and/or in one occupation may be over.

The shamrock organisation
An example of Handy's changing perception of organisations is provided by his use (in *The Age of Unreason*) of the shamrock. He uses this symbol to demonstrate three

bases on which people are often employed by organisations today. The people linked to an organisation are beginning to fall into three groups, each with different expectations of it, each managed and rewarded differently.

The first group is a core of qualified professional technicians and managers. They are essential to the continuity of the organisation, and have detailed knowledge of it, and of its aims, objectives, and practices. They are rewarded with high salaries and associated benefits, in return for which they must be prepared to give commitment, to work hard, and, if necessary, to work long hours. They must be mobile. They work within a task culture, one within which there is a constant effort to reduce their numbers.

The second group consists of contracted specialists who may be used, for example, for advertising, R&D, computing, catering, or mailing services. They operate in an existential culture; and are rewarded with fees rather than with salaries or wages. Their contribution to the organisation is measured in output rather than in hours, in results rather than in time.

The third group—the third leaf of Handy's shamrock—consists of a flexible labour force, discharging part-time, temporary, and seasonal roles. They operate within a role culture; but, Handy observes, while they may be employed on a casual basis, they must not be managed casually but in a way that recognises their worth to the organisation.

The federal organisation and the inverted doughnut

The concept of the federal organisation was first explored in *The Age of Unreason* and expanded in *The Empty Raincoat*. In it, subsidiaries federate to gain benefits of scale. Federal organisations should not be confused with decentralised organisations, in which power lies in the centre and is exerted downwards and outwards. In the federal organisation the role of top management is redefined as that of providing vision, motivating, inspiring, and coordinating; initiative comes from the components of the organisation. Handy observes and describes the principle of 'subsidiarity'—not handing out or delegating power, but ruling and unifying only with the consent and agreement of equal partners.

In *The Empty Raincoat* Handy uses the metaphor of the inverted doughnut to demonstrate how those in the subsidiaries must constantly seek to extend their roles and associated activities. The hole in the conventional doughnut is filled by the core activities of the subsidiary; the substance of the doughnut represents a diminishing vacuum into which the subsidiary can expand its activities given the necessary drive, will, and ability.

Portfolio working and downshifting

Following on from his work on organisational change, Handy studied the effects of such change on the individual. He coined the concept 'portfolio working', based on the assumption that full-time working for one employer will soon be a thing of the past. Embedded in this is the notion of downshifting—the idea that it is possible to exchange some part of income for a better quality of life.

Although Handy has gone on record as saying that more and more individuals will opt out of formal organisations and sell their services at a pace and at a price to suit themselves, he has also admitted that comparatively few may find themselves in a position to take real advantage of this. He argues, however, that there is much that the organisation can do to help the individual to get to grips with the new uncertainty. It was in discussion with the Japanese that Handy coined the 'theory of horizontal fast track'. In Japan, the most talented people are moved around from experience to experience as quickly as possible, so that their talents can be tested in different situations, with different managers and different cultures. This ensures that they discover what they are really good at and provides a lot of experience.

CONTEXT AND CONCLUSIONS
With his imaginative use of analogy and metaphor, the Handy of the 1990s moved us from the past into the future. He argues that federalist and shamrock organisations can really be successful only if businesses are prepared to invest in their workforces and build relationships of trust.

While he is as much concerned with individuals as organisations, his messages are sometimes disquieting. In *The Hungry Spirit*, he assesses the effects of the competitiveness of capitalism on the individual, suggesting that people can become not only stressed but also selfish and insensitive. But his message is not confined to pessimism about the future. On the contrary, the new capitalism consists of intellectual property—know-how, not merely physical and financial resources; the new knowledge markets enable low-cost entry to those with 'a bit of wit and a bit of imagination' and the new products of the knowledge world are not nearly so destructive on the environment as the industrial products of the past.

Handy stands apart from many other management writers by his breadth of vision, his setting of management in a wide social and economic context, and the sheer readability of his writing. He is also ready to modify his views in the light of experience and further thought (he has admitted that some of his expectations have been proved wrong). He is not merely an observer of change but increasingly a catalyst, who forces people to stand back from their daily routine, take stock, and view the future through different glasses, acknowledging change, and addressing its implications.

THE BEST SOURCES OF HELP
Books:
Handy, Charles. *Understanding Organizations*. London: Penguin Books, 1985.
Handy, Charles. *The Gods of Management*. London: Souvenir Press, 1985.
Handy, Charles. *The Age of Unreason*. London: Business Books, 1989.
Handy, Charles. *The Empty Raincoat*. London: Hutchinson, 1994.
Handy, Charles. *Beyond Certainty*. London: Hutchinson, 1995.
Handy, Charles. *The Hungry Spirit: Beyond Capitalism—A Quest for Purpose in the Modern World*. London: Hutchinson, 1997.
Handy, Charles. *The Elephant and the Flea*. London: Hutchinson, 2001.

FREDERICK HERZBERG

1923	Born.
1945	Enters Dachau concentration camp with US liberating forces.
1946	Graduates from City College of New York.
1951–1957	Research director of psychological services in Pittsburgh, Pennsylvania.
1957	Appointed professor of management at Case Western Reserve University, Cleveland, Ohio.
1959	*The Motivation to Work* published.
1966	*Work and the Nature of Man* published.
1968	'One more time: how do you motivate employees?' published in the *Harvard Business Review*.
1972	Joins University of Utah's College of Business.
2000	Dies.

> **SUMMARY**
>
> Herzberg is best known for his 'hygiene-motivation' or 'two factor' theory of what motivates workers. He invented the acronym KITA (Kick In The Ass) and also coined the term 'job enrichment' to describe a process in which positively motivating factors are built into the design of jobs. Herzberg's work focused on the individual in the workplace and the attitude of individuals to their jobs, but it also has been popular with managers as it emphasises the importance of management knowledge and expertise.

LIFE AND CAREER

Frederick Herzberg (1923–2000) was a US clinical psychologist who became an influential management thinker through his work on the nature of motivation and the most effective ways of motivating people. The 'overriding interest in mental health' that led him into a career in psychology stemmed from a belief that 'mental health is the core issue of our times', a conviction prompted by his posting, while serving in the American forces during the Second World War, to the Dachau concentration camp very soon after its liberation. On his return to America, he worked for the US Public Health Service before beginning an academic career. His 'hygiene-motivation' theory was first set out in *The Motivation to Work*, published in 1959. From 1972 until his retirement he worked at the University of Utah Business School.

CONTRIBUTION
The hygiene-motivation theory

The 'hygiene-motivation' or 'two factor' theory that made Herzberg's name grew out of research he undertook with two hundred Pittsburgh engineers and accountants in the late 1950s.

He asked his subjects to recall times when they had felt exceptionally good about their jobs; then why they had had these positive feelings, and also what effect those feelings had had both on their performance at work and on their lives outside work. In a second question, he asked them to recall times when their experiences at work had resulted in negative feelings.

Herzberg was struck by the fact that, in the answers to his questionnaire, the positive things that the respondents had to say about their work experiences were not the opposite of the negative ones. From this, he concluded that there were two factors at work.

He postulated first of all that human beings have two sets of needs:

- lower-level needs as an animal to avoid pain and deprivation
- higher-level needs as a human being to grow psychologically

These needs have to be satisfied at work as much as in any other sphere of life. He concluded from the results of his survey that some factors in the workplace meet the first set of needs but not the second, and vice versa. The former group of factors he called 'hygiene factors' and the latter, 'motivators'.

'Hygiene factors' have to do with the context or environment in which a person works. They include:

- company policy and administration
- supervision
- working relationships
- working conditions
- status
- security
- pay

The most important thing about these factors is that they do not in themselves promote job satisfaction; they serve primarily to prevent job dissatisfaction, in the same way that good hygiene does not in itself produce good health, but a lack of it will usually cause disease. Herzberg also spoke of them as 'dissatisfiers' or 'maintenance factors', because their absence or inadequacy causes dissatisfaction at work, while their presence simply keeps workers reasonably happy without motivating them to better themselves or their performance. Some factors are also not to be regarded as true motivators because they need constant reinforcement. Once introduced, they increasingly come to be regarded as rights to be expected, rather than incentives to greater satisfaction and achievement.

'Motivators' (also referred to as 'growth factors') relate to what a person does at work, rather than to the context in which it is done. They include:

- achievement
- recognition
- the work itself
- responsibility
- advancement
- growth

Herzberg explains that the two sets of factors are separate and distinct because they are concerned with two different sets of needs. They are not opposites.

Herzberg's hygiene-motivation theory is derived from the outcomes of several investigations into job satisfaction and job dissatisfaction, studies that replicated his original research in Pittsburgh. The theory proposes that most of the factors that contribute to job satisfaction are motivators, while most of the factors that contribute to job dissatisfaction are hygiene factors.

Most of the evidence on which Herzberg based his theory is relatively clear-cut. This is particularly the case with regard to achievement and promotion prospects as potential job satisfiers and with regard to supervision and job insecurity as factors that contribute principally to dissatisfaction.

The element that continues to cause some debate is salary/pay, which seems as if it might belong in either group. Herzberg himself placed salary with the dissatisfiers, although the evidence was not so clear in this instance. This would seem to be the more appropriate classification. Although pay may have some short-term motivational value, it is difficult to conceive of it as a long-term motivator of the same order as responsibility and achievement. Most experience (and the history of industrial relations) would point to pay as a dissatisfier and therefore a hygiene factor along with supervision, status, and security.

KITA
In his extremely influential 1968 article for the *Harvard Business Review*, 'One more time: how do you motivate employees?', Herzberg basically lumped all the hygiene factors together with the less pleasant aspects of work experience under the heading KITA (Kick In The Ass). To explain why managers are unable to motivate employees, he demonstrated again that employees are not motivated by being kicked (figuratively speaking), or by being given more money or benefits, or by a comfortable environment, or by reducing the time they spend at work. These things merely produce movement, the avoidance of pain. What genuinely motivates are things that are intangible, or intrinsic to the work.

Adam and Abraham
Herzberg used biblical allusions to illustrate his theory, especially in his book *Work and the Nature of Man*, first published in 1966 and intended as a psychological underpinning to his workplace-oriented studies. He depicted humanity's basic needs as two parallel arrows pointing in opposite directions. One arrow represents the 'Animal-Adam' nature of human beings, concerned with the basic need to avoid physical deprivation (the hygiene factors); the other represents their 'Human-Abraham' nature, which is driven by a need to realise their potential for perfection (the motivation factors).

Job enrichment
Job enrichment was a logical extension of Herzberg's hygiene-motivation theory. Still working on the basic premise that a satisfied workforce is a productive workforce, he proposed that motivators of the type he had always advocated should be built into job design. They included:

- self-scheduling
- control of resources
- accountability
- undertaking specialised tasks in order to become expert in them

He saw it as a continuous function of management to ensure that people were given the opportunity to become more and more responsibly and creatively involved in their jobs.

CONTEXT AND CONCLUSIONS

Herzberg's work—in common with that of Elton Mayo (known for the Hawthorne experiments), Abraham Maslow (developer of the hierarchy of needs), and Douglas McGregor (creator of Theory X and Theory Y)—can be seen as a reaction to F.W. Taylor's scientific management theories. These last focused on techniques which could be used to maximise the productivity of manual workers and on the division of mental and physical work between management and workers. In contrast, Herzberg and his contemporaries believed that workers wanted the opportunity to feel part of a team and to grow and develop.

Although Herzberg's theory is not highly regarded by psychologists today, managers have found in it useful guidelines for action. Its basic tenets are easy to understand and can be applied to all types of organisation. Furthermore, it appears to support the position and influence of management.

More specifically, it has had a considerable impact on reward systems, first, in a move away from payment-by-results systems, and today in the growing proportion of cafeteria benefits schemes, which allow individual employees to choose the fringe benefits which best suit them.

Job enrichment was more theorised about than put into practice. Many schemes that were tried resulted only in cosmetic changes or led to demands for increased worker control and were therefore terminated. Nowadays the concept is more one of people enrichment, although this still owes a great deal to Herzberg's original work. His greatest contribution has been the knowledge that motivation comes mainly from within the individual; it cannot be imposed from the outside by an organisation in accordance with some formula. Many of today's trends—career management, self-managed learning, and empowerment—have their basis in Herzberg's insights.

THE BEST SOURCES OF HELP
Books:
Herzberg, Frederick. *Work and the Nature of Man*. London: Staples Press, 1968.
Herzberg, Frederick. *The Managerial Choice: To Be Efficient and To Be Human*. Homewood, Illinois: Dow Jones-Irwin, 1976.
Herzberg, Frederick, Bernard Mausner, and Barbara Bloch Snyderman. *The Motivation to Work*. 2nd ed. New York: John Wiley, 1959.
Journal Articles:
Cameron, Donald. 'Herzberg–Still a key to understanding motivation.' *Training Officer*, Jul./Aug. 1996, pp. 184–186.
Herzberg, Frederick. 'One more time: how do you motivate employees?' *Harvard Business Review*, Jan./Feb. 1968, pp. 53–62.
(This article was republished, in *Harvard Business Review*, Sept./Oct. 1987, pp. 109–120, with a retrospective commentary by the author. By the time of this republication, the article had sold over one million reprints, making it the most requested article in the *Harvard Business Review*'s history)

GEERT HOFSTEDE

1928	Born.
1953	Graduates from Delft Institute of Technology.
1967	Receives PhD from University of Groningen.
1967–1973	Undertakes massive research project into IBM.
1980	*Culture's Consequences* published.
1991	*Culture and Organizations* published.

> **SUMMARY**
> Hofstede identified four 'dimensions' (commonly known as 'Hofstede's dimensions') for defining work-related values associated with national culture: power distance; individualism/collectivism; masculinity/femininity; and uncertainty avoidance. He also devised the 'values survey module' for use in researching cultural differences, which has been adopted by many other researchers in their work.

LIFE AND CAREER

Geert Hofstede (b. 1928) is a Dutch academic who has also spent long periods in industry, most notably at IBM. He is emeritus professor of organisational anthropology and international management at the University of Limburg in Maastricht in the Netherlands, and he founded the Institute for Research on Intercultural Cooperation. He has become known for pioneering research on national and organisational cultures. Much of his subsequent thinking was based on a monumental six-year research project in the late 1960s and early 1970s into the workings of a giant international corporation, originally known by the pseudonym HERMES and later revealed as IBM.

The management of cultural diversity is becoming a significant issue for companies of all sizes, not just multinationals. The rise of global business—leading to an increase in the number of joint ventures and cross-border partnerships, greater co-operation within the European Union, and business's need to embrace people from a variety of ethnic backgrounds and cultures, have all contributed to the need to develop cultural sensitivity. Ignorance or insensitivity in cultural matters can cause serious problems to international operations. The transfer of Western values to the East, for example, may be inappropriate, and corporate culture and management practices may need modifying to suit local conditions. Hofstede's work has provided a framework for understanding cultural differences.

CONTRIBUTION
Theory of culture

Hofstede defines culture as being collective, but often intangible. Nonetheless, it is what distinguishes one group, organisation, or nation from another. In his view, it is made up of two main elements: internal values, which are invisible, and external elements, which are more visible and are known as practices. The latter include rituals (such as greetings), heroes (a broad concept that includes not only people but also such things as television shows), and symbols (such as words and gestures). The cultures of different organisations can be distinguished from one other by their practices, while national cultures can be differentiated by their values.

Values are among the first things that are programmed into children. These are reinforced by the local environment at school and at work. It is, therefore, difficult for an individual to change them in later life, and this is the reason why expatriate workers often experience difficulties when faced with another national culture.

The dimensions of national culture

Hofstede carried out his research using a questionnaire called the 'values survey module'. From the results, he drew up indices that reflected the national cultural characteristics or dimensions of a country. (All the quotations in this section are taken from Hofstede's *Cultures and Organizations*, 1991.)

Power distance — how a society handles inequalities

Power distance is defined by Hofstede as 'the extent to which the less powerful members of institutions and organisations within a country expect and accept that power is distributed unequally'.

In nations with a low power distance, such as the United Kingdom, inequalities among people will tend to be minimised, decentralisation of activities is more likely, subordinates will expect to be consulted by superiors, and privileges and status symbols are less evident. In high-power-distance nations, conversely, inequalities among people are considered desirable, there is greater reliance by the less powerful on those who hold power, centralisation is more normal, and subordinates are likely to be separated from their bosses by wide differentials in salary, privileges, and status symbols.

Individualism/collectivism: behaviour towards the group

'Individualism pertains to societies in which the ties between individuals are loose: everyone is expected to look after himself or herself and his or her immediate family. Collectivism as its opposite pertains to societies in which people from birth onwards are integrated into strong, cohesive in-groups, which throughout people's lifetime continue to protect them in exchange for unquestioning loyalty.'

In some societies, people need to belong to a group and have a loyalty to the group. Children learn to say 'we'. This is true of countries such as Japan, India, and China. In other societies, such as in the United Kingdom, individualism is more important, and there is a lower emphasis on loyalty and protection. Children learn to say 'I'. In strong collectivist countries, there tend to be greater expectations of the employer's obligations towards the employee and his or her family.

Masculinity/femininity: behaviour according to gender

'Masculinity pertains to societies in which social gender roles are clearly distinct; femininity pertains to societies in which social gender roles overlap.'

In a masculine society (Hofstede gives the United Kingdom as an example), there is a division of labour in which the more assertive tasks are given to men. There is a stress on academic success, competition, and achievement in careers. In a feminine society such as France (according to Hofstede), there is a stress on relationships, compromise, life skills, and social performance.

The last 10 to 15 years have seen enormous changes—a 'feminisation' process—in the behaviour of Western democracies. It has also been said that the emergence of developing countries is as much about feminisation as it is about dealing with harder business and economic realities.

Uncertainty avoidance: the need for structure
Uncertainty is 'the extent to which the members of a culture feel threatened by uncertain or unknown situations'.

In some societies there is a pronounced need for structure. This is because those societies tend to fear the unknown and to possess a high degree of uncertainty. Countries characterised by a low level of uncertainty (such as the United Kingdom) do not perceive something different to be dangerous, whereas, in strong uncertainty-avoidance societies, people will seek to reduce their exposure to the unknown and limit risk by imposing rules and systems to bring about order and coherence. The same thing can be seen in organisations: for example, where there is a need for rules and dependence there will tend to be a pyramidal organisational structure.

Dimensions in practice
Hofstede is keen to emphasise that his 'dimensions' are not a prescription or formula but merely a concept or framework. They equip us with an analytical tool to help us understand intercultural differences, and a very useful one now that, with the rise of global business, many people are working with, or managing, individuals and groups from cultures other than their own. Multinational companies, for instance, building international teams, can make use of Hofstede's framework to make sense of the cultural differences they encounter in their practical experience. Knowing about such differences can help to avoid conflict in international management. Using the framework shows that it is always not safe to assume that apparently similar countries in the same region, for example Holland and Belgium or Austria and Hungary, have similar cultures.

The dimensions also provide us with a convenient shorthand method of defining the cultural characteristics of a particular organisation or country. For example, if someone refers to a country as having a 'high feminine index', it suggests that its inhabitants characteristically value having a good working relationship with their supervisor and with their co-workers, living somewhere they and their family want to live, and having job security.

CONTEXT AND CONCLUSIONS
Hofstede's theory has been extensively validated, although the point needs to be made that cultures change and the specific country examples that Hofstede used in the past may no longer be valid today. His framework has been used by other researchers to determine the suitability of certain management techniques for various countries or to make comparisons between countries to understand cultural differences in various areas of management. Mo Yuet-Ha used Hofstede's framework to assess the cultural differences and similarities between East Asian countries. The findings were then used to underpin the understanding of competency-based behaviours in these countries.

Hofstede's original research focused on middle-class workers. Other writers have extended his work by looking at different groups of workers and different countries. Michael Bond took Hofstede's work into Hong Kong and Taiwan, using a Chinese values module devised by Chinese social scientists to test whether Hofstede's work was conditioned by his Western outlook and methods. The cultural dimensions were confirmed, except that of uncertainty avoidance, which may be a theory applicable only to the West. (Other researchers have also cast doubt on this dimension, suggesting that it may have been merely a product of the time at which Hofstede did his original research and may not be as relevant today.) Bond's work led to the discovery of a fifth dimension, long-term/short-term orientation. This dimension measures the extent to which a country takes a long- or short-term view of life. The long-term orientation of Confucian dynamism and thrift correlated strongly with economic growth.

Fons Trompenaars, another noted writer on cultural diversity, has carried out work that shows how national culture influences corporate culture. For Trompenaars, the major types of culture—the Family (a power-oriented culture), the Eiffel Tower (a role-oriented culture), the Guided Missile (a project-oriented culture), and the Incubator (a fulfilment-oriented culture)—are comparable with Hofstede's model. Hofstede himself has also extended his work into this area by collaborating with Henry Mintzberg, linking Mintzberg's five organisational structures with his own cultural dimensions. This link is intended to show that some organisational structures fit better in some national cultures that in others.

THE BEST SOURCES OF HELP
Books:
Hofstede, Geert. *Culture's Consequences: International Differences in Work-Related Values.* Beverly Hills: Sage, 1980.
Hofstede, Geert. *Cultures and Organizations: Software of the Mind.* London: McGraw-Hill, 1991.
Hofstede has pointed out that *Culture's Consequences* was a scholarly book, whereas *Culture and Organizations* was written for practising managers and students. The latter book revisited the basic material of the former and also included some new information.

Journal Articles:
Brown, Andrew D., and Michael Humphreys. 'International cultural differences in public sector management: Lessons from a survey of British and Egyptian technical managers.' *International Journal of Public Sector Management*, vol. 8 no. 3, 1995, pp. 5–23.
Hofstede, Geert, and M.H. Bond. 'Confucius and economic growth: new trends in culture's consequences.' *Organisational Dynamics*, vol. 16 no. 4, pp. 4–21.
Morden, Tony. 'National culture and the culture of the organisation.' *Cross-Cultural Management: An International Journal*, vol. 2 no. 2, 1995, pp. 3–12.
Mo Yuet-Ha. 'Orienting values with Eastern ways.' *People Management*, 25 July 1996, pp. 28–30.

JOSEPH JURAN

1904	Born.
1912	Family joins father in United States.
1920	Enrols at University of Minnesota.
1924	Goes to work for Western Electric at Hawthorne Works in Chicago.
1926	Chosen for inspection training programme by visiting Bell Laboratories team.
1928	Produces first work on quality, the training pamphlet *Statistical Methods Applied to Manufacturing Problems*.
1937	Head of industrial engineering at Western Electric's corporate headquarters in New York.
1941	Assistant administrator for Lend-Lease programme.
1945	Leaves Western Electric for New York University.
1951	Publication of *Quality Control Handbook*.
1954	Invited to lecture in Japan.
1964	*Managerial Breakthrough* first published.
1979	Founds the Juran Institute.

> **SUMMARY**
>
> Joseph Juran is a charismatic figure and a legend in his own time, recognised worldwide for his extensive contribution to quality management. He has been instrumental in shaping many of our current ideas about quality. While he is often referred to as one of the leading figures of total quality management, much of his work actually preceded the total quality concept. Regarded as one of the architects of the quality movement in Japan, his influence on manufacturing throughout the world has been substantial.

LIFE AND CAREER

Juran was born in 1904 in a small village in part of the Austro-Hungarian Empire that is now Romania. He was the third of four children and lived in poverty for much of his childhood. His father left the family in 1909 to find work in America and some three years later there was enough money for the rest of the family to join him in Minnesota.

Juran excelled at school in America and his affinity for mathematics and science meant that he was soon advanced the equivalent of three year-grades. He enrolled at the University of Minnesota in 1920 and became the first member of his family to enter higher education. By 1924 he had earned himself a BSc in electrical engineering and in 1936 a JD in law at Loyola University. During his career Juran has produced many leading international handbooks, training courses, and training books that have all been widely read and have collectively been translated into 16 languages. He has been awarded more than 40 honorary doctorates, honorary memberships, medals, and plaques around the world. For his work on quality in Japan he was awarded the Second Order of the Sacred Treasure for 'the development of quality control in Japan and the facilitation of US and Japanese friendship', and in the United States he has been awarded the National Medal of Technology.

Starting out as a professional engineer in 1924, Juran worked in the inspection department of the famous Hawthorne works of Western Electric, and this first job stimulated his interest in quality. The plant was vast, with some 40,000 workers, 5,000 of whom were in inspection. Juran's unfailing memory soon allowed him to develop an encyclopaedic knowledge of the place. His intellectual and analytical abilities were recognised early and he quickly progressed through a series of line management and staff jobs.

In 1926 a team of statistical quality-control pioneers from Bell Laboratories came to the Hawthorne plant to apply some of their methods and techniques. Juran was selected as one of twenty trainees to participate in the training programme and was later appointed as one of the two engineers in the newly formed inspection statistical department. It was while in this role that he authored his first work, *Statistical Methods Applied to Manufacturing Problems*.

By 1937, Juran was head of industrial engineering at Western Electric's head office in New York. He became the equivalent of an in-house consultant, visiting other companies and discussing ideas about quality and industrial engineering. Indeed, it was on one such visit to General Motors in Detroit that he realised how relevant Pareto's idea of 'the vital few and the trivial many' was to quality management. He eventually described this idea as the 'Pareto Principle' (see below).

In 1941 Juran was seconded as an assistant administrator to the Lend-Lease Administration in Washington. This assignment was to last for four years, during which he streamlined the shipment process to reduce the number of documents required and to cut costs significantly. Today such an approach might be called business process re-engineering; Juran has long claimed that there is nothing new about BPR!

Juran left Washington and Western Electric in 1945 with the aim of writing, lecturing and consulting. In 1951 he published his *Quality Control Handbook*, and this established his reputation as an authority on quality and increased the demand for his lecturing and consulting services. In 1954 he delivered a series of lectures in Japan at the invitation of the Union of Japanese Scientists and Engineers. Though Juran himself plays down their significance, in Japan it is widely held that these lectures formed the basis of the country's shift towards an economy based on quality principles. The ideas from these lectures were published in his book *Managerial Breakthrough*, in 1964.

In 1979 Juran founded the Juran Institute with the aim of increasing awareness of his ideas. It was through this Institute that the widely acclaimed video series *Juran on Quality Improvement* was produced, and he continued to write and publish into the 1990s. He played a part in setting up the Malcolm Baldrige National Quality Award and only retired from leading the Institute in 1987.

CONTRIBUTION
Pareto Principle
In his early days as a young engineer Juran noted that when defects were listed in the order of the frequency with which they occurred, a relatively small number of types of defect accounted for the bulk of those found. As his career in management progressed he noted the occurrence of this phenomenon in other areas. The idea of 'the vital few and the trivial many' was forming. In the 1930s Juran was introduced to the work of Vilfredo Pareto, an Italian economist, who had produced a mathematical model to explain the unequal distribution of wealth. Pareto had not promoted his model as a universal one and did not talk of an 80:20 split, but in preparing the first edition of the *Quality Control Handbook* Juran needed a form of shorthand to describe his idea. Remembering Pareto's work he captioned his description 'Pareto's

principle of unequal distribution'. Since then the 'Pareto Principle' has become a standard term to describe any situation where a relatively small percentage of factors are responsible for the substantial percentage of effect. Juran later published an explanation of his error in attributing more to Pareto than the latter had originally claimed, at the same time recognising the contribution of another economist, M.O. Lorenz. Juran was, in reality, the first to identify and popularise the 80:20 rule (as it has colloquially become known) as a universal principle.

Breakthrough

In his classic work *Managerial Breakthrough* Juran presents his general theory of quality control. Central to this is the idea of an improvement breakthrough.

Juran defines a breakthrough as 'change, a dynamic, decisive movement to new, higher levels of performance' (Juran 1994, p. 3). This he contrasts with control, which means 'staying on course, adherence to standard, prevention of change' (Juran 1994, p. 1). Not all control is viewed as negative, and not all breakthroughs are expected to be for the good. Breakthrough and control are seen as part of a continuing cycle of events. Juran highlights the importance of managers' understanding of the attitudes, the organisation, and the methodology used to achieve breakthrough, and of how they differ from those used to achieve control.

The Juran trilogy and quality planning road map

Juran's message on quality covers a number of different aspects. He focused on the wider issues of planning and organisation, managerial responsibility for quality, and the importance of setting targets for improvement. Intrinsic to these, however, was his belief that quality does not happen by accident and needs to be planned. The process of quality improvement is best summarised in his 'trilogy' concept, based on the three financial management processes of financial planning, financial control, and financial improvement. Various interpretations of the trilogy have been published, and the following represents one version.

Quality planning
- Identify who the customers are.
- Determine the needs of those customers.
- Translate those needs into our language.

Quality control
- Optimise the product features so as to meet our needs and customer needs.
- Develop a process which is able to produce the product.

Quality improvement
- Optimise the process.
- Prove that the process can produce the product under operating conditions.
- Transfer the process to operations.

Juran's 'road map' provides a more detailed approach to the steps within the quality planning element of the trilogy. It is made up of a series of actions with corresponding outputs, and emphasises the need for measurement throughout. In his book *Juran on Quality by Design* Juran describes six activities in the road map: establish quality goals; identify the customer; determine customer needs; develop product features; develop process features; establish process controls; and transfer to operations.

Quality campaigns

Juran has never been a fan of quality campaigns based on slogans and praise. He viewed the Western quality crisis of the early 1980s as being a result of too many quality initiatives based on campaigns with too little planning and substance. In his view, planning and action should make up 90% of an initiative, with the remaining 10% being exhortation.

Juran's formula for success is as follows.

- Establish specific goals to be reached.
- Establish plans for reaching those goals.
- Assign clear responsibility for meeting the goals.
- Base the rewards on the results achieved.

CONTEXT AND CONCLUSIONS

Juran's contribution to the revolution in Japanese quality philosophy helped to transform that country into a market leader. Add to this his influence on Western manufacturing and management in general, and you emerge with a guru who has been influential for more than half a century.

Juran has had a varied career in management and, while his fame centres upon his ideas and thinking on quality issues, his influence in the field of management is far wider. He has played a number of roles—writer, teacher, trainer, and consultant—and has contributed a great deal, over many years, to the field of management. Many of the thousands of managers who have learned from him hold him in near reverence, and management today is infused with his techniques and ideas, even though the name of their creator is not always recognised.

THE BEST SOURCES OF HELP
Books:
Butman, John. *Juran: A Lifetime of Influence*. New York: John Wiley, 1997
Juran, Joseph. *Managerial Breakthrough*. New York: McGraw-Hill, 1964.
Juran, Joseph. *Juran's Quality Control Handbook*. New York: McGraw-Hill, 1988.
Juran, Joseph. *Juran on Planning for Quality*. New York: Free Press, 1988.
Juran, Joseph. *Juran on Leadership for Quality*. New York: Free Press, 1989.
Juran, Joseph. *Juran on Quality by Design*. New York: Free Press, 1992.
Juran, Joseph, and Frank M. Gryna. *Quality Planning and Analysis*. New York: McGraw-Hill, 1993.
Juran, Joseph. *Managerial Breakthrough*. Revised ed. New York: McGraw-Hill, 1994.

ROSABETH MOSS KANTER

1943	Born.
1977	Publication of *Men and Women of the Corporation*.
1983	Publication of *The Change Masters: Corporate Entrepreneurs at Work*.
1983–Present	Professor of business administration, Harvard Business School.
1989	Publication of *When Giants Learn to Dance: Master the Challenge of Strategy, Management, and Careers in the 1990s*.
1989–1992	Editor, *Harvard Business Review*.

SUMMARY

It is difficult to classify Rosabeth Moss Kanter as a specialist in any particular area, as her prolific writings encompass a wide range of topics. She views herself, however, as a thought leader and developer of ideas, and is best known for her work on change management and innovation.

Much of Kanter's success is due to a combination of rigorous research, practical experience, and her ability to write in a clear and concrete way, using many illustrative examples.

LIFE AND CAREER

Kanter was born in 1943, in Cleveland, Ohio, and attended the top women's academy, Bryn Mawr. She took her PhD at the University of Michigan and was associate professor of sociology at Brandeis University from 1966 to 1977. Between 1973 and 1974 she was on the Organization Behavior Program at Harvard, and she was a fellow and visiting scholar of Harvard Law School between 1975 and 1976.

From 1977 to 1986 Kanter was professor of sociology and professor of organisational management at Yale, and from 1979 to 1986, she was a visiting professor at the Sloan School of Management, Massachusetts Institute of Technology (MIT). In 1986, she returned to Harvard as the 'class of 1960' professor of entrepreneurship and innovation, and she still holds the post of professor of business administration at Harvard Business School.

Between 1989 and 1992 Kanter was editor of the *Harvard Business Review*, and she acted as a key economic adviser to Michael Dukakis during his 1988 presidential campaign. She has travelled widely as a public speaker, lecturer, and international consultant. In 1977, she and her future husband, Barry Stein, set up a management consultancy called Goodmeasure, which has some large and well-known multinational companies as clients.

CONTRIBUTION

Kanter has authored or co-authored several books and well over 150 major articles. Her doctoral thesis was on communes, and her first books, written during the early 1970s, were sociological. The three books for which she is best known are *Men and Women of the Corporation*, *The Change Masters* and *When Giants Learn to Dance*. There is a logical progression in them, in that the first studies the stifling effects of bureaucratic organisation on individuals, while the subsequent titles go on to explore ways in which 'post-entrepreneurial' organisations release, and make use of, individuals' talents and abilities. Later books include *The Challenge of Organizational Change* (with Barry A. Stein and Todd D. Jick), *World Class: Thriving Locally in the Global Economy*, *The Frontiers of Management*, and *Evolve*.

Men and Women of the Corporation

Men and Women of the Corporation won the C. Wright Mills Award in 1977 as the year's best book on social issues. It is a detailed analysis of the nature and effects of the distribution of power and powerlessness within the headquarters of one large, bureaucratic, multinational corporation (called Industrial Supply Corporation, or Indsco, in the book). The effects of powerlessness on behaviour are explored and the detrimental effects of disempowerment, both for the organisation and individual employees, are made clear. Women were the most obvious group affected by lack of power, though Kanter emphasises that other groups outside the white, male norm, such as ethnic minority members, were also affected.

Three main structural variables explained the behaviours observed within Indsco:

- the structure of opportunity
- the structure of power
- the proportional distribution of people of different kinds

Before this book was published, it was generally assumed that behavioural differences underlay women's general lack of career progress. Kanter's findings made structural issues central, however, and the implications for change management were significant. If all employees were to become more empowered, organisations rather than people would need to change. Accordingly, the book ends with practical policy suggestions to create appropriate structural changes.

While working on this book, Kanter identified the need for organisational change to improve working life, create more equal opportunities, and make more use of employees' talents within organisations.

The Change Masters

The Change Masters puts forward various approaches to achieving these ends. Kanter compares four traditional corporations like Indsco with six competitive and successful organisations, described as 'change masters'. All findings were weighed against the experiences of many other companies and much other material. From the six innovative organisations, Kanter derives a model for encouraging innovation.

Innovative companies were found to have an 'integrative' approach to management, while firms unlikely to innovate were described as 'segmentalist' insofar as they were compartmentalised by units or departments. The difference begins with a company's approach to problem-solving, and extends through its structure and culture. Entrepreneurial organisations:

- operate at the edge of their competence, focusing on exploring the unknown rather than on controlling the known
- measure themselves by future-focused visions (how far they have to go) rather than by past standards (how far they have come)

Three clusters of structures and processes are identified as factors that encourage power circulation and access to power: open communication systems, network-forming arrangements, and decentralisation of resources. Their practical implementation is discussed.

Individuals can also be change masters. 'New entrepreneurs' are people who improve existing businesses rather than start new ones. They can be found in any functional area and are described as, literally, the right people, in the right place, at the right time:

- the right people—those with vision and ideas extending beyond the organisation's normal practice
- the right place—an integrative environment fostering proactive vision, coalitions, and teams
- the right time—a moment in the historical flow when change becomes most possible

The ultimate change masters are corporate leaders, who translate their vision into a new organisational reality.

The Change Masters advocates 'participation management' as the means to greater empowerment. Some major 'building blocks' for productive change are identified, and practical measures to remove 'road blocks' to innovation are discussed.

When Giants Learn to Dance

When Giants Learn to Dance completes Kanter's trilogy on the need for change, which, she considered, US corporations had to confront in order to compete more effectively. The global economy is likened to a 'corporate Olympics' of competing businesses, with results determining which nations, as well as organisations, are winners.

The games differ, but successful teams share some characteristics, such as strength, skill, discipline, good organisation, and focus on individual excellence. To win, American companies would have to become progressively more entrepreneurial and less bureaucratic. Kanter suggested as a model for the 1990s the 'post-entrepreneurial' corporation, in which three shaping forces would play the key roles:

- the context set at the top
- top management values
- project ideas and approaches coming up through the organisation

An 'athletic' organisation of this kind would be lean, flexible, and would seek to create synergies through the use of team and partnership approaches. The organisation would be built on empowerment, and employees would be highly valued within team-based or partnership relationships.

Kanter picks out seven skills or sensibilities that characterise individual 'business athletes'. These are:

- the ability to operate and get results without depending on hierarchical authority, position, or status
- the ability to compete in a way that enhances co-operation, and aims to achieve high standards rather than destroy competitors
- the high ethical standards needed to support the trust that is crucial for co-operative approaches when competing in the corporate Olympics

- a dose of humility, basic self-confidence being tempered by the understanding that new things will always need to be learnt
- process focus, that is, respect for the process of implementation as well as for the substance of what is implemented
- a multifaceted and ambidextrous approach that makes possible cross-functional or cross-departmental work, the forming of alliances where appropriate, and the cutting of ties where necessary
- a temperament that derives satisfaction from results, and a willingness to be rewarded according to achievements

World Class: Thriving Locally in the Global Economy
World Class: Thriving Locally in the Global Economy focuses on world class companies with employees described as 'cosmopolitan' in type. These people are rich in the 'three Cs'—concepts, competence, and connections—and carry a more universal culture to all the places in which their company operates.

This knowledge-rich breed is set against 'locals', who are set in their ways, and the two groups are viewed as the main classes in modern society. The book is optimistic, in that Kanter believes stakeholders can influence world-class companies to spread best practice around the world.

Globalisation, it is argued, offers an opportunity to develop businesses and give new life to the regions. From her studies of regenerative areas, Kanter suggests that business and local government leaders can work together to draw in the right sort of companies to create prosperity.

Later works
The Challenge of Organizational Change: How Companies Experience It and Leaders Guide It, co-authored with Barry Stein and Todd Jick, draws a distinction between evolutionary and revolutionary change, here described as the 'long march' and 'bold stroke' approaches.

Rosabeth Moss Kanter on The Frontiers of Management collects Kanter's essays and research articles for the *Harvard Business Review* together into one volume.

CONTEXT AND CONCLUSIONS
Overall, Kanter's books present some fairly complex ideas in a way that many people seem to find approachable. They are well-argued and supported with a wealth of practical research evidence. Some of her central ideas, once viewed by some as unrealistic, have now become absorbed into general management wisdom. These include empowerment, participative management, and employee involvement. In *The Frontiers of Management*, she is presented as a ground-breaking explorer who has initiated a revolution in terms of new ways of working. It is also pointed out, however, that some managers have still not crossed the frontiers, or do so in aspiration rather than actuality.

THE BEST SOURCES OF HELP
Books:
Moss Kanter, Rosabeth. *Men and Women of the Corporation*. New York: Basic Books, 1977.

Moss Kanter, Rosabeth. *The Change Masters: Corporate Entrepreneurs at Work*. London: George Allen & Unwin, 1983.

Moss Kanter, Rosabeth. *When Giants Learn to Dance: Master the Challenge of Strategy, Management, and Careers in the 1990s*. London: Simon & Schuster, 1989.

Moss Kanter, Rosabeth, Barry Stein, and Todd Jick. *The Challenge of Organizational Change: How Companies Experience It and Leaders Guide It*. New York: Free Press, 1992.

Moss Kanter, Rosabeth. *World Class: Thriving Locally in the Global Economy*. New York: Simon & Schuster, 1995.

Moss Kanter, Rosabeth. *Rosabeth Moss Kanter on the Frontiers of Management*. Boston: Harvard Business School Press, 1997.

Journal Article:

Dickson, Tim. 'Interview with Rosabeth Moss Kanter.' *Financial Times*, 17th May 1996, p. 17.

KAPLAN AND NORTON

> **SUMMARY**
>
> The name of Robert Kaplan is almost invariably linked with that of his co-author, David Norton, and with the assessment tool they jointly introduced to the business world in the early 1990s—the 'balanced scorecard'. Kaplan and Norton argued that adherence to quarterly financial returns and the bottom line alone could not provide the organisation with an overall strategic view. The balanced scorecard was a breakthrough precisely because it enables the organisation to describe its strategy adequately. It shows how non-financial factors—intangible assets—tied in with the financial ones.

LIFE AND CAREER

Robert Kaplan is Marvin Bower Professor of Leadership Development at Harvard Business School in Boston. He was previously based at Carnegie Mellon University, where he was dean of the Graduate School of Industrial Administration, in Pittsburgh. Kaplan's research work has focused on performance measurement systems, in particular activity-based costing and the balanced scorecard.

David Norton is a founder and president of the Balanced Scorecard Collaborative, based in Lincoln, Massachusetts. He also founded and was president of Renaissance Solutions, a balanced scorecard consulting firm.

They are jointly recognised as the popularisers of the balanced scorecard concept. Their approach to it was first introduced in a 1992 *Harvard Business Review* article ('The balanced scorecard: Measures that drive performance'), which began with a variation of the saying 'What gets measured gets done'; Kaplan and Norton took as their starting point 'What you measure is what you get'.

As the story goes, David Norton coined the term 'balanced scorecard' after a conversation with John Thompson, who was then president of IBM Canada. John Thompson, returning from a round of golf, announced he needed a scorecard just like the one he used during his game to measure the performance of his company. The balanced scorecard grew out of that conversation.

CONTRIBUTION

Setting up the balanced scorecard, Kaplan and Norton argued that strategies often fail because they are not converted successfully into actions that employees can understand and apply in their everyday work. The problem comes with the search for realistic measures that are meaningful to those doing the work, relate visibly to strategic direction, and provide a balanced picture of what is happening throughout the organisation, not just of one facet of it. It is this aspect that the balanced scorecard addresses.

It concentrates on measures in four key strategic areas—finance, customers, internal business processes, and learning and innovation—and requires the implementing organisation to identify goals and measures for each of them. Research and experimentation have come up with the following, which seem to be regularly applied in many organisations.

Financial perspective
- Goals: Survival, success/growth, prosperity.

- Measures: Return on capital, cash flow, revenue growth, liquidity, cost reduction, project profitability, performance reliability.

Customer perspective
- Goals: Customer acquisition, retention, profitability, and satisfaction.
- Measures: Market share, transaction cost ratios, customer loyalty satisfaction surveys/index, supplier relationships, key accounts.

Internal business process perspective
- Goals: Core competencies, critical technologies, business processes, key skills.
- Measures: Efficiency measures of working practices and production processes, cycle times, unit costs, defect rates, time to market.

Learning and innovation perspective
- Goals: Continuous improvement, new product development.
- Measures: Productivity of intrapreneurship, new ideas and suggestions from employees, employee satisfaction, skill levels, staff attitude, retention, and profitability, rate of improvement.

The scorecard provides a description of the organisation's strategy. It will indicate where problems lie because it shows the interrelationships between goals and the activities that are linked to their achievement. It creates an understanding of what is going on elsewhere in the organisation and shows all employees how they are contributing. As Kaplan has said: 'The business scorecard seeks to empower all levels of the workforce by educating them about their company's strategy and the small steps they can take to achieve their goals.' Providing that accurate and timely information is fed into the system, the scorecard also helps to focus attention where change and learning are needed through the cause and effect relationships it can reveal. Examples of the types of insight achieved were detailed in 'Linking the balanced scorecard to strategy'.

- If we increase employee training about products, then they will become more knowledgeable about the full range of products they can sell.
- If employees are more knowledgeable about products, then their sales effectiveness will improve.
- If their sales effectiveness improves, then the average margins of products they sell will increase.

Implementing the balanced scorecard
In 'Putting the balanced scorecard to work' Kaplan and Norton identify eight steps towards building a scorecard:

1. Preparation. Select/define the strategy/business unit to which to apply the scorecard. Think in terms of the appropriateness of the four main perspectives defined above.

2. First interviews. Distribute information about the scorecard to senior managers along with the organisation's vision, mission, and strategy. A facilitator will interview each manager on the organisation's strategic objectives and ask for initial thoughts on scorecard measures.

3. First executive workshop. Match measures to strategy. The management team

is brought together to develop the scorecard. After agreeing the vision statement, the team debates each of the four key strategic areas, addressing the following questions:

- If my vision succeeds, how will I differ?
- What are the critical success factors?
- What are the critical measurements?

These questions help to focus attention on the impact of turning the vision into reality and what has to be done to make it happen. It is important to represent the views of customers and shareholders, and to gain a number of measures for each critical success factor.

4. Second interviews. The facilitator reviews and consolidates the findings of the workshop and interviews each of the managers individually about the emerging scorecard.

5. Second workshop. Hold a team debate on the proposed scorecard; the participants should discuss the proposed measures, link ongoing change programmes to the measures, and set targets or rates of improvement for each of the measures. Start outlining the communication and implementation processes.

6. Third workshop. Final consensus on vision, goals, measures, and targets. The team devises an implementation programme to communicate the scorecard to employees, integrate it into management philosophy, and develop an information system to support it.

7. Implementation. The implementation team links the measures to information support systems and databases and communicates the what, why, where, and who of the scorecard throughout the organisation. The end product should be a management information system that links strategy to shop-floor activity.

8. Periodic review. Balanced scorecard measures can be prepared for review by senior management at appropriate intervals.

CONTEXT AND CONCLUSIONS

Kaplan and Norton published their first article on the balanced scorecard in early 1992. Since then, elaborating, explaining, and applying the basic concept seems to have become a small industry. The jury is, nevertheless, still out on whether it will be an innovation of lasting importance or merely a passing fad. But an increasing number of organisations are trying it out. David Norton has claimed that 60% of large US companies are now using some sort of scorecard that combines financial with nonfinancial measures.

The balanced scorecard should not be regarded as a panacea. In 'The design and implementation of the balanced business scorecard: an analysis of three companies in practice', Stephen Letza states that the balanced scorecard should highlight performance as a dynamic, continuous, and integrated process, act as an integrating tool, function as the pivotal tool determining the organisation's current and future direction, and deliver information that forms the backbone of its strategy. He also highlights some of the major drawbacks that may be encountered when using the balanced scorecard and points out the need to:

- avoid being swamped by the minutiae of too many detailed measures and make sure that measures do genuinely relate to the strategic goals of the organisation

- make sure all the organisation's activities are included in the assessment—this ensures that everyone is contributing to the organisation's strategic goals
- watch out for conflict as information becomes accessible to those who were not formerly in a position to see it or act on it, and try to harness conflict constructively

The balanced scorecard can be seen as the latest in a long line of attempts at management control, descending from Taylor through to work measurement systems, quality assurance systems, and performance indicators. Commentators claim that the balanced scorecard could become the management tool of the early 21st century, given that it is flexible and adaptable to each organisation's use, and that it is practical, straightforward, and devoid of obscure theory. Most importantly, it responds to many organisations' requirements to expand strategically on traditional financial measures and points to areas for change.

THE BEST SOURCES OF HELP
Books:
Kaplan, Robert, and David Norton. *The Balanced Scorecard: Translating Strategy into Action*. Boston, Massachusetts: Harvard Business School Press, 1996.
Kaplan, Robert, and David Norton. *The Strategy-Focused Organization*. Boston, Massachusetts: Harvard Business School Press, 2000.
Journal Articles:
Kaplan, Robert, and David Norton. 'The balanced scorecard: measures that drive performance.' *Harvard Business Review*, Jan./Feb. 1992, pp. 71–79.
Kaplan, Robert, and David Norton. 'Putting the balanced scorecard to work.' *Harvard Business Review*, Sept./Oct. 1993, pp. 134–147.
Kaplan, Robert, and David Norton. 'Using the balanced scorecard as a strategic management system.' *Harvard Business Review*, Jan./Feb. 1996, pp. 75–85.
Kaplan, Robert, and David Norton. 'Linking the balanced scorecard to strategy.' *California Management Review*, Fall 1996, pp. 53–79.
Kaplan, Robert, and David Norton. 'Strategic learning and the balanced scorecard.' *Strategy and Leadership*, Sept./Oct. 1996, pp. 18–24.

THEODORE LEVITT

1925	Born.
1935	Leaves Germany for the United States.
1959	Lecturer in business administration at Harvard Business School.
1960	'Marketing myopia' appears in *Harvard Business Review*.
1965	Edward W. Carter Professor of Business Administration, Harvard Business School.
1990	Resigns post as editor of *Harvard Business Review*.

SUMMARY

Theodore Levitt has made a key contribution to management theory in the marketing field, stimulating debate on the importance of a pervasive marketing mindset within an organisation. Having encouraged an awareness of the marketing concept, Levitt proceeded to further analyse the benefits and shortfalls of marketing in a series of journal articles and books over four decades. His talent for expounding his views clearly and for illustrating his arguments with company examples and metaphors makes his work highly accessible.

LIFE AND CAREER

Born in Volmerz in Germany, Levitt moved with his parents to the United States in 1935, where he later studied economics. In the late 1950s he worked as a consultant in Chicago, before being approached by the Harvard Business School. In his very first year there he began to teach marketing, although at the time he had reportedly never read a book on the subject.

Levitt's first article was published in 1956. His tenure at Harvard as an academic lasted for more than 30 years. This period included a spell as a somewhat controversial editor of the *Harvard Business Review*, a post from which he resigned in 1990 following an argument over an article on women in management.

CONTRIBUTION

Levitt emphasises the need for a company to achieve a balanced orientation by including marketing in its strategy; he focuses on the need for a marketing outlook to pervade an organisation and provide a necessary counterbalance to a preoccupation with production. His landmark article expounding this theory, 'Marketing myopia', appeared in the *Harvard Business Review* in 1960 and is one of the most requested reprints from that journal, having sold over 500,000 copies. Subsequently, Levitt reiterated and expanded his theory in several articles and books. These partly focus on the methodology of implementing the marketing mode, including the proposition of a 'marketing matrix' for assessing the degree of marketing orientation existing in a company. They also explore the theory behind the marketing concept and delineate some of its limitations and problems. Other works concentrate on such topics as 'the industrialization of service' (examining the potential benefits of applying the production line and quality control methods of industry to service provision), the nature of the product, advertising, and globalisation.

'Marketing myopia' explored

Levitt himself described his article 'Marketing myopia' as a manifesto. It challenged the conventional thinking of the time by putting forward a persuasive case for the importance of the marketing approach and the shortsightedness of failing to incorporate it into business strategy.

In an era in which postwar shortages contributed to a concentration on production, most companies had developed a product orientation, which, Levitt believed, was too narrow a philosophy to allow continued business success. A drive to increase the efficiency and volume of production took place at the expense of monitoring whether the company was actually producing what the customer wanted. The article stressed that 'customer wants and desires should be a central consideration of any business. The organisation must learn to think of itself not as producing goods or services but as buying customers, as doing the things that will make people want to do business with it'.

In order to achieve this, 'the entire corporation must be viewed as a customer-creating and customer-satisfying organism. Management must think of itself not as providing products but as providing customer-creating value satisfactions. It must push this idea (and everything it means and requires) into every nook and cranny of the organisation'.

Levitt highlighted the need for companies to define what business they are in, as this concentrates attention on customer needs. He used the now famous example of the railways, which, rather than thinking of themselves as being in the business of running trains, should instead have defined themselves as providing transportation. Self-definition along those lines would have helped the railway companies to be aware of changing customer demand; if they had had that awareness, they might not have suffered so greatly from the rise of road and air transport. Focusing on the satisfaction of customer needs, Levitt argues, is a better path to continued business success than concentration on the actual product on offer.

Also presented in 'Marketing myopia', as a warning against complacency, is Levitt's belief that 'in truth there is no such thing as a growth industry'. There are growth opportunities, which can be created or capitalised on, but those companies which believe they are 'riding some automatic growth escalator invariably descend into stagnation'. The belief that a company is in a growth industry and is therefore secure must never be allowed to overshadow or replace awareness of the need to practise marketing and assert a customer orientation. This is the only route through which a company can hope to achieve sustained expansion.

Of a more practical nature is the 'marketing matrix', a device presented by Levitt in *Marketing for Business Growth* to aid the measurement of a company's marketing orientation. A horizontal scale of 1–9 records the degree of customer orientation, and a vertical scale of 1–9 records the degree of company orientation. A score of 9 on both scales is the ideal. Using this method, organisations can assess their incorporation of marketing thinking and determine where steps are needed to improve their strategy and to become more marketing-oriented.

Ways of doing this include the 'industrialisation of service', which involves the measuring and standardising of customer service to a predetermined quality level, in other words, applying industrial-style quality controls to the service process. For example, a production line can be set up for service delivery, and service encounters can be standardised and monitored to ensure that they are of a similar quality. This has been accomplished with great success by the McDonald's fast food chain ('The industrialisation of service'). To recognise this concept is, writes Levitt, '...to introduce a potentially emancipating new cognitive mode and operating style into modern enterprise' (*The Marketing Imagination*). Another factor that is important in enhancing a marketing orientation is relationship marketing. (See 'After the sale is over'.) This revolves around the need not only to acquire customers, but also to keep them and form mutually beneficial long-term relationships with them.

In a 1983 article, 'The globalization of markets', Levitt once more produced a forward-looking 'manifesto' with a view of the changing nature of the marketplace and the trend, fuelled by technological advances, towards globalisation. His thesis is that, in order to survive and prosper, companies must offer standardised products around the world, products that incorporate the best in design, reliability, and price. The efficiency of such an approach will outweigh, in his opinion, the benefits of taking into account varying cultural preferences and tailoring products to different national markets. The reason for this is the overlying trend towards world homogenisation. 'Two vectors shape the world—technology and globalisation. The first helps determine human preferences; the second, economic realities. Regardless of how much preferences evolve and diverge, they also gradually converge and form markets where economies of scale lead to reduction of costs and prices.'

Thinking about Management, Levitt's 1991 book, contains a distillation of his thinking on effective management, presented in nuggets in the three categories of thinking, changing, and operating. Many of his theories are here reiterated, and the work forms a useful guide to his collected thought.

CONTEXT AND CONCLUSIONS
A major influence on Levitt's work was the writing of Peter Drucker, who was among the first to see marketing as all-pervasive: 'Marketing is not a function, it is the whole business seen from the customer's point of view.' (*The Practice of Management*)

However, although influenced by academic thought, Levitt seems to have drawn his greatest inspiration from the real world, examining the companies around him and distilling the examples of good and bad practice that illustrate much of his writing.

Levitt's influence contributed to the rise of the marketing concept in the 1960s and its increasing incorporation into management thinking, initially in the United States, but later also in Europe. His subsequent works may not have achieved the fame of 'Marketing myopia', but they are nevertheless an important part of the evolving pattern of marketing writing that has gathered impetus through recent decades. By pointing out the myopic vision of many managers, Levitt set in motion a vigorous new way of thinking that was taken up by other management writers and practitioners and culminated in the rebirth of marketing in the 1980s. Other marketing gurus such as Philip Kotler acknowledge the influence of Levitt's work, and he is regularly quoted.

In retrospect, Levitt has been proven to have had remarkable foresight in his anticipation of the importance of marketing to organisations, his initial work predating the marketing boom by two decades. He also successfully predicted the value of relationship marketing, a topic which only became an identifiable discipline in the early 1990s, and the concept of the global village, which is now commonplace.

Levitt's assertion that there is no such thing as a growth industry is another tenet that proved influential, and was taken up by writers such as Tom Peters and Richard Pascale in the 1990s.

THE BEST SOURCES OF HELP
Books:
Levitt, Theodore. *Innovation in Marketing: New Perspectives for Profit and Growth.* New York: McGraw-Hill, 1962.

Levitt, Theodore. *Marketing for Business Growth.* New York: McGraw-Hill, 1974. (First published in 1969 as *The Marketing Mode: Pathways to Corporate Growth.*)

Levitt, Theodore. *The Marketing Imagination.* New York: Free Press, 1983.

Levitt, Theodore. *Thinking about Management.* New York: Free Press, 1991.

Journal Articles:
Levitt, Theodore. 'Marketing myopia.' *Harvard Business Review*, Jul./Aug. 1960, pp. 45–56.

Levitt, Theodore. 'The industrialization of service.' *Harvard Business Review*, Sept./Oct. 1976, pp. 63–74.

Levitt, Theodore. 'After the sale is over.' *Harvard Business Review*, Sept./Oct. 1983, pp. 87–93.

Levitt, Theodore. 'The Globalization of Markets.' *Harvard Business Review*, May/Jun. 1983, pp. 92–102.

KURT LEWIN

1890	Born.
1910	Begins formal training in psychology in Berlin.
1914	Graduates as PhD from the University of Berlin.
1914–1916	Active service with the German army; is wounded and awarded the Iron Cross.
1916–1932	Teaches at the University of Berlin.
1932	Leaves Germany to escape persecution by the Nazis.
1935	Appointed professor of child psychology at the University of Iowa.
1944	Co-founds the Research Center for Group Dynamics at MIT. Mother killed in Nazi extermination camp.
1947	Dies.

SUMMARY

Kurt Lewin (1890–1947) is often called 'the father of social psychology'. His extensive output included studies of leadership styles and their effects and work on group decision-making, and he was responsible for the development of force field theory, the 'unfreeze—change—refreeze' model of change management, the 'action research' approach to research, and the group dynamics approach to training (especially in the form of T Groups). He was behind the founding of the Center for Group Dynamics in the United States.

LIFE AND CAREER
German-born, Lewin was professor of philosophy and psychology at Berlin University until he fled to the United States in 1932 to escape from the Nazis. There, he taught at Cornell University, and then at Iowa, becoming professor of child psychology at the latter's Child Research Station. In 1944 he went on to found, with Douglas McGregor and others, a research centre for group dynamics at the Massachusetts Institute of Technology.

CONTRIBUTION
Leadership styles and their effects
With his colleagues L. Lippitt and R. White, Lewin studied the effects of three different leadership styles on the outcomes of boys' activity groups in Iowa (1939). Those three styles were classified as 'democratic', 'autocratic', and 'laissez-faire'. It was found that in the group with an autocratic leader, there was more dissatisfaction and behaviours became either more aggressive or apathetic. In the group with a democratic leader, there was more co-operation and enjoyment, while those in the laissez-faire group showed no particular dissatisfaction, although they were not particularly productive, either.

Significantly, when the respective leaders were asked to change their styles, the effects produced by each leadership style remained similar. Lewin was aiming to show that the democratic style achieved better results. The possibility of social and cultural factors influencing the results undermined his findings to some extent; nevertheless, the studies suggested the benefits of a democratic style in an American context. They also showed that it is possible for leaders and managers to change their approach, to improve their leadership through training, and to adopt management styles appropriate for their situation and context.

Group decision-making
After the Second World War, Lewin carried out research for the US government, exploring ways of influencing people to change their dietary habits and eat less popular cuts of meat. He found that, if group members were encouraged to become involved, discussed the issues themselves, and were then able to make their own decisions as a group, they were far more likely to change their habits than if they simply attended lectures where they were given information, recipes, and advice.

Force field analysis
Lewin put forward the theory that people's activity is affected by forces in their surrounding environment, or 'field'. Its three main principles are that:

- behaviour is a function of the existing field
- analysis starts from the complete situation and distinguishes its component parts
- a concrete person in a concrete situation can be mathematically represented

A particular feature of Lewin's method of analysing behaviour within a given field, for example, within a situation or an organisation, is its identification of the forces at work there as either 'driving forces', which will tend to promote change, or 'restraining forces', which will tend to hinder it. Such things as ambitions, goals, needs, or fears, that drive a person towards or away from something, constitute driving forces. Restraining forces are different in nature, according to Lewin, in that they act to oppose driving forces rather than constituting independent forces in themselves.

Force field analysis is used extensively for purposes of organisational and human resources development, because it can help to indicate when the driving and restraining forces affecting people are not in balance, thus creating a situation in which change can occur.

The interplay of the two types of force can produce either stability or instability. Where activities and situations go on from day to day in a regular, stable routine—that is, in what Lewin calls 'quasi-stationary processes'—the forces are more or less balanced out and equalised; they fluctuate around a state of equilibrium. Achieving change, therefore, involves altering the forces that maintain this equilibrium. To bring about an increase in productivity, for example, the forces currently keeping production at its existing quasi-stationary levels would have to be changed. This can be done by taking one of two alternative routes:

- strengthening the driving forces, for example, paying more money for more productivity
- restraining inhibiting factors, for example, simplifying production processes

Strengthening the drives would seem the obvious route to take, but analysis would show that this could lead to the development of countervailing forces, concern among employees about tiredness, or worry about new targets becoming a standard expectation. Reducing restraining forces, for example, through investment in machinery or training to make the process easier, might be a less obvious, but more rewarding approach, bringing about change with less resistance or demoralisation.

Lewin identified two questions to ask when seeking to make changes within the framework of force field analysis:

- Why does a process continue at its current level under the present circumstances?
- What conditions would change these circumstances?

For Lewin, 'circumstances' is a concept with a very broad meaning; it covers anything from the social context and wider environment to subgroups and communication barriers between groups. The position of each of these factors determines a group's structure and 'ecological setting' while the structure and setting together determine a range of possible changes that are dependent on, and can to some degree be controlled by, the pacing and interaction of forces across the entire field.

Model of change: unfreeze—change—refreeze

Lewin believed that, to achieve change effectively, it was necessary to look at all the options for moving from the existing state to a desired future one, then to evaluate the possibilities of each option and decide on the best one, rather than simply identifying a desired goal and taking the straightest and easiest route to it. His change management model is linked to force field analysis and encourages managers to beware of two kinds of force of resistance, the first deriving from 'social habit' or 'custom', and the second from the creation of an 'inner resistance'. These two different kinds of force are rooted in the interplay between a group as a whole and the individuals within it, and only driving forces that are strong enough to break the habits, challenge the interests, or 'unfreeze' the customs of the group will overcome them. As most members will want to stay within the behavioural norms of the group, individual resistance to change will increase as a person is induced to move further away from current group values. In Lewin's view, this type of resistance can be lowered either by reducing the value the group attaches to something, or by fundamentally changing what the group values. He considered that a complex, stepped process of unfreezing, changing, and refreezing beliefs, attitudes, and values was required to achieve change, with the initial phase of unfreezing normally involving group discussions in which individuals experience others' views and begin to adapt their own.

Since Lewin's death, 'unfreeze—change—refreeze' has sometimes been applied more rigidly than he intended, for example by discarding an old structure, setting up a new one, and then 'fixing' the latter into place. Such an inflexible course of action fits badly with more modern attitudes to change as a continuous and flowing process of evolution. Lewin's change model is now often criticised for its linearity, especially from the perspective of more recent research on non-linear, 'chaotic' systems and complexity theory. The model was, however, process-oriented originally. Lewin himself viewed change as a continuing process, recognising that extremely complex forces are at work in group and organisational dynamics.

T-Groups

What is now known as the 'T-Group' (or Training Group) approach was pioneered by Lewin when, in 1946, he was called in to try to develop better relations between

Jewish and black communities in Connecticut. Bringing such groups of people together was, Lewin found, a powerful way of exposing areas of conflict, so that established behaviour patterns could 'unfreeze' before potentially changing and 'refreezing'. He called these learning groups T-Groups. This training approach became particularly popular during the 1970s. Some interpreters of the method, however, have used it in a more confrontational way than Lewin may have intended.

Action research
Lewin's 'action research' approach is linked to T-groups. Introduced during the 1940s, it was seen as an important innovation in research methods and was especially used in industry and education. Action research involves experimenting by making changes and simultaneously studying the results, in a cyclic process of planning, action, and fact-gathering. Lewin's approach emphasised the power relationship between the researcher and those researched, and he sought to involve the latter, encouraging their participation in studying the effects of their own actions, identifying their own biases, and working to transform relationships within their communities.

'Action research' centred on the involvement of participants from the community under research and on the pursuit of separate but simultaneous processes of action and evaluation. Different variations of this approach have evolved since Lewin's day, and its validity as a scientific research method for psychology is often questioned. Its strengths, however, in offering groups or communities an involving, self-evaluative, collaborative, and decision-making role are widely accepted.

CONTEXT AND CONCLUSIONS
Lewin is widely recognised as a seminal figure in social psychology, although his early death obscured his central role in the development of the managerial human relations movement. In the United States and the United Kingdom (especially through the work of the Tavistock Institute), much subsequent management thinking and research has been influenced by Lewin's approaches and ideas. These, following in the tradition of Mayo's 1920s and 1930s Hawthorne studies, underlie the whole current field of organisational development and change management.

THE BEST SOURCES OF HELP
Books:
Lewin, Kurt. *Resolving Social Conflicts: Selected Papers on Group Dynamics*. New York: Harper and Brothers, 1948.
Lewin, Kurt. *Field Theory in Social Science*, edited by Dorwin Cartwright. London: Tavistock Publications Ltd, 1952, reprinted 1963.
Journal Articles:
Lewin, Kurt, R. Lippitt, and R. White. 'Patterns of aggressive behaviour in experimentally created "social climates".' *Journal of Social Psychology*, vol. 10, 1939, pp. 271-99.
Lewin, Kurt. 'Action research and minority problems.' *Journal of Social Issues*, vol. 2, 1946, p. 65.
Lewin, Kurt. 'Frontiers in group dynamics.' *Human Relations*, vol. 1, 1947, pp. 5-41.

NICCOLÒ MACHIAVELLI

1469	Born.
1498	Secretary of Second Chancery, Florence.
1512	Falls from grace as Medici family returns to power.
1513	Publication of *The Prince*.
1527	Dies.

> **SUMMARY**
>
> Throughout most of the five centuries since his death Niccolò Machiavelli has not been a popular figure. There have always been a few people who appreciated his genius, but most have so closely associated him with intrigue and dark deeds. Fortunately, in the last 100 years or so, a more reasoned view of his work has developed and the enormous value of Machiavelli's philosophy and its remarkable relevance to modern society has emerged progressively.

LIFE AND CAREER

Niccolò Machiavelli was born in 1469, the son of a Florentine lawyer. He first came to public notice when in 1498, aged 29, he was appointed Secretary of the Second Chancery—part of the complex bureaucracy that ran Florence as a city state. His appointment came after the execution of Savonarola, the friar-politician who, after leading a revolt that expelled the Medicis and established a democratic republic, dominated Florentine life until he fell foul of the papacy and was burned for heresy.

Machiavelli held the post of Secretary for 14 years, during which time his influence was significant. He took part in 30 foreign missions, meeting most of Europe's key politicians and rulers. This opportunity to learn about government, politics, and economics must have been unique. Unfortunately, it was not to last. In 1512 the Medicis returned to power, and Machiavelli lost his post immediately. He was then suspected, quite wrongly, of plotting against the Medicis, for which he was arrested, imprisoned, and tortured. Although eventually found innocent, he was expelled from Florence and forced to spend the rest of his life in exile on an isolated farm. His many attempts to re-enter political life failed and he died in 1527, still struggling to regain his lost influence. It was more than 300 years later that Italy became unified, as Machiavelli had wanted it to be.

Whilst Machiavelli may not have enjoyed his time in exile, the world has gained immeasurably from it. The enforced idleness allowed him to write prodigiously about his experiences and ideas.

His written works include a history of Florence, several plays, and two books that established him as a great authority on power politics: *The Prince* and *The Discourses*. Professor Max Lerner, in his introduction to the 1950 Random House edition of *The Prince* describes the book as 'a grammar of power'. There can be no more fitting description of this seminal work.

CONTRIBUTION

Machiavelli presents no instant management theories, no clever techniques for solving day-to-day problems. He deals mainly with broad strategies, and to get value from his writing one needs to interpret it and make comparisons. Perhaps the best approach is to first read Jay's introduction on the art of making such comparisons

(1967) and then to read Machiavelli with a personal checklist of interests and questions.

Some pertinent insights

The following examples show how certain passages in Machiavelli's writing bridge the seemingly huge gap between sixteenth-century politics and twentieth-century business.

Leadership

Machiavelli provides several examples of good leaders and leaves his readers in no doubt about the importance of skilful leadership to the success of any enterprise. He dismisses luck and genius as the key to successful leadership and goes for 'shrewdness'. The dangers and risks a leader faces are dramatically illustrated (happily for us these are less terrifying today than in Renaissance Italy), and comparison is made between the relative ease of getting to a position of leadership and the difficult task of staying there.

Centralisation versus decentralisation

Anyone who thinks that the problem of choosing between centralised or decentralised control is a modern dilemma will be quickly persuaded otherwise by reading *The Prince*. Machiavelli's examples are drawn entirely from government and from military history, but the comparisons with today's business world are easy to make. Perhaps his best advice comes when he is talking about the government of colonies and outposts.

Poor communications in Renaissance times usually made decentralisation the only option in such cases, and Machiavelli's recommendations centre on what today we would call selection and training. A colonial governor must be carefully selected for his experience and loyalty, trained thoroughly in the state's way of doing things, and made so familiar with 'best practice' that, however isolated from 'head office' guidance he may be, the job will still get done in a highly predictable way. Shades of William Whyte's *Organization Man*?

Takeovers

The equivalent of a takeover in Machiavelli's world was the conquest of another country or the establishment of a colony. In such matters his advice is very clear. One either totally subjugates the original inhabitants, so that rebellion is unlikely and the cost of garrisoning the place reduced to a minimum, or, and Machiavelli makes clear this is his preference, the conqueror puts in a small team of 'key managers'.

This team will displace only a small number of the original inhabitants, who being scattered cannot rebel, and the remainder will quickly toe the new management line since they have everything to gain from co-operation and a clear indication of what happens to those who do not co-operate. Parallels with business takeovers are frighteningly stark.

Change

Machiavelli has little to offer in the way of ideas for coping with change, but shows very clearly that the problems of introducing change were just as awesome and hazardous in the sixteenth century as they are today. In *The Prince* he says: 'It must be considered that there is nothing more difficult to carry out, nor more doubtful of success, nor more dangerous to handle, than to initiate a new order of things.'

Federations and bureaucracies
Machiavelli compared the 'management' of sixteenth-century France and Turkey. He saw France as a 'federal organisation'; a collection of independent baronies in which the retainers regarded their baron, and not the king, as the 'key manager'. Such organisations are difficult to control, impossible to change, and the ruler is easily overthrown. Turkey, on the other hand, was in Machiavelli's time a classic bureaucracy with a highly trained civil service. Civil servants were frequently moved around, hence they developed no local loyalties, and had a strict, hierarchical relationship with 'top management'. The ruler in such a state, being appointed by the 'system', was secure, respected, and powerful. The points of comparison with today's large organisations need little emphasising.

CONTEXT AND CONCLUSIONS
The impact of Machiavelli's writing on politics has been accepted for some time, but the relevance of his ideas to business had to wait until the second half of the nineteenth century, when companies began to operate as large, complex organisations—the equivalent in Machiavelli's terms of a move from a tribal society to a corporate state. An English parson, writing in 1820, compares Machiavelli unfavourably with the devil, yet by the 1860s Victor Hugo was able to say, 'Machiavelli is not an evil genius, nor a cowardly writer, he is nothing but the fact...not merely the Italian fact, he is the European fact.'

Machiavelli's image is not helped by what many see as an amoral attitude towards power. It is easy to take offence when he unashamedly says, 'A prudent ruler ought not to keep faith when by so doing it would be against his interest, and when the reasons which made him bind himself no longer exist.'

Such statements are easier to accept if we remember they were made in times very different from our own. They were also the words of a man who was a true observer; he reported what he saw and measured results dispassionately in terms of practical success or failure. He had moral views, as can be seen in his other writing, but on political issues he is a cold realist. He had, as Professor Lerner so aptly observed, 'the clear-eyed capacity to distinguish between man as he ought to be and man as he actually is—between the ideal form of institutions and the pragmatic conditions under which they operate'.

By being so linked with intrigue, cruelty, and opportunism, Machiavelli remains rooted in his own age. However, if we set him aside from the harsh realities of sixteenth-century Europe and look at how he observes human nature and organisations, we see a man who was centuries ahead of his time.

THE BEST SOURCES OF HELP
Books:
Jay, Antony. *Management and Machiavelli*. London: Hodder and Stoughton, 1967.
Machiavelli, Niccolò. *The Prince and The Discourses* (introduced by Max Lerner). New York: Random House, 1950.
(A number of editions of *The Prince* and *The Discourses* are currently in print.)
Whyte, William. *The Organization Man*. Philadelphia: University of Pennsylvania Press, 2002.

ABRAHAM MASLOW

1908	Born.
1934	Receives PhD from the University of Wisconsin.
1935	Returns to New York to work at Columbia University.
1937–1951	On the faculty of Brooklyn College.
1943	'Hierarchy of needs' first presented in an article in the *US Psychological Review*.
1951	Becomes head of the psychology department at Brandeis University.
1954	*Motivation and Personality* published.
1970	Dies.

> **SUMMARY**
>
> Maslow, known principally for his theory of the 'hierarchy of needs', was one of the first people to be associated with the humanistic—as opposed to task-based—approach to management. As people have increasingly come to be appreciated as a key resource in successful companies, Maslow's model has remained a valuable management concept.

LIFE AND CAREER

Abraham Maslow (1908–1970) was a US psychologist and behavioural scientist. He spent part of his career in industry as well as working as an academic. He liked to say that, whereas most early psychologists studied people with psychological problems, he devoted his attention to successful people. The 'hierarchy of needs' theory, on which his fame chiefly rests, was first presented in 1943 in the *US Psychological Review*, and later developed in his book *Motivation and Personality*, first published in 1954. His concepts were originally offered as general explanations of human behaviour, but quickly came to be regarded as a significant contribution to workplace motivation theory. They are still used by managers today to understand, predict, and influence employee motivation.

CONTRIBUTION

Maslow grouped human needs into classes and arranged these classes in the form of a hierarchy, ascending from the lowest to the highest. When one set of needs is satisfied, it ceases to be a motivator; motivation is then generated by the unsatisfied needs further up the hierarchy. The classes of needs identified by Maslow are: survival or physiological needs, safety or security needs, social needs, ego-status needs, and self-actualisation needs, and they appear in that order in the hierarchy. Today the hierarchy is usually represented as a pyramid, although Maslow himself did not present it in that way.

The five levels within the hierarchy can be broken down as follows.

- Survival or physiological needs. These are the most primitive of all needs, comprising all the basic animal requirements such as food, water, shelter, warmth, and sleep.
- Security or safety needs. In earlier times, these needs expressed themselves in the form of a desire to be free of physical danger. In the modern context, they have been refined and are now felt in mainly social and financial terms; purely physical requirements have been replaced by the need for things such as job security or a living wage.
- Social needs. Most humans need to belong and to be accepted by others. They are

essentially social beings and therefore seek membership of social groups, such as work groups.
- Ego-status needs. Most humans also need to be held in esteem by both themselves and others. This kind of need is satisfied by power, prestige, and self-confidence.
- Self-actualisation needs. The most sophisticated type of need is the desire to maximise one's skills and talents. This embraces self-realisation, self-expression, and self-fulfilment.

There are certain conditions, Maslow wrote, that are immediate prerequisites for satisfying needs, such as the freedom to speak, the freedom to express oneself in other ways, the freedom to defend oneself, justice, fairness, and honesty. Any danger threatening these is perceived almost as if it were a danger to the satisfaction of the needs themselves.

The hierarchy is usually referred to as if it were a fixed order, but Maslow explained that it is not necessarily rigid or universally applicable in its usual form. While most people do experience their basic needs in the order indicated, there are a number of exceptions. Creative people, for example, are often driven by a desire for self-actualisation and give it precedence over the satisfaction of 'lower' needs in a way that the average person perhaps would not. The hierarchy is often presented in simplified terms, giving the false impression that one need must be fully satisfied before the next need emerges. In fact, as Maslow pointed out, man is a continually wanting animal, whose basic needs are for the most part partially satisfied and partially unsatisfied at the same time. Needs continually overlap; for example, social needs are felt by almost everyone, including those people whose basic physiological needs are not being met. As soon as a need is satisfied, however, it will drop out of the equation and cease to be a motivator.

Maslow's intention all along was to define an aspect of the human condition, but his insights are obviously applicable within a business context. If, for example, a manager is able to recognise which level of the hierarchy a worker has reached, then he or she can motivate the employee in the most appropriate way. Peter Drucker, in his book *Management: Tasks, Responsibilities, Practices* (London: Heinemann, 1973), pointed out that although it becomes less satisfying to obtain economic rewards as one moves up the hierarchy, the need for economic reward does not necessarily become less important. This is because, as their impact as a positive incentive decreases, their ability to create dissatisfaction and act as a disincentive increases. Economic rewards come to be seen as entitlements and, if they are not looked after, can act as deterrents.

CONTEXT AND CONCLUSIONS
Maslow is often mentioned in connection with his contemporaries, Douglas McGregor and Frederick Herzberg, who were also developing motivation theories at about the same time. Maslow admired McGregor, the author of Theory X and Theory Y, although he had strong reservations about the validity of Theory Y. Herzberg suggested that hygiene factors—those that may be causes of job dissatisfaction (for example, working conditions, salary, job security, or company policy) but are not in themselves incentives to improve performance—should be separated from motivators—those that lead to positive job satisfaction (such as achievement, recognition, responsibility, or advancement). Herzberg's hygiene factors can be

compared with Maslow's levels one, two, and three, and the motivators to levels four and five.

Maslow's influence continues through the work of later psychologists and writers, such as Chris Argyris and Blake and Mouton. Argyris looked at how individual initiatives and creativity can coexist with organisational rules. Blake and Mouton were the authors of the *Managerial Grid*, which created the concept of the manager who balanced a concern for people with a concern for the task.

Practising managers have also, on the whole, found Maslow's concept a valuable and sensible one, which helps to clarify their thoughts. It is often used as a basis for questionnaires and checklists to discover an individual's level of motivation, or cited in support of the idea of empowerment. Twyla Dell, in *How to Motivate People* (London: Kogan Page, 1988), listed the ten qualities that people most want from their jobs and included two questionnaires to help readers judge how many of the ten qualities they were receiving and giving in their work. She then matched the ten qualities to Maslow's hierarchy.

Maslow's theory fully makes sense only when applied, as he originally intended, to life in general rather than to the workplace in particular. This is because some of the needs of the individual, particularly the higher needs, may be satisfied outside the workplace. This holistic view is nonetheless important within the workplace, as employers increasingly come to realise that individuals have a life outside their job that impinges on their performance at work. Although Maslow's theory is now over 50 years old, it is still referred to by managers and it offers them useful insights. Along with Herzberg and McGregor, he is recognised as one of the founding fathers of motivation theory.

THE BEST SOURCES OF HELP
Books:
Frick, Willard B. *Humanistic Psychology: Interviews with Maslow, Murphy, and Rogers*. Columbus, Ohio: Charles E. Merrill, 1971.

Hoffman, Edward. *The Right to be Human: a Biography of Abraham Maslow*. Wellingborough: Crucible, 1989.

Lowry, Richard J. *A. H. Maslow: An Intellectual Portrait*. Monterey, California: Brookes Cole, 1973.

Maslow, Abraham. *Motivation and Personality*. 2nd ed. New York: Harper and Row, 1970.

Maslow, Abraham. *The Farther Reaches of Human Nature*. New York: Viking Press, 1971.

Further Reading
Journal Article:
Berman Brown, Reva. 'Abraham Maslow and self-actualisation'. *Organizations and People*, Jan. 1994, vol. 1 no. 1, pp. 42–45.

ELTON MAYO

1880	Born.
1911	Appointed lecturer in logic, ethics, and psychology (later professor of philosophy) at University of Queensland.
1923	Moves to United States and takes a post at Pennsylvania University; conducts experiments on productivity in a spinning mill, related to working conditions.
1924–1932	Experiments are carried out at the Hawthorne plant.
1928	Moves to Harvard as associate professor of industrial research; becomes involved with Hawthorne experiments.
1929–1930	Deduces that a more listening, caring style of supervision raises morale and boosts productivity.
1930–c1945	Develops TWI programme.
1947	Retires from Harvard.
1947–1949	Adviser to British government on problems within industry.
1949	Dies.

> **SUMMARY**
>
> George Elton Mayo (1880–1949) has secured fame as the leader in a series of experiments that became one of the great turning points in management thinking. At the Hawthorne plant of Western Electric, he discovered that job satisfaction increased through employee participation in decisions, rather than through short-term incentives.

LIFE AND CAREER

An Australian by birth, Mayo read psychology at Adelaide University and, in 1911, was appointed lecturer in logic, ethics, and psychology (and later professor of philosophy) at the University of Queensland.

Anxious to move to the United States for professional reasons, he took a post at Pennsylvania University in 1923. Here, he became involved in one of the investigations that acted as a dry run for Hawthorne. In one department at a spinning mill in Philadelphia, labour turnover was 250%, compared with an average of 6% in other parts of the company. A series of experimental changes in working conditions was introduced in the department, most notably rest pauses. These changes led to successive increases in productivity and the raising of morale. After one year, labour turnover was down to the average level for the company. It was assumed that this improvement was due to the introduction of rest pauses—a conclusion that was to undergo substantial modification as a result of Hawthorne.

The Hawthorne experiments began in 1924 and Mayo's involvement in them in 1928, after he had moved to the Harvard University School of Business Administration as associate professor of industrial research. Later awarded a chair, he remained at Harvard until his retirement in 1947. During the Second World War, Mayo contributed to the development of supervisor training with his Training Within Industry (TWI) programme, which was widely adopted in the United States.

The last two years of his life were spent in the United Kingdom, as an adviser to the British government on problems within industry.

CONTRIBUTION

Mayo wrote about democracy and freedom, and the social problems of industrialised civilisation. It is as the author of *Human Problems of an Industrial Civilisation*, which reports on the Hawthorne experiments, that he is known for his contribution to management thinking, even though he disclaimed responsibility for the design and direction of the project.

The Hawthorne experiments

The Hawthorne plant of Western Electric was located in Chicago. It had some 29,000 employees and manufactured telephones and telephone equipment, principally for AT&T. The company had a reputation for advanced personnel policies and had welcomed a study by the National Research Council into the relationship between workplace lighting and the efficiency of individual workers. The study began in 1924 by isolating two groups of workers in order to test the impact of various incentives on their productivity. Improvements to levels of lighting produced increases in productivity, but so too did reversion to standard lighting and even below-standard lighting in both groups. The initial assumption therefore was that increased output stemmed from variation alone.

Other incentives, including payment incentives and rest pauses, were manipulated at regular intervals and, although output levels varied, the trend was inexorably upwards. Whatever experimentation was applied, output went up. Although it had been fairly conclusively determined that lighting had little to do with output levels, the assistant works manager (George Pennock) agreed that something peculiar was going on, and that experimentation should continue.

Early deductions—supervision and employee attitudes

In the winter of 1927, Pennock invited Clair Turner, professor of biology and public health at Massachusetts Institute of Technology (MIT), to contribute. Turner quickly resolved that rest pauses in themselves were not the cause for increased output, although longer rest pauses gave rise to more social interaction, which in turn affected mental attitudes. Turner attributed the rise in output to the small group; the type of supervision; earnings; the novelty of the experiment; and the increased attention to the workers generated by the experiment itself.

Pennock had been among the first to note that supervisory style was important. The supervisor involved in the illumination experiment had been relaxed and friendly; he got to know the operators well and was not too worried about company policies and procedures. Discipline was secured through enlightened leadership, and an esprit de corps grew up within the group. This was in stark contrast to standard practice before the experiment.

When Pennock invited Turner to participate, he also invited Mayo—although it is not known whether this was as a result of Mayo's achievements at the Philadelphian spinning mill, or because of a desire to involve Harvard. Visits in 1929 and 1930 indicated to Mayo 'a remarkable change of attitude in the group'. Mayo's view was that the test room workers had turned into a social unit, enjoyed all the attention they were getting, and had developed a sense of participation in the project.

In order to understand this further, Mayo instituted a series of interviews. These provided the workers with an opportunity to express their views. It emerged that they would feel better for discussing a situation, even if it did not change. Further exploration revealed that some complaints had little or no basis in fact, but were actually indicators of personal situations causing distress.

By focusing on a more open, listening and caring interview approach, Mayo had struck a key which linked the style of supervision and the level of morale to levels of productivity.

Further research — social groups

A third stage in the research took place in the bank wiring room, with a similar application of incentives to productivity. Here it emerged that output was restricted:

- the group had a standard for output that was respected by individuals in the group
- the group was indifferent to the employer's financial incentive scheme
- the group developed a code of behaviour of its own, based on solidarity in opposition to the management
- output was determined by informal social groups rather than by management

Mayo had read the work of F.W. Taylor, who had already established that social groups were capable of exercising very strong control over the work behaviour of individual members (Taylor had called it 'systematic soldiering'). The interesting development that Mayo noted, however, was that whereas in the first set of experiments productivity went up as the project progressed, in the other — the bank wiring room — productivity was restricted.

In *The Human Problems of an Industrial Civilization,* Mayo wrote: 'Human collaboration in work...has always depended for its perpetuation upon the evolution of a non-logical social code which regulates the relations between persons and their attitudes to one another. Insistence upon a merely economic logic of production...interferes with the development of such a code and consequently gives rise in the group to a sense of human defeat. This...results in the formation of a social code at a lower level and in opposition to the economic logic. One of its symptoms is "restriction".'

The question which needed to be asked, therefore, was, 'What was different between the two groups?' The answer was found to lie with the attitude of the observer — where the observer encouraged participation and took the workers into his confidence, productivity went up; where the observer merely watched and adopted the trappings of traditional supervisory practice, output was restricted.

Interpreting Hawthorne

For industry to benefit from the experiments at Hawthorne, Mayo first concluded that supervisors needed training in understanding the personal problems of workers, and also in listening and interviewing techniques. He held that the new supervisor should be less aloof, more people-oriented, more concerned, and skilled in handling personal and social situations.

It was only later, after a period of reflection, that Mayo was able to conclude that:

- job satisfaction increased as workers were given more freedom to determine the conditions of their working environment and to set their own standards of output
- intensified interaction and co-operation created a high level of group cohesion

- job satisfaction and output depended more on co-operation and a feeling of worth than on physical working conditions

In Mayo's view, workers had been unable to find satisfactory outlets for expressing personal problems and dissatisfactions in their work life. The problem was that managers thought the answers to industrial problems resided in technical efficiency, when actually the answer was a human and social one.

Mayo's contribution lies in recognising that the formality of strict rules and procedures spawns informal approaches and groups with their base in human emotions, problems, and interactions. The manager, therefore, should strive for an equilibrium between the technical organisation and the human one, and hence should develop skills in handling human relations and situations. These include diagnostic skills in understanding human behaviour and interpersonal skills in counselling, motivating, leading, and communicating.

CONTEXT AND CONCLUSIONS

Mayo has been acclaimed by his followers as the founder of the human relations school of management, and criticised by sociologists for not going far enough in his interpretations. Reading Mayo's conclusions causes no surprise, let alone discovery, at the end of the 20th century; his attitudes are increasingly commonplace among social scientists, trade unionists, and managers alike. But that is perhaps a measure of his achievement, because most commentators agree that he was the first to demonstrate, infer, and provide evidence for the benefits of a shift in management thinking away from the widespread dominance of Taylor's scientific management.

F.J. Roethlisberger said of Mayo that the data were not his; the results were not his; but the interpretations of both were indeed his. Without those interpretations, the results of Hawthorne might still be collecting dust in the archives.

The experiment also gave rise to the term 'Hawthorne effect': a situation which arose because people were 'singled out' for special treatment or because a 'special situation' was created in which workers could feel free to air their problems.

Mayo's ideas on the emergence of 'informal' organisations were read by Argyris and others as they developed theories about how organisations learned and developed. The discrediting of the 'rabble hypothesis' theory led directly to the work of McGregor. The Hawthorne studies established the beginnings of recognition that management style is a major contributor to industrial productivity; that interpersonal skills are as important as monetary incentives or target-setting, and that a more humanistic approach is an important means of satisfying the organisation's economic and social needs.

THE BEST SOURCES OF HELP
Books:
Mayo, Elton. *The Human Problems of an Industrial Civilization* 2nd ed. Boston: Harvard University Press, 1946.
Mayo, Elton. *The Social Problems of an Industrial Civilization*. London: Routledge and Kegan Paul, 1949.

DOUGLAS McGREGOR

1906	Born.
1932	Graduates from Wayne University.
1935	Receives PhD in experimental psychology from Harvard University.
1948–1954	President, Antioch College.
1954	Professor of management, Massachusetts Institute of Technology.
1960	Publication of *The Human Side of Enterprise*.
1964	Dies.
1993	Listed as one of the most popular management writers alongside Henri Fayol.

> **SUMMARY**
>
> Developer of Theory X and Theory Y, which describe two views of people at work and two opposing management styles, Douglas McGregor's relatively short career has been a key influence for many of today's management commentators. *The Human Side of Enterprise* marked a watershed in management thinking, and laid the foundations for the modern, people-centred view of management.

LIFE AND CAREER

Douglas McGregor (1906-1964) followed a mostly academic career, lecturing at Harvard University, Massachusetts Institute of Technology (MIT) and Antioch College and becoming the first Sloan Fellows professor at MIT. Although, because of his early death, he wrote only a few publications, they have had a great impact.

In 1993 McGregor was listed as one of the most popular management writers, alongside Henri Fayol (in *Management Gurus—What Makes Them and How to Become One*). Major American writers such as Rosabeth Moss Kanter, Warren Bennis, and Tom Peters, whose writings have much influence on current learning and practice, agree that much of modern management thinking goes back to McGregor, especially the implications of his writing for theories on leadership.

CONTRIBUTION

McGregor believed that managers' basic beliefs have a dominant influence on the way that organisations are run, and central to this are managers' assumptions about the behaviour of people. McGregor argues that these assumptions fall into two broad categories—Theory X and Theory Y. His findings were detailed in *The Human Side of Enterprise*, first published in 1960.

Theory X and Theory Y describe two views of people at work and may be used to describe two opposing management styles.

Theory X: the traditional view of direction and control

Theory X is based on the assumptions that:

- the average human being has an inherent dislike of work and will avoid it if at all possible
- because of this human dislike of work, most people must be coerced, controlled, directed, and threatened with punishment to get them to make adequate effort towards the achievement of organisational objectives

- the average human being prefers to be directed; wishes to avoid responsibility; has relatively little ambition; wants security above all else.

A Theory X management style therefore requires close, firm supervision with clearly specified tasks and the threat of punishment or the promise of greater pay as motivating factors. Managers working under these assumptions will employ autocratic controls that can lead to mistrust and resentment from those they manage. McGregor acknowledges that this approach constitutes a damning statement about the 'mediocrity of the masses'. He acknowledges, too, that the 'carrot and stick' approach can have a place but will not work when the needs of people are predominantly social and egoistic.

Theory Y: the integration of individual and organisational goals

Theory Y is based on the assumptions that:

- the expenditure of physical and mental effort in work is as natural as play or rest. The average human being does not inherently dislike work. Depending upon controllable conditions, work may be a source of satisfaction, or a source of punishment
- external control and the threat of punishment are not the only means for bringing about effort towards achieving organisational objectives. People will exercise self-direction and self-control in the service of objectives to which they are committed
- commitment to objectives is a result of the rewards associated with their achievement. The most significant of such rewards, such as the satisfaction of ego and self-actualisation needs, can be direct products of effort directed towards organisational objectives
- under proper conditions, the average human being learns not only to accept but to seek responsibility. Avoidance of responsibility, lack of ambition, and emphasis on security are generally consequences of experience, not inherent human characteristics
- the capacity to exercise a relatively high degree of imagination, ingenuity, and creativity in the solution of organisational problems is widely, not narrowly, distributed in the population
- under the conditions of modern industrial life, the intellectual potential of the average human being is used only partially.

Theory Y assumptions can lead to more co-operative relationships between managers and workers. A Theory Y management style seeks to establish a working environment in which the personal needs and objectives of individuals can relate to, and harmonise with, the objectives of the organisation.

In *The Human Side of Enterprise,* McGregor recognises that Theory Y is not a panacea for all ills. But by highlighting such ideas, he hopes instead to achieve an abandonment by management of the limiting assumptions of Theory X and a consideration of the techniques involved in Theory Y.

Theory into practice

Abraham Maslow viewed McGregor as a mentor, and was a strong supporter of theories X and Y. So he decided to put Theory Y (that people want to work, achieve, and take responsibility) into practice in a Californian electronics factory. However, he found that an organisation driven solely by Theory Y could not succeed, as some sense of direction and structure was required. Instead, Maslow advocated an improved version of Theory Y that involved an element of structured security and direction taken from Theory X.

Maslow's negative experience with implementing Theory Y must be balanced against that of McGregor himself at a Procter & Gamble plant in Georgia, where he introduced Theory Y through the concept of self-directed teams. This plant was found to be a third more profitable than any other Procter & Gamble plant; it was kept a trade secret until the mid-1990s.

Before he died, McGregor began to develop a further theory that addressed the criticisms made of theories X and Y—that they were mutually incompatible. Ideas he proposed as part of this theory included lifetime employment; concern for employees (both inside and outside the working environment); decision by consensus; and commitment to quality. He tentatively called it Theory Z. Before it could be widely published, McGregor died and the ideas faded.

Theory Z

The work on Theory Z that McGregor began was not completely forgotten. During the 1970s, William Ouchi began to expound its principles by comparing and contrasting Japanese (Type J) and American (Type A) organisations.

Type A organisations, he proposed, tend to offer short-term employment, specialised careers (with rapid promotion), and individual decision-making and responsibility. Type J firms, on the other hand, mirror the ethos of Japanese society—collectivism and stability rather than individuality. Those American firms that share Type J characteristics, and indeed have more in common with Type J organisations, were described as Type Z (examples included Hewlett-Packard and Procter & Gamble).

Leadership

Before McGregor, the thrust of writing about leadership focused on the qualities and characteristics of 'great people', in the hope that, if those qualities were identified, they could be emulated.

McGregor argued that there were other variables involved in leadership, including the attitudes and needs of the followers, the nature and structure of the organisation itself, and the social, economic, and political environment. For McGregor, leadership was not a property of the individual but a complex relationship among these variables. He was one of the first to argue that leadership was more about the relationship between the leader and the situation he or she faced, than merely the characteristics of the leader alone.

CONTEXT AND CONCLUSIONS

The Human Side of Enterprise marked a watershed in management thinking, that had previously been dominated by the scientific approach of Taylor, and formed the foundations for the current, people-centred view of management.

Theory Y has been criticised for being too idealistic, but if we examine each of the six tenets of Theory Y in turn, we can trace much modern thinking back to McGregor:

1. Work, as a source of satisfaction, means accepting that people need to know not just what or how, but why; the adoption of meaningful objectives is one of the keys to self-motivation.

2–4. Ownership, commitment, and responsibility are three of the cornerstones of empowerment.

5–6. The encouragement for people to be fully exercised in the solution of organisational problems is central to action learning, total quality management, strategic thinking, and knowledge exploitation.

As mentioned above, Moss Kanter (writing on empowerment), Bennis (on leadership), and Peters (on excellence as well as chaos) all acknowledge their debt to McGregor.

Contemporary and subsequent commentaries on McGregor's theories have tended to see them as black and white. Harold Geneen, former president and CEO of ITT, commented that although Theories X and Y propose a neat summary of business management, no company is run in strict accordance with either one or the other. Peter Drucker said that Theory X sees people as immature, whereas Theory Y sees them striving towards adulthood.

The two contrasting theories are best seen perhaps as two polarising forces with which managers have to grapple. Blake and Mouton expressed this in terms of the managerial grid, where managers constantly have to balance the drives and forces between task—getting things done—and people—how best to get them done for the benefit of the organisation and the individuals doing them.

Although Theory Y has been held up as an unachievable aim—with the individual and the organisation having convergent aspirations—the successful cases in which this aim is being attempted are growing. It is precisely such a goal that organisations are hoping to achieve through continuous improvement, continuous professional development, and participation schemes operating in climates of empowerment.

It is not going too far to say that *The Human Side of Enterprise* recognises that although we cannot actually motivate people, we do have a responsibility to acknowledge the elements involved in motivation. What we can do is to attempt to create the right climate, environment, or working conditions for motivation to be enabled.

THE BEST SOURCES OF HELP
Books:
Huczynski, Andreas. *Management Gurus—What Makes Them and How to Become One*. London: Routledge, 1992.
McGregor, Douglas. *The Human Side of Enterprise*. New York: McGraw-Hill, 1960.
McGregor, Douglas. *Leadership and Motivation*: MIT Press, 1966.
McGregor, Douglas. *The Professional Manager*. New York: McGraw-Hill, 1967.
Ouchi, William G. *Theory Z: How American Business Can Meet the Japanese Challenge*. Reading, Massachusetts: Addison Wesley, 1981.

HENRY MINTZBERG

1939	Born.
1961	Receives a B Eng from McGill University.
1961–1963	Operational research with Canadian National Railways.
1968	Receives a PhD and becomes professor at McGill University; also subsequently becomes director of the Center for Strategic Studies.
1973	Publication of *The Nature of Managerial Work*.
1975	Wins the McKinsey Prize for best article.
1988–1991	President of the Strategic Management Society.
1991–	Holds other positions in management institutions, including that of visiting professor at INSEAD in France.
1995	*The Rise and Fall of Strategic Planning* receives the George R. Terry best book of the year award.
1995–2000	Director of International Masters Program in Practicing Management.
1996	Appointed Cleghorn Professor of Management Studies at McGill University.

> **SUMMARY**
> Often regarded as an iconoclast and a rebel, Henry Mintzberg has certainly challenged many traditional ideas. But he does not attack people with whom he disagrees; he simply sets about proving them wrong, with devastating clarity. Devoted to understanding how people actually manage, he resists every temptation to pontificate about how anyone *ought* to manage.

LIFE AND CAREER

Henry Mintzberg was born in Canada and has spent virtually all his working life there. He studied at McGill University and, after further study at MIT, returned to Canada to take up an appointment with Canadian National Railways in 1961. In 1963 he moved into the academic world and by 1968 was back at McGill University as a professor, a post he holds to the present day. He is also director of the Center for Strategic Studies in Organization at McGill and has held several important positions in other management institutions, including that of visiting professor at INSEAD, the international business school at Fontainebleau in France. He has been a consultant to many organisations throughout the world and from 1988 to 1991 he was president of the Strategic Management Society.

Mintzberg's major impact on the management world began with his book *The Nature of Managerial Work*, published in 1973, and a seminal article in the *Harvard Business Review*, 'The manager's job: folklore and fact', written two years later. Based on detailed research and thoughtful observation, these two works established Mintzberg's reputation by showing that what managers did, when successfully carrying out their responsibilities, was substantially different from much business theory.

CONTRIBUTION

Unlike many gurus, Mintzberg's contribution to management thinking is not based on one or two clever theories within some narrow discipline. His approach is broad, involving the study of virtually everything managers do and how they do it. His general appeal is further enhanced by a fundamental belief that management is about applying human skills to systems, not applying systems to people, a belief that is demonstrated throughout his writing.

How managers work

In 'The manager's job: folklore and fact', Mintzberg sets out the stark reality of what managers do. 'If there is a simple theme that runs through this article, it is that the pressures of his job drive the manager to be superficial in his actions—to overload himself with work, encourage interruption, respond quickly to every stimulus, seek the tangible and avoid the abstract, make decisions in small increments, and do everything abruptly,' he writes.

Mintzberg uses the article to stress the importance of the manager's role and the need to understand it thoroughly before attempting to train and develop those engaged in carrying it out.

'No job is more vital to our society than that of the manager. It is the manager who determines whether our social institutions serve us well or whether they squander our talents and resources. It is time to strip away the folklore about managerial work, and time to study it realistically so that we can begin the difficult task of making significant improvements in its performance.' In *The Nature of Managerial Work*, Mintzberg proposes six characteristics of management work and ten basic management roles.

- The manager's job is a mixture of regular, programmed jobs and unprogrammed tasks.
- A manager is both a generalist and a specialist.
- Managers rely on information from all sources but show a preference for that which is transmitted orally.
- Managerial work is made up of activities that are characterised by brevity, variety and fragmentation.
- Management work is more an art than a science and is reliant on intuitive processes and a 'feel' for what is right.
- Management work is becoming more complex.

Mintzberg places the ten roles that he believes make up the content of the manager's job into three categories.

Interpersonal
- Figurehead—performing symbolic duties as a representative of the organisation.
- Leader—establishing the atmosphere and motivating the subordinates.
- Liaiser—developing and maintaining webs of contacts outside the organisation.

Information
- Monitor—collecting all types of information that are relevant and useful to the organisation.
- Disseminator—transmitting information from outside the organisation to those inside.
- Spokesperson—transmitting information from inside the organisation to outsiders.

Decision-making
- Entrepreneur—initiating change and adapting to the environment.
- Disturbance Handler—dealing with unexpected events.
- Resource Allocator—deciding on the use of the organisation's resources.
- Negotiator—negotiating with individuals and dealing with other organisations.

The Structuring of Organizations
In his 1979 book, *The Structuring of Organizations*, Mintzberg identified five types of 'ideal' organisation structures. These were: simple structure; machine bureaucracy; professional bureaucracy; divisional; and adhocracy. The classification was re-examined and expanded ten years later in *Mintzberg on Management* and the following, more detailed, view of organisation types drawn up:

- the Entrepreneurial Organisation—small staff, loose division of labour, little management hierarchy, informal, with power focused on the chief executive
- the Machine Organisation—highly specialised, routine operating tasks, formal communication, large operating units, tasks grouped under functions, elaborate administrative systems, central decision making, and a sharp distinction between line and staff
- the Diversified Organisation—a set of semi-autonomous units under a central administrative structure. The units are usually called divisions and the central administration referred to as the headquarters
- the Professional Organisation—commonly found in hospitals, universities, public agencies, and firms doing routine work, this structure relies on the skills and knowledge of professional staff in order to function. All such organisations produce standardised products or services
- the Innovative Organisation—this is what Mintzberg sees as the modern organisation: one that is flexible, rejecting any form of bureaucracy and avoiding emphasis on planning and control systems. Innovation is achieved by hiring experts; giving them power; training and developing them; and employing them in multi-disciplinary teams that work in an atmosphere unbounded by conventional specialisms and differentiation
- the Missionary Organisation—it is the mission that counts above all else in such organisations, and the mission is clear, focused, distinctive, and inspiring. Employees readily identify with the mission, share common values and are motivated by their own zeal and enthusiasm.

Strategy and planning
The relationship between strategy and planning is a constant theme in Mintzberg's writing and his views on the subject are perhaps his most important contribution to current management thinking.

In his 1994 book, *The Rise and Fall of Strategic Planning*, Mintzberg produces a masterly criticism of conventional theory. His main concern is with what he sees as basic failings in our approach to planning. These failings are:

- processes—the elaborate processes used create bureaucracy and suppress innovation and originality
- data—'hard' data (the raw material of all strategists) provides information, but 'soft' data provides wisdom. 'Hard information can be no better and is often at times far worse than soft information.'

- detachment—it is no use producing strategies in 'ivory towers'. Effective strategists are not people who distance themselves from the detail of a business 'but quite the opposite: they are the ones who immerse themselves in it, while being able to abstract the strategic messages from it.'
- strategy is not 'the consequence of planning but the opposite: its starting point'. Mintzberg has coined the phrase 'crafting strategies' to illustrate his concept of the delicate, painstaking process of developing strategy—a process of emergence that is far removed from the classical picture of strategists grouped around a table predicting the future. He argues that while an organisation needs a strategy, strategic plans are generally useless as one cannot predict two to three years ahead.

CONTEXT AND CONCLUSIONS

Henry Mintzberg remains one of the few truly generalist management writers of today. Different readers see him as an expert in different areas. For some people, he is an authority on time management, and he has written some of the most thoughtful and practical advice on this subject; for others he is the champion of the hard-pressed manager, surrounded by management theorists telling him or her how to do his or her job; and for yet another group, he is a leading authority on strategic planning.

For most people, however, Mintzberg is the man who dared to challenge orthodox beliefs and who has changed our ideas about many key business activities.

THE BEST SOURCES OF HELP
Books:
Mintzberg, Henry. *The Nature of Managerial Work*. New York: Harper & Row, 1973.
Mintzberg, Henry. *The Structuring of Organizations: a Synthesis of the Research*. Englewood Cliffs, New Jersey: Prentice Hall, 1979.
Mintzberg, Henry. *Structures in Fives: Designing Effective Organizations*. Englewood Cliffs, New Jersey: Prentice Hall, 1983.
Mintzberg, Henry. *Power In and Around Organizations*. Englewood Cliffs, New Jersey: Prentice Hall, 1983.
Mintzberg, Henry. *Mintzberg on Management: Inside our Strange World of Organizations*. New York: Free Press, 1989.
Mintzberg, Henry. *The Rise and Fall of Strategic Planning*. Hemel Hempstead: Prentice Hall International, 1994.
Mintzberg, Henry, and J. B. Quinn. *The Strategy Process: Concepts, Contexts, Cases*. 3rd ed. London: Prentice Hall International, 1996.
Journal Articles:
Mintzberg, Henry. 'The manager's job: folklore and fact.' *Harvard Business Review*, Mar./Apr., pp. 163-176. (Originally published in 1975, the article includes a retrospective commentary by the author.)
Mintzberg, Henry. 'Crafting strategy.' *Harvard Business Review*, Jul./Aug. 1987, pp. 66-75.
Mintzberg, Henry. 'The fall and rise of strategic planning.' *Harvard Business Review*, Jan./Feb. 1994, pp. 107-114.
Mintzberg, Henry. 'Rounding out the manager's job.' *Sloan Management Review*, Autumn 1994, pp. 11-26.
Mintzberg, Henry. 'Musings on management.' *Harvard Business Review*, Jul./Aug. 1996, pp. 61-67.

IKUJIRO NONAKA

1935	Born.
1958	Graduates from Waseda University
1995	Publication of *The Knowledge-Creating Company*.
1995	Joins Japan Advanced Institute of Science and Technology (JAIST).
1997	Becomes dean of the School of Knowledge Science at JAIST.

> **SUMMARY**
> The work of Ikujiro Nonaka is best known for its focus on the creation of knowledge within organisations. Nonaka believes that this is the most meaningful core capability for a company, particularly because it leads to innovation. He argues that the knowledge generated becomes the key source of competitive advantage for the firm.

LIFE AND CAREER

Ikujiro Nonaka (born 1935) is the first professor of knowledge at the Haas School of Business, University of California, where he previously received his MBA and PhD degrees. He is also dean of the graduate School of Knowledge Science at the Japan Advanced Institute of Science and Technology (JAIST) in Japan. He was formerly a professor and director of the Institute of Innovation Research at Hitotsubashi University, Tokyo.

Professor Nonaka has described his work as comparative research on knowledge-creating processes in companies around the world, and also research on the characteristics of innovative activities in Japanese companies. He seeks to answer questions about what knowledge is, how organisations create knowledge, and how we can promote knowledge creation.

CONTRIBUTION
The knowledge-creating company

In their book *The Knowledge-Creating Company: How Japanese Companies Create the Dynamics of Innovation*, Ikujiro Nonaka and Hirotaka Takeuchi argue that the success of Japanese companies is due to their skill and expertise in organisational knowledge creation, especially with respect to bringing about continuous business innovation. They use the metaphor of a journey, warning that there are new and foreign road signs to follow on the way. The book, which combines theoretical and philosophical analysis with practical case studies, attempts to convey the complex forces at work within creative organisational systems. It is not straightforward to read, but the authors justify this with the declaration that '...managers can no longer afford to be satisfied with simplistic ideas about knowledge and its creation'.

Explicit and implicit knowledge

Nonaka and Takeuchi's starting point is a contrast between Western and Eastern philosophies. In the West knowledge is formal, unambiguous, systematic, falsifiable, and scientific, and a quest for knowledge normally involves the analysis and interpretation of data and information. New knowledge is documented and then transferred by means of formal training. The authors describe this form of knowledge as 'explicit'. It is primarily managed through databases and manuals. Human expertise, experience, and insights are, they claim, generally ignored as sources of knowledge.

In the East, however, knowledge is intuitive, interpretative, ambiguous, non-linear, and difficult to reduce to scientific equations. Instead of being created through data analysis and interpretation, it grows from the expertise and experience of many people, whose minds are probed for insights. New knowledge is distributed and retained through experience. The resulting Eastern form of knowledge is described as 'implicit'.

In the authors' view, implicit and explicit knowledge are not totally separate but mutually complementary entities. Successful Japanese companies are able to convert implicit knowledge to explicit knowledge, so that knowledge acquired by individuals becomes organisational knowledge shared among colleagues, and explicit knowledge is converted into implicit knowledge by individuals. Nonaka and Takeuchi refer to this interaction between implicit and explicit knowledge as knowledge conversion. They suggest four methods of knowledge conversion, otherwise known as the SECI process:

- socialisation
- externalisation
- combination
- internalisation

These are described as the mechanisms by which implicit knowledge is 'amplified' throughout the organisation, creating a spiral model of knowledge creation.

Middle-up-down management style

Nonaka and Takeuchi argue that the two traditional Western management styles, 'top-down' and 'bottom-up', fail to foster the dynamic interaction necessary to create organisational knowledge.

Successful Japanese companies acknowledge the vital role played by middle managers in taking the top management vision of 'what should be' and the frontline employees' realistic sense of 'what is', and developing midrange concepts. Middle managers are, in effect, the real 'knowledge engineers' of the knowledge-creating company, serving as facilitators between top and bottom as well as between theory and reality, and playing a key role in innovation.

A 'hypertext' organisation consisting of interconnected layers is put forward as the ideal structure for knowledge creation. It combines two traditional structures—the hierarchy and the task force. Surprisingly, the model for this organisational form is the US military, which is bureaucratic in peacetime but highly task-oriented in war. Nonaka and Takeuchi provide two case studies of Japanese companies that have attempted to implement a hypertext structure—Kao and Sharp.

Transferring knowledge

The Knowledge-Creating Company is rich in case studies, which are mostly based on large, well-established Japanese companies, including Matsushita, NEC, Canon, Honda, and Nissan. Many of the case studies describe a 'transferring process', in which the organisational knowledge created during new product development in one division becomes transferred to other parts of the company. For example, the knowledge created within Canon while developing the mini-copier in the early 1980s was subsequently used in other areas. The product knowledge generated was applied to other equipment such as printers; the knowledge gained from the manufacturing process led to the automation of copier production; and the organisational knowledge gleaned influenced the way the company was managed.

The transfer of knowledge can also take place at a global level across national boundaries, and one example given is of Nissan's experience of developing a car in the United Kingdom. The case of Shin Caterpillar Mitsubishi, a US–Japanese alliance, shows how knowledge creation can cut across company as well as national boundaries. It refers to the experience of Mitsubishi of Japan and Caterpillar of the United States when they pooled their resources to develop and market hydraulic shovels. Nonaka and Takeuchi demonstrate that using the four stages of knowledge conversion within the alliance averted potentially damaging clashes of culture, overcame the weaknesses of both sides in knowledge creation, and led to effective knowledge creation and innovation.

Practical implications

The authors finish with some recommendations as to what Western companies can do to become knowledge-creating companies. They should:

- create a knowledge vision (top management should define the boundaries of organisational knowledge and outline what kind of knowledge ought to be created)
- develop a knowledge crew (of employees with diverse talents)
- build a high-density field of interaction (an environment in which frequent and intensive interactions take place) at the front-line
- piggyback on the new product development process
- adopt middle-up-down management
- switch to a hypertext organisation
- construct a knowledge network with the outside world (meaning external stakeholders such as customers)

The concept of 'Ba' or shared spaces

Since the publication of *The Knowledge-Creating Company*, Nonaka has developed the theory of 'Ba', which provides a platform for creating knowledge. Ba means 'place' or 'shared spaces' and can be physical (for example, an office), virtual (for example, e-mail) or mental (for example, shared experiences, ideas, and, by extension, organisation culture). Nonaka argues that knowledge cannot be separated from its context and is embedded in these shared spaces.

Nonaka describes four kinds of platform corresponding to the four stages of knowledge conversion mentioned above. Each space supports a particular conversion process and thereby speeds up overall knowledge creation.

- Originating (supports the socialisation stage)—physical face-to-face experiences which provide the environment in which individuals share feelings and experiences. These are the key to the transfer of tacit knowledge.
- Interacting (supports the externalisation stage)—a team-based environment, where individuals' mental models and skills are converted into common terms and concepts. This assists the process in which tacit knowledge is made explicit.

- Cyber (supports the combination stage)—interaction in the virtual world of cyberspace. This facilitates the exchanging and combining of different forms of explicit knowledge.
- Exercising (supports the internalisation stage)—focused training with senior mentors and colleagues which assists the conversion of explicit knowledge into tacit knowledge.

'Knowledge activists'
Knowledge activists support platforms and cultures by enabling knowledge creation. A knowledge activist can be an individual, group, or department that takes on a particular responsibility for energising and co-ordinating knowledge creation throughout the organisation. The activist has three roles: to act as a catalyst of knowledge creation, to co-ordinate knowledge creation initiatives, and to provide overall direction to these efforts.

CONTEXT AND CONCLUSIONS

Peter Drucker first used the terms 'knowledge worker' and 'knowledge society' in the 1960s and more recently stated that knowledge has become the only meaningful resource. Nonaka acknowledges Drucker's contribution and takes it a stage further by looking at how knowledge is created and examining the processes involved.

The second half of the 1990s saw a huge surge of business interest in knowledge, led primarily by practitioners rather than academics. Nonaka, while not responsible for the attention given to knowledge management, provided ideas that gave purpose and direction to practitioner initiatives. No other writer in this field has made such a forceful business case for knowledge creation. Also Nonaka reminds us that information technology is not enough and that human experience and implicit knowledge are important in creating new knowledge. Lastly, Nonaka emphasised the importance of the role of middle management in organisation information creation as early as 1988, and this was a significant departure from the Western view of middle management as a deadweight, potentially expendable part of the corporate structure.

In these respects Nonaka's ideas have been absorbed into the mainstream of management thinking and are almost taken for granted. Few organisations, however, have embraced his vision in its entirety, or attempted the kind of cultural and organisational restructuring to improve knowledge creation which he advocates.

THE BEST SOURCES OF HELP
Book:
Nonaka, Ikujiro, and Hirotaka Takeuchi. *The Knowledge-Creating Company: How Japanese Companies Create the Dynamics of Innovation*. New York: Oxford University Press, 1995.
Journal Articles:
Nonaka, Ikujiro. 'The knowledge-creating company.' *Harvard Business Review*, Nov./Dec. 1991, vol. 69 no. 6, pp. 96–104.
Nonaka, Ikujiro, Georg Von Krogh, and Kazuo Ichijo. 'Develop knowledge activists!' *European Management Journal*, Oct. 1997, vol. 15 no. 5, pp. 475–483.
Nonaka, Ikujiro, and Noboru Konno.'The concept of 'Ba': Building a foundation for knowledge creation.' *California Management Review*, Spring 1998, vol. 40 no. 3, pp. 40–54
Nonaka, Ikujiro, Ryoko Toyama, and Noboru Konno. 'SEC ba and leadership: a unified model of dynamic knowledge creation.' *Long Range Planning*, Feb. 2000, vol. 33 no. 1, pp. 5–34.

KENICHI OHMAE

1943	Born.
1972	Joins McKinsey & Co.
1975	Publication of *The Mind of the Strategist*.
1987	Publication of *Beyond National Boundaries*.
1990	Publication of *The Borderless World*.
1995	Stands as candidate for governorship of Tokyo.
1995	Publication of *The End of the Nation State*.

SUMMARY

Ohmae's fresh approach to business strategy challenged business leaders to think in innovative, simple, and unconventional terms. His work in the late 1970s and 1980s heralded the arrival of Japanese management techniques in the West. Ohmae was the messenger for the Japanese way of doing business, urging managers to think 'out of the box', and challenge accepted norms with clear, simple ideas in order to gain, and sustain, competitive advantage.

LIFE AND CAREER

Kenichi Ohmae was born in 1943 on the island of Kyushu, and graduated from Waseda University and the Tokyo Institute of Technology before obtaining a PhD in nuclear engineering from the Massachusetts Institute of Technology. In 1972 he joined the consultancy firm McKinsey & Co, becoming managing director of their Tokyo office. As well as being a nuclear physicist, he is an accomplished clarinettist and a politician. In 1995, he stood for election as governor of Tokyo and also acted as an adviser to Japan's then prime minister, Nakasone.

Ohmae lives in Yokohama and advises some of Japan's most successful international companies in a wide spectrum of industries. His special interest and area of expertise is in formulating creative strategies and developing organisational concepts to implement them.

Ohmae's seminal book, *The Mind of the Strategist*, was published in Japan in 1975. It was, however, only when interest in Japanese management methods increased during the early 1980s that the book was published in the United States. This 1982 American edition was given the subtitle *The Art of Japanese Business*. In *The Mind of the Strategist* Ohmae argues that the success of Japanese companies can be attributed to the nature of Japanese strategic thinking. This, contrary to the Western stereotype of Japanese management, was largely creative, intuitive, and vision-driven. Ohmae went on to explain what this creativity involved and how it could be learnt.

The view presented by Ohmae overturned traditional Western perceptions of Japanese managers and the idea that their success was founded on brilliantly rational, far-sighted thinking. Ohmae heralded a revolution based on creativity and innovation, and showed how, in the hands of a single, talented strategist, creativity could transform a major corporation.

In 1990, Ohmae's book *The Borderless World* challenged Japanese companies and corporations around the world to take account of globalisation in their strategic planning. He urged businesses to focus less on the competitive aspects of strategy (promoted so effectively by Porter and others), and instead to give greater focus to 'country' and 'currency', two key elements that in an interdependent world economy can make or break a business strategy. This approach reflected Ohmae's increasing focus on global business and the relationship between business and the nation state. The latter was also the subject of two other books, *Beyond National Boundaries* (1987) and *The End of the Nation State* (1995).

Just as *The Mind of the Strategist* had encouraged innovation in strategy in the 1980s, so *The Borderless World* highlighted the importance of the global interdependence that dominated trade in the 1990s.

CONTRIBUTION
The role of the strategist
Ohmae has explored a number of features of successful business strategies (usually Japanese), and compared them with their typical counterparts in the West. He identified several key differences including:

- *vision and dynamic leadership*. Japanese businesses tend to have a single, driving force in the form of an effective strategist, a leader or visionary who possesses what Ohmae has described as an idiosyncratic mode of thinking. Through this, company, customers, and competition (described as the strategic triangle) merge into a dynamic interaction from which, eventually, a comprehensive set of objectives and plans for action emerges. This approach was in marked contrast to the large, strategic planning bureaucracies that were typical of many large Western corporations of the time (the early 1980s).
- *customer focus*. The customer is at the heart of Japanese strategy and is virtually enshrined as central to corporate values. The focus of the business needs to be on delivering what the customer wants, or there will be no business.
- *methodology*. Ohmae perceived that to develop effective strategies, managers must first gain a detailed understanding of the characteristics of each element in a situation, and then develop a holistic plan tying each part of the business, each separate resource, into a competitive and efficient operation. This is not a systems approach based on linear thinking, but instead relies on detailed analysis ('the starting point') and knowledge, combined with innovation, intuition, and creativity.

The strategic triangle
Ohmae claimed that, in constructing any business strategy, the three main players to be taken into account are the corporation itself, the customer, and the competition. Each of these three Cs is a living entity with its own interests and objectives, while collectively they form the strategic triangle. The three Cs influence strategy and planning in a number of important ways.

1. *Strategic business units (SBUs)*. The need for strategic business units that understand all three elements and to which strategic decisions can be delegated is held to be essential, in order to take adequate account of the strategic triangle. This is particularly the case for a large company made up of a number of different businesses selling to different customer groups (probably with different competitors). The definition of a business unit is always likely to be in dispute, so Ohmae suggests asking three key questions as a test:

- Are customer wants well-defined and understood by the industry, and is the market segmented so that differences in those wants are treated differently?
- Is the business unit (an aspect of the corporation) equipped to respond easily to customer wants and needs?

- Do competitors have different sets of conditions that give them a relative advantage over the business unit?

If the business unit seems unable to compete effectively, then it should be redefined to better meet customer needs and competitive threats.

2. *Freedom of operation.* For Ohmae, the SBU must have full freedom of operation across the strategic triangle in order to develop and implement an effective strategy. In devising a strategy the SBU must be able to:

- address the total market for its customers
- encompass all of the critical functions of the corporation, i.e., procurement, design, manufacturing, sales, marketing, distribution, and service, in order to respond with maximum freedom to the total needs of the customer
- understand all key aspects of the competitor so that the corporation can seize an advantage when opportunities arise, and exploit any unexpected sources of strength

3. *Matching the corporation with the market.* In the context of the strategic triangle, Ohmae sees the role of the strategist as matching the strengths of the corporation to the needs of a clearly defined market. Such matching, however, is relative to the capabilities of the competition. For this reason, Ohmae defines a successful strategy as one that ensures a better or stronger matching of corporate strengths to customer needs than that provided by competitors.

Four routes to strategic advantage

In *The Mind of the Strategist* Ohmae identifies four ways in which a corporation can gain advantage over its competitors.

- A business strategy based on key factors for success (KFS). The business is required to identify what it does to give it an advantage over its competitors, or where the potential for advantage is greatest, and then concentrate resources there.
- Relative superiority. If a business is still unable to gain an advantage over its competitors and the KFS struggle is being waged equally, then any difference between the two competing businesses can be exploited. This might, for example, mean linking products together through the sales network to provide customers with better offers.
- Aggressive initiatives. When a competitor is established in a stagnant, low-growth industry, then Ohmae advocates an unconventional strategy aimed at upsetting the competitor's KFS. This can be achieved by challenging the accepted ways of doing business in the industry—upsetting the status quo.
- Strategic degrees of freedom. Success in the competitive struggle can be achieved by a business strategy based on the use of innovations. This may involve the vigorous opening up of new markets or the development of new products in areas untouched by the competition.

In each case, Ohmae believes that the main concern is to avoid taking the same approach in the same market as the competition.

CONTEXT AND CONCLUSIONS

Gary Hamel, among others, has recognised Ohmae's immense influence and contribution, emphasising the impact of his challenge to managers to think in new and unconventional ways. It is a testament to the strength and appeal of Ohmae's work that, although the growth of the Japanese economy faltered during the 1990s, his ideas are still regarded as fundamental contributions to strategic management.

It might be argued that Ohmae's emphasis on strategic creativity helped to lay the foundations for the radical, transforming management approaches of the 1980s and 1990s. Certainly, if one accepts the need for an intuitive, innovative strategist, then it seems likely that there will be widespread changes in the ways that organisations are managed. So it was with the arrival of lean production, business process re-engineering, and strategies for innovation and empowerment. Ohmae's view of the strategist, in fact, is now the widely accepted norm, and the need for a questioning approach that is not constrained by tradition, fear, or habitual patterns of behaviour has filtered down from the strategists themselves to all layers of organisations.

Later works by Ohmae have focused on the rise of the global business and the relationships between business and governments. In a sense, Ohmae has grown away from his starting point and now prefers to write about a time when the end of the nation state is imminent. For many this emphasis on the distant future—rather than on business approaches for the medium-term—is of more relevance to politicians and academics than companies competing today. Even so, his legacy of startlingly simple, unconventional, and effective approaches is still required reading for many executives.

THE BEST SOURCES OF HELP
Books:
Ohmae, Kenichi. *The Mind of the Strategist*. New York: McGraw Hill, 1982.

Ohmae, Kenichi. *Japan Business: Obstacles and Opportunities*. New York: John Wiley, 1983.

Ohmae, Kenichi. *Triad Power: The Coming Shape of Global Competition*. New York: Free Press, 1985.

Ohmae, Kenichi. *The Borderless World: Power and Strategy in the Interlinked Economy*. London: William Collins, 1990.

Ohmae, Kenichi. *The End of the Nation State: The Rise of Regional Economics*. London: Harper Collins, 1995.

TAIICHI OHNO

1902	Sakichi Toyoda invents power loom.
1912	Taiichi Ohno born.
1932	Ohno joins Toyoda Automatic Loom Works.
1936–1937	Toyoda starts manufacturing automobiles.
1945–1973	Development of Toyota Production System.
1947	Toyota producing 100,000 vehicles per year.
1956	Ohno visits United States to study production methods.
1990	Dies.
2000	Toyota produces 5.8 million vehicles internationally.

> **SUMMARY**
> Japanese manufacturing has gained a reputation for innovative thinking and developments, and the current Western focus on quality, just-in-time delivery, waste and defect reduction, and kanban systems all have their origins in Japanese manufacturing companies. Taiichi Ohno was responsible for much of the background work and thinking that created the now widely recognised and much copied Toyota Production System.

LIFE AND CAREER

The history of the Toyota Production System goes back to the Toyoda Spinning and Weaving Company, set up by Sakichi Toyoda in 1918. This company later became the Toyota Automatic Loom Works. From the outset Sakichi recognised that his main competitors were based in the United Kingdom—an early observation of global competition. By 1929 the company had gained a reputation for innovative looms that stopped when there was a quality problem, such as a break in the thread. A British company, Platt Brothers, bought the production and sales rights for this loom for £100,000, a deal that was to have far-reaching consequences. This money was given to Sakichi's son Kiichiro to expand the company and to develop automotive technology. The Model AA was launched in 1936. A year later the Toyota Motor Company was formed.

Kiichiro travelled widely in his search for the best infrastructure for his company and Detroit was a place where he learnt a great deal. Ford's assembly line system provided the framework upon which Kiichiro based his early car production, but he recognised the need to adapt it to the particular market conditions in Japan. Toyota was producing cars solely for the internal market, which meant supplying small numbers with high variety. This contrasted with the Ford approach of large numbers 'in any colour you like as long as it is black'. Operating with only limited funds, Toyota was forced to work with supplier partners to generate the necessary capital investment.

It was under these conditions that Taiichi Ohno was brought into the company and one of his initial assignments was to increase the productivity of the Japanese company, which was behind that of Ford by a factor of ten. At the end of the Second World War Kiichiro had decreed that the company must 'catch up with America in three years'. Ohno realised that Japanese workers could not realistically be working ten times less effectively than their American counterparts. Waste and inefficiency must be prevalent and if they could be eliminated from the system productivity could increase by a factor of ten—or even more! The elimination of waste marked the start of the Toyota Production System and remains the basis from which it has evolved to this day.

CONTRIBUTION
Ohno's early experiments in waste elimination were based within the manufacturing machine shops of which he was in charge. The 'one man one machine' approach was seen as the only cost-effective system that a heavily unionised American industry could adopt. The production of large quantities of parts on high-speed, expensive machines creates the potential for an abundance of waste. Ohno experimented with different machine layouts, encouraging workers to become multiskilled and stopping machines when a job was finished. He encountered many problems during these early stages and learnt the need for patience to allow workers to adapt to change.

Later he travelled widely in the United States looking at car plants. The knowledge he gained about Ford's assembly line was later to be applied in his ideas on continuously flowing processes. However, according to company lore, his 'most important discovery in the US was the supermarket'. This has been explained by the fact that he came from a country that, at the time, was unused to self-service. The way customers chose exactly what they wanted impressed Ohno, as did the way stores supplied goods in a simple, efficient, and timely manner.

In his later years Ohno often described his production system in terms of a supermarket. Like a supermarket, each production line sets out its produce for the next line to choose from. Each line becomes the customer for the preceding one and a 'supermarket' for the following one. Such an approach represents a radical rethink of the production systems of the time. These were primarily 'push' systems, where the rate of output of the preceding line governed the running rate of the factory. Ohno's ideas amount to a 'pull' system, whereby demand pulls through resources from the previous line.

The Toyota Production System was developed between 1945 and 1973 and is still evolving. Its basic elements are *muda* (waste control), just-in-time, *ninben no tsuita jidoka* (automation with a human touch), *jidoka* (the quality principle), *heijunka* (production levelling), and *kanban* (the 'signboard'—a stock-control system).

Muda
The philosophy of the Toyota Production System is based on obtaining cost reductions through the elimination of wasteful operations. Ohno divides waste into the following seven categories:

- overproduction
- transporting
- unnecessary stock on hand
- producing defective goods
- waiting (idle/non-productive time)
- processing itself
- unnecessary motion

The key to eliminating waste is first to find it and then to ensure that it is recognised as waste by all.

Just-in-time
The concept of just-in-time (often shortened to JIT) was invented by Kiichiro Toyoda, but it was Ohno who developed its full potential and made it into the system we know today. JIT means supplying to each process what it needs when it needs it and in the quantity that it needs.

Ohno's ideas about just-in-time implementation flowed once again from his experience of the supermarket. Customers visit the supermarket to buy as much of what they want as they happen to need. When he arrived at Toyota he found that, as in most assembly production at the time, lines producing an item usually pushed their output on to the next stage, whether the next stage needed it or not. Ohno proposed turning this around so that the 'process that needs the parts [goes] to get what is needed, when it is needed and in the quantity needed'. Thus, the output of a process is replaced as it is transported and consumed by the next process. Storage (inventory) becomes the responsibility of the producer, not the user. Thus workers and their supervisors can clearly see whether they are working too fast or too slow and can act to reduce the waste.

Ninben no tsuita jidoka
'Autonomation' is the second pillar of the Toyota Production System and results from Sakichi Toyoda's earlier invention of the auto-activated weaving machine. The machine would automatically stop if a problem occurred, thus preventing the production of defective products. At Toyota the same principle was carried forward so that all machines were equipped with various safety devices, fixed-position stopping, and poka-yoke foolproofing systems to eliminate defective products.

The concept, however, is applied not only to machinery, but also to the production line and workers. It basically allows workers to stop the production line if a problem occurs. This enables each problem to be fully explored using Ohno's 'five whys' (asking the question 'Why?' five times to get to the heart of a problem), and makes sure that everyone understands the reason why it has arisen. In the long term this creates an efficient production line.

Jidoka
Jidoka means building quality into the process itself and is a natural extension of autonomation. Inspection teams were the traditional answer to quality control in most manufacturing systems. Ohno believed that quality must flow from production and not inspection. He achieved this by developing the most efficient and safest method of doing every task and training each team member to carry it out in this manner.

Heijunka
Work levelling or load smoothing is the major basis for the elimination of waste. Peaks and troughs in demand create waste capacity; it should be possible to rearrange the production plan and schedule to level out its effects. In this way a process with less work can help out another process that has excess work. In the

complex production systems of the car industry the only viable solution, which most manufacturers adopted, was to maintain inventory, itself a waste.

A production line may have cars with different engine sizes, of different colours, and with a mix of left- and right-hand drives. Toyota's solution was to equalise not only the quantities but also the types of parts used. This creates an even demand for the different types of components throughout the production cycle. Peaks and troughs are avoided, even in the most minute parts of the process.

Kanban
The kanban system evolved at the same time that Toyota was experimenting with just-in-time and is the method by which the system runs smoothly. Ohno recognised the need for a method of exchanging information between processes in a pull manufacturing environment. By taking the finished product as the starting point, Ohno developed a system of tags or signboards for controlling the transportation of a finished assembly and the production of replacement parts.

A kanban is used for managing and assuring just-in-time production. It is a simple and direct form of communication that is always located at the point where it is needed. Kanbans can be of various shapes as designed by the particular plant. Normally they are a small piece of paper on which is recorded how many of what part to pick up or which parts to manufacture. Ohno built the Toyota kanban system around six rules.

- Do not send defective products to the next process.
- Subsequent processes come to withdraw only what is needed.
- Produce only the exact quantity withdrawn by the subsequent process.
- Equalise production (load smoothing).
- Use *kanban* as a means of fine tuning.
- Stabilise and rationalise the process.

CONTEXT AND CONCLUSIONS
Taiichi Ohno was an excellent originator of new ideas with his own unique management style. The Toyota Production System is remarkable because it was developed in completely the opposite direction to the traditional ways of thinking about production at the time. Ohno was able to build in the quality and the flexibility required in a small but demanding home marketplace by developing a 'pull' manufacturing system. The combination of the early example set by his senior managers, his own conscientious research and study of the best of America's assembly line production systems, and his Japanese patience and logic enabled the fledgling Toyota motor company to survive, against its large American competitors.

THE BEST SOURCES OF HELP
Books:
Ohno, Taiichi. *Workplace Management*. (Translated by Andrew P. Dillon.) Cambridge, Massachusetts: Productivity Press, 1982.

Ohno, Taiichi. *Toyota Production System: Beyond Large-Scale Production*. Cambridge, Massachusetts: Productivity Press, 1988.

Ohno, Taiichi, and Setsuo Mito. *Just-in-Time for Today and Tomorrow*. Cambridge, Massachusetts: Productivity Press, 1988.

ROBERT OWEN

1771	Born.
1781–1790	Works in various drapery businesses in Stamford, London, and Manchester.
1790	Becomes joint owner of textile factory in Manchester.
1799	Purchases mill in New Lanark from his father-in-law, David Dale, and sets about creating a 'model' mill and village.
1808	Keeps the mill open, in spite of the US trade embargo on British goods; mass unemployment elsewhere.
1813–	Tries to persuade other manufacturers to follow his example in employment practices.
1815	Attempts to introduce a bill to legislate on working conditions in factories.
1819	Legislation finally introduced, although limited to banning employment of children under nine.
1825	Leaves for the United States; founds New Harmony in Indiana.
1828	Returns to England after project fails due to internal disagreements and bad planning, leaving the settlement in his sons' hands.
1834	Founds the Grand National Consolidated Trades Union.
1858	Dies.

> **SUMMARY**
>
> Robert Owen is perhaps best known for his model textile factory and village at New Lanark in Scotland. Conditions in early factories were harsh, with hazardous working conditions. Long working hours were the norm, with children as young as five or six working under the same conditions as adults. Factory owners placed more importance on the care of their expensive machines than on the well-being (or otherwise) of their expendable employees. Owen's strength was that he saw his employees as every bit as important to the success of his enterprise as the machines he owned.

LIFE AND CAREER
Owen the factory owner

By the age of 19, Owen was joint owner of a textile factory in Manchester. Being new to the responsibilities of management, he learnt about the workings of the factory by observing his employees as they carried out their work. He wrote: 'I looked very wisely at the men in their different departments, although I really knew nothing. By intensely observing everything, I maintained order and regularity throughout the establishment, which proceeded under such circumstances much better than I had anticipated.'

In 1799, Owen (with a group of partners) purchased the New Lanark mill from his father-in-law, David Dale. Even though Dale was recognised as a progressive employer, conditions in and around the factory were still very poor. Children from five or six years old were employed through contracts with the local poorhouse, and working for 15 hours per day was common. Owen immediately withdrew from accepting any further children from the poorhouse and raised the minimum age of employment to ten. He also banned the beating of children.

Robert Owen

CONTRIBUTION

Although a paternalistic employer, Owen was a businessperson above all else. He made no changes to employment conditions that could not be justified on economic grounds—all social improvements at New Lanark were funded through the profits of the factory. To achieve this, he required improved productivity from his workforce through changes to the working practices and methods of the factory.

For a workforce that was already working very hard, this was not popular. Owen (uniquely for the time) realised he had to gain the trust of his employees in order to get them to co-operate with the changes to the working environment he wished to achieve. He did this (in the language of today) by persuading 'champions'. He wrote: 'I...sought out the individuals who had most influence among [the workforce] from their natural powers or position, and to these I took pains to explain what were my intentions for the changes I wished to effect.'

Owen further won the trust of his employees when, in 1808, the United States passed a trade embargo on British goods. Most mills closed and mass unemployment occurred. Unlike other mill owners of the time, Owen kept his employees on full pay just to maintain the factory machinery in a clean, working condition.

This approach of fair management proved to be successful and, as returns from the business grew, Owen began to alter the working environment. Employment of children gradually ceased (as no further children were indentured from the poorhouse) and those still in employment were sent to a purpose-built school in New Lanark. The housing available to his workers was gradually improved, the environment was freed from gin shops, and crime decreased. The first adult night school anywhere in the world also operated in New Lanark. Finally, Owen set up a shop at New Lanark, and the principles behind this laid the basis for the later retail co-operative movement.

Owen the innovator

Owen's innovations, however, did not merely extend to improving working conditions for his employees. The Industrial Revolution (which began in the mid-to-late 1700s) led to a belief in the supremacy of machines. Owen opposed this growing view by seeking to humanise work.

'Many of you have long experiences in your manufacturing operations of the advantage of substantial, well-contrived and well-executed machinery. If, then, due care as to the state of your inanimate machines can produce such beneficial results, what may not be expected if you devote equal attention to your vital machines, which are far more wonderfully constructed,' he wrote.

As already indicated, Owen was one of the first to 'manage' rather than order his workforce, and the first to attempt to gain agreement for his ideas rather than impose them on others (a worker could not be sacked for disagreeing with Owen). Additionally, he required his managers to behave with some autonomy (possibly the first example of empowerment at work); managers (or superintendents) were selected carefully and trained to be able to act in Owen's absence.

Owen developed an aid to motivation and discipline: the silent monitor system, which could be described as a distant ancestor of the appraisal schemes in practice today. Each machine within the factory had a block of wood mounted on it with a different colour—black, blue, yellow, or white—painted on each face. Each day, the superintendents rated the work of their subordinates and awarded each a colour that was then turned to face the aisle so that everyone was able to see all ratings. The intention of this scheme was that high achievers were rewarded and slackers were motivated to improve.

Owen the reformer
The factory at New Lanark was spectacularly profitable, with returns of over 50% on investment, and Owen held this to be proof of the validity and importance of his theories. Strengthened by his profitability, he tried to persuade other manufacturers to follow his example in employment practices. This was first attempted through those of influence who visited New Lanark (estimates put the number of visitors at 20,000 between 1815 and 1825) and then, in 1815, via his attempt to introduce a bill to legislate on basic working conditions in factories.

The aims of the bill were to ban the employment of those aged under ten; to ban night shifts for all children; to provide 30 minutes' education a day for those under 18; and to limit the working day to ten and a half hours. This would have been enforced by a system of government factory inspectors. The bill failed to be introduced in its intended form, as its opponents argued that it would be bad for business and that in any case most employers were voluntarily doing what the bill would require. By the time it was finally introduced in 1819, the legislation was limited to banning the employment of those under nine.

In 1825, disillusioned with his failure successfully to introduce far-reaching employment legislation but still enthusiastic about his ideals, Owen left for the United States, where he founded New Harmony in Indiana. This, along with other projects, failed because of internal disagreements and bad planning. He returned to England, where in 1834 he founded (and briefly chaired) the Grand National Consolidated Trades Union and continued to push for social reform and the growth of the co-operative movement. Robert Owen died, aged 87, in 1858.

CONTEXT AND CONCLUSIONS
Owen occupies a curious position in the history of management thinking. Dismissed by his contemporaries and now little recognised apart from the linking of his name with that of New Lanark, his vision and foresight place him as the pioneer of management practices that are taken for granted today.

Although many influential people visited the sites of New Lanark and New Harmony, the ideas Owen propounded failed to win him immediate followers. There is much debate about the reasons behind this. The New Lanark factory was obviously very profitable (although, as Frank Podmore argued, almost any personnel policy could have been profitable then because profits in the cotton spinning industry at the time were so large), but still none of his factory-owning contemporaries adopted his ideas. Possibly the radical nature of his views contributed to this—if he had instead advocated a step-by-step approach towards improving working conditions and relations with employees instead of an 'all-or-nothing' approach, he might have been more successful.

Although it is not too surprising that resistance to his ideas came from factory owners (who may indeed have felt they had much to lose from following them), antipathy was also expressed from across the political spectrum. Some of the most long-lasting criticism was expressed by Marx and Engels in their Communist manifesto. The label of 'Utopian' that they applied to Owen is one by which he is still well known. The manifesto expressed the view that his ideas could not work in practice; his success at New Lanark was, they argued, due to luck rather than judgment.

Against these negative views must be set the experiences of those followers Owen did inspire. Although Owen's own partnership with Quakers and Nonconformists at the end of his time at New Lanark failed (because of their wish to impose religious instruction on all), it was this sector of society that produced the people who were most influenced by his ideas. They included Titus Salt, George Palmer, and Joseph Rowntree.

The foresight Owen demonstrated in areas such as motivation of employees, industrial relations, and management by observation was not appreciated until a century later, in the work of F.W. Taylor and Mary Parker Follett, among others. In 1949, Urwick and Brech wrote of Owen: 'Generations ahead of his time, he preached and practised a conception of industrial relations which is, even now, accepted in only a few of the most progressive undertakings.'

Owen's lasting contribution may be best seen in the fact that it would be unthinkable for modern employers not to meet the practices he advocated.

THE BEST SOURCES OF HELP
Books:
Clutterbuck, David, and Stuart Crainer. *Makers of Management: Men and Women Who Changed the Business World*. London: Macmillan, 1990.

O'Toole, James. *Leading Change: Overcoming the Ideology of Comfort and the Tyranny of Custom*. San Francisco: Jossey-Bass, 1995.

Owen, Robert. *A New View of Society*. London: n.p. 1817.

Podmore, Frank. *Robert Owen*. London: Appleton, 1906.

Urwick, Lionel, and Edward Brech. *Making of Scientific Management: volume ii, Management in British Industry*. London: Management Publications Trust, 1949.

Wren, Daniel. *Evolution of Management Thought*. New York: John Wiley, 1987.

RICHARD TANNER PASCALE

1938	Born.
1982	Publication of *The Art of Japanese Management*.
1984	Publication of 'Perspectives on strategy: the real story behind Honda's success', *California Management Review*.
1999	Publication of 'Surfing the edge of chaos', *Sloan Management Review*.

> **SUMMARY**
>
> Richard Tanner Pascale came to prominence in the early 1980s at the time when Peters and Waterman's *In Search of Excellence*, published in 1982, was aiming to redefine the route to corporate success. His *The Art of Japanese Management* (co-authored with Anthony Athos), expounding the virtues of the McKinsey 7-S model, has become a classic, and he has remained at the forefront of management thinking ever since.

LIFE AND CAREER

Born in 1938, Pascale was educated at the Harvard Business School. In the late 1970s he was heavily involved in the evolution of the Seven-S model developed by Peters and Waterman at McKinsey. As a member of faculty at Stanford's Graduate School of Business, Pascale acted as an advisor to the White House and as a consultant to many Fortune 500 companies. More recently he became an associate fellow at Templeton College, Oxford .

A critic of fads, Pascale, like many of his contemporaries, does not want to be known as a 'guru' or 'expert'. Such labels, he believes, evoke the image of a 'hero with all the answers', and he would rather be recognised as someone who keeps addressing questions as they occur and recur. To that end, Pascale spends a number of days every year focusing on questioning, and learning from discussions with, business leaders.

CONTRIBUTION
Japanese management and the 7 Ss

A spirit of enquiry brought Pascale and Athos into contact with Peters and Waterman in the late 1970s, when Waterman was driving a McKinsey initiative to seek out new models of corporate success. Peters and Waterman went on to cite American examples of success in their 1981 bestseller, while Pascale and Athos looked at lessons from Japan and how they were being applied in corporate America. What brought the four of them together was the accelerating pace of business change and the increasing inadequacy of corporate information systems that had been sufficient in the past. Both *In Search of Excellence* and *The Art of Japanese Management* expounded the 7-S theory, but it was Pascale and Athos who explored it in greater depth, tracing many of its origins to working practice in Japanese organisations, and particularly in the Matsushita Electric Company.

Comparing Matsushita to ITT, Pascale and Athos found that the two organisations were differentiated more by 'softer' elements of management style, staffing policies, skills, and shared values than by their systems, structure, or strategy.

In the early 1980s, the 7 Ss—usually presented in the shape of a circle or diamond—were as original for their juxtaposition of concepts not previously trumpeted as important, as for their communicability through alliteration.

- Strategy—how the organisation gets from where it is to where it wants to be.
- Structure—how the firm is organised.
- Systems—how information moves around.
- Style—the patterns of behaviour of senior management.
- Staff—not just numbers, but the characteristics of those who live and work at the organic centre of the organisation.
- Skills—the distinctive capabilities of individuals or of the organisation as a whole.
- Superordinate goals (shared values)—not so much bottom-line targets as the meanings and values that are pervasive throughout the organisation and 'genuinely knit together individual and organisational purposes'.

Ambiguity and uncertainty

In *The Art of Japanese Management* Pascale and Athos describe how managers are increasingly faced with situations which are neither clear-cut nor susceptible to resolution by the application of rational analysis. These situations are born out of the conflicts, ambiguities, and uncertainties that stem from the four Ss of style, staff, skills, and shared values. In such circumstances, the East has something to teach us. Rather than forcing a final solution, the authors suggest, it may be better to accept the lack of clarity in the situation, and simply 'decide' to proceed. 'Proceeding' should yield further information, and the best course may be to move toward the goal by a sequence of tentative steps rather than by bold, striking actions.

The Honda effect

Pascale published 'Perspectives on strategy: the real story behind Honda's success' in the Spring 1984 issue of *California Management Review*. This article juxtaposed two contrasting views on the rise of Honda in the United States: the Boston Consulting Group's (BCG's) account and the Honda executives' own explanation. The article stimulated much debate, which was later summarised in 'The Honda effect revisited', another *California Management Review* article (Summer 1996, vol. 38, no. 4) by Henry Mintzberg and others.

BCG attributed Honda's success to long-term investment in technology and economies of scale instead of in short-term profitability. Pascale did not aggressively dispute this, but found it did not explain why the then still young Honda had embarked on an apparently reckless US strategy in the first place. Interviewing a number of Honda executives, Pascale became aware that the story was characterised more by miscalculation, chance, and learning-on-the-spot than by a logical, analytical progression of the sort that emerges from BCG's rationalised account.

Pascale explained BCG's interpretation of the 'Honda effect' as the result of a Western preference for the oversimplification of reality and linear explanations of events, an approach that overlooked the process through which organisations experiment, adapt, and learn. This preference leads to a failure to appreciate that the ways in which an organisation deals with miscalculation, mistakes, and chance events outside its defined plan are often crucial to its success over time.

The key to Honda's success, concluded Pascale, was organisational agility. He continually returns to this theme, believing agility to be a core organisational competence.

Agility
Pascale's five conclusions summarising the Honda debate propose the following.

- Organisational agility is increasingly important as a source of renewable competitive advantage.
- Agility resides in what an organisation is rather than what it does. In *The Art of Japanese Management*, Pascale cites Harold Geneen's attempt, while chief executive at ITT, to reduce uncertainty through quantification and controls. Matsushita, on the other hand, he pictures as a Pied Piper, more in tune with the uncertainty and imperfection that exist in all organisations, and operating on a basis of shared values and beliefs created by a philosophy linking work to social as well as productive ends.
- The interaction of four key dimensions makes an organisation what it is:
  (i) power—can employees really influence the course of events?
  (ii) identity—do individuals identify with the organisation as a whole?
  (iii) contention—how is conflict brought out into the open and used creatively?
  (iv) learning—how does the organisation handle and develop new ideas?
  Within Honda, for example, employees are empowered to take pioneering action and they share an enterprise-wide identity in cross-functional teams, while debate, experimentation, and enquiring attitudes are actively encouraged.
- Strategic intent and agility depend on the norms, values, and behaviours inculcated within the social system of the organisation. Pascale refers to Honda's efforts to institutionalise responsiveness, adaptability, and external focus.
- Agility depends on certain organisational disciplines, such as continuing dissatisfaction with the status quo, managing back from the future, uncompromising straight talk and the bringing of differences out into the open, and harnessing adversity by learning from setbacks and adapting to move forward.

Complexity, chaos, and letting go
In an article called 'Surfing the edge of chaos' in *Sloan Management Review* (Spring 1999, vol. 40, no. 3), Pascale addresses what he considers to be the biggest challenge facing organisations today—how to increase the number of workable and winning strategic initiatives. He builds on the principles of the science of complexity.

- A complex adaptive system is at risk when it is interfered with and controlled. Equilibrium precedes extinction.
- Complex adaptive systems are capable of self-organisation and of generating new methods of operating.
- Some complex adaptive systems can move towards the brink of chaos before new patterns emerge and new forms of organisation take shape.
- Complex adaptive systems cannot be directed or strictly controlled.

In drawing parallels between the world of complex scientific systems and the world of organisations, Pascale tests out these four principles against a period of change at Shell, through interviews with Steve Miller, the director driving Shell's renewal initiative. He concludes the article by quoting Miller's words—that is, not by summarising and generalising, but by going into the depth and individuality of the organisational context itself. It is interesting to look at some of Miller's comments (quoted below) and relate them to the above four principles:

- 'You have to recognise that the top can't possibly have all the answers.'
- 'The actual solutions about how to best meet the challenges of the moment, those thousands of strategic challenges...have to be made by the people closest to the action.'
- 'The leader becomes a context setter.'
- 'Once the grassroots realise they own the problem, they also discover that they can help create and own the answers.'
- 'There's another kind of risk to the leaders...the risk of exposure. Before, you were remote from them, now, you're very accessible.'
- 'Finally, the scariest part is letting go...you get more feedback than before...you know more through your own people about what's going on in the marketplace...but you still have to let go of the old sense of control.'

CONTEXT AND CONCLUSIONS

Pascale's research, consulting, and exploration continue to lead him to redefine what makes organisations tick, at a time when uncertainties grow at an accelerating pace. He does not fit easily into any predefined category of management theorist and remains both at the front and at the edge in seeking new ways of understanding organisations. Pascale has sought to explore the processes of change by trying to understand their complexities and interdependencies, and not by trying to reduce his findings to mechanistic formulas. In line with his own advice to organisations, he himself exhibits a lack of complacency in his efforts to understand the right pieces, before fitting them into the organisational jigsaw.

He describes his recent work on complexity as a 'big idea' and, although it builds on established principles of complexity theory, it will no doubt seem a little strange at first, particularly to those who want to eradicate uncertainty.

THE BEST SOURCES OF HELP
Books:
Pascale, Richard Tanner, and Anthony Athos. *The Art of Japanese Management*. London: Penguin Books, 1982.

Pascale, Richard Tanner. *Managing on the Edge: How Successful Companies Use Conflict to Stay Ahead*. London: Viking, 1990.

Journal Articles:
Pascale, Richard Tanner, Mark Millemann, and Linda Gioja. 'Changing the way we change.' *Harvard Business Review*, Nov./Dec. 1997, pp. 127–139.

Pascale, Richard Tanner, Tracy Goss and Anthony Athos. 'The reinvention roller coaster: risking the present for a powerful future.' *Harvard Business Review*, Nov./Dec. 1993, pp. 97–108.

TOM PETERS

1942	Born.
1966–1970	Naval service, including a term of duty in Vietnam and being assigned to the Pentagon.
1973	Leaves Stanford with PhD in organisational behaviour; works for White House as senior drug abuse adviser.
1974–1981	Joins consultancy firm, McKinsey, becoming a partner in 1977.
Late 1970s	Various collaborative research projects; development of the McKinsey 7-S Model.
1982	Publication of *In Search of Excellence*.
1982–present	Writing, lecturing, touring, and changing his mind; formulates ideas for a management agenda for the 1990s and beyond.

SUMMARY

Tom Peters has probably done more than anyone else to shift the debate on management from the confines of boardrooms, academia, and consultancies to a broader, worldwide audience, where it has become the staple diet of the media and managers alike. Peter Drucker has written more and his ideas have withstood a longer test of time, but it is Peters—as consultant, writer, columnist, seminar lecturer, and stage performer—whose energy, style, influence, and ideas have shaped new management thinking.

LIFE AND CAREER

Born in Baltimore in 1942, Peters repaid a navy scholarship to Cornell with a degree in civil engineering and four years' service in the navy, spending a term of duty in Vietnam in 1966 before being assigned to the Pentagon in 1968. He left Stanford in 1973 with a PhD in organisational behaviour and worked for the White House for a short while as senior drug abuse advisor. In 1974 he joined the top consultancy firm, McKinsey.

Exposed to consulting assignments in America's blue-chip companies, Peters's curiosity and imagination led him in the late 1970s into various aspects of collaborative research, which brought about the development of the McKinsey 7-S Model. This model focuses on shared values, staff, systems, strategy, structure, skills, and style. It was in fact the first expression of the shift—characterising all of Peters's work—away from the traditional numbers-centred, rational, analytical, and bureaucratic notion of management of McKinsey and many others towards a more innovative, intuitive, and people-centred approach.

In 1982, Peters co-published with Bob Waterman *In Search of Excellence*, which brought him worldwide fame, and set him off on a new career expounding his theories of excellence. Since then, his life has been a whirlwind of writing, lecturing, touring, and changing his mind.

Peters describes himself as gadfly, curmudgeon, champion of bold failures, prince of disorder, maestro of zest, corporate cheerleader, and irritator. *Fortune Magazine* calls him the Ur-guru (the original guru) and *The Economist* the Über-guru. He is the founder of the Tom Peters Group and lives on his farm in Vermont, or on American Airlines, or on an island off the Massachusetts coast.

CONTRIBUTION

In Search of Excellence resulted from the application of the 7-S model in an attempt to discover models of excellence in corporate America. Peters and Waterman identified eight lessons from their research.

- a bias for action—excellent companies got on with doing the job, unconstrained by the bureaucratic trappings
- be close to the customer—this has since become a key business 'must'
- autonomy and entrepreneurship—the entrepreneur has freedom to think, act and invest effort in the organisation
- productivity through people—it was previously believed that large organisations held the key to productivity because only they could handle the economies of scale required for profitability
- be driven by hands-on values—the shared values of the 7-S model that matter to employees, as well as making the business tick with managers who are not afraid to get their hands dirty
- stick to the knitting—companies should stay with their core competencies, not diversifying for the sake of it
- simple form, lean staff—successful companies were not preoccupied with their size or procedures but with keeping things simple
- simultaneous loose-tight properties—examples of excellence derived from the faster-moving, more flexible features of smaller organisations, not the more cumbersome aspects of large ones

When Peters declared in 1987, at the beginning of *Thriving on Chaos*, that there are no excellent companies, it was not only in recognition of the fact that many of the companies he had cited earlier had foundered. It was also because the rules had changed again: there was no single consistent route to excellence. Times change, so companies need to change their approach in order to continue to be successful. Peters has argued consistently that the eight lessons from *In Search of Excellence* remain valid—the companies he cited that later foundered merely failed to follow the lessons through.

A Passion for Excellence was published in 1985, intended as a sequel to *In Search of Excellence*, but this time with the focus on leadership. According to Peters (and his coauthor Nancy Austin) the successful leader becomes passionate about getting the most out of people, takes to heart the full people-centred implications of the 7 Ss, and lays the basis for the culture of empowerment. It is also in this book that Peters starts to return time and again to the centrality of the customer.

In *Thriving on Chaos*, Peters was one of the first to describe the emerging world of uncertainty and accelerating change. He was lucky with his timing: it was published in the same month (October 1987) that the stock-market crashes in Wall Street, London, and Tokyo brought chaos to the world's money markets. The book was in fact a rejection of the secure world of the past, and a description of the uncertain world of the future. Some of the book's themes were already there in *In Search of Excellence*: customer responsiveness and flexibility through empowerment, for example. But already in 1987, the world was a fast-changing place where increased competition meant speed to market, and that meant fast-paced innovation. Most of all, Peters understood that organisations would need flexible systems to deal with a topsy-turvy world.

Thriving on Chaos encouraged managers to cast off their old thinking and be prepared for a world of change and uncertainty. But Peters had not yet drawn a map of how to get there. *Liberation Management* was his attempt to draw such a map. He advocated flexible, flowing structures that are anti-hierarchical and based on building up relationships with customers. As he had done in *Thriving on Chaos*, Peters quoted examples of companies that represent the lean, flatter, and responsive organisation required now that the old rule-book had been torn up. Again, he focused on the need to innovate, on closeness to customers, and on empowerment. In *Liberation Management* Peters asserted that knowledge is becoming the key asset, the working capital of the organisation.

Peters the writer

Drucker may have written more, but Peters is beginning to catch him up. *Thriving on Chaos* is over 500 pages long; *Liberation Management* is over 800. In addition, Peters wrote a column for 10 years as a channel for his thoughts, ideas, observations, and continuing flow of examples of companies.

His style of writing, as well as the content of his work, has changed over the years. One of the attractive features of *In Search of Excellence* was its accessible style. Peters's later works take this style to an extreme and reduce the language of management to monosyllabic expressions designed to shock, excite, provoke, and stir the reader out of conventional thinking. Hence his 1994 title—*The Pursuit of Wow!*

The guru as performer

This is an area that Tom Peters has made his own. Many gurus are academics or writers, but few would claim to have the impact of Peters on stage. He has been universally described as a brilliant performer, with great stage presence and unbeatable delivery technique. Sometimes delivering two seminars a day in different cities, Peters is acknowledged for his genuine interest, concern, even passion for getting people to reflect on the way they manage.

The Tom Peters seminar: *The Circle of Innovation*

The message that comes over in *The Circle of Innovation* is one that has taken between 15 and 20 years to develop. The book attempts to push the management of organisations to anticipate the topsy-turvy markets that are emerging with global markets, the Internet, and the ever greater closeness of customer and producer.

- Beyond change—be prepared to try things out, but do not expect to get things right first time. Peters acknowledges the role of stability and regularity but attaches far greater importance to agility.
- Beyond downsizing—aim to be big and small at the same time, so that you get the benefits of a large organisation (economies of scale, networking, and knowledge-sharing) along with those of the small (speed, independence, and responding to opportunities).
- Beyond empowerment—make every job entrepreneurial.
- Beyond loyalty—everybody learns to think about the future, the customer, and the bottom-line.
- Beyond re-engineering—the conversion of units or departments into full professional service firms with responsibility and accountability.

- Beyond disorganisation—as the organisation spots and responds to opportunities, it becomes a network of partners, distributors, suppliers, and customers with boundaries that are transparent to outsiders.
- Beyond the learning organisation—stimulating curiosity and creativity everywhere in the organisation.
- Beyond TQM—towards sustainable product/service differentiation to escape the sameness of today's markets through design.
- Beyond management—from management to revolutionary leadership.

CONTEXT AND CONCLUSIONS

Peters did not actually discover the concept of customers with *In Search of Excellence*, but he and Waterman bucked the dominance of strategy to remind management that customers come first. If he seems all for discontinuity and disorganisation, it is principally to remind people not to get stuck in the rut of procedures and routine.

Peters has been criticised for not being thorough or academic enough in support of his assertions, for relying too much on his charisma as a performer, and for 'dumbing down' management to a level of mundaneness and banality. But one of the widely agreed achievements of Tom Peters is that, for a period of 15 years or more, his antennae have sensed where the world of business is heading before it arrives. It is also widely acknowledged that his approach, style, and energy have popularised management ideas to a wider audience than ever before.

Managers from all levels and from all types of organisation say that Peters's influence has been positive rather than negative, and he is spoken of in the same league as Porter, Ohmae, Hamel, Handy, and even Drucker. If he has changed his mind, it is because the world of the 1990s and 2000s has altered radically from that of the 1970s. If he has been inconsistent, he has nonetheless stayed ahead of the management times and foreseen—or helped to set—the management agenda for the fast-changing world of the future.

THE BEST SOURCES OF HELP
Books:
Crainer, Stuart. *Corporate Man to Corporate Skunk: The Tom Peters Phenomenon, A Biography*. Oxford: Capstone Publishing, 2001.
Peters, Tom, and Bob Waterman. *In Search of Excellence: Lessons from America's Best-run Companies*. New York: Harper & Row, 1982.
Peters, Tom, and Nancy Austin. *A Passion for Excellence: The Leadership Difference*. New York: Harper Collins, 1985.
Peters, Tom. *Thriving on Chaos: Handbook for a Management Revolution*. New York: A. Knopf, 1987.
Peters, Tom. *Liberation Management*. New York: A. Knopf, 1992.
Peters, Tom. *The Tom Peters Seminar: Crazy Times for Crazy Organisations*. New York: Vintage Books, 1994.
Peters, Tom. *The Pursuit of Wow! Every Person's Guide to Topsy-Turvy Times*. New York: Vintage Books, 1994.
Peters, Tom. *The Circle of Innovation: You Can't Shrink Your Way to Greatness*. London: Hodder & Stoughton, 1997.

MICHAEL PORTER

1947	Born.
1969	Completes a degree in aeronautical engineering at Princeton University.
1971	Receives an MBA from Harvard Business School.
1973	Receives a PhD from Harvard University. Joins the Harvard Business School faculty.
1980	Publishes *Competitive Strategy*, which sets him at leading edge of strategic thinking.
1994	Founds The Initiative for a Competitive Inner City, and becomes chairman and CEO.

SUMMARY

In an age when management gurus are both lauded by the faithful and hounded by the critics, Michael Porter seems to be one of the few who is both academically fire-proof and largely without criticism from the business world. Porter has been at the leading edge of strategic thinking since his first major publication, *Competitive Strategy*, in 1980.

LIFE AND CAREER

Born in 1947, Porter completed a degree in aeronautical engineering in 1969 and joined the Harvard Business School faculty at the age of 26. Like many academics, he has set up a consulting company, Monitor, advising both leading-edge companies and governments on strategy.

His thinking on strategy has been supported by precision research into industries and companies. Over a period of almost 20 years, his thinking remains consistent as well as developmental—it has not stood still since *Competitive Strategy* became a corporate bible for many in the early 1980s.

CONTRIBUTION

Before *Competitive Strategy*, most strategic thinking focused on either the organisation of a company's internal resources and their adaptation to meet particular circumstances in the marketplace, or improving an organisation's competitiveness by lowering prices to increase market share. These approaches, derived from the work of Igor Ansoff, were bundled into systems or processes that provided strategy with its place in the organisation.

In *Competitive Strategy*, Porter managed to reconcile these approaches and provide management with a fresh way of looking at strategy—not just from the point of view of markets or of organisational capabilities, but from the point of view of industry itself.

Internal capability for competitiveness—the value chain

Porter describes two different types of business activity—primary and secondary. Primary activities are concerned with transforming inputs (raw materials) into outputs (products), and in delivery and after-sales support. These are usually the main 'line management' activities and include:

- inbound logistics—materials handling, warehousing
- operations—turning raw materials into finished products
- outbound logistics—order processing and distribution
- marketing and sales—communication and pricing
- service—installation and after-sales service

Secondary activities support the primary and include:

- procurement—purchasing and supply
- technology development—know-how, procedures and skills
- human resource management—recruitment, promotion, appraisal, reward and development
- firm infrastructure—general and quality management, finance, planning

To survive competition and supply what customers want to buy, the company has to ensure that all these value-chain activities link together, even if some of the activities take place outside the organisation. A weakness in any one of the activities will impact on the chain as a whole and affect competitiveness.

The five forces

Porter argued that in order to examine its competitive capability in the marketplace, an organisation must choose between three generic strategies:

- cost leadership—becoming the lowest-cost producer in the market
- differentiation—offering something different, extra, or special
- focus—achieving dominance in a niche market

The skill is to choose the right one at the right time. These generic strategies are driven by five competitive forces that the organisation has to take into account. These are the:

- power of customers to affect pricing and reduce margins
- power of suppliers to influence the organisation's pricing
- threat of similar products to limit market freedom and reduce prices and thus profits
- level of existing competition that impacts on investment in marketing and research and thus erodes profits
- threat of new market entrants to intensify competition and further impact on pricing and profitability

In recent years, Porter has revisited his earlier work. Such is the acceleration of market change that companies now have to compete not on a choice of strategic front, but on all fronts at once. Porter has also said that it is a misconception of his approach for a company to try to position itself in relation to the five competitive forces. Positioning is not enough. What companies have to do is ask how the five forces can help to rewrite industry rules in the organisation's favour.

Diversification

Instead of going it alone, an organisation can spread risk and attain growth by diversification and acquisition. While the blue-chip consulting companies such as Boston Consulting Group (market growth/market share matrix) and McKinsey (7-S framework) have developed analytical models for discovering which companies will rise and fall, Porter prefers three critical tests for success.

- The attractiveness test. Industries chosen for diversification must be structurally attractive. An attractive industry will yield a high return on investment, but entry barriers will be high; customers and suppliers will have only moderate bargaining power, and there will be only a few substitute products. An unattractive industry will be swamped by a range of alternative products, high rivalry, and high fixed costs.

- The cost-of-entry test. If the cost of entry is so high that it prejudices the potential return on investment, profitability is eroded before the game has started.
- The better-off test. How will the acquisition provide advantage to either the acquirer or the acquired? One must offer significant advantage to the other.

Porter devised seven steps to tackle these questions.

- As competition takes place at the business unit level, identify the interrelationships among the existing business units.
- Identify the core business that is to be the foundation of the strategy. Core businesses are those in attractive industries and in which competitive advantage can be sustained.
- Create horizontal organisational mechanisms to facilitate interrelationships among core businesses.
- Pursue diversification opportunities that allow shared activities and pass all three critical tests.
- Pursue diversification through a transfer of skills, if opportunities for sharing activities are limited or exhausted.
- Pursue a strategy of restructuring if this fits the skills of management, or if no good opportunities exist for forging corporate partnerships.
- Pay dividends so that shareholders can become portfolio managers.

The national diamond

Why do some companies achieve consistent improvement in innovation, seeking an ever more sophisticated source of competitive advantage? For Porter, the answer lies in four attributes that affect industries. These attributes are:

- factor conditions—the nation's skills and infrastructure capable of enabling a competitive position
- demand conditions—the nature of home-market demand
- related and supporting industries—presence or absence of supplier/feeder industries
- firm strategy, structure and rivalry—the national conditions under which companies are created, grow, organise, and manage

These are the chief determinants that create the environment in which businesses flourish and compete. The points on the diamond constitute a self-reinforcing system, in which the effect of one point often depends on the state of the others, and any weakness at one point will impact adversely on an industry's capability to compete.

The new strategic wave

Sometime between 1980 and 1990 a new wave of more subversive strategic thinking—with Gary Hamel and *Strategy as Revolution*, and Mintzberg with 'The fall and rise of strategic planning' (*Harvard Business Review*)—emerged to replace the old rule-book. Porter's main contribution to date, *Competitive Strategy*, argues that strategic planning lost its way because managers failed to distinguish between strategic and operational effectiveness and confused the two.

The old strategic model was based on productivity, increasing market share, and lowering costs. Hence, total quality management, benchmarking, outsourcing, and re-engineering were all at the forefront of change in the 1980s as the key drivers of operational improvements. But continuing incremental improvements to the way things are done tend to bring different players up to the same level, rather than differentiating them. To achieve differentiation therefore means that:

- strategy rests on unique activities, based on customers' needs, customers' accessibility, or the variety of a company's products or services
- the company's activities must fit and link together. In terms of the value chain, one link is prone to imitation, but with a chain, imitation is very difficult
- it is important to make trade-offs. Excelling at some things means making a conscious choice not to do others—it's a question of being a 'master of one trade' to stand out from the crowd, as opposed to being a 'jack of all trades' and lost in the mass. Trade-offs deliberately limit what a company offers. The essence of strategy lies in what not to do.

CONTEXT AND CONCLUSIONS

It is a mark of Porter's achievement that much of his work on *Competitive Strategy*, researched in the 1970s, still has high value and relevance and still shapes mainstream thinking on competition and strategy.

While his work is academically rigorous, his ability to abstract his thinking into digestible chunks for the business world has given him wide appeal to both the academic and business communities. It is now standard practice for organisations to think and talk about 'value chains', and the five forces have entered the curriculum of every management programme.

THE BEST SOURCES OF HELP
Books:
Crainer, Stuart. *Key Management Ideas: Thinking That Changed the Management World*. 3rd ed. London: Financial Times Prentice Hall, 1998.

Porter, Michael. *Competitive Strategy: Techniques for Analyzing Industries and Competitors*. New York: Free Press, 1980.

Porter, Michael. *Cases in Competitive Strategy*. New York: Free Press, 1983.

Porter, Michael. *Competitive Advantage: Creating and Sustaining Superior Performance*. Rev. ed. New York: Free Press, 1985.

Porter, Michael, ed. *Competition in Global Industries*. Boston: Harvard Business School Press, 1986.

Porter, Michael. *The Competitive Advantage of Nations*. Rev. ed. New York: Free Press, 1998.

Journal Articles:
Porter, Michael. 'Corporate strategy: the state of strategic thinking.' *The Economist*, 23 May 1998, pp. 21–22, 27–28.

Porter, Michael. 'The competitive advantage of nations.' *Harvard Business Review*, Mar./Apr. 1990, pp. 73–93.

Porter, Michael. 'From competitive advantage to corporate strategy.' *Harvard Business Review*, May/Jun. 1987, pp. 43–59.

Porter, Michael. 'What is strategy?' *Harvard Business Review*, Nov./Dec. 1996, pp. 61–78.

C.K. PRAHALAD

1941	Born.
1960–1964	Works as an industrial engineer.
1966	Completes an MBA at the Indian Institute of Management.
1975	Completes a DBA at Harvard Business School.
1975	Visiting Research Fellow, Harvard Business School.
1975–1977	Professor and chairman, Management Education Programme, Indian Institute of Management.
1981	Visiting professor, INSEAD, Fontainebleau, France.
1986-	Professor, University of Michigan Business School
1994	Co-writes *Competing for the Future* with Gary Hamel.
1994	Receives award from Indo-American Society for promoting goodwill, understanding, and friendship between India and the United States.
1995	American Society for Competitiveness recognises his contribution to competitiveness in business.

> **SUMMARY**
>
> C.K. Prahalad is regarded as one of the most influential thinkers on strategy in the United States. His work stems from a deep concern with the ability of large organisations to maintain competitive vitality when faced with international competition and changing business environments. Many of his ideas on competitive analysis argue against the supremacy of traditional strategic thinking and focus upon the concepts of 'strategic intent', 'core competence', and 'strategy as stretch and leverage'.

LIFE AND CAREER

Prahalad came to management thinking from the field of physics—entering the world of the fuzziest of sciences from one of the most precise. He worked as an industrial engineer before completing an MBA at the Indian Institute of Management in 1966 and a DBA at Harvard Business School in 1975. Since then he has been a visiting research fellow at Harvard, a professor at the Indian Institute of Management, and a visiting professor at the European Institute of Business Administration (INSEAD). He is Harvey C. Fruehauf Professor of Corporate Strategy and International Business at the Graduate School of Business Administration, University of Michigan. Over the years he has been a consultant for many large, multinational firms, including Eastman Kodak, AT&T, Honeywell, Philips, Motorola, and Ahlstrom.

Prahalad's contributions to strategic thinking have been widely acknowledged. *BusinessWeek* wrote '...a brilliant teacher at the University of Michigan, Prahalad may well be the most influential thinker on corporate strategy today.' In September 1993 the *Wall Street Journal*'s Special Report on Management Education named him as one of the top ten teachers in the world. In 1994 he received the annual award presented by the Indo-American Society for his outstanding contribution towards the promotion of Indo-American goodwill, understanding, and friendship, and in 1995 the American Society for Competitiveness recognised his outstanding academic contribution to competitiveness in business.

CONTRIBUTION
Competing for the Future
Prahalad sees this book as presenting a new view of competitiveness, strategy and organisations. It takes the ideas of strategic intent, core competence, and strategy as stretch and leverage, and builds on them to create a new strategy model.

Strategic intent
Strategic intent is described as a way of creating an obsession with winning at all levels and across all functions of the organisation. It is a shared competitive agenda for global leadership. Strategic intent uses stretch targets to create competitive advantage. For example, landing a man on the moon by the end of the 1960s provided the stretch target that gave the United States global leadership in space. It is the role of senior management to develop the organisation in a way that closes the gap between ambition and ability. This involves active management processes, which include focusing the organisation's attention on the urgency of winning; motivating people with challenges that require personal effort and commitment; using these challenges to create mid-term competitive advantage, and applying intent consistently to guide resource allocation. Strategic intent provides the focus for 'barrier-breaking' initiatives.

Core competencies
Core competencies are often confused with core capabilities and core technologies. A core competence is an ability that transcends products and markets, and it results when an organisation learns to harmonise multiple technologies, learning, and relationships across levels and functions. Core competencies feed into core products, which themselves can become business units. A core competence provides access to a wide variety of markets, makes a significant contribution to the customer's perceived benefit, and is difficult for competitors to imitate. Examples include Sony's competence in miniaturisation, Philips's optical-media expertise, and Black & Decker's knowledge of small electrical engines. Viewing the organisation as a portfolio of competencies is seen to lead to strategic advantage.

Strategic architecture
A strategic architecture is a framework for leveraging corporate resources towards the strategic intent. It draws upon a variety of information to present a view of the evolution of an industry. A strategic architecture identifies the core competencies to build, and their constituent technologies. It provides a framework within which innovation can be planned and managed.

Corporate imagination
In order to realise the potential that core competencies create, organisations must have the imagination to visualise new markets and the ability to move into them ahead of the competition. The key to competitive advantage is the process through which organisations release corporate imagination, identify and explore new competitive space, and consolidate control over emerging markets. Prahalad suggests that four elements combine to quicken an organisation's imagination:

- escaping the focus on served markets
- searching for innovative product concepts
- overturning assumptions about price and performance relationships
- leading customers rather than following them

Escaping served markets
Traditionally, organisational concern for existing markets blurs the view of new markets. Such a defensive policy is fine up to a point, but it should not be at the expense of new and potentially lucrative markets.

Innovative product concepts
Dramatic innovations in product concepts reshape markets and industry boundaries, creating new competitive space. Such innovations take one of three forms:

- the addition of a new function to a successful product
- the development of a new form for delivering a proven functionality
- the delivery of a proven functionality through an entirely new product concept

Product innovations flow from organisations that view a market in terms of needs and functionalities. This logical process of dissecting a product or service into its functional components is rare in most organisations.

Price/performance trade-off
Most organisations view products and services as price/performance trade-offs. Radical innovation can be achieved where an organisation pursues those products labelled 'unattainable dreams'. New competitive space can be created by understanding how emerging technologies might allow customers' unmet needs to be satisfied, or their existing needs to be better satisfied.

Leading customers
Leading customers requires a deep insight into the lifestyles, needs, and aspirations of today's and tomorrow's customers. Traditional modes of market research fail to provide such insights: it is through creative human science studies that such an understanding can be gained. Leading customers to where they want to go, before they know it themselves, provides a huge competitive advantage. This approach involves all functions of the organisation. It creates marketeers with technological imagination and technologists with marketing imagination, overcoming the debate about whether an organisation should be market- or technology-led.

Expeditionary marketing
On the premise that being first to market provides a competitive advantage, expeditionary marketing is identified as a tool used by organisations that create competitive space. Expeditionary marketing helps organisations gain an understanding of the particular features, price, and performance of new products that will successfully penetrate the market. Such learning can be gained only when a product—imperfect as it might be—is launched. Expeditionary marketing increases the number of successful products an organisation achieves by increasing the number of market opportunities, niches, and product variations explored.

CONTEXT AND CONCLUSIONS

The strength of Prahalad's writing lies in the fact that much of it has resulted from debate and development with his joint authors. His belief that there was more to strategy than existing theories portrayed caught the attention of academics and practising managers alike. Couple this with a strong belief in the need for business school research to have a strong managerial significance, and you begin to realise why Prahalad is held in such high regard.

Consultancy work in corporate America and beyond continually raised the question of how smaller rivals, new to a market, could prevail against much larger, richer organisations. 'Existing theories of strategy and organisation, while providing a solid base for discovery, do not fully answer these questions,' Prahalad argues. These theories help us to understand the structure of an industry, identify the attributes of a transformational leader, and provide a scorecard for monitoring relative competitive advantage. But they do not provide insight into what it takes to redesign an industry, help us understand the role of the leadership team in visualising the future, or explain the process of competence-building. *Competing for the Future* is a work which aims to fill the gap between theory and reality.

Prahalad's ideas developed at a time when corporate strategy was in crisis and in need of a new face. Organisations were more concerned with improving operational efficiency than focusing on the future, and downsizing for short-term gain meant that many businesses were failing to focus on the potential of tomorrow. It was the recognition that such an approach could not continue that has made large organisations receptive to Prahalad's thinking.

THE BEST SOURCES OF HELP
Book:
Prahalad, C.K., and Gary Hamel. *Competing for the Future*. Boston: Harvard Business School Press, 1994.

Journal Articles:
Prahalad, C.K., and Yves Doz. 'An approach to strategic control in MNCs.' *Sloan Management Review*, 1981, vol. 22 no. 4, pp. 5–13.

Prahalad, C.K., and Gary Hamel. 'Do you really have a global strategy?' *McKinsey Quarterly*, Summer 1986, pp. 34–59.

Prahalad, C.K., Gary Hamel, and Yves Doz. 'Collaborate with your competitors and win.' *Harvard Business Review*, Jan./Feb. 1989, pp. 133–139.

Prahalad, C.K., and Gary Hamel. 'Strategic intent.' *McKinsey Quarterly*, Spring 1990, pp. 36–61.

Prahalad, C.K., and Gary Hamel. 'Core competence of the corporation.' *Harvard Business Review*, May/Jun. 1990, pp. 79–91.

Prahalad, C.K., and Gary Hamel. 'Corporate imagination and expeditionary marketing.' *Harvard Business Review*, Jul./Aug. 1991, pp. 81–92.

Prahalad, C.K., and Gary Hamel. 'A strategy for growth: The role of core competencies in the corporation.' *EFMD Forum*, no. 3-4 1993, pp. 3–9.

Prahalad, C.K., and Gary Hamel. 'Competing for the future.' *Harvard Business Review*, Jul./Aug. 1994, vol. 72 no. 4, pp. 122–128.

Prahalad, C.K., and Gary Hamel. 'Competing in the new economy: managing out of bounds.' *Strategic Management Journal*, Mar. 1996, pp. 237–242.

REG REVANS

1907	Born.
1926–1929	Studies at Cambridge.
1928	Represents Great Britain in the long jump at the Olympics.
1929	Sets undergraduate long jump record; held until 1962.
1935	Appointed chief education officer for Essex.
1938	Becomes director of education for the mining industry (later the National Coal Board).
1950	Returns to academia to research management of coal mines; develops theories of action learning.
1950–present	Holds range of professorial positions in the fields of industrial administration and management; campaigns around the world to spread his ideas and has had influence in countries as diverse as Belgium, India, and Egypt.
1970s–1980s	National output in Belgium surpasses that of many major competitors; credit laid at Revans's feet.
2003	Dies.

> **SUMMARY**
> Reginald Revans (1907–2003) was involved in education throughout his long and varied career. Scathing about the value of traditional 'chalk and talk' management education that prevailed during the 1960s and 1970s, he argued that people learned most effectively not from books, lecturers, or teachers, but from sharing real problems with others.

LIFE AND CAREER

Revans studied at Cambridge (where he held the undergraduate long jump record between 1929 and 1962) and, during his time there, represented Great Britain in the long jump at the 1928 Olympics. After he obtained his degree, Revans became a research fellow at Emmanuel College and in 1935 he was appointed chief education officer for Essex. At the end of the Second World War, he became director of education for the mining industry (later the National Coal Board), but by 1950 he had returned to academia to research the management of coal mines. From the mid-1950s, Revans held a range of professorial positions in the fields of industrial administration and management. In 1995 he gave his backing to the establishment of the Centre for Action Learning and Research at Salford University.

CONTRIBUTION
Action learning processes

While director of education for the National Coal Board, Revans spent two years living and working with miners, trying to identify what their problems really were (rather than what people thought they were). His experiences led him to understand that people learn most effectively through 'doing' in groups, and this realisation helped him develop the theories to support 'action learning'.

The learning process may be expressed as:

Learning = Programmed knowledge + the ability to ask 'insightful' Questions or $L = P + Q$.

Programmed knowledge (P) is conveyed through books, lectures, and other structured learning mechanisms. It is an accessible format for knowledge, but it may take time to find exactly what we need, and in isolation is not sufficient to fulfil all learning needs. Revans argued that it is overvalued in management learning.

Insightful questions (Q) are those questions that are asked at the right time and are based on experiences or an attitude about ongoing work projects, as well as on creativity that goes beyond acceptance of ready-made solutions. Revans maintained that P is the domain of experts, while Q is the domain of leaders who wish to drive projects forward by getting answers. Revans noted also that P was the initial letter of poppycock, platitude, and professor, while Q initiates query and quiz.

Insightful questions are the key to Revans's process. P will not take you very far unless you focus on the reflective side of what you do. Revans argued that it is not just 'doing' but learning to learn by doing—Q—that is much more important.

Revans suggested that each participant should have the following (deceptively simple) questions at the forefront of his or her thinking.

- What are we really trying to do?
- What is stopping us from doing it?
- What can we do about it?
- Who knows about (understands) the problem being tackled?
- Who cares (genuinely wants something done) about the problem?
- Who can (has enough power to) get something done about it?

Action learning requires solutions to be implemented, not just recommended. Because it demands probing and sensitive questions, it can also require levels of tact and diplomacy.

Principles of action learning

Action learning is a process that, if it is to work, must be owned by its participants. This is because, Revans argued, the participants need to make their own decisions about tasks, in order to learn how to help each other. Besides the important issues of ownership, action learning has other principles that must be adhered to.

- The learning context must be a real working situation, or a defined project meaningful to the participants—not a simulation. Learning to take action involves taking it, not merely making a recommendation on someone else's problem.
- Members of the learning set (the group or team involved) should all be able to make a contribution from their experience.
- The team members need to be ready to continue to learn from one another as they discuss problems and test out ideas through regular meetings. The learning process is not one of isolation: managers learn best from each other.
- Scheduled input of knowledge (P) should be kept to a minimum.
- An adviser needs to be present for the life of the team to facilitate, help, steer, or guide when needed, but not to teach or lecture.
- Top management support must be available to respond to the team's findings.

To be successful, action learning also requires:

- commitment from the top—no hidden agendas in which time spent will produce an outcome that has been rejected before it is announced
- the full commitment of everyone involved—action learning must be voluntarily embraced; it cannot be imposed

- time for meetings and questions, which necessitates flexibility in terms of scheduling
- good communication to facilitate enthusiasm and commitment from all participants
- an atmosphere of trust and openness—team members should be able to feel relaxed about confronting sensitive internal issues

These are onerous requirements for a learning programme, but the benefits offered through action learning make the undertaking worthwhile. Action learning:

- encourages self-reliance and develops people, especially in times of uncertainty and discontinuity
- is an aid to management development because it helps individuals to prepare for the future by helping themselves
- develops the organisation by changing the way it behaves
- produces results because it requires team members to take decisions
- can be a powerful problem-solving tool

CONTEXT AND CONCLUSIONS

Accepting Revans's distinction between knowledge or didactic learning (P) and insightful questioning (Q), research has revealed those situations in which action learning may be most appropriate. These are where:

- knowledge is changing rapidly
- a body of knowledge is applied to specific problems
- the individual is acquiring self-knowledge
- processes and concepts for thinking and learning are applied

By contrast, action learning may prove less appropriate where knowledge is relatively stable; when you are building up a body of knowledge, or where the body of uncontested knowledge is well-established.

Revans's position of influence on modern-day management remains undefined, and he varied from being underestimated and ignored to being described as a management genius. He campaigned around the world to spread his ideas and had influence in countries as diverse as Belgium, India, and Egypt. In Belgium, his ideas were applied with particular success—national output during the 1970s and 1980s surpassed that of many major competitors, and credit for this was laid at Revans's feet. He had his detractors as well as his devotees, and this is probably as much for his uncompromising style as for his apparently simplistic thinking. But it is on his thinking that posterity should judge him, and there are a number of discernible developments in the domain of business learning that have been influenced by Revans.

Learning cycle
Developed by David Kolb, this ensures that a learner cannot assume a passive role. Instead, learning is active, following a continuous, cyclical process of experience, evaluation, conceptualisation, and experimentation.

Learning preferences
All learners have different levels of comfort or difficulty in relation to the phases of Kolb's learning cycle. Some may need to practise more than others; some may

prefer reading; some observation. Peter Honey and Alan Mumford have identified four basic styles of learning—the activist, the theorist, the reflector, and the pragmatist—which take account of Revans's great emphasis on learning to learn by doing.

Competence movement
The competence movement in management education is principally about being able to do things better in the workplace, by using work-based problems and situations for projects and assignments. Along with the growth of National Vocational Qualifications and the rise of mentoring schemes, the movement must surely acknowledge Revans as one of its main forerunners.

THE BEST SOURCES OF HELP
Books:
Bennett, R., and J. Oliver. *How to Get the Best from Action Research—A Guidebook*. Bradford: MCB University Press, 1988.

Honey, Peter, and Alan Mumford. *Manual of Learning Styles*. 3rd ed. Maidenhead: Peter Honey Publications, 1992.

Kolb, David. *Experiential Learning: Experience as the Source of Learning and Development*. London: Prentice Hall, 1984.

Revans, Reg. *Action Learning: New Techniques for Management*. London: Blond & Briggs, 1980.

Revans, Reg. *The ABC of Action Learning: a Review of 30 Years of Experience*. Bromley: Chartwell-Bratt, 1983.

EDGAR SCHEIN

1928	Born.
1949	Masters degree in psychology, Stanford.
1972–1982	Chairman of the Organization Studies Group of Sloan School of Management, Massachusetts Institute of Technology.
1978–1990	Sloan Fellows Professor of Management, Massachusetts Institute of Technology.
1985	Publication of *Organizational Culture and Leadership*.

> **SUMMARY**
>
> Edgar Schein pioneered the concept of corporate culture with his landmark book *Organizational Culture and Leadership* (1985), which sparked off much research into the subject. He also coined the now much-used phrases 'psychological contract' and 'career anchor'.

LIFE AND CAREER

Currently the Sloan Fellows Professor of Management Emeritus and part-time senior lecturer at the MIT Sloan School of Management, Edgar Schein has had a long and distinguished academic career. He received his PhD in social psychology from Harvard University, collaborated with Douglas McGregor at MIT, and worked for many years with the National Training Laboratory. In addition, he has made a strong contribution to the 'helping' professions, mainly in the areas of organisation development, career development, and organisational culture.

Schein has researched and written extensively about the factors that influence individual and organisational performance. The main themes underlying his work are the identification of culture(s) in the organisation, the relationship between organisational culture and individual behaviour, and the importance of organisational culture for organisational learning. Douglas McGregor invited him to MIT on the basis of his work on the repatriation of POWs following the end of the Korean War. This work strongly influenced Schein's whole career, and re-emerged forcefully in 1999 in an article for the *Learning Organization* on brainwashing and organisational persuasion techniques ('Empowerment, coercive persuasion, and organizational learning: Do they connect?', vol. 6, no. 4, pp. 163–172).

CONTRIBUTION
Corporate culture

Early in his career Schein found traditional approaches to understanding work behaviour and motivation firstly too simplistic to explain the range of experiences of individuals in organisations and secondly too restrictive, since human and organisational needs vary widely from person to person, place to place, and time to time. In *Organizational Culture and Leadership*, he became the first management theorist to define corporate culture and suggest ways in which culture is the dominant force within an organisation.

In his view, culture is a mix of many different factors, such as:

- observed behavioural regularities when people interact
- norms that evolve in working groups

- dominant values pushed by the organisation
- the philosophy guiding the attitudes of senior management to staff and customers
- organisational rules, procedures, and processes
- the feeling or climate that is conveyed without a word being spoken

In *Organizational Culture and Leadership,* Schein defines culture as a pattern of basic assumptions, and discusses how these fall into five, often oppositional, categories:

- humanity's relationship to nature—some organisations seem to want to dominate the external environment, while others accept its domination
- the nature of reality and truth—the ways and means by which organisations arrive at the 'truth'
- the nature of human nature—some people seem to avoid work if they possibly can, while others embrace it as a way of fulfilling their potential, to both their own and the organisation's benefit
- the nature of human activity—a focus on the completion of tasks on the one hand, and on self-fulfilment and personal development on the other
- the nature of human relationships—some organisations seem to facilitate social interaction, others to regard it as an unnecessary distraction

Organisational socialisation

Schein's thoughts on organisational socialisation were triggered when, after arriving at MIT, he asked McGregor for guidance in the form of previous outlines and notes for a course he was preparing. McGregor politely refused, saying there was no need to rely on history and that Schein should make up his own mind. This lesson in acclimatising to MIT led Schein to argue that companies should be conversant with their socialisation practices and recognise the conflicts they can create for new recruits.

In 'Organizational socialization and the profession of management' (*Sloan Management Review*, Fall 1988, pp. 53–65) Schein discusses how, when a new recruit enters the organisation, a process of socialisation—adaptation or 'fit'—takes place. He argues that this process has more to do with recruits' past experience and values than their qualifications or formal training.

Usually, Schein suggested, organisations create a series of events that work to undo the new recruit's old values to some extent, so that he or she is more open to learning new values. This process of 'undoing' or 'unfreezing' can be unpleasant, and its success may therefore depend upon either a recruit's strong motivation to endure it, or the organisation's perseverance in making recruits endure it. There are three basic responses to this socialisation process:

- rebellion—outright rejection of the organisation's norms and values
- creative individualism—selective adoption of key values and norms
- conformity—acceptance of the organisation's norms and values

Noting similarities between brainwashing experienced by servicemen captured during the Korean War and the socialisation of executives on programmes at MIT, Schein argues that many forms of organisational development involve restructuring and change, and have serious implications for the way people work and their relationship with management.

Schein likens such processes to a form of coercive persuasion, or brainwashing, giving people little choice but to abandon, for example, older norms and values that fit badly with the new learning. If we are in tune with the goals and values of the change this will not be a problem, but if we dislike the values, we are likely to disapprove of the brainwashing. Schein concludes that, because the very concept of organisation involves some restriction of individual freedom to achieve a joint purpose, the concept of a continually learning, innovative organisation is something of a paradox, since creativity and learning are related to individual freedom and growth.

Organisational learning

Organisational learning, Schein considers, needs to be fast in order to cope with growing market pressures, yet seems to be obstructed by a fear of, or anxiety about, facing change, particularly on the part of senior executives. This feeling is associated with reluctance to learn what is new, because it appears too difficult or disruptive. Schein argues that only a new anxiety greater than the existing one can overcome this, and his 'anxiety 2' is the fear, shame, or guilt associated with not learning anything new.

Schein emphasises the need for people to feel psychologically safe, if change is to happen. Achieving organisational learning and transformation therefore depends upon creating a feeling of safety and overcoming the negative effects of past incentives and past punishments—especially the latter. To learn, people need to feel motivated and free to try out new things.

Psychological contract and career anchors

In *Organizational Psychology* Schein highlights a 'psychological contract' (attributing the original concept to Chris Argyris), which he defines as an unwritten set of expectations operating between employees and employing managers and others in an organisation. He stresses how essential it is that both parties' expectations of a contract should match, if a long-term relationship that will benefit both parties is to develop.

Closely linked to the notion of the psychological contract is the concept of the 'career anchor', a guiding force that influences individuals' career choices and is based on their self-perceptions. Schein proposes that, from their varying aspirations and motivations, individuals—perhaps unconsciously—develop one underlying career anchor, which they are unwilling to surrender. On the basis of 44 cases, he distinguishes career anchor groups such as technical/functional competence, managerial competence, creativity, security or stability, and autonomy.

The three cultures of management

Rather than a single culture, Schein identifies three cultures (or communities of interest) within an organisation: the operator culture, which evolves locally within organisations and within operational units; the engineering culture of technicians in search of 'people-free' solutions; and the executive culture, which is focused on financial survival.

The three often conflict rather than work in harmony. For example, while the executive culture requires systems and reporting relationships for evidence that operations are on track, the engineering culture attempts to design systems that cut across lines of control and the people manning these.

In his article 'Three cultures of management: The key to organizational learning' (*Sloan Management Review*, Fall 1996, pp. 9–20) Schein suggests that, in many cases, either operators assume executives and engineers do not understand their work needs and covertly do things in their own way; or executives or engineers assume a need for tighter control over operators and force them to follow policies and procedure manuals. In either case, there is no commonly understood plan, and efficiency and effectiveness suffer.

Schein stresses the need to take the concept of culture more seriously and accept how deeply embedded are the assumptions of executives, engineers, and employees. He proposes that helping executives and engineers learn how to learn about, analyse, and evolve their cultures may be central to organisational learning.

CONTEXT AND CONCLUSIONS

Schein's work now spans more than four decades and his great contribution has been in linking culture with individual development and growth, putting the accent on organisations as complex systems and on individuals as whole beings.

Schein was aware that the concept of corporate culture was no cure-all for ailing organisations. The fact, however, that culture is now generally recognised as a central factor in organisational change and development is largely attributable to his work.

THE BEST SOURCES OF HELP
Books:
Schein, Edgar. *Career Dynamics: Matching Individual and Organizational Needs*. Reading, Massachusetts: Addison-Wesley, 1978.
Schein, Edgar. *Organizational Psychology*. 3rd ed. Englewood Cliffs, New Jersey: Prentice Hall, 1980.
Schein, Edgar. *Organizational Culture and Leadership*. 2nd ed. San Francisco: Jossey-Bass, 1997.
Schein, Edgar. *The Corporate Culture Survival Guide*. San Francisco: Jossey-Bass, 1999.
Journal Article:
Schein, Edgar. 'How can organizations learn faster? The challenge of entering the green room.' *Sloan Management Review*, Winter 1993, pp. 85–92.

PETER SENGE

1947	Born.
1975–1990	Research at the Sloan School of Management into ways of learning.
1990	Publication of *The Fifth Discipline*.
Present	Director of the Center for Organizational Learning at the Sloan School of Management, MIT.

SUMMARY Populariser of the theory of the learning organisation, first suggested by Chris Argyris and Donald Schon, Peter Senge studied how organisations develop adaptive capabilities in a world of increasing complexity and change. His work culminated in the publication of *The Fifth Discipline: The Art and Practice of the Learning Organisation*.

LIFE AND CAREER
Peter Senge is the director of the Center for Organizational Learning at the Sloan School of Management, Massachusetts Institute of Technology (MIT). He graduated in engineering from Stanford before doing a PhD in social systems modelling at MIT. For many years, Senge studied how businesses and organisations develop adaptive capabilities in a world of increasing complexity and change, but the success of his book *The Fifth Discipline* popularised the concept of the 'learning organisation'.

Published in 1990, *The Fifth Discipline* brought the attention of the world to bear on this rather unassuming man, who suddenly found himself the modern equivalent of a medieval crusader seeking dramatically to change corporate America, and indeed the rest of the world, against all the odds. Senge's message was simple—the learning organisation believes that competitive advantage derives from continued learning, both individual and collective. Furthermore, the new challenges of the information age demand that not only businesses, but also educational institutions and governments, transform themselves radically. Senge describes himself as an 'idealistic pragmatist' and spends much time building learning organisations with the top leaders of companies, education, and government.

Although Senge's ideas are utopian, his Center for Organizational Learning has attracted an impressive list of corporate sponsors who have dug deep into their pockets to fund pilot programmes.

CONTRIBUTION
The Fifth Discipline
In *The Fifth Discipline*, Senge suggests that there are five basic ingredients for a learning organisation.

Systems thinking: Senge's whole approach to organisations is a 'systems' approach that views the organisation as a living entity, with its own behaviour and learning patterns. He introduces the idea of 'systems archetypes' to help managers spot repetitive patterns that lead to recurrent problems or limits to growth.

Personal mastery: every modern manager recognises the importance of developing skills and competencies in individuals, but Senge takes this notion further by stressing the importance of spiritual growth in the learning organisation. True spiritual growth exposes us to a deeper reality; it teaches us to see the current reality more clearly and, by highlighting the difference between vision and the current reality, generates a creative tension, out of which successful learning arises. In Senge's own words, a learning organisation is 'a group of people who are continually enhancing their capability to create their future' by 'changing individuals so that they produce results they care about, accomplish things that are important to them'.

Mental models: the systems approach is continued with Senge's emphasis on mental models. This discipline requires managers to construct mental models for the driving forces behind the organisation's values and principles. Senge alerts his readers to the impact of acquired patterns of thinking at the organisational level and the need to develop non-defensive mechanisms for examining the nature of these patterns.

Shared vision: according to Senge, true creativity and innovation are based on group creativity, and the shared vision the group depends on can only be built on the personal vision of its members. Shared vision occurs when the vision is no longer seen by the team members as separate from the self.

Team learning: effective team learning involves alternating processes for dialogue and discussion. Dialogue is exploratory and widens possibilities, whereas discussion narrows down the options to find the best alternatives for future decisions. Although these two processes are complementary, they need to be separated. Unfortunately, most teams lack the ability to distinguish between these two modes and to move consciously between them.

Senge's basic premise can be stated very simply: people should put aside their old ways of thinking (mental models); learn to be open with others (personal mastery); understand how the company really works (systems thinking); form a plan everyone can agree on (shared vision); and then work together to achieve that vision (team learning).

Practical tools — *The Fifth Discipline Fieldbook*

Recognising that the ideas contained in *The Fifth Discipline* needed to be made more accessible to practising managers, Senge and his colleagues produced a more practical guide — *The Fifth Discipline Fieldbook*. Throughout the book, the authors stress that anyone who wants to be part of a learning organisation must be willing to go through a personal change. To help this process, Senge and his co-authors provide a set of elaborate personal awareness exercises. The *Fieldbook* was designed as a resource for dipping into and it contains many good ideas and case studies. Even if you find Senge's thinking too general, the *Fieldbook* is well worth scrutinising for references and new ideas. Here are just a few:

System archetypes and causal loops: the *Fieldbook* devotes a lot of time to mapping processes in organisations, analysing feedback loops and identifying typical organisational problems (the system archetypes). This process-mapping tool can help employees to work out how complex systems interact, and to develop their 'mental models' of the organisation. The 'beer game' described in *The Fifth Discipline* is a simulation based on these models.

Left- and right-hand columns: by writing down in meetings what you really think (left-hand column) and what you actually said (right-hand column), you can analyse and identify those personal prejudices that get in the way of really productive work.

The ladder of inference: this exercise provides a step model for analysing our values, beliefs, and actions. Climbing down the ladder helps us to discover why we behave the way we do, and helps us to avoid jumping to dangerous conclusions. The steps on the ladder are as follows:

- I take ACTIONS based on my beliefs
- I adopt BELIEFS about the world
- I draw CONCLUSIONS
- I make ASSUMPTIONS based on the meanings added to my mental models
- I add MEANINGS (cultural and personal)
- I select DATA from what I observe
- I OBSERVE data and experiences.

The container: this is a dialogue tool that has proved very effective (if not explosive!) in some organisations. People at a meeting are encouraged to imagine a container that holds everyone's hostile thoughts and feelings. As everyone speaks out, putting their fears, prejudices, and anger on the table, the hostility between different factions is neutralised, because it is exposed in a safe place for all to discuss. In the early days of such experiments, a good facilitator is probably essential.

Learning labs and flight simulators: the *Fieldbook* provides useful references for all those who wish to design effective simulations for training sessions.

CONTEXT AND CONCLUSIONS

Although Senge's *The Fifth Discipline* was a bestseller, its basic concepts had emerged from extensive research carried out at the influential Sloan School of Management at MIT over 15 years. The success of the 'learning organisation' concept is a reflection of the times. None of the book's concepts is new, but Senge was able to put them all together and to create a simple but very powerful concept.

Senge is a product of his age, probably greatly influenced by the culture of the 1960s in the United States. His systems approach towards organisations shows the same maturity displayed in the systems analysis tools developed by thinkers such as Peter Checkland at Lancaster University. Here the organisation is viewed as a 'superorganism' with its own behaviour patterns, but also profoundly influenced by the nature of its constituent members. The sad fact is that Senge was one of the first management gurus to make the accepted beliefs of a whole generation of social scientists, biologists, and environmentalists credible to the corporate world.

In his own words, Senge says: 'We live under a massive illusion of separation from one another, from nature, from the universe, from everything. We're depleting the earth and we're fragmenting our spirit. The symptoms are pollution, anger, and fear. Everything in our culture is about the management of impressions and appearances, from physical fitness to the way we dress. And yet on another level we know it's all bullshit.' Even having just passed the millennium, there is little evidence that the change in attitude needed to achieve Senge's ideals—of long-term corporate sustainability and freedom for all to achieve personal mastery—is in sight: there are very few organisations that have been able to implement his ideas successfully.

The main criticism that can be levelled at Senge's work is the inherent difficulty of applying his models. Senge was trained as an engineer and then became involved in social research. Both require a systems approach, but this cannot be developed easily. In fact systems thinking is about as easy as learning brain surgery on a three-day seminar. Nor can most companies afford the luxury of their top executives learning to 'crash land' for too long.

Breaking old corporate habits is very hard, and therefore transforming an enterprise into a learning organisation is highly problematical and not for the faint-hearted. The reason for this is simple—in order to move forward to a new, co-operative learning model, managers have to give up their traditional areas of power and control. They have to hand over power to the learners and allow them to make mistakes. In a blame-orientated culture, this change in attitude remains a major obstacle.

Despite the elusiveness of its ideals, *The Fifth Discipline* has proved highly influential. Its concepts have stimulated the debate and acceptance of issues such as self-managed development, empowerment, and creativity. Its practical impact can be seen in modern human resource management strategies, teamwork principles, and in quality models.

It is more important perhaps to recognise that in life all the most profound truths are deceptively simple, yet almost impossible to apply in practice. The difficulty experienced in applying Senge's ideas does not invalidate them—if anything, it confirms their importance for companies in the next millennium.

THE BEST SOURCES OF HELP
Books:
Checkland, Peter. *Systems Thinking, Systems Practice!* Chichester: John Wiley, 1981.
Gibson, Rowan, ed. *Rethinking the Future.* London: Nicholas Brealey, 1997.
Kleiner, Art. *The Age of Heretics: Heroes, Outlaws, and the Forerunners of Corporate Change.* London: Nicholas Brealey, 1996.
Senge, Peter. *The Fifth Discipline: The Art and Practice of the Learning Organization.* London: Century Business, 1990.
Senge, Peter, et al. *The Fifth Discipline Fieldbook: Strategies and Tools for Building a Learning Organization.* London: Nicholas Brealey, 1994.
Journal Articles:
Senge, Peter. 'The future of workplace learning and performance.' *Training and Development USA*, vol. 48 no. 5, 1994, pp. S36-S47.
Senge, Peter. 'Mr Learning Organization.' *Fortune International*, 17 Oct. 1994, pp. 75-81.
Senge, Peter. 'Looking ahead: implications of the present.' *Harvard Business Review*, Sept./Oct. 1997, pp. 18-32.

ADAM SMITH

1723	Born.
1748	Appointed lecturer in literature at Edinburgh University.
1751	Appointed professor of literature at Glasgow University.
1763	Publication of *The Theory of Moral Sentiments*.
1776	Publication of *The Wealth of Nations*.
1778	Accepts post of commissioner of customs in Scotland.
1787	Elected lord rector at Glasgow University.
1790	Dies.

SUMMARY

Adam Smith (1723–1790) published his best-known book, fully entitled *An Inquiry into the Nature and Causes of the Wealth of Nations* but commonly known as *The Wealth of Nations*, in 1776. This is often described as one of the most important texts of our time, and its two main philosophical points stressed the supreme value of individual liberty, and the pursuit of self-interest as ultimately beneficial for society as a whole.

LIFE AND CAREER

Smith was brought up in Kirkcaldy by his widowed mother. He went, on a scholarship, to Glasgow University at 14, to study mathematics and moral philosophy; and then, at 17, to Balliol College, Oxford. In 1748, he was appointed to a lectureship in literature at Edinburgh, and in 1751, became professor of literature at Glasgow University. One year later, he was appointed professor of moral philosophy and, despite a nervous disorder, faltering speech, and a tendency to forgetfulness, became a teacher of high repute. His lectures focused on theology, ethics, and jurisprudence.

In 1763, following the publication of his first book, *The Theory of Moral Sentiments*, Smith was asked to act as tutor and companion to the young Duke of Buccleuch during his 'grand tour' of Europe. Through this he met several great philosophers and thinkers, including Voltaire and Rousseau, and his own ideas took firmer shape. On his return from Europe he retired to Kirkcaldy to concentrate on writing *The Wealth of Nations*.

In 1778, Smith accepted the post of commissioner of customs in Scotland, and was elected lord rector at Glasgow University in 1787. Although Smith had plans to add a third volume (on jurisprudence) to follow the other two, his writings remained limited to reissuing editions of *The Wealth of Nations*.

Smith never married and, despite his impressive mind, became known as somewhat eccentric, largely due to his tendency to forget everyday things, such as changing from his nightclothes into day wear. After the death of Smith's mother, he was looked after by an aunt until his death in 1790.

HISTORICAL BACKGROUND

To understand Smith's thinking fully, it is helpful to know a little about his background. He knew many of the most influential contemporary thinkers, and spent much time debating in the gentlemen's clubs of London. He was a friend of both John Locke and David Hume and was, for a time, a disciple of Quesnay, the leading

French physiocrat. *The Wealth of Nations* undoubtedly drew ideas from many such sources.

In the later 17th and 18th centuries, there was increasing interest in the theory of 'natural' law. The natural sciences had become established since the publication of Newton's *Philosophiae Naturalis Principia Mathematica* (1687) and there was a strong drive to uncover the natural laws that were thought to guide people's actions.

At the same time, burdensome government regulations were increasingly criticised, and the theory of natural order was being drawn into ideas about society and government. For example, John Locke's *Treatise on Civil Government* (1691) proposed that men are born free and equal, and are governed by 'natural laws', arguing that, while executive power is necessary, this should be only by consent.

Such revolutionary ideas were taken up by many great thinkers, including Hume, Hutchison, the French physiocrats, and Smith himself. It was, however, impossible to prove the existence of a benevolent 'natural order', ordained by God for men's happiness. While proponents of the concept considered it to be self-evident, it was always, in fact, an intangible hypothesis wide open to challenge.

The idea that human society should be based on a natural order encouraged ideas about individualism to develop further. The concept of an economic system founded on individual self-interest rather than government control is central to *The Wealth of Nations*, and to later social, political, and economic change.

THE WEALTH OF NATIONS
Natural law and 'laissez faire'

The Wealth of Nations followed the French physiocrats in arguing that all human powers are subject to immutable, natural moral and physical laws. These laws, divine in origin, were thought to offer a basis for government that could leave things to work naturally, with results that would satisfy both individual and state interests.

Smith never actually used the term 'laissez faire', but his book popularised associated arguments for government non-intervention in social, economic, and commercial matters. 'Laissez faire' was first used by the French, and essentially meant that the government should let things alone, specifically in terms of trade, production of goods, and quantities or quality of products. This philosophy dominated much 18th and 19th century government, and assumed that:

- natural laws, if left to work freely, would create the best possible society
- enlightened individual selfishness was ultimately in the public interest
- men are born equal

The Wealth of Nations took ten years to write, and the ideas within it challenged Smith's contemporary, mercantilist government and its protectionist laws. The author realised that his book would outrage those with vested interests in business or government, because of its arguments for government-enforced competition and against price-fixing.

Although often castigated as such, Smith was neither inhumane nor a proponent of 'the law of the jungle' as an approach to social organisation. He recognised the worst tendencies of some businessmen who 'love to reap where they never sowed', and was extremely aware of how greed could lead to excesses of monopoly and corruption. Smith did, in fact, support some forms of intervention, especially in public areas such as defence. He did not, however, have our benefit of hindsight, or know how the Industrial Revolution would change society, creating some extremely wealthy businessmen, and a mass of extremely poor industrial workers, who would suffer greatly because of their lack of protection from regulatory laws.

The law of labour
Natural law was considered by Smith to encompass a 'law of labour'. According to this, the external environment could provide men with the products necessary for subsistence, in return for their labour, and all men should therefore have the right to carry out activities to preserve their existence. Government's only role should be to promote the existence of natural law and to enable its free working.

The natural laws were assumed to work in the same exacting way as mathematical laws. Left to themselves, they should establish an order that would benefit both individuals and society. Individualism, for Smith and the other economists and philosophers of his time, meant relief from the constraints of mercantilism, the right to economic freedom, and the right of a people to legislate for themselves and be taxed by the government they chose.

The division of labour
Smith gives many examples of the advantages of the division of labour, with each worker focusing upon a single stage of manufacture rather than, as in traditional crafts, being involved in every stage. His ideas were based on life before 1760, and he did not foresee how the introduction of machinery would make the division of labour even more logical and sometimes a harsh necessity.

The free market
Smith's main thesis throughout *The Wealth of Nations* was the inefficiency of government interference, which he demonstrates with reference to the markets for both national and international trade. He envisions a free market as a customer-driven, democratic mechanism through which, by exercising their free choices about purchase or sale prices, people would act to regulate resources fairly. Although it was Dudley North who first related supply to demand and extolled the benefits of free trade, Smith recognised that buyers as well as sellers profit from trade, and saw international commerce as a source of wealth for both importers and exporters.

Smith had a very positive vision of how a free market would eventually realise a state of 'universal opulence' for everyone. He argued that each nation should concentrate on those industrial areas where it enjoyed a 'comparative advantage'. These ideas were taken up by subsequent economists such as Ricardo and Malthus, and can be traced within the thinking of some contemporary strategists, particularly in Michael Porter's work on competitive advantage.

Morality
Smith is often criticised for a lack of moral focus in *The Wealth of Nations*, but he did assume that its readers would already know of the moral base given in *The Theory of Moral Sentiments*. The earlier book sought to explore moral judgements within the context of Smith's assumption that people are essentially driven by self-interest,

and proposed that we all have 'social propensities' for sympathy, justice, and benevolence.

CONTEXT AND CONCLUSIONS
The Wealth of Nations had a profound influence on English history, leading to the end of the mercantilist era and catalysing a social and economic order based on individualism and the 'natural laws' supposedly underlying competition and free market forces.

Smith's ideas have often been castigated for the support they gave to later businessmen who grew very rich while rejecting any regulations to protect industrial workers. He wrote his masterpiece, however, before the Industrial Revolution began to take effect, and it was intended as a polemic against restrictive government policies and monopolistic abuses, rather than as a panegyric for unregulated business. Also, just as Smith's first book, *The Theory of Moral Sentiments*, supplies a moral aspect to complement *The Wealth of Nations*, it is probable that his intended, but unwritten, third volume on jurisprudence could have contributed ideas for legal safeguards to protect the public from abuses resulting from greed and collusion, since he considered these typically to arise out of people's business activities and contacts.

For his time, Smith was actually a social radical, promoting liberty and equality and denouncing various pillars of the existing establishment. From our modern perspective, it is clear there was no factual base for his ideas about natural law and harmony, and that perfect competition could not erase social problems, particularly when factors from a future that Smith could not have imagined (including giant corporations, economic cycles and depressions, mass unemployment, and mechanical warfare) became more pertinent. Despite this, however, *The Wealth of Nations* remains a 'milestone' book, offering a composite analysis that shaped our social and economic world.

THE BEST SOURCES OF HELP
Books:
Haakonssen, Knud, ed. *The Theory of Moral Sentiments*. Cambridge: Cambridge University Press, 2002.
Smith, Kathryn, ed. *Wealth of Nations*. Oxford: Oxford University Press, 1998.

SUN TZU

c. 400 BC	Sun Tzu lived and wrote.
1780	First European translation of *The Art of War* published.
1910	English translation published.

> **SUMMARY**
> The quality management techniques used by Japanese companies enabled them to put cheaper and better products into American and British shops than their domestic rivals. The search to discover how they achieved this led to an understanding that Japanese business people have a different perspective on the marketplace from their Western counterparts. Further studies showed that Asian business leaders appeared to attach great significance to classical Chinese military strategy and to believe that the principles underpinning it are embedded in various aspects of daily life.

LIFE AND CAREER

Although the precise dates of his birth and death are not known, Sun Tzu is thought to have lived over 2,400 years ago, at roughly the same time as Confucius. Brought up in a family of army officers, he became familiar with, and eventually expert in, military affairs. Historians are generally agreed that he was a general who led a number of successful military campaigns in the region currently known as the Anhui Province. It is recorded that the state of Wu, under whose sovereign he served, became a dominant power at that time. Since then, it has become standard practice for Chinese military chiefs to familiarise themselves with Sun Tzu's writings.

CONTRIBUTION
The Art of War

Sun Tzu's *The Art of War* (the book's actual title is *Sun Tzu Ping Fa*, literally 'The Military Method of Mr Sun') is a compilation of his thinking on the strategies that underlie success in war. It has been translated into many languages, and there are several English versions. This account is based on the translation by Thomas Cleary, published by Shambhala Pocket Classics and available on the Internet. Two further editions, published by Tuttle and Wordsworth Editions respectively, also were consulted.

Sun Tzu's anecdotes and thoughts, which fill no more than about 25 pages of text in all, are divided into 13 sections:

1. strategic assessments
2. doing battle
3. offensive strategy
4. formation
5. force
6. emptiness and fullness
7. armed struggle
8. adaptations
9. manoeuvring armies

10 terrain
11 nine grounds
12 attack by fire
13 use of spies

Some of these have less current relevance than others, but they are all worth at least a glance. Hidden among advice such as not to dally in salt marshes when retreating or attacking (11), there is the odd gem that is striking in its modernity. For example: 'when a leader enters deeply into enemy territory with the troops, he brings out their potential.' (11) The advice given in section 10 on how to proceed in narrow or steep terrain (occupy the high and sunny side to await your opponent) can be quickly passed over, but a little further on in the same section Sun Tzu's castigation of poor leadership is much more pertinent: 'When generals are weak and lack authority, instructions are not clear, officers and soldiers lack consistency, and they form battle lines every which way; this is riot.'

On strategy

Many commentaries focus on the first section, strategic assessments, at the expense of the others. It is certainly there that, helped by a little lateral thinking, Sun Tzu seems best to relate to the spirit of modern business. He refers initially to five key factors that determine the result of war:

- politics—that which causes people to be in harmony with their ruler
- weather—the seasons
- terrain—distances, difficulty or ease of travel, opportunities or safety
- leadership—a matter of intelligence, trustworthiness, humanity, courage, and strictness
- discipline—organisation, chain of command, logistics

There are also seven issues to be appraised (the postscript following each question has been added to indicate the line most interpretations take).

- Whose moral influence is the stronger? (Whose followers are more willing to subscribe to common goals?)
- Which leader is the more able? (Who has the ability to combine benevolence and compassion with boldness and strict discipline?)
- Which army has greater advantage of nature and terrain? (Whom do politics, economic cycles, investment, and social and cultural factors favour? Who understands the bigger picture?)
- Whose laws and rules are more effective? (Do people understand what is expected as a result of clear instructions and procedures?)
- Whose troops are stronger? (How can things be arranged so that small can compete effectively with large?)
- Whose soldiers are better trained? (Who uses delegation and training for organisational effectiveness?)
- Whose system of rewards and punishments is clearer? (Who is therefore able to generate higher performance and a better competitive position?)

The theme of strategy is picked up again and again, apparently at random. One interpretation stretches section 6 to make it relate to market presence and strategies of deception employed to fool competitor intelligence. Sun Tzu argues that 'there is no constant good or bad, right or wrong: therefore victory in war is not repetitious, but adapts its form endlessly...so a military force has no constant formation, water has no constant shape: the ability to gain victory by changing and adapting according to the opponent is called genius'. (6)

On information and intelligence
'...to fail to know the conditions of opponents because of reluctance to give rewards for intelligence is extremely inhuman, uncharacteristic of a true military leader... so what enables an intelligent government and a wise military leadership to overcome others and achieve extraordinary accomplishments is foreknowledge...[which] must be obtained from people who know the conditions of the enemy.' (13)

On tactics
'Making the armies able to take on opponents without being defeated is a matter of unorthodox and orthodox methods.' (5)

'The difficulty of armed struggle is to make long distances near and make problems into advantages.' (7)

On competition and competitor intelligence
'So if you do not know the plans of your competitors, you cannot make informed alliances.' (7)

'So the rule of military operations is not to count on opponents not coming, but to rely on having ways of dealing with them; not to count on opponents not attacking, but to rely on having what cannot be attacked.' (8)

On leadership and people management
'If they rule armies without knowing the arts of complete adaptivity, even if they know what there is to gain, they cannot get people to work for them.' (8)

'If soldiers are punished before a personal attachment to the leadership is formed, they will not submit, and if they do not submit, they are hard to employ.' (9)

'Look upon your soldiers as you do infants, and they willingly go into deep valleys with you; look upon your soldiers as beloved children, and they willingly die with you.' (10)

'If you are so nice to them that you cannot employ them, so kind to them that you cannot command them, so casual with them that you cannot establish order, they are like spoiled children, useless.' (10)

On communication
'When directives are consistently issued to edify the populace, the populace accepts ... when directives are consistently issued, there is mutual satisfaction between the leadership and the group.' (9)

CONTEXT AND CONCLUSIONS
Historians tell us that the *Sun Tzu Ping Fa* is the oldest existing military treatise in the world, predating von Clausewitz by 2,200 years. But so what? Stuart Crainer asks how *The Art of War* can have any relevance to running a crisp factory in Ipswich. It

is a fair question. How can the thoughts of a Chinese general who lived two and a half millennia ago possibly inform, enlighten, or inspire a modern manager, or have any bearing on his or her day-to-day concerns? And even if there are interesting links, do they do any more than show us that ancient Chinese strategists did not differ fundamentally from modern business-people?

Sun Tzu's supporters, however, insist that his concepts are ageless. Although it is easy to stretch interpretation too far and find meaning anywhere if you look hard enough, such things as strategic intelligence, planning, attention to detail, cunning, deception, and theories of leadership in which the leader earns authority with the led, have universal value and are appropriate to any human arena and any period.

If part of Sun Tzu's modern appeal derives from the constant search for any nuggets of intelligence that may give an organisation an edge over the competition, another part lies in the fact that the *Ping Fa* offers an opportunity to gain insights into the Oriental mind that do not come from someone with a modern axe to grind or reputation to make. In addition, the insights are couched in direct, no-nonsense, hard-hitting language that makes them seem more, not less, pregnant with meaning.

As globalisation brings East closer to West, business relationships will hinge on understanding cultures and attitudes that may appear strange at first. And if the managers of Crainer's crisp factory in Ipswich set strategic goals, sell their goods abroad, or interrelate with their workforce, *The Art of War* may still have something to say to them. It is finding its way into many MBA programmes.

THE BEST SOURCES OF HELP
Books:
Kaufman, Stephen F. *The Art of War: The Definitive Interpretation of Sun Tzu's Classic Book of Strategy for the Martial Artist*. Rutland, Vermont: Charles E. Tuttle, 1996.
Sun Tzu. *The Art of War*. (Translated by Yuan Shibing, interpretation Tao Hanzhang, foreword Norman Stone.) Ware: Wordsworth Editions, 1993.
Sun Tzu. *The Art of War*. (Translated by Thomas Cleary.) Boston, Massachusetts: Shambhala Pocket Classics, 1991.
Journal Articles:
Crainer, Stuart. 'Braingain.' *Management Today*, April 1998, pp. 68–70.
Min Chen. 'Sun Tzu's strategic thinking and contemporary business.' *Business Horizons*, Mar./Apr. 1994, pp. 42–48.

GENICHI TAGUCHI

1924	Born.
1942–1945	Serves in Japanese navy during the Second World War.
1945	Works in Ministry of Public Health and Welfare and Ministry of Education.
1950	Joins Electrical Communication Laboratory (ECL) of Nippon Telephone and Telegraph Company.
1960	Wins Deming prize for contribution to field of quality engineering (later wins it three more times).
1962	Awarded doctorate by Kyushsu University.
1964	Takes up professorship at Aoyamagokuin University in Japan.
1970s	Develops concept of the quality loss function.
1980s	Visits AT&T Bell Laboratories in the United States; American interest in his methodology established.
1983	Becomes executive director of the Ford Supplier Institute.
1986	Receives Indigo Ribbon from the emperor of Japan for contribution to economics and industry; medal from International Technology Institute for work on statistical methods to achieve cost and quality improvements.
1986	Institute of Statisticians organises conference in London; Taguchi's ideas become known in Europe.
1987	UK Taguchi Club formed (now the Quality Methods Association); ideas adopted widely in the West.
1998	Honorary member of the American Society for Quality (ASQ).

SUMMARY

Taguchi is famous for his pioneering methods of modern quality control and low-cost quality engineering. He is the founder of what has come to be known as the Taguchi method, which seeks to improve product quality at the design stage by integrating quality control into product design, using experiment and statistical analysis. His methods have been said fundamentally to change the philosophy and practice of quality control.

LIFE AND CAREER

Genichi Taguchi, born in Japan in 1924, served in the Navigation Institute of the Japanese navy during the Second World War. He then worked in the Ministry of Public Health and Welfare and in the Institute of Statistical Mathematics of the Ministry of Education, meeting the renowned statistician, Matosaburo Masuyame, who nurtured his statistical skills.

In 1950, Taguchi joined the Electrical Communication Laboratory (ECL) of Nippon Telephone and Telegraph Company, gaining six years' experience in experimentation and data analysis while developing telephone switching systems. The commercial benefits resulting from his ECL work helped Taguchi to earn the Deming prize in 1960, for his contribution to the field of quality engineering. He went on to win this award, one of Japan's most prestigious commendations, a further three times.

In 1962, Taguchi was awarded a doctorate by Kyushu University, after working with industrial statisticians (and beginning his work on the signal-to-noise ratio) at Bell Laboratories in the United States. He continued working for ECL in a consulting role and became part of the associate research staff of the Japanese Standards Association, where he founded the Quality Research Group. In 1964, he took up a professorship at Aoyamagokuin University in Japan, where he spent the next 17 years developing his methods.

Throughout this time, Taguchi was largely unheard of outside Japan. He developed his concept of the quality loss function in the early 1970s, but it was during the 1980s that Taguchi's methods became established, when he revisited AT&T Bell Laboratories in the United States, as director of the Japanese Academy of Quality.

After that, interest from US companies such as Xerox, Ford, and ITT in Taguchi's methodology increased. In 1982, Taguchi was involved in seminars for Ford executives, and the following year he became executive director of the Ford Supplier Institute (later known as the American Supplier Institute). He was also further honoured in 1986, receiving the Indigo Ribbon from the emperor of Japan for his contribution to Japanese economics and industry, and the International Technology Institute's medal for his work on statistical methods to achieve cost and quality improvements.

Throughout much of this time, Taguchi was also operating as a full-time consultant to various major companies in the United States, Japan, China, and India. Apart from occasional work with, for example, Lucas Industries, Taguchi's ideas only became known in Europe from 1986, when the Institute of Statisticians organised a conference in London. The UK Taguchi Club (now the Quality Methods Association) was formed the following year and, since then, Taguchi methods have been in regular and widespread use in the West, particularly in the car industry. Taguchi himself is now in semi-retirement.

CONTRIBUTION
Taguchi methods
Taguchi developed methods for both online (process) and offline (design) quality control, which formed the basis of his approach to total quality control and assurance within a product's development life cycle. His approach emphasised improving the quality of product and process prior to manufacture (that is, at the design stage) rather than the more traditional approach of achieving quality through inspection.

Quality loss function
Taguchi's approach differed from the traditional one of manufacturing a product within a specification based on tolerances, equally spaced around a target value. He developed a concept of 'quality loss' occurring as soon as there is a deviation away from the target value, and worked in terms of quality loss rather than just quality. He defined quality loss as 'the loss imparted to society from the time the product is shipped', and this related the loss to society as a whole. Thus, it included both company costs, such as reworking, scrapping, and maintenance, and any loss to the customer through poor product performance and reduced reliability.

A loss function curve can be calibrated by using information from the customer.

A target value is identified as being the best possible value of a quality characteristic. Taguchi associates a simple, quadratic loss function with deviations from the target. Thus:

- the smaller the performance variation, the better the quality of the product
- the larger the deviation from the target value, the larger the loss to society

A loss will occur even when the product is within the specification allowed, although it is minimal when the product is on target.

After the design engineer has determined the cost of parts being manufactured out of specification, this information can be used to justify expenditure on quality improvement, enabling decisions to be made on firm cost and quality grounds. Thus, it is possible to estimate whether the 'quality gain' from changing a design is worthwhile—although ensuring that a product is produced at a quality level acceptable to the customer remains an important consideration.

Signal-to-noise ratio

One of Taguchi's most innovative ideas was to use a quality measure called the 'signal-to-noise ratio', which communications engineers could employ to find the strength of an electrical signal. Taguchi applied this measure to everyday products, and used it as a measure to choose control levels that could best cope with changes in operating and environmental conditions, or noise.

Robust quality of design

On the basis of the signal-to-noise measure, Taguchi was able to develop the concept of robustness, which enables a product to be designed to be less affected by noise. Given normal variations in process operations, the product in question would be less likely to fail acceptable quality criteria.

Product design improvement

During the product design and production engineering phases, Taguchi set out three steps that must be followed.

1. System design: this may involve the development of a prototype design, and will determine the materials, parts, and assembly system to be used. The manufacturing process has also to be considered.

2. Parameter design: Taguchi's parameter design aimed to find the most cost-effective way of controlling noise. Taguchi process and design improvements are gained by identifying easily controllable factors and settings that minimise performance variation. Controllable factors are design factors that a designer can set or easily adjust. The specified value becomes the signal. Uncontrollable factors are noise, or external variations, and a higher signal-to-noise ratio means better quality. Taguchi found that if controllable factors were set at optimal levels, the product would be robust to external changes. This was achieved through parameter design applied at the design (offline) stage to reduce or remove the effect of noise factors.

Experiments were designed using orthogonal arrays that (rather simply described) were a series of rows and columns allowing the effects of different factors to be extracted and separated out. Taguchi was not the inventor of the orthogonal array, but this type of experimentation moved away from the traditional approach of testing one factor at a time. His new approach dramatically reduced the number of experiments and prototypes required and, in consequence, costs were much lower. He developed various experimental designs that allowed the variability of the noise factors on each controllable factor setting to be simulated. The settings that minimised variability could then be determined.

3. Tolerance design: if parameter design failed, Taguchi suggested using tolerance design to identify the most crucial noise factors. Tolerances could be reassigned so that the overall variability was reduced to acceptable levels.

Invest last not first
Taguchi placed much emphasis on optimising the product and process at the beginning, in order to engineer product quality (parameter design) into the system. Using low cost materials and components was a vital feature of this, and money was spent on higher cost items only when necessary (tolerance design).

CONTEXT AND CONCLUSIONS
It was W. E. Deming who first recognised the importance of moving quality control backwards from inspection to proper process control, notably via statistical process control (SPC). Taguchi moved quality control even further back, to the design stage, thus completing the total quality loop. Taguchi's techniques and statistical experimental designs for offline quality improvement complemented SPC, to achieve online quality improvement. Deming's philosophy regarding management quality improvement encompassed both.

It has been said that Deming's work inspired a revolution in the old management culture, while Taguchi inspired evolution. Certainly Deming provided a theory mainly for management, while Taguchi provided important techniques for improving a process at every stage, from design to production, and for keeping the improved processes under control.

THE BEST SOURCES OF HELP
Books:
Bendell, A., et al. *Taguchi Methods: Applications in World Industry*. Kempston: IFS Publications, 1990.
Logothetis, Nickolas. *Managing for Total Quality: from Deming to Taguchi and SPC*. New York: Prentice Hall, 1992.
Ohno, Taiichi, Elsayed Elsayed, and Thomas Hsiang. *Quality Engineering in Production Systems*. New York: McGraw Hill, 1989.
Taguchi, Genichi. *Offline Quality Control*. Nagoya: Central Japan Quality Control Association, 1980.
Taguchi, Genichi. *Introduction to Quality Engineering: Designing Quality into Product and Processes*. Tokyo: Asian Productivity Organization, 1986.
Taguchi, Genichi. *Online Quality Control*. Tokyo: Japanese Standards Association, 1986.
Taguchi, Genichi. *The System of Experimental Design, vols. 1 & 2*. New York: Kraus International Publications, 1987.

FREDERICK WINSLOW TAYLOR

1856	Born.
1874	Becomes an apprentice pattern-maker and machinist at Enterprise Hydraulic Works.
1878	Takes unskilled job at the Midvale Steel Works.
1881	Gains master's degree in mechanical engineering.
1890	Becomes general manager of Manufacturing Investment Company (MIC).
1898	Becomes joint discoverer of the Taylor-White process, a method of tempering steel.
1911	Publication of *The Principles of Scientific Management*.
1915	Dies.

> **SUMMARY**
>
> Peter Drucker is often called 'the guru's guru'. Drucker himself would suggest that the accolade should be given to Frederick Winslow Taylor (1856–1917). 'On Taylor's "scientific management" rests, above all, the tremendous surge of affluence in the last 75 years which has lifted the working masses in the developed countries well above any level recorded, even for the well-to-do,' Drucker wrote in *Management: Tasks, Responsibilities, Practices*.

LIFE AND CAREER

Although Taylor passed the entrance examination for Harvard College, failing eyesight meant that he could not take up his place. Instead he took the unusual step for someone of his background of becoming an apprentice pattern-maker and machinist at the Enterprise Hydraulic Works.

Following his apprenticeship, Taylor took up an unskilled job at the Midvale Steel Works. After several different jobs and a master's degree in mechanical engineering, he was appointed chief engineer there. In 1890 he became general manager of Manufacturing Investment Company (MIC), eventually becoming an independent consulting engineer to management.

In 1881, Taylor won the doubles championships of the United States Lawn Tennis Association and a year later, the doubles in the Young American C.C. Lawn Tennis Tournament. Later in his career he developed a passion for golf and, in keeping with his love of experiment, attempted to make a putting green that was reliant on water below the surface rather than on natural rainfall. By the time of his death, Taylor's experiments had led to him filing at least 50 patents and had made him an extremely wealthy man.

CONTRIBUTION

Scientific management

Taylor's seminal work—*The Principles of Scientific Management*—was published six years before his death. In it, he put forward his ideas of 'scientific management' (sometimes referred to today as 'Taylorism'), which differed from traditional 'initiative and incentive' methods of management. These ideas were an accumulation from his life's work, and included several examples from his places of employment. The four overriding principles of scientific management are as follows.

- Each part of a job is analysed 'scientifically', and the most efficient method for undertaking it is devised—the 'one best way' of working. This consists of examining the implements needed to carry out the work, and measuring the maximum amount a

'first-class' worker can do in a day. Workers are then expected to do this much work every day.
- The most suitable person to undertake the job is chosen, again 'scientifically'. The individual is taught to do the job in the exact way devised. Everyone, according to Taylor, has the ability to be 'first-class' at some job. It is management's role to find out which job suits each employee and train them until they are first-class.
- Managers must co-operate with workers to ensure the job is done in the scientific way.
- There is a clear 'division' of work and responsibility between management and workers. Managers concern themselves with the planning and supervision of the work, and workers carry it out.

Taylor summed up the differences between his principles of management and the traditional method as follows: 'Under the management of "initiative and incentive", practically the whole problem is "up to the workman"; while under the scientific management, fully one-half of the problem is "up to the management"...The principal object of management should be to secure the maximum prosperity for the employer, coupled with the maximum prosperity for each employee.' Taylor could justify his methods because he felt that his long-term goal would lead to 'diminution of poverty, and the alleviation of suffering'.

His main reason for developing scientific management was that he wished to do away with 'soldiering' or 'natural laziness', as he believed that all workers spent little time putting in full effort. To do this, Taylor aimed to analyse every job in a scientific way so that no one could be in any doubt about how much work could and should be done in a day. He felt that 'every single act of every workman can be reduced to a science'. Much inconclusive argument has ensued as to whether he was the pioneer of time and motion study. Certainly, time study played as important a part in Taylor's scientific job and task analysis as the examination of a worker's movements and the implements he used.

Inherent in Taylor's management style was the setting up of planning departments, staffed by clerks who ensured that 'every laborer's work was planned out well in advance, and the workmen were moved from place to place...very much as chessmen are moved on a chessboard, a telephone and messenger system having been installed for this purpose'. He concluded that, in this way, 'a large amount of the time lost through having too many men in one place and too few in another, and through waiting between jobs, was entirely eliminated'. Such a policy did, however, require the setting up of a more 'elaborate organisation and system', which sowed the seeds for Max Weber's bureaucratic organisation structure. Taylor's approach constituted one of the first formal divisions between those who do the work (workers) and those who supervise and plan it (managers).

Management and workers

For workers on the shopfloor, scientific management brought a dramatic loss in skill level and autonomy. As well as being subject to increased supervision, workers were no longer able to use their own tools, which they might have spent many years modifying to suit their own style. In many cases, however, Taylor's ideas were extremely effective. In the case of shovellers at the Bethlehem Steel Works, workers earned higher wages and the company saved between $75,000 and $80,000 per year through greater efficiency.

Although Taylor believed that disputes between managers and workers would be eliminated because what 'constitutes a fair day's work will be a question for scientific investigation, instead of a subject to be bargained and haggled over', there were numerous occasions when his ideas came into conflict with labour organisations. His opinion of such unions was invariably derogatory, as he was convinced that their objective was to limit the output of their members. Because of this, Taylor focused on the individual, believing that where a group of workers was formed, peer pressure would be used to ensure each man did not work to his full capacity. In the Bethlehem Steel Works, he decreed that no more than four men could work together in a gang without a special permit.

Even the way he wrote about unskilled workers was condescending. 'Now one of the very first requirements for a man who is fit to handle pig iron as a regular occupation is that he shall be so stupid and phlegmatic that he more nearly resembles in his mental make-up the ox than any other type' is a typical example.

Although Taylor's manner often appeared inhumane, he also wrote: 'If the workman fails to do his task, some competent teacher should be sent to show him exactly how his work can best be done, to guide, help, and to encourage him and, at the same time, to study his possibilities as a workman. So that, under the plan which individualizes each workman, instead of brutally discharging the man or lowering his wages to make good at once, he is given the time and the help required to make him proficient at his present job, or he is shifted to another class of work for which he is either mentally or physically better suited.'

Contemporary reaction to scientific management
It is easy to see why Taylor's work was regarded as inhumane. However good his motives of bringing about the greater good for the worker on the shopfloor, the alleviation of poverty, and the elimination of waste, his methods were extremely hard and sometimes had the opposite effect.

It took him three years to implement some of his methods in the Midvale Steel Works. The men resorted to breaking their machines in an attempt to prove to management that Taylor was overworking them. In response, he fined any man whose machine broke, until eventually 'they got sick of being fined, their opposition broke down, and they promised to do a fair day's work'.

CONTEXT AND CONCLUSIONS
Many of Taylor's ideas are relevant to the modern day. Three in particular, taken from *The Principles of Scientific Management*, stand out:

- Rewards: 'A reward, if it is to be most effective in stimulating men to do their best work, must come soon after the work has been done...The average workman must be able to measure what he has accomplished and clearly see his reward at the end of each day if he is to do his best.' In Taylor's view, it was pointless to involve the shopfloor workers in end-of-year profit-sharing schemes.
- Quality standards: The use of written documentation for each part of a worker's job, inherent in scientific management, is strikingly prescient of the procedural documentation used in the ISO 9000 series of quality standards. 'In the case of a

machine-shop which is managed under the modern system, detailed written instructions as to the best way of doing each piece of work are prepared in advance, by men in the planning department. These instructions represent the combined work of several men in the planning room, each of whom has his own speciality, or function...The directions of all of these men, however, are written on a single instruction card, or sheet.' The main difference is that today's best practice means involving staff in drawing up their own procedures.

- Suggestion schemes: Taylor proposed a form of incentive for employees to make suggestions if they felt an improvement could be made, either to the method or the implement used to undertake a task. If, after analysis, the suggestion was introduced into the workplace, the person suggesting it 'should be given the full credit for the improvement, and should be paid a cash premium as a reward for his ingenuity. In this way the true initiative of the workmen is better attained under scientific management than under the old individual plan.'

At the time of his death in 1917, Taylor's work was the subject of much debate, both for and against it. His approach is now frowned upon as 'Victorian', but it should not be forgotten that he was a man of his times and sought solutions to the problems of his times. The main criticism of Taylor is that his approach was too mechanistic—treating people like machines or as unthinking creatures to be trained like dogs, rather than as human beings.

However, he was one of the first true pioneers of management through his scientific examination of the way work is done, and his thinking led directly to the achievements of other management gurus such as Max Weber and Henry Ford.

THE BEST SOURCES OF HELP
Books:
Kakar, Sudhir. *Frederick Taylor: A Study in Personality and Innovation*. Cambridge, Massachusetts: MIT Press, 1970.

Nelson, Daniel. *Frederick W. Taylor and the Rise of Scientific Management*. Madison, Wisconsin: Wisconsin University Press, 1980.

Taylor, Frederick Winslow. *Shop Management* in *Scientific Management* (comprising *Shop Management, The Principles of Scientific Management, Testimony before the Special House Committee*). New York: Harper, 1947.

Taylor, Frederick Winslow. *The Principles of Scientific Management*. New York: W.W. Norton, 1967.

ALVIN TOFFLER

1928	Born.
1965	Coins the term 'future shock' in an article in *Horizon*.
1969–1970	Works as consultant for AT&T.
1970	Publication of *Future Shock*.
1977	Co-founds Institute for Alternative Futures with Clement Bezold and James Dator.
1980	Publication of *The Third Wave*.
1986	Helps set up Issyk-Kul Forum, the first non-Communist, non-governmental organisation in the former USSR.
1990	Publication of *Powershift*.
1993	Publication of *War and Anti-War*.
1996	Founds Toffler Associates, an executive advisory firm.

SUMMARY

Widely recognised as one of the world's leading authorities on change, Alvin Toffler is anything but the classical soothsayer. He very carefully avoids words like 'trend' and 'prediction' in his writing, and insists that nobody can tell for certain what will happen in the future. His special gift is an understanding of the effects of change. It comes from a broad and deep knowledge of science, technology, and the arts, and a capacity to deduce from detailed analysis what might result when complex technological and social changes impact on entrenched attitudes and vested interests.

LIFE AND CAREER

Alvin Toffler was born in 1928. Though he has travelled widely, he gained all his education and working experience in the United States. He has been a visiting fellow at the Russell Sage Foundation, a visiting professor at Cornell University, a faculty member of the New School for Social Research, and a highly successful business consultant. He has several honorary degrees, and his books have won many awards.

Much of Toffler's work has been created in collaboration with his wife Heidi—as he is always the first to point out. Theirs is a long-standing partnership: both studied English at New York University and then entered the heady Bohemian world of post-war Greenwich Village, where their interests were mainly in writing poetry and planning novels.

Not a scientist by first choice, Toffler understood from a very young age the importance of science and technology in the modern world and took a course in the history of technology.

The Tofflers spent several years in journalism, writing for publications ranging from *Fortune* and *Playboy* to the leading political, scientific, and economic journals of the day. In 1960 an invitation from IBM to write a paper on the long-term social and organisational implications of the computer gave them a lengthy exposure to high technology. From this seminal experience grew the all-consuming interest in change, for which they are now world-famous. *Future Shock*, the first book in Toffler's great trilogy on change, was begun shortly after completing the IBM paper.

Alvin Toffler

CONTRIBUTION
Though he has published many books and countless articles and papers, Toffler's philosophy, and most of his key ideas, are encapsulated in three books: *Future Shock* (1970), *The Third Wave* (1980), and *Powershift* (1990). Each is a self-standing work in its own right, but they combine to form a trilogy that develops Toffler's ideas about change in a seamless dialogue.

Toffler gives his own brief summation of what the trilogy is all about in the preface to *Powershift*: '...the central subject is change—what happens to people when their entire society abruptly transforms itself into something new and unexpected. *Future Shock* looks at the process of change—how change affects people and organisations. *The Third Wave* focuses on the directions of change—where today's changes are taking us. *Powershift* deals with the control of changes still to come—who will shape them and how.'

Besides giving a painstaking analysis of change and the many challenges and problems it brings, the trilogy is full of hope. The books argue, convincingly, that the rapid change all around us is not so chaotic or random as it first appears; there are patterns and recognisable forces behind it. Understanding these patterns and forces will allow us to cope 'strategically' with change, and to avoid haphazard responses to individual events as they are encountered.

The Trilogy: *Future Shock*
Toffler has described the effect of too much change occurring too quickly so well, that the expression 'future shock' has entered the world's vocabulary and is now widely used to define the disorientation, confusion, and breakdown of decision-making capacity that afflicts individuals, groups, and whole societies when they are overwhelmed by change.

In his preface to *Powershift*, Toffler contends that 'the acceleration of history carries consequences of its own, independent of the actual direction of change. The simple speed-up of events and reaction times produces its own effects, whether the changes are perceived as good or bad'.

Future Shock was written over 30 years ago, and we are now able to test the accuracy of Toffler's foresight. What we find is quite remarkable; he anticipated the break-up of the nuclear family, the genetic revolution, the 'throwaway' society, the resurgence of emphasis on education, and the increased importance of knowledge in society.

The Third Wave
This book explores perhaps Toffler's most elegant theory, adding a 'third wave' to the other two great and generally recognised surges in human development.

The first came with the introduction of agriculture, and humankind's revolutionary shift from hunter-gatherer to settled farmer. This released it from the constant struggle for subsistence, providing the stability and security needed to develop the arts and technology that are the basis of civilisation as we know it today.

The second was the industrial revolution, the remarkable leap forward in manufacturing methods and the organisation of labour that created the industrialised world. The exploitation of raw materials, mass production, and an ever more ingenious application of technology brought prosperity and comfort to those countries that could embrace the necessary changes.

Toffler's third wave is the post-industrial, information-based revolution that began, he suggests, in the 1950s, with a number of major technological and social changes.

In *The Third Wave*, Toffler predicted with an uncanny foresight both the profound effects of information technology and biotechnology on the economy, and the changes we can now see taking place in manufacturing methods, marketing, and working patterns. He showed particular prescience in foreseeing the development of niche marketing and the increased power of the consumer. He even invented a new word—'prosumer'—to designate the fusion of producer and consumer.

In his introduction to the book, Toffler talks of the seemingly chaotic changes of the 1960s that produced 'a culture of warring specialisms, drowned in fragmented data and fine-toothed analysis', and a climate in which synthesis 'is not merely useful—it is crucial'. It was to address this need for synthesis that Toffler conceived *The Third Wave*. It is, he claims, 'a book of large-scale synthesis [that] describes the old civilisation in which many of us grew up, and presents a careful, comprehensive picture of the new civilisation bursting into being in our midst'.

He goes on to say: '...the world that is fast emerging from the clash of new values and technologies, new geophysical relationships, new life-styles and modes of communication, demands wholly new ideas and analogies, classifications and concepts. We cannot cram the embryonic world of tomorrow into yesterday's conventional cubby holes.'

Powershift

In this, the final book of the trilogy, Toffler carries forward his earlier analysis with an exploration of how individuals, organisations, and nations will be affected by inevitable changes in the way power is perceived and applied. He talks of a 'new power system replacing that of the industrial past'.

The word 'powershift' in the title means something very different from the usual two-word term 'power shift'. Toffler says that, while a power shift is a transfer of power, a 'powershift' is 'a deep-level change in the very nature of power'. A powershift does not merely transfer power, but also transforms it.

In *Powershift* we are reminded of the three basic sources of power: violence, wealth, and knowledge. All businesses work in what Toffler describes as a 'powerfield', where these three 'tools of power' constantly operate. The rising importance of knowledge, so eloquently argued throughout the trilogy, has brought about a profound change in the balance between them.

Powershift gives no hint of an early solution to the problems associated with change. Toffler talks about the struggles to come as individuals, businesses, and national economies move away from their traditional sources of power towards a new dependence on knowledge. In his view, the problems will not be over when these power conflicts are resolved. He sees even greater challenges ahead as divisions develop between 'fast' and 'slow' economies.

Another idea, explored throughout the trilogy but most strongly in *Powershift*, is what Toffler calls 'de-massification'. By this he means a reversal of the trend towards 'mass' solutions prevalent in the late 20th century. He sees mass marketing giving way to niche and micro-marketing; mass production being replaced by increasingly customised production; and large corporations being broken down into small, autonomous units. Even politics and the concept of nationhood, Toffler believes, will be affected by the pressure to 'de-massify', created by the increasing awareness of better-informed individuals and made effective by the unstoppable development of information technology.

CONTEXT AND CONCLUSIONS

Influential as Toffler's trilogy continues to be, it must be remembered that the last of the three books was published in 1990; it would be misleading to imply that Toffler's work started or finished at that point. *The Adaptive Corporation*, for example, published in 1985, was built around the report resulting from Toffler's 1969–70 consultancy work for AT&T. Ignored by senior management at the time, this report became influential later, at the time of the Bell divestiture. The book deals with questions of organisational change and adaptation through focusing on the case of AT&T.

Other books and articles have appeared since the trilogy and, from the time of the publication of *Powershift*, Heidi Toffler has allowed her role to be more formally acknowledged; the Tofflers' more recent publications have been under explicit joint authorship.

Their contribution to world politics is something many management commentators neglect. Respected by many world leaders, they have played a significant part in improving East-West relations. Mikhail Gorbachev is an admirer whom they have met several times and greatly influenced.

The Tofflers also visited China and were having a positive effect on Chinese politics until the disastrous reversals following the Tiananmen Square episode. Their books are now banned in China though, of course, banning books often merely serves to increase their influence.

Of the Tofflers' major publications in the last ten years, *War and Anti-War* is usually regarded as the most important. It focuses on warfare, suggesting that changes in the way we do business are matched by a parallel revolution in how we make war — and that, like so many in commerce and manufacturing, these military changes derive directly from advances in information technology. Their ideas have already been proved correct in the Gulf War and elsewhere, but Alvin Toffler's most chillingly accurate prediction came in an interview he gave for the *New Scientist* magazine of March 1994, where he spoke of the inadequacy of conventional military force in controlling terrorist action. To illustrate his point, he quoted a former US intelligence officer as saying that, if he had 20 people and a million dollars, he could shut down America. Seven years later the events of 11 September 2001 provided appalling evidence of this statement's credibility.

THE BEST SOURCES OF HELP
Books:
Toffler, Alvin. *Future Shock*. London: Bodley Head, 1970.
Toffler, Alvin. *The Third Wave*. London: Collins, 1980.
Toffler, Alvin. *Powershift*. New York: Bantam Books, 1990.
Toffler, Alvin, and Heidi Toffler. *War and Anti-War*. New York: Little, Brown & Company, 1993.

VICTOR VROOM

1932	Born.
1955	Receives MA from McGill University.
1958	Receives PhD from the University of Michigan.
1964	Publication of *Work and Motivation*.
1972	Appointed chairman of the department of administrative science at Yale.
1973	Publication of *Leadership and Decision-Making*, coauthored by Philip Yetton and containing the Vroom/Yetton model.

> **SUMMARY**
>
> Victor Vroom (1932–) is acknowledged as a leading authority on the psychological analysis of behaviour in organisations. His major contributions include work on motivation in the workplace, illustrated by his expectancy model, and research into leadership styles and decision-making. From the latter, he and Philip Yetton developed a model for selecting appropriate methods of problem-solving for different situations.

LIFE AND CAREER

Born in Canada in 1932, Victor Vroom gained his bachelor's and master's degrees at McGill University and a PhD at the University of Michigan. He taught at the universities of Michigan and Pennsylvania and the Carnegie Institute of Technology before being appointed John G. Scarle professor of organisation and management and professor of psychology at Yale University's school of management. He has also acted as a consultant to many large organisations.

Vroom's work spans the two disciplines of management and psychology. He first applied psychology to organisations in a prize-winning doctoral dissertation in 1960. This examined the effects of personality on participation in decision-making. His theories were further developed in a 1964 book, *Work and Motivation*, which applied expectancy theory to work for the first time. Expectancy theory maintains that people will be motivated to behave in certain ways if they believe that doing so will bring them rewards they seek and value.

Vroom's study of the causes of people's decisions to act in certain ways at work continued with his collaboration with Philip Yetton to develop what became known as the Vroom/Yetton model of leadership decision-making (*Leadership and Decision-Making*, 1973). This is a contingency model that identifies styles of leadership appropriate to different situations. Specifically, it can be used by managers to assess the degree to which they should encourage people to participate in the decision-making process. With Arthur Jago, Vroom further developed this model in *The New Leadership: Managing Participation in Organizations*.

CONTRIBUTION

Expectancy theory

In *Work and Motivation* Vroom defines the central problem of motivation as 'the explanation of choices made by organisms among different voluntary responses' (p. 9). To understand how these choices are made, he defines the three concepts—valence, expectancy, and force—and describes how these work in conjunction to determine how people will decide to act, given possible routes of behaviour leading to possible outcomes.

Valence is a term referring to a preference for one outcome over another. An outcome is said to have positive valence when a person prefers attaining it to not attaining it; when he or she prefers not to attain an outcome, then it has a negative valence; and when he or she is indifferent to whether an outcome is attained or not, it has a valence of zero. If a manager particularly wants a promotion, for example, and thinks that successful completion of a certain project will earn that promotion, then he or she will attach a positive valence to completing the project, and be motivated to do so by the perceived value of the reward.

A person's behaviour, however, is affected not only by preference for one outcome over another, but also by how likely he or she believes these outcomes to be. Vroom defines expectancy as 'a momentary belief concerning the likelihood that a particular act will be followed by a particular outcome' (p. 17). Expectancy can be assigned a value from zero (the belief that the outcome will not follow on from the action) to one (the belief that the outcome certainly will follow on from the action). If someone wants a cup of coffee, for example, and knows that there is a drinks machine in the staff room, that person will walk straight there. The act of walking there has a high expectancy value in terms of obtaining coffee, whereas the act of walking to, say, the post room has a low expectancy value, as the person does not expect to find coffee there.

The third concept that Vroom outlines is force. He argues that a person's behaviour is the result of a field of forces, each of which has direction and magnitude. Mathematical values assigned to the valences and expectancies for acts are combined to produce their hypothetical force, and the act that produces the highest level of force is assumed to be the one that the person will choose. The highest levels of force will be produced by actions with high levels of both valence and expectation.

Vroom's model is summed up in an equation:

$M = (E \times V)$

where M is the motivational force resulting from the sum of expectancy and valence, E is the expectancy measure and V represents the valence for the individual of a particular outcome. (Source: Martin, J. *Organizational Behaviour*. London: International Thompson Business Press, 1998.)

Vroom's theory can be put into practice by interviewing individuals or giving them questionnaires to assess their expectancies and valences. These are then scored, and the expectancy score is multiplied by the valence score. The results for all outcomes that could be produced by a particular behavioural alternative are added together to give the expected value (EV) of that alternative. Each possible course of behaviour can be assigned an EV in this way, and the model predicts that the one with the highest EV will be a subject's most likely choice.

The primary implication for managers is that, since motivation is closely tied to reward, they should aim to encourage high work performance by tailoring rewards to those things which employees value most—and some research will be needed here to find out just what these might be for each individual. Incentives and benefits should be explicitly linked to actions which are in line with the organisation's strategy and which will contribute to its success.

This is a normative model: it can only predict how people should make decisions to act, rather than how they actually do make such decisions. In reality, few people are well enough informed about all the possible choices and all the possible outcomes to make balanced judgments as to which behaviour it would be best for them to adopt. As a theory explaining a general approximation of an individual's behaviour, however, it has gained much support.

In 1968 Vroom's expectancy theory was extended by L.W. Porter and E.E. Lawler in their book *Managerial Attitudes and Performance* (Homewood: Richard D. Irwin, 1968). Their model emphasised that performance is also affected by factors other than motivation.

Subsequent research has focused on showing that expectancy models can be used quite accurately to predict choice of occupation, levels of job satisfaction, and levels of work effort. An extensive review of recent research on expectancy theory can be found in 'Old friends, new faces: motivation research in the 1990s', by Maureen L. Ambrose and Carol T. Kulik (*Journal of Management*, May/June 1999).

Vroom/Yetton model of leadership decision-making

Vroom's second major model, developed with Philip Yetton, shows how different leadership styles can be harnessed in solving different types of problems.

In *Leadership and Decision-Making* (1973), he and Yetton looked further into the issue of participation in decision-making by subordinates. They developed a set of rules that can be used to determine the level and form of participation in the decision-making process that will support the best solution in different problem-solving situations. New managers may think they must make decisions alone, but Vroom clearly believes that this is not the case. He outlines types of decision-making involved in both group problems that affect a manager's workgroup, and in individual problems that affect only the manager. The following list from *Leadership and Decision-Making* (p. 13) shows the types of management decision methods for group problems:

- authority decisions—made by the manager alone without involving others. A1—the manager makes the decision on his own using information available at the time. A2—the manager makes the decision alone but obtains his information from subordinates or other group members first.
- consultative decisions—made by the manager after consultation with a group. C1—the manager approaches several other people individually to obtain their suggestions, then makes his own decision. C2—the manager brings several other people together at the same time as a group and collectively obtains their suggestions, then makes his own decision.
- group decisions—made by a whole group in consensus. G2—the manager brings together several other people at the same time and they discuss the problem to arrive at a consensus decision between them.

Five similar methods are defined for individual problems. The Vroom/Yetton model then proposes a decision tree based on seven rules, which managers can use to pinpoint the most appropriate method for a given situation.

By means of a sequence of questions, each requiring a yes/no answer that advances the manager along a decision tree path, the problem is ultimately defined as one of 14 types. Vroom and Yetton then recommend suitable methods of decision-making (from methods A1-G2 above) for each problem type.

Since some types of problem can be solved by more than one method, further means of choosing between them are needed. When Vroom and Arthur Jago revised the model in 1988, they suggested that time is one important factor to consider: person-hours carry a financial cost, and a swiftly made decision may be best; also, a decision might be required urgently, and participative processes may slow down the decision-making process.

The Vroom/Yetton model has been progressively developed by its original authors, and by Vroom and Jago, since its inception. Further factors examined include:

- the extent to which participation benefits the organisation by offering development opportunities for participants
- the influence of a manager's position in the organisational hierarchy on his or her problem-handling style
- the styles adopted by women managers

CONTEXT AND CONCLUSIONS

Vroom has made valuable contributions in the fields of both management and psychology. His models have been tested and extended, and remain important landmarks in the discipline of industrial psychology. Vroom has explored other, neighbouring aspects of industrial psychology, but the two theories outlined above remain his most famous and enduring work. The models proposed by Vroom, and by Vroom and Yetton, have contributed much to managers' understanding of behaviour, and to their ability to mould behaviour to produce the most favourable outcomes, and so to manage more effectively.

The Vroom/Yetton model of leadership decision-making, however, was at the height of its fame a quarter of a century ago and management thinking has changed since then. There is now more emphasis on delegation, empowerment, flatter structures, and matrix management, all of which have implications for managers' choices of leadership style. Vroom himself is not oblivious to change and development, and has actually used it to justify the relevance of his work on the Yale website: 'Managers seldom live in a static world. They change jobs, change organisations, move from one country to another, from sector to sector. [Such changes]...spur new challenges, new opportunities, and place new situational demands on leadership...Old habits must be discarded if one is to respond to today's challenges and opportunities.'

THE BEST SOURCES OF HELP
Books:
Vroom, Victor. *Work and Motivation*. New York: John Wiley, 1964.
Vroom, Victor, and Philip Yetton. *Leadership and Decision-Making*. Pittsburgh: University of Pittsburgh Press, 1973.
Vroom, Victor, and Arthur Jago. *The New Leadership: Managing Participation in Organizations*. Englewood Cliffs, New Jersey: Prentice Hall, 1988.
Journal Article:
Vroom, Victor. 'Reflections on leadership and decision-making.' *Journal of General Management*, Spring 1984, vol. 9 no. 3, pp. 18–36.

MAX WEBER

1864	Born.
1894	Professor of political economy, University of Freiburg, Germany.
1897	Professor of political economy, University of Heidelberg, Germany.
1904	First publication of *The Protestant Ethic and the Spirit of Capitalism*.
1919	Professor of Political Economy, University of Munich, Germany.
1920	Dies.

> **SUMMARY**
>
> Since the early 1980s it has become fashionable to criticise bureaucracies for being out of touch with rapidly changing market conditions. As he was the first to develop the concept of bureaucratic organisation any understanding of the way modern organisations work would be incomplete without at least a cursory study of Weber, who is commonly described as a founding father of sociology and whose work is also of historic importance from a managerial viewpoint. Weber's thoughts on the concepts of leadership, power, and authority are closely linked to his description of bureaucracy.

LIFE AND CAREER

Max Weber was born on April 21, 1864, the eldest of seven children, and grew up in a cultured bourgeois household, ruled by a strong authoritarian father. At university in Heidelberg, Weber studied economics, medieval history, and philosophy as well as law. A period of military service brought him under the care of his uncle, Hermann Baumgarten, a historian, and his wife. Both uncle and aunt acted as mentors to Weber, the former as a liberal who treated him as an intellectual peer, the latter as a person who impressed him with her deep sense of social responsibility towards her charitable work. Both offered a stark contrast to Weber's father, who treated his son with patronising authoritarianism.

It was probably during this formative period that Weber developed an aversion to the way people then most often gained positions of power and authority—through nepotism and accident of birth—factors he considered were lacking in legitimacy. He started to think of ways to free the individual as much as possible from personal judgments or from judgments clouded by emotion or self-interest.

After periods as a legal scholar at Heidelberg and then at the University of Berlin, Weber became professor of political economy, first at the University of Freiburg, and later at Heidelberg.

His principal contribution to the study of organisations stemmed from his interest in understanding why people obeyed commands. This interest led him to distinguish between power as the ability to force obedience, irrespective of resistance, and authority as the ability to get orders obeyed as a matter of course, apparently voluntarily.

CONTRIBUTION

Weber describes power as the probability of carrying out one's own will despite resistance or, at its extreme, as the ability to force people to obey. It is not necessarily the same as leadership or authority, but is invariably linked to them. Organisational power he links to structure and authority and considers inherent in any hierarchy or bureaucracy. Invariably the effects of power depend upon who has it, how that person is perceived, and the particular situation in which power is invoked. Weber identified three types of legitimate authority.

Charismatic authority

The leader is obeyed because of followers' faith in his or her special, 'supernatural' qualities. Weber proposed in his *Theory of Social and Economic Organization* that the term 'charisma' was associated with someone who possesses exceptional, supernatural qualities and who is thus set apart from ordinary people. These qualities constitute the basis on which that individual is considered to be, and is treated as, a leader.

Commentators at the beginning of the 21st century might conclude that very few business leaders could be said to have supernatural qualities. We must remember, however, that Weber was arguing from a philosophical standpoint, not a current, pragmatic management one; we may therefore understand 'supernatural' as being 'supernormal' and at the opposite end of a scale balanced by 'rational'. Although not considered supernatural, many business leaders have been deemed special in some way, and have had attributed to them qualities that set them apart from 'ordinary people'. Indeed, research in the 1970s and 1980s by Warren Bennis suggested that leaders do have qualities which set them apart, although he did not use the word 'supernatural' and went on to suggest that leadership qualities can be developed.

Of his three models of legitimate authority Weber thought charisma the least stable because its inspirational and motivational qualities disappear when the leader relinquishes the post. For Weber, charisma was not a sustainable option as the basis for authority. He advocated locating legitimacy in something more lasting and systematic.

Traditional authority

Leaders have authority by virtue of the status they have inherited; the extent of their authority is determined by birth, custom, precedent, and usage. Although Weber derives his theory from a study of history, we can still sometimes witness today how many positions of authority are handed from one generation to another, as firms establish dynasties, and appointments have more to do with family ties than competence. Another characteristic of organisations based on traditional authority is that things tend to be done in a particular way just because 'they have always been done like that'.

In the competitive world of today, the dangers of this approach are only too apparent: larger organisations get caught up in their own systems and either fail to spot when competitors are catching them up or markets are slipping away, or else simply become trapped by their own inertia. Precedent, rather than rational analysis, becomes the reason in itself for doing things.

Weber's search for a sustainable form of organisational authority based on rational analysis led him to distinguish a third authority system.

Rational-legal authority

Authority within a bureaucracy is both legal and rational when it is exercised through a system of rules and procedures attached to the 'office'—the job role—which an individual occupies.

Weber described how bureaucracy-based, rational-legal authority works:

- the organisation is structured around official functions that are bound by rules, each area having its own specified competence
- functions are structured into offices organised into a hierarchy that follows technical rules and norms for which training is provided
- the administration is separated from the ownership of the means of production
- the rules, decisions, and actions of the administration are recorded in writing

Weber stated that the bureaucracy was technically the most efficient form of organisation because, within it, work is conducted with precision, knowledge of files, continuity, discretion, unity, strict subordination, and reduction of friction.

Bureaucracies

Within bureaucracies organised along rational lines, the abuse of power by leaders is minimised because:

- offices are ranked in hierarchical order
- operations are conducted in accordance with impersonal rules
- officials are allocated specific duties and areas of responsibility
- appointments are made on the basis of qualifications and suitability for the post

Weber was, however, also aware of the shortcomings of bureaucracy, inasmuch as:

- their characteristic information processing and filtering to the top makes them cumbersome and slow to react
- their machinery makes it difficult to handle individual cases, because rules and procedures require all individuals to be treated as if they were the same
- bureaucratisation leads to depersonalisation, because the roles of officials are circumscribed by written definitions of their authority, and there is a set of rules and procedures to cater for every contingency

Weber recognised that the more efficient a bureaucracy becomes, the more it succeeds in excluding the personal, the irrational, and the incalculable in favour of emotional detachment and 'professionalism'. Perhaps this goes a long way towards explaining why Weber is held in low esteem in today's business climate of change and uncertainty.

CONTEXT AND CONCLUSIONS

Weber recognised the dangers of bureaucratisation and spoke of how measurement processes could turn people into cogs in a machine. In this respect his reflections are not too distant from Marx's theories of alienation. Although organisational bureaucratisation increases efficiency and productive capability, its mechanical efficiency also threatens to dehumanise its participants. Weber also believed, however, that the only way people could make a significant contribution was to subjugate their personalities and desires to the impersonal goals and procedures of large scale organisations. Paradoxically, he believed that the only way to escape such a mechanical future was for a charismatic leader to transform the organisation into something new.

Bureaucracy became the model for the 20th-century organisation, and was encapsulated in Alfred Sloan's General Motors and Harold Geneen's ITT. Perhaps the mundaneness and regularity of bureaucratic, corporate life was best described in William Whyte's *The Organization Man* (1956), in which the individual is taken over by the bureaucratic machine, in the name of efficiency. A more recent and humorous interpretation of life in a bureaucracy has been depicted by Scott Adams in *The Dilbert Principle*.

The bureaucracy may have outlived its age of supremacy, but it is still hard to foresee a future without any need for the order, procedures, levels of authority, and controls that constitute a bureaucracy. The problem is how to develop systems that combine necessary bureaucratic features with a people-centred, flexible, and imaginative style.

As the foremost social scientist of his day—with little interest in management— Weber would have found it hard to believe that he was to exercise such a dominant influence on the way organisations have been managed. He would have also found it hard to credit the notion that he would be quoted as one of a trinity of management pioneers, along with Henri Fayol and F.W. Taylor, contemporaries whom he would not have known or read.

THE BEST SOURCES OF HELP
Books:
Pugh, Derek S., and David J. Hickson. *Great Writers on Organizations*. Aldershot: Ashgate Publishing, 2000.

Weber, Max. *The Protestant Ethic and the Spirit of Capitalism*. London: Allen & Unwin, 1950.

Weber, Max. *Theory of Social and Economic Organization*. Trans. A.M. Henderson and T. Parsons. New York: Free Press, 1947.

BUSINESS GIANTS

JOHN JACOB ASTOR

1763	Born.
1783	Sets sail for America. Takes $24 and seven flutes.
1784	Arrives in New York.
1785	Marries.
1786	Opens shop selling pianos and buying furs.
1808	Consolidates holdings and incorporates American Fur Company.
1810	Founds Pacific Fur Company.
1811	Establishes Astoria at the mouth of the Columbia River.
1820s	Fur trade begins to slow down.
1834	Sells entire holdings in fur trade and retires. Develops property.
1848	Dies.

> **SUMMARY**
>
> Born in Germany, John Jacob Astor emigrated to America in 1780. Arriving with a few dollars and seven flutes, he amassed a fur and property empire that made him one of the richest men of his day. Astor's story is a lesson for all entrepreneurs: provide excellent customer service; be close to markets; buy cheap, and sell wherever the price is best. In a battle with Astor, the state-subsidised fur trade looked as if it would surely be the winner, but Astor won easily.
>
> Then, in his canniest career move, Astor dumped his fur trading interests, just before fur became old hat. Moving onto something more fashionable, he bought up property—lots of it—in the way that most people buy household goods. In doing so, he helped shape the development of one of the greatest cities on the planet—New York. When he died in 1848, he was worth over $20 million.

LIFE AND CAREER

Born in Walldorf, Germany in 1763, John Jacob Astor was the third son of a butcher. His brother George, the eldest son, left Germany for England to establish a business making and selling musical instruments. His brother Henry departed for New York. In 1780, John Jacob too left the family farm, made his way down the Rhine Valley, and set sail for England, where he joined his brother in business.

In London, Astor learned to speak English, assisted his brother, and saved enough money to take a ship across the Atlantic. In November 1783, at the end of the War of American Independence, he set sail for the United States. With him he took $24 and seven flutes. The journey took the standard eight weeks, arriving in Chesapeake Bay in January. Astor's berth was in the crew's quarters and on the crossing, so the story goes, he befriended another German emigrant who told him about the fur trade and the opportunities it offered.

CONTRIBUTION

Arriving in New York in March 1784, aged 21, Astor soon married and set up a shop selling pianos and buying furs. His wife would look after the store while Astor ventured into the northern territories, building a network of contacts among the fur traders.

The lucrative fur trade was important not only commercially, but also politically. Canada's patronage from France was dependent on its revenues. American,

John Jacob Astor

French-Canadian, and British companies—like the Hudson Bay Company and the Northwest Company—dominated the fur trade. In 1796 a treaty between the United States and Great Britain demarcated trading boundaries along national borders, excluding the Canadians from American territories. Into the vacuum left by the Canadians moved Astor.

By 1800, Astor was the leading American fur trader. It was a considerable achievement. As well as dealing with competition from other private traders, Astor was competing with the American government. Keen to make a show of strength to the Native Americans and to keep out the French and English, President George Washington had approved funds to set up the Office of Indian Affairs and a series of state-sponsored fur factories. The problem was that when it came to the actual trading, private traders won hands down. Government representatives like Thomas McKenney insisted on foisting ploughs and other implements that were deemed to be intrinsically good or useful on the Native Americans, who, uninterested in sanctimony or agricultural equipment, wanted kettles and muskets. Like all good entrepreneurs, Astor gave them what they wanted and got what he wanted in return—furs. He refused to sell the Native Americans liquor, reasoning that they were unlikely to make good trappers if inebriated. Astor also out-competed on service. The government maintained trading posts some distance from the Native Americans, so Astor's men went upriver to deal with them directly. It was customer service at its best.

> *By 1800, Astor was the leading American fur trader. It was a considerable achievement.*

At the other end of the supply chain, Astor got better prices for his furs than the government did. While the government sold the furs straight away on the local market, regardless of demand or over supply, Astor shipped his furs around the world to whatever market paid the best price. The folly of the government's attempts to control the fur trade was revealed when it passed legislation to close down the fur factories and sell their assets. The sales realised $50,000 against an investment of $300,000.

Already wealthy, Astor expanded his commercial horizons. He obtained permission to trade through ports owned by the East India Company; sent a ship to China in a joint venture, and pocketed $50,000 in profit. The profit was ploughed into New York property.

In 1808 Astor consolidated his holdings and incorporated the American Fur Company. This was a precursor to an attempt to control the developing fur trade in the West. Most companies planned to extend their territories to the West. The key would be finding and controlling a route through to the Pacific. A Canadian expedition had set out cross-country and was rumoured to be making good progress. Astor thought it would be more sensible to make his way around the Cape of Good Hope by ship and head for the mouth of the Columbia River. To finance his enterprise, he joined forces with some of the members of the Northwest Company and founded the Pacific Fur Company in 1810.

Astor's party arrived at the Columbia River in 1811. Six weeks after they raised the US flag over a hastily-erected stockade, christened Astoria, the Canadian expedition arrived. Astoria was to be an essential cog in Astor's international trading plans. No one could accuse him of lacking ambition. His intention was to send goods from New York to Astoria; trade them for furs with the Indians; ship the furs to the Orient to be traded for goods; ship the Oriental goods to Europe and trade them for European goods, and ship the European goods to America, taking a profit at every stage. It was a brilliant plan that fell at the first hurdle, when one of his ships sank and the 1812 war between the United States and England broke out. The British forced Astor to hand over his fort in Astoria for $58,000.

Other than this setback, Astor did well out of the war. Even in his worst year during the war, his revenues were $50,000. By the end of the conflict he had substantially increased his property holdings. After the war, with the help of some friendly government officials and some useful legislation that forbade Canadian involvement in the American fur trade, Astor gained control of all the Northwest Company's holdings that lay within American borders. He continued to take over the interests of other companies, inching his way West. But by the late 1820s, fashions had changed, silk was all the rage, and profits were falling. Never failing to spot a trend, Astor got out while he could. In June 1834, he sold all his fur-trading holdings and retired.

For the rest of his years, Astor dabbled in property speculation. He had long bought parcels of land in New York; now he bought up vast tracts of land on the urban fringes of New York, calculating—correctly—that at the current rate of population growth, the city would soon swallow up his plots; he became one of the largest property owners in New York and, as a by-product, one of the main landlords. He died in 1848, the richest man in America. His fortune was some $20 million.

CONTEXT AND CONCLUSIONS
What Astor considered legitimate trade, modern sentiment labels amoral and unethical. The fur trade, an industry of considerable commercial and political importance at the time, is now considered anathema in many parts of the world. Astor's dealings with the indigenous Indian population and the tenants of his property empire also left much to be desired by today's standards. Nevertheless, Astor is an important figure in business history for a number of reasons. As a champion of private enterprise, his endeavours clearly illustrated the shortcomings of state monopolies. Ultimately he demonstrated that the disincentivised, bureaucracy-ridden, heavily subsidised, state-run fur factories were no match for an agile private enterprise that paid close attention to its customers' needs and promoted innovation as a means to increasing profitability. Astor's actions also helped open the western frontiers of America for development. Finally, regardless of his motivation, he was responsible for shaping the development of Manhattan and New York.

THE BEST SOURCES OF HELP
Books:
Houghton, Walter. *Kings of Fortune or the Triumphs and Achievements of Noble, Self-made Men*. Chicago: The Loomis National Library Association, 1888.
Irving, Washington. *Astoria; or, Enterprise Beyond the Rocky Mountains*. London: Richard Bentley, 1839.
Smith, Arthur Howden. *John Jacob Astor: Landlord of New York*. Philadelphia: Lippincott, 1929.
Terrell, John Upton. *Furs by Astor (John Jacob Astor)*. London: William Morrow & Co, 1963.

PHILEAS TAYLOR BARNUM

1810	Born.
1841	Opens American Museum in New York.
1842	Introduces General Tom Thumb.
1850	Creates first American superstar, singer Jenny Lind.
1853	Starts New York's first illustrated newspaper.
1870	Starts The Greatest Show on Earth.
1875	Serves as mayor of Bridgeport, Connecticut.
1877	Elected to first of two terms in the state General Assembly.
1882	Purchases Jumbo the elephant from London Zoo.
1888	Proposed as a potential presidential candidate.
1891	Dies.

> **SUMMARY**
>
> A consummate showman and raconteur, P.T. Barnum was one of the most colourful figures to grace the business stage. He started out as a clerk and became a newspaper editor. His media career was cut short, however, when he was sued for libel and ended up in prison for 60 days. It was the nature of his release—40 horsemen, a carriage, and a band—that convinced him of the power of spectacle.
>
> Barnum went on to stage a series of extravaganzas, backed by astounding claims, each a little more superlative than the last. He paraded a woman called Joice Heth as the 161-year-old nurse of George Washington; exhibited '500,000 natural and artificial curiosities from every corner of the globe' in the American Museum on Broadway, New York; showed an embalmed mermaid to a mixed reception; and in 1842 hired the diminutive Charles Stratton as General Tom Thumb, who earned him an audience with Queen Victoria in England.
>
> Towards the end of his career as a showman, he teamed up with James Bailey to take the Barnum and Bailey Greatest Show on Earth on tour across America. Fittingly for a man with such great powers of persuasion, he also tried his hand at politics. In 1875 he was elected mayor of Bridgeport, Connecticut, and went on to serve two terms on the state General Assembly. He was even touted as a potential presidential candidate.

LIFE AND CAREER

There is no proof that Phileas Taylor Barnum ever said, 'There's a sucker born every minute.' If he did, he was certainly not among their number. Born on 5 July 1810 in Bethel, Connecticut, Barnum was the eldest of five children. He was a bright child who excelled at maths. At the age of ten, he was woken one night by his teacher who had bet a neighbour that Barnum could calculate the height of a pile of wood in five minutes. He did it in less than two. He also demonstrated a flair for salesmanship, selling lottery tickets at the age of 12.

After his father died, Barnum travelled to Brooklyn, New York, where he found work at a general store. Captivated by the hustle and bustle of the city, he left the general store, but stayed on in New York, working at a weekly newspaper. His journalistic career was short-lived. Although promoted to the role of editor, he was successfully sued for libel and sentenced to serve 60 days in jail. In a sign of things to come, Barnum was greeted on his release by a band, a troop of 40 horses, and a horse and carriage.

Phileas Taylor Barnum

CONTRIBUTION

Barnum's career as showman and huckster extraordinaire started in earnest when he was 25. He paid the then considerable sum of $1,000 for the services of Joice Heth, who claimed to be both 161 years old and the nurse of the first US president, George Washington. To a man with an innate sense of the dramatic, Heth was too good a business opportunity to pass up. 'Unquestionably the most astonishing and interesting curiosity in the world!' was Barnum's handbill slogan. His investment in Heth paid off handsomely. Exhibiting in New York and New England, he pulled in $1,500 a week. When interest in Heth began to flag, he spread a rumour that she was not a living person but an automaton. It worked, drawing crowds who wished to see if it was true. Heth was exhibited until her death in February 1836. Even then, Barnum refused to allow her death to restrict his cash flow, arranging a public autopsy to verify her age. When the stunt backfired—the doctor said the woman was no older than 80—Barnum successfully spun the story in his own favour.

Building on the success he enjoyed with Heth, Barnum bought Scudder's American Museum on Broadway in New York, and populated it with '500,000 natural and artificial curiosities from every corner of the globe'. In a wonderful example of his characteristic audacity, he put up a sign in the Museum bearing the words 'This way to the egress'. Unsuspecting visitors would follow the directions in pursuit of the mysterious 'egress', only to learn that 'egress' meant 'exit' and they would then have to pay another quarter to get back in. Barnum's famous attractions included 'The Feejee Mermaid', an embalmed mermaid (in reality half monkey, half dried fish), and in 1842 Charles Stratton, aka General Tom Thumb, the world's smallest man. Measuring just 25 inches in height, Tom Thumb was a worldwide hit, and earned Barnum an audience with Queen Victoria in England.

In 1850 Barnum conducted perhaps his most profitable business venture of all. He introduced America to the European opera star Jenny Lind, popularly known as 'the Swedish Nightingale'. When Lind disembarked at New York harbour in 1850, she was greeted by a crowd of 30,000, drawn by Barnum's publicity machine. He turned her into one of the first entertainment superstars. She performed over 90 concerts in all in the United States. When they parted company in 1852, Barnum had grossed over $700,000 from her performances.

Barnum ran the American Museum in New York for 27 years. As well as dealing with the constant stream of visitors and sourcing new exhibits, he also had to deal with three major fires, which burned down the building. After the last of these in 1868, he retired from the museum business.

At the age of 60, Barnum started the business that he is probably most closely

> *At the age of 60, Barnum started the business that he is probably most closely associated with— P.T. Barnum's Grand Travelling Museum, Menagerie, Caravan, and Circus, or The Greatest Show on Earth, as it became known.*

associated with—P.T. Barnum's Grand Travelling Museum, Menagerie, Caravan, and Circus, or The Greatest Show on Earth, as it became known. 'We ought to have a big show,' said Barnum, 'the public expects it, and will appreciate it.' Barnum's show was the biggest circus in America, grossing $400,000 in its first year. On the road, Barnum teamed up with James Bailey and James Hutchinson, both Englishmen, and in 1881 toured as the Barnum and London Circus.

In a promotional tour de force, he arranged for Jumbo to walk across the brand-new Brooklyn Bridge in 1883 to test its strength. Both survived. Sadly, however, Jumbo didn't survive a collision with a freight train in St Thomas, Ontario.

'The Towering Monarch of His Mighty Race, Whose Like the World Will Never See Again'—or Jumbo, as he was better known—was another of Barnum's acquisitions. Purchased from London Zoo in 1882 for $10,000, the elephant became the subject of a transatlantic tug-of-war when, in an outbreak of Jumbomania, the English public objected to his departure. As usual, Barnum got his way, shipping the creature to the United States. In a promotional tour de force, he arranged for Jumbo to walk across the brand-new Brooklyn Bridge in 1883 to test its strength. Both survived. Sadly, however, Jumbo didn't survive a collision with a freight train in St Thomas, Ontario. Undaunted, Barnum had him stuffed and continued to display both the elephant and its skeleton. In 1888 he teamed up once again with Bailey to tour as Barnum and Bailey's Greatest Show On Earth.

Throughout the years of his circus triumphs, the irrepressible Barnum also dabbled in politics. Not surprisingly, for a man with such consummate PR skills, he had some success. In 1875 he was elected as mayor of Bridgeport, Connecticut, and in 1877 he was elected to the first of two terms in Connecticut's General Assembly. He was even put forward as a potential presidential candidate in 1888, although this came to nothing.

In 1891 Barnum made a light-hearted remark to the effect that the press only said nice things about people when they were dead. Picking up on his comments, the *New York Sun* printed his obituary on the front page with the headline 'Great and Only Barnum—He Wanted to Read His Obituary—Here It Is'. Ironically, several weeks later Barnum was dead. He died quietly in his sleep on 7 April 1891. Professional to the last, his final words were reportedly about the show he was promoting at New York's Madison Square Garden: 'Ask Bailey what the box office was at the Garden last night.'

CONTEXT AND CONCLUSIONS

Huckster, showman, impresario, and entrepreneur—P.T. Barnum was all these and more. The man who could justifiably be considered the father of advertising and public relations was the king of hyperbole. He invented the beauty contest, the baby contest, and the travelling show. He persuaded thousands to pay to see a 'mermaid', which was in reality half monkey, half fish. In a manner that would make the most Svengali-like of pop managers blush, he discovered the diminutive Tom Thumb, aged four, and groomed him for stardom, teaching him to sing and dance live (no lip-synching in the 1800s). A man who knew the value of contacts, he hunted buffalo with General Custer and was friends with General Grant. He was said to be the United States's second millionaire and was so famous around the world that a letter sent from New Zealand addressed to 'Mr Barnum, America' still found its way to him. When he died *The Times* printed the following leader: 'Barnum is gone. That fine flower of Western civilization, that *arbiter elegantiarum* to Demos, has lived. At the age of 80, after a life of restless energy and incessant publicity, the great showman has lain down to rest. He gave, in the eyes of the seekers after amusement, a lustre to America.' A fitting epitaph.

CLOSE BUT NO CIGAR
DON KING
The shock-haired boxing promoter monopolised the money-spinning heavyweight division of the boxing world. Larger than life—although not quite as outsize as Barnum—King was especially noted for speaking at breakneck speed, quoting Shakespeare at press conferences, and having a Teflon-coated ability to deflect criticism and bad publicity.

THE BEST SOURCES OF HELP
Books:
Barnum, P.T. *The Life of P.T. Barnum: Written by Himself*. Champaign, Illinois: University of Illinois Press, 2000 (originally published in 1854).
Barnum, P.T. *Struggles and Triumphs, or, Forty Years' Recollections of P.T. Barnum, Written by Himself*. Abridged ed. London: Penguin, 1982 (originally published in 1869).
Werner, M.R. *Barnum*. New York: Harcourt, Brace & Co, 1923.
Fitzsimons, Raymond. *Barnum in London*. New York: St Martin's Press, 1970.
Saxon, A.H., ed. *Selected Letters of P.T. Barnum*. New York: Columbia University Press, 1983.

JEFF BEZOS

1964	Born.
1986	Graduates from Princeton.
1990	Youngest vice-president at Bankers Trust.
1992	Senior vice-president at D.E. Shaw & Co.
1995	Amazon.com opens for business.
1998	Net sales of $252.9 million, an increase of 283% over the same period in 1997.
1999	Amazon.com, Inc. has a market capitalisation of $6 billion. Voted *Time* magazine's person of the year.
2000	Adds toys and electronics to product range.
2001	Amazon.com, Inc. posts first quarterly profit and achieves highest ever score for service business in American Customer Satisfaction Index. Industry protest as Amazon.com seeks patents to protect systems for online payments and advertisement allocation.

SUMMARY

Jeff Bezos, the founder and CEO of Amazon.com, is the most famous son of the e-commerce revolution. The company he created became the best-known online brand in the world.

After graduating from Princeton University in 1986, Bezos worked for a variety of investment firms, notably D.E. Shaw & Co, where he helped establish one of the most successful quantitative hedge funds on Wall Street. By 1992 he had made it to vice-president, yet he gave up this glittering career to chase a dream. Amazon.com opened for business on the Internet in July 1995, and with relentless hype soon became the flagship for the New Economy. When the tide turned against dot-com stocks in 2000, Amazon.com looked as if it might be washed up. Yet Bezos rode the storm and is floating high once more, with growing additional business in toys and electronic products.

LIFE AND CAREER

Born on 12 January 1964 in Albuquerque, New Mexico, Jeffrey Preston Bezos was a clever child. At a very early age he took a screwdriver to his cot and dismantled it into its component parts. This set a pattern. A few years later, when his grandfather bought him a Radio Shack electronics kit, he concocted a 'burglar alarm' to keep his siblings (one brother, one sister) out of his bedroom. Moving on to the garage, the venue of choice for so many budding entrepreneurs, the ingenious Bezos proceeded to build a microwave oven driven by solar power. There is no record of how well it cooked.

> *Amazon.com opened for business on the Internet in July 1995, and with relentless hype soon became the flagship for the New Economy.*

Mike Bezos was an engineer with Exxon, and the family moved several times because of his work. Jeff attended high school in Miami and spent most summers on his grandfather's ranch, living the life of a cattle farmer and driving the tractors.

CONTRIBUTION

In 1986, after graduating in electrical engineering and computer science from Princeton, Bezos headed for Fitel, a high-tech start-up company in New York, where he built a computer network for financial trading. After Fitel Bezos joined Bankers Trust, becoming their youngest vice-president in February 1990. From there he moved to D.E. Shaw & Co. The Wall Street firm interviewed him on the strength of a recommendation from one of its partners, who suggested, 'he is going to make someone a lot of money someday.' At Shaw, Bezos described his role as 'sort of an entrepreneurial odd-jobs kind of a person', effectively looking for business opportunities in the insurance, software, and Internet sectors. He excelled in the role, helping to establish one of the most successful quantitative hedge funds on Wall Street, and becoming senior vice-president in 1992.

Then came his epiphany. Sitting at his computer in the office one day surfing the Internet, Bezos came across an astounding fact. According to usage statistics, the Internet was growing at a rate of 2,300% a year. He sensed an opportunity. Online commerce, he realised, was a natural next step. Being a combination of Wall Street insider and computer nerd, he was perfectly positioned to cash in.

Bezos compiled a list of 20 products that were suitable for selling online. On the list were items such as CDs, magazines, PC software and hardware—and books. The shortlist was quickly whittled down to two contenders: books and music. In the end, he plumped for books. His logic was twofold. With more than 1.3 million books in print as against 300,000 music titles, there was simply more to sell. And, perhaps more important, the major book publishers appeared less intimidating than their record company counterparts. The six major record companies had a stranglehold on the popular music distribution business, but the biggest book chain, Barnes & Noble, had only 12% of the industry's total sales.

Quitting his job, Bezos headed out to Seattle. 'I will change the economics of the book industry,' he is reputed to have told one venture capitalist. Ironically, some of the fundraising took place in the coffee shop of a Barnes & Noble bookstore.

With no state tax, a wealth of high-tech talent, and a major book distributor on the doorstep—Ingram's warehouse, Oregon—Seattle seemed a perfect place to start his new business. In the garage of his rented home, Bezos and his first three employees set up their computers and began writing software for the new business. He originally planned to call the company Cadabra, a reference to the magic incantation. Fortunately for him, his friends convinced him that, while the name might have spellbinding connotations, it also sounded very similar to 'cadaver'. Instead, Bezos opted for Amazon, after the world's largest river.

The company, according to its website, 'opened its virtual doors in July 1995 with a mission to use the Internet to transform book buying into the fastest, easiest, and most enjoyable shopping experience possible.' By the beginning of 1999, Amazon.com, Inc. had a market capitalisation of an astonishing $6 billion—more than the combined value of Barnes & Noble and Borders, its two largest bookstore competitors. The fourth quarter of 1998 brought net sales of $252.9 million, an increase of 283% over the same period in 1997. With Amazon awash with revenue, analysts and e-commerce commentators seemed unperturbed by the absence of profits.

Bezos, meanwhile, was a model of reassurance. Amazon would reach $1 billion in sales by 2000, he confidently asserted, and sure enough it did. Yet details about when Amazon would make a profit were hazier. Amazon was, said Bezos, in 'an investment phase', as might be expected of a company that had only just celebrated its fourth birthday. For a while, investors were more than happy to go along for the ride.

Then, in June 2000, cracks began to appear in the almost unanimous support enjoyed by the star child of the Internet revolution. Holly Becker, e-commerce analyst at Lehman Brothers and a long-time Amazon believer, switched her recommendation on the company from a buy to a neutral. She was, she said, 'throwing in the towel on Amazon'. Many saw Becker's change of heart as a turning point in the company's fortunes.

Yet Bezos may well have the last laugh. With some 21 million satisfied customers in the year to June 2001, revenue over the same period up by 16%, and a strategic alliance with Internet service provider AOL in the bag, Warren Jenson, Amazon.com's chief financial officer, correctly predicted operating profitability in the fourth quarter of 2001. Customer satisfaction was officially recognized when Amazon achieved the highest ever scores for a service industry in 2001 and 2002. The Amazon range is growing too, with the introduction of toys and electronics in 2000. Bezos, however, came under fire for holding back the broader development of e-commerce when he applied for patents to protect Amazon's Honour online payment system and the company's system for allocating advertising space from multiple bidders. Whether, in the final analysis, Bezos will go down in the business history books as the creator of a viable and long-lived Internet business, or simply as an e-business pioneer, remains to be seen.

> Holly Becker, e-commerce analyst at Lehman Brothers and a long-time Amazon believer, switched her recommendation on the company from a buy to a neutral. She was, she said, 'throwing in the towel on Amazon'.

CONTEXT AND CONCLUSIONS

Amazon is the totem stock of the Internet generation. What the critics will tell you is that through smoke and mirrors, PR, and puff, one man has succeeded in making a fortune through hyping his online business to previously unthought-of heights. What he has created, after all, is nothing more or less than a virtual bookshop, and one that in its first five years didn't turn a profit. But Amazon.com isn't a bellwether stock without reason. Bezos is the quintessential dot-com icon. He proved to the business world that the Internet was about more than the dissemination and exchange of knowledge. He proved that it was possible to overcome fears about purchasing online, that it was possible to drive down transaction costs, and that it was feasible to build an international e-commerce business over the Internet. Bezos is one of the great business pioneers. He had the courage to attempt something that people doubted could be done. Amazon has firmly entrenched itself as a dominant force in e-commerce and as a result of product additions and strategic alliances is now a virtual marketplace. The question is whether it can profitably exploit its position.

CLOSE BUT NO CIGAR
SCOTT BLUM

A colourful character, Blum survived a brush with the US Securities and Exchange Commission while at his company Pinnacle Micro and went on to found buy.com. buy.com epitomised the gung-ho, blindly optimistic philosophy of dot-com mania with its 'make money by losing money' strategy. The idea was to sell goods on the Internet at a loss and make money through advertising. Critics sniggered. The 'losing money' part went well; unfortunately the 'make money' element was lacking. Critics laughed openly. Meanwhile Blum stepped down as CEO in March 1999, and as chairman in October of the same year. He put his less than 50% of shares into a blind trust, raised $100 million in finance, and moved on to Enfrastructure.com, providing 'scalable, full-service technology and infrastructure for high-growth companies'.

THE BEST SOURCES OF HELP
Books:
Saunders, Rebecca. *Business the Amazon.com Way: Secrets of the World's Most Astonishing Web Business*. Oxford: Capstone, 1999.
Spector, Robert. *Amazon.com: Get Big Fast—Inside the Revolutionary Business Model That Changed the World*. London: Random House Business Books, 2000.
Website:
Amazon: **www.amazon.co.uk**

WILLIAM BOEING

1881	Born.
1908	Travels to Seattle.
1915	Takes first plane flight.
1916	Pacific Aero Products Company incorporated for $100,000.
1917	Pacific Aero Products changes name to the Boeing Airplane Company.
1919	Eddie Hubbard flies 60 letters from Vancouver to Seattle.
1922	Becomes Boeing Airplane Company chairman.
1927	Signs contract to fly airmail from Chicago to San Francisco.
1928	Consolidates business as Boeing Airplane and Transport Company.
1929	Boeing Airplane and Transport Company becomes United Aircraft and Transport.
1930	Ellen Church, a registered nurse, is first female flight attendant.
1934	United Aircraft and Transport broken up. William Boeing resigns as board chairman.
1956	Dies.

> **SUMMARY**
>
> William Boeing soared to dizzying heights with his aircraft manufacturing company and airline, founded in 1916 as Pacific Aero Products. Son of a wealthy timber merchant, Boeing looked set to carve out a business in timber, until the day he first saw a manned aeroplane. From that point onwards, until his retirement from the aircraft industry in 1934, he strove to turn his obsession with flight into a profitable business. For the most part he succeeded. With the help of some brilliant engineers, he designed and built a biplane that no longer required the pilot to sit on the wing. Incorporating his first company, he turned out aircraft for the military, always improving the technology.
>
> When the end of the First World War temporarily dampened orders for military aircraft, Boeing switched to commercial planes. He secured contracts to supply airmail and, with the help of pilot and entrepreneur Eddie Hubbard, built a successful airmail operation. But, in 1934, his dreams crashed to the ground when the government of the day accused him of monopolistic practices and ordered the break up of his company into three separate companies. Disillusioned, Boeing retired and spent the remainder of his years in property development and thoroughbred horse breeding.

LIFE AND CAREER

The birth of William Boeing in Detroit, Michigan on the first day of October 1881 goes down in history as one of the most significant days in the development of air travel. After an education in Detroit and Switzerland, Boeing studied at Yale Engineering College. His father was a wealthy timber merchant, so in 1902 Boeing went to work for the family timber interests in Aberdeen, Washington, working his way up to become president of Greenwood Logging Company.

In 1908, he travelled to Seattle. It was here that Boeing became interested in aeronautics. On the University of Washington campus during the Alaska-Yukon-Pacific Exposition in 1909, he saw a manned flying machine for the first time. To the modern eye, the contraption in which J.C. 'Bud' Mars took to the skies seems laughable, as well as downright dangerous. To Boeing, the sight of the small petrol-powered dirigible ascending above the university buildings was a marvel.

CONTRIBUTION

Boeing's next view of the wonders of aeronautical engineering came at the American air show held in Los Angeles in 1910. At the show, 'barnstormers'—stunt pilots who performed (hopefully) death-defying tricks—entertained an astonished crowd. Boeing left for the return journey to Seattle filled with a burning curiosity about aviation. In the next few years he discovered all he could about aeronautics. He joined the Seattle University Club, where he picked the brains of students like navy engineer Conrad Westervelt. As far as Boeing was concerned, Westervelt—who had taken a few aeronautics courses at the Massachusetts Institute of Technology—was as good as an expert on the subject.

Together, Boeing and Westervelt made a study of biplanes, sometimes from close quarters. The unflappable Boeing was a passenger in early biplanes made by firms such as the Curtiss Aeroplane and Motor Company, in which both the pilot and passenger were required to sit on the wing during flight—not an undertaking for the faint-hearted. The more he found out, the more Boeing was convinced that it was possible to design a better biplane than any that existed at the time.

> *Together, Boeing and Westervelt made a study of biplanes, sometimes from close quarters.*

In 1915, with the help of Westervelt and another engineer, Herb Munter, Boeing established the Pacific Aero club in a boathouse at Lake Union. Together they began work on the B & W—a new twin-float seaplane.

Boeing was wildly enthusiastic about the prospects of his new enterprise. He anticipated that the First World War would mean the US government would need more planes. He produced two prototype seaplanes, 'Bluebill' and 'Mallard', taking the controls of 'Bluebill' on its maiden flight. Encouraged by the trials, Boeing founded Pacific Aero Products Co in July 1916. But things didn't go as planned. Lieutenant Westervelt was reassigned and consequently unable to continue working with Boeing. Worse still, the navy rejected Boeing's prototypes. Undaunted, he hired another engineer, Tsu Wong, and built a new improved 'Model C' seaplane. When America entered the war in April 1917, Boeing changed the name of Pacific Aero Products to Boeing Airplane Co, and obtained orders from the navy for 50 planes. A workforce of over 300 was assembled to construct the new planes in the 'Red Barn' on the Duwamish River.

The end of the First World War was celebrated throughout the allied nations. For Boeing, it was a bittersweet moment. Victory in Europe meant the end of an intense period of activity and without the war to fuel production, prospects looked bleak. Orders dried up. To keep the factory open, Boeing turned to speedboat and furniture manufacture. To all his ventures, Boeing applied exacting standards. The boats were so good that Canadian smugglers used them to evade the authorities. Small military contracts kept the company ticking over, but it was an entirely different type of business that was to save Boeing from bankruptcy.

Although Boeing didn't know it at the time, his future lay in the hands of a man called Eddie Hubbard. Hubbard was Boeing's chief test pilot, the second Seattle man to win a licence from the Aero Club of America. Hubbard was convinced that the future of the aeroplane lay in transporting passengers and goods. In March 1919 he delivered the first international airmail to America, flying in from Vancouver, Canada. While Boeing struggled for survival, Hubbard organised an aerial taxi offshoot of the company. In 1920, Hubbard was awarded a contract to carry mail between Seattle and Canada. He left Boeing and started his own firm, buying a Boeing B1 seaplane to use as the delivery plane. It was Boeing's first commercial aircraft sale.

If this was good news for Boeing, the Kelly Act, passed in 1925, was even better. Until then, domestic airmail was carried under a virtual government monopoly. The Kelly Act allowed the Post Office to grant contracts to carry airmail on certain routes to private operators. In 1926, the Post Office invited tenders for its Chicago–San Francisco route. Hubbard personally persuaded Boeing to bid. Boeing won, founded a new subsidiary—the Boeing Air Transport Corporation—and welcomed Hubbard back into the fold to help organise the new company.

When it was clear that the transport of passengers by airline, as Hubbard suggested, promised to be the saviour of Boeing's airline manufacturing company, Boeing put all his energy into expanding that side of the business. He rushed out over 20 Model 40s in time to start the new airmail contracts on 1 July 1927. In 1928, he brought airline and aircraft manufacturing operations under the aegis of a new company—the Boeing Airplane and Transport Company—and then bought out one of his main rivals, Gorst's Pacific Air Transport. He introduced larger planes that were capable of carrying up to 18 passengers, attended by registered nurses—the first air stewardesses. In 1929, Boeing changed the name of his company to United Aircraft Transport and proceeded to buy out most of the competition. When the balance of the Post Office mail contracts was handed out to private carriers, United picked up the northern routes.

> *As a stopgap measure the routes were handed over to the army which, ill-equipped to handle the airmail routes, lost ten pilots in two weeks.*

Boeing's acquisitive activities had, however, brought him onto the radar of President Franklin Roosevelt and a new Democratic administration. The US government, in a show of strength, was determined to rid the country of the monopolistic practices that had dominated industry throughout the late 19th and early 20th centuries. Boeing was bang in the government's firing line. All airmail franchises were cancelled with effect from 10 March 1934. As a stopgap measure the routes were handed over to the army which, ill-equipped to handle the airmail routes, lost ten pilots in two weeks. When the contracts were offered to private carriers again, aircraft manufacturers were prevented from bidding. This was a poorly disguised move to restrain Boeing's power. As a result of the government's actions, United Aircraft and Transport was divided into three separate companies: United Aircraft Co, Boeing Airplane Company, and United Air Lines.

The mail contracts arrived just in time to save Boeing. His company might have survived long enough to pick up lucrative military supply contracts, but the break up of the government monopoly on airmail distribution made it a certainty and allowed Boeing to bring in much-needed cash and to rebuild the manufacturing business. When the airmail contracts were subsequently withdrawn, Boeing's company was in a strong enough position to survive without them.

Boeing, however, was appalled with the government's actions. The loss of the mail contracts sapped his resolve. After the break up of United Aircraft and Transport, the prospect of restructuring and steering his company through another difficult period depressed him. In 1934, at the age of 50 he retired from the company he had founded and had little more to do with it, other than acting as a consultant during the Second World War.

After retirement he concentrated on property deals, buying tracts of land to the north of Seattle. These became the Blue Ridge housing development. Ironically the first houses erected were bought by Boeing Company managers. Boeing also became a successful breeder of thoroughbred horses. He died in 1956.

CONTEXT AND CONCLUSIONS

Boeing was one of the great business pioneers of the 20th century. Fascinated by aviation as a young man, he turned a passion for flying into a business. Although he was a competent pilot, his skill lay in spotting talented people and getting them to produce results. Navy Lieutenant Conrad Westervelt taught Boeing aviation and introduced him to other enthusiasts. Herb Munter, a brilliant engineer, helped Boeing build his first plane. Another engineer, Tsu Wong, helped improve it. Eddie Hubbard persuaded Boeing of the merits of the airmail industry and passenger airlines. By motivating these and other employees and colleagues and inspiring them with his leadership, Boeing built the first major commercial aeroplane manufacturer. After the government intervened to clip his company's wings, he left the industry a dispirited and bitter man. But, before he died, he witnessed the introduction of the jet airliner, by the company he founded over 50 years before.

THE BEST SOURCES OF HELP
Books:
Cleveland, Carl. *Boeing Trivia*. Seattle, Washington: CMC Books, 1989.
Serling, Robert. *Legend & Legacy: The Story of Boeing and Its People*. New York: St Martin's Press, 1992.

WARREN BUFFETT

1930	Born.
1934	Publication of *Security Analysis* by Ben Graham and David Dodd.
1950	Attends Columbia Business School.
1951	Graduates from Columbia, starts to invest for a living.
1965	Acquires Berkshire Hathaway (invests $10,000; it is worth $51 million by 1999).
1967	Berkshire Hathaway buys National Indemnity Company and National Fire & Marine Insurance Company.
1969	Winds up investment partnership to concentrate on Berkshire.
1995	Buys major stake in McDonald's.
1996	Acquires GEICO, the sixth-largest US automobile insurer.
1998	Buys Executive Jet Corporation.
2001	Becomes the United States's second richest man behind Bill Gates.
2001	Announces 21st century investment strategy focusing on bricks, paints, and housewares.
2002	Berkshire Hathaway announces first ever negative coupon security.
2003	Continues investment strategy by acquiring furnishing goods giant, Burlington Industries.

SUMMARY

Warren Buffett (1930–) had an eye for a deal from an early age. He progressed from childhood race tipster and paper-round king to property owner and stock picker extraordinaire. By the age of 14 the young Buffett had already accumulated enough money to buy 40 acres of farmland. Now in his seventies, he is a multibillionaire—though not one to flaunt his wealth. The Coca-Cola-swilling, ukulele-playing Buffett lives a modest life, occupying an average house and preferring to drive an older car rather than the latest model even though his personal fortune makes him one of the richest men in the world. He is justly one of the most influential people in the finance world.

LIFE AND CAREER

In 1952, an aspiring 21-year-old money manager placed a small advertisement in an Omaha newspaper, inviting people to attend a class on investing. He reckoned it would be a good way to accustom himself to appearing before audiences. His preparation even involved investing $100 for a Dale Carnegie course on public speaking. Twenty others turned up that day. If that same young man were speaking today, the building would be besieged. He was Warren Buffett, one of the greatest investors of all time.

Born on 30 August 1930, in Omaha, Nebraska, Warren Buffett exhibited the talents that were to make him wealthy at an early age. At the age of six, he would buy six-packs of Coca-Cola for a quarter, break them up, and sell the individual bottles for

At the age of six, he would buy six-packs of Coca-Cola for a quarter, break them up, and sell the individual bottles for a nickel each.

a nickel each. When the young Buffett was stricken with a mysterious illness, he lay in bed working out how to get rich. On his recovery he roped his friends into a number of money-making enterprises he had thought up.

He looked for lost golf balls, packaged up those he found, and sold them. He also became one of the youngest racing tipsters in the United States when he published *Stable Boy Selections*—his information on the hot horses of the moment. His record for picking winners is not known, but if it was anything like his later talent for picking stocks, he must have made a few punters very rich.

When Warren was 12 his father, Howard Buffett, won a seat in Congress and the family moved to Washington, DC. The move was initially unpopular with Buffett. However, he changed his mind when he realised the commercial potential of the US capital. He took on five paper rounds at once, delivering a staggering 500 papers each morning and earning the equivalent of a man's full-time salary of $175. When he was still only 14 he had earned $1,200—enough to enable him to buy 40 acres of farmland in Nebraska and rent it out for farming.

CONTRIBUTION

After another business foray at senior school, installing renovated arcade games in barbers' shops, Buffett decided to enhance his natural flair for commerce with a formal business education. He landed a place at the prestigious Wharton School of Finance and Commerce at the University of Pennsylvania.

But Buffett did not complete his studies at Wharton. He found the theoretical aspects of business dull and discovered nothing in the curriculum to slake his thirst for practical knowledge. He finished his studies in business and economics at the University of Nebraska, in the meantime organising paper rounds for the *Lincoln Journal* on the side. At 19 he applied to Harvard Business School, but was refused admission. He turned to Columbia Business School, where he studied finance under investment guru Ben Graham.

It was in reading the stock market that Buffett found his true vocation. His first foray into stocks had been as a boy aged 11 (of course it helped that his father was a stockbroker). Young Buffett bought three shares in Cities Service preferred at $38 a share; the stock promptly fell to $27. When it had recovered to $40 he sold, making a small profit. The stock then rose to $200, leaving the boy kicking himself and teaching him the value of long-term investment.

Determined to make a living by investing, Buffett ploughed his energy and all the savings amassed from his various schemes into the stock market. From 1951 to 1956 he turned $9,800 into $140,000. News spread about the new whiz kid investor, and more and more people asked him to invest their money for them. What started with friends spread to the general public, and soon Buffett was forming limited partnerships and taking a 25% cut of any return above 4%.

Once Buffett started investing as a career, he developed his own personal investment strategy. He began by looking for stocks that offered outstanding value—those that were relatively cheap given their asset value—and then holding those shares for the long term. 'Lethargy, bordering on sloth, should remain the cornerstone of an investment style,' he has said. He was heavily influenced by the theories of Ben Graham, his former tutor at Columbia and the co-author of the investment classic *Security Analysis* (1934). Buffett eventually took Graham's investing strategies a step further by seeking out companies whose shares were inexpensive compared to their growth prospects. This approach required assessing a company's intangible assets, such as brand value. In this Buffett was ahead of his time. The area of intangible assets is now the subject of growing interest from business academics, but in the 1950s it was largely neglected. Buffett, however, was not unduly interested in theoretical niceties.

Theory was all very well, as Buffett had noted at Wharton, but how would his strategy work in practice? The answer proved to be, phenomenally well. Between 1957 and 1966 the investment partnership that Buffett managed posted an amazing 1,156% return—against 122.9% over the same period for the Dow Jones Industrial Average. A partner's investment of $10,000 would, after deducting Buffett's share, have returned $80,420. Buffett continued to out-perform the market, making a 36% return in 1967 and a 59% return in 1968 in a speculative market, which was not particularly suited to his particular investment strategy.

In 1969, to the surprise of his managers, Buffett called it a day. Concerned about maintaining his performance in an uncongenial investment climate, he decided to wind up the partnership.

Since 1969 his attentions have been focused entirely on his investment vehicle Berkshire Hathaway, the publicly-listed company he acquired in 1965. The markets may go up or down, but over time Buffett has delivered consistently for his shareholders. His legendary, almost uncanny, knack of picking stocks has earned him the epithet 'the Sage of Omaha'. On the strength of his company's performance, it's a tag he undoubtedly deserves. A $10,000 investment in Berkshire Hathaway in 1965 would have been worth over $50 million by the end of 2000. Investors who backed the S&P 500 Index would have accumulated some $500,000, a paltry amount by comparison. Along the way, Buffett has picked stocks such as Coca-Cola and American Express when they were at a low ebb. The only downside, so far, has been investments into insurance companies, which have hit problems since 2002. On the other hand, he has resisted the temptation to be drawn into media-fuelled stock bubbles such as the Internet boom of the 1990s. 'As a group, lemmings have a rotten image,' notes Buffett, 'but no individual lemming has ever received bad press.'

He remains determined to avoid the technology sector, 'We have embraced the 21st century by entering such cutting edge industries as bricks, carpets, insulation, and paint—try to control your excitement.' From 2001, he has invested in companies like Fruit of the Loom, Pampered Chef and Burlington Industries, part of that 'household' portfolio.

Buffett himself has remained relatively unaffected by the plaudits heaped upon him. A modest man, he has few indulgences other than a corporate jet. Even then he bought a small, used plane for Berkshire; when he traded up to a more expensive model, he named it 'the Indefensible'. Modesty apart, he moved into the position of the United States's second richest person in 2001 behind Bill Gates. He lives in an average home in Omaha, famously drives an old car, and maintains a fairly small office with few staff. His main hobby, it seems, is reading company reports, in which he reportedly maintains an avid interest despite the many thousands he's undoubtedly ploughed through.

CONTEXT AND CONCLUSIONS
Warren Buffett is one of the greatest investors of all time. What lifts him above his peers is a determination to stick to his investment principles. Companies have risen and fallen, one minute at the height of fashion, the next on the bankruptcy pile. Buffett has steadfastly refused to jump on any bandwagon. Unlike so many other investors who are nursing burnt fingers, Buffett let the dot-com train roll on by. Famously, he refuses to invest in businesses that he doesn't understand—which includes most high-tech companies. Instead Buffett has made a fortune for himself and his shareholders by investing in undervalued companies for the long-term. It's Buffett's willingness to buck the trend that makes him worth his 'Sage of Omaha' tag.

THE BEST SOURCES OF HELP
Book:
Lowenstein, Roger. *Buffett: The Making of an American Capitalist*. New York: Doubleday, 1996.

LEO BURNETT

1891	Born.
1930	Joins Erwin Wasey as creative vice-president.
1935	Borrows $50,000 and starts his own agency.
1940	Leo Burnett agency lands first major new client, the American Meat Institute.
1950	Proctor and Gamble appoints Leo Burnett for an institutional campaign.
1955	Retained by Philip Morris to develop a campaign for Marlboro cigarettes.
1967	Retires—although he continues to work at his agency part-time.
1971	Dies.

> **SUMMARY**
>
> Leo Burnett (1891–1971) changed the face of advertising in the United States. After working his way through a number of agencies, including Homer McKee and Erwin Wasey, he resisted the lure of the Madison Avenue agencies in New York and in 1935 set up his own business in Chicago. After a hesitant start, Burnett's distinctive style of advertising soon attracted major clients such as Procter & Gamble. The Leo Burnett advertising agency went on to produce some of the most striking advertising of its time, including the 'Marlboro Man' campaign. Burnett's advertising philosophy gave rise to the Chicago School of advertising, and by his death in 1971 he was universally acknowledged as one of the most influential figures in his industry.

LIFE AND CAREER

Leo Burnett was born George Noble Burnett in St Johns, Michigan, on 21 October 1891. The name Leo was a result of hospital officials mistaking the abbreviated Geo for Leo. The name stuck.

Burnett started out in advertising young. His father owned a dry-goods store and Burnett would design and draw the display cards, little realising that advertising would come to play such an important part in his life. He attended the local high school, moonlighting as a reporter for several weekly newspapers in the area. Immediately after graduation he briefly took up a position as a teacher in St Johns's single-classroom village school before heading for the University of Michigan at Ann Arbor.

At university, Burnett took a degree in journalism. Once again he continued to work throughout his studies, this time both as a night editor at the *Michigan Daily* and producing display cards for a department store. Leaving university he worked at the *Peoria [Illinois] Journal* as a reporter for $18 a week. He remained there for about a year, until the lure of the burgeoning automobile industry proved too great and he set off for Detroit.

In Detroit Burnett joined the Cadillac Motor Car Company as editor of an in-house magazine. He had been tipped off about the job by one of his old college professors and, as part of his application, wrote an essay on neatness that sufficiently impressed the people at Cadillac to win him the job. Soon Burnett had been handed responsibility for Cadillac's advertising. The pattern for his social and professional life was set.

CONTRIBUTION

After a brief stint in the US Navy during the First World War—much of it spent building a breakwater in Lake Michigan—Burnett, with several other Cadillac employees, broke away to form LaFayette Motors. He followed LaFayette to Indianapolis but when the company moved to Wisconsin he remained in Indianapolis as creative head at the Homer McKee advertising agency.

He settled at Homer McKee for ten years as a copywriter. In 1929 the stock market crash affected advertising agencies badly. Homer McKee was no exception, losing one of its major automobile accounts. Now with a young family, Burnett needed a secure job and decided to move on. The family moved to Chicago in 1930, and Burnett signed up for Erwin Wasey as creative vice-president. At the time Erwin Wasey was one of the leading advertising agencies in the world. Shortly after Burnett joined, the firm moved its headquarters to New York. The New York advertising agencies had developed a reputation for a hard-sell approach. They were also perceived by their western and mid-western clients as favouring companies based on the East Coast.

Several of Burnett's clients approached him and suggested he open his own agency. Initially Burnett's loyalty prevailed. Then Art Kudner left Wasey to start his own agency, taking several automobile clients, including General Motors, with him. Burnett relented. It was 1935, Burnett was 44, and on 5 August his own agency opened for business.

The Marlboro campaign with its imagery of the rugged Marlboro Man was one of the most memorable of the 20th century.

Burnett borrowed $50,000 to start Leo Burnett Company, Inc. He was joined by a friend, Jack O'Kieffe, as well as three clients—Green Giant, Hoover, and Realsilk Hosiery—who brought in revenues of some $900,000. The agency's first year was a tough one. Despite attempts to win accounts from both Hershey and Wrigley Gum, Burnett ended the year with the same clients he started with.

The second year went the same way. Burnett had briefly recruited Dick Heath, who brought in some business. Unfortunately Burnett and Heath fell out within the year and Heath left. It wasn't until O'Kieffe persuaded Burnett to bring Heath back that things began to improve. In 1940 Leo Burnett landed its first major new client, the American Meat Institute. Thereafter the agency gathered momentum, picking up prestigious accounts such as the Pillsbury Family Flour account, Kellogg's Cereals, and—the account that brought Burnett onto the radar of the Madison Avenue agencies—the Tea Council, a New York-based organisation.

Burnett's agency made a name for itself through its distinctive style of advertising—what Burnett called 'stressing the inherent drama in the product'. The trickle of clients became a flood after Proctor and Gamble appointed Burnett's for an institutional campaign in 1950.

In 1955 Burnett's was retained by Philip Morris to develop a campaign for Marlboro cigarettes. The Marlboro campaign with its imagery of the rugged Marlboro Man was one of the most memorable of the 20th century. There were many other notable campaigns in the years that followed.

Burnett's influence on the advertising industry was so great that the term 'the Chicago School of advertising' was coined to describe his and his followers' distinctive approach. It was a style that tried to capture the essence of the product in its advertising rather than just use clever words. It was also an inclusive approach that didn't try to play to either East or West Coast America in particular.

In the late 1960s, suffering increasingly from illness, Burnett took a back seat in the business he had created. In 1967 he 'retired', although he continued to come into the office at least twice a week. On 7 June 1971 after a spell in the office, Burnett suffered a heart attack at his home and died that night. He was 79.

CONTEXT AND CONCLUSIONS

Praised by competitors and clients alike, Leo Burnett made a unique contribution to the advertising industry. He created his own, highly influential school of advertising—the Chicago School. He was driven by a consuming passion for excellence and creativity that shone through in the work of his agency. He also adopted a socially responsible approach to business, demonstrated through the firm's pro bono work, carried out in part under the auspices of the Advertising Council.

Unlike some other agencies, the pressures of winning business never drove Burnett's company to employ unscrupulous or cut-throat practices. It was a testimony to its founder's even-handed approach that he was often praised by his closest rivals.

THE BEST SOURCES OF HELP
Book:
Broadbent, Simon. *The Leo Burnett Book of Advertising*. London: Business Books, 1984.
Website:
Leo Burnett: **www.leoburnett.com**

ANDREW CARNEGIE

1835	Born.
1848	Family moves to Allegheny near Pittsburgh, Pennsylvania. Carnegie, aged 12, takes job in cotton mill.
1870	Builds first blast furnace. Experiments with the Bessemer process.
1874	Opens steel furnace at Braddock.
1880	Plant operating for 24 hours a day with profits of $2 million.
1881	Company reorganises as Carnegie Bros & Co.
1882	Carnegie acquires coke-producing interests of Henry C. Frick.
1886	Writes *Triumphant Democracy*.
1889	Moves to New York to conduct R&D into the steel manufacturing process. 'Gospel of wealth' article published. Steel production 332,111 tons.
1899	Steel production 2,663,412 tons. Carnegie buys out Frick.
1901	Frick and J. Pierpont Morgan purchase the Carnegie Company for $500 million.
1919	Dies.

> **SUMMARY**
>
> Andrew Carnegie (1835–1919) only just merits consideration as one of the top hundred business leaders of the 20th century. This is not because his talents as a businessman are suspect—he was one of the finest businessmen of his generation—but because a significant proportion of his achievements fell within the 19th century. That Carnegie has made it into this select group is testimony to his impact on the commercial revolution that took place in the United States as the 19th century gave way to the 20th. Carnegie was arguably the first of a generation of businessmen who pioneered industrial growth in the United States and throughout the world on the back of steel manufacturing and the building of railways. At the end of his long career he had built the largest steel company in the United States and amassed a vast personal fortune.

LIFE AND CAREER

Andrew Carnegie was born in Dunfermline on 25 November 1835. In 1848 economic depression persuaded Carnegie's father to emigrate with his family to the United States. The family settled in a colony of Scots gathered at Slabtown, Allegheny, near Pittsburgh, and the 12-year-old Andrew took work in a local cotton mill.

Leaving the cotton mill, he got a job at the Pittsburgh Telegraph Office as a messenger boy. Thomas A. Scott, superintendent of the western division of the Pennsylvania Railroad at the time, spotted Carnegie's potential and appointed him as his secretary at $50 a month, in those days a handsome salary for one so young. It was Scott who set Carnegie on the path to riches by showing him the likely gains of investing in start-up companies. Acting on a tip from Scott, Carnegie bought stock in the Adams Express Company using money from his mother, who remortgaged her house. Shortly afterwards he borrowed money to invest in a venture commercially exploiting the invention of the sleeping car for the railway.

During the American Civil War, Carnegie served with Scott in Washington. Then, with the Union victory secured, he took Scott's old position as superintendent of the western division of the Pennsylvania Railroad. But his entrepreneurial instincts were not satisfied, and he soon left the railways to set up an iron bridge building firm, the Keystone Bridge Company. He was also involved in several other speculative ventures that proved successful.

CONTRIBUTION
While Carnegie was busy hustling in the United States, Henry Bessemer, an inventor and businessman, was working on a manufacturing process in England that would change industry the world over. The Bessemer process allowed the industrialised production of steel from iron. Carnegie often visited the United Kingdom, and on one visit he came across the Bessemer converter. It was a revelation.

Carnegie was arguably the first of a generation of businessmen who pioneered industrial growth in the United States and throughout the world on the back of steel manufacturing and the building of railways.

Hurrying back to the United States, Carnegie formed Carnegie, McCandless, & Co, built his first blast furnace in 1870, and began experimenting with the Bessemer process. He opened a steel furnace at Braddock and, by 1880, the plant was operating 24 hours a day and producing annual profits of $2 million. In 1881 the company reorganised, becoming Carnegie Bros & Co. Carnegie held the controlling interest. In 1882 he acquired the coke-producing interests of Henry C. Frick, who became his most trusted associate.

In 1889 Carnegie moved to New York to continue his research into the steel manufacturing process. He also spent six months of the year with his family in Scotland. In his absence Carnegie left Frick, as chair of Carnegie Bros, in charge of the day-to-day running of the company. When Frick took over, the company was a collection of disparate threads—the threads being individual mills and furnaces dotted about Pittsburgh. Frick wove these threads together into a fabric: an organisation that would become the biggest steel-making enterprise in the world. He centralised the management structure and integrated production. The firm was transformed into the Carnegie Steel Company, valued at $25 million.

Unfortunately for Carnegie, Frick also presided over one of the most notorious incidents in US corporate history. In an attempt to drive down costs and boost profits, Frick reduced piecework rates. Incensed, the Amalgamated Iron and Steel Workers Union called its members at the Carnegie Homestead plant out on strike. Instead of settling through negotiation, Frick inflamed the situation by arranging to bring in 300 strikebreakers.

When the day came and the strikebreakers arrived on barges down the Monongahela River, complete with armed guard, all hell broke loose. At the end of a day of pitched battle, ten men lay dead and a further 60 were wounded. Homestead was placed under martial law.

Carnegie, in Scotland at the time, was irate. It was not just the disruption to the company that he rued; Frick had gone against his explicit instructions not to use strikebreakers. For Carnegie it was a matter of personal ethics. Nevertheless, being the controlling owner and, as such, ultimately responsible, he had to bear the dark stain of the workers' blood on his reputation for many years after the debacle.

Although Carnegie refrained from criticising Frick in public, their relationship never recovered. The company continued to thrive, improving annual production of steel from 332,111 tons in 1889 to 2,663,412 in 1899, and profits from $2 million to $40 million. But, because of the deteriorating relationship between them, Carnegie took the opportunity to buy Frick out for a handsome $15 million in 1889. Even this act of severance failed to quell the personal animosity between the two men. In 1901 Frick returned with the backing of the notorious J. Pierpont Morgan and purchased the Carnegie Company for $500 million, establishing the US Steel Corporation which, valued at $1.4 billion, was the biggest steel company in the world.

Some saw him as a smug, tyrannical, autocratic, arrogant slave-driver; others as a wise, benevolent, enlightened entrepreneur.

CONTEXT AND CONCLUSIONS

Carnegie played a leading role in the industrialisation of the United States. As a poor Scottish boy who became one of the wealthiest men in the world, his rise from rags to riches was extraordinary. In his time he was criticised and praised in equal measure. Some saw him as a smug, tyrannical, autocratic, arrogant slave-driver; others as a wise, benevolent, enlightened entrepreneur. Of the many qualities Carnegie possessed, one in particular stands out: he was an opportunist who acted on his instincts. He took any opportunity to promote his business interests. When he invited the Prince of Wales to ride a Pennsylvania Railway engine, for example, he did it to secure business favours rather than to increase his social standing.

Carnegie will be remembered as much for his philanthropy as for his business adventures. In later life, guided by his ethical beliefs, he gave away the greater part of his fortune. He set up a trust fund 'for the improvement of mankind'. The Carnegie Institute of Pittsburgh, the Carnegie Institute of Technology, the Carnegie Institution of Washington, and three thousand public libraries were built with this trust money.

When the 'King of Steel' died in August 1919, he had already given away $350 million of his fortune.

THE BEST SOURCES OF HELP
Books:
Carnegie, Andrew. *The Empire of Business*. New York: Doubleday, Doran, & Co, 1902.
Mackay, James. *Andrew Carnegie: His Life and Times*. Chichester: John Wiley, 1998.
Website:
Carnegie Corporation of New York: **www.carnegie.org**

WILLIS HAVILAND CARRIER

1876	Born.
1901	Graduates from Cornell University. Joins Buffalo Forge Company.
1906	Patents 'apparatus for treating air'.
1914	Buffalo Forge closes air-conditioning subsidiary.
1915	Forms Carrier Engineering Corporation.
1922	Invents the centrifugal refrigeration machine.
1924	Detroit's J.L. Hudson Co becomes first air-conditioned department store.
1925	Installs air conditioning into Rivoli Theater in New York.
1928	San Antonio's Milam Building the first air-conditioned office tower.
1930	Air conditioning installed into over 300 theatres.
1940s	Turns over company facilities and expertise to war effort.
1950	Dies.

SUMMARY

Willis Haviland Carrier invented his air-conditioning machine early in his career. He spent the rest of his life improving his product and building and leading the company that sold it. A brilliant student, he graduated from Cornell University in 1901 and carried his natural inquisitiveness into his first job. His initial research into heating and cooling devices resulted in one of the first commercial air-conditioning machines. When his company dropped the technology, Carrier started his own company. Then, with a mixture of charm, persuasion, and inventiveness, he set about selling his idea to America. He was so successful that by the time of his death in 1950, air conditioning was taken for granted by millions of Americans.

LIFE AND CAREER

Willis Haviland Carrier was born and raised on a farm, on the eastern shores of Lake Erie in Angola, New York. Born on 26 November 1876, he was an only child. In later years it was said that Carrier had been something of a mathematical prodigy, but the reality was more mundane. As many children do, he struggled with maths, especially fractions. His mother insisted on a novel way of teaching him. 'My mother told me to bring up a pan of apples from the cellar,' said Carrier. 'She had me cut them into halves, quarters and eighths, and add and subtract the parts. Fractions took on a new meaning, and I felt as if no problems would be too hard for me—I'd simply break them down to something simple and they would be easy to solve.'

Carrier put his problem-solving skills to good use studying for a mechanical engineering degree at Cornell University in Ithaca, New York. He was an exceptional student. 'Carrier would start explaining an idea in class, and he was soon so far ahead of us in his thinking that not even the professor could keep up with him,' said a fellow undergraduate.

Theoretical engineering came easily. Money didn't. Despite a four-year scholarship Carrier still struggled to survive, taking on a string of odd jobs so he could afford to eat and pay the rent. When he graduated in 1901, he went to work for the Buffalo Forge Company, designing heating systems.

CONTRIBUTION

At Buffalo Forge, Carrier started at the bottom on the draftsman's board. He soon discovered a serious flaw in the design process. There was insufficient data available on the science of heating and cooling air to allow the design of well-engineered heating and drying systems. Carrier spent his evenings poring over books, compiling his own data tables. Finally he summoned the courage to ask his boss for funds to research the subject, requesting $3,000. His boss misheard the sum as $30,000. When he found out the true figure, he was so relieved that he agreed to Carrier's request on the spot.

Carrier set up his own research team to investigate the basic engineering principles involved in heating buildings. The research, which enabled the company to calculate how much heating surface area is required to heat a building of a particular size, led to savings of $40,000. His research efforts paid off in other ways too. Carrier was promoted to head up the company's experimental engineering department.

In the sultry summer of 1901, the Brooklyn-based company of Sackett-Wilhelms Lithographing and Publishing had problems. The humidity affected its business badly. The ink ran and the moist paper swelled, costing the company money. Representatives came to see Carrier. Could he do something to regulate the humidity? He said he'd try.

Carrier didn't invent room-cooling machines. Primitive devices, aimed at making buildings more comfortable to live in during hot humid summers, had been around for some time, especially in America's Deep South. Most were variations on a theme—air blown by a fan over a block of ice. Crude and impracticable, these devices did little to abate the oppressive heat, and even less to combat the humidity. In addition, the transport of ice—an industry in itself—was difficult and expensive.

In 1928, San Antonio's Milam Building opened the first air-conditioned office tower. An unexpected bonus was a staggering 51% increase in productivity among white-collar workers during the summer months.

It didn't take long for the inventive Carrier to improve upon the ice machines. Inspiration for his new work came to him out of a fog that enveloped him as he stood in a damp Pittsburgh railway station. The paradoxical solution to the problem of how to control humidity in a room lay in creating an artificial fog, in which Carrier determined the amount of air saturation. His first design was a contraption that pulled moist air through a filter, passed it over chilled coils, and then redirected it to where it was needed. It was the equivalent of melting 54 tons of ice a day. In 1906 he patented an improved version of the design to which he gave the name 'apparatus for treating air'. A competitor, Stuart Cramer, coined the term 'air conditioner'.

Carrier had hit the jackpot. Buffalo Forge, however, was blind to the opportunity. With the outbreak of the First World War in 1914, the company shut down its small but growing air-conditioning subsidiary. Undaunted Carrier took his invention and, in 1915, with several friends and $32,600, formed Carrier Engineering Corporation. The company's slogan was 'Every Day a Good Day'.

In its first year the company was awarded 40 contracts for air conditioning systems. In 1922 Carrier produced another improvement to his system—the centrifugal refrigeration machine. This invention made it practical to introduce air conditioning into large spaces. Industry snapped up the company's new product. Carrier's air conditioning brought comfort to shoppers at Detroit's J.L. Hudson Co, when it became the first air-conditioned department store in 1924. Relief was in sight too for the millions of office workers slogging through summer days in their sweat-drenched shirts. In 1928, San Antonio's Milam Building opened the first air-conditioned office tower. An unexpected bonus was a staggering 51% increase in productivity among white-collar workers during the summer months.

> *The government even removed the company's chillers from department stores such as Macy's to install them in war production plants.*

Carrier's air conditioning also proved popular with theatregoers. Stifling heat in the summer left New York's theatres either empty or closed. In 1925, the owner of the famous Rivoli Theater in New York took a risk and asked Carrier to install air conditioning. Passers-by reading the advertising would have been forgiven for thinking that the air conditioning was a bigger attraction than the play. So it proved. The queue snaked around the block for the first air-conditioned performance which, after a sticky beginning when the 133-ton air conditioning machine was late starting up, was a great success. By 1930, Carrier had installed air conditioning into 300 theatres. With the benefit of air conditioning at work and at play, it wasn't long before the American public was demanding it in their homes.

In the 1920s, Carrier started to supply home air-conditioning units—the small 'Weathermaker'—for residential use. But when the chill wind of the Great Depression blew, plans for air-conditioned homes were shelved. The Second World War further delayed the mass introduction of air conditioning into homes, when Carrier's production facilities were given over to the war effort. The government even removed the company's chillers from department stores such as Macy's to install them in war production plants.

Carrier never got to grips with the domestic market, failing to produce a small and reliable enough product to bring to the consumer mass market. It wasn't until the 1950s that companies like Westinghouse would introduce home air-conditioning on a large scale. Carrier never lived to see it—he died of a heart attack in September 1950.

CONTEXT AND CONCLUSIONS

Known as 'the Chief' by his workers, Carrier was both an inventor and a leader. Although he relied on the business skills of colleague Irvine Lyle to help build his company, Carrier was the driving force behind its success. Other people were investigating the means of controlling air temperature and humidity—Stuart Cramer, for example, was on the right track but failed to see the bigger picture. But Carrier realised the potential of his invention and, by installing it in theatres and offices, brought it to the public's attention, thus creating a growing tide of demand.

Air conditioning made new industrial processes possible and increased productivity and, more importantly, it made life comfortable for millions of people. It is difficult for anyone who lives in temperate climes to understand the significance of Carrier's achievement, but for those who step outdoors in the summer to the blast of hot air and the closeness of 80% humidity there is no need to explain.

CLOSE BUT NO CIGAR
STUART CRAMER

Carrier may be the man known for bringing air conditioning to the people of the United States, but he didn't invent the term. The man who did was Stuart Cramer of Charlotte, North Carolina. Trained as an engineer, Cramer built up substantial holdings in the textile industry of the southern states in the early 1900s. Driven by necessity, he designed a device to moisten the air in his textile factories and filed a patent for the 'Cramer System of Air Conditioning'. However he seemed to lack Carrier's vision, as the Parks-Cramer Company aimed its humidification primarily at the cotton industry rather than at a wider audience.

THE BEST SOURCES OF HELP
Books:
Ingels, Margaret. *Willis Haviland Carrier: Father of Air Conditioning*. Reprint ed. Manchester, New Hampshire: Ayer Company Publishing, 1972.
Wampler, Dr Cloud. *Willis H. Carrier, Father of Air Conditioning*. New York: Newcomen Society, 1949.

STEVE CASE

1958	Born.
1979	Graduates from Williams College; joins Procter & Gamble.
1983	Gets job at Control Video.
1989	Quantum Computers renamed America Online (AOL).
1991	Case becomes CEO of AOL.
1992	America Online IPO.
1996	4.6 million subscribers.
1998	Acquires CompuServe.
1999	Acquires Netscape.
2000	Announces merger with Time Warner.
2001	AOL has 30 million subscribers. Launches new improved AOL 7.0.
2002	AOL launches broadband services. Restates pre-merger profits prompting US Justice Department enquiry into accounting practices. AOL TimeWarner posts record charges of $54 billion.
2003	Case resigns as CEO.

> **SUMMARY**
>
> Steve Case, born in 1958, is cofounder and former CEO America Online (AOL). A political science graduate, he worked in various marketing and sales positions before eventually starting up Quantum Computers, which offered online services to users of Commodore computers.
>
> Renamed America Online (AOL) in 1989, the company went public in 1992 with 150,000 subscribers. By 1996 that figure was 4.6 million. In 1998 Case wiped out a chunk of the competition by buying CompuServe and its 2.5 million subscribers, as well as Netscape. By 2001 AOL had 30 million subscribers worldwide.
>
> The pinnacle of Case's deal-making came in early 2000 with the shock announcement of a $166 billion merger with media giant Time Warner. However, the merger was slow to succeed and continuing poor results led to his resignation in 2003.

LIFE AND CAREER

Steve Case, born 21 August 1958 in Honolulu, Hawaii, is a world apart from the Marc Andreessens (Netscape) and David Filos (Yahoo!) of the New Economy. Instead of taking the standard geekster's path to billionaire status—studying computer sciences or engineering in some West Coast tech hotspot like Stanford—he graduated in political science at Williams College, Massachusetts.

He followed this by working in marketing and sales, first at Procter & Gamble (hair-care products) and then at PepsiCo (the Pizza Hut division). It was only then that Case paid any attention to the Internet.

Recalling the first time he logged on, Case said, 'I thought it was magical then, I still think it's magical today. The centre of my world is consumers. Every day I wake up and say, "How can we make America Online more interesting, more useful, more fun, more affordable, so that it will attract a broader audience?" Because I still remember that excitement 13 years ago when I first connected to an online service.'

After his taste of the corporate world, Case joined a small video-games service company, Control Video, in 1983. He had always had a touch of the entrepreneur about him. As a child he sold lime juice from his back yard at two cents a cup, took charge of the obligatory paper round, and started a mail-order company, Case Enterprises, with his brother Dan.

While the video company wasn't a storming success, it did introduce Case to Jim Kinsey and Mark Seriff. It was the perfect combination: Seriff had technology in his blood (he had worked on Arpanet, the forerunner of the Internet), Kinsey was a finance man, and Case provided the sales and marketing know-how. Together the trio founded Quantum Computers. The company provided online services to users of the soon-to-be-defunct Commodore computer. Commodore imploded, but America Online (AOL), as the Quantum business was renamed in 1989, went from strength to strength.

'Consumers want one place where they can find good Internet content and meet interesting people. And they want someone to make it easy for them.'

CONTRIBUTION

Case instinctively knew what the customer wanted. Not burdened with a technological background, he could pitch the product at the average consumer, and make the consumer experience as simple and as user-friendly as possible. 'Our strategy has always been crystal clear,' he said in a 1998 interview. 'Consumers want one place where they can find good Internet content and meet interesting people. And they want someone to make it easy for them.'

America Online entered the market in 1992. At the time it had a membership of some 150,000. By 1996, with the help of an innovative marketing strategy involving the shipping of AOL CDs offering a free trial, 4.6 million had signed up. The company's marketing guru, Jan Brandt, even put disks on the office wall bearing the message, 'Resistance is futile'.

AOL dominated its main rivals, CompuServe and Prodigy, although Microsoft's MSN was still a distant threat. Yet success brought its problems. AOL replaced usage charges with a flat-fee structure and usage figures shot up. People spent more time online, the systems couldn't cope, and the service caved in under the pressure.

Case hired Bob Pittman, cofounder of MTV, to take over the day-to-day running of the company. Pittman was a media man who understood content delivery. He also knew how to deal with a corporation the size of AOL. Making money out of the subscriptions, however, proved a tough nut to crack. The more users AOL signed up, the more AOL spent on infrastructure and maintaining quality of service. Case and Pittman formulated a business model in which content sucked in subscribers who then spent money. Surely if they had a captive audience, advertisers would be falling over themselves to get onto AOL. That's what they figured, and they were right.

Pittman attacked costs, driving down customer acquisition costs from close to $400 per new subscriber to below $100. Concessions were sold to bring in money: 1-800-Flowers bought the flower concession for $25 million; Amazon paid $19 million to be the exclusive bookseller on the external aol.com website; Barnes & Noble went one better, paying $40 million to be the exclusive bookseller inside.

> *The pinnacle of Case's deal-making came in early 2000 with the shock announcement of a $166 billion merger with media giant Time Warner.*

Active on the acquisitions trail, Case engineered a takeover of rival CompuServe in 1998 (adding 2.5 million subscribers), and in the same year took the opportunity to acquire Netscape for $4.2 billion. Then, in early 2000, AOL made the shock announcement of a planned $166 billion merger with media giant Time Warner. However, the merger failed to produce instant success and in 2002, posted record charges of $54 billion. Further financial troubles hit the company in 2002 when it re-stated pre-merger profits, prompting a US Justice Department enquiry into accounting practices.

AOL, meanwhile, continued to expand its operations, adding broadband services in 2002 to broaden its appeal. Roughly 80% of the world's online users log on to AOL in some way. And while they are there, traipsing around the online shopping malls, they part with over $10 billion dollars a year. By 2002, more than 35 million subscribers worldwide were spending an average of 70 minutes a day on AOL, adding up to more than 1 billion subscriber hours each month. Despite that success, Case's position had become untenable and he resigned from AOL Time-Warner in January 2003. A high-profile figurehead, Case felt that he had become a 'distraction'—'Some shareholders continue to focus their disappointment with the company's post-merger performance on me personally.'

CONTEXT AND CONCLUSIONS
Not for Steve Case the 'poring over circuit boards in the garage' approach to building a tech empire! He took an alternative route to IT stardom. When he saw the Internet, he figured there would be plenty of people who would struggle to get to grips with the technology. Until the advent of the Internet, most home entertainment involved turning on a switch and choosing a channel. If you could read the television schedules, then you had pretty much mastered the art of TV use. The Internet changed the rules. For a start, access was via a computer, which had to be correctly configured, and then there were the browser and the URLs, the server addresses, the e-mail protocols, and much, much more. For the uninitiated, logging onto and navigating the Internet was the equivalent of string theory and quantum mechanics. Case changed all that with the AOL CD. He made the Internet experience easy for millions worldwide, and in so doing built a company that was effectively able to take over one of the world's largest media companies, Time Warner.

THE BEST SOURCES OF HELP
Book:
Swisher, Kara. *Aol.com: How Steve Case Beat Bill Gates, Nailed the Netheads, and Made Millions in the War for the Web*. London: Century, 1998.
Website:
Aol Anywhere: **www.aol.com**

JOHN CHAMBERS

1949	Born.
1974	Obtains law degree from West Virginia University.
1975	Graduates from Indiana University with an MBA.
1983	Moves to Wang.
1984	Cisco founded in San Jose, California, by Sandra Lerner and Len Bosack.
1995–2000	Chambers arrives at Cisco as CEO. Market capitalisation increases from $9 billion to $550 billion.
December 2000	Chambers detects sharp drop in sales.
January 2000	Company goes from 70% growth to minus 30% in 45 days.
2001	Company posts first ever loss, of $2.69 billion.

> **SUMMARY**
>
> John Chambers is best known for his management of Cisco Systems, which dominates the market for routers—the boxes that direct data traffic on the Internet—and his evangelising of the Internet. When he arrived at Cisco it was a growing, but still small, company worth $9 billion. In the space of five years, Chambers turned it into a networking colossus with a market cap that touched $555 billion. He achieved this by taking measures that included focusing on teams; promoting excellent customer service; instilling a distinctive corporate culture; and ravenously acquiring other companies. One of his distinctive talents is the ability to assimilate acquired companies into the Cisco fold. More than 70 companies have been seamlessly integrated into Cisco, with a much better talent retention rate than is usual. Cisco, like most other tech companies, stumbled in 2001. The company posted its first loss in its eleven-year history and shed thousands of employees. Since then, however, he has re-energised Cisco and returned it to profit.

LIFE AND CAREER

Born on 23 August 1949, John Thomas Chambers graduated from West Virginia University with a law degree, despite having mild dyslexia. Then he studied for an MBA at Indiana University, graduating in 1975.

He is best known for his association with Cisco, but his career has included stints at two other major IT companies. At IBM in the early 1980s, he witnessed at first hand how bureaucracy and uniformity could slow a company down and kill creativity. In 1983 Chambers moved to the now defunct computer company, Wang. At Wang he learned how risky betting the company on proprietary technology can be. It was an unpleasant experience for Chambers, who was assigned the task of implementing the downsizing. He made over 4,000 employees redundant. Later he recalled the pain and vowed never to repeat the experience: 'The bleeding went on for 15 months. One person after another would sit across the desk from me and ask, "What did I do wrong?" And the honest answer is they didn't do anything wrong—it was management acting more like Santa Claus than like business leaders. It was the most painful thing I have ever gone through. I never want to go through it again. I will do anything to avoid it.'

In early 2001, however, Chambers experienced déjà vu. He announced large-scale redundancies at Cisco, shedding 8,500 people—18% of its workforce.

CONTRIBUTION
Husband and wife team Sandra Lerner and Len Bosack founded Cisco Systems in San Jose, California, in 1984. They started the company to market the router, a device they developed to allow incompatible computer systems to communicate with each other. Today Cisco dominates the router market, providing 80% of the devices that power the Internet. Routers direct packets of data along the Internet, making sure they take the quickest route. The company started with routers, but the product line soon evolved to encompass firewalls, web servers, web caches, ethernets, and other essential Internet products.

Cisco's strategy involves concentrating on three key markets: corporations and other organisations with complex networking needs, covering different locations and computer platforms; service providers such as ISPs (Internet Service Providers); and small and medium-sized businesses that need data networks with connection to the Internet or each other. The company describes itself as 'global networked business'. The global networked business model, according to Cisco, uses the network to gain competitive advantage by 'opening up the corporate information infrastructure to all key constituencies'.

Chambers arrived as CEO at Cisco in 1995. Having learned how not to run a business during spells at IBM and Wang, he put his own management theories into practice. Through the late 1990s, he made Cisco one of the most valuable companies in the world. When he started, market cap was some $9 billion. By April 2000 the company was valued at $500 billion. It briefly touched $555 billion, making it the most valuable company in the world. Chambers also delivered impressive earnings growth. For the majority of the 1990s, Cisco's revenue growth was between 30% and 50%.

One the reasons for Chambers's success is his obsessive pursuit of the customer. Customer satisfaction is paramount. When he arrived in 1995, he assumed the self-styled mantle of consumer advocate. Other industry players concur with this view of Chambers as a consumer champion. John Doerr, celebrated venture capitalist at Kleiner Perkins Caufield & Byers, noted: 'John Chambers is the most customer-focused human being you will ever meet.' Whether keeping customers happy or securing a deal, Chambers is attentive and charming. A man with old-school manners, the story goes that he is happy to take a handshake over a contract.

> *He has shaken a lot of hands. Cisco likes to grow through acquisition.*

He has shaken a lot of hands. Cisco likes to grow through acquisition. It has swallowed over 70 companies, representing an investment of more than $30 billion. 'The companies who emerge as industry leaders will be those who understand how to partner and those who understand how to acquire,' says Chambers. 'Customers today are not just looking for pinpoint products, but end-to-end solutions. A horizontal business model always beats a vertical business model. So you've got to be able to provide that horizontal capability in your product line, either through your own R&D, or through acquisitions.' Chambers prefers to integrate the staff of the acquired company into Cisco rather than lose them. This way he saves on R&D costs and adds to the Cisco talent pool.

Chambers has been banging the Internet drum across the globe. Increased productivity, cost reduction, democratisation, the dissemination of knowledge—all this and more can be yours, promises Silicon Valley's Internet evangelist. All you need to do is get connected—preferably with Cisco products. It's a convincing pitch from a man who truly believes in the power of the Net.

Cisco practises networking on a grand scale. Close to 90% of the company's business is done online. 'At Cisco we've learned there are ways to achieve productivity gains in the way that the company interfaces with its employees, customers, and suppliers, using the power of the Internet. We have changed almost every aspect of the way people work, and the average productivity increase we've experienced per Internet application we've implemented has been over 50%,' Chambers has said. 'We call this phenomenon the "network effect".'

The company says that its Internet-based customer and employee support gave it the productivity boost which helped it become one of the most profitable companies in history. An application that has attracted attention at Cisco is 'virtual close'—the ability to close the books on the company accounts every working day. It relies on integrating employees and suppliers so that they appear as one virtual company. Every evening Chambers receives a summary of the financial company's performance.

It was one such summary that set the alarm bells ringing in December 2000. Chambers, sitting at his desk, noticed a blip in the sales figures. The blip extended over the next few days. He rang round his CEOs and discovered the news was consistently grim. 'Exactly three weeks later,' says Chambers, 'we hit the wall.' It was a hard wall and Cisco was travelling fast. The company went from 70% growth to minus 30% in 45 days. Chambers was wearing his safety belt. He survived to fight on, unlike 8,500 company employees. The firing was 'the worst thing I ever had to do', says Chambers. Sounds familiar. Still, he is taking the medicine along with the remnants of the Cisco staff. He doesn't travel first class, and during 2001 he took a salary of $1.

> *Chambers, sitting at his desk, noticed a blip in the sales figures. The blip extended over the next few days.*

Cisco's main competitors have also been hit by the sudden downturn in the market. In mid-2001 Lucent Technologies, Juniper, and Sycamore were all suffering as badly or worse. Some fingers have pointed at Chambers and his management of the company. He has been blamed for the accumulation of inventory stockpiled in the warehouse. Chambers counters by explaining that he was attempting to improve delivery times. On a 5-point scale, customer satisfaction was an unheard of 4.4. The one flaw was poor delivery. But Chambers is a risk taker and likes to foster a risk-taking environment. 'Anyone who takes risks and does not make mistakes is kidding themselves—they're not taking a risk,' he has said. The company posted its first ever loss in the third quarter of 2001—$2.69 billion.

'We have learned that the peaks will be much higher in this new economy than people realised and the valleys will be much lower. And they will occur much quicker and closer together,' Chambers notes. 'Changes that used to occur in ten years now occur in one or two quarters, and changes that used to occur in one or two quarters now occur in a couple of weeks.'

Despite the most difficult trading conditions, Cisco returned to profit in 2002. The company had reorganized in recognition of its customers' changing needs and introduced an Internet Business Roadmap that gave customers a clear growth path for the future. During 2002, Cisco was very active in rolling out a product called Metropolitan Ethernet that was designed to bring the next generation of broadband services to homes and businesses in densely-populated areas. In 2003, the company announced that it was moving into the small office/home office (SOHO) market in a serious way.

CONTEXT AND CONCLUSIONS

The jury is out on John Chambers. For five years, his management of Cisco seemed exemplary. Market cap was up from $9 billion to $500 billion, with consistent revenue growth of over 30%. Then in 2001, in Chambers's own words, the company 'hit the wall'. Cue a round of savage cost cutting, including a parting of the ways with over 8,000 employees that restored profitability in 2002. On the plus side, Chambers is not alone. Countless CEOs were left wringing their hands in the wake of the dot-com meltdown and economic slowdown that ushered in the new millennium. On the minus side, Chambers had built up surplus inventory to the tune of $1 billion, sitting in the warehouse waiting for a buyer. And the less faithful might say that the market for Cisco's products will never be as buoyant again, given the more circumspect attitude taken by financiers towards Internet start-ups. The test will be over the next few years, either at Cisco or elsewhere (although Chambers has said he intends to stay at Cisco). If Chambers revives Cisco's fortunes or holds his own in a poor market, he may deserve a place in the ranks of the great CEOs.

CLOSE BUT NO CIGAR
CARLY FIORINA

Chairman and CEO of $50 billion IT company Hewlett-Packard, the world's second-largest computer maker, Fiorina's rise to the top has been a steady one. Before HP she spent 20 years at AT&T and Lucent. She spearheaded the planning and execution of Lucent's 1996 initial public offering and spin-off from AT&T. Then, as president of Lucent's global service provider business, she dramatically increased growth rate, rapidly expanded international revenues, and gained market share in every region across every product line.

She managed HP's mega merger with Compaq in 2002, once regulators and family shareholders of both companies had given it the green light.

THE BEST SOURCES OF HELP
Book:
Bunnell, David, and Adam Brate. *Making the Cisco Connection*. New York: John Wiley, 2000.

WALTER CHRYSLER

1875	Born.
1905	Attends the Chicago Auto Show.
1908	William Crapo Durant founds General Motors.
1911	Employed as works manager at Buick, part of General Motors.
1916–1919	To prevent him leaving, Durant ups his salary from $50,000 to $500,000.
1920	Leaves GM and retires.
1921–1923	Rescues Willy's-Overland, then Maxwell-Chalmers, and builds the Chrysler Six.
1924	Chrysler Six car shown during New York Auto show. Chrysler Six goes into production.
1925	Maxwell Motors becomes the Chrysler Corporation. Chrysler is president and chairman. Company turns in a profit of $17 million.
1928	Chrysler Corporation buys Dodge Brothers' dealership network. Renamed Chrysler Motors. The 1,048ft Chrysler building constructed in midtown Manhattan.
1940	Dies.

> **SUMMARY**
>
> Walter Chrysler (1875–1940) was the founder of one of the largest US automobile corporations of the 20th century, the eponymous Chrysler Motors. Even as a teenager Chrysler demonstrated a natural ability for engineering. His formidable engineering talents were later matched by his organisational and management skills. From Buick and General Motors in 1908 to the Chrysler Corporation in 1925, via Willys-Overland and Maxwell-Chalmers, Chrysler proved to be something of an automobile company doctor transforming ailing firms into healthy ones. By his death in 1940 he had put Chrysler firmly alongside Ford and General Motors as one of the big three US automobile companies.

LIFE AND CAREER

Shortly after Chrysler was born, his family moved from Wamego, Kansas, to Ellis, Kansas, where his father worked as an engineer for the Kansas Pacific Railroad. Chrysler attended the local school in Ellis, but also spent a great deal of time with his father in the engineering workshops of the Kansas Pacific Railroad, where he developed a fascination with engineering.

Upon leaving school he became an engineer with the Union Pacific Railroad (previously the Kansas Pacific Railroad) and by the age of 18 had already designed and built a miniature steam engine that ran on a homemade track.

When, aged 22, Chrysler finished his apprenticeship, he set out across the United States looking for work. He moved from job to job, working for the Rio Grande & Western Railroad, the Colorado & Southern Railroad, and the Chicago & Great Western Railroad, all the while enhancing his reputation as a skilled engineer.

It was in Oelwein, Iowa, while working as the Superintendent of Motive Power for the Chicago & Great Western Railroad, that Chrysler first saw the contraption that would change his life. Walking the streets of Oelwein one day, he came across several horseless carriages. Curiosity aroused, he made a point of attending the 1905 Chicago Auto Show.

Walter Chrysler

CONTRIBUTION

At the Auto Show Chrysler was entranced by a Locomobile Phaeton, with its red leather upholstery and white bodywork. Putting $700 down and financing the balance, Chrysler bought the car, had it shipped home, and then proceeded to take it to pieces—not once but several times. By the time Chrysler had finished dismantling and reassembling his new car he had a perfect understanding of how it was engineered.

His next career move took him to Pittsburgh, Pennsylvania, as works manager for the American Locomotive Company. It was an executive there who tipped him off about a job at the Buick automobile company. Chrysler met Buick's president, Charles W. Nash, and was taken on as works manager. It was 1911—Chrysler had entered the automobile industry.

The Buick plant in Flint, Michigan was the cornerstone of William Crapo Durant's General Motors, founded in 1908. Durant was ousted as president of GM in 1910, but staged a comeback, regaining the presidency in 1916 and firing Charles W. Nash. As Durant's fortunes rose so to did Chrysler's. Chrysler began by sorting out production at the Buick plant. Before long he was president and general manager of Buick. When Durant got wind of a rumour that Chrysler was planning to take over another auto company, Packard Motors, Durant made Chrysler an offer he couldn't refuse. He increased his salary from $50,000 a year to an astonishing $500,000.

Chrysler's meteoric ascent continued. As General Motors' vice-president in charge of production and then executive vice-president, Chrysler worked alongside Durant. But Chrysler wasn't impressed with Durant's handling of the company. Predicting disaster, he left GM in 1920. Shortly after, Durant was forced out by GM's financiers over the company's $80 million debt. Chrysler, however, had restored the good name of Buick and increased production from 40 to over 500 cars a day. In 1920, aged 45 and financially secure, he put away his desk diary and retired.

It was a brief retirement. He was approached by a group of bankers and asked to rescue the ailing Willy's-Overland company. He would have a two-year contract, the position of executive vice-president, and a free hand. Chrysler asked for one extra thing—an annual salary of $1 million. The desperate bankers agreed; Chrysler set about saving the company.

His strategy was to build a brand new car—new design, new engineering—to revive W-O's fortunes. He assembled a team of automotive experts that included the independent engineering team of Carl Breer, Owen Skelton, and Fred Zeder. Work was well advanced on the new car when the bankers got cold feet and withdrew their support. Chrysler, however, motored on, forming the Chrysler Corporation as a separate entity within W-O and retaining the original design team at the production facility in Elizabeth, New Jersey. The new car was christened the Chrysler Six.

Before long Chrysler was on the move again when bankers called him in to save yet another automobile company in trouble—Maxwell-Chalmers. Chrysler negotiated with W-O to be allowed to work with Maxwell and took a $100,000 salary and stock options. When his two-year contract was up at W-O, Chrysler left for Maxwell-Chalmers.

When he arrived, Maxwell-Chalmers was in a mess. After some wheeling and dealing Chrysler merged Maxwell and Chalmers. Then, at the helm of the new Maxwell Motors, Chrysler refocused his attention on the Chrysler Six. He brought the Chrysler Six engineering team to Maxwell, and in 1923 the new car appeared in prototype. With its fast top speed, high-compression engine, and hydraulic brakes, the Chrysler Six was truly revolutionary.

For once Chrysler struggled to raise the finance to put the car into production. Bankers were reluctant to bankroll an unproven and experimental product. Undaunted, Chrysler took the car to the 1924 New York Auto show. On discovering that, as a prototype, the car was ineligible for the show, he displayed it in the foyer of the Hotel Commodore—the show's headquarters—creating enough interest to persuade financiers Chase Securities to put up production money.

The Chrysler Six was in production in the same year. In that year alone 32,000 were sold. Maxwell Motors was restructured in 1925, emerging as the Chrysler Corporation with Chrysler as president and chairman of the board. In 1925 the company turned in a profit of $17 million. New models rolled off the Chrysler production line. In 1928 Chrysler Corporation bought Dodge Brothers with its extensive dealership network and changed its name to Chrysler Motors. With Chrysler in command, the company flourished, survived the Great Depression, and outlasted many competitors by a combination of astute management and innovative products. Chrysler remained president until 1935 and chairman until his death in 1940.

> *Maxwell Motors was restructured in 1925, emerging as the Chrysler Corporation with Chrysler as president and chairman of the board. In 1925 the company turned in a profit of $17 million.*

CONTEXT AND CONCLUSIONS

The list of recipients of *Time* magazine's Man of the Year award is dominated by politicians and statesmen, with a few notable exceptions. One of those exceptions is the *Time* magazine Man of the Year in 1928—Walter Chrysler. Alongside Henry Ford and William Crapo Durant, Chrysler was one of the greatest automobile industrialists of the first half of the 20th century.

Of the three men, Chrysler arguably represented the most complete combination of technical, entrepreneurial, and managerial ability. Few men have taken on such demanding corporate challenges so frequently. It was no coincidence that, whenever an automobile company was ailing, the man the bankers called in to save it was Chrysler.

THE BEST SOURCES OF HELP
Books:
Chrysler, Walter P., with Boyden Sparkes. *Life of an American Workman*. New York: Dodd, Mead & Co, 1950.
Breer, Carl, ed. Anthony J. Yanik. *The Birth of the Chrysler Corporation and its Engineering Legacy*. Warrendale, Pennsylvania: Society of Automotive Engineers, 1995.
Curcio, Vincent. *Chrysler: The Life and Times of an Automotive Genius*. Oxford: Oxford University Press, 2001.
Website:
Chrysler: **www.chrysler.com**

JIM CLARK

1944	Born.
1961	Joins the Navy.
1971	Gains MS in physics from Louisiana State University.
1974	Gains PhD in computing from University of Utah.
1978	Starts teaching at Stanford University.
1982	Founds Silicon Graphics.
1994	Leaves Silicon Graphics and founds Netscape.
1998	AOL acquires Netscape.
1999	Founds myCFO.com
2001	Healtheon Services becomes the third multi-billion dollar business founded by Clark.
2001	Starts project to remotely control luxury yacht Hyperion via Internet.
2002	Sells myCFO.com.

> **SUMMARY**
>
> When it comes to technology start-ups, Jim Clark is a man with the Midas touch. His companies have created billions of dollars of shareholder value. He epitomises the restless, pioneering spirit of the new economy.
>
> After a spell in the Navy, Clark embarked on a teaching career at Stanford University, expanding his interest in computer graphics research. When no one would invest in the technology he invented, he established his own company, Silicon Graphics. During his time at Silicon Graphics from 1982 to 1994, the company was at the forefront of computer graphics technology and its machines set the standard.
>
> With one success behind him and already a wealthy man, Clark teamed up in 1994 with the cherubic-faced Marc Andreessen to found Netscape. It was another huge success: the Netscape browser dominated the market for several years. With a number of other start-ups to his credit, Clark marches on. His subsequent ventures, myCFO.com, a Web-based financial adviser for high-net-worth individuals, and Healtheon services, an online healthcare business, have kept him busy since 1999.

LIFE AND CAREER

James H. Clark was born in 1944 in Plainview, Texas. Initially he showed little interest in gaining an education and at the age of 16 dropped out of school. It was 1961. One story has it that Clark was suspended for telling a teacher to 'go to hell' after being reprimanded for failing to read Samuel Taylor Coleridge's *Rime of the Ancient Mariner*. Had Clark read the poem, it might have appealed to his nautical impulse: after leaving school he promptly joined the US Navy.

Clark's lack of interest in school wasn't due to a lack of aptitude. He had a gift for maths and technology but simply wasn't ready to study at that point in his life. Military service changed that. While in the Navy Clark was required to take a standard maths test. His score was so high that the administrators suspected him of cheating and insisted he retake the test. When he repeated the feat they moved him into an area that might tax his mind a little more: computers. The Navy was also the proving ground for Clark's shrewd business brain. He ran a surreptitious loans business on the side, lending money to other sailors to tide them over until payday. At 40% interest it was a lucrative enterprise.

CONTRIBUTION

After the Navy Clark went to Louisiana State University and excelled, earning an MS in physics in 1971. In 1974 he earned a PhD in computer science at the University of Utah. At Utah Clark met Ivan Sutherland, widely regarded as the man behind interactive computer graphics. It was a field in which Clark was to have a major impact.

The pattern of Clark's early working life was that of a bright, if somewhat restless, individual seeking a challenge that would hold his attention. Seduced by a romantic notion of academic life, he embarked on a teaching career at the University of California, Santa Cruz. The romance soon wore off and he left to take up consultancy, which he found even less to his liking.

Returning to academia in 1978, Clark joined the faculty of Stanford University. In addition to his teaching duties, he had obtained funding from the US Defense Advanced Research Projects Agency (DARPA) to lead a team of students conducting research into computer graphics technology.

Clark worked with his team for three years. During that time they made several important technological breakthroughs. The team created a 'geometry engine' that shifted 3-D graphics processing from software to hardware, with the instruction set embedded into a computer chip. Clark attempted to sell the technology to established computer companies.

When no one showed any interest, Clark determined to go it alone. 'I concluded after talking to DEC and IBM and all these companies,' he said, 'that they didn't understand how to use what we had in the first place, so they would surely screw it up.' Taking six of the Stanford team with him, he left Stanford in 1982 to found Silicon Graphics (now SGI).

At Silicon Graphics the ambitious Clark drove his team to create the ultimate 3-D engine, delivering interactive, real-time 3-D computer graphics to the humble PC. When Clark resigned from SGI in 1994, the company had had eight years of an astonishing 40% annual growth, with annual revenues reaching the $2 billion mark. The company employed more than 5,000 people; the name Silicon Graphics was synonymous with the high-end computer graphics market.

SGI machines enabled designers to visualise objects by rendering them onscreen using a computer. They could then rotate them, morph them, and manipulate them to give an accurate representation of how the object would appear and behave in the real world. SGI had an impressive list of clients: NASA, British Aerospace, and the US military all used Silicon Graphics machines. When the Hollywood film industry caught on to the potential of the SGI technology, the studios used it to create out-of-this-world special effects in films such as *Jurassic Park* and *Terminator II*, as well as entirely computer-generated movies, including *Toy Story*.

In February 1994 Clark left the company that had made him rich. The split was the result of his growing frustration. SGI had become a large company: it was no longer able to move at the speed Clark wanted. His vision was to bring expensive SGI technology within the reach of the average consumer. Others at the company were unconvinced. Clark left.

He was unemployed for approximately 24 hours. On the morning he resigned, he sent an e-mail to Marc Andreessen, a brilliant young computer programmer. Clark thought that an invention of Andreessen's, the NCSA Mosaic browser, would be perfect for interactive television. At the time the Internet was in its infancy, and many saw interactive television as 'the next big thing'. Andreessen persuaded Clark that the Internet was the best market for the browser, and in 1994 they established Mosaic Communications Corporation with $6 million of Clark's money and $6 million of venture capital. It was the company that became Netscape.

Clark's genius was evident in the business plan. The strategy was a radical one: give the product—the Netscape browser—away. It was a masterstroke, and it worked. Soon the Netscape Navigator browser was familiar to virtually every Internet user. By 1996 Clark and Andreessen's company had captured over 80% of the market. If the browser was given away to noncorporate users, Clark made sure corporations paid for it and the compatible server software. At the company's IPO in August 1995 it was valued at some $2 billion, making Clark the first Internet billionaire. Had it not been for Microsoft, Netscape would have become the dominant browser on the Internet. Although initially slow to recognise the potential of the Internet, Microsoft moved decisively into the browser market. Up against the might of the Redmond-based computer giant, Netscape eventually lost ground and was sold to America Online. Despite the fall, Clark, commenting on the move to split Microsoft, argued that Microsoft should be allowed to keep its own browser as part of the Windows operating system. Having played a significant role in making the Internet the pervasive means of communication it is, Clark became even wealthier after the AOL deal.

Since then Clark's enterprising spirit has seen him involved in several start-ups, including Healtheon, Shutterfly.com, and myCFO.com. Healtheon was Clark's vehicle to overhaul the ailing US health service, and its success made it the third multi-billion dollar business he had founded. MyCFO.com, a web-based financial advisory service for high-net-worth individuals, proved successful before he sold it in 2002. And when Clark is not working hard he's playing hard, flying his stunt plane or crewing his $30 million 155-foot sailboat *Hyperion*. Since 2001, he has been working on a project to control *Hyperion* remotely via the Internet.

CONTEXT AND CONCLUSIONS
In the space of two decades Jim Clark built three incredibly successful companies. The first, Silicon Graphics, was part of the personal computer revolution; the second, Netscape, played a pivotal role in the development of the Internet; the third, Healtheon, is helping to reshape the US health service. How did he do it? Clark attributes his fortune to 'a combination of being persuasive, believing in what you're doing, having integrity...and knowing how to judge good people, because you can't afford to have anything but good people early on in a company'.

Clark knows the value of a good team, surrounding himself with the right people. 'I look for intelligence and a certain measure of humility,' he observes. 'People who are boastful or too proud may be really good, but they're not my kind of people. A business is about teams, and teams mean getting along with people. There's just not enough room for a lot of superegos in a company.' Clark then acts as a catalyst, fomenting the creativity and hard work necessary in a start-up. It is a formula that has made him one of the stars of the new economy.

THE BEST SOURCES OF HELP
Website:
myCFO.com: **www.myCFO.com**

CHRISTOS COTSAKOS

1948	Born.
1973	Receives BA in communications from Paterson State College.
1983	Graduates as MBA from Pepperdine University.
1967–1968	Serves as a rifleman in the 101st Airborne Division in Vietnam.
1973	Starts as a package handler at Federal Express in Los Angeles.
1988	Becomes vice-president for European operations.
1995	Becomes co-CEO at ACNielsen.
1996	Appointed CEO at E*Trade.
1998	Implements bold strategic plan.
1999	E*Trade reaches 1.5 million accounts, with $28 billion under management.
2000	E*Trade second largest web-based broker.
2002	Despite posting $240 million loss, Cotsakos pays himself $80 million.
2003	Resigns from E*Trade.

SUMMARY

There are few leading companies that can boast a decorated war hero as CEO: E*Trade is one of them. Christos Cotsakos made the transition from errant schoolboy to successful businessman, with the help of a few wise words from a Greek Orthodox priest. In between, he served in the US military during the Vietnam War and was decorated for his bravery. A stint at the marketing research firm of ACNielsen proved he had the management nous to succeed in business. Hired by Bill Porter in 1996 to put some fizz into the Internet operations of E*Trade Securities, a stock-brokerage firm, Cotsakos had, by 2000, built the company into the number two web-based brokerage. However, major losses in 2002, coupled with a massive and controversial $80 million personal bonus, put the pressure on Cotsakos and he resigned in 2003.

LIFE AND CAREER

The second youngest of five children, Christopher Cotsakos was born to a family of poor Greek immigrants on 29 July 1948. He grew up on the streets of Paterson, New Jersey, and, like many of the children in his neighbourhood, he was an unruly child. Caught helping himself to the communion wine at St Athanasios's Greek Orthodox church, he received a timely lecture from the priest on the responsibility of leadership. It was an incident that shaped his life thereafter. The priest's words stayed with him, as Cotsakos was both surprised and impressed to hear that he had leadership potential.

Although he may not have realised it at the time, he was already displaying the qualities that would serve him so well in business. His natural authority had already secured him the incongruous dual responsibilities of ringleader of the local gang and captain of the altar boys at St Athanasios's. It became even more evident during military service in the Vietnam War. When in March 1968 his unit was pinned down by enemy fire, Cotsakos, then aged only 19, single-handedly fought his way out, receiving a Purple Heart and Bronze Star for his heroic actions.

CONTRIBUTION

When he returned home from the war, Cotsakos attended Paterson State College in New Jersey, majoring in communications. In 1973, after graduating, he went to work for Federal Express as a package handler. It was a good time to join the company, which was undergoing a period of rapid expansion. He rose quickly through the ranks and by 1988 was in charge of European operations. Choosing to remain in Europe, he switched from FedEx to the market research company AC Nielsen, at the time a unit of the Dun & Bradstreet Corporation.

When in March 1968 his unit was pinned down by enemy fire, Cotsakos, then aged only 19, single-handedly fought his way out, receiving a Purple Heart and Bronze Star for his heroic actions.

At ACNielsen, Cotsakos was once again swiftly promoted, although his management style put a few noses out of joint along the way. 'Christos didn't follow the rules,' noted Robert Weissman, D&B's former CEO. 'He made people feel unsafe.' Weissman liked his style, however. In 1995 he promoted Cotsakos to the position of co-CEO, handing him the responsibility for putting the company in shape before it was sold by Dun & Bradstreet. It was a difficult period for Cotsakos, who struggled to find common ground with his fellow co-CEO Robert J. Lievense. In the end he left ACNielsen for another challenge at E*Trade.

This Internet share-trading company had started life as an electronic trading network, Trade Plus & Co. Trade Plus had been founded in 1982 by Bill Porter, an MIT MBA graduate, to provide trading services to the stock brokerages Fidelity, Charles Schwab, and Quick & Reilly. By 1992 it had changed its name to the E*Trade Group, and, under the name of E*Trade Securities, was providing share-dealing services to the public via AOL and CompuServe. Porter's aim was to offer a low-cost service on the back of high-volume business. Economies of scale allowed E*Trade to reduce its commission charge seven times between 1991 and 1995. In 1996 things really took off when Porter saw the potential of Internet trading, and launched E*Trade.com. He brought in Cotsakos to manage the new venture.

Although E*Trade had stolen a march on its competitors, the advantage did not last long. To survive, Cotsakos had to fight a battle on two fronts. On one side were the deep-discount brokers swarming onto the Internet and undercutting E*Trade on price. On the other were the traditional broking services such as Charles Schwab & Co, Morgan Stanley, Merrill Lynch, Prudential, and PaineWebber, pursuing a clicks-and-bricks strategy. The established brokerages charged more but provided an added-value service, and possessed strong brand image.

Luckily for E*Trade, Cotsakos was no stranger to a fight. In 1998 he decided the time was right for drastic action. The company was doing well—turning in a $7 million profit on $72 million sales—but Cotsakos believed that this belied the company's shortsighted strategy. Being a major player in the share-trading market, he realised, was not enough to secure the future of E*Trade. What was required was a bigger vision: transformation into a financial portal covering insurance, financial news, banking, and other financial sectors. The company had to become the obvious destination for anyone with an interest in online financial information and products. Such a strategy required an investment of billions of dollars in technology and marketing, at the expense of profits for some time to come. But the end, in Cotsakos's view, would justify the means. It was a bold move and carrying it off would require special qualities—resolve, single-mindedness, and excellent managerial skills. But he was confident he could see it through.

To deliver on his ambitions, Cotsakos employed his own idiosyncratic, unconventional management style. It was an approach that owed more to his experiences in the army than to conventional management textbooks. He deployed an array of unusual methods to instil his own particular brand of company culture at E*Trade. His unorthodox tactics included subjecting new members of staff to an initiation ritual in which each had to stand on a chair and reveal something 'insightful' about himself or herself. To lighten the mood, employees tended to carry around rubber chickens. Executives also were subjected to some unusual management development experiences—being sent off for some team building at a cookery school, for example.

Motivating employees and building teams is Cotsakos's speciality. Employees who aren't a good fit with the E*Trade culture are swiftly rejected by it. One new recruit who didn't last, for example, balked at standing on a chair. 'It's all about getting people excited about how they can make a difference as a person and as a team,' says Cotsakos.

To deliver on his ambitions, Cotsakos employed his own idiosyncratic, unconventional management style. It was an approach that owed more to his experiences in the army than to conventional management textbooks.

Cotsakos leads from the front, and he's a tough act to follow. He crams more into a day than many executives manage in a week. He serves on the boards of a number of leading technology companies, and even managed to juggle his job as CEO with studying for a PhD in economics at London University. He demands the same uncompromising standards from his employees. 'My job is to make people do the impossible,' says Cotsakos. 'I push people hard and I don't tolerate excuses.'

Between 1998 and 2000 Cotsakos and E*Trade made progress, but at a price. As he predicted, the company bled money and posted mounting losses. Yet it also rapidly expanded its consumer base from fewer than 100,000 to more than two million, placing it third behind Schwab and Fidelity Investments in terms of online accounts. By 1999, it had 1.5 million accounts and funds of $28 billion dollars under management. Despite terrible trading conditions in 2001, the company still managed a small second quarter operating profit, with revenues down by less than 10%—helped by drastic cuts in the marketing budget. With its customer base

Rubber chickens, standing on chairs, and cookery courses may seem strange tools with which to build a world-beating business, but so far they seem to have worked.

approaching four million, it was now the second biggest web-based stockbroker and appeared to be in good shape to bounce back even higher when stock buying picked up again. However, 2002 proved to be a disastrous year with losses of $240 million. Despite that Cotsakos paid himself a package worth $80 billion, causing outrage amongst shareholders. Although he backed down and agreed to just a token salary, it was too late and he was forced to resign in 2003.

CONTEXT AND CONCLUSIONS

Christos Cotsakos is an example of what strong leadership and force of personality can achieve in business. After a successful career at ACNielsen, he has hauled E*Trade up by its bootstraps with bold vision and unorthodox management. Rubber chickens, standing on chairs, and cookery courses may seem strange tools with which to build a world-beating business, but so far they seem to have worked. During his tenure as CEO, Cotsakos wasn't coy about his plans for E*Trade. Business is a war and he wanted to be on the winning side. As he observed in an interview: 'It's all about loyalty and trust and who you have in the foxhole with you. At E*Trade, we're an attacker, we're predatory. We believe we have a God-given right to market share.'

THE BEST SOURCES OF HELP
Website:
E*Trade: **www.etrade.com**

MICHAEL DELL

1965	Born.
1977	Aged 12, sells stamps by catalogue.
1983	Enters the University of Texas at Austin.
1984	Drops out of university to found Dell Computer.
1988	Dell Computer's first-year revenues $257.8 million.
1994	www.dell.com launched.
1997	Dell's online sales, begun in 1996, exceed $3 million a day.
2000	Online sales reach $50 million.
2000	Problems with supply of Intel chips, Dell stock price falls.
2000	Accelerates investment strategy of acquiring companies in networking and storage.
2000	Introduces computers with open-source Linux operating system.
2002	Launches managed networking services.

SUMMARY

Michael Dell (1965–) was always going to be a winner. After all, how many high school students earn more than their teachers? Dell progressed from selling newspaper subscriptions to selling computers.

Yet it wasn't the product that made him wealthy, it was the way he sold it. The Dell corporation pioneered direct selling of computers. It is also an excellent example of a company succeeding by sticking to its founding principles: build to order, keep low stocks, sell direct, understand your customer. And the Internet was a godsend for Dell. What better way of reaching the global consumer? Dell's success with the direct selling business model has made him the youngest CEO ever of a *Fortune* 500 company.

LIFE AND CAREER

Michael Dell started his business career as a boy. Born in Houston, Texas, on 23 February 1965, he came across his first commercial opportunity when he was just 12 years old. Like many children of his age, Dell was a keen collector of stamps. Where he differed from his peers was in his approach. Dell didn't swap stamps with his friends from school, he contacted the auction houses and sent them his catalogue. When anyone placed an order he went out to find the required stamps. His direct sales method and entrepreneurial acumen were an early sign of what was to come.

Dell brought new focus and intensity to his early commercial forays. As a summer job he sold newspaper subscriptions for the *Houston Post*. He quickly realised that calling people randomly using the list of telephone numbers supplied by the company was not the best way to win new business. Instead he targeted two distinct groups, newly-weds and new home-owners. He obtained lists of applicants for wedding licences from the local courthouse. From another source he compiled a list of people who had recently applied for mortgages. He then wrote a personalised message and carried out his own direct mail campaign. Subscriptions poured in. When the new school term began Dell was asked as part of an economics assignment to complete a tax return. After calculating his profits Dell estimated his income at $18,000. His teacher, assuming a mistake, corrected his return by moving the decimal point. She was dismayed to discover that the mistake was hers. Dell earned more than she did.

CONTRIBUTION

Dell's career really started while studying at the University of Texas at Austin. By then the boy who had dismantled and reassembled the motherboard of his Apple II computer at 13 had grown into a fledgling entrepreneur, making money from his computing hobby. Dell would rebuild computers and sell them. Still at university, he started a company called PCs Limited, headquartered in his dormitory room. Ignoring his parents' advice to concentrate on his studies, he decided the lure of business was too great and concentrated his efforts on his PC company.

In 1984 the Dell Computer Corporation was founded with just $1,000 in capital. With such a small investment Dell was forced to develop a business model that required little capital outlay. He decided to build to order. This eliminated the need to tie up working capital in inventory. The company carried only around 11 days' stock—and still does. Compare this to the 45 days' worth of inventory in an average, nondirect sales channel and the cost savings are obvious. Building to order also allowed Dell to cut out the middleman, retaining more profit and reducing selling costs from a typical 12% of revenue to a mere 4–6% of revenue.

Low costs and high profit margins are a recipe for an exceptional business. In its first eight years Dell Computer grew at an astonishing annual rate of 80%.

Low costs and high profit margins are a recipe for an exceptional business. In its first eight years Dell Computer grew at an astonishing annual rate of 80%. Even when it slowed down, it was still growing at over 50% a year. By the middle of 2000 its yearly revenues were up to $27 billion.

Such a successful business model has attracted its imitators. Companies such as Compaq and Gateway have adopted a similar model. None, however, seem to be able to capture the Dell magic. 'There is a popular idea now that if you reduce your inventory and build to order, you'll be just like Dell. Well, that's one part of the puzzle, but there are other parts too,' Dell has said. He explains the company's success as 'a disciplined approach to understanding how we create value in the PC industry, selecting the right markets, staying focused on a clear business model, and just executing.'

Dell has built more than a simple direct-selling company. His company's success is closely linked to its relationship with the customer. He knows that the company must not only sell but deliver. Dell Computer has made good use of its direct communication with the consumer. The result? A strong brand, low customer acquisition costs, and high customer loyalty. Dell asks his customers to complain so that he can keep the company at the cutting edge of consumer needs. The company once ran an ad that said, 'to all our nit-picky, over-demanding, ask-awkward-questions customers. Thank you, and keep up the good work'. Few computer companies—or any other company, come to that—would have the confidence to run a similarly worded ad.

With his innate enthusiasm for technology Dell was quick to realise the potential of the Internet. Harnessing its power to reach a wide audience at little cost, the company swiftly moved its selling operations online. 'The Internet for us is a dream come true,' Dell has said. 'It's like zero-variable-cost transaction. The only thing better would be mental telepathy.' The figures support the point. Dell began e-commerce in 1996. By 1997 the company's online sales exceeded $3 million a day. The comparable figure for 2000 was $50 million. Half the company's sales are Web-enabled.

When it comes to strategy Dell is no slouch. In the run-up to 2000 all the talk in the industry (apart from the Y2K worries) was about the imminent demise of the PC. Analysts predicted that PC sales would slump as consumers sought mobile computing solutions. Donald Selkin, chief investment strategist at Joseph Gunnar, the New York securities and banking firm, said of Dell Computer, 'I believe its glory days are over; I hate to say it, but it's old technology.'

Others believe that Dell's success is founded on a business model rather than a particular product. As if to prove the point, Dell has expanded into areas such as servers and storage network devices. In the quarter ending 3 April 2000, for example, sales of these products accounted for 48% of the systems sales total. There was a 100% increase in sales of storage products, and Dell's machines accounted for 40% of the worldwide industry growth in the server market. Michael Dell says, 'I believe we have the right business model for the Internet age. We have a significant lead in dealing direct with customers and suppliers.'

In 2000, he re-affirmed the company's commitment to its core strategy of beating components on price and performance, but also indicated that he was accelerating investment into networking and storage companies. He also started to offer Linux open-source operating systems on PCs, broadening the appeal of the range. In 2003, he launched Dell-managed network services to strengthen the company's position in corporate computing. Despite those changes, the company was damaged by a shortage of Intel chips in 2000 and suffered its first stock price fall.

The Dell Computer Corporation had been consistently ranked number two in the world in terms of liquidity, profitability, and growth among all computer systems companies, and number one in the United States. With that sort of performance, many a CEO would be pleased to take a bow and enjoy the applause. Michael Dell merely describes it as 'a great start'.

CONTEXT AND CONCLUSIONS

The youngest CEO ever to run a *Fortune* 500 company, Michael Dell has joined the ranks of the most revered entrepreneurs in America. He is credited as the man who took the direct sales model and elevated it to an art form. Dell Computer may not be the biggest company in the world—yet. Nor are its products the most innovative. Yet Dell has built a benchmark company, demonstrating how best to structure a business in order to reap the most reward from new technologies.

THE BEST SOURCES OF HELP
Book:
Dell, Michael, and Catherine Fredman. *Direct from Dell: Strategies That Revolutionized an Industry*. New York: HarperInformation, 2000.
Website:
Dell: **www.euro.dell.com**

WALT DISNEY

1901	Born.
1918	Tries to enlist for the First World War, aged 16, but is rejected.
1920	Creates his first original animated characters.
1925	Marries employee Lillian Bounds.
1928	Creates Mickey Mouse.
1937	First feature-length musical animation, *Snow White and the Seven Dwarfs*, premiers.
1940	Disney and over 1,000 staff occupy the Burbank Studios.
1955	Disneyland opens.
1964	Conceives Experimental Prototype Community of Tomorrow (Epcot).
1966	Dies.
1971	Disney World opens in Orlando, Florida, with Epcot to follow in 1982.

> **SUMMARY**
>
> Walt Disney (1901–1966) started with an idea for a cartoon and finished with a film studio. Over a 43-year career in Hollywood, he and his studio won 48 Academy Awards and 7 Emmys as well as a host of other awards. He pioneered the cartoon as an entertainment medium with full-length cartoon features like *Snow White and the Seven Dwarfs*, *Dumbo*, and *Fantasia*. Under his guidance the Disney entertainment machine also produced family film favourites such as *Mary Poppins* and wildlife features such as *The Vanishing Prairie* among its 100-plus films. Today the company that Disney created spans a huge entertainment industry that even his, the most fertile of imaginations, could never have conceived.

LIFE AND CAREER

Born in Chicago, Illinois, on 5 December 1901, Walt Disney was brought up on a farm near Marceline, Missouri. As a child he showed above-average ability. At the tender age of seven he sold sketches to neighbours. His interest in the arts continued at McKinley High School in Chicago where he concentrated on drawing and photography. In the evenings he studied at the Chicago Academy of Fine Arts.

When the First World War arrived, Disney tried to enlist in the US Army. Unable to produce his birth certificate, he was rejected as being too young. Instead he travelled to France with the Red Cross and spent his time driving an ambulance decorated with his own cartoons.

Settling in Kansas City after the war, Disney embarked on a career as a cartoonist. In 1920, while working for Kansas City Film Ads, he created his first original animated characters. In May 1922 he started his own company, Laugh-O-Grams. The laughs were short-lived as the company quickly ran into financial difficulties, and Disney decided to leave. Emboldened by the spirit of youth, he left for Hollywood armed only with his drawing equipment, an idea for a cartoon, and the suit he stood up in.

CONTRIBUTION

Disney's new venture began where so many great US corporate dreams have started: in a garage. Together with his brother Roy, Disney launched Disney Brothers Studio. He started out with $500 borrowed from his uncle, $200 from Roy, and $2,500 from his parents, who mortgaged their house to find the money. Before long Disney was out of the garage and into the back of a Hollywood real estate office. The first work that he sold was a series of featurettes based on Lewis Carroll's Alice character.

Mickey Mouse was born in 1928. There are several versions of how Disney came up with the idea of the little mouse. The most frequently recounted story is that a flash of inspiration came to him on the way home from a disastrous business meeting in which he was forced to relinquish control of his most successful character at the time—Oswald the Rabbit. Daydreaming on the train to Hollywood, he recalled the mice that had been frequent visitors to his old office. Disney wanted to call his new character Mortimer. His wife—displaying a more acute instinct for marketing—persuaded him to christen his creation Mickey Mouse. Mickey made his debut in the first-ever sound cartoon *Steamboat Willie*. It was November 1928 and Disney was just 26.

Disney continued to innovate within the cartoon medium. *Silly Symphonies* introduced Technicolor to cartoons, and in 1937 he premiered the first feature-length musical animation, *Snow White and the Seven Dwarfs*. Disney took a huge risk with *Snow White*. The film was the first of its kind. The $2 million it cost to make was a huge amount in the 1930s, particularly in the middle of the Great Depression. Fortunately for Disney, the gamble paid off, and the studios followed *Snow White* with other full-length animated classics including *Pinocchio*, *Dumbo*, and *Bambi*.

By 1940 Disney and over 1,000 staff had occupied the Burbank Studios. For some time Disney's role had been that of a catalyst; he no longer drew any of the studio's output, nor had he done so since the early 1920s. In his own words he was 'a little bee. I go from one area to another, and gather pollen and sort of stimulate everyone'. The worker bees in Disney's hive weren't always impressed with him. Many resented his reluctance to acknowledge the contribution of the studio artists. Indeed, he wasn't an easy man to work for. Frequently neurotic and obsessive, he imposed strict rules at his studio. Anyone heard swearing in mixed company was sacked on the spot, and despite Disney's own preference for a pencil moustache, facial hair was forbidden for all male employees.

During the 1940s the Disney studio became embroiled in a series of labour disputes. Disney was also a member of the Motion Picture Alliance for the Preservation of American Ideals—an organisation which sought out 'communists, radicals, and crackpots' in the movie business. In 1947 he testified before the House Un-American Activities Committee, denouncing a number of employees at his studios as communist sympathisers. The fallout from these events took years to dissipate.

The Second World War had temporarily sidelined the Walt Disney studio's output. During the war most of the Disney facilities were given over to the making of propaganda and health films commissioned by the US government. The studio's small nongovernmental output consisted of comedy shorts to pep up morale. After the war Disney continued to hone his craft and vary the studio's productions. Cartoons were joined by films combining live action and animation, and 'true-life adventures' portraying animals in their natural habitat.

In 1955 Disney took his brand in a new direction. The Disneyland theme park in Anaheim, California, was to be a living embodiment of the Disney movies; a magical land where children and adults could mingle with their favourite cartoon stars from the big screen. Disney's investment was $17 million. It was another big risk for him, but Disneyland was a great hit, with Mickey and his friends greeting a million people in its first seven weeks and many millions more since.

At the same time, Disney continued to push his products on television. He supplied television with the *Wonderful World of Color*, exploiting the lack of programming in what was still a comparatively new medium, colour television.

> *The Disneyland theme park in Anaheim, California, was to be a living embodiment of the Disney movies; a magical land where children and adults could mingle with their favourite cartoon stars from the big screen.*

From the mid-1960s onwards one project consumed the final years of Disney's life. The plan was to build a Disney World with a social dimension. Disney was interested in solving the problems afflicting urban living in America. His answer was the Experimental Prototype Community of Tomorrow (Epcot) — the equivalent of a gigantic Ideal Home Exhibition for urban life.

Disney World opened in October 1971. Located in Florida, it was built over 43 square miles and included an amusement theme park, hotel complex, airport, and, 11 years later, the futuristic Epcot Center. Like its Californian relation, Disney World was a success. Disney, however, was not present to witness the fruition of his plans. He died on 15 December 1966.

CONTEXT AND CONCLUSIONS

Walt Disney is an icon of the 20th century and an American folk hero. To many, his name conjures up an image of wholesome homespun entertainment laced with good old-fashioned American family values. While this may have been true of his studio's output, Disney himself was a tough, tenacious, and driven businessman with a sizeable ego.

His innovative work ranged from celebrated animated feature films to futuristic amusement parks. The magic of Disney is, however, nowhere more evident than in the fact that such a complicated and often difficult man could attract such talented individuals to his studios and somehow persuade them to produce their very best work. Critics may carp about his management style, but the vision and drive that spawned a billion-dollar international entertainment company was down to one man: Walt Disney.

THE BEST SOURCES OF HELP
Books:
Byrne, Eleanor, and Martin McQuillan. *Deconstructing Disney*. London: Pluto Press, 1999.
Nardo, Don. *Walt Disney*. San Diego, California: Lucent Books, 2000.
Schickel, Richard. *The Disney Version: The Life, Times, Art, and Commerce of Walt Disney*. Chicago: Ivan R. Dee, 1997.
Website:
Disney.co.uk: **www.disney.co.uk**

JAMES BUCHANAN DUKE

1856	Born.
1881	Family business starts cigarette production.
1890	The big five tobacco companies merge to form the American Tobacco Company.
1905	Duke brothers start their own hydroelectric generating business, the Southern Power Company (becomes Duke Power in 1927).
1911	The American Tobacco Company is trustbusted and broken up into a new American Tobacco Company, Liggett and Myers, P. Lorillard, and R.J. Reynolds.
1924	Duke Endowment fund established.
1925	Dies.

SUMMARY

James Buchanan Duke (1856–1925), or 'Buck', as he was commonly known, was born into a tobacco business dynasty. His father, Washington Duke, had over many years and despite the interruption of the American Civil War built up a thriving tobacco business in Orange County, North Carolina. Had it not been for Buck Duke the business might well have remained a successful but parochial tobacco company. Under his guidance, however, W. Duke, Sons and Company swiftly rose to cultivate a global tobacco empire culminating in victory in the 'tobacco wars' and Duke's elevation to president of the American Tobacco Company. When the US government dissolved the tobacco trust in 1911, a major setback for Duke, he merely switched his attentions to the energy business. The Southern Power Company, which he founded with his brothers in 1905, subsequently became Duke Power and remains so to this day.

LIFE AND CAREER

Duke was born near Durham, North Carolina. His education—his academic education, that is—took place at New Garden School in Greensboro, North Carolina, and the Eastman Business College in Poughkeepsie, New York. A more direct form of education took place in the family business. The Duke family farmed and produced tobacco products, chiefly smoking tobacco. Under pressure from local competition, however, they eventually shifted to the production of cigarettes in 1881.

Initially this manufacturing process was carried out by hand and was a slow and cumbersome one. Even an expert could roll only four cigarettes a minute. As cigarettes became more popular the tobacco companies sought to mechanise the process. The Allen and Ginter Company of Richmond, Virginia, offered $75,000 to any person who could invent a practical cigarette-making machine. The offer was taken up in 1880 by 18-year-old James Bonsack, who developed a machine of this type. However, Allen and Ginter discarded it after a trial period.

Sensing an opportunity, W. Duke, Sons and Company took up the machine (two, in fact). Once again the invention disappointed, but Buck Duke and a young engineer, William O'Brien, were able to alter it and make it reliable, cutting the cost of manufacturing cigarettes in half.

CONTRIBUTION

At the age of 28 the young Buck Duke was called upon to open a branch of the family business in New York. Within five years the New York factory was rolling out half the entire country's total production of cigarettes. His talent for marketing helped. According to later commentators, Duke 'was always an aggressive advertiser, devising new and startling methods which dismayed his competitors, and was always willing to spend in advertising a proportion of his profits which seemed appalling to more conservative manufacturers'.

Duke wasn't allowed to celebrate his success for long as the 'tobacco wars' loomed. Fought between the five principal cigarette manufacturers, the tobacco wars were a bitterly contested struggle for supremacy in the market. The four main combatants were the Allen and Ginter Company of Richmond, the F.S. Kinney Company and the Goodwin Company, both of New York, and William S. Kimball and Company of Rochester. Together with the Duke company these manufacturers produced 90% of North America's cigarettes in the 1880s. Each company thought that it could dominate the market, and an advertising war ensued. When no clear winner emerged, it became apparent that the most sensible approach would be to staunch the flow of spending and merge the five companies.

Although James Duke founded a power company that still survives to this day, as well as an endowment trust that has handed out billions of dollars to its beneficiaries, he is best remembered for the part he played in establishing the tobacco industry.

When the smoke cleared in 1890, the five companies had gone. In their place stood the result of the merger—the American Tobacco Company—with Duke at its helm as president. This tobacco giant became known as the 'tobacco trust'. During the following decade the victorious Duke steered the American Tobacco Company to global dominance.

In 1901 he visited Britain to thwart the transatlantic competition. In the space of a few days he bid for both Players and Ogdens, two large cigarette manufacturers. He succeeded in buying Ogdens, and this prompted the formation of the Imperial Tobacco Company to fight off Duke's unwanted attentions. Duke in turn formed the British American Tobacco company.

Eventually, the American Tobacco Company fell victim to its own burning ambition. In 1911 the United States Supreme Court, in the trust-busting spirit of the times, ordered the dissolution of the tobacco trust as a 'combination in restraint of trade'. At the time of its break-up, American Tobacco had 80% of the market and revenues of some $325 million. From the ashes of the tobacco trust grew four major tobacco corporations: a new American Tobacco Company, Liggett and Myers, P. Lorillard, and R.J. Reynolds.

While Buck Duke was conquering the tobacco markets, his eldest brother, Benjamin Newton, was wrapping up the textile market. The Duke family had been involved in textiles as far back as 1892. As the textile empire grew, so too did the need for cheap power. This encouraged the Dukes, including Buck, to start up their own hydroelectric generating business, the Southern Power Company (subsequently renamed Duke Power), in 1905. As with everything else the Dukes touched, the energy business became very successful and before long was supplying electricity to over 300 cotton mills, plus factories, towns, and cities in the Piedmont region of North and South Carolina.

Duke was an ardent Methodist and conducted his professional life in a manner befitting his religious beliefs. He was the richest member of the Duke dynasty, and in later life he embarked on a philanthropic spree. In 1924 he established the Duke Endowment as a permanent trust fund. The prime beneficiary of the fund was Trinity College, a Methodist-related institution founded in part by Duke's father. A new university was built around Trinity College and renamed Duke University. The Duke Endowment, with offices in Charlotte, North Carolina, remains to this day one of the largest foundations in the United States. It has distributed more than one billion dollars.

James Duke died in New York on 10 October 1925, and is interred on the campus of Duke University.

CONTEXT AND CONCLUSIONS

Although James Duke founded a power company that still survives to this day, as well as an endowment trust that has handed out billions of dollars to its beneficiaries, he is best remembered for the part he played in establishing the tobacco industry. With the benefit of hindsight, it is clear that Buck Duke was successful in producing and marketing what turned out to be a pernicious product. Even so, he was a tenacious and formidable businessman with considerable marketing acumen.

Duke summed it up: 'I have succeeded in business not because I have more natural ability than many people who have not succeeded, but because I have applied myself harder and stuck to it longer.'

THE BEST SOURCES OF HELP
Book:
Nall, James O. *The Tobacco Night Riders of Kentucky and Tennessee, 1905–1909*. Kuttawa, Kentucky: McClanahan Publishing House, 1991.
Websites:
The Duke Endowment Non-Profit Foundation: **www.dukeendowment.org**
Duke Energy: **www.duke-energy.com**

WILLIAM CRAPO DURANT

1861	Born.
1905	Takes control of Buick Motor Company.
1908	Founds General Motors.
1910	Loses control of General Motors but remains as vice-president.
1911	Founds Chevrolet Motor Company.
1920	Ousted from General Motors.
1921	Founds Durant Motors.
1933	Durant Motors files for bankruptcy.
1936	Personally bankrupted.
1947	Dies.

> **SUMMARY**
>
> William Crapo Durant (1861–1947) was one of the most fascinating characters in the history of the automobile industry. He was a brilliant entrepreneur whose life was a commercial roller-coaster ride.
>
> Not long out of school, Durant went to work for the Flint City Waterworks and ended up saving it from financial ruin. He made a million-dollar fortune in his thirties and took control of the year-old Buick Motor Company in 1905. The remainder of Durant's life was a series of triumphant highs and desperate lows. He formed General Motors in 1908, lost control in 1910, founded the Chevrolet Motor Company in 1911, and regained control of General Motors in 1917—but by 1920 he had been ousted once more. He set up Durant Motors in 1921, lost control following the Wall Street crash, and was declared personally bankrupt in 1936. In all, it was an extraordinary career befitting an extraordinary man.

LIFE AND CAREER

Durant was born in Boston, Massachusetts, in 1861. In 1875 he moved with his mother and sister to Flint in Michigan, a town that would be at the heart of the emerging US automobile industry.

Although bright, Durant compiled an undistinguished academic record—he left school at 16 over a dispute with the school headmaster. He obtained work in a lumberyard owned by a relative and soon moved on, selling medicine, then cigars. After a series of jobs in real estate, book-keeping, fire insurance, and, improbably, a spell as co-owner of an ice-rink, he came to rest at the Flint City Waterworks. The waterworks at the time was an ailing business, but Durant soon turned it around and restored it to profitability. He was barely 25.

Having cut his teeth on this initial enterprise, Durant went into business with another young man, Dallas Dort. The two bought out a local businessman with $1,500 borrowed from the bank and in 1886 founded the Flint Road Cart Company (later Durant-Dort Carriage Company). Their main product, a new two-wheeled horse-drawn carriage, proved spectacularly popular, with sales peaking at 75,000 in 1895. Durant and Dort earned enough money to retire, but for Durant, still in his thirties, it was just the beginning.

Between 1901 and 1904 the newly wealthy Durant spent much of his time in New York learning the finer points of finance and stockbroking. It was an interest that was to cost him dear in future years.

In 1905, sensing that the days of the horse-drawn cart might be coming to an end, Durant bought into the year-old Buick Motor Company. On the strength of the automobile designed by David Buick, he raised $1.5 million in investment. David Buick, the Scottish-born inventor, left the company prematurely in 1906 and died a poor man.

CONTRIBUTION

Durant adopted an autocratic management style from the start. As it turned out, his drive, energy, and domineering approach to business would be the perfect recipe to grow companies, but proved ineffective at moving those companies on to the next stage of development.

Buick survived the national economic crisis of 1907 which bankrupted many other small automobile companies. To protect the business Durant sought mergers with his competitors, and approached the automobile manufacturers Henry Ford and Ransom Olds. Both were interested, but only if Durant put his own money up-front. This Durant was reluctant to do. Instead he bought up a disparate collection of smaller companies, and, incorporating Buick, he formed General Motors (GM) in September 1908.

As Durant continued to acquire automobile companies, including Oldsmobile and Cadillac, GM took on more debt. By 1910 the company owned over 20% of the industry, but it had also run into financial difficulties. Bankers refused to finance the acquisition of Ford, and loaned GM the capital it needed to continue operations only on the condition that Durant stepped down from management. A board of five trustees replaced him; Durant remained as vice-president.

The resilient Durant merely moved on to his next deal. In August 1911 he formed Mason Motor Corporation and the Little Motor Car Company. Then, having persuaded founder William Little and racing driver associate Louis Chevrolet to stay with the firm, he incorporated the Chevrolet Motor Company in November 1911. Soon the Chevrolet car was in production; by 1915 Chevrolet Motor Company's net profit was some $1.3 million.

While Durant was building his new company, his old one was in trouble. General Motors was fighting for market share in an industry in which its rivals were undercutting it substantially. Incredibly, by 1917—with the assistance of the du Pont brothers—Durant had wrested back the presidency of General Motors by acquiring 450,000 of GM's 768,733 shares. Durant was also fortunate to meet a rising star of the automobile industry, Alfred Sloan Jr, who was also to become a business legend.

General Motors Company was renamed the General Motors Corporation, and Durant once more assumed dictatorial command of his disparate collection of companies. General Motors continued to prosper, and during the First World War Durant signed a deal with the US government to supply equipment for the war effort. Despite the company's success, however, Durant was approaching the end of his on-off relationship with General Motors. When the US post-war economy hit the buffers, Durant once more found himself and GM in financial difficulties. GM stock, which had risen 5,500% between 1914 and early 1920, nose-dived. In the nine months from March to November 1920, GM stock fell by 68%, losing over 30% of its value in one month alone. Durant tried to support the share price by buying GM stock on the market, as well as from friends whom he had persuaded to invest in the company. The result for Durant was disaster. Not only did he lose control of his beloved company, being replaced by Pierre du Pont in 1920, he also lost most of his personal fortune.

Durant bounced back one last time, founding the eponymous Durant Motors in 1921 with the help of money from friends—including, ironically, the du Pont family. By May 1921 the Durant Four was on the market, and by the middle of the year the company had received 30,000 orders, worth $31 million. The company went on to produce innovative vehicles such as the four-cylinder Star. Now in his sixties, Durant steered his company successfully through the 1920s, negotiating personal setbacks such as the death of his mother and his own illness resulting from a train crash. During this time he also campaigned in favour of prohibition and developed an interest in politics.

> *It was the Wall Street crash of 1929 that finally put paid to Durant's career in business. Once again the bankers came knocking on his door, and once again he found himself over-extended.*

It was the Wall Street crash of 1929 that finally put paid to Durant's career in business. Once again the bankers came knocking on his door, and once again he found himself over-extended. This time, his personal fortune exhausted, he was forced to sell the shares in his company, and in 1933 Durant Motors filed for bankruptcy. Finally, in February 1936, Durant filed for personal bankruptcy, declaring debts of $914,000. Although he tried to get other ventures off the ground, Durant's entrepreneurial days were over. He died on 18 March 1947, in New York, in the same year as his great rival Henry Ford.

CONTEXT AND CONCLUSIONS

Durant was entertainingly reckless and sometimes brilliant. His idiosyncratic approach is summed up in one story. Oldsmobile was not planning any new models when it was taken over by GM. Then Durant arrived at the Oldsmobile factory in Lansing in a Buick Model 10. He ordered that its body be removed and sawed in half and then he reassembled the pieces, placed them a little further apart, and announced his plans: 'We'll make a car a little wider than this Buick. We'll have it a little longer: more leg room. Put your regular hood and radiator on it. It will look like an Olds and it will run. Paint it, upholster it—and there's your Oldsmobile for the coming year.'

Durant's seat-of-the-pants management style suited the fledgling days of the car industry, but it was increasingly ill-suited when the going became corporate. 'In bringing General Motors into existence, Mr Durant had operated as a dictator,' said Alfred Sloan Jr. 'But such an institution could not grow into a successful organization under a dictatorship. Dictatorship is the most effective way of administration, provided the dictator knows the complete answers to all questions. But he never does and he never will. That is why dictatorships eventually fail. If General Motors were to capitalize on its wonderful opportunity, it would have to be guided by an organization of intellects. A great industrial organization requires the best of many minds.'

In many ways Durant was the archetypal entrepreneur. He loved the deal, he loved selling, and he loved making things happen. His management style, however, was autocratic, dictatorial, and problematical when he was trying to move his companies on from the start-up stage. His life was the perfect example of the tightrope entrepreneurs tread between success and failure. It was his maverick streak that made him brilliant and led to the creation of the largest automobile manufacturer in the world, General Motors. And it was the same maverick streak that finally bankrupted him.

THE BEST SOURCES OF HELP
Book:
Madsen, Axel. *The Deal Makers: How William C. Durant Made General Motors*. Chichester: John Wiley, 1999.
Website:
General Motors: **www.gm.com**

GEORGE EASTMAN

1854	Born.
1874	Starts work at the Rochester Savings Bank on $15 per week.
1878	Takes up photography.
1880	Patents a dry plate and a machine for mass-producing it.
1881	Takes Henry Strong as partner.
1884	The Eastman Dry Plate and Film Company incorporated.
1885	Advertises his revolutionary new photographic film.
1888	The word KODAK registered as a trademark.
1899	'Wage dividend' strategy implemented.
1919	Hands one third of his company holdings—$10 million—to his employees.
1932	Dies.

> **SUMMARY**
>
> 'You push the button, we do the rest.' The well-known advertising phrase was coined by George Eastman (1854–1932), the US industrialist who brought photography to the masses. Before Eastman's intervention, photography was the province of a small number of specialists who could both understand and physically manoeuvre the cumbersome technical machinery necessary to take a small picture. Eastman reduced photography to a simple process, making it accessible to all. In addition to his role as an innovator, he brought enlightened management practices to his company, the Eastman Kodak Company—practices that were far ahead of their time. During his tenure the Eastman photographic empire grew from one assistant to over 13,000 employees and from a small room to the 55-acre, 95-building Kodak Park Works in Rochester, New York State.

LIFE AND CAREER

The youngest of three children, Eastman was born in the village of Waterville, 20 miles south-west of Utica, in upstate New York. Aged five, Eastman moved with his family to Rochester. Sadly, his father died unexpectedly, leaving the Eastman family in financial straits.

Finishing school at 14, Eastman was forced to get a job to contribute to the family finances. After a period with an insurance firm, he decided to study accounting at home in the evenings to increase his chances of earning more than $5 a week. In 1874, five years after starting in insurance, his studies paid off when he was offered a position as a junior clerk at the Rochester Savings Bank on a weekly salary of over $15.

CONTRIBUTION

Eastman's life-changing moment came at the age of 24. He was planning a holiday to Santo Domingo when a colleague suggested making a photographic record of the trip. Eastman bought the equipment needed to take a photograph using state-of-the-art wet-plate technology. This comprised a camera the size of a 21-inch computer monitor and tripod, together with the glass plates on which the images were captured, and the chemicals, glass tanks, plate holder, and other paraphernalia required for developing them. There was also a tent in which the developing had to take place before the wet plates with the photographic emulsion on could dry out.

George Eastman

To learn how to use all the equipment cost $5 — a week's wages for Eastman only a few years earlier.

Eastman never made it to Santo Domingo. Instead he became obsessed with photography. Before long he was busy perfecting a dry-plate process in which a photographic plate was covered with a veneer of a special gelatin emulsion. This emulsion remained sensitive even when it was dry, enabling the plate to be exposed whenever the photographer wished, unlike the wet-plate process in which the print had to be developed immediately. It was an idea that Eastman had read about in a British magazine. He took the idea, perfected it, and in 1880, after three years of experimentation, patented a dry plate and a machine for mass-producing it. He gave up his job at the bank and at the beginning of 1881 took on a partner, Henry Strong.

> *Eastman never made it to Santo Domingo. Instead he became obsessed with photography.*

Quick to recognise the commercial possibilities of his innovation, Eastman leased a building on State Street, Rochester, and began to turn out dry plates for other photographers. Early on the company was faced with a crisis when the dry plates provided to dealers proved defective. Eastman recalled all the faulty plates and replaced them with good ones. 'Making good on those plates took our last dollar,' he later said. 'But what we had left was more important — reputation.' In 1884 the Eastman Dry Plate and Film Company was incorporated.

It dawned on Eastman that he could do more than make life easier for professional photographers. He could, in his own words, 'make the camera as convenient as the pencil'.

When Eastman perfected the transparent roll film and roll holder, the days of cumbersome plate photography were numbered. Photography was at last within reach of the amateur. Eastman took a hand in all aspects of promoting his new photographic film. He wrote the ads and came up with the famous slogan: 'You push the button, we do the rest.' He even dreamt up the word Kodak, registering the trademark in 1888, and devised the yellow colour scheme associated with it. Its origins have been a subject of speculation ever since, but Eastman appears to have invented the name out of thin air. 'I devised the name myself,' he told his biographer. 'The letter "K" had been a favourite with me — it seems a strong incisive sort of letter. It became a question of trying out a great number of combinations of letters that made words starting and ending with K. The word Kodak is the result.'

The KODAK camera was released in 1888 and before long KODAK advertising was inescapable. One of the first electric advertising signs in London's Piccadilly bore the legend KODAK. In 1892 the company was renamed the Eastman Kodak company of New York.

Eastman built his business using an enlightened humanitarian management style far removed from that of some of his contemporaries. In 1899 he distributed to his entire workforce a substantial sum from his own pocket. It was the first act of Eastman's 'wage dividend' strategy, a plan to reward employees in proportion to the dividend paid on the company stock. Continuing in the same vein, in 1919 he handed a third of his company holdings — worth some $10 million — to his employees. At the same time he instituted retirement annuities, life insurance, and disability benefits.

George Eastman

George Eastman's philanthropy extended beyond the confines of his corporation. The Massachusetts Institute of Technology (MIT) was particularly favoured as two of its graduates, Frank Lovejoy and Darragh de Lancey, had become valued assistants to Eastman. He gave the institute $20 million under the name of 'Mr Smith'— and for years after there was intense speculation over the identity of the mysterious benefactor. Eastman was confident enough of his anonymity to join in a toast to Mr Smith at an annual MIT alumni dinner.

On one day alone in 1924 Eastman signed away $30 million to the University of Rochester, MIT, Hampton University, and Tuskegee Institute. As he laid down the pen he said, 'Now I feel better.'

In his final years Eastman was plagued by disability resulting from damage to the lower spinal cord. His inability to lead an active life frustrated him so much that he shot himself on 14 March 1932. He was 77.

CONTEXT AND CONCLUSIONS

Eastman took a cumbersome scientific process and turned it into a commercial mass-market product. Through his pioneering and innovative work on photographic technology he brought the means of capturing the moment on film to the general public at a price it could afford. Eastman was also the father of a particular type of 'trust what's in the box' branding. With its suggestion that consumers simply need to provide their imagination to complement its technology, Microsoft's 'Where do you want to go today?', for instance, is a modern echo of that first Kodak promise, as is 'Intel Inside'. Both draw on Eastman's early inspiration that consumers could be persuaded to trust the brand to take care of the technological side, leaving them free to personalise the product to suit their own lives.

Eastman's slogan captured a turning point in the history of consumerism unlike any other. Previously consumers had understood—even if only at a rudimentary level—how the products they bought worked. But in the late 19th and early 20th century, an explosion of new and technically complex inventions—which included the telephone, the electric light bulb, and film processing—changed the situation forever.

An enlightened manager, Eastman introduced business practices well ahead of his time. He recognised the importance of crisis management when faced with complaints from customers. He also understood that acknowledging the contributions of the workforce with remuneration above and beyond their basic salary would in turn benefit the company. Few companies the size of Eastman Kodak were forward-thinking enough to implement employee share-ownership schemes and the variety of employment benefits he instituted.

THE BEST SOURCES OF HELP
Books:
Ackerman, Carl W., and Edwin R. Seligman. *George Eastman: Founder of Kodak and the Photography Business*. Boston: Houghton Mifflin Co, 1930.

Brayer, Elizabeth. *George Eastman: A Biography*. Baltimore, Maryland: Johns Hopkins University Press, 1996.

Collins, Douglas. *The Story of Kodak*. New York: H.N. Abrams, 1990.
Website:
Kodak.co.uk: **www.kodak.co.uk**

THOMAS ALVA EDISON

1847	Born.
1854	Family moves to Port Huron, Michigan.
1859–62	Sells newspapers on the Grand Trunk Railway.
1863	Works as a telegraph operator; travels across the United States.
1868	Patents his first invention, an electric vote recorder.
1869	Takes up inventing full time, moves to New York, and starts his first business, making telegraph equipment.
1871	Opens a factory and laboratory in Newark, New Jersey.
1874	Develops a quadruplex system for the telegraph.
1876	Moves to Menlo Park, New Jersey.
1877	Invents the phonograph.
1879	Develops the first commercially viable electric light bulb.
1882	Opens Pearl Street Central Power Station in New York.
1889	Forms Edison General Electric, and invents the kinetograph (an early motion picture camera).
1892	Edison General Electric merges with Thomson-Houston to create General Electric. Edison sells his interest.
1910	Invents a nickel–iron–alkaline storage battery.
1931	Dies.

> **SUMMARY**
>
> 'Genius is 1% inspiration and 99% perspiration,' declared Thomas Alva Edison (1847–1931), the US inventor and entrepreneur. It was a maxim he clearly lived by. Unlike many inventors, Edison was a great businessman. By the end of his extraordinary career he had accumulated 1,093 US and 1,300 foreign patents. The inventor of the phonograph and the incandescent light bulb also found time to start up or control 13 major companies. Directly or indirectly, his endeavours led to the creation of well-known corporations like General Electric and RCA. Consolidated Edison is still listed on the New York Stock Exchange.

LIFE AND CAREER

Thomas Edison was born in the town of Milan, Erie County, Ohio, of Dutch and Scottish extraction. The youngest of seven children, he was effectively an only child since his siblings were much older. His schoolteacher mother was loath to let the young Edison out of her sight and educated him mainly at home.

He was a voracious reader. Newton's *Principia Mathematica*, Parker's *Natural and Experimental Philosophy*, and Gibbon's *Decline and Fall of the Roman Empire* had all been devoured before he reached the age of 12. It was a pattern that continued as Edison embarked on a lifetime of discovery and self-education.

From an early age he displayed an entrepreneurial spirit. When, due to economic hardship, the family was forced to move to Port Huron, near Detroit, he sold vegetables from his home garden, operated a newspaper concession on the Grand Trunk Railroad, and eventually printed his own paper, the *Grand Trunk Herald*. In his spare time he conducted chemical experiments. In one particular episode, he set fire to a train's boxcar. This mishap aroused such anger in the guard, who had to put out the fire and burnt his hands in the process, that he struck Edison on the ear, bursting his eardrum and leaving him partially deaf.

CONTRIBUTION
Telegraphy turned out to be the catalyst for Edison's greatness. He was a natural with the Morse key, becoming one of the fastest transcribers of his day. As a night-duty telegrapher, he was required to key the number six every hour to confirm he was still manning the wire. Instead he invented a machine that automatically keyed the number and he spent the nights indulging himself at local bars. Sacked from a succession of jobs, he crossed the United States working as a freelance telegrapher, finally coming to rest in New York. He had by this time filed for his first patent: an automatic vote recorder for the Massachusetts Legislature.

It was in New York that Edison formed his first partnership, with Frank Pope, a noted telegraphic engineer, to exploit the potential of their inventions. The partnership was subsequently absorbed by Gold & Stock, a company controlled by Marshall Lefferts, former president of the American Telegraph Company, who paid $20,000 to the two partners for this privilege. Recognising Edison's ingenuity, Lefferts conducted a side-deal with him, securing Edison's independent patents for the then princely sum of $30,000.

In 1870, with the benefit of some financial security, Edison hired the talents of Charles Batchelor, an English mathematician, and John Kruesi, a Swiss machinist. He signed patent agreements with Gold & Stock and Western Union, took on a business partner, William Unger, moved into a four-storey building at Ward Street, Newark, New Jersey, and started inventing on a grand scale. The fertile mix of minds at Ward Street quickly produced a stock printer, quadruplex telegraphy, and a machine to enable the rapid decoding of Morse.

By 1876 the 29-year-old Edison had 45 inventions to his name and was worth some $400,000. He was also married to Mary Stilwell. Domestic life did little to change his work habits. Indeed he appeared to work even longer hours. Edison was notorious for his devotion to seeking a solution to the problem in hand. Not only would he work, sleep, and eat at the company premises, but he would lock the lab doors and tell his staff they were staying until they arrived at an answer.

The 1870s were the most creative phase of Edison's life. Needing to expand his premises he moved into buildings at Menlo Park, New Jersey. It was there that he and his team perfected the phonograph. The patents were filed in December 1877, but developing a commercially viable product proved difficult. Finally the phonograph came to market in a selection of models from large to miniature, motor-driven or hand-cranked. The product was a huge success—so much so that Edison's creditors began creeping out of the woodwork.

Barely pausing to draw breath, Edison continued to invent. In early 1877 he began experimenting with incandescent filaments and glass bulbs. Some time before developing the light bulb, he managed to persuade a consortium that he could design a marketable lighting system based on such a product. As a result he signed a rights and remuneration agreement that laid the foundation for the Edison Electric Light Company.

In reality he was far from developing this product. Time passed with Edison making favourable noises about progress while actually making little headway in the lab. Feeling the pressure, at one point he retired to a cupboard under the stairs, took a dose of morphine, and slept for 36 hours.

It was on Wednesday 12 November 1879 that Edison finally lit a bulb that lasted long enough to be considered of commercial value. It lasted for 40 hours 20 minutes and within two months Edison had extended its lifetime to 600 hours. Countless visitors trekked to Menlo Park to gaze in wonder at the lights that lit the roadway. Sadly, what followed for Edison was not the triumph of invention but a period of protracted patent litigation that lasted over ten years.

The invention of the light bulb and the formation of the Edison Electric Light Company mark the pinnacle of Edison's achievements. He did continue to invent. In the years that followed, a succession of innovations emerged: DC generators, the first electric lighting system, electrical metering systems, alkaline storage batteries, cement manufacturing equipment, synchronised sound and moving pictures, and submarine detection by sound. His labs also hosted a great number of prodigious minds, most notably Nikola Tesla, famed for his work on the Tesla coil and AC induction motors. The wizard of Menlo Park, however, never quite recaptured the brilliance of his earlier years. Edison died, working to the last, on Sunday 18 October 1931.

CONTEXT AND CONCLUSIONS

Part of Edison's genius lay in the realisation that innovation alone was insufficient for commercial success. Edison focused on creating a commercially viable product. To do so, he assembled a team of brilliant minds at Menlo Park. In effect he created the first product research lab—a forerunner of facilities such as the celebrated Xerox PARC at Palo Alto, California. It was a practical and commercial approach to invention that proved immensely successful.

Edison's pragmatism also extended to patenting his ideas. He understood the value of intellectual property and the importance of being able to assert ownership of ideas.

A legend in his own lifetime, his achievements were acknowledged shortly before his death in a nationwide celebration attended by luminaries such as President Hoover, Henry Ford, John Rockefeller, and George Eastman. He remains an inspiration for inventors and entrepreneurs to this day.

THE BEST SOURCES OF HELP
Books:
Baldwin, Neil. *Edison, Inventing the Century*. New York: Hyperion, 1995.
Israel, Paul. *Edison: A Life of Invention*. Chichester: John Wiley, 1998.
Jenkins, Reese V., et al., eds. *The Papers of Thomas A. Edison*. Baltimore, Maryland: Johns Hopkins University Press, 1989.
Josephson, Matthew. *Edison: A Biography*. Chichester: John Wiley, 1992.
Millard, Andre. *Edison and the Business of Innovation*. Baltimore, Maryland: Johns Hopkins University Press, 1990.
Website:
Con Edison Inc.: **www.conedison.com**

MICHAEL EISNER

1942	Born.
1960	Starts at Denison University, Granville, Ohio.
1966	Works with Barry Diller at ABC.
1969	Joins Diller as director of feature films and programme development.
1971	Becomes head of daytime and children's programming at ABC.
1976	Becomes president of Paramount.
1984	Appointed CEO of Disney Productions.
1987	*Three Men and a Baby* grosses over $100 million at the box office.
1992	Disneyland Paris opens.
1994	Katzenberg leaves. Shelves Disney America plans.
2000	Disney posts profit of $1.9 billion on revenues of $25 billion.
2002	Attacks IT industry for failing to adequately protect digital content.

> **SUMMARY**
>
> Michael Eisner, chairman and CEO of Disney, is what the famous company lacked for many years: a true successor to Walt Disney himself. The big cheese that made the mouse roar, he breathed life into a moribund Disney when he joined it in 1984, with his own personal team of 'mouseketeers', to work alongside president and chief operating officer Frank Wells. Eisner and Wells resurrected the magic kingdom. Eisner's insight was that Disney should be in the family entertainment business in all its manifestations, so the Disney brand was stretched to encompass a mountain of merchandising, stores, books, videos, games, movies, and theme parks. His other claim to fame is the size of his pay cheque.
>
> Born during the Second World War, Eisner got an early taste of the entertainment business when, still a student, he spent three months at NBC studios. With the help of his father's contacts, he obtained a job as a clerk at NBC. Next he worked at ABC (a company he later bought) with Barry Diller. In 1973, aged 34, he followed Diller to Paramount as president. Together with young, thrusting executives such as Jeffrey Katzenberg, Eisner helped make Paramount a hit factory. Katzenberg followed him when he moved to Disney to rejuvenate the ailing studio and make it an entertainment powerhouse once again. In the mid-1990s, however, the Disney magic lost its sparkle temporarily as Eisner contended with executive fallouts and the aborted Disney America project, and had heart bypass surgery. But by 2000 the company was back on track, and Eisner's status as one of the highest paid executives in the United States looked to be deserved.

LIFE AND CAREER

Michael Eisner was born in Mt Kisco, New York on 7 March 1942. An affluent family, the Eisners lived in a large apartment on Park Avenue on the Upper East Side of Manhattan, where Michael attended a local private school, Allen-Stevenson. More interested in sport than studies, he soon discovered he had a strong competitive drive and preferred to be a leader rather than a follower. He displayed a self-confident streak that belied his young age and that remained with him all his life. Attending a reunion of a summer camp many years later, he arrived at the hotel, joined the others, sat down to a slap-up meal, and even sang the camp song at the appropriate moment. It was only when the director of his camp walked into the room, sidled over to him, and explained that he was attending the wrong reunion, that Eisner realised self-confidence could sometimes be misplaced.

After Allen-Stevenson came boarding school, and then, in 1960, Eisner started at Denison University in Granville, Ohio. The dissection class put paid to his idea of studying medicine so he switched to English as his major. During one summer vacation he managed to wangle a job at NBC; his father knew Robert Sarnoff, the son of RCA founder, David Sarnoff. Although he spent his three months at NBC as nothing more than a runner, working on the sets of shows such as *The Price Is Right*, he fell in love with the entertainment business.

CONTRIBUTION

Despite his persistence and enthusiasm, however, and help of his father's contacts, Eisner struggled to find a job in entertainment. Eventually, he was offered the job of a clerk for $65 a week at NBC. He accepted immediately. Shortly afterwards, he took a weekend job at WNBC radio as traffic researcher. His job was to 'borrow' other radio stations' traffic reports and pass them on to the morning DJ. Eisner was in no position to argue about the ethics of the situation and did as he was told, although he occasionally embellished his traffic bulletins with imaginary streets named after past girlfriends.

By 1966 he had obtained a job working as Barry Diller's assistant at ABC (Diller was to become one of the most respected executives in the entertainment business). ABC proved an excellent training ground for the ambitious Eisner, who became involved in all aspects of the television business and quickly learnt that hit TV shows were like gold dust. Eisner estimates the odds of achieving even an average success at only one in 4,000. In 1968 he turned down a job offer from the advertising agency Foote, Cone, & Belding, but recommended one of his superiors, who landed the job. Eisner promptly took up the position that had been vacated.

Diller, meanwhile, had been promoted to work on a partnership with Universal Studios to produce made-for-television films. In 1969 Eisner joined him as director of feature films and programme development. In 1971 Eisner became head of daytime and children's programming at ABC. With ABC's daytime ratings languishing at the bottom of the table, it was a win-win situation for him. Sure enough, daytime television improved considerably under his control, so that, several Eisner-instigated shows later, he was back with prime-time development, this time as vice-president.

> *Eisner was in no position to argue about the ethics of the situation and did as he was told, although he occasionally embellished his traffic bulletins with imaginary streets named after past girlfriends.*

In 1976 Eisner decided to move out to Los Angeles. After a string of successes, including *Happy Days* and *Starsky & Hutch*, he was headhunted by Barry Diller, now at Paramount, and offered the job of president of Paramount. He was only 34.

Between 1977 and 1982, profits at Paramount increased from $30 million to over $100 million, largely due to the new culture of aggressive creative risk-taking

Michael Eisner

introduced under Diller and Eisner. Hit TV shows such as *Taxi* and *Mork & Mindy*, together with films such as *Saturday Night Fever, Elephant Man, Grease, Star Trek, Ordinary People, Airplane*, and *Raiders of the Lost Ark* brought the dollars flooding into the Paramount coffers. In 1984, after some political infighting at Paramount, Eisner, by now one of the top film executives in the country, moved on to become CEO of Disney.

When Eisner joined Disney in 1984 the company was in the doldrums. He set about transforming the declining film and theme park company into an entertainment giant. Key to this transformation was an injection of new blood in the form of Jeffrey Katzenberg, still in his early thirties.

Under the labels Touchstone Pictures and Hollywood Pictures, Katzenberg gave the go-ahead to a string of hit feature films including *Down and Out in Beverly Hills* and *Three Men and a Baby*, a film that grossed over $100 million at the box office, the first Disney film ever to do so. Of their first 17 films, 15 made money.

Eisner, with his tremendous experience in television, also rejuvenated Disney's TV output with top ten shows such as *Ellen* and *Home Improvement*. Eisner and Disney were attacking on all fronts. Eisner repackaged classic Disney animation for home video. Titles such as *Bambi, Cinderella*, and the more modern *Aladdin* and *The Lion King* elevated Disney to the number one Hollywood studio in home video sales.

By the early 1990s Disney, now trading as the more commercial-sounding Walt Disney Company rather than Walt Disney Productions, was posting revenues of over $5 billion and profits close to $1 billion. The days of Disney being built on the fortunes of a small mouse were long gone. From 1985 right through to 1990 the company posted record profits for 20 quarters in a row.

It was only in the mid-1990s that the Disney magic began to lose a little of its sparkle. Although Eisner pulled off a major coup when he acquired the ABC broadcast network, this was counterbalanced by a spectacular and acrimonious falling-out with his longtime co-worker, both at Paramount and Disney, Katzenberg. This followed Katzenberg's departure to found DreamWorks with industry luminaries Steven Spielberg and David Geffen. Eisner got angry, reportedly, because of leaks of financial information to the media, which he attributed to Katzenberg. Katzenberg in turn claimed he was owed substantial bonuses, worth several hundreds of millions of dollars. In court, Eisner admitted he might have said of the diminutive Katzenberg, 'I hate the little midget', and that he believed his one-time associate had a 'dark side'. The dispute rumbled on for several years before it was settled privately. It was an unfortunate end to what had been such a profitable partnership. A little later, Eisner had more executive problems when he hired Mike Ovitz, talent agent, as his number two, only to see him depart just over a year later.

On top of the problems following Katzenberg's departure, Eisner also had to handle the ongoing saga of Disney America. The plan was to build a park that provided a historical experience focusing on America's past. The problem was the proposed site for the venture—outside the town of Haymarket, Virginia. What Eisner hadn't factored into his decision to locate Disney America in Virginia was the proximity of some of the richest families in the United States. Only hours after being publicly announced in November 1993, the project was facing a barrage of criticism. Up against some of most powerful and effective lobbyists in the country, Eisner eventually had to back down, despite the money and time spent on the planning. Then, to cap it all, he had to undergo heart bypass surgery.

Eisner's troubles were reflected in the balance sheet: profits dropped 28% from 1998 to 1999. But by 2000 Disney was back on track with a profit of $1.9 billion on revenues of $25 billion. And Eisner benefited personally from Disney's recovery; his base salary rose from $750,000 to $1 million, securing his position as one of the highest-paid CEOs in the United States.

Eisner watched the growth of digital media distribution with some trepidation, fearing that it could harm revenues and profitability. In 2002, he provoked anger by suggesting to a US Senate Committee that IT and software companies had failed to provide adequate protection for digital media because 'piracy helps sell computers'.

CONTEXT AND CONCLUSIONS

Michael Eisner has had three extraordinary careers. At ABC and Paramount he earned a reputation as a producer of hit shows. He carried that reputation to Disney and added to it by demonstrating an ability to revitalise a corporation. His instinct for what an audience wants was honed in the screening rooms of ABC where he nurtured hit shows such as *Happy Days*. And by surrounding himself with the best talent in the industry, he managed to stay in touch with viewer tastes. Hollywood can be incestuous, backbiting, and an extremely difficult environment to work in. It is testimony to Eisner's political skills and entertainment instincts that he has managed to stay at the top for so long and recover from potentially knockout blows such as the abortive Disney America scheme.

CLOSE BUT NO CIGAR
DAVID GEFFEN

Very close in this case, since David Geffen is undoubtedly one of the major powers in Hollywood. Like Mike Ovitz, Geffen started out in the mailroom at the William Morris talent agency. Working his way up, he made big money boosting the careers of rock acts such as The Eagles and Jackson Browne. At Warner Brothers, he discovered that life in a big studio didn't suit him, but he still managed to persuade them to help finance his own record label, Geffen Records, which had hits with artists such as Aerosmith, Guns 'n Roses, and Cher. At the same time, he enjoyed success with the Geffen Film Company and films such as *After Hours* and *Beetlejuice*. He sold his record company to MCA. It in turn was sold to Matsushita, at which time his stock was worth some $700 million. In 1994 Geffen made his biggest claim yet for media moguldom when he linked up with Jeffrey Katzenberg and Steven Spielberg to found DreamWorks SKG, a new Hollywood studio.

THE BEST SOURCES OF HELP
Books:
Eisner, Michael, and Tony Schwartz. *Work in Progress*. Harmondsworth: Penguin, 1988.
Flower, Joe. *Prince of the Magic Kingdom: Michael Eisner and the Re-making of Disney*. Chichester: John Wiley, 1991.

LARRY ELLISON

1944	Born.
1964	Leaves University of Illinois, attends University of Chicago.
1969	Moves to Berkeley, California.
1976	IBM publishes System R. Project research paper.
1977	Co-founds Oracle with Bob Miner and Ed Oates.
1986	Oracle IPO. Company revenues circa $55 million.
1989	Oracle revenues circa $571 million.
1990	Oracle hits financial difficulties.
Mid-1990s	Focuses Oracle on Internet-related products.
1998	Wins Sydney–Hobart boat race.
1999	Launches first electronic exchange for the automotive industry.
2000	Oracle praised for financial performance. Oracle admits spying on Microsoft.
2001	Proposes Oracle solution for controversial US national identity card scheme. Loses position as the United States's second richest man.
2002	Oracle launches first fully-integrated relational database.

> **SUMMARY**
>
> The man behind Oracle, Larry Ellison, was responsible for his company's transformation from a small software company in the 1970s to what is now a new-economy, Net-centric powerhouse. Raised on Chicago's South Side, Ellison was a self-taught computer programmer. Travelling out West, he struck the software equivalent of gold when he developed the Oracle database program.
>
> At its IPO in 1986, Oracle's revenues were some $55 million. Three years later that figure was $571 million. The company's early success owes a good deal to Ellison's leadership. At the time critics carped about his playboy lifestyle, flashy cars, and girlfriends, embellishing their stories with tales of his owning fighter aircraft. Ellison, in the meantime, worked like a driven man, making important decisions such as dropping his company's flagship product and betting the future of Oracle on the Internet. In 2001, his reputation was damaged when he admitted spying on Microsoft and he provoked further controversy when he proposed a US national identity card scheme after the September 11th terrorist attack. Despite that, it's a brave person who bets against Ellison, the samurai warrior of Silicon Valley.

LIFE AND CAREER

Born in 1944, Lawrence J. Ellison was raised on Chicago's South Side. Parts of the neighbourhood were tough, and the district was described by *Look* magazine as the oldest and worst black ghetto in the United States. Ellison says he was unaware that it was a 'bad neighbourhood' until some years after he left.

Ellison's childhood dream was to become an architect. Gifted at maths and science, he attended the University of Chicago to study maths; there he taught himself computer programming. Then, like another computer billionaire, Bill Gates, Ellison dropped out of university and headed in 1969 for California and the nascent computer industry. Arriving armed with little more than his self-taught computing skills, Ellison took a job as a computer programmer.

CONTRIBUTION

It was Ellison's good fortune to obtain a job with Amdahl. Founded by Gene Amdahl, the company was 45% owned by Fujitsu, so Ellison had the opportunity to travel to Japan on business. It was a trip that was to change his perspective on life and have a long-lasting influence on his approach to business.

Japanese culture, Ellison realised, was fundamentally different from that in the United States. He was intrigued by the apparent contradictions: the Japanese were aggressive yet incredibly polite; they were arrogant yet humble. He was also interested in the emphasis they placed on the group rather than the individual. This attitude, the antithesis of the individualistic, entrepreneurial ideals he had grown up with, pervaded Japanese corporations and society. Ellison's observations of Japan made a profound impression on him.

In 1976, IBM developed SQL (sequel), a computer language for accessing databases. Popular opinion at that time said that database programs were not commercially viable. Ellison didn't agree. He was quick to recognise the commercial possibilities. If he moved fast, he thought he could beat IBM to market with a database product.

Ellison was not a man to doubt his instincts, and he sought financing for a new company that would specialise in databases. Venture capitalists were less enthusiastic than he was about his business prospects. 'They wouldn't even meet with you,' said Ellison of the VCs. 'They would just leave you waiting in the waiting room for 45 minutes, until you finally got the idea they were not going to see you. And then the receptionist would search your briefcase to make sure you were not stealing copies of *BusinessWeek* from the coffee table. We were persona non grata in the venture capital community.'

In 1976, IBM developed SQL (sequel), a computer language for accessing databases. Popular opinion at that time said that database programs were not commercially viable. Ellison didn't agree.

Frustrated, Ellison and his partners Bob Miner and Ed Oates invested $2,000 of their own money into the start-up. The company was named System Development Laboratories and was later renamed Oracle Corporation. The company's first product was two years in the making, with Ellison and colleagues supporting themselves through consultancy work.

Once news got out about Oracle's new software, the company never looked back. Profitable from day one, in the period up to the millennium the company lost money for only one quarter, in 1990. Its rate of growth was incredible. When Oracle was publicly floated in March 1986, revenues were some $55 million. By 1989, when the company moved to its new campus-style location at Redwood Shores, California, revenues were approximately $571 million.

Oracle's success has been built on the strength of the product, coupled with an aggressive pursuit of market share. Ellison recalls that his attitude to competitors was informed by his experiences in Japan. On a business trip he got talking to a Japanese executive about competition. 'We believe,' said the executive, 'that our competitors are stealing the rice out of the mouths of our children. In Japan we think anything less than 100% market share is not enough. In Japan we believe it is not sufficient that I succeed; everyone else must fail. We must destroy our competition.'

After recounting the tale to a newspaper reporter, Ellison was greeted with a story featuring his picture accompanied by the words 'It's not sufficient that I succeed; everyone else must fail'. Whether or not he needed any lessons in competitive drive is a moot point: his competitive instincts appear to be well developed. Oracle has for the most part shown itself unwilling to co-exist peacefully with its rivals and has capitalised on its market position.

One element of corporate make-up Ellison did adopt from the Japanese is his fervour for building a team culture. He has said that he would 'never hire anybody I wouldn't enjoy having lunch with three times a week'. If everyone at Oracle gets on, Ellison reasons there will then be less destructive internal conflict. This is one of his greatest strengths: an innate understanding of what motivates people and makes them tick.

In his private life Ellison has always liked to live life to the full. He has flown fast planes, driven fast cars, and sailed fast yachts. Like media mogul Ted Turner, Ellison is a world-class yachtsman and was first across the line in the Sydney–Hobart race in 1998, a race in which six lives were lost due to the appalling weather. A good tennis player and a man who likes to be seen with attractive women, Ellison's playboy lifestyle has proved a target for critics who have accused him of neglecting his corporate responsibilities.

It is a charge that under-estimates Ellison's commitment to his business empire. His shrewd judgment is illustrated by his decision in the mid-1990s to refocus the company away from its flagship client-server software products to products that can run via a browser over the Internet. Ellison virtually bet the future of the company on this vision. His comment was, 'If the Internet turns out not to be the future of computing, we're toast. But if it is, we're golden.'

To date, Oracle9i—the company's new Internet database software—has sold well, and the company has continued to launch a series of 'firsts'. In 1999, Oracle was involved in establishing the first industry electronic business exchange—Autoxchange. 2000 saw the first Internet file system, 2001 the first database with a built-in web server, and 2002 the first fully-integrated relational database. However, 'off the field' incidents have also accompanied Ellison. In 2000, the company admitted to employing private investigators to spy on Microsoft and, in 2001 following the September 11th terrorist attacks, the company provoked controversy by proposing detailed recommendations for a US national identity card scheme.

Although Oracle was hit along with other technical companies by the slowdown in 2000–2001, Ellison continues to remain one of the richest men in the world. However, he slipped from second place to fourth in 2001 and ninth in 2002.

CONTEXT AND CONCLUSIONS

Ellison is one of a select band of first-wave computer tycoons. In the same way that technological advances made the likes of Edison, Schwab, Gillette, and Ford rich at the beginning of the 20th century, so computers and the Internet have created a small group of billionaires in the final decades of the century.

A man who likes to play harder and work harder than most, Ellison is in the mould of those earlier moguls. Critics have accused him of arrogance. They fail to appreciate the self-belief required to succeed. Ellison, like one of his heroes, Winston Churchill, is a man with the courage of his own convictions, the courage to stand alone and ignore conventional wisdom. It is not that he is beyond humility— he has, for example, learnt much from Japanese culture and incorporated that knowledge into Oracle. But Larry Ellison is a man who sees his self-belief as integral to his success.

THE BEST SOURCES OF HELP

Book:
Wilson, Mike. *The Difference between God & Larry Ellison, God Doesn't Think He's Larry Ellison: Inside Oracle Corporation.* New York: HarperTrade, 1998.

Website:
Oracle Corporation UK Limited: **www.oracle.com/uk**

HENRY FORD

1863	Born.
1884	Attends business school for three months.
1896	Chief engineer at Edison electrical factory in Detroit. Drives first vehicle out of garden shed.
1901	Ford drives to victory in Grosse Point car races.
1903	Founds Ford Motor Co.
1905	Model A Fordsmobile produced.
1908	The first Model T rolls off the production line.
1914	Ford introduces wages for unskilled workers at a minimum of $5.
1918	The River Rouge plant built.
1919	Ford's son, Edsel, becomes president of the company.
1924	Ten millionth Model T produced.
1928	Brings out second Model A.
1945	Hands over power to his grandson Henry Ford II.
1947	Dies.

> **SUMMARY**
>
> Henry Ford (1863–1947) was part engineer, part inventor, and part entrepreneur. A talent for engineering and curiosity drove Ford to develop a prototype automobile in his garden. His flair helped him found the Ford Motor Company to develop his prototype. By 1924 Ford had sold ten million Model T Fords—the car famously available in a choice of colours so long as it was black. On his way to ten million sales Ford broke the land speed record and the mould of manufacturing. During his lifetime his introduction of mass-production assembly line methods irrevocably changed the nature of manufacturing, something for which, for once, the use of the phrase 'paradigm shift' is wholly justified.

LIFE AND CAREER

Ford was born in 1863 on his father's farm at Greenfield, near Detroit, Michigan. As a boy he showed great interest in mechanics and engineering. He delighted in dismantling his friends' watches and then reassembling them, and while still a schoolboy built an engine from junk. He was always looking for ways to improve things. 'Even when I was very young I suspected that much might somehow be done in a better way,' he later observed. 'That is what took me into mechanics.'

Leaving school at 16, Ford went to work as an engineer for James Flower & Co in Detroit. To supplement his meagre $2.50 a week, he worked at a jewellers in the evenings. Nine months of gruelling hours later, Ford moved to the Dry Dock Engine Works to try his hand at a different type of engineering. By 1896, he was chief engineer at the Edison electrical factory in Detroit, but finding himself unable to confine his engineering to work, Ford continued to tinker with engineering projects at home.

His first prototype automobile was the Quadricycle, built in his garden shed.

Ford's strategic planning skills appear to have been underdeveloped at this early stage in his career. His first prototype automobile was the Quadricycle, built in his garden shed. The Quadricycle was too big to drive out of the shed, which forced him to dismantle part of the shed to remove the innovative horseless carriage.

For eight years Ford continued to work 12-hour days and then come home to improve his invention. Yet despite the potential of his automobile, no one could be persuaded to invest in it. The turning point came when Ford built a car for the Grosse Point automobile races. Although inexperienced, Ford entered the races, drove the car himself, and won emphatically. He repeated the feat the following year, in 1902. The victory attracted financiers and, after a couple of corporate false starts, the Ford Motor Company was up and running. On the way Ford broke the world land speed record for a four-cylinder automobile, driving a mile over the frozen Lake Sinclair in 39.2 seconds, seven seconds faster than the existing record.

CONTRIBUTION

Ford's idea was to produce a car for 'everyday wear and tear', suitable for the masses. 'Anything founded on the idea of the greatest good for the greatest number will win in the end,' he said. Competitors like Cadillac were expensive, at many thousands of dollars, and so beyond the reach of the majority of ordinary people. Ford's first commercial automobile was the Model A Fordmobile, in 1905. Priced at $850, it undercut its rivals and, in its basic but solid design, it appealed to the mass market. It was followed in 1908 by the Model T.

The overwhelming demand for the Model T forced Ford to modify the production process and make it more efficient. Initially the cars moved along the production line on cradles. At each stop, men climbed over the cars attending to different tasks. Ford simplified the process and made it more predictable. First, he delineated tasks so that one man performed one task repeatedly, instead of several. Second, he roped the cars together so that they travelled at a steady speed through the plant. These simple but effective measures resulted in an increase in production from 100,000 to 200,000 with, at the same time, a reduction in the workforce of nearly 1,500 men.

Production-line work was arduous and monotonous; staff turnover was high. In 1914 Ford reluctantly increased wages for unskilled workers to a minimum of $5, a move that brought in workers from far and wide. Tens of thousands joined the Ford automobile company. So many prospective employees queued up at the factory gates that the fire brigade had to use its hoses to disperse the crowd.

Ford's management style was not, however, benevolent. The company had its own Sociological Department to nanny the workers—making sure, among other things, that they practised good personal hygiene. Ford's coercive managerial style grated among the workforce. To sweeten this he introduced profit sharing and an extensive welfare programme.

So many prospective employees queued up at the factory gates that the fire brigade had to use its hoses to disperse the crowd.

He stopped short of allowing the workers to form a union, however. When Roosevelt introduced the Wagner Act of 1935, allowing the unionisation of the motor companies, Ford resisted the legislation bitterly, refusing to let unions operate at Ford auto plants. It was only after adverse publicity as a result of the infamous Battle of the Overpass in May 1937, when several United Auto Workers' officials were badly beaten, allegedly by Ford employees outside the River Rouge plant, that Ford was forced to back down and permit union organisation at the company.

By 1924 Ford had manufactured 10 million Model Ts and built a new plant at River Rouge, with wages raised to $6 a day. Increasingly he spent less time managing—his son, Edsel, had become president in 1919—and more time pursuing his socially idealistic interests. He built an experimental rural idyll, a model US village named Greenfield Village. He also launched the Peace Ship in an attempt to end the First World War and hobnobbed with other magnates and entrepreneurs such as his good friend Henry Firestone. Although a pacifist, Ford was drawn into war manufacturing after Pearl Harbour when the Willow Plant was built to produce B-24 bombers. This gigantic production works, with its mile-long assembly line, produced one plane every hour, with a total of 86,865 aircraft between May 1942 and the end of the war. In 1943 Ford returned as CEO after Edsel died.

More at home on the factory floor addressing engineering problems, Ford lacked the managerial skills and flexibility necessary to keep the company ahead of the competition. He was unable to keep pace with the beast he had created. Fixated on the Model T, he waited too long to develop the company's next model, the revamped Model A (launched in 1927), and so lost the initiative forever to General Motors. Like many entrepreneurs Ford was reluctant to give up his company. A poorly-managed succession further damaged the company, with Ford finally handing power to his grandson Henry II in 1945. Ford died at the age of 84 on 7 April 1947.

CONTEXT AND CONCLUSIONS

Henry Ford is frequently cited as one of the most important and influential businessmen of the 20th century. Although he didn't invent that icon of modern society, the motor car, he was responsible for turning it into a mass-market commodity. Once the sole province of the wealthy, the car was, in its pre-Ford incarnations, a toy—unreliable, poorly engineered, impractical, and above all expensive. Ford changed all that. The champion of mass production, he started an entire industrial revolution of his own, founded on his Model T. It was a revolution that made Ford $1 billion richer and made travel a reality for millions.

THE BEST SOURCES OF HELP
Books:
Doubleday, Ralph H. *The Triumph of an Idea: The Story of Henry Ford*. New York: Graves, Doran & Company, Inc., 1934.
Ford, Henry, and Samuel Crowther. *My Life and Work*. New York: Doubleday, Page & Co, 1923.
Website:
Ford Motor Company: **www.ford.co.uk**

BILL GATES

1955	Born.
1977	Drops out of Harvard to start up computer software company with Paul Allen.
1980	Agrees to license operating system to IBM.
1995	Windows 9X series introduced.
1997	Microsoft ordered to supply Windows 95 without a browser.
2000	Microsoft found guilty of anti-competitive behaviour. Judge orders break-up of Microsoft.
2001	Break-up ruling set aside by appeal court. Launch of XP generation of OS and X-Box game console.
2002	Gates Foundation donates $300 million to world health research.
2003	Major focus on security of Windows operating system. Commitment to mobile computing. Microsoft passes $200 billion market capitalisation.

SUMMARY

Bill Gates's contribution to the development of computer technology is beyond dispute. At the age of 13 he was already plotting his business future, forming the Lakeside Programmers Group with some school friends. Its aim was to seek commercial opportunities for their computer skills. His early programming brilliance, his alliance with Microsoft cofounder Paul Allen, and his departure from Harvard to start Microsoft are well known.

Microsoft went on to become one of the most successful companies the world has ever seen. As the Internet market exploded, he beat off Netscape in the browser wars. But perhaps his biggest challenge to date has come from the Department of Justice and its anti-trust lawyers. Despite protracted litigation Gates has so far managed to keep Microsoft intact, and enabled it to hold on to its dominant position.

LIFE AND CAREER

William Henry Gates III was born in Seattle on 28 October 1955. He was a precociously brilliant boy. Before his tenth birthday he had read the family's encyclopaedia from beginning to end.

At Lakeside, the exclusive private school he attended in Seattle, he developed an obsession with computers. Gates, then still only 13 years old, and some of his computer friends formed the Lakeside Programmers Group, dedicated to using their programming skills to make money.

At Lakeside he developed a friendship with another boy two years his senior. The boy, whose obsession with computers matched Gates's, was Paul Allen.

The intellectually driven Gates left Lakeside in 1973 to study law at Harvard. Law was a lot less appealing to him, however, than computing. He contacted Allen and the two teamed up to develop a version of an early computer language—BASIC. Gates dropped out of Harvard in 1977 to start up a small computer software company with Allen. They called it Microsoft.

He was a precociously brilliant boy. Before his tenth birthday he had read the family's encyclopaedia from beginning to end.

Bill Gates

CONTRIBUTION

A brilliant strategic decision in 1980 set Microsoft on the road to global dominance. At that time IBM dominated the IT industry through its mainframe business. By the late 1970s Microsoft was licensing its software to a number of customers. But the prevailing wisdom was that hardware was the business to be in and software merely an adjunct. Apple at the time was developing a proprietary in-house operating system (OS) that would provide a competitive advantage. Its strategy was to maintain control over what it regarded as its superior hardware by running it with its own software. Gates thought differently. As far as he was concerned the more people that used Microsoft software on their machines the better. So when IBM approached Microsoft to develop the operating system for its first PC, Gates recognised what an enormous opportunity this presented. IBM's dominance of the IT market meant that its PCs were destined to set the standard—both for hardware and for the OS. IBM failed to realise that, when the end-user switched on the machine, the part of the computer he or she interacted with would be the OS, supplied by Microsoft. Gates capitalised on the situation, cannily retaining the right to license its OS to other PC manufacturers.

The decision by IBM to use Microsoft's MS-DOS was a turning point for both companies. From that point onwards, the fortunes of IBM, which singularly failed to grasp the significance of the OS, would inexorably decline, until Lou Gerstner came to its rescue as CEO in 1993. For Microsoft the only way was up. Endorsed by IBM, MS-DOS displaced other competing OS offerings regardless of their technical merits, in much the same way that VHS had vanquished Betamax in the battle of the video standards.

Yet in those early days the rest of the world still failed to understand the importance of Gates's coup. Even in 1984, Fortune magazine was criticising Gates for failing to develop the management depth that would turn a temporary victory into long-term dominance.

Yet in those early days the rest of the world still failed to understand the importance of Gates's coup. Even in 1984, *Fortune* magazine was criticising Gates for failing to develop the management depth that would turn a temporary victory into long-term dominance. Not for the last time the media underestimated Gates's drive, ambition, and strategic vision.

When ill health forced Allen to leave Microsoft, Gates's position as leader was confirmed. Microsoft's rapid growth soon made it the darling of Wall Street. From a share price of $2 in 1986, Microsoft stock had soared to $105 by the first half of 1996, making Gates a billionaire.

Microsoft has launched a succession of successful Windows products. But Gates hasn't had things all his own way. When the Internet revolution took off in the early 1990s, Microsoft was momentarily caught off balance. A company called Netscape sprang up, giving away a nifty piece of software called a browser that transformed the Web from a techie's playground to a mass-market phenomenon. Microsoft desperately responded by licensing Mosaic browser technology from a company called Spyglass, tweaking it, and repackaging it as the Microsoft browser Internet Explorer. To cover all the bases, Microsoft also bought WebTV, eShops, Hotmail, and Vermeer, the original developers of the Front Page HTML editing software.

Critics regularly deride the company for buying technology rather than developing its own solutions. Microsoft has countered that it has developed a number of important technologies and is still doing so.

Criticism has also constantly been levelled at Microsoft, alleging that it abuses its dominant market position. Matters came to a head when the US Justice Department investigated Microsoft to establish whether the company was in breach of anti-trust law. In June 2000, after a lengthy trial and a mountain of depositions, US District Judge Thomas Penfield Jackson ordered Microsoft to be split into two companies, holding that it had violated the nation's anti-trust laws by using monopoly power to push aside potential competitors to the detriment of consumers. Microsoft took the case to the appeal court in February 2001, and in June of that year the court decided to overturn part of the original decision, withdrawing the requirement for Microsoft to be broken up. In May 2003, Microsoft undertook to pay over £450 million to AOL Time Warner to settle claims of unfair market dominance. Despite these hurdles, the company continues to grow and, in 2003, it passed $200 billion market capitalisation.

Ultimately it may not be the anti-trust ruling that poses the biggest threat to Microsoft's bottom line. Microsoft risks being sidelined by the sheer pace of technological progress. Handhelds and mobile phones may be the PCs of the future, and those markets are not dominated by Microsoft. Even on its home ground of PC operating systems, open-source software such as Linux poses a threat. Gates hit back with the launch of Microsoft's next-generation XP operating system towards the end of 2001. On this occasion it was the closer integration with the Internet and, in particular, the 'smart tags' feature that worried some commentators. In the event, the feature was dropped, although that doesn't mean it won't resurface. Another big product for Gates in 2001 was the X-box. This new gaming system, released in time for Christmas 2001, was Microsoft's shot at breaking into a lucrative market on the hardware side. It is too early to tell, however, whether the combined forces of XP and the X-box, plus the numerous partnership agreements Microsoft has forged with dot-com companies, will be enough to preserve its hegemony. But Gates, the architect of the world's greatest software company, won't go down without a fight.

Since 2000, Gates has moved from CEO to Chief Software Architect to concentrate even more on the company's future direction. Software security is a major focus and Microsoft launched an initiative in 2003 called Trustworthy Software. The company is also targeting mobile computing as an important arena for future development.

CONTEXT AND CONCLUSIONS

Bill Gates is lauded and reviled in almost equal measure. His charitable work, which tends to be overlooked, has grown rapidly and, in 2002, the Gates Foundation gave more than $300 million to tackle Aids and other global health challenges. The secrets that lie behind Microsoft's spiral of success have been dissected from every possible angle. Whatever you think of the dominance of Microsoft or Gates's methods, it cannot be doubted that when it comes to building and retaining a competitive advantage he has few peers. His technical skills, while not to be underrated, are not his greatest attribute. Far more important is his strategic thinking. It is this that has enabled him to outsmart his opponents at every turn. His other great attribute is the ability to hire the best talent and then motivate it to work at a fast tempo. He may appear awkward, geeky even, in public, but Gates is as sharp as a box of razors.

CLOSE BUT NO CIGAR
KEN OLSEN
Olsen was once hailed by *Fortune* magazine as the 'most successful entrepreneur in the history of American business'. Founding Digital Equipment Corporation (DEC) in 1959, he spent the next 35 years riding the IT rollercoaster at the helm of his company. Olsen, the man who pioneered the minicomputer, was heavily influenced by the writings of Alfred Sloan and organised DEC along similar lines to GM (small business units) when under Sloan's control. He left in 1992 to found Advanced Modular Solutions Inc. After a disastrous spell in the early 1990s, DEC was finally bought by Compaq in 1998.

THE BEST SOURCES OF HELP
Books:
Dearlove, Des. *Business the Bill Gates Way*. Oxford: Capstone, 1998.
Gates, Bill. *Business @ the Speed of Thought: Succeeding in the Digital Economy*. London: Penguin, 1999.
Wallace, James, and Jim Erickson. *Hard Drive: Bill Gates and the Making of the Microsoft Empire*. Chichester: John Wiley, 1992.
Website:
Microsoft: **www.microsoft.com/uk**

HAROLD GENEEN

1910	Born.
1934	Obtains a degree in accounting.
1934–1959	Works for number of firms including American Can, Bell and Howell, Jones and Laughlin Steel, and Raytheon.
1959	Joins ITT.
1966	ABC merger blocked.
1971	Acquires Hartford Insurance.
1977	Steps down as chief executive.
1979	Steps down as chairman.
1983	Resigns as director.
1997	Dies.

> **SUMMARY**
>
> Harold Geneen is the classic example of the CEO as analyst. He joined the board of ITT in 1959 and set about turning the company into the world's greatest conglomerate. His basic organisational strategy was that diversification was a source of strength. Under Geneen, ITT's spending spree amassed a total of 350 companies. By 1970, ITT was composed of 400 separate companies operating in 70 countries.
>
> By sheer force of personality, Geneen's approach worked. Between 1959 and 1977, ITT's sales went from $765 million to nearly $28 billion and earnings per share rose from $1 to $4.20. Geneen stepped down as chairman in 1979. But a company built around the drive and energy of one man will not last longer than that man's career. His followers were unable to sustain Geneen's uniquely driven working style. In the month of Harold Geneen's death, ITT was taken over.

LIFE AND CAREER

Son of a Russian Jewish father and an Italian Catholic mother, Harold Geneen was born in Bournemouth in 1910. His family moved to the United States before his first birthday, but his parents separated soon after they arrived. As a result, Geneen's childhood was spent at boarding schools and summer camps. When Geneen started work as a runner for the New York Stock Exchange, he continued to study at night at New York University. In 1934 his hard work was rewarded with a degree in accounting.

For the next 25 years his career took in a string of companies, starting with the forerunners of Coopers & Lybrand, followed by Montgomery (an accounting firm), then the American Can Co, Bell and Howell Co, Jones and Laughlin Steel Co, and Raytheon. After Raytheon, where Geneen was vice-president, came the biggest challenge of his career and the job that made him famous: the International Telegraph and Telephone Company, more commonly known as ITT.

CONTRIBUTION

When Geneen arrived at ITT in 1959, the corporation was a ragbag collection of businesses, loosely focused around telecommunications, with revenues of $800,000. During the 1960s the predominant organisational trend was one of diversification and conglomeration. CEOs went into a purchasing frenzy, raiding the corporate aisles for any company, no matter what business it was in, so long as it turned a profit. Geneen was no exception.

Over the ensuing decade Geneen purchased over 300 companies, operating in over 60 different countries. There was no rationale to these purchases, no common thread, other than that of profit. Sheraton hotels, Avis car hire, Continental Baking were all tucked away in ITT's roomy locker. 'I never met a business that I didn't find interesting,' said Geneen, and the ITT balance sheet certainly bore him out.

It was a mammoth undertaking to manage so many disparate companies. Fortunately for ITT, Geneen was no slouch; on the contrary, he was a fiercely driven workaholic. His ITT office in New York was equipped with eight telephones and a clock that showed which parts of the world were in daylight and which were in darkness. Ten suitcase-sized leather attaché cases crammed full of documents were stacked along the window ledges. Six of the cases, stuffed with reports, communiqués, and memos from over 400 reporting corporations, followed Geneen around the country and the world. 'If I had enough arms and legs and time, I would do it all myself,' said Geneen. Well into his eighties, long after he left ITT, Geneen was still working a ten-hour day at his office in New York's Waldorf-Astoria hotel. A typical Geneen story is recounted by an old ITT executive. Dragging a group of executives in for an evening meeting, Geneen worked them late into the night. At 11.45 p.m., the last of the executives made his way out of the office, pausing to wait for Geneen. Instead the CEO peeled off his jacket, pulled on a sweater and carried on working—the last executive in the building.

Fortunately for ITT, Geneen was no slouch; on the contrary, he was a fiercely driven workaholic.

Even so, it required all his energy to control the ITT conglomerate. To keep it together, Geneen employed rigorous financial accounting methods. Each month, 50 or more executives flew to Brussels to spend several days examining the figures. 'I want no surprises,' was one of Geneen's mantras. Full information was paramount, as was the ability to tell real facts from details masquerading as facts. 'The highest art of professional management requires the literal ability to smell a real fact from all others,' asserted Geneen.

And his approach seemed to work. From 1959 to 1977, ITT sales rocketed from some $765 million to approaching $28 billion, with earnings up from $29 million to $562 million. It was a success by most people's standards, not just Geneen's. Yet the more companies he acquired, the harder it was to keep all the plates spinning in the air. In 1974 and 1975 profits fell: Geneen may have been able to keep up a relentless pace, but his followers were either unable or unwilling to match it.

Geneen's efforts to support his company's share price sometimes strayed outside the boundaries of acceptable practice. In 1972, America's Securities and Exchange Commission discovered $8.7 million had been sunk into nefarious and illegal activities around the world. This allegedly included bribery, and colluding with the CIA in an attempt to undermine the Allende government in Chile.

Geneen stepped down as chief executive in 1977, as chairman in 1979, and as a director four years later—not that such a relentless man could ever retire to a life of quiet contemplation and gentle pastimes. He carried on working in a number of different companies of his own creation until his death from a heart attack in 1997.

ITT, however, was a different proposition. Without Geneen to support it, the house of cards collapsed. ITT limped on but eventually, after selling many of the companies acquired by Geneen, it was split up into three separate companies.

CONTEXT AND CONCLUSIONS

Harold Geneen was one of the last of his breed. He came to power at ITT at the height of the mania for conglomerates. Size mattered, and if size mattered then Geneen was very, very important. It is doubtful if any other CEO in corporate history acquired more companies—over 300—with less rationale. Of course acquisition is one way to grow earnings, but eventually the relentless growth has to stop and increased earnings must come from existing operations. Even a man with Geneen's drive and boundless energy will struggle to keep 300 plates in the air, and so it proved. In the decade following his departure from ITT, the cry from the boardroom was 'stick to the knitting'. Companies slimmed down, shed noncore business, and left ITT looking like a bloated dinosaur. Yet Geneen deserves his place in the pantheon of business greats. Why? Because he was the best of his type, the paragon of his age, the king of the conglomerates.

> *Harold Geneen was one of the last of his breed.*

CLOSE BUT NO CIGAR
CHARLES BLUDHORN

Who today remembers Charlie Bludhorn? Yet in the 1960s and 1970s, Bludhorn—then head of conglomerate Gulf and Western—was one of the most fashionable CEOs of his time. Along with conglomerate kings such as James Ling, Henry Singleton, Charles 'Tex' Thornton, and of course Harold Geneen, Bludhorn was fêted as a business visionary. Among the many corporate baubles he accumulated were Music Corporation of America, Madison Square Garden, and Paramount Studios. When conglomerates fell out of fashion, so did Bludhorn. Gulf and Western was whittled down to size until Paramount was pretty much all that remained.

THE BEST SOURCES OF HELP
Books:
Sampson, Anthony. *The Sovereign State of ITT*. New York: Stein and Day, 1973.
Shoenberg, Robert. *Geneen*. New York: Norton, 1985.

LOU GERSTNER

1942	Born.
1964	Joins McKinsey & Company.
1978	Joins American Express.
1985–1989	President of American Express.
1991–1993	IBM's cumulative losses pass $15 billion, a new record for corporate misery.
1993	Joins IBM as new CEO and chairman of the board.
1993–1995	Restructuring means over 80,000 jobs go.
1994	IBM posts $3 billion profit on sales of $60 billion.
1995	Buys Lotus Notes.
2000	Revenues $88.4 billion with net profits of $8.1 billion.
2001	Stock price breaks through $100 barrier. Company valued at $178 billion.
2002	Steps down as CEO, but remains chairman of the board.

> **SUMMARY**
>
> Lou Gerstner's business career seems almost too good to be true. After a broad education, taking in engineering and business, Gerstner went to work for the management consultancy McKinsey. He was appointed senior partner at 31—the youngest ever. There followed an equally impressive progression through blue chips American Express and RJR Nabisco. At Amex, Gerstner revitalised the fledgling credit card business. At RJR he made inroads into a mountain of debt, preparing the company for the megamerger of the century. The IBM job seemed like a no-win scenario: the once-great company, holed below the waterline, looked to be sinking faster than the Titanic. Gerstner reportedly took the job only after head-hunters Heidrick & Struggles persuaded him it was 'for the good of the country'. With Gerstner's ingredients in the mix, an apparently poisoned chalice turned out to be a refreshing brew. Eight years on and IBM was back, holding its own with the best of the IT heavyweights, both young and old. Much of the credit went to Gerstner.

LIFE AND CAREER

Born in Mineola on 1 March 1942, Louis Frederick Gerstner was the second of four sons. His early education was courtesy of the local Catholic school. His higher education is a textbook progression for many of today's top executives. First he mastered a specialised discipline, in his case engineering science at Dartmouth, graduating in 1963. After Dartmouth he went on to obtain an MBA from Harvard Business School. Then he joined management consulting firm McKinsey & Company in 1964.

At McKinsey, Gerstner made rapid progress and was appointed director at the age of 28. His early career post-McKinsey was no less impressive. At American Express during the 1980s, he revitalised the company's credit card division and saw net income grow by 66%. Then he went on to RJR Nabisco Holdings, where he cut a debt mountain of $26 billion to $14 billion, preparing the company for the largest leveraged buyout in corporate history.

When IBM cast around for an executive to replace CEO John Akers and pull the company out of the mire, they chose Gerstner. The surprise was that Gerstner, with a glittering career ahead of him, entertained the offer to chase an apparently lost cause. But, to the relief of 'Big Blue' and head-hunters Heidrick & Struggles, in 1993 Gerstner joined IBM as its new CEO.

CONTRIBUTION

When Gerstner arrived at IBM, it was in big trouble. For years 'Big Blue' had been the dominant company in the information technology industry, reaping massive profits through sales of its mainframe computers. But by the late 1980s the company had become complacent, lazy, and slow. Full of its own self-importance, it ceased to innovate and lagged behind a rapidly changing IT market. Although it had introduced an IBM-badged PC, by outsourcing the two key components—the operating system and the processing chip—the company had handed the advantage to Microsoft and Intel. Bogged down in bureaucracy and bloated with top-heavy management, IBM ground to a halt. In 1990 gross profit margins were a healthy 55%, but by 1993 they had slumped to 38%. There was no sign of an end to the downward trend. Gerstner's response was immediate, dramatic, and effective. His recovery checklist was: cut costs; get customers back again; find strategic direction; and restore employee morale.

Cutting costs was comparatively easy, if painful. Gerstner budgeted for a restructuring cost of $8.9 billion, and set about laying off 35,000 employees before the end of 1995. The figure ended closer to 85,000. Elsewhere, measures such as centralised purchasing, better inventory management, and the eradication of duplication in areas like product development, all contributed to improving the balance sheet position. In a move to improve customer relations, Gerstner made a special effort to get out and see the customers in person. The feedback from thousands of customer contacts persuaded him to retrain his generalist workforce to become the product specialists that customers demanded.

As Gerstner got rid of staff, he also took the opportunity to get rid of some of the ingrained corporate culture. Out went the traditional IBM executive look of blue suits and white shirts. 'This is a company that was very successful for several decades, but the curse of success is that people try to codify it,' he said pointedly in an interview with the *Financial Times*. 'My view is that you perpetuate success by continuing to run scared, not by looking back at what made you great, but looking forward at what is going to make you ungreat, so that you are constantly focusing on the challenges that keep you humble, hungry, and nimble.'

When Gerstner landed at IBM, much was made of his lack of technological background. 'He won't be able to spot technological opportunity,' the critics said. And, when he gave a speech early on which included the line 'the last thing IBM needs now is a vision', there was a chorus of disapproval from the media Cassandras. With hindsight, worries over a paucity of vision were unfounded. For a man with no vision, Gerstner has been remarkably consistent in his strategy for IBM.

Innovation is a central plank of Gerstner's strategy. In the year that he arrived, IBM filed for more patents than any other company in the United States. Thereafter, each year brought new innovative technologies from the supposedly directionless IT giant. Voice recognition technology, the world's fastest supercomputer, copper-wired semiconductors, promising new technology to replace silicon chips, nanotechnology...the list of IBM innovation under Gerstner runs on.

Much of IBM's creativity is aimed at e-business, an area Gerstner believes is vital to the future success of 'Big Blue'. By the beginning of 2001, the fastest-growing segment of the roughly $90-billion company was its services business. Gerstner has repositioned the company as a major e-business company while hanging on to core business such as servers, storage, networking, and middleware. It's a neat trick. Cleverly, he has also abandoned the IBM closed, proprietary approach to technology and embraced the philosophy of the open source movement, opening up IBM's technologies to other companies in a flurry of partnering deals.

So what impact has Gerstner had on the bottom line? In 1994, nearly two years after his arrival, the company posted a $3 billion profit on sales of $60 billion. This came after three consecutive years of losses, totalling $15 billion. On the strength of the recovery in profits, the share price had improved to $89 by early 1994. Since then it's mostly been an upward trend, although IBM stock has been susceptible to the same sorts of fluctuation as other technology stocks. Performance has also looked solid. Revenues for 2000 were $88.4 billion, with net profits of $8.1 billion. By October 2001 the stock price had broken through the $100 barrier, and the company was valued at $178 billion. Whichever measure you use, Gerstner's performance is impressive. Some even believe it justifies his $14 million salary.

The challenge facing Gerstner and IBM now is to sustain the transformation. For a company of IBM's size, perpetual motion is a necessary but elusive quality. Gerstner seems to have confounded the critics by creating an agile and innovative company from a stagnant behemoth without, as was predicted, splitting it into smaller units. Despite stepping down as CEO in 2002, Gerstner is still chairman of the board at IBM. After his lengthy stint in the hot seat, and with IBM in such good shape, who would blame him for spending a few more hours on the golf course?

CONTEXT AND CONCLUSIONS

By reputation, Lou Gerstner sits alongside management heavyweights of the post-Second World War period such as Jack Welch and Andy Grove. Is such exalted standing merited? The answer is unquestionably yes. Gerstner's timely arrival saved one of the largest and most famous IT companies in the world from extinction. He rediscovered the tradition of innovation and customer service, ingrained in the organisation by its founder Thomas Watson Sr. He was the right leader, in the right place, at the right time. In the late 1980s and early 1990s, IBM needed a manager who could make an unwieldy, bureaucratic, and tired company agile and hungry again. It took some painful restructuring, but Gerstner steered the company through its bad times and altered its course. The company emerged with a new focus that embraced e-business and IT services, while retaining its core manufacturing business and corporate values. The transformation was reflected in the bottom line as IBM regained favour among investors, analysts, and media alike. After a stellar career at companies such as McKinsey, American Express, and RJR Nabisco, Gerstner's triumph at IBM was a fitting capstone for one of the finest managers of his generation.

THE BEST SOURCES OF HELP
Book:
Garr, Doug. *IBM Redux: Lou Gerstner and the Business Turnaround of the Decade*. New York: HarperBusiness, 2000.

KING CAMP GILLETTE

1855	Born.
1871	Gillette family hardware business burns down.
1890	Holds four patents.
1894	Writes *The Human Drift*.
1895	Works for the inventor of cork-lined bottle caps.
1901	Gillette and Nickerson form the American Safety Razor Company.
1903	Production begins on the new safety razor.
1904	The renamed Gillette company is awarded the patent for the new invention. Invents the double-edged blade—a concept still used to this day.
1905	Twelve million blades sold to date, generating revenues of $90,000.
1915	Sales of seven million blades a year.
1932	Dies.

SUMMARY

King Camp Gillette, the US safety-razor entrepreneur, made his fortune by taking a mundane everyday product and improving it. So confident was he of his invention that he formed the American Safety Razor Company in 1901 and persuaded investors to back him before he even had a commercial product. In the first year of production Gillette sold 51 razor sets and 168 blades. By 1905 the figure was 250,000 razor sets and 100,000 blade packages. Part of the secret of Gillette's success was his modern attitude towards branding. With his picture on the wrappers of his disposable blades, he was soon known the world over. By the time he had moved on to improving the world through his social theories, the Gillette safety razor was a permanent fixture in the grooming habits of a large proportion of the world's male population.

LIFE AND CAREER

King Camp Gillette was born in Fond du Lac, Wisconsin, into a family of innovators. His father was a patent agent and small-time inventor. His mother wrote a cookery book based on a lifetime of culinary experimentation; the book was still in print a century later. When Gillette was four, his family moved to Chicago to start up a hardware business. Unfortunately, the business was ravaged by the Great Fire, and in 1871 the family moved once again, this time to New York.

Gillette took a job as a travelling salesman. Not content with merely selling his products, he couldn't resist improving them. By 1890 he had accumulated four patents. In 1895 he was working for the man who had invented cork-lined bottle caps. He had some simple advice for Gillette: 'Invent something people use and throw away.' Gillette took his words to heart and turned his attention to the safety razor.

His father was a patent agent and small-time inventor. His mother wrote a cookery book based on a lifetime of culinary experimentation; the book was still in print a century later.

King Camp Gillette

Traditionally, men of the time used the straight-handled razor blade to shave. The increasing use of the railway, however, had prompted a rethinking of the design of this basic implement. The swaying of the carriages made it downright dangerous to use the traditional cut-throat. Safety razors had been invented—a heavy blade fitted at right angles to a short handle—but they still had major shortcomings. Gillette used a Star safety razor. This required continual sharpening on a leather strap just as the traditional razor did. Eventually the blade wore out.

Gillette had an idea. What if it were possible to take a small square of sheet steel and put a permanently sharp edge on it? Such a product would be sufficiently affordable to throw away when it became dull.

CONTRIBUTION

To help him in his quest for a new improved safety razor, Gillette turned to metallurgists at the Massachusetts Institute of Technology. They assured Gillette that his idea was impossible. Undaunted, Gillette continued to search for someone who shared his belief and vision. That person was William Emery Nickerson, an inventor who, ironically, had been educated at MIT.

Gillette's search had taken six years. His doggedness was rewarded in 1901 when, together with Nickerson, he formed the American Safety Razor Company. Then in 1903 production began on the new safety razor. Razor blades were bundled up and sold as a package. The razor handle was sold as a one-off purchase. In 1904 the renamed Gillette Safety Razor Company was awarded the patent for the new invention. Initial sales were disappointing. After an intensive advertising campaign in men's magazines and newspapers in the United States and Europe, however, things improved. By 1906 12 million blades had been sold, generating revenues of $90,000.

The inevitable patent battles ensued. With a large proportion of the world's population as a potential market, sharp practices were rife. Competitors came to the market with modified versions of Gillette's product. Gillette responded with litigation or, in many cases, by buying the competition. And all the while he continued to tinker with his invention. In 1904 he came up with the double-edged blade, a concept used to this day. With his face plastered over the wrappers of his razor blades, Gillette became a celebrity.

Although the Gillette razor made King Camp Gillette a millionaire, he remained unfulfilled. He had strong philosophical and political beliefs. With his newly made millions he was now a powerful figure in North American commerce. He had an idealistic vision of a utopian society based on universal co-operation, and he now had the means to attempt to make it a reality.

Gillette wrote several books outlining his vision, beginning with *The Human Drift* (1894) that predated the invention of the Gillette razor. In a reaction against the mass pollution and sprawling urban development of the Industrial Revolution, he planned pollution-free cities contained in giant glass domes. In this new Utopia, one company would carry out all production with the citizens as the shareholders. 'Selfishness would be unknown, and war would be a barbarism of the past,' he wrote.

One interesting by-product of Gillette's obsession was his meeting with Henry Ford. In the years before the First World War Gillette attempted to set the wheels of his World Corporation in motion. First he asked Teddy Roosevelt to be president. When Roosevelt unsurprisingly declined, Gillette approached the writer Sinclair

Lewis, who in turn arranged a meeting between Gillette and Ford. The outcome of this meeting between two dogmatic, strong-willed millionaires should have been no surprise. At first the two merely talked over each other then, growing angrier, they began to shout at one another.

CONTEXT AND CONCLUSIONS

Gillette's attempts at social engineering came to nothing. The Wall Street Crash of 1929, coupled with boardroom machinations and constant patent litigation, put paid to his personal fortune. He spent a lot of time during his final years trying unsuccessfully to extract oil from shale. In the end he died, unfulfilled and frustrated, in 1932. The Gillette Safety Razor Company, however, thrived, carrying on its founder's tradition of innovation and remaining at the cutting edge of safety razor development. The company introduced foam shaving cream (Foamy), antiperspirant (Right Guard), and continued to do what Gillette had always done—improve the safety razor with the twin-blade, pivoting-head, disposable, and triple-blade razors.

> *The Wall Street Crash of 1929, coupled with boardroom machinations and constant patent litigation, put paid to his personal fortune.*

King Camp Gillette will be remembered for creating a product used daily by people the world over. Not only did he pioneer the market for disposable products, but he also showed an early and prescient awareness of the power of both celebrity and the brand. His image on the packaging of his product made him famous and helped reassure the consumer about the product's quality. This in turn boosted sales and helped make the Gillette Safety Razor Company the leader in its market.

THE BEST SOURCES OF HELP
Book:
Adams, Russell B., Jr. *King C. Gillette: The Man and His Wonderful Shaving Device.* Boston: Little, Brown & Co, 1978.
Website:
The Gillette Company: **www.gillette.com**

ROBERTO GOIZUETA

1931	Born.
1953	Graduates from Yale University.
1954	Starts work for Coca-Cola in Cuba.
1959	Castro takes power in Cuba.
1960	Flees Cuba for Miami.
1964	Moves to Coca-Cola HQ in Atlanta.
1974	Made senior vice-president. Is told Coca-Cola's secret formula.
1979	Appointed vice-chairman of Coca-Cola.
1980	Becomes CEO and chairman of Coca-Cola.
1981–1997	Coca-Cola's stockmarket value leaps 3,500%.
1982	Oversees launch of Diet Coke and purchase of Columbia Pictures.
1985	Launches and withdraws New Coke.
1996	Coca-Cola plays unofficial host to the 1996 Olympic games in Atlanta.
1997	Dies.

> **SUMMARY**
>
> Roberto Goizueta (1931–1997) could have been the owner of his family's sugar refinery business. Instead he became head of Coca-Cola, one of the world's largest and most valuable companies. Fleeing from communist Cuba after Fidel Castro came to power in 1959, Goizueta arrived in Miami in 1960 and began working for Coca-Cola. He moved to the corporate headquarters in Atlanta in 1964. With the support of company legend Robert Woodruff, Goizueta worked his way steadily up through the management ranks until he was made CEO in 1980.
>
> During his tenure Goizueta improved Coca-Cola's stagnating share price and took the company into noncore but profitable areas such as entertainment. Despite his considerable successes, however, he is likely to be remembered as the man who authorised one of the biggest marketing gaffes of all time—the switch from the traditional Coca-Cola formula to New Coke in 1985. New Coke was a commercial and public relations disaster, but at least Goizueta was brave enough to admit his mistake. And there's no question that Goizueta was good for Coca-Cola. In hospital, fighting the cancer that was eventually to kill him, he commented, 'It's all right if people want to worry about me. But they shouldn't worry about the company, because it's in better shape than it's ever been.'

LIFE AND CAREER

Roberto Crispulo Goizueta was born in Havana, Cuba, on 18 November 1931. He was a bright child who had a privileged upbringing. He attended a private school, the Cheshire Academy in Connecticut, where he mastered the English language through an unusual combination of formal tuition and sitting through countless hours of American films.

He earned a degree in chemical engineering at Yale University in 1953, graduating tenth in his class, and returned to Cuba to work at his family's sugar refining business. He wanted to carve out a career for himself, however, and on an off-chance answered an advert in a Havana newspaper for a bilingual chemical engineer. He got the job and started work on 4 July 1954, with the Coca-Cola Company.

In 1959, after leading a communist revolution, Fidel Castro seized power in Cuba. Eighteen months later Goizueta, his wife Olga, and their three children left for the United States, leaving everything behind except a suitcase, $200 in cash, and 100 Coca-Cola shares.

CONTRIBUTION

Goizueta and his family settled in Miami, where he worked for Coca-Cola's Latin American division. In 1964 he was reassigned to the technical research and development department at the company's headquarters in Atlanta.

He was a hard worker known for his tidiness and sharp dress sense. In Atlanta he found himself working closely with a company legend, Robert Woodruff. Woodruff had organised the syndicate that in 1923 bought out the Candler family's interests in Coca-Cola. He had overseen the company's global expansion and Coke's growth into one of the world's most valuable brands, and he was still a major player. Goizueta clearly made a good impression on Woodruff: in 1966 he was made company vice-president. Aged just 35, he was the youngest-ever executive to have held the post.

Goizueta's meteoric rise continued. He became senior vice-president in 1974 and a vice-chairman in 1979. Finally, in May 1980, he became CEO and chairman of Coca-Cola. At the time he was one of only two people who knew the formula for Coca-Cola, then, as now, one of the most closely held industrial secrets in the world. It was a long way from the family sugar refinery in Cuba.

When Goizueta took the helm, Coca-Cola was facing one of the toughest challenges in its history. Its chief rival, PepsiCo, was using a taste test dubbed the 'Pepsi Challenge' to turn soda drinkers into Pepsi purchasers. Worryingly, in Pepsi's blind taste test it turned out that many consumers preferred Pepsi to Coke. Goizueta had promised that he was prepared to take risks in an effort to revitalise the company and in April 1985 he proved true to his word when he announced that Coca-Cola was replacing its traditional recipe cola. The switch to New Coke was, according to Goizueta, 'the boldest single marketing move in the history of the consumer goods business'. Unfortunately, it also proved one of the major marketing mistakes of the 20th century.

When Goizueta took the helm, Coca-Cola was facing one of the toughest challenges in its history. Its chief rival, PepsiCo, was using a taste test dubbed the 'Pepsi Challenge' to turn soda drinkers into Pepsi purchasers.

Detailed market research conducted by Coca-Cola had supported the move, indicating that most consumers preferred the new formula. But New Coke failed miserably on the shelves. After it was introduced, not only did Pepsi remain a threat, but the old-formula Coke was still selling in millions of units every day. The move weakened the Coca-Cola brand. Instead of shrugging off Pepsi's threat in the manner of the market leader it was, Coca-Cola appeared worried. Furthermore, by producing a drink named 'New Coke' the company dislocated its established brand values of tradition and authenticity from its new product. To call this the marketing own goal of the century would be to understate the effect. Goizueta was buried under an avalanche of criticism. Some Coke fans uncharitably said that the new formula tasted like 'furniture polish'; others said 'sewer water'.

To his credit, Goizueta didn't let pride or stubbornness get in the way of good marketing. Realising that the introduction of New Coke had been a disaster, he backtracked, and in July, after only 90 days, he reintroduced the original formula as Classic Coke. It has not been tinkered with since.

With the exception of the New Coke debacle, Goizueta's period at the helm of Coca-Cola was a huge success. In 1982 he oversaw the successful product launch of Diet Coke. That same year he led the company in a new direction, agreeing to purchase Columbia Pictures. Though a nightmare to manage, the acquisition turned out to be a smart financial deal: seven years later Coca-Cola sold Columbia to Sony, making a profit of nearly $1 billion.

Goizueta died in 1997, aged 65, leaving a personal fortune of $1.3 billion. When he died Coca-Cola was valued at $145 billion, compared with a value of $4 billion when he became chief executive.

CONTEXT AND CONCLUSIONS

When Goizueta was appointed CEO of Coca-Cola, the soft drinks manufacturer was beginning to show signs of vulnerability in a market it had dominated since it was first founded. Pepsi Cola was posing a threat to Coca-Cola through the Pepsi Taste Challenge. Pepsi's blind taste-test results favouring Pepsi over Coke had the Coca-Cola executives rattled. Goizueta, a man willing to take risks, played Russian roulette with the Coke brand and lost: fortunately he only shot the company in the foot. Yet his response merely reinforced what a brilliant CEO he was. Rather than try to tough it out, he acceded to public demand. His prompt action prevented a marketing mishap from becoming a full scale corporate disaster. It also re-energised the brand, reminding the public how much they loved 'classic' Coke.

THE BEST SOURCES OF HELP
Book:
Greising, David. *I'd Like the World to Buy a Coke: The Life and Leadership of Roberto Goizueta*. Chichester: John Wiley, 1999.
Website:
Coca-Cola: **www.cocacola.com**

ANDY GROVE

1936	Born.
1957	'Traitorous eight' start Fairchild Semiconductor. Grove escapes to United States.
1963	Gains PhD from University of California, Berkeley.
1968	Gordon Moore and Bob Noyce start Intel.
1979	Becomes Intel's president and chief operating officer.
1981	IBM decides to use Intel microprocessors.
1985	Shifts Intel's focus to microprocessors.
1987	Becomes CEO of Intel.
1994	Flawed Pentium microprocessors recalled.
1998	Steps down as Intel's CEO.
1999	Intel launches Pentium 3 processors.
	Grove, a former journalist, warns media to adapt to threat of web publications.
2001	Intel experiences product shortages and delays. 500 job cuts.
	Launch of Itanium high-end processor.
	European Commission launches antitrust case against Intel.

> **SUMMARY**
>
> Andy Grove managed to survive a childhood in Nazi-occupied Hungary only to find himself a victim of the cold war. He escaped to the United States in 1957. After educating himself in New York and California, Grove joined Fairchild Semiconductor. In 1968 he followed colleagues Bob Noyce and Gordon Moore to form a new company, Intel. By 1979 he was chief operating officer.
>
> In the 1980s Grove concentrated the company's efforts on manufacturing microprocessors. He was made CEO in 1987. In 1994 he faced a crisis when a flaw was discovered in the company's flagship product, the Pentium processor. Under pressure, Grove made the decision to replace the chips rather than try to tough it out, reinforcing Intel's reputation. During his tenure as CEO Grove presided over a 24-fold increase in the company's stock value.

LIFE AND CAREER

Illness, discrimination, poverty: Andy Grove, born Andras Grof in pre-war Hungary on 2 September 1936, suffered them all as a child. At the age of four he fell ill with scarlet fever which left him with impaired hearing. Then another, more sinister, threat cast its shadow: as the Nazis swept to power in Europe, the Jewish Grof family feared for their lives. Grof and his mother assumed false identities and were sheltered by friends. The young Grof became Andras Malesevics.

Miraculously he and his family avoided the death camps and survived the war. Their celebrations were short-lived however, as in 1956 communist Russia invaded Hungary; Grof and the rest of his family found themselves on the wrong side of the iron curtain. Weighing up his options Grof, by now used to playing for high stakes, decided to escape.

He fled to Austria and from there to the United States, changing his name to Andrew Grove along the way. Arriving in the United States in 1957, he enrolled at City College of New York, graduating in 1960 with a first in chemical engineering. After City College, he studied at the University of California, Berkeley, receiving his PhD in 1963.

Andy Grove

His first job after graduation was at Fairchild Semiconductor, a young company formed by several research scientists including Robert Noyce and Gordon Moore.

CONTRIBUTION

Fairchild Semiconductor was the cradle of the computing revolution. It was formed by a disaffected group of researchers from William Shockley's research team at Shockley Semiconductor Laboratory in Palo Alto, California. Shockley had received the Nobel Prize for his work developing the transistor, and his academic reputation attracted some of the finest minds in electronics to his company, including Bob Noyce, Gordon Moore (of Moore's Law fame), Julius Blank, Victor Grinich, Eugene Kleiner, Jean Hoerni, Jay Last, and Sheldon Roberts.

Shockley's poor management style bred disaffection among his research team. The eventual exodus from his company of the so-called 'traitorous eight' was one of the landmarks of computing history. The company they founded, Fairchild Semiconductor, revolutionised the world of computing through its work on the silicon transistor. The drain of talent from Shockley's lab went on after Fairchild to start up some of the best-known companies in Silicon Valley. Intel (Bob Noyce and Gordon Moore), Advanced Micro Devices (Jerry Sanders), and National Semiconductor (Charlie Sporck) were all spin-offs from Fairchild.

When Gordon Moore and Bob Noyce left Fairchild in 1968 to set up Intel, they asked Grove to come with them. Noyce and Moore's original business plan involved manufacturing a new kind of computer memory using semiconductor technology, and in 1970 the first dynamic random-access memory (DRAM) for commercial use rolled off Intel's production lines. Intel had also been approached by a Japanese company, the Nippon Calculating Machine Corporation (NCM), to produce logic chips. Intel had already been working on a smaller single-chip, general-purpose logic device and offered its own solution. A chip was eventually developed. Instead of the patent rights passing to NCM, Intel retained ownership and licensed manufacturing and selling rights. It was this key decision by Grove and the management team that paved the way for Intel to become the microprocessor giant it is today.

Intel's success was founded not only on its innovative skills but also on its skilful repositioning of what had previously been a commodity computer component into a household-name brand. TV commercials elevated the mundane microchip to an aspirational product. Encouraged by the 'Intel Inside' campaign, consumers insisted on having an Intel chip inside their PCs. The Intel Pentium processor became as strongly associated with PCs as Microsoft's Windows operating system, another marketing success story.

Andy Grove's vision was instrumental in Intel's success. Grove steered the company from a fledgling producer of memory chips into a giant of the microprocessor industry. He got things done. In the early days he was the man who organised the office space and manufacturing capacity. He played a key role in the 1981 negotiations with IBM that saw Intel beat off competition from Motorola to supply the microprocessors for IBM's PCs.

In many ways Grove's childhood experiences in war-torn Europe had prepared him well for business life. He was a man who didn't avoid tough decisions. In the 1980s, when microprocessors looked as if they might be a better bet than memory, Grove made the bold and risky decision to refocus the company's efforts. It was a difficult decision that meant making thousands of employees redundant. In 1987 Grove became CEO of Intel. The decisions didn't get any easier. Grove averted a potential crisis when a flaw was discovered in the company's flagship Pentium microprocessor. With a technical problem probably discernible only by mathematicians threatening to balloon into a PR disaster of epic proportions, Grove acted decisively. He could have used Intel's muscle to pass on the burden of replacement to the retailers and consumers. Instead Grove offered to replace the processors. The move may have cost a fortune—$475 million—but it safeguarded the Intel brand. Profits went up.

Grove was a godsend to the company's shareholders. During his tenure as CEO Intel's stock value increased 24-fold. In May 1998 Grove stood down as CEO, remaining as chairman of the board. Since stepping down he has focused on strategic thinking. Drawing on his experience as a journalist, he advised the media in 1999 to change its approach in light of the growing strength of web publications.

Since Grove took a back seat at Intel the company has been wrestling with a number of difficult issues, not least a likely future decline in demand for microchips. Moore's Law (originated by Intel co-founder Gordon Moore) states that microprocessing power will double every 18 months. It has held true for over a decade, delivering revenue growth to Intel through consumer chip upgrades. Eventually, though, Moore believes that the rate of increase will slow, and he should know. Grove appears to be prepared for this. He is on record as saying that 'all companies will be Internet companies'. Backing this view, Intel has diversified its operations to embrace the Internet. Technical innovation continued after Grove's departure with the launch of the Pentium 3 processor in 1999, Pentium 4 in 2000, and the Itanium high-end 4-bit processor in 2001. However supply problems hit the company hard in 2000, leading to the loss of 500 jobs that year. In 2001, the company hit further problems when the European Commission launched an antitrust case against Intel for alleged abuse of a dominant position to stifle competition.

CONTEXT AND CONCLUSIONS

Just as all companies need an entrepreneur to make things happen in the formative stages of a new venture, so too they need an organiser and steady hand to help guide a company from start-up through the growth phase and beyond. Andy Grove is such a man. With resolve, vision, and an ability to take risks based on hard facts, Grove came from behind the iron curtain to become CEO of one of America's technology bellwether stocks. As a child in war-torn Europe, Grove learned to assess a situation using all available information and then make a decision. It is a skill that has served him well throughout his life, both business and personal. Whatever his future achievements, his accomplishments at Intel alone merit a place alongside the great business leaders of the 20th century.

THE BEST SOURCES OF HELP
Books:
Grove, Andrew S. *Only the Paranoid Survive: How to Achieve a Success That's Just a Disaster Away.* New York: Doubleday, 1999.
Grove, Andrew S. *Swimming Across: A Memoir.* New York: Warner Books, 2001.
Jackson, Tim. *Inside Intel: Andy Grove and the Rise of the World's Most Powerful Chip Company.* Collingdale, Pennsylvania: DIANE, 2001.
Website:
Intel UK: **www.intel.co.uk**

WILLIAM RANDOLPH HEARST

1863	Born.
1887	Takes control of the *San Francisco Examiner*.
1889	The *San Francisco Examiner* makes a profit.
1895	Heads for New York to save the *New York Morning Journal*.
1896	Acquires New York's *Evening Journal*.
1902	Becomes a Democratic congressional representative for New York.
1920s	Builds a fabulous castle on San Simeon estate.
1930s	Forced to consolidate empire following the Great Depression.
1951	Dies.

SUMMARY

Arguably the most famous media mogul of the 20th century, William Randolph Hearst (1863–1951) took the silver spoon of his inheritance and fashioned it into a gold one. Despite his patrician upbringing, he succeeded in keeping his finger on the pulse. Through a combination of media savvy and extraordinary stamina and persistence, he built an ailing newspaper, the *San Francisco Examiner*, into a billion-dollar media empire. At his peak, Hearst owned over 40 major newspapers and magazines, not to mention a handful of radio stations and film companies. In 1951 he died an immensely wealthy and powerful man, immortalised ten years previously, and much to his chagrin, in Orson Welles's film, *Citizen Kane*.

LIFE AND CAREER

Hearst was born in San Francisco on 29 April 1863. His father was a wealthy industrialist and speculator, and his mother a socialite and philanthropist. It was a potent cocktail of wealth, commerce, and culture that was to have a profound effect on him. An only child, he spent his early years shuttling between the family's huge estate at San Simeon, California, and their home in New York.

> *An only child, he spent his early years shuttling between the family's huge estate at San Simeon, California, and their home in New York.*

The classical academic route for the privileged awaited: a first-class prep school—St Paul's Preparatory School in Concord, New Hampshire—followed by an Ivy League university—Harvard. At Harvard Hearst excelled in social activities. He was a member of the Hasty Pudding Theatre and, more notably, business manager for the college magazine, the *Harvard Lampoon*. So much energy was put into his social life that he neglected his academic work. Hearst was eventually expelled and he never received his degree.

Shrugging off his academic failure, he took a job instead at the *New York World*. Joseph Pulitzer's newspaper was one of the leading newspapers in New York at the time. Hearst may not have paid attention in his Harvard classes, but at the *New York World* he received a first-class education in how to run a newspaper. However, he was soon summoned back to San Francisco by his father.

CONTRIBUTION

In contrast to media moguls like Louis Mayer who worked their way up from the bottom of the pile, Hearst was handed his first newspaper as a gift. The *San Francisco Examiner* had been purchased by Hearst's father to provide him with a voice when he was running for the US Senate. With the senate seat secured, the paper was surplus to requirements. Neglected, its circulation dwindled. The younger Hearst was desperate to take charge of it. His father was less keen and offered him as alternative inducements a one-million-acre ranch in Chihuahua, the 275,000-acre San Simeon ranch north of San Luis Obsipo, the Anaconda copper mines in Montana, and the Homestake gold mine in South Dakota. Hearst refused them all saying: 'You are very kind but I would rather have the *Examiner*.' Reluctantly, his father relented.

On 4 March 1887 Hearst took up residence at the *San Francisco Examiner*. He had discovered his métier. He was a brilliant newspaper proprietor. Thanks to a radical overhaul, by 1889 the *Examiner* was in profit. The staid format Hearst had inherited was replaced with hard-hitting investigative reporting, coupled with sensationalist, attention-grabbing headlines. Increased sports coverage, serialised stories by well-known authors, banner headlines like 'Huge Frantic Flames', biographical sketches, and exposés of the seedy underbelly of Californian life all contributed to the heady populist mix.

As circulation and profits rose, Hearst expanded the business. In 1895 he returned to his old hunting ground on the East Coast to save the *New York Morning Journal*. It was a decision that put him in direct competition with his one-time mentor, Joseph Pulitzer. Hearst pulled no punches in the ensuing circulation war. He added the *Evening Journal* to his collection in 1896 and poached some of Pulitzer's top writers. It was a period that gave rise to the term 'yellow journalism', where newspapers assumed the role of opinion-formers and determiners of morals. In scenes commonplace today, rival newspapers vied for scoops and used their front pages to boast of their achievements.

The most famous example of Hearst's proactive stance to newspaper reporting is the comment attributed to him when the illustrator Frederick Remington informed him that he wished to return from an uneventful Havana. Hearst supposedly responded: 'Please remain. You furnish the pictures and I'll furnish the war.'

His methods may have been controversial, but they worked. Hearst was unstoppable. He soon acquired newspapers in major cities throughout America. Following in his father's footsteps he became involved in politics. In 1902 Congress welcomed Hearst as a Democratic representative for New York. In all he served two terms in Congress and also became Mayor of New York.

With his newspaper empire firmly established, Hearst expanded into other areas of the media. As a publisher he produced titles that included *Cosmopolitan*, *Good Housekeeping*, and *Harper's Bazaar*. He also moved into the film-making business, cutting his teeth with Hearst-Metronome News. Ultimately it was the film industry, coupled with his infatuation for the actress Marion Davies, that was to prove his downfall.

He formed W. R. Hearst's Cosmopolitan Productions as a vehicle for Davies, his Brooklyn-born mistress and a former Ziegfeld Follies girl. Abandoning his political career after failed attempts at the Senate and the presidency, Hearst focused solely on films. Of the hundred films he sanctioned over the next 20 years, half featured his mistress. As well as sinking millions of dollars into making films, Hearst spent more millions on a Beverly Hills mansion for Davies. Finally he embarked on the folly that was to prove his undoing, the construction of the Hearst Castle estate at San Simeon. The 25,000 acres of the estate and castle contained rare and priceless works of art, antiquities, a zoo, an airfield, and guest houses which were chateaux dismantled in Europe and flown to California to be reassembled stone by stone.

> *His final years were spent trying to prevent the release of Orson Welles's film* Citizen Kane, *a thinly disguised biopic of him. He failed.*

Hearst might have survived such profligate extravagance had it not been for the Great Depression. During the 1930s he was forced to consolidate his empire, selling newspapers and works of art to remain afloat. By the end of the decade he had halved his business interests and plundered the treasures at San Simeon. Marion Davies too, liquidated her personal assets and pumped $1 million into her lover's business. His final years were spent trying to prevent the release of Orson Welles's film *Citizen Kane*, a thinly disguised biopic of him. He failed. In the end, in ill health and bitter at the Welles episode, he retreated to San Simeon, handing over control of his empire to lawyers and managers. He died at the home of Marion Davies on 14 August 1951.

CONTEXT AND CONCLUSIONS

Although Hearst's final years were marred by what must have been for him a humiliating fall from grace, he will still be remembered as one of the greatest media barons of all time. While he was born with all the advantages wealth brings, Hearst turned around the *San Francisco Examiner*, invented a new style of popular journalism, and fashioned a media empire through hard-nosed determination, incredible stamina, and a common touch that belied his background. Hearst was truly a paradox. A man with wealth beyond the dreams and understanding of most, he was blessed nevertheless with the innate ability to appreciate the hopes and fears of ordinary people.

To the last he saw himself as the people's champion. He believed that the criticism and misfortunes that had befallen him were the result of his willingness to take a stand on behalf of the masses. 'Any man who has the brains to think and the nerve to act for the benefit of the people of the country,' he said, 'is considered a radical by those who are content with stagnation and willing to endure disaster.'

THE BEST SOURCES OF HELP
Books:
Davies, Marion. *The Times We Had: Life with William Randolph Hearst*. New York: Ballantine Books, 1975.
Nasaw, David. *The Chief: The Life of William Randolph Hearst*. Boston: Houghton Mifflin Co, 2000.
Proctor, Ben. *William Randolph Hearst: The Early Years 1866–1910*. Oxford: Oxford University Press, 1998.
Website:
The William Randolph Hearst Foundations: **www.hearstfdn.org**

HUGH HEFNER

1926	Born.
1944	Joins US Army as cartoonist.
1949	Joins the Chicago Cartoon Company.
1950	Works as an advertising copywriter for the Carson, Pirie, Scott department store.
1951	Joins *Esquire* magazine.
1953	First issue of *Playboy* goes on sale.
1959	Buys 70-room Playboy Mansion on Chicago's Gold Coast.
1959	One-hour, syndicated 'Playboy's Penthouse' premiered.
1971	Moves to the Mansion West in Holmby Hills, California.
1977	Hosts *Saturday Night Live* show.
1982	Hands over control of Playboy empire to daughter Christie.

SUMMARY

Hugh Hefner has built a publishing empire on the backs of naked women and bunny rabbits. A man who likes to dress in pyjamas and who has a rare species of marsh rabbit named after him (*Sylvilagus palustris hefneri*), Hefner broke the boundaries of sexual permissiveness in US society when he launched *Playboy* magazine in 1953. It started with a circulation of 53,000; 20 years later it was over 6 million. When Hefner handed the control to his daughter Christie in 1982, Playboy was an industry comprising magazines, cable television, videos, and clothes. More than that, it was part of the fabric of US male culture.

LIFE AND CAREER

Born in Chicago, Illinois, on 9 April 1926, Hugh Hefner attended Sayre Elementary School and Steinmetz High on the West Side of Chicago. He was no great academic—not that he was a dunce, either (according to the Playboy website he has an IQ of 152)—he just preferred to channel his energies into other activities. At school he served as student council president, launched a school newspaper, and spent a lot of time drawing cartoons.

He graduated from high school in 1944 and joined the US Army as an infantry clerk. His job was a little unusual: it entailed drawing cartoons for the Army press. When the Second World War was over, he was discharged from the army and, wishing to continue his education, enrolled at the University of Illinois in Champaign/Urbana. There he continued to display a capacity for multi-tasking that set him apart from his peers. Not only did he get through his degree in two and a half years, he also found time to draw cartoons for the *Daily Illinois* and edit a campus magazine called *Shaft*. As a sign of things to come, he was responsible for the introduction of 'Coed of the Month', a new feature in *Shaft*.

When he left university, Hefner embarked on a career as a cartoonist. In 1949 he joined the Chicago Cartoon Company as an assistant personnel manager, and a year later worked as an advertising copywriter for the Carson, Pirie, Scott department store. By 1951 he was working

> *When he left university, Hefner embarked on a career as a cartoonist.*

for *Esquire* magazine as a promotion copywriter. He looked set for an ordinary uneventful working life, when the company announced that it was relocating to New York. Hefner was happy in Chicago, so he decided to stay and set up his own magazine.

CONTRIBUTION

The days of glamorous offices and lavish mansions were still a long a way off. The first issue of *Playboy* magazine was put together on the kitchen table in Hefner's South Side flat. The magazine featured a calendar photo of Marilyn Monroe. Unsure about how his revolutionary publication would be received and whether he would be able to produce another, Hefner left the cover date off. The first issue went on sale in December 1953.

Hefner's publishing instincts were vindicated when the first issue sold 50,000 copies. The revenue from this edition alone allowed him to cover his costs and produce another. The magazine that would bring the world the Playboy bunny was up and running.

Part of the reason for the magazine's phenomenal success during the 1950s and 1960s were the ideals espoused by Hefner and reflected in his magazine. *Playboy*, he insisted, was never intended to be a smutty publication. Instead it aimed to bring pictures of naked women out from under the bed and onto the coffee tables. 'It was never my intention to be a revolutionary,' he says. 'My intention was to try to create a mainstream men's magazine that included sex in it. That turned out to be a very revolutionary idea. That's because we lived in what I then and now viewed as a very repressive, sick society.'

With a mixture of photo sets featuring perfect-looking, scantily dressed women and articles addressing issues of the time, Hefner tapped into an undercurrent of thought that looked to break away from the prudish mentality of the 1950s. The heady mixture of liberal journalism and eroticism brought sales of over 6 million in the 1970s. It also bought Hefner a Playboy jet, and a hedonistic lifestyle that was the envy of many a red-blooded male.

> *In just a few years Hefner had amassed enough wealth to fund the purchase of the 70-room Playboy Mansion on Chicago's Gold Coast.*

In just a few years Hefner had amassed enough wealth to fund the purchase of the 70-room Playboy Mansion on Chicago's Gold Coast. He moved out of the Playboy headquarters and into the mansion, living and working there for the best part of a decade. In 1971 he moved again, this time to the Mansion West in Holmby Hills, California. The old Playboy mansion was donated to the Art Institute of Chicago and subsequently converted into flats.

During his years at the helm of the Playboy business, Hefner gained a reputation for eccentricity. His dress sense is a little unconventional. Way ahead of his time, Hefner anticipated 'dress down Fridays' with his own version of dressing down every day. Unless venturing outside the substantial gates of his mansion, he likes to spend the whole day in his pyjamas. This sartorial quirkiness dates back to the early days of *Playboy*, when, working long hours, he just never got around to getting dressed. Once the whole operation was being run behind closed doors in the Chicago Playboy mansion, he saw no need to change his ways and so continued to wear a fresh pair of pyjamas every day—putting on a different pair for the evening. If he had company, he simply donned a smoking jacket.

CONTEXT AND CONCLUSIONS
To some, Hugh Hefner is one of the 20th century's greatest pornographers. To others, he is a business icon—a man who, in the spirit of all great entrepreneurs, saw an opportunity and exploited it. It takes tremendous skill to expand a business rapidly, retain control over it, continue to manage it effectively, and protect the brand. Hefner succeeded in building a multi-million-dollar empire and brand a recognised the world over. Unlike many founders of big businesses, he even managed a painless succession, handing control over to his daughter Christie.

In answer to moral criticisms, Hefner is on record as saying that with Playboy, he is merely combating hypocrisy over attitudes towards sex in society, bridging 'the gap between what we said and what we actually did'. Morality aside, though, there is no denying Hefner's genius for business.

THE BEST SOURCES OF HELP
Books:
Brady, Frank. *Hefner*. New York: Macmillan, 1974.
Miller, Russell. *Bunny: the Real Story of Playboy*. Austin, Texas: Holt, Rinehart and Winston, 1985.
Website:
Playboy Enterprises, Inc.: **www.playboyenterprises.com**

MILTON SNAVELY HERSHEY

1857	Born.
1871	Drops out of school, aged 13.
1872	Apprenticed at Joe Royer's Ice Cream Parlour and Garden.
1876	Opens a shop making and selling sweets in Philadelphia.
1882	Closes business in Philadelphia; opens and fails in Chicago.
1883	Opens sweet shop in New York, which closes in 1886.
1886	Starts the Lancaster Caramel Company.
1893	Visits Chicago World's Fair and orders chocolate-making equipment.
1895	Starts selling chocolate.
1900	Hershey's Chocolate Bar introduced. Lancaster Caramel Company sold for $1 million.
1906	Derry Church becomes Hershey Town.
1916	Builds sugar mill in Cuba.
1920	Loses $2.5 million on sugar futures. Forced to borrow from banks.
1942	US Army asks Hershey to develop chocolate bar for field rations.
1945	Dies.

> **SUMMARY**
>
> Milton Snavely Hershey (1857–1945) is the entrepreneur who brought the world the Hershey chocolate bar. He was a late starter in business, his first attempts in the confectionery industry ending in failure. Real success finally came in his late thirties with the Lancaster Caramel Company, a business he eventually sold to a rival for a large sum. The break that put Hershey in the history books came in 1893 when he stumbled across chocolate-manufacturing equipment at the World's Fair in Chicago. Hershey concentrated on chocolate, perfected a recipe for milk chocolate, introduced mass production, and built a thriving chocolate business as well as a town called Hershey.

LIFE AND CAREER

Born on 13 September 1857, Milton Snavely Hershey was brought up in Hockersville, Pennsylvania. It was a small rural town and he was educated in a one-room schoolhouse. His parents were farmers and, from a very early age, Hershey was expected to help out on the farm tending the livestock and doing other chores.

After attending a string of schools—including a private high school, the Village Academy of Green Tree, where he did not do well—Hershey gave up on education and took a position as an apprentice with a German-language newspaper based in Gap, Lancaster County. It was soon clear that his talents did not lie with either journalism or publishing. He left the paper and joined Joseph H. Royer of Lancaster as an apprentice confectioner.

He was an ambitious young man. Aged 19 he founded his own company, M.S. Hershey, Wholesale and Retail Confectioner. The business failed and was sold in 1882. Over the following few years Hershey travelled the country trying to set himself up in the sweet-making business. In Denver, Colorado, he learnt how to make caramels. In New York he sold his sweets on the street. None of these ventures prospered, so he headed back to Lancaster. It was in Lancaster, the scene of his first business failure, that Hershey finally met with some success.

CONTRIBUTION

Hershey put his caramel-making skills to work. From the outset his business was based on quality of product. 'Give them the quality, that's the best kind of advertising in the world' was his motto. The business took off when Hershey's caramels came to the attention of a sweet importer who bought some to sell in England.

In 1893, however, while visiting Chicago, Hershey met the manufacturer of a German-made chocolate-making machine. He ordered one of the machines and had it shipped to Lancaster. The eventual result was a change of direction and the development of his most famous product, Hershey Chocolate.

With the caramel business, Hershey had excelled in creating a diverse range of sweets. Now he concentrated on perfecting a single product: chocolate. In 1900 he sold his caramel business for $1 million to the American Caramel Company of Philadelphia. With the proceeds, he invested in a new chocolate factory near his family home—he was married by now—in Derry Church.

> *Hershey put his caramel-making skills to work. From the outset his business was based on quality of product.*

When it came to making chocolate, Hershey had no recipe book or magic formula to rely on. Together with a few trusted colleagues he locked himself away and laboured over the perfect milk chocolate recipe. 'Nobody told Mr Hershey how to make milk chocolate. He just found out the hard way,' recalled one of his employees. Hard work though it was, Hershey struck chocolate gold. The result of his research—the Hershey chocolate bar—soon became a byword for quality in the United States.

Hershey continued to consolidate his chocolate business. He produced variations on the standard bar including: Mr Goodbar, a milk chocolate and peanut bar, in 1925; Krackel, a chocolate bar filled with crisped rice, in 1938; and Hershey miniatures—small versions of all Hershey's chocolate bars—in 1939. To secure his sugar supply and ensure its quality he built a sugar mill and small town in Cuba along the lines of Hershey, Pennsylvania.

In 1920 Hershey suffered a setback when he lost $2.5 million on the sugar futures market. He was forced to borrow from the bank, and, as a condition of the loan, the bank put a representative in Hershey's factory. It took him two years to pay the loan off and eject the overseer.

As Hershey's business grew, so too did the town surrounding the factory. Hershey wanted to build a town in keeping with his social philosophy in the same way that other chocolate philanthropists, like Joseph Rowntree and George Cadbury, had done in England. He drew up plans for an idyllic community that would not only house its inhabitants but provide for their every need, including employment at the Hershey chocolate factory. When the town was completed it contained parks, churches, a school, a hotel, a golf course, and even a zoo. Inhabitants would walk along streets such as Areba, Caracus, and Para, all named after cocoa bean producing regions. Hershey held a competition to name the new town. The winning entry, Hersheyoko, was vetoed by the US Post Office, so he

> *Hershey wanted to build a town in keeping with his social philosophy in the same way that other chocolate philanthropists, like Joseph Rowntree and George Cadbury, had done in England.*

settled for plain old Hershey Town. He also constructed a mansion, High Point, overlooking the chocolate factory, to house his family.

Shortly before his death, one last act assured the name of Hershey a place in business history. When the United States entered the Second World War, the US military instructed him to develop a chocolate bar for the troops—one that wouldn't melt. He once again set about chocolate innovation. The resulting Field Ration D Chocolate Bar formed an essential part of the army's personal kit. Not only was it a great favourite of the US personnel, but with the stationing of American troops in England and the subsequent D-Day invasion of Europe, it became part of Second World War folklore. Hershey died on 13 October 1945, aged 88.

CONTEXT AND CONCLUSIONS

First and foremost Hershey pioneered the mass production of food and, in particular, chocolate. It may only have been milk chocolate, but Hershey manufactured it on an unprecedented scale. Besides his single-minded approach, Hershey possessed a number of other qualities that contributed to his success. He was innovative, creating the Hershey Kiss and inventing his own recipe for milk chocolate. He was a bold risk-taker, making decisions like the one to build a sugar plant in Cuba. Perhaps his defining characteristic, however, was his enlightened attitude towards corporate social responsibility. It makes sense to keep the workforce happy, but few can claim to have gone to such lengths as Hershey to do so. The business history books tell how successful the Hershey chocolate bar was and still is. Hershey Town with its schools, parks, churches, and chocolate factory is a more permanent record.

THE BEST SOURCES OF HELP
Books:
Brenner, Joël Glenn. *The Emperors of Chocolate: Inside the Secret World of Hershey and Mars*. New York: Random House, 1999.
McMahon, James D. *Built on Chocolate: The Story of the Hershey Chocolate Company*. Santa Monica, California: General Publishing Group, 1999.
Website:
Hershey Foods Corporation: **www.hersheys.com**

SOICHIRO HONDA

1906	Born.
1937	Founds Tokai Seiki Heavy Industry (TSHI).
1948	Co-founds Honda with Takeo Fujisawa.
1949	D Type motorcycle—the Dream—manufactured.
1952	Production of Cub begins.
1954	Honda motorcycle team is founded.
1959	Opens dealership in United States. Super Cub goes into production.
1963	Honda becomes top-selling motorcycle brand in United States.
1973	Officially retires.
1984	Ten million Honda 50s sold in United States.
1992	Dies.

> **SUMMARY**
>
> Soichiro Honda started in business as a car mechanic and then, bypassing the time-honoured Japanese networking system or *gakubatsa*, he made his own way in business with no help from cronies. The Honda Company was founded in 1948 and its first motorcycle, the Dream, was produced a year later. Success followed success. In 1959 Honda became the leading motorcycle manufacturer in Japan, and the Honda sports motorcycle team won the team prize at the Isle of Man TT races. In the same year the first Honda motorcycles were sold in the United States; soon they were out-selling every other brand. The company went into the automobile business in the 1960s. Until Soichiro Honda's death in 1992, the company continued to be the most popular motorcycle manufacturer in the world and remained high in the international rankings of leading automobile manufacturers.

LIFE AND CAREER

Born in the small Japanese town of Komyo in 1906, Soichiro Honda spent his early childhood helping his father with his bicycle repair business. At 15, without the benefit of a formal education, Honda travelled to Tokyo to look for work. He obtained an apprenticeship at a garage, but ended up baby-sitting for the garage owner. Frustrated and dispirited, he returned home, only to be called back within six months. This time he stayed for six years, working as car mechanic before returning home once more to start his own car mechanic business. He was 22.

Honda's love of cars extended to racing them, and he set a new average speed record in 1936. Unfortunately he suffered a bad crash, breaking several bones, including both wrists. His wife, fearing for his safety, persuaded him to give up his hobby. Without the distraction of racing, Honda concentrated his energies on his business, and in 1937 he expanded into piston-ring manufacture, setting up Tokai Seiki Heavy Industry (TSHI). He was still

> *Born in the small Japanese town of Komyo in 1906, Soichiro Honda spent his early childhood helping his father with his bicycle repair business.*

conscious of his lack of education, however, and enrolled at the Hamamatsu School of Technology. As it turned out, he needn't have bothered.

Honda made a poor student. The demands of his business made it difficult to keep up with his class work. He was reluctant to pay attention to engineering lectures that didn't involve piston rings, and he refused to take notes or attend written examinations. When the school's principal warned Honda that if he did not submit to examination he would not receive his diploma, Honda was unrepentant. 'I am not impressed by diplomas. They don't do the work,' he later said. 'My marks were not as good as those of others, and I didn't take the final examination. The principal called me in and said I should leave. I told him that I didn't want a diploma—it had less value than a cinema ticket. A ticket at least guaranteed you would get in. A diploma guaranteed nothing.'

Giving up on the diploma and therefore shunning the *gakubatsa*, the Japanese old-boy networking system, the maverick Honda set out to make his fortune on his own terms.

CONTRIBUTION

By 1948 Honda had sold TSHI to Toyota for 450,000 yen (worth about $1 million today). He had established the Honda Technical Research Institute in 1946 and had tried to retire but found he couldn't resist the lure of engineering.

In 1948 Honda met a kindred spirit in financier Takeo Fujisawa. The two men had similar opinions on Japan's post-war industrial strategy. Both believed in long-term investment, and in partnership with Honda, Fujisawa agreed to invest in a new company to manufacture engines. Honda retained responsibility for engineering, while Fujisawa dealt with marketing and sales.

> *Honda was a perfectionist when it came to product design. He travelled the world conducting market research in person.*

By the 1950s Honda had signed a contract to sell the company's entire output of motorcycle engines to a company called Kitagawa. This wasn't as good a deal as it first appeared: Honda was geared up to produce 100 engines a month, while Kitagawa only produced 80 motorcycles at the most during the same period. Honda addressed the resulting cash-flow problem by tearing up his contract with Kitagawa and replacing it with deals to supply complete motorcycles to distributors.

The company's first big hit was the Cub, which offered customers the choice either of buying an engine to fit to their bicycles or buying a complete motorcycle. In less than a year the Cub was selling 6,500 units a month and had captured over 70% of the Japanese domestic motorcycle market.

While Honda's reluctance to play by the rules caused problems in some areas, particularly with the Japanese Ministry of International Trade and Industry (MITI), it served the company well in others. Honda adopted a refreshingly open recruitment policy. Although the company had problems recruiting graduate students because of Honda's unwillingness to play the *gakubatsa* game, it attracted many high-calibre employees who had been rejected by other Japanese corporations.

Honda was a perfectionist when it came to product design. He travelled the world conducting market research in person. He attended motorcycle races, taking notes on the competition. By using the best of the competition as a benchmark, Honda managed to turn the Honda motorcycle from an average product into the best racing motorcycle in the world. Success in motorcycle racing (Honda launched its own motorcycle racing team in 1954) raised the public profile of the company, added to the brand value, and enabled racing technology to filter down to the standard production model.

A big year for Honda came in 1959, when the company went into large-scale production of a new model that would sweep all before it, the Super Cub. To manufacture it Honda constructed the world's largest motorcycle plant in Suzuka City, which turned out 30,000 machines a month. In the same year the Honda team won first prize in the Isle of Man motorcycle races. Success on the track translated into sales.

In 1959 Honda Motorcycles opened its first dealership in the United States. Rather than sell through the existing US motorcycle distributors, Honda went for a more unconventional approach. He sold the small Honda motorcycles wherever he thought he might attract customers. At the time, total motorcycle sales in the United States were less than 5,000 per month. But by 1963 the company was selling 7,800 units; by 1984 Honda had sold some ten million Honda 50s. This remarkable success was due to the quality of the product and a brilliant advertising campaign. Instead of targeting its product at conventional motorcycle enthusiasts, Honda authorised a campaign with the slogan 'You meet the nicest people on a Honda'. The campaign targeted the family market and was a huge success.

The company Honda built went on to dominate the motorcycle market and make a big impact in the car market. At the end of the 20th century the company was still the world's number one motorcycle manufacturer. Honda retired in October 1973, taking an office in Tokyo where he busied himself with work connected with the Honda Foundation. He died in 1992.

CONTEXT AND CONCLUSIONS
Along with Konosuke Matsushita, Akio Morita, and Eiji Toyoda, Soichiro Honda was one of Japan's greatest industrialists. Notable for his independent streak, Honda spurned the traditional methods of building a business, deciding instead to go it alone. Turning a hobby into a business, he built a billion-dollar company that produced the best-selling motorcycle in the world. So good were their design and build quality that Honda motorcycles were soon outselling Triumph and Harley-Davidson in the UK and US markets. To achieve this Honda used a combination of excellent engineering and clever marketing. By making a sports motorcycle that was faster than its competitors, the Honda company gained cachet for its consumer models and stayed at the cutting edge of technological development.

Above all, Soichiro Honda was determined to make his dreams a reality. 'Many people dream of success,' he said. 'To me success can only be achieved through repeated failure and introspection. In fact, success represents 1% of your work which results from the 99% that is called failure.'

THE BEST SOURCES OF HELP
Website:
Honda: **www.honda.co.uk**

HOWARD HUGHES

1905	Born.
1909	Father forms Sharp-Hughes Tool Company.
1925	Hughes moves to Hollywood, California. Starts making films.
1927	*Two Arabian Knights* wins the Academy Award for comedy.
1934	Sets up Hughes Aircraft Company.
1935	Breaks airspeed record.
1936	Aged 30, breaks US transcontinental speed record in a self-built plane.
1938	Smashes record for New York–Paris flight with time of 16 hours and 35 minutes.
1939	Obtains majority share in Transcontinental & West Airline.
1948	Saves airline (now renamed Trans World Airlines) from bankruptcy.
1954	Sells large part of RKO and concentrates on TWA.
1955	Establishes the Howard Hughes Medical Institute in Miami, Florida.
1966	Sells TWA shares for $750 million.
1975	Dies.

SUMMARY

Howard Robard Hughes Jr (1905–1975) was born into wealth. His father founded a company that exploited a new design of oil drill. The Sharp-Hughes Tool Company was to provide a safety net of wealth throughout Hughes's life that made it possible for him to indulge his every whim. Indulge he did. Before the age of 25 he had moved to Hollywood and made several successful films, founded a new drill bit company, bought over a hundred cinemas, and learned to fly. By the time of his death in 1975, he had a built a successful airline (TWA), run a film business, bought a piece of the gaming action on the Strip in Las Vegas, broken several airspeed records, survived three plane crashes, and become a legendary recluse. Few people have packed as much into one lifetime as Howard Hughes.

LIFE AND CAREER

There is much disagreement about the facts surrounding the life of Howard Hughes. The disagreement even extends to his birthplace. Was it the city of Houston or the oil town of Humble? But there is no argument that Hughes was born on 24 December 1905 in Texas. His father was a wealthy man with a business degree from Harvard and a law degree from Iowa State University. In 1909 Howard Sr formed the Sharp-Hughes Tool Company, manufacturing drilling bits for the oil industry. It was his invention of a new oil drill bit that propelled the Hughes family to the kind of wealth that even his noted profligacy could not dent.

As a boy, Howard Jr was especially interested in engineering. He showed an impressive knack for building machines, constructing his own radio set as well as his own motorcycle. Away from engineering, Hughes's Uncle Rupert, a novelist and playwright, would take the boy to visit the Goldwyn studio where he developed a fascination with cinema.

Both Hughes's parents died before he was 20. Upon the death of his father, he somehow persuaded his relatives to sell him the Hughes Tool Company. Then, in 1925, he married a wealthy woman, Ella Rice, and moved to Hollywood, California.

In Hollywood Hughes began to exhibit the almost maniacal energy and drive that sustained him throughout his varied career.

CONTRIBUTION

By 1925 Hughes had created the Caddo Rock Drill Bit Company, bought a controlling interest in Multi-Color, Inc., moved into a house on Muirfield Road in Los Angeles, and employed Noah Dietrich, ostensibly as an assistant. Dietrich was to become the 'fixer' for the Hughes empire in the coming years. Hughes also purchased over a hundred cinemas to assist him in his latest venture: film-making.

Hughes's first film, *Swell Hogan*, was a flop. His third, *Two Arabian Knights*, made money and won the 1927 Academy Award for comedy. Hughes had another hit with *Scarface* and followed it with *The Front Page*. The difficulties involved in making *Scarface*, which stemmed partly from antagonism towards his anti-Semitic beliefs, took their toll on him and he temporarily abandoned film-making. For a time he restricted his interest in the film world to dating some of the most beautiful women of the time, including Ida Lupino, Katharine Hepburn, Ginger Rogers, Ava Gardner, and Lana Turner. Instead of making films he turned his attention to the aviation business.

> *Hughes's first film,* Swell Hogan, *was a flop. His third,* Two Arabian Knights, *made money and won the 1927 Academy Award for comedy.*

Hughes decided to form an aircraft company, so he employed a brilliant aeronautical engineer, Glen Odekirk, and set up business in a hangar in California. In the interval between filming *The Front Page*, and setting up the Hughes Aircraft Company in 1934, he disappeared from sight. At about the same time, however, there appeared on the scene a gangly employee of American Airways, 6 feet 3 inches tall, called Charles Howard, who, irritatingly, asked endless questions about the airline's operations. Charles Howard, it transpired, was none other than Howard Hughes himself. Hughes also spent some of this 'missing' period travelling as a hobo, and as a society photographer, a business he started from scratch in Huntsville, Texas, under the name R. Wayne Rector.

In 1939 Hughes helped finance Transcontinental & West Airline, obtaining a majority share in the process. The airline was later renamed Trans World Airlines (TWA). By 1940 the dynamic Hughes was running several businesses simultaneously, in different fields. He still owned the tool-manufacturing company he had bought from his father's estate, which made him $2 million a month. In addition he was back in the film business, running an airline, and gearing up for wartime manufacturing.

In the first half of the 1940s Hughes ordered commercial aircraft from Lockheed, made and released the film *The Outlaw*, created a new starlet in Jane Russell, opened a manufacturing plant to assist the US war effort, and crashed yet another aircraft. He had already crashed two planes, killing two passengers.

In 1946, after another period of absence, Hughes reappeared to test his experimental reconnaissance aircraft, the XF-11. At 400 mph the plane became unstable. To the consternation of the members, he tried to land on the Los Angeles Country Club golf course. Luckily for the club, but unluckily for him, he didn't make it, ploughing into a house on the way down. He was admitted to the Cedars of Lebanon

Hospital, and the doctors predicted he would not last through the night. His injuries were extensive: a crushed chest, 12 broken ribs, a collapsed left lung, fractured shoulder, crushed vertebrae, and third-degree burns. Remarkably, the apparently indestructible Hughes made a good recovery. He was left with burn scars and a deformed left hand, but very much alive.

Discharged from hospital, he set about turning TWA around. He saved the ailing airline by obtaining a subsidy from the Civil Aeronautics Board in 1948, and a $10 million loan from the Reconstruction Finance Corporation. He also bolstered his film business, buying the struggling RKO studio (Radio-Keith Orpheum) for $9 million. In 1954 Hughes sold most of RKO to concentrate on TWA. In 1955 he established the Howard Hughes Medical Institute in Miami, Florida, in an attempt to reduce his tax liabilities. On 3 May 1966 he sold 78% of his TWA stock for $750 million. It made him, temporarily, the richest man in the world.

The remainder of Hughes's career, until his death in 1975, was characterised by obsessive-neurotic behaviour and flight from the IRS. Yet, despite his continual dislocation—moving from one hotel to another, one country to another—his increasingly bizarre behaviour, and his dependence on pain-killing drugs, Hughes somehow managed to control his businesses from the end of a phone. He even expanded into hotels and casinos, buying the Desert Inn, Sands, Castaways, New Frontier, and Silver Slipper on the Strip in Las Vegas, as well as thousands of acres of land and over 500 mining concessions in a gigantic spending spree.

The fact that Hughes's disparate collection of companies fell apart within 12 years of his death is evidence, if any were needed, that his bizarre personality was the glue that bound his business empire together.

CONTEXT AND CONCLUSIONS
Of all the business leaders and entrepreneurs of the 20th century, Howard Hughes is one of the most colourful, controversial, and bizarre. An examination of his life reveals a man driven by the most basic of instincts: power, greed, lust, enmity. He ended his days a compulsive-obsessive, drug-dependent hypochondriac, but consistently conducted business deals with a shrewdness beyond most of his peers. His achievements encompass film-making, aviation, and the hotel and gambling industry. In cinema Hughes notoriously pushed back the boundaries of decency and showed that it was possible to make successful films outside the studio system. In Nevada he succeeded in loosening the Mob's grip on Las Vegas. In aviation he was among those who pioneered commercial airflight.

THE BEST SOURCES OF HELP
Books:
Brown, Peter Harry, and Pat H. Broeske. *Howard Hughes: The Untold Story*. Brentwood, California: Dutton, 1996.
Keats, John. *Howard Hughes*. New York: Random House, 1972.
Rummel, Robert W. *Howard Hughes and TWA*. Washington, DC: Smithsonian Institution Press, 1991.
Thomas, Tony. *Howard Hughes in Hollywood*. Sacramento, California: Citadel Press, 1985.

LEE IACOCCA

1924	Born.
1946	Joins Ford as a trainee engineer.
1949	Becomes sales manager.
1956	Introduces a new finance scheme called the '56 for '56'.
1970	Becomes president of Ford.
1978	Fired by Henry Ford II.
1979	Iacocca becomes chairman and CEO of Chrysler.
1983	Writes out cheque for $813,487,500 to clear Chrysler's federal debt.
1992	Retires from Chrysler.
1999	Starts EV Global Motors.

SUMMARY

The lionisation of chief executive officers began in earnest with Lee Iacocca. In the 1980s his remarkable turnaround of car giant Chrysler made him a corporate hero. The myth he helped to create culminated in the extraordinary worship of GE's Jack Welch in recent years. Arriving at the Ford Motor Corporation as a trainee engineer in 1946, in the 1980s his remarkable turnaround of car giant Chrysler made him a corporate hero. Iacocca always claimed he wasn't a natural salesman, but he made a big impact at Ford with his revolutionary financing plan. He introduced the Ford Mustang, and was promoted to president of the company. After an internal power struggle, instigated by Henry Ford II, Iacocca was fired in 1978. He switched sides, joining Chrysler and becoming CEO in 1979. Since retirement in 1992, he has concentrated on the healthy lifestyle, launching electric-powered vehicles and supporting healthy foods.

LIFE AND CAREER

Lee Iacocca was born on 15 October 1924 in Allentown, Pennsylvania. Iacocca's father ran a small hot-dog business. For the Iacoccas, as for many other families during the late 1920s and 1930s, times were hard. Iacocca Sr lost all his money and nearly lost the family home. Even though Lee Iacocca was only seven at the time, the harshness of the Depression ingrained frugality so deeply that, while he may not have been risk-averse in his business dealings, he always invested money conservatively and to this day dislikes waste.

In the 1980s his remarkable turnaround of car giant Chrysler made him a corporate hero.

CONTRIBUTION

As a trainee at Ford's famous River Rouge plant, Iacocca got to see every stage of car production, from the extraction of coal and limestone, through the production of steel, to the manufacturing of the cars on the assembly line. It represented the best training the auto industry had to offer. Graduating from his trainee course, Iacocca decided against engineering and instead went to work in the Ford sales office in Chester, Pennsylvania. He was not a born salesman, yet through practice and experience he improved quickly, moving from a bashful, stammering sales clerk to become sales manager in 1949.

The 1950s were good years for Iacocca. In 1956, to combat poor sales of Ford motor cars, he introduced a new finance scheme called the '56 for '56'. Credit financing was just beginning to take hold as a way of purchasing cars. The scheme allowed the cash-strapped purchaser to make a modest down payment of 20% and then follow up with three further payments of $56. The scheme was a success, and was adopted companywide, making Iacocca an overnight star within the Ford ranks. One promotion quickly followed another. By 1960 he was head of the Ford division. Aged 36, Iacocca was general manager of the largest division in the world's second biggest automobile company.

He soon stamped his authority on the company, playing an influential role in the decision to abandon a proposed new model, the Cardinal, which was dropped despite the company incurring a $35 million loss. In its place, the first Ford Mustang rolled off the assembly line. The new car had been designed from scratch and was priced at an affordable level. Its launch created a wave of publicity, simultaneously featuring on the covers of *Time* and *Newsweek* magazines. The Mustang was the car the market had been waiting for. In its first year it sold a record 418,812, making a profit of $1.1 billion.

The Mustang was the car the market had been waiting for. In its first year it sold a record 418,812, making a profit of $1.1 billion.

For Iacocca, who had championed the Mustang, the car's popularity had certain unwelcome side effects. There was no such thing as a private life any more for the man who had brought Ford's most popular car to market. When Iacocca was returning from a trip to Europe on the Ford company plane, the pilot was contacted by two other pilots and a radio operator from a ship below, all of them wanting to speak to his celebrated passenger. 'Is nothing sacred? It's Sunday morning. I am in the middle of nowhere, and I can't get away from this Mustang mania!' was Iacocca's reply. But Iacocca had much to thank the Mustang for. In January 1965 he was promoted to vice-president of the corporate car/truck group, and on 10 December 1970 he became president of the Ford empire.

President he may have been, but Iacocca was not the most powerful person at Ford. That honour was reserved for the founder's grandson, Henry Ford II. Ford operated an unorthodox management style: he ruled through fear; executives could find themselves clearing their desks for the most unlikely reasons. For several years Iacocca managed to walk the tightrope, on the one hand not seeming to threaten Ford's authority yet, on the other, doing a good enough job to avoid being fired. It is to his credit that Iacocca managed to stay in the job as long as he did.

In ill health, with his marriage strained, Ford became increasingly paranoid and his decisions increasingly bizarre. There was even an internal investigation within the company at Ford's request into Iacocca's activities, which allegedly cost over $1,500,000 and came up with nothing damaging. Then, in 1977, Ford turned to the management consulting firm McKinsey & Company, calling them in to reorganise the company's management structure. McKinsey recommended a new structure with a chairman/CEO, vice-chairman, and president at the top. Iacocca now became number three in the ruling triumvirate, and to humiliate him further, Ford insisted on parading this apparent demotion in public. Then in 1978 Ford fired Iacocca. The reason—in Ford's own words—was: 'Sometimes you just don't like somebody.'

Iacocca was 54. He could have retired. Yet a few months later he joined the Chrysler Motor Corporation, becoming chairman and CEO in September 1979. During his time at Chrysler Iacocca executed one of the most impressive turnarounds in automobile history. When he arrived, the Detroit press was full of gloomy headlines such as 'Chrysler losses are worst ever'. The company was struggling, but, when he joined, Iacocca had not realised how serious its problems were. He soon found out: Chrysler was running out of money, and fast. Iacocca took swift remedial action: he eradicated excess inventory, renegotiated contracts with car rental companies Hertz and Avis, recruited a slew of top talent, and made substantial lay-offs. Most important of all, he went cap in hand to the government and applied for a loan guarantee for $1.2 billion. It required new legislation. To secure government support Iacocca had to give testimony in Washington before the House of Representatives and Senate hearings. But the request was granted.

That it was attests to Iacocca's powers as a salesman. As he cut costs at Chrysler (he cut his own salary to $1), and the automobile market picked up, Chrysler's flagging fortunes revived. In 1983 Chrysler made a profit of $925 million and not long after a new stock offering, Iacocca wrote out an historic cheque for $813,487,500 to clear the balance of the debt outstanding on the government loan.

Iacocca went on to steer Chrysler to greater success. He engineered the company's $1.5 billion acquisition of American Motors, and incorporated the Jeep into Chrysler's product offering. Iacocca retired from Chrysler in 1992, but his enthusiasm for business remained undiminished. Leaving the motor giants behind him, he founded a small start-up company, EV Global Motors, selling electric-powered bicycles. In 2001, he took 'clean transport' a stage further by launching the LIDO, an electric-powered vehicle designed for local driving, that resembled a cross between a golf buggy and Chrysler's retro PT Cruiser. Critics claimed that he had spent his career putting polluting vehicles on driveways and now it was payback time. Iacocca also invested in diabetes research through his support for Olivio Premium Products, a company marketing products based on olive oil. Iacocca pledged the equivalent of 25% of Olivio sales to research.

CONTEXT AND CONCLUSIONS

Brilliant businessmen such as Henry Ford, Walter Chrysler, and Billy Durant long ago earned their place in the auto hall of fame. But among the post-war generation, few deserve to sit alongside the founding fathers. Lee Iacocca is one of them, successfully running not one but two of the big three US motor manufacturers.

A rare combination of talented salesman and empathetic man-manager, Iacocca had an instinctive feeling for which models would sell and which would not. He introduced the Ford Mustang and revitalised Ford's prospects when the company was drifting directionless following the death of the first Henry Ford. At Chrysler Iacocca performed one of the most breathtaking turnarounds in corporate history; in the process he became a corporate icon.

CLOSE BUT NO CIGAR
BOB LUTZ

Ex-Marine fighter pilot Lutz paid his dues in the motor business, working his way through General Motors, BMW, and, finally, Ford, where he was vice-president. After Ford he became Iacocca's right-hand man at Chrysler and played a big part in the company's revival. Many think he should have got the CEO job when Iacocca left. In 2001 he left Chrysler to join General Motors as vice-president.

THE BEST SOURCES OF HELP
Books:
Iacocca, Lee, with William Novak. *IACOCCA—An Autobiography*. London: Sidgwick & Jackson, 1985.
Iacocca, Lee, with Sonny Kleinfield. *Talking Straight*. London: Sidgwick & Jackson, 1988.
Wyden, Peter. *The Unknown Iacocca*. London: Sidgwick & Jackson, 1988.
Website:
Chrysler: **www.chrysler.com**

STEVE JOBS

1955	Born.
1974	Takes a job with Atari.
1976	First product, the Apple I, marketed.
1977	Apple II. Apple incorporated; Mike Markkula buys shares in the company and becomes chairman.
1980	Apple goes public.
1982	$1 billion sales; John Sculley becomes CEO.
1984	Launch of Apple Macintosh.
1985	Jobs leaves Apple.
1986	Founds NeXT. Co-founds Pixar.
1993	Sculley leaves Apple.
1996	Jobs returns as consultant.
1997	Becomes 'interim CEO'.
1998	iMac launched.
2000	Drops 'interim' from job title.
2001	Apple launches iPhoto to move into digital photography.
2003	New iMac launched. Launch of world's first 17-inch portable computer. Oracle announces it may buy into Apple.

SUMMARY

Steve Jobs, cofounder of Apple Computer, is one of the folk-hero CEOs. The company was started in a garage—by Jobs and his cofounder Steve Wozniak—and its Apple PCs changed the face of computing. Unfortunately, Apple got its strategy wrong, tying the Mac operating system software to Apple hardware. Microsoft went in the opposite direction, licensing the MS-DOS operating system to any and every PC manufacturer. The rest is history.

In 1985, former Pepsi chairman John Sculley, brought in to add beef to Apple, removed Jobs from the company he had founded. Sculley himself was removed in 1993, and Jobs was eventually asked to return.

Since his comeback, Jobs has breathed new life into the company. To his many fans, Apple's revival confirms Jobs's status as one of the greatest technology entrepreneurs ever.

LIFE AND CAREER

In February 1955 Paul and Clara Jobs adopted an orphan, Stephen Jobs. Jobs was brought up in Los Altos, California.

Out of school, Jobs attended lectures at the Hewlett-Packard electronics company, and it was while working at Hewlett-Packard one summer that he met Stephen Wozniak, a University of California dropout. Wozniak was an engineering whiz kid who was continually inventing gadgets.

Once again he hooked up with Wozniak, attending meetings of the 'Homebrew Computer Club'. Most of the members were geeks, interested only in diodes, transistors, and the electronic gadgets they built from them. Jobs was different; he had an eye for style, utility, and marketability. Jobs persuaded Wozniak to work with

Steve Jobs

him to build a personal computer. The Apple I computer was designed in Jobs's bedroom and the prototype constructed in his garage.

After moderate success selling their first computer, a local electronics retailer ordered 25. Some helpful advice from a retired CEO of Intel inspired Jobs and Wozniak to start their own company. To do so they sold their most treasured possessions, in Jobs's case his Volkswagen microbus. For Wozniak it was his prized Hewlett-Packard calculator. With the $1,300 they raised, the two started a new company, which they named Apple.

> *The Apple I computer was designed in Jobs's bedroom and the prototype constructed in his garage.*

CONTRIBUTION

The company's first product, the Apple I, was marketed in 1976, priced at $666. As members of the local computing fraternity, Jobs and Wozniak were well positioned to drum up interest in their new machine. Sales of the Apple I brought in $774,000 and soon the two entrepreneurs were working on the Apple II. The second incarnation of the Apple computer was a resounding success. This was not just down to its engineering; it was also due in large part to Jobs's marketing savvy. In an inspired move he brought in Regis McKenna, the best public relations man in Silicon Valley, the man who went on to popularise relationship marketing.

In 1980 Apple went public. Originally priced at $22 per share, the stock rose on the first day to $29, capitalising the company at $1.2 billion. Between 1978 and 1983, in the absence of any real competition, Apple forged ahead in the personal computer market; its compound growth rate was over 150% per annum. Then, in 1981, IBM introduced its first PC, using an operating system called MS-DOS, licensed from a small software company called Microsoft. Within two years, IBM had exceeded Apple's dollar sales of PCs. Furthermore, Microsoft was causing a stir in the PC market, even though it didn't manufacture PC hardware. Microsoft licensed its operating software to PC producers. Jobs realised that if IBM and Microsoft were allowed to dominate the market then Apple could become marginalised.

To restore Apple's fortunes, Jobs turned to John Sculley, CEO at Pepsi.

The result of this unlikely alliance between the corporate suit, Sculley, and the counterculture kid, Jobs, was the personal computer that cemented Apple Computer's status as the computer enthusiast's favourite computer company—the Apple Macintosh.

Instead of writing commands in computerese, Macintosh owners used a mouse to click on easily recognisable icons—a rubbish bin and file folders, for example. Suddenly, you didn't need a degree in computer science to operate a personal computer. Other companies followed where Apple led, most significantly Microsoft. Apple became the darling of the creative world with an iconic status that Bill Gates and his crew never achieved. But what Microsoft did do was to dominate the PC software industry, commanding 80% market share as against Apple's 20%. In the end that proved critical.

The Apple fairy tale came to a sticky end in 1985 when white knight Sculley did the unthinkable and removed Jobs from the company he had founded. A fired-up

Jobs proceeded to plough $250 million of investors' money into another start-up—NeXT Computer. It disappointed, selling only 50,000 units. Pixar Animation Studios, in which he invested $60 million of his own fortune, was a different story, however. This investment eventually paid out with the computer-animated blockbusters *Toy Story* and *A Bug's Life*. Back at Apple, Sculley himself was booted out in 1993 after a disastrous period that saw Apple's market share plummet from 20% to just 8%. He was replaced by Michael Spindler, who lasted until 1996, by which time Apple's market share had fallen to just over 5%. Apple was staring oblivion in the face; even its long-term devotees began to switch to the Microsoft-powered PCs in droves. Spindler was shown the door; Gil Amelio took over in the hot seat. After 500 days in the job, and with Apple's market share unmoved, Amelio invited Jobs back to help in a consulting role. It wasn't long before Amelio was on his way out too, and Jobs, now Apple's self-styled interim CEO, was back where he started.

With Jobs back at the helm, Apple looked more like its old self. He dumped the NeXT operating system that he had sold to Apple, ditched loss-making licensing contracts, and most significantly launched the new iMac. The iMac was the embodiment of everything Jobs believed in: eye-catching design and simple operation. It was also the product of a different vision of the computer itself. It had no disk drive—Jobs believed they had been superseded by external storage devices such as zip drives and the Internet. The stylish Internet-ready machine, which Jobs hoped would restore the company's fading fortunes, was launched with the slogan 'Chic Not Geek' blazed across advertising posters. The iMac, a vision in translucent blue, sold 278,000 units in the first six weeks, an achievement that had *Fortune* magazine describing it as 'one of the hottest computer launches ever'. Wall Street, too, recovered its confidence in Apple: the company's share price doubled in less than a year. Revenues for the fiscal year 2000 were some $7.98 billion, with net earnings of $786 million, and Apple has started to open a series of retail stores across the United States. Since then Apple's share price has been caught up in the same vortex as other technology companies. Product development has continued to follow the Steve Jobs theme of cool computing. 2001 saw the launch of iPhoto, Apple's strategy to win a strong position in digital photography. This was followed in 2003 by an even more powerful version of the iMac plus the world's first 17-inch portable, the latest version of the Powerbook. However, despite the continuing innovation, Apple's financial performance remained poor and, in 2003, Oracle announced that it might buy into the ailing company. What the future holds is not clear, but with Jobs back on the Apple throne, at least the company looks more like its old successful trailblazing self.

> *The iMac was the embodiment of everything Jobs believed in: eye-catching design and simple operation.*

CONTEXT AND CONCLUSIONS

Described by one newspaper as a 'corporate Huckleberry Finn', Steve Jobs is one of a select group of IT whiz kids that includes Bill Gates, Larry Ellison, and Scott McNealy. Where Jobs differs from his tech peers is in his sense of style. IBM brought computers to the business world, Microsoft gave the PC its MS-DOS operating system, but Jobs made computing easy. By taking the graphical user interface that he had first seen in a Xerox PARC laboratory and incorporating it into the Apple Mac, Jobs enabled the technologically nonliterate to use a computer by simply pointing and clicking.

And if that wasn't a sufficient contribution to the history of the PC, Jobs developed one of the first computer animation film studios, Pixar, and then returned to Apple just in time to save it from rotting. With the introduction of the iMac, Jobs once again demonstrated the imagination and design flair that made him a multimillionaire and made Apple the computer of choice for millions of devoted followers.

THE BEST SOURCES OF HELP
Books:
Carlton, Jim. *Apple: The Inside Story of Intrigue, Egomania, and Business Blunders.* New York: Random House, 1997.
Deutschman, Alan. *The Second Coming of Steve Jobs.* New York: Broadway Books, 2000.
Young, Jeffrey S. *Steve Jobs: The Journey Is the Reward.* New York: Lynx Books, 1988.
Website:
Apple: **www.apple.com**

INGVAR KAMPRAD

1926	Born.
1943	Registers company, Ikéa (letters don't become uppercase until much later).
1948	Advertises furniture for the first time.
1951	Publishes first catalogue. Revenue exceeds one million kronor ($95,000).
1953	Opens factory combined with furniture exhibition centre in Älmhult.
1956	Introduces flat packaging.
1958	Opens first store in Älmhult.
1965	Introduces self-service in stores.
1982	Ownership transferred to Dutch Foundation—Stichting INGKA.
1986	Officially retires, handing day-to-day running to Anders Moberg.
1995	Stichting INGKA buys Habitat chain.
1999	150th store opens. Turnover reaches Kr60 billion ($5.689 billion).
2002	Becomes the United Kingdom's largest furniture retailer. Announces sons will take over running of IKEA.
	Bombs planted outside Dutch stores.
2003	Apologises for past involvement in Nazi activities. IKEA announces opening of first Israeli store in 2004.
	Opens first Russian store.

SUMMARY

The flat-pack king of furniture, Kamprad is a brilliant if unorthodox businessman. Like Richard Branson, Kamprad enjoys challenging the establishment and upsetting the odds. Industrious from an early age, Kamprad took on the furniture cartel in Sweden and neatly out-manoeuvred it. In the end, as he always predicted they would, customers got what they demanded: low prices and good quality. Kamprad continued to deliver value for money to ordinary people through innovations such as flat-pack furniture and self-service. Shopping the IKEA way became a family day out, a fun experience, long before the advent of the out-of-town shopping centre. When Kamprad officially took a back seat from line management at IKEA in 1986, he had changed the nature of retailing and provided inspiration for thousands of entrepreneurs.

LIFE AND CAREER

Ingvar Kamprad was born on the family farm, Elmtaryd, in 1926, in the harsh countryside of Smland, Sweden. His was a tough upbringing. Sweden in the late 1920s and early 1930s was a difficult place in which to grow up. Outside the Swedish cities, the cold unforgiving landscape of the country offered few opportunities for advancement. Yet Kamprad was resourceful and full of the enthusiasm of youth.

He began in a small way by selling matches to neighbours. He was five years old. He graduated to catching fish and selling them, as well as picking lingonberries which he dispatched by bus to a local buyer. He made his first real money selling garden seed. It was enough to buy a new racing bike and a typewriter.

CONTRIBUTION

Kamprad was still only 17 when, in 1943, he started his own company. He called it Ikéa: IK from his initials, E for Elmtaryd, the farm he grew up on, and A for

Agunnaryd, his home village. By 1945 Kamprad was selling a hotchpotch of products. His business had outgrown local delivery and he began to sell by mail order. Newspaper advertisements stimulated demand and the local milk van and train network solved his distribution problems. Soon pens, pencils, picture frames, wallets, watches and other assorted goods were wending their way across Sweden, courtesy of IKEA. Astonishingly Kamprad was still working full time, as well as running this business. It was only after completing his national service in 1946 that he began to focus solely on his business.

Kamprad advertised furniture for the first time in 1948. His decision to sell furniture was initially a result of matching his main competitor. The furniture was sourced from local manufacturers; it was cheap, and sales were promising—so much so that four years later he abandoned his other products to concentrate on affordably priced furniture and domestic articles.

> He made his first real money selling garden seed. It was enough to buy a new racing bike and a typewriter.

Until 1953 the business had operated as a mail order business only. The problem was that competition in the mail order industry was driving down prices and product quality. Kamprad was engaged in a vicious and unsustainable price war on several fronts, and delivery of shoddy goods by competitors was also adversely affecting the reputation of the industry. The solution was to allow the customers to see and touch the products themselves. Kamprad bought a local joinery in Älmhult that was about to close and informed his customers that IKEA was now a furniture company. If the customers wished to see the products in the catalogue close up, then they could visit IKEA's furniture exhibition when it opened on 18 March 1953. It was a gamble. On the opening day, nervously Kamprad threw back the doors of his new display-store-cum-furniture factory. The sight that greeted him took his breath away. There were at least 1,000 people waiting patiently outside. Maybe it was the coffee and buns that he had rashly promised to all first-day visitors.

It was in those early days that the principles that underpin IKEA's business today were developed. Cost awareness was one fundamental rule. Kamprad saved on string, boxes, paper, and whatever he could. Another feature was the provision of food. IKEA's stores may have progressed from the provision of buns and coffee to restaurants with extensive menus, but the idea that you can get something tasty to eat remains. For Kamprad it was always a practical decision to provide food, since people were travelling long distances to reach the Ämhult factory.

In 1955, Kamprad encountered his first major setback. IKEA was doing well; but business was too good, as it turned out. Unable to compete fairly with Kamprad, competitors turned to less savoury methods. Suppliers suddenly found themselves under pressure not to supply IKEA. The company was mysteriously banned from trade fairs. On one occasion, Kamprad had to resort to entering a trade fair hidden under a carpet, in the back of a friend's Volvo. But he had the last laugh. Facing difficulties in obtaining supplies, Kamprad decided to build and design his own furniture. Banned from trade exhibitions, he bought his own exhibition centres. Whatever the competition did, Kamprad outfoxed them.

IKEA milestones followed swiftly, one after another. Flat packaging was introduced in 1956, so customers could get the furniture into their cars more easily. A 6,700 square metre IKEA store was opened in Älmhult in 1958, and the company signed on its 100th employee. Self-service was introduced in 1965. By the 1970s, IKEA was an international company with stores right across Europe. By 1999 the company had 150 stores in 30 countries, employing 44,000 people. Revenues were over $7 billion and the IKEA catalogue's circulation was a staggering 100 million.

Although Kamprad is officially retired from day-to-day management, he is still seen by many as the company's totemic leader. Despite his phenomenal wealth—taxation and legal issues mean that he resides in Switzerland—Kamprad appears to be fundamentally the same person who started out selling matches all those years ago. He is still famously cost-conscious—he once described himself as a 'Swedish Scotsman'. He flies economy, eats modestly, dresses casually, and has been known to haggle at his local market. IKEA is the same: suits are conspicuously absent, there is minimal hierarchy, the advertising is a little eccentric.

IKEA's international expansion continues. In 2002, IKEA became the UK's largest furniture retailer and, in 2003, they opened a shopping centre in Leningrad. The announcement of the planned opening of the first store in Israel in 2004 followed Kamprad's public apology for his Nazi sympathies in early life. And controversy also hit the company in the Netherlands with bombs found outside several stores in December 2002.

> *He flies economy, eats modestly, dresses casually, and has been known to haggle at his local market.*

As for succession, Kamprad finally agreed that his sons should take over the company in 2002. Earlier he had shown no signs of acceding to his sons—he has three. Statements such as 'I don't think any of my sons are capable of running the company, at least not yet,' reinforced the impression that Kamprad believes there is still an important role for him to play at IKEA. As does his biography, *Leading by Design*, in which he says, 'The demon in me says that there is so much to do...I'm never satisfied.'

CONTEXT AND CONCLUSIONS

Kamprad's unique approach to management is encapsulated in 'A Furniture Dealer's Testament', the list of concepts Kamprad wrote down for his co-workers before he emigrated from Sweden. This creed says as much about Kamprad himself as it does about his company. It is based on some simple statements: 'The product range is our identity; the IKEA spirit is a strong and living reality; profits give us resources; reaching good results with small means; simplicity is a virtue; doing it a different way; concentration is important to our success; taking responsibility is our privilege, and many things remain to be done—a glorious future.' IKEA is a company made in Kamprad's own image. He has taken his values, carved from the harsh terrain of Smland, and assembled them into an international furniture company. He has done things his way, the different way. He has taken the road less travelled. It is a lesson for all entrepreneurs.

CLOSE BUT NO CIGAR
TERENCE CONRAN
With a similar idea at a similar time, Conran first started selling furniture from his basement in London's Notting Hill in 1952, just as Kamprad was about to open his factory-store. The first shop in the Habitat chain opened on the Fulham Road in 1964. Conran was always strongly design-led. The Conran Design Group was founded in 1956, and he was instrumental in shaping the look and feel of London's 'swinging sixties'. Selling affordable, stylish furniture, Habitat stores flourished and were joined by The Conran Shop. In the early 1990s, Conran sold the Habitat chain to IKEA. He continues to control the chain of Conran Shops and has successfully branched out into restaurants.

THE BEST SOURCES OF HELP
Books:
Grant, John. *IKEA Magic: 20 Business Lessons*. London: Texere, 2000.
Torekull, Bertil. *Leading by Design: The IKEA Story*. New York: HarperBusiness, 1999.
Website:
Ikea: **www.ikea.com**

HERB KELLEHER

1932	Born.
1956	Graduates from New York University.
1960	Starts to practise law in San Antonio, Texas.
1966	Discusses plan to start airline with Rollin King.
1968	Competing airlines sue Southwest.
1971	Southwest starts flying in Texas. Has its IPO.
1973	Southwest turns first profit.
1978	Becomes chairman.
1982	Becomes president and CEO.
1989	$1 billion in revenues.
1992	Arm wrestles Kurt Herwald.
2001	Steps down as CEO.
	Donates $4 million to University of Texas Center for Entrepreneurship.
2002	Named CEO of the Year.

SUMMARY

It was 1966 when lawyer Herb Kelleher sketched the plans for a low-price, no-frills airline on the back of a napkin. It was another five years until the first Southwest Airlines plane taxied down the runway carrying passengers. Ever since, Kelleher has been tearing up the management rule book. With singing flight attendants, practical jokes, and fancy dress, a Southwest ticket is worth its price just for the onboard entertainment— never mind the fast turnarounds, reliability, convenience, and low cost. But what else would you expect from a Harley-riding, bourbon-drinking CEO, who dresses up as Elvis and arm wrestles executives from competing carriers? From nowhere, Kelleher has created a company with $5 billion in annual revenues and a record of over 25 years of profitability. Maybe it doesn't seem so crazy after all.

LIFE AND CAREER

Born on 12 March 1932 in New Jersey, Herb Kelleher was an exceptional scholar. An undergraduate at Wesleyan University in Connecticut, he was one of those lucky students who excel at both sports and academic work, and he racked up an impressive list of achievements. From Wesleyan, Kelleher went on to New York University where he studied law, graduating in 1956.

After law school, Kelleher had a stint as a clerk in the Supreme Court of New Jersey and then practised law in San Antonio, Texas, starting in 1960. Over the next six years he built his law practice up, until in 1966 a chance conversation with one of his clients set him on an entirely new career path.

In a downtown bar—the St Anthony's Club—Kelleher's client Rollin King explained his idea for a budget airline service to connect three of Texas's main cities, Dallas, Houston, and San Antonio. The two of them drew up a business plan and jotted down the flight pattern on the back of a paper napkin: it was the outline for Southwest Airlines. The napkin is now framed and hanging on the wall in the company HQ. Kelleher put in $10,000 (for a stake worth over $200 million by 2001), and the company was incorporated in March 1967.

Herb Kelleher

CONTRIBUTION

With three airlines dominating the air traffic in Texas—Braniff, Texas International, and Continental—breaking up the cosy status quo was no easy task. Neither was it cheap. Over the next four years, Kelleher and Southwest Airlines sunk over a million dollars into fighting moves to block the company's application for airline certification. It was a bitter fight. A newspaper reported, 'Don't bother spending your money on a movie or going to see a play or attending a concert. Just come over and watch Herb Kelleher and the lawyers for Braniff and Texas International cut each other into little bits and pieces.' Colleagues and friends told Kelleher to give up, but Kelleher, a born fighter, won a final appeal to the Texas Supreme Court.

With Kelleher as chief legal counsel and Lamar Muse, a veteran of the airline business, as CEO, Southwest Airlines opened for business in 1971. Under intense pressure from the competition, Southwest toughed out the early years. Smarting from their legal defeat, the competing airlines embarked on a savage price war, which at times turned into physical violence. 'We were the bar-room brawlers of the airline industry,' said Kelleher. It wasn't until the third year in business that the company turned a profit. But, in 1978, Southwest Airlines flew into more turbulence when Muse resigned. In hindsight, the resignation of Muse was the making of Southwest: it brought Kelleher in as president. In 1982 he became CEO. He was to prove one of the most unorthodox, innovative, and successful CEOs of any major American corporation.

In hindsight, the resignation of Muse was the making of Southwest: it brought Kelleher in as president.

Kelleher had no time for existing airline business practice unless it supported his two principal aims: keeping the customer happy, and keeping costs down. He instigated a raft of measures designed to keep costs to a minimum. For example, customers choose seats on a first-come, first-served basis. And those hoping for a slap-up meal will be disappointed, as there are no in-flight meals—only peanuts—thus saving time and speeding up turnaround.

Kelleher's no-frills service is backed up with excellent customer care, driven by even better employee care. The key to this is the corporate culture that Kelleher has inspired. As far as he is concerned, working for Southwest Airlines should, above all else, be fun. At Southwest headquarters, casual dress is the norm, practical jokes are encouraged, employee birthdays are celebrated, and any excuse to have a party is a good one. It is no different on the planes. Passengers are likely to be greeted by flight attendants dressed as leprechauns on St Patrick's Day, have their safety instructions delivered in a Southwest Airlines version of stand-up comedy, and jump when the flight attendants pop out of the overhead luggage compartments.

Nor is Kelleher above these bizarre pranks either. There can be few CEOs of major American companies who have settled a high-level dispute with another corporation by arm wrestling their opposite number (Kelleher arm wrestled Kurt Herwald, chairman of Stevens Aviation, instead of going to court over an advertisement; he lost). Or who, when faced with a complaining customer who was clearly in the wrong, authorised a letter to the offending party advising them to fly with another airline. Or who have dressed up as Elvis for a recruitment ad that helpfully suggests CVs should be marked 'Attention Elvis'.

But despite what many may think, there is method in Kelleher's madness. The staff turnover rate at Southwest—below 7%—is one of lowest in the industry. And the company has never lost at any time because of union disputes. When Kelleher took over as CEO in 1982, revenues were $270 million, there were 2,000 employees and 27 planes. By 2001, revenues had soared to over $5 billion, with 30,000 employees and 344 planes.

Kelleher's unique brand of management continues to dazzle in an intensely competitive business.

Kelleher's unique brand of management continues to dazzle in an intensely competitive business. There is no doubt that Southwest Airlines' success is principally down to its CEO...The question is, what happens when Kelleher steps down? Southwest is about to find out. In 2001, Kelleher retired as CEO. When asked what he would be doing with his new-found free time he replied, in his characteristic but offbeat style, 'I might write about science. I might write about astronomy.'

Shortly after he retired, Kelleher was named as CEO of the Year. In 2002, he set out to encourage other entrepreneurs by donating $4 million dollars to the University of Texas Herb Kelleher Center for Entrepreneurial Excellence. He remains involved with Southwest Airlines as chairman of the board, but will finally cut all links in 2005

CONTEXT AND CONCLUSIONS

Southwest took a risk when it named a lawyer with no practical airline experience as president, and then CEO. The gamble paid off. Kelleher has inspired a unique corporate culture of fun and family at Southwest. Employees want to work for Southwest, and don't want to leave. Passengers want to fly Southwest because they know that, as well as a quick, on-time, low-cost flight, the likelihood is they will have a light-hearted, amusing journey.

Success didn't come overnight. Kelleher had to do battle with the competing carriers in the courts. He then had to convince the people at Southwest that the eccentric and offbeat can work, if it is underpinned by sound business practice. It may seem a little crazy on board, but the planes are full and the company is turning a profit every year. Along with CEOs such as IKEA's Ingvar Kamprad, and Virgin's Richard Branson, Kelleher has pioneered unconventional management practices and shown you can 'do it differently' and win.

THE BEST SOURCES OF HELP
Books:
Freiberg, Kevin, and Jackie Freiberg. *NUTS! Southwest Airlines' Crazy Recipe for Business and Personal Success*. Austin, Texas: Bard Press, Inc., 1996.

Goddard, Larry, and David Brown. *The Turbocharged Company: Igniting Your Business to Soar Ahead of the Competition*. Collingdale, Pennsylvania: DIANE, 1995.
Website:
Southwest Airlines: **www.southwest.com**

PHIL KNIGHT

1938	Born.
1959	Gains BS in Business Administration at University of Oregon.
1962	Travels to Japan in search of an athletics shoe manufacturer.
1964	Forms Blue Ribbon Sports with his old athletics coach, Bowerman.
1971	Company brand renamed Nike (after the Greek goddess of victory).
1972	Carolyn Davidson paid $35 for designing the 'swoosh' logo adopted by Nike. The Cortez, the first shoe to appear under the Nike brand, arrives.
1975	Steve Prefontaine dies in a car crash. Introduction of the waffle sole.
1978	Blue Ribbon Sports renamed Nike Inc. Revenues of $71 million.
1980	Nike goes public.
1983	Revenues of $149 million.
1985	Launch of the Air Jordan.
1986	Revenues hit $1 billion.
1993–1994	Company rethinks strategy.
1998	Commits company to responsible employment practices.
1999	Nike co-founder Bill Bowerman dies.
2000	Nike designs uniforms for Sydney Olympics. Withdraws donation of $30 million to University of Oregon.
2001	Nike admits to worker exploitation. US Congress briefing on Nike employment practices.

> **SUMMARY**
>
> Phil Knight (1938–) followed his early promise on the running track at the University of Oregon with an equal talent for running a successful business. The product was, fittingly, the athletics shoe, which Knight, along with his partner and ex-athletics coach Bill Bowerman, revolutionised, transforming a basic accessory into a high-tech piece of athletics equipment. With a stroke of marketing genius, Knight chose the name Nike, Greek goddess of victory, for his brand in 1971, and the 'swoosh' as his logo in 1972. Nike really hit the big time in the 1980s when its athletics shoes, starting with the Air Jordan in 1985, ran off the track and into mainstream fashion. The issue of child labour and Nike's manufacturing processes threatened to tarnish Knight's and the brand's reputation in the late 1990s, but strong management and a willingness to face ethical issues has seen Nike emerge in a better shape than some other multi-nationals.

LIFE AND CAREER

Philip H. Knight was born in Portland, Oregon. At high school he played a lot of sport as well as becoming a roving reporter for the school paper. After high school he attended Oregon University where he took a BS in Business Administration. A keen runner throughout his childhood, Knight also joined the university athletics team. His athletics coach at university was Bill Bowerman, a man who, in coaching terms, was way ahead of his time. As well as training his athletes, he would experiment with their equipment to try and reduce their times. As part of that experimentation he constructed prototype athletics shoes with lightweight leather and, later, nylon uppers. The shoes may have only made a difference measurable in fractions of seconds, but in athletics a fraction of a second makes the difference between a gold medal and a silver.

After graduating from Oregon, Knight went to Stanford Graduate Business School to study for an MBA. As part of his master's degree he wrote a marketing paper. The thrust of his argument in the paper was that cheaper labour coupled with efficient manufacturing processes could threaten the dominance of German companies, such as Adidas and Puma, in the athletics shoe market. When Knight graduated, he decided to back his hunch and in 1962 travelled to Japan in search of an athletics shoe manufacturer. He found a small factory run by the Onitsuki Tiger Company and convinced them to supply him with shoes to import to the United States.

Back in America in 1964, Knight teamed up again with Bowerman to form Blue Ribbon Sports. They each invested $500 in the new company. Knight's first retail outlet for the shoes was the back of his car, from which he would sell athletics shoes at high school athletics events.

CONTRIBUTION

Knight was unable to earn enough income from his shoe enterprise to support himself. Instead he was forced to take a job teaching accounting at Portland State University. In 1971 Knight and Bowerman decided to rename the company's brand. They chose Nike as the new name. Bowerman's bizarre experimentation with shoe design paid off when he made an outsole by pouring rubber into a waffle iron. Sports shoe technology would never be the same again.

Later that year Knight was looking for a designer to prepare some charts for a business meeting when he came across graphic design student Carolyn Davidson, who was working on an assignment in the hallway at the university. Knight commissioned her to produce some work for his company. Pleased with the results, he asked her if she could design a logo for the company. The brief was simply that the logo should suggest movement. From a selection of designs, Knight chose the 'swoosh' sign, adopting it as the brand logo in 1972. Davidson was paid $35 for her endeavours. Today the 'swoosh' logo is synonymous with Nike and recognised throughout the world. The Nike brand was no. 30 in the Interbrand Most Valuable Brands 2000 survey, valued at $3,015 million.

Knight's marketing savvy helped the Nike brand gain public recognition. Before trainers became mainstream fashionwear, Knight had the idea of associating the Nike product with top sports stars. The first star selected was middle-distance runner Steve Prefontaine, who was paid by Nike to wear its sports shoes. Prefontaine won a series of races wearing Nike shoes and narrowly failed to capture a medal in the 1972 Olympics. Tragically, he died in a car crash in 1975. By this time, however, Nike products were firmly associated with outstanding sporting achievement in the mind of the consumer.

By 1978 Blue Ribbon Sports had been officially renamed Nike Inc. In the same year Nike's revenues were $71 million. The company went public in 1980. In 1983 revenues were $149 million and by 1986 a massive $1 billion.

Chicago Bulls superstar Michael Jordan succeeded Steve Prefontaine as the Nike sports personality. This association helped propel Nike to even greater heights as Jordan became a US sports icon, and Nike sports shoes became everyday wear for devotees of hip and happening youth culture. Knight continued to push technical innovation in Nike products with the launch of the Air Jordan in 1985. Whether the revolutionary product's air cushioning was a gimmick or actually increased performance didn't appear to matter, as the trendy trainer outstripped the competition, becoming Nike's best-selling shoe.

In the early 1990s the company's phenomenal growth slowed. Nike had profited up to then thanks to the popularity of jogging and basketball in the United States. But by 1993 these markets were flagging, and Knight decided to broaden the company's appeal: 'We decided we're a sports company, not just a shoe company'. By extending the appeal of Nike across a greater range of sports, the company managed to stay ahead of the pack. The strategy involved: more stars, such as golfer Tiger Woods and tennis star André Agassi; more sports, and more innovations, including the Predator football boot.

The biggest threat to Nike's continuing success in the late 1990s was the issue of worker exploitation and child labour. Knight looked to head off the protests. In a statement to the National Press Club in May 1998 he said that 'the Nike product had become synonymous with slave wages, forced overtime, and arbitrary abuse', and pledged to change things. He implemented a series of high-profile initiatives at the company to commit Nike to responsible employment policies. These measures sit uneasily, however, with Knight's cancellation of a financial contribution to his old university because of its decision to join the Workers' Rights Consortium. However, the criticism continued. In 2001, the company admitted to exploiting workers, but tried to regain some ground by committing to continued production in Indonesia. It was also the subject of a US Congress briefing on its 'sweatshop' practices.

In product terms, the range continued to grow. The death of co-founder Bill Bowerman in 1999 was a blow, but Nike responded by launching the successful 'Bowerman' range of running shoes. Nike golf equipment sales soared in 2000 when Tiger Woods won a succession of titles. The 2000 Sydney Olympics proved a valuable platform for a new generation of high-tech sports equipment.

CONTEXT AND CONCLUSIONS

Phil Knight's is one of the great marketing stories of the 20th century. Turning the humble athletics shoe into a must-have street fashion item was a masterstroke of marketing genius. It was a leap that he had to make in order to take Nike from a niche manufacturer of sporting footwear to a clothing and footwear giant and internationally recognised brand. No mere marketer, Knight has also proved an astute strategist, guiding Nike in a different direction where necessary and facing up to the issue of the exploitation of foreign workers that threatened to elbow Nike off the track.

THE BEST SOURCES OF HELP
Books:
Strasser, J.B., and Laurie Becklund. *Swoosh: The Unauthorized Story of Nike, and the Men Who Played There*. Orlando, Florida: Harcourt Brace Jovanovich, 1991.
Katz, Donald. *Just Do It: The Nike Spirit in the Corporate World*. New York: Random House, 1994.
Goldman, Robert, and Stephen Papson. *Nike Culture: The Sign of the Swoosh*. Thousand Oaks, California: Sage Publications, 1998.
Website:
Nike: **www.nike.com/europe/english**

RAY KROC

1902	Born.
1922	Begins work as sales representative for Lily Tulip Cup.
1954	Visits McDonald's burger restaurant in San Bernardino, California.
1955	Opens his first McDonald's in Des Plaines, Illinois.
1961	Buys out the McDonald brothers for $2.7 million.
1963	Number of hamburgers sold reaches one billion.
1965	Ronald McDonald introduced.
1967	First overseas branch opened.
1974	Buys the San Diego Padres baseball club.
1984	Dies.

> **SUMMARY**
>
> Ray Kroc (1902–1984) was looking forward to retiring after a comfortable career selling milkshake mixers. All that changed one day in 1954 when he walked into a small restaurant in San Bernardino, California. It was called McDonald's Famous Hamburgers, and Kroc's visit was the catalyst for a global food revolution. He made a deal with the McDonald brothers and set about creating a franchise network. In 1961 he bought out the brothers for a bargain $2.7 million.
>
> The company went public in 1965. By the 1970s Kroc had turned a $2.7 million investment into a $500 million fortune. The public bought McDonald's burgers by the million. By the time of Kroc's death in 1984, the McDonald's golden arches were recognised the world over as a symbol for convenient and cheap fast food.

LIFE AND CAREER

Raymond Kroc was born in Oak Park, Illinois, on 5 October 1902. His life and career can be divided up into two periods: before McDonald's and after it. Before McDonald's Kroc tried a variety of jobs before carving out a role as a milkshake-mixer sales rep.

At 15 he lied about his age so he could take part in the First World War as a Red Cross ambulance driver. Disappointingly for him, the nearest he got to Europe was Connecticut. He was still finishing his training the day the war ended.

Having missed out on the war, Kroc looked for a job. He spent some time playing the piano for a living, and in 1922 landed a job selling paper cups for the Lily Tulip Cup Company. Kroc was good at sales and had an eye for business. When one of his customers, Earl Prince, patron of Prince Multimixers, showed Kroc the five-spindle mixer he had invented, Kroc switched companies. He got a contract to sell the mixers nationally, and for the next 17 years that was exactly what he did. At 52 Kroc had spent most of his working life selling mixers. He was comfortably off and, like most of men of his age, was thinking about his retirement, until, that is, the fateful day in 1954 when he walked into the small burger restaurant in San Bernardino run by the McDonald brothers.

CONTRIBUTION

What impressed Kroc about the burger restaurant run by brothers Dick and Mac McDonald, apart from the large number of mixers they ordered and the queues down the street, was the way the business was run. It was as if Henry Ford had applied his mass-production formula to the food business. The brothers ran a burger assembly line. There were eight five-milkshake mixers churning out 40 milkshakes at a time. To speed up the cleaning, the brothers dispensed plastic utensils and paper napkins. So efficient was the McDonalds' operation that customers received their meal within 60 seconds. Furthermore, the brothers offered a very limited menu at extremely competitive prices. For Kroc it was commercial love at first sight. 'I felt like some latter-day Newton who'd just had an Idaho potato caromed off his skull,' he later wrote.

Kroc was convinced that fast food, McDonald's style, could be the next restaurant revolution. Using all the skills he had acquired in 25-plus years of selling, he sold himself to the McDonald brothers, persuading them to license their name to him. In return they would receive a percentage of the sales for each franchise he created. To the McDonald's model Kroc brought dynamism and a homespun business philosophy. 'Luck is a dividend of sweat,' he once observed. 'The more you sweat, the luckier you get.'

Kroc was convinced that fast food, McDonald's style, could be the next restaurant revolution.

The four pillars on which Kroc built the McDonald's empire were quality, service, cleanliness, and value. He introduced some innovations of his own such as standardising the size of the burger and the amount of onions served with each one. He even built a laboratory in Chicago to research the ultimate french fry. Kroc's obsession with perfecting the McDonald's business formula cost him his marriage.

Kroc's first restaurant opened in Des Plaines, Illinois, in 1955. Several others quickly followed. Kroc insisted franchisees ran their restaurants according to his strict guidelines. Although he had little trouble convincing franchisees to open McDonald's restaurants, Kroc still encountered severe financial problems that nearly bankrupted him in the early years. In 1960 revenues of $75 million translated into profits of $139,000. His solution was to buy the land where the restaurants were to be located and then lease them to the franchisees. In this way Kroc retained closer control over the business and made more money.

Soon Kroc's financial problems were a thing of the past and he was eyeing a bigger prize. In 1961 he bought out the McDonald brothers for just $2.7 million. It was one of the best deals in business history—for Kroc at least. He then embarked on a massive advertising campaign. The McDonald's landmarks kept coming: a billion hamburgers by 1963; the five hundredth restaurant; the brilliant concept of the burger clown, Ronald McDonald, universally appealing to children. In fact, so popular was Ronald McDonald that not long after his first national ad appearance in 1965, more children knew his name than that of the US president.

When the company went public in 1965, Kroc was $3 million richer. It was a fortune that grew to $500 million by the mid-1970s as McDonald's franchises sprang up everywhere. With the company firmly established in the United States, Kroc expanded overseas. In 1967 he took the golden arches to Canada, followed by Europe, Asia, and the rest of the world.

Kroc's great wealth affected him very little, as he spent much of his time ensuring the McDonald's franchises maintained his high standards. One small indulgence was his acquisition of the San Diego Padres baseball team in 1974. He died at the age of 81 in San Diego, California.

CONTEXT AND CONCLUSIONS
Few people can claim to have changed the way the world eats. Ray Kroc is one such individual. It took vision and courage to turn his back on a comfortable retirement for a new business opportunity at the age of 52. Kroc's idea was perfect for his time. The United States was suburbanising, prospering, and depending more and more on the automobile; Kroc provided an increasingly mobile nation with fast, cheap, convenient food. His genius was not only to spot the opportunity but to package the experience carefully. Through franchises, strictly-regulated service and food production values, and innovative marketing, Kroc single-handedly invented the modern concept of fast food. He also pioneered the global brand, cooking up a McDonald's-style food revolution across the world.

> *Few people can claim to have changed the way the world eats. Ray Kroc is one such individual.*

THE BEST SOURCES OF HELP
Books:
Kroc, Ray, with Robert Anderson. *Grinding it Out: The Making of McDonald's*. New York: St Martin's Press, 1992.
Love, John F. *McDonald's: Behind the Arches*. Rev. ed. New York: Bantam, 1995.
Website:
McDonald's: **www.mcdonalds.co.uk**

EDWIN LAND

1909	Born.
1926	Leaves Harvard University after his first year.
1928	Invents the first synthetic sheet polariser.
1929	Files for a patent.
1933	Forms Land-Wheelwright Laboratories.
1937	Forms Polaroid Corporation, Boston. Polaroid day glasses are introduced.
1939	Polaroid moves its offices from Boston to Cambridge, Massachusetts.
1948	First instant camera and film go on sale.
1957	Polaroid lists on the New York Stock Exchange. Awarded honorary doctorate by Harvard.
1963	Colour instant camera goes on sale.
1977	Invention of Polaroid Instant Movie Camera.
1982	Retires as president of Polaroid.
1991	Dies.

> **SUMMARY**
>
> Edwin Land (1909–1991) pioneered instant photography for the masses with his invention of the Polaroid camera. The original idea was inspired by a question from his daughter on a sunny day in 1944 and a leisurely walk around the dusty streets of Santa Fe. Other important enterprises such as Land's groundbreaking work into light polarisation at his Harvard University laboratories during the 1930s are less well known. And few people realise that it was a friend's fishing trip that led to the invention of Polaroid sunglasses, or that Land released a revolutionary new instant movie camera at the same time as Sony was introducing videotape in 1977.
>
> Land's life was a synthesis of invention and business. 'An essential aspect of creativity is not being afraid to fail,' he observed. Even after he retired from Polaroid in 1982, he devoted his time to his hobby, inventing. He built a research laboratory complex and filled it with like-minded people.

LIFE AND CAREER

Born in Bridgeport, Connecticut, on 7 May 1909, Edwin Herbert Land was the only son of Harry and Martha Land. Theirs was a comfortable household; Harry Land owned property and ran a scrap-metal yard. As a boy Land was a keen scholar, albeit a tired one—he is said to have slept with a copy of R.W. Wood's *Physical Optics* beneath his pillow. According to his high school yearbook, the young Land was a 'star in his studies'. He was a student first at Norwich Free Academy, from which he graduated with honours, and later at Harvard University.

Land's academic interests weren't sufficient to keep him at Harvard. As a first-year student he was already developing a cheap, effective polariser of light that he called 'Polaroid'. In 1926, after that first year, he abandoned his formal physics studies, continuing his education instead at the New York Public Library. Although he didn't graduate, Harvard University awarded him an honorary doctorate in 1957, one of many honorary degrees.

CONTRIBUTION

Land is best known for the invention of the Polaroid camera. Although the idea came to him in a moment of inspiration, he had already laid the foundations for instant photography with his advances in the field of light polarisation.

When Land began to apply his mind to the subject, the main tool in use was the Nicol prism. Developed in 1828, it was a bulky and expensive piece of equipment. Land was convinced that he could improve on William Nicol's invention. His idea, following observations based on his studies in the New York Public Library, was to place a large number of aligned crystals in transparent plastic. The plastic would then be set, fixing the position of the crystals. Land gave a lecture on his idea at Harvard after a few preliminary experiments.

He patented his invention in 1929 and then set up companies to develop and exploit it. The first, in 1933, was Land-Wheelwright Laboratories, established with Land's Harvard physics instructor George Wheelwright III. Next came the Polaroid Corporation, founded in Boston in 1937. The next task was to find commercial applications for the invention.

Land's original idea had been to use the technology to reduce glare in car headlights. Because this application involved an increase in wattage with a commensurate increase in fuel consumption, however, Land was unable to persuade automobile manufacturers of its benefits. This rejection led him to develop a string of products that used the new technology. Many of them were inspired by chance discoveries.

The world has a trout fisherman to thank for the invention of Polaroid sunglasses. One of Land's colleagues went on a fishing trip and took a piece of Polaroid film with him. When he returned he told Land that looking through the Polaroid reduced the surface glare from the water and enabled him to spot the fish. This discovery led to the manufacture of Polaroid glasses. At first these were sold in specialist hunting and fishing shops, but eventually they became the ubiquitous Polaroid sunglasses. The sunglasses led to the development of other products such as camera filters and antiglare screens.

Land attracted the finest minds he could find to his Boston laboratories and led his research team in developing a range of products. He invented a new method of 3-D photography that was used extensively for reconnaissance during the Second World War. Then there were inventions such as night-time goggles and the polarising ring sight. Land also contributed to the technology used during the cold war, including the surveillance equipment employed in the high-altitude U2 spy planes and spy satellites.

Land is probably best known for his invention of instant photography and the Polaroid camera. The idea came from a conversation with his three-year-old daughter Jennifer in 1944. It was a sunny day in Santa Fe, New Mexico, and Land took a snapshot of her. Why, she asked, couldn't she see the picture he had taken of her immediately? This set Land thinking, and after pacing round the town for an hour he arrived at a solution.

The first demonstration of Land's revolutionary new instant camera took place in February 1947, at a meeting of the Optical Society of America. The commercial model was on sale within two years at a retail price of $89.50. Land was well aware that correct pricing was a key to the camera's success, and he priced it for the mass market.

> *The Polaroid camera was a phenomenal success. Land could easily have retired to a life of luxury. Instead he continued to conduct his research into the nature of light.*

The Polaroid camera was a phenomenal success. Land could easily have retired to a life of luxury. Instead he continued to conduct his research into the nature of light. He also invented a number of other products, including the Polavision instant movie camera, which hit the shops in 1977. Unfortunately it was an advanced product in a soon-to-be-defunct technology: the invention of magnetic videotape spelt the beginning of the end for 8mm film.

Land retired as president of Polaroid in 1982, but he continued his research. He built himself a research institute, the Rowland Institute for Science in Cambridge, Massachusetts, where he continued to experiment along with a group of fellow researchers until his death in 1991.

CONTEXT AND CONCLUSIONS

Edwin Land was an inventor/business executive in the tradition of Thomas Edison. He possessed the rare combination of an inventive mind and the discipline to address the often mundane but challenging demands of running a big corporation. In a world in which commercial research is often jealously guarded, Land profited from his openness. He was happy to show friends and colleagues his research, and to challenge them to find commercial applications for his work. This led to the development of a number of new products, most famously Polaroid sunglasses. Had it not been for the advent of Betamax and VHS video tape, Land's invention of the instant movie camera might have been his crowning achievement.

Sadly, with Land gone, the company he founded struggled. In 2001, faced with debts of $950 million, the company made some 25% of its workforce redundant and was fighting to avoid bankruptcy.

THE BEST SOURCES OF HELP
Book:
Olshaker, Mark. *The Polaroid Story: Edwin Land and the Polaroid Experience*. Lanham, Maryland: Madison, 1983.

ALLEN LANE

1902	Born.
1919	Joins The Bodley Head.
1934	Has the idea for Penguin on a train journey to London.
1935	First Penguin books come off the presses.
1936	Resigns from The Bodley Head and founds Penguin Books Ltd with just £100.
1937	The Bodley Head goes into voluntary liquidation.
1940–45	Lane produces books for the troops with the Forces Book Club.
1961	Penguin Books Ltd becomes a publicly listed company.
1970	Dies.
1970	S. Pearson & Co buys Penguin for £15 million.

SUMMARY

Allen Lane changed the reading habits of a nation. Born into a publishing family—his uncle John owned The Bodley Head—Lane had a head start in the business. He joined in 1919 aged 17, spurning the role of publisher of limited and select editions to plough a populist furrow. In 1935, on an inspired hunch (courtesy of a dull train journey), Lane embarked on a radical change of direction, as a publisher of mass-market paperbacks under the imprint Penguin. Stylish, printed on quality paper, pocket-sized, featuring popular authors, and affordable, they were an astonishing success. Leaving The Bodley Head, which subsequently went into liquidation, he founded Penguin Books Ltd in 1936. From that moment onward it was one success after another. Pelicans, Penguin Specials, Puffin Picture Books, and many other series followed. Lane even managed to monopolise the provision of paperback books to the armed services during the Second World War. By the time of his death in 1970, the word 'penguin' had become synonymous with the paperback book, and Penguin Books, by then a publicly listed company, had become a major force in publishing.

LIFE AND CAREER

Born on 21 September 1902, in Bristol, Lane was the eldest of four children. He acquired his early education at Bristol Grammar School, largely unnoticed. He was neither a brilliant scholar nor a poor one. Sixty years after his attendance, the school was asked to provide a list of its most distinguished alumni; no one remembered Lane.

At 17 Allen Lane went to work for The Bodley Head publishing house. It was April 1919, and Lane had secured a job at the once prosperous publishers through his uncle John Lane, who owned the firm. By then, however, The Bodley Head had run into financial difficulties. Moving out of its niche market of limited editions, it found itself burdened with the expensive reprinting of successful titles.

Lane started in the lowly position of office boy. But his uncle was keen to increase his responsibilities, encouraging him to find new authors, discuss contracts, and act in every way as if he was a director, even though he was not. In 1924 Lane, the heir-apparent, was promoted to the board. His uncle died soon after, having caught a chill waiting to catch a train from London to Brighton.

Allen Lane

CONTRIBUTION

Assuming his natural position as head of the firm, Lane was immediately launched into a publishing controversy. A friend offered the salacious memoirs of a distinguished diplomat. Lane eagerly signed up, advancing £100 to his friend, who was to be the editor. When the book came out its scandalous contents caused an uproar. Dragged before the board, Lane was asked to reveal the author. When he named the gentleman as the British ambassador in Rome, Sir Rennell Rodd, the astonished board asked Lane whether he had in fact spoken to Rodd in person, and suggested that he make further investigations as to the veracity of his source. When Lane quizzed his friend and go-between more closely, the latter ruefully admitted that he had made the whole thing up. There followed many letters of grovelling apology, punctuated with appearances in court. For Lane it was a chastening introduction into the world of publishing.

> *When Lane quizzed his friend and go-between more closely, the latter ruefully admitted that he had made the whole thing up. There followed many letters of grovelling apology, punctuated with appearances in court. For Lane it was a chastening introduction into the world of publishing.*

But his luck was about to change. Sometime in 1934 he took a train to London, returning from a weekend in Devon with the crime author Agatha Christie and her husband. Not having taken any reading matter to occupy his mind, Lane lamented the lack of reasonably priced, portable, well-presented literature. Back in London he tried to persuade his brothers Richard and John, who had joined him at The Bodley Head, that the principles of Woolworth's mass-market, mass-production, and mass-distribution retail operation could be applied to publishing.

Spotting the gap in the market, Lane and his brothers decided to go ahead with a new imprint for the mass market, even though the rest of The Bodley Head directors were unsupportive. First they had to choose a name. A shortlist was drawn up with Dolphin first, followed by Porpoise, and Penguin as the third choice. The first two proved unavailable, so they settled on Penguin. The new Penguin imprint would publish reprints of popular fiction. Lane knew that it was essential to the success of the new venture that the new books should have an eye-catching design and be small, lightweight paperbacks. This enabled him to price the books at sixpence each. After a poor showing from retailers, Lane managed to interest Woolworth, who saved Penguin from an early demise by ordering 63,000 copies.

In July 1935 the first books came off the Penguin presses, financed by the strength of Bodley Head's credit. There were 10 titles, beginning with *Ariel*, a biography of Percy Bysshe Shelley by André Maurois. This first batch of paperbacks also included titles such as *The Mysterious Affair at Styles* by Agatha Christie and Ernest Hemingway's *A Farewell to Arms*. The books had an eye-catching appearance. Lane designed the covers himself, using strong bold colours to indicate the type of book:

orange, for example, was used for general literature, green for crime, and pink for travel. The books also were numbered—from 1 to 3,224, published in 1974. On the spine and on the front cover of the paperbacks was the distinctive Penguin logo, designed by Edward Young, an amateur artist who worked for The Bodley Head.

In 1936, convinced he had found the future of book publishing, Lane resigned from The Bodley Head and founded Penguin Books Ltd with just £100 of capital. Lane's new offices were in the crypt of Holy Trinity Church, Marylebone Road, previously used as a store by The Bodley Head. In 1937, The Bodley Head went into voluntary liquidation. In the same year, Penguin moved out of its office in the bowels of the earth to a three and a half acre plot at Harmondsworth, Middlesex. The property cost £2,000—plus an additional £200 for the crop of cabbages already planted on the land.

The popularity of Lane's Penguin paperbacks was astonishing. Within six months over one million copies had been sold. By the end of 1936 there were 70 titles on the Penguin list. This spurred Lane on to develop new series. In 1937 the Pelican series was introduced. These books were designed for the knowledge-hungry masses who had missed out on higher education. In pre-war England, they constituted a sizeable majority of the population. Another new series swiftly followed. Penguin Specials focused on current affairs and were designed to feed the increasing appetite for social and political information and analysis during the Depression and in the run-up to the Second World War. These also were a huge success, selling a quarter of a million copies in just a few weeks.

> *In 1937, The Bodley Head went into voluntary liquidation. In the same year, Penguin moved out of its office in the bowels of the earth to a three and a half acre plot at Harmondsworth, Middlesex. The property cost £2,000—plus an additional £200 for the crop of cabbages already planted on the land.*

The outbreak of war presented a challenging problem for Lane. Like most other materials, paper was rationed, severely restricting the output of publishers. Fortunately for Lane, paper quotas were assessed on sales during the year before the outbreak of the war, assuring Penguin a substantial supply of raw materials. Also he was friendly with the director of Army Welfare and managed to secure a monopoly for supplying service personnel with books. Ironically, the war, which had threatened to destroy the rapidly growing publishing company, turned out to be a boon. The name of Penguin Books and its logo became familiar to armed forces across the world. Troops with time on their hands applied to the Forces Book Club for light relief. Penguin Specials also proved popular, keeping the population informed on issues related to the war and serving as a morale-boosting form of propaganda. They also provided practical advice—for example, like the book on aircraft recognition that enabled those on the ground to know whether to run and take shelter, or simply wave. Also launched during the war years was the Puffin Picture Books series for children. Thus the war period brought not only financial success for Penguin but also a huge marketing success.

As a company that before the war had produced ten million books for readers worldwide and that had prospered during it, Penguin Books should have easily gone on to dominate post-war publishing. For once, though, Lane seemed to miss a trick by allowing competitors such as Pan to steal market share in the popular paperback arena. Lane had made what he regarded as an ethical as well as a commercial decision to publish less popular fiction and more nonfiction during the war years. The gap this left in the market, however, was rapidly filled by Corgi, Pan, and Panther. Of these, Pan was arguably the most successful, with its striking cover artwork and extensive backlist of mass-market popular titles. It wasn't long before Pan was pushing Penguin for the number one spot. By 1955 Pan was selling eight million books a year compared to Penguin's 10 million, with 150 titles in print against Penguin's 1,000.

On 20 April 1961 Penguin Books Ltd became a publicly listed company. Until the 1960s, it had managed to survive, even prosper, as a private company. But the publishing world was changing. Lane signed a seven-year contract to serve as chairman and managing director of the new company. He spent his final years at the business planning his succession, working on a hardback imprint, The Penguin Press, and fighting a guerrilla war against an increasingly vocal board of directors. When the board seemed to favour the publication of a book, Sine's *Massacre*, which the company's founder strongly disapproved of, Lane, the man who fought through the courts for the right to publish *Lady Chatterley's Lover*, sneaked off with a trusted employee, loaded up a van with all the copies of *Massacre*, drove them to his farm, and burnt the lot. In 1968 Lane also entered into negotiations with the publisher Longman with a view to merging the two companies so as to inject some badly needed capital into Penguin. During the negotiations Longman was swallowed by S. Pearson & Co to form Pearson Longman. It was S. Pearson & Co that finally bought Penguin for £15 million in 1970. By then Lane was dead. He died of cancer on 7 July 1970.

CONTEXT AND CONCLUSIONS

Allen Lane didn't invent the paperback, but he did popularise it. Moving from the small but select publisher The Bodley Head, where he made his mark by publishing James Joyce's *Ulysses*, Lane, together with his brothers Richard and John, founded a publishing company predicated on Frank Woolworth's mass-market, low-cost business model. The established publishers may have sneered at the time, but Lane had the last laugh. With the 6d (sixpence) Penguin paperbacks Lane democratised book-buying, and with it reading, in the United Kingdom. Through being supplied to the troops during the Second World War, the Penguin brand became both recognised throughout the world and synonymous with the paperback. Often difficult to work with, divisive, and politicking, Lane still inspired his workforce with an almost fanatical loyalty. Although Lane has gone, the Penguin imprint lives on to remind us of his outstanding contribution to publishing.

THE BEST SOURCES OF HELP
Website:
Penguin UK: **www.penguin.co.uk**

ESTÉE LAUDER

1908	Born.
1924	Uncle founds New Way Laboratories.
1944	Lauder sets up her own office.
1947	Estée Lauder, Inc. founded.
1948	First retail account at Saks Fifth Avenue, New York.
1953	Launch of Youth-Dew.
1960	First international account at Harrods, London.
1968	Revenues of $40 million.
1972	Son Leonard made president. Lauder becomes chair.
1980s	Lauder steps back from running the company.
1995	Company IPO.

> **SUMMARY**
>
> Much of the US cosmetic queen Estée Lauder's (1908–) early life is shrouded in mystery. What is known is that she started in the cosmetics business selling her uncle's Six-in-One Cold Cream in 1924. By 1944 she had acquired a husband, an office in New York, and a cosmetics concession in Saks Fifth Avenue. Lauder formally incorporated Estée Lauder Inc. in 1947. Resisting calls to go public, she kept her company in family hands and used her formidable sales and marketing talents to drive the business forward. In 1968 revenues were an estimated $40 million with profits of $4 million. Lauder ceded control to her son Leonard in 1972. By 1999, Estée Lauder, Inc. was earning over $3 billion in revenue from over a hundred products.

LIFE AND CAREER

Estée Lauder was born Josephine Esther Mentzer in Queens, New York, in 1908, the youngest of nine children. Her father ran a hardware store, and Lauder went to school nearby.

The young Lauder was introduced to the cosmetics business through her uncle Dr Schotz, a chemist. His business, New Way Laboratories, was founded in 1924. Among the various potions and lotions he made—which included a poultry-lice killer, paint stripper, varnish, and embalming fluid—were several beauty treatments. Lauder helped her uncle out by selling products with names like Six-in-One Cold Cream and Dr Schotz Viennese Cream.

In 1930 she married Joe Lauder, but by 1939 the couple had separated. A subsequent reconciliation led to their remarriage in 1942, at which time Lauder vowed to direct all her energies to selling cosmetics products. She continued to sell her uncle's products, setting up her own office at 39 East 60th St in February 1944.

Soon afterwards Lauder won a sales concession in the Bonwit Teller department store. She then set her sights higher. The prize concession was in Saks Fifth Avenue. When she told Bob Fiske, cosmetics buyer at Saks, that the department store should give her a concession, Fiske demurred, explaining that there was no demand for her products from his customers. Undeterred, Lauder created a demand by giving her products away at a talk at the Waldorf-Astoria Hotel. When she returned to Fiske, he relented.

In the late 1940s, with $60,000 or so at her disposal, Lauder was unable to persuade the BBD&O advertising agency to create a campaign for Estée Lauder. Instead she chose a more direct route to her customers. Using Saks's mailing list, Lauder sent out samples and gifts as an enticement for customers to visit her store concessions.

CONTRIBUTION

Lauder's breakthrough came with the invention of her first fragrance, the bath oil Youth-Dew. Her principal competition, firms like Arden and Rubenstein, had all started with skin-care products and gravitated to fragrances.

Accounts of how Lauder created her first fragrance differ. It seems that an old friend, A.L. van Amerigan, president of van Amerigan-Haebler (which subsequently became International Flavors and Fragrances), was involved. Similarly Ernest Shiftan, an employee of IFF and one of America's top perfumers, may well have been responsible for the development of the fragrance. Whether Amerigan gave the fragrance to Lauder is unclear. What is certain is that Youth-Dew, introduced in 1953 at Bonwit's department store as bath oil, was an instant success. For $8.50 customers got a perfume that lasted a whole day.

Shrewdly, Lauder used the demand for the new perfume to sell her other cosmetics. The Youth-Dew line was eventually extended across a range of cosmetics including a pure fragrance. With Lauder shamelessly promoting it at every opportunity, it wasn't long before Estée Lauder was the third-largest cosmetics business in the United States behind Arden and Rubenstein.

Lauder's marketing acumen was again evident when a new breed of skin-care products making dubious scientific claims began to spread from Europe to the United States. In France an emphasis on 'feeding' the skin had given rise to products that made various health claims about their effects. The Food and Drug Administration in the United States, however, imposed tough regulations on products making any such claims. There were, for example, a host of placental-based products that fell foul of the FDA and were withdrawn. Lauder, instead of making scientific claims for her new skin product, simply named it Re-Nutriv. The product's health-enhancing attributes were implied in the name. She was also careful not to cross the line in her advertising. It focused instead on the high price of the product, and how a price of $115 a pound was justified by the inclusion of the 'costliest' ingredients.

At the time Estée Lauder's headquarters were at 666 Fifth Avenue, on the second floor—Lauder had a fear of heights. Competitors were close at hand. Charles Revson, founder of Revlon, was on the top floor of the same building and Helena Rubenstein was across the street. As Lauder made progress commercially she was also climbing socially. Her house in Palm Beach, Florida, afforded her the opportunity to meet rich people from the upper echelons of US society. Lauder's efforts at networking were not entirely without mishap. One story has it that, arriving for dinner at the home of Dorothy Munn, wife of financier Charles Munn, she gave a box of cosmetics (presumably her own) to her hostess. This was viewed as a gauche gesture as Dorothy Munn was wealthy enough to have her cosmetics made privately—a kind of haute-perfume.

By the 1970s Estée Lauder had seen off its corporate competition and added the Clinique brand to its beautifying armoury. Lauder herself had outlasted her personal rivals as both Elizabeth Arden and Helena Rubenstein had died within a year of each other in the 1960s. Lauder had since moved her headquarters to the new General Motors Building (with the ever-present Revlon camped on the top floors); she had also, by virtue of her friendship with the Duchess of Windsor, firmly placed herself at the pinnacle of the social scene. Her son Leonard became president of the company in 1972 with Lauder becoming chair.

The 'little business' that Leonard Lauder once said his mother was growing now controls over 40% of the cosmetics market in US department stores. Available in 118 countries, Estée Lauder products bring in over $3 billion in revenue.

CONTEXT AND CONCLUSIONS
Estée Lauder, Inc. is an astonishing example of how an international business can be built up from humble beginnings through one woman's relentless drive, networking, belief in her own products, and brilliant marketing. In particular, Lauder was responsible for a number of innovative marketing techniques for the cosmetics business, most notably the free gift with purchase.

Her strength of leadership was emphasised through her determination to keep the company in the control of her family. Estée Lauder remained an entirely private company until its IPO in 1995. The Lauder family still holds a significant proportion of the shares. Although Lauder has progressively taken a back seat since the 1980s, her sons Leonard and Ronald, daughter-in-law Evelyn, grandson William, and great-granddaughter Aerin remain actively involved in the company.

> *The 'little business' that Leonard Lauder once said his mother was growing now controls over 40% of the cosmetics market in US department stores.*

THE BEST SOURCES OF HELP
Books:
Israel, Lee. *Estée Lauder: Beyond the Magic: An Unauthorized Biography*. New York: Macmillan, 1985.
Lauder, Estée. *Estée: A Success Story*. New York: Random House, 1985.
Website:
Estée Lauder: **www.esteelauder.co.uk**

RALPH LAUREN

1939	Born.
1962–1964	Serves in the US Army.
1968	Forms Polo.
1971	First shop opens.
1986	Flagship shop opens on Madison Avenue, New York.
1993	The Polo Sport shop opens.
1997	Awarded 1996 Menswear Designer of the Year by the Council of Fashion Designers of America.
1997	Polo Ralph Lauren IPO.
2000	Revenues of $1.6 billion.

> **SUMMARY**
>
> Today designer shops are commonplace, and designer brands sell everything from sunglasses to perfume. But it wasn't always like that. In the days before DKNY, CK, and Armani, there was Polo by the American designer Ralph Lauren.
>
> Lauren's early life suggested little of the success that lay ahead, other than a predilection for expensive suits. But, in the late 1960s, after persuading the New York shop Bloomingdale's to sell his unfashionably wide ties, Lauren never looked back. From a single shop in 1971, the Lauren fashion empire now numbers over 130 shops with revenues of over $1 billion. As Lauren designs on into a new millennium, the Polo brand continues to reflect his ability to capture the essence of a certain American way of life.

LIFE AND CAREER

Born in New York in 1939, Ralph Lauren always had an eye for fashion. The youngest of four children, his fashion flair and sense of colour may have been inherited from his father, who was a mural painter. His education was highly conventional. After high school it wasn't fashion college that awaited him but City College, Manhattan, and a business degree. As a teenager Lauren was a snappy dresser. He didn't stint on quality, preferring to pay $100 for a suit (at that time a lot of money), rather than buy a cheaper, less well-made one. This was not always a popular policy with his parents.

Two years into his business degree, Lauren took a job as a salesman at a glove company. This was followed by a similar job at a tie manufacturer's. It was while still at the tie firm, A. Rivetz & Co, that Lauren took the first tentative steps towards building his fashion empire. He began to create his own tie designs. With $50,000 and his designs, Lauren left Rivetz to form his own company, Polo, with his older brother. It was 1968.

CONTRIBUTION

Lauren chose the name Polo because of its sporty, upper-class connotations. Polo began life as a tie shop. His ties were distinctively wide—wider than was fashionable at the time. While the customers appreciated the new designs, the shops weren't convinced. Lauren tried to get the famous New York shop Bloomingdale's to stock his products. Bloomingdale's was interested but asked if he would modify his designs by narrowing the ties to make them more in keeping with the fashion of the day. They also insisted he remove his brand label. The plucky Lauren called the store's bluff and refused. It wasn't long before Bloomingdale's was back, agreeing to stock Polo designer ties on Lauren's terms.

Lauren could never have succeeded without an innate sense of style and an innovative eye for fashion. Equally important was his understanding of how to build a brand. Lauren made Polo and its associated brands a lifestyle, as well as a design choice. Throughout the 1980s the Polo brand was backed by distinctive advertising that conjured up a range of associations, from safaris to the English aristocracy.

Ralph Lauren's first shop opened in 1971. In the seventies the concept of the designer shop was still in its infancy. Lauren was one of the first men's fashion designers to open a shop in his own name. With the help of his brother Jerry, he continued to establish the brand with season after season of clothes that aimed to be stylish, classic, and timeless. As more shops opened, Lauren extended his range to women's wear, and then to his 'home collection' line, comprising linen, towels, furniture, and other similar products. The flagship shop, Rhinelander Mansion on Madison Avenue, was opened in 1986, and in 1993 the Polo Sport shop opened across the street.

While the 1980s saw an extension of the Polo brand into new areas, it also brought new competition. Suddenly businessmen were wearing a new brand of suit: the Giorgio Armani power suit. Lauren modified his designs to produce crisp-looking sophisticated suits. What he would not do was abandon the ethos of the Polo brand for short-term gain. 'I'm a long-term person,' he has said. 'I'm long-term about my work. I'm a builder. Everything I do is an extension of my life.' Lauren's long-term perspective proved astute. What was considered the height of fashion in the 1980s seemed unduly ostentatious in the altogether more reserved 1990s.

In June 1997 the company went public. The IPO raised $767 million for Polo Ralph Lauren and made Lauren a very wealthy man. As befits the man behind one of the hottest fashion properties of the 20th century, Lauren lives a stylish life. He has properties in Jamaica, Long Island, and Fifth Avenue, as well as an estate in Bedford, New York, and a ranch in Colorado. A keen driver, Lauren has amassed a collection of prestigious cars that includes a 1937 Alfa Romeo and a 1938 Bugatti. In 1998 he showed his patriotic side by donating $10 million towards the cost of restoring and displaying the original version of the American flag, fashioned in 1813.

CONTEXT AND CONCLUSIONS

Ralph Lauren led where many have since followed. His concept of the men's designer shop was adopted by many other famous names, including Giorgio Armani and Calvin Klein. Lauren built Polo into a global brand with its quintessential, clean-cut, 'preppy' look. His success was in selling not only clothes, but

> *Lauren could never have succeeded without an innate sense of style and an innovative eye for fashion. Equally important was his understanding of how to build a brand.*

a way of life—a glimpse of which was revealed through stylised advertising. As Lauren says: 'I don't design clothes, I design dreams.' Today the company's brand names include Polo, Polo by Ralph Lauren, Polo Sport, Ralph Lauren, Lauren, RALPH, Ralph Lauren Purple Label Polo Jeans Co, and many others. There are now over 130 Polo/Ralph Lauren shops around the world selling a range of products from fragrances to footwear, fabric to furniture, as well as the classic menswear Lauren made his name designing. For $150,000 you can even buy a Ralph Lauren caravan: a gleaming silver Airstream with a choice of four differently themed interiors.

THE BEST SOURCES OF HELP
Books:
Gross, Michael. *Genuine Authentic: The Real Life of Ralph Lauren*. New York: HarperCollins, 2003.
McDowell, Colin. *Ralph Lauren and the Spirit of America*. London: Cassell, 2002.
Trachtenberg, Jeffrey A. *Ralph Lauren: The Man behind the Mystique*. New York: Little, Brown, 1981.
Website:
Polo.com Ralph Lauren: **www.polo.com**

WILLIAM LEVITT

1906	Born.
1927	Works in his father's law firm.
1944	Serves with the navy construction unit in Oahu, Hawaii.
1947	Starts construction on Levittown in Nassau County, Long Island.
1950	Featured on cover of July edition of *Time* magazine.
1954	Brothers separate.
1958	Builds 12,000-home project in Willingboro, New Jersey.
1960	Company goes public.
1961	Posts a loss of $1.4 million.
1967	Sells company for $92 million to ITT.
1978	Attempts a comeback.
1994	Dies.

> **SUMMARY**
>
> Bill Levitt never intended to go into the construction business. Neither did his father. But when one of his father's property deals went awry, the family was left with 40 half-built houses that needed finishing to recoup their investment. The young Levitt was press-ganged into helping, and ended up as president of the family construction business, Levitt & Sons. Custom-built houses for wealthy execs followed. Then, in post-Second World War America, Levitt struck gold. Buying up vast tracts of farm land on Long Island with the help of his father and brother, he constructed Levittown—a seminal milestone in US construction history. It marked a transition to mass-constructed, low-cost housing. More Levitt-style suburban housing followed. Levitt's empire survived a rift with his brother in the 1950s, but it didn't survive a change in consumer tastes, a scarcity of building land and public censure over some of his business practices. Levitt sold his business to Harold Geneen's ITT in 1967 for $92 million, was virtually bankrupted in the 1970s, and made a failed comeback in the 1980s. He died in 1993, with a tarnished reputation, but is still remembered fondly by many of the original residents of Levittown.

LIFE AND CAREER

William Levitt was born on 9 January 1906, the son of a New York-based lawyer. After the Boys High School at Bedford-Stuyvesant, he went on to New York University to study maths and English. It's not clear whether he ever graduated. He is reported to have said, 'I got itchy. I wanted to make a lot of money. I wanted a big car and a lot of clothes.' Years later, he claimed that he graduated in 1927.

While Levitt was at college, his father was representing clients in property deals and buying and selling properties on the side. In one deal, Levitt senior bought 100 building plots from a bankrupt client and financed a builder, who bought the land to build houses. When the builder's business went under, he handed back the land with 40 half-finished houses. Bill and his brother were recruited to help complete them. The houses were built and Levitt's father, encouraged by their efforts, formed Levitt & Sons to develop the rest of the plots.

William Levitt

CONTRIBUTION

At 22, Levitt was president of the newly-formed building firm, with control of marketing, sales, and financing. His brother Alfred took charge of design. It was in the depths of the great depression, but Levitt's flamboyant sales patter helped sell Levitt houses to the upper middle classes. After Levitt sold 18 houses from the development, the firm committed to build another 600 over a four-year period.

A 200-house development in Manhasset, Long Island followed. Then another 1,200. The wealthy were beating a path to Levitt's door to snap up his $18,000 houses. But the cracks in the Levitt business philosophy were already apparent. Levitt, the grandson of a rabbi, restricted the purchasers of his new houses. No Jewish or black people were allowed. It was a practice that would stain Levitt's reputation.

Before the United States entered the Second World War, Levitt & Sons shifted its focus from housing for the well-off to mass-market housing. US builders traditionally built three or four houses a year. Levitt planned to build up to 40 a day. It was a new approach to house building, based on assembly-line production. Construction was broken down into its constituent parts: 27 of them. A specialist team was assigned to each process. There was a team for carpentry, for tiling, and for roofing. There was even a team for red paint and one for white paint. Another group of men spent their days bolting washing machines to the floors. In the first development of this kind, 2,350 houses were erected for the navy in Norfolk, Virginia, and in 1944 Levitt was called up to serve with the navy construction unit in Oahu, Hawaii. Levitt was just biding time until he could get back to building. 'Beg, borrow, or steal the money and then build and build,' he told his navy colleagues, explaining how postwar America would be crying out for low-cost housing. He was right. During the war years, housing production had stalled. Later, with the troops returning from the war and low-cost mortgages available from the government, there was a huge pent-up demand.

While Levitt was in the navy, his brother and father were buying tracts of potato farmers' land on the Hempstead Plains in Nassau County, Long Island. The plan was to build a self-contained community of 6,000 homes.

While Levitt was in the navy, his brother and father were buying tracts of potato farmers' land on the Hempstead Plains in Nassau County, Long Island. The plan was to build a self-contained community of 6,000 homes. It was by far the largest-ever planned housing development in the United States. Levitt's brother and father planned the uniform houses and bought the land, but it was Levitt's financing and promotion skills that made Levittown, as it is known, possible. He got on the right side of the politicians and persuaded them to rewrite the planning laws. Construction started in 1947 on 7.3 square miles of land in Nassau County, and became the most celebrated (and at times criticised) development in the United States. By 1951 there were over 17,400 homes.

By the early 1950s, the relationship between Levitt and his brother had become strained. Flamboyant Levitt liked to live it up. With a swish Manhattan apartment and celebrity friends, he grew accustomed to the high life. *Time* magazine put him on its cover in July 1950, calling him a 'cocky rambunctious hustler'. His brother Alfred, always the quiet one, was embarrassed by his brother's taste for the limelight. In 1954, the tension became unbearable and the brothers agreed to go their separate ways.

It was a difficult time for Levitt. Demand for housing was falling, and land suitable for building was becoming scarce. His company, which went public in 1960, posted a loss of $1.4 million in 1961. But Levitt was a survivor. He spread his projects, undertaking small developments both in the United States and abroad. In Puerto Rico he successfully completed a 12,000-home development. By the end of the 1960s, the business was back on track and making profits.

> Time *magazine put him on its cover in July 1950, calling him a 'cocky rambunctious hustler'*

Levitt's biggest coup came in 1967, when he negotiated the sale of his building firm to Harold Geneen's International Telephone & Telegraph Corporation (ITT). With a sale price of $92 million, it appeared a staggeringly good deal for Levitt, especially as the company had been posting a loss only a few years before. It made Levitt phenomenally wealthy, with $62 million worth of ITT stock. Under the terms of the deal, Levitt gave up the right to build housing in the United States for ten years.

But in a sense it was a bad deal for Levitt. His life was defined by his work, and Geneen wanted him to play no part in the company's future. Cold-shouldered by ITT executives, Levitt spent his time frittering away his money. He acquired paintings by Degas and Monet, a 237-foot yacht, and built a chateau. None of these compensated him for the loss of his vocation. Worse was to come when, in the 1970s, ITT shares slumped. For tax reasons Levitt chose not to sell his ITT shares, borrowing against them instead to raise cash. When the shares dipped to 10% of their original value, Chase Manhattan bank seized the stock as security.

In 1978 when the restrictive clause preventing him from building in the United States expired, Levitt attempted a comeback. But through the 1980s he was a shadow of his former self. He became involved in suspect financial practices and diverted funds from his business to feed his extravagant lifestyle. He was barred from doing business in New York, accused of siphoning $70 million from his family's charities, and was forced to sell his mansion. However, he remained flamboyant to the end. He died in 1994, still talking about his imminent comeback. 'I have a regular organisation ready to punch in full-time. I need another six months,' he said in his last interview. He died three months later.

CONTEXT AND CONCLUSIONS

Over a 64-year career in the construction business, William Levitt sold a slice of the American Dream to thousands of would-be homeowners. Following the Second World War, on just over seven acres of land in Nassau County, Long Island, Levitt financed and oversaw the mass production of suburban houses in artificially-created communities. The original $50 million development is still going strong, as

Levitt spent his time frittering away his money. He acquired paintings by Degas and Monet, a 237-foot yacht, and built a chateau. are the dozens that followed. Later in his career, Levitt attracted criticism for the racist restrictions he imposed on purchasers. His extravagant lifestyle distracted him from his business affairs. He failed to adapt to modern sensibilities. He became mired in a scandal of financial irregularities. But for all his failings, he merits inclusion in the business hall of fame for his vision of a new kind of housing development, his brilliant marketing of the concept, and the clever financing that enabled the completion of Levittown. Asked late in life what he would like to be remembered for, he answered with characteristic rumbustiousness: 'I would like to stay alive. I don't want to be remembered.' Pressed further he continued, 'I'd like to be remembered as a guy that I suppose gave value for low-cost housing. Not somebody that gave value for half-million dollar houses. Anybody can do that.'

CLOSE BUT NO CIGAR
LE CORBUSIER

Le Corbusier (Charles-Edouard Jeanneret-Gris) was born in La Chaux de Fonds, Switzerland in 1887. Perhaps the greatest architect of the 20th century, he invented the 'international style' and influenced Mies Van Der Rohe and Walter Gropius, among many others. He also tried his hand at social planning, although less successfully than Levitt. Nothing could be farther apart than Levittown, chock-full of small box houses, and Brasilia, the incarnation of Le Corbusier's 'Radiant City'. Yet Le Corbusier's stark and functional attempts at urban planning, with distinct zones for leisure, working and living, were a failure. In the United States, Le Corbusier inspired urban renewal and public housing projects that damaged the social fabric of the cities. Many have since been torn down. Levittown, on the other hand, despite the authoritarian approach and the restrictive covenants imposed on inhabitants ('thou shalt mow the lawn'; 'thou shalt not use a washing line') is still a thriving community.

THE BEST SOURCES OF HELP
Books:
Ferrer, Margaret Lundrigan, and Tova Navarra. *Levittown: The First 50 Years*. Dover, New Hampshire: Arcadia Publishing, 1997.
Gans, Herbert. *The Levittowners: Ways of Life and Politics in a New Suburban Community*. New York: Alfred Knopf, 1967.

HENRY ROBINSON LUCE

1898	Born.
1920	Graduates from Yale. Voted 'most brilliant student'.
1922	Leaves Baltimore for New York. Time, Inc. incorporated on 28 November.
1923	The first issue of *Time* hits the stands.
1927	First profit posted—$3,860.
1928	Profits of $126,000.
1929	*Fortune* magazine launched.
1936	*Life* magazine launched.
1954	*Sports Illustrated* magazine launched.
1958	Suffers heart attack.
1967	Dies.

> **SUMMARY**
>
> Henry Robinson Luce's strict Presbyterian upbringing at a missionary station in China seemed to do him no harm. His early academic record was outstanding, and his performance at Yale University no less impressive. When he graduated in 1920 he had already shown a talent for editing by radically overhauling the Yale newspaper, the *Daily News*. Following a whistle-stop tour of Europe, he worked on the *Chicago Daily News* and then the *Baltimore News*, where he linked up with fellow Yale alumnus Briton Hadden. Together they were unstoppable, launching a new publication *Time: The Weekly News Magazine* in March 1923 and nursing it from a paltry circulation to one of 118,000 in its third year. In 1929 they followed this success with the launch of the business magazine *Fortune* to chronicle the ups and downs of the Wall Street crash and the ensuing Great Depression.

LIFE AND CAREER

Henry Robinson Luce was born on 3 April 1898 in Tengchow, China, where his Presbyterian missionary parents were teaching at a Christian mission. The first of four children, Luce's upbringing was an austere one. His daily routine began at six in the morning with a cold bath, followed by half an hour of Bible study. With six hours of Chinese lessons a day, the young Luce was fluent in the local tongue before he was able to speak English.

Barring a brief visit to America in 1906, Luce was to remain in China until he was 14. A precocious scholar, he attended the British-run boarding school in Chefoo. It was a tough environment with strict discipline. Fortunately for Luce, a strong work ethic, combined with a keen mind, kept him at the top of the class and away from the master's cane. The school's pupils were predominantly English, and Luce frequently found himself sticking up for the United States. 'My Anglo-Americanism is deeper than any words,' he once said. 'Indeed, it is written in the blood of that shameful, and futile, endless two hours one Saturday afternoon, when I rolled around the unspeakably dirty floor of the main schoolroom with a British boy who had insulted my country.'

After Chefoo in China came the Hotchkiss School in Connecticut, America, with a brief three-week tour of Europe in between. There Luce continued his excellent scholastic record: outstanding marks in his Greek exams, the honour roll, and leader of the class in most subjects. Outside his lessons he discovered a new talent as editor-in-chief of the *Hotchkiss Literary Monthly* and assistant managing editor of the weekly school newspaper, the *Record*. Luce had found his vocation.

CONTRIBUTION

It was at Yale that Luce started his career in publishing in earnest. Together with fellow student and ex-Hotchkiss pupil Briton Hadden, Luce revolutionised the Yale newspaper, the *Daily News*. On graduation in 1920 Luce was voted 'most brilliant' and Hadden 'most likely to succeed'. The combination proved irresistible. After Yale, Luce continued his tour of the world's most prestigious educational establishments, heading for Oxford University, where he studied history. Then, after a whistle-stop tour of Europe, he returned to the United States, obtaining work first on the *Chicago Daily News* and then on the *Baltimore News*. It was in Baltimore that Luce rejoined his old friend Hadden and together they developed a plan to launch a new weekly news magazine called *Facts*. When the magazine was finally launched it was called *Time: The Weekly News Magazine*.

The pair left Baltimore for New York in February 1922. There they rented a small one-room office, acquired a third partner in Culbrith Sudler, who was reportedly an expert at selling advertising, and spent the next few months seeking advice and capital. Advice was forthcoming—mostly along the lines of 'don't do it'—but capital was less plentiful. Eventually, however, they managed to raise sufficient funds (partly through a share issue) and incorporated the business on 28 November 1922, having moved to a small loft in the printing trades building on Eighth Avenue. To decide who should edit the magazine and who should manage the business side of things, Hadden and Luce tossed a coin. It was to Luce's everlasting chagrin that he lost and, in the intervening three-year period before he was able to take up the post of editor, Hadden had the opportunity to stamp his mark on *Time* magazine. The first issue of *Time* hit the newsstands in March 1923, with a cover price of 15 cents. With the law stating that any news over 24 hours old belonged in the public domain, news elements of the magazine came almost entirely from the *New York Times*.

> *With catastrophic timing, the first issue of* Fortune, *30,000 copies in all, rolled off the presses just three months after the spectacular stock market crash of October 1929.*

The distribution of the first issues was farcical. A string of debutante acquaintances was entrusted with the task of addressing the first three issues and dispatching them to subscribers, who could read all three before making a financial commitment. In the ensuing mix-up some subscribers received three copies of the same issue, only one issue, or no issue at all. Of the 25,000 who agreed to take a look, only 9,000 ever received a copy. And of the 5,000 sent to the newsstands, 3,000 were returned unsold.

After this inauspicious start, however, circulation grew steadily. By the third year it had reached 110,000, with advertising revenue of $283,000, yet a profit remained elusive. Indeed, it wasn't until 1927 that the new magazine made a profit, and then it was just $3,860. In 1928 a more respectable figure of $126,000 was posted, and from that point onwards figures improved rapidly. By then, Luce was editor. He ensnared his readers with an array of literary devices: compound words such as 'sexational' and the more successful 'socialite' made their debut on the pages of *Time*. Foreign words such as 'tycoon' (from the Japanese *taikun*, meaning prince) and 'pundit'(from the Hindu *pandit*, meaning sage) were popularised by Luce; and he also made common the use of euphemisms such as 'great and good friend'—meaning mistress—to skirt around potentially libellous issues.

By 1927 *Time* had moved again, not once but twice, coming to rest eventually in Manhattan, just off Fifth Avenue. Luce's lifelong friend Hadden had always said his aim was to make one million dollars by the age of 30. As it turned out he made more than that, but in February 1929, nine days after his 31st birthday, he died from a streptococcus infection. Luce was left in full charge of the magazine.

Fortune magazine was the second major venture under the Time, Inc. banner. Founded in 1929, it was Luce's idea, based on his instinct that 'business is obviously the greatest single common denominator of interest among the active leading citizens of the United States—our best men are in business'. *Fortune* was two years in the planning. The magazine owes its name to Luce's wife Lila, who preferred *Fortune* to *Power*. To head up the editorial staff, Luce chose Parker Lloyd Smith, a brilliant Oxford graduate who did an excellent job in the magazine's early days, until in 1931 he threw himself to his death from a hotel window, for no apparent reason.

With catastrophic timing, the first issue of *Fortune*, 30,000 copies in all, rolled off the presses just three months after the spectacular stock market crash of October 1929. In spite of, or perhaps because of, its timing, the first issue was well received, and the magazine managed to survive the economic depression that followed. By 1937 revenues were up to $500,000 and circulation in excess of 460,000. Through the ensuing decades *Fortune* magazine catalogued the ups and downs of US business life.

Over the next 30 years, Luce built a publishing business with a worldwide circulation of over 13 million. To *Time* and *Fortune* he added the even more successful *Life* magazine, founded in 1936. In 1954, when *Sports Illustrated* was introduced, it broke the circulation records set by *Life*. Luce successfully steered the company through the Second World War, adroitly negotiated the communist witch-hunts that swept post-war America, and fended off hundreds of threats to sue the company for invasion of privacy or libel each year.

In 1967 the circulation of Luce's flagship magazine was some 7,500,000. Advertising, which was twice as much as for any other magazine, brought in $170 million to Time, Inc. *Time* magazine itself sold some 3,500,000, yielding $86 million in advertising revenue. The company that Luce founded on a budget of $86,000 had total revenues in excess of $500 million, with profits of $37 million. For much of his later career Luce regularly threatened to retire. 'At 40 I will retire and let the young take

> *Over the next 30 years, Luce built a publishing business with a worldwide circulation of over 13 million. To* Time *and* Fortune *he added the even more successful* Life *magazine, founded in 1936.*

over,' he used to say. But it was always the same story; even after his heart attack in 1958, he could not drag himself away. In February 1967 he was still in command of his empire, when he finally succumbed to another heart attack.

CONTEXT AND CONCLUSIONS
Flamboyant media moguls such as William Randolph Hearst, Lord Beaverbrook, and Lord Thomson are better remembered today than Henry Robinson Luce, especially outside the United States. Luce, the man with a Presbyterian upbringing, was content to remain in the shadows. He neither sought political power, as Beaverbrook did, nor did he go in for ostentatious shows of wealth like Hearst's mansion in San Simeon. Yet Luce's contribution to publishing was just as important, if not more so, as that of his peers. He created a number of magazines that have survived him and gone on to become national institutions. A brilliant scholar, a brilliant editor, Luce did much to change the nature of reporting. There is no question that the achievement of the man who brought the world *Time*, *Life*, and *Fortune* magazines deserves greater recognition.

THE BEST SOURCES OF HELP
Books:
Cort, David. *The Sin of Henry R. Luce: An Anatomy of Journalism*. Secaucus, New Jersey: Carol Publishing Group, 1974.
Swanberg, W.A. *Luce and His Empire*. New York: Scribner, 1972.
Websites:
Time.com: **www.time.com/time**
Fortune.com: **www.fortune.com**

KONOSUKE MATSUSHITA

1894	Born.
1918	Starts Matsushita Electric Appliance Factory.
1929	Formulates the 'basic management objective'.
1933	Introduces the 'five guiding principles'.
1935	Matsushita Electric Appliance renamed Matsushita Electric Industrial Company (MEI).
1937	Adds two more guiding principles.
1946	Founds the Peace and Happiness through Prosperity (PHP) Institute.
1950	Returns to the company.
1961	Becomes chairman of MEI.
1965	Introduces five-day working week.
1973	Steps down as chairman.
1989	Dies.

> **SUMMARY**
>
> For a man who never left his native country before the age of 56, Konosuke Matsushita made a big impact on the world. Matsushita started work at the age of nine. After spells at an electrical engineering company, Matsushita started his own company, Matsushita Electric Appliance (later Matsushita Electric Industrial, or MEI) in 1918. Through a combination of product innovation, clever marketing, and forward-thinking management, Matsushita developed the company into one of the largest of its kind in pre-war Japan.
>
> After a difficult post-war period, Matsushita rejoined his company in 1950. Reasserting his business values, he transformed MEI into an industrial giant that today consists of over 300 subsidiaries.

LIFE AND CAREER

The youngest of eight children, Konosuke Matsushita was born in 1894 in the farming village of Wasa in Wakayama Prefecture, Japan. His father was a landlord who received income from the local tenant farmers, enabling the family to live in reasonable comfort. That changed in 1898 when Matsushita's father decided to speculate on the rice market. The investment was spectacularly unsuccessful and left the family in financial ruin. The changed circumstances spelled the end of Matsushita's rudimentary schooling. At the tender age of nine, he was asked by his father to go to Osaka to work in a charcoal brazier shop. This was followed by an apprenticeship in a bicycle shop.

In 1910 the young Matsushita was taken on as a wiring assistant at the Osaka Electric Light Company (OELC). He was a quick learner and despite his age, just 16, his skill at wiring earned him rapid promotion. But in 1917 he decided to leave OELC, partly due to health problems. Matsushita suffered from a debilitating lung condition and frequently took days off work to rest. He reasoned that if he could start his own business he would be able to accommodate his poor health. He also wanted to market a new light socket he had invented, and his employers at OELC had done little to encourage his inventiveness.

CONTRIBUTION

In 1918, at the age of 23, he founded Matsushita Electric Appliance Factory (the company became Matsushita Electric Industrial Company, MEI, in 1935). He had three employees, the equivalent of $50, and a prototype for a new type of electrical socket. Business was tough to begin with. Matsushita's first socket design turned out to be a dud. But the next product, an electrical attachment plug, sold well, especially as Matsushita under-cut the competition by up to a third. The product that kept the company going, though, was a battery-powered bicycle lamp shaped like a bullet. The lamp was unique in being able to run for up to 40 hours. Some Japanese even used it to light their houses.

Matsushita was a good engineer, but he was even better at marketing. He used the demand for his bicycle lamp to build a sales network throughout Japan. Once he had established countrywide distribution, he put the trademark 'National' on Matsushita products and lowered prices to make his lamp a mass-market product. He also pioneered the use of national newspaper advertising, a relatively rare sight in Japan in the 1920s.

In 1929, with the company firmly established, Matsushita put into practice the management practices and philosophy for which he was to become famous. He was an extremely enlightened manager for his time. This much is evident from the slogan he adopted for the company: 'harmony between corporate profit and social justice'. Matsushita followed this in 1933 with his 'five guiding principles' (two more were added in 1937), which shaped the conduct of the company. The principles, still adhered to today, are service to the public, fairness and honesty, teamwork for the common cause, untiring effort for improvement, courtesy and humility, accord with natural laws, and gratitude for blessings.

Matsushita's first socket design turned out to be a dud. But the next product, an electrical attachment plug, sold well, especially as Matsushita under-cut the competition by up to a third.

During the 1930s Matsushita took a number of decisions illustrating the leadership style that was to earn him the nickname 'the god of management'. During the recession of 1930 Matsushita refused to make wholesale lay-offs. Instead he recruited under-employed factory workers to go out and sell stockpiled inventory. Later in 1931 he bought the rights to a radio patent, which he then made freely available to the market. This was an expensive ploy, but it had the effect of stimulating the market and so ultimately profited the company. It presaged a similar move by David Sarnoff, head of RCA, with the patent for building colour television sets, and anticipated the stance taken much later by the open source movement in computing. In 1932 Matsushita declared that entrepreneurs and manufacturers should aim 'to make all products as inexhaustible and as cheap as tap water'.

Somehow Matsushita managed to hold the company together during the Second World War. In post-war Japan, MEI came under the severe restrictions imposed on certain Japanese companies by the Allies. Matsushita was almost removed as president, but was saved in part by a petition from 15,000 employees. For a time he devoted his energies to the Peace and Happiness through Prosperity Institute, which he founded in 1946, returning to his company duties only in 1950. He reinvigorated the company, reorganising it along divisional lines. At the same time he reassessed processes to make them more efficient and refocused the company on the core values he had expressed in the 1930s.

From 1950 to his retirement as chairman in 1973, Matsushita oversaw a huge expansion of the company as its 'three treasures'—washing machines, refrigerators, and televisions—as well as other electrical goods were exported around the world. The company grew to become one of the world's largest manufacturers of electrical goods, controlling a stable of global brand names including Panasonic, Technics, and JVC.

A measure of the man's attention to his business is revealed by an incident at the Matsushita Pavilion during the Osaka world exposition in 1970. The exposition had been open for a few days when the pavilion's staff were surprised to see Matsushita waiting in the queue outside. When they rushed out to usher the founder of their company indoors, he told them that he had stood in the queue to find out how long visitors had to wait before they were admitted. Later that day he ordered that the queuing system be re-appraised to speed up admission and that shade from the sun be provided for the people waiting outside.

From the 1970s onwards Matsushita concentrated much of his time on developing and explaining his social and commercial philosophies, mainly through his 44 published books. His most popular title, *Developing a Road to Peace and Happiness Through Prosperity*, sold over four million copies. He continued to teach his unique concept of management until his chronic lung problems claimed his life. He died of pneumonia on 27 April 1989. He was 94.

CONTEXT AND CONCLUSIONS

Konosuke Matsushita founded one of Japan's greatest corporations, Matsushita Electric Industrial. Yet he is remembered for much more than the creation of an electrical goods empire. At MEI Matsushita implemented management practices that were far ahead of their time. He abandoned the conventional centralised management structure. He drew up a corporate creed and identified corporate values. He pioneered advertising in the press and competed both on price and quality.

Matsushita's philosophy can best be summed up by the 'basic management objective' he formulated in 1929: 'Recognising our responsibilities as industrialists, we will devote ourselves to the progress and development of society and the well-being of people through our business activities, thereby enhancing the quality of life throughout the world.' It was something Matsushita did to great effect.

THE BEST SOURCES OF HELP
Books:
Gould, Rowland. *The Matsushita Phenomenon*. Tokyo: Diamond Sha, 1970.
Kotter, John P. *Matsushita: Leadership Lessons from the Life of the 20th Century's Most Remarkable Entrepreneur*. New York: Free Press, 1997.
Matsushita, Konosuke. *Quest for Prosperity—The Life of a Japanese Industrialist*. Tokyo: PHP Institute, 1988.
Website:
Panasonic: **www.panasonic.co.uk**

LOUIS MAYER

1885	Born.
1907	Buys rundown cinema in Haverhill, Massachusetts.
1915	Shows D.W. Griffith's *Birth of a Nation* at his cinemas.
1918	Starts film production firm in Los Angeles: Louis B. Mayer Pictures.
1924	Louis B. Mayer Productions, the Samuel Goldwyn Company, and Metro merge to form Metro Goldwyn Mayer, or MGM.
1926	*Ben Hur*.
1927	Formation of the Academy of Motion Pictures Arts and Sciences.
1932	*Grand Hotel*.
1936	Rival Irving Thalberg dies.
1951	Ousted from MGM after a power struggle with Dore Schary.
1957	Dies.

SUMMARY

The real-life story of film tycoon Louis Mayer (1885–1957) reads like a script from one of his films. Mayer hauled himself up from his humble beginnings as the son of an immigrant scrap-metal dealer to become a Hollywood legend. Starting in 1907 with a small chain of cinemas, by 1924 he was vice-president of Metro Goldwyn Mayer, arguably the greatest studio in Hollywood history.

Over the following decades the studio with the famous lion emblem was a roaring success as Mayer exerted his despotic influence over every aspect of the film-making process. Like many dictators, benign or otherwise, Mayer was ousted from MGM in 1951 after a bitter power struggle.

LIFE AND CAREER

Louis Mayer was born Eliezar Mayer on 4 July 1885 in Minsk, Russia (now in Belarus). In 1888 Mayer emigrated with his family to New Brunswick, Canada. In Canada Mayer's father built a small junk-dealing business into a profitable scrap-metal organisation. After elementary school Mayer joined his father's business, preferring the world of commerce to that of academia. Soon he had his own scrap business in Boston.

> *In 1907 Mayer took his first small step on the road to Hollywood. Relinquishing his position in the family business, he bought a small dilapidated cinema in Haverhill, Massachusetts at a knock-down price.*

In 1907 Mayer took his first small step on the road to Hollywood. Relinquishing his position in the family business, he bought a small dilapidated cinema in Haverhill, Massachusetts at a knock-down price. He completely overhauled the cinema and made a decision to show only quality films. His gamble paid off. Soon he was the owner of the largest cinema chain in New England. Film exhibitors fought to show new films at Mayer's cinemas. In 1915 he showed D.W. Griffith's *Birth of a Nation*, one of the most popular films of its time. The huge profit Mayer made from showing the film helped finance his ensuing adventures in Hollywood.

CONTRIBUTION

By 1918 Mayer was camped out in Los Angeles, operating as a film promoter through his company, Louis B. Mayer Pictures. It was the start of his biggest adventure. At first productions were funded from the proceeds of the cinema-chain business. He made a star of the actress Anita Stewart and, fired up by the acclaim received for his first production, *Virtuous Wives*, continued to use her as his main attraction for the following five years.

Hollywood was still in its infancy. For aspiring moguls there remained a once-in-a-lifetime opportunity to stake a claim in the city of celluloid. Mayer may have been wealthy because of his cinema business, but his fortune was small change in an industry dominated by fabulously rich powerbrokers. And the mogul of all moguls was Marcus Loew. He commanded his fiefdom from the East Coast; 3,000 miles away in his New York office Loew pulled the strings that made Hollywood dance.

In 1924 Mayer hit the jackpot. Loew decided that he wanted his own studio, Metro, to merge with Louis B. Mayer Pictures and the Samuel Goldwyn Company. What Loew wanted, he generally got, to the point that when Samuel Goldwyn backed out of the deal, Loew retained the Goldwyn name, calling the newly-formed company Metro Goldwyn Mayer (MGM). Mayer was appointed vice-president. With his inherited stable of stars he was finally in a position to dominate Hollywood.

> *Mayer ruled MGM 'as one big family, rewarding obedience, punishing insubordination, and regarding opposition as personal betrayal'.*

At MGM Mayer ostensibly shared his power with Irving Thalberg, hired in from Universal by Loew. In reality, Mayer ruled the roost, conducting a bitter battle behind the scenes with Thalberg that ended only with Thalberg's death in 1936.

By all accounts Mayer was an autocratic, manipulative despot who ruled MGM using extreme cunning. He was described by Ephraim Katz, the late respected film scholar and author of the classic resource, *The Film Encyclopedia*, as 'a ruthless, quick-tempered, paternalistically tyrannical executive'. Mayer ruled MGM 'as one big family, rewarding obedience, punishing insubordination, and regarding opposition as personal betrayal'. His political acumen must truly have been brilliant to control the egos of film stars such as Lon Chaney and Greta Garbo, as well as directors like King Vidor and Erich von Stroheim.

Unashamedly populist, Mayer was said to abhor intellectualism. Like many other media moguls he had an innate sense of what the masses wanted. He was also a hands-on operator. To the frequent annoyance of the studio employees, who considered themselves the true auteurs, Mayer not only constantly intervened in film-making but also managed to take many of the plaudits.

Inexorably MGM's power grew, and with it, Mayer's. The studio churned out a film a week and created its own town, Culver City, where thousands of studio employees participated in the American dream. Off screen, Mayer was as ruthless as ever. He was equally adept at cutting film or cutting staff. He used the rise of the talkies as an excuse for a purge of the studio stars. Names that Mayer had helped make he now discarded: Buster Keaton, Erich von Stroheim, even Greta Garbo, were swept off the scene as Mayer and MGM marched on through the 1930s and 1940s.

Mayer cleverly managed to thwart objections to MGM's increasing dominance of the film industry by forming an alliance of sorts under the banner of the Academy of Motion Pictures Arts and Sciences. Mayer, along with Douglas Fairbanks Sr, was a prime mover behind the Academy's creation in 1927.

As with most dictatorial leaders, however, his ruthlessness eventually caught up with him. In the 1950s, lacking the energy of the emerging generation of would-be studio executives, he was finally ground down by the behind-the-scenes scheming. Outmanoeuvred, he was ejected from MGM in 1951 to be replaced by Dore Schary. Grittily determined to the last, Mayer spent his final years failing to persuade the shareholders of MGM's parent company, Loew, to reinstate him and dump Schary. He died of leukaemia in 1957.

CONTEXT AND CONCLUSIONS

In many ways Mayer's life was a drama in which he himself played the roles of both hero and villain. On his journey to moguldom he made countless enemies. It was said at the time of his death that the reason that half of Hollywood attended his funeral was to check that the great man was indeed dead. Mayer also earned the grudging respect of his competitors, who harboured a sneaking admiration for his commercial acumen.

At MGM Mayer presided over a golden age of film-making. He was responsible for a host of hits like *Ben Hur* (1926) and *Dinner at Eight* (1933). At his zenith he commanded the highest salary in the world: over a million dollars a year. Bob Hope said of Mayer that he 'came out west with 28 dollars, a box camera, and an old lion. He built a monument to himself—the Bank of America.'

Perhaps Mayer's most fitting epitaph is one of his own observations. Commenting on survival in the film business, the combative son of a scrap-dealer who became the most powerful man in Hollywood eloquently put it thus: 'Look out for yourself or they'll pee on your grave.'

THE BEST SOURCES OF HELP
Books:
Altman, Diana. *Hollywood East: Louis B. Mayer and the Origins of the Studio System*. Secaucus, New Jersey: Carol Publishing Group, 1992.
Gabler, Neal. *An Empire of Their Own: How the Jews Invented Hollywood*. New York: Doubleday, 1988.
Schulberg, Budd. *Moving Pictures*. New York: Stein and Day, 1982.
Zierold, Norman. *The Moguls*. Los Angeles: Avon Books, 1972.
Website:
MGM: **www.mgm.com**

CYRUS HALL McCORMICK

1809	Born.
1830	Given ownership of his father's prototype reaper invention.
1831	Produces viable working machine.
1834	Receives 14-year patent for the threshing machine.
1843	Head-to-head showdown with rival Obed Hussey.
1847	Moves business to Chicago.
1851	Awarded prize at Crystal Palace Grand Exhibition.
1859	Production at 4,119 machines a year.
1861	Beginning of American Civil War.
1870	Production of 10,000 machines a year.
1871	Great fire of Chicago destroys McCormick's manufacturing plant.
1873	New production plant opens.
1884	Dies.

SUMMARY

Cyrus Hall McCormick had invention in his blood. He grew up with a father who was constantly inventing strange contraptions. On the family farm in Virginia, McCormick perfected the design of one of his father's crazy ideas—the mechanised reaping machine. Aged only 22, he started a small-scale home-manufacturing operation in Virginia Valley, producing two machines in 1840. It ended up as a massive manufacturing concern, based in Chicago. In 1884, the McCormick Harvesting Machine Company sold 54,841 harvesting machines to farmers from the United States to Australia.

A millionaire by the age of 50, McCormick paved the way for an agrarian revolution through the invention of his reaping machine and a host of innovative marketing techniques, from the instalment plan to the money-back guarantee.

LIFE AND CAREER

The son of a farmer and inventor, Cyrus Hall McCormick was the oldest of eight children. Born on 15 February 1809 in Rockbridge County, Virginia, McCormick grew up on the 532 rolling acres of farmland belonging to the family. His father Robert, in addition to running the farm, spent a lot of time tinkering with inventions aimed at easing the burden of farming. The most significant of his inventions was a horse-drawn reaping device, abandoned when he failed to perfect it. McCormick's father lacked the business sense, the will, and the drive necessary to turn any of his various inventions into a commercial venture.

The young McCormick had already demonstrated an ability for invention when, at the age of 15, he built a light-weight cradle for harvesting grain. When he was still 21, his father gave him a head start in life, handing over the ownership of his reaper invention. In 1831, McCormick worked six weeks non-stop to perfect the invention, to produce a viable working machine.

CONTRIBUTION

In the summer of 1831, the 22-year-old McCormick used his horse-drawn reaper to mow down the field of wheat at John Steele's farm in Rockbridge County, Virginia.

Cyrus Hall McCormick

The assembled audience—farmers, labourers, and slaves—had witnessed the beginning of the mechanisation of agriculture. Quality control would come later.

McCormick wasn't the first to invent the reaper. Others, such as Obed Hussey, were also thinking along the same lines. In 1834, McCormick applied for and received a 14-year patent for his threshing machine. Hussey had obtained a patent for his reaping device a year earlier. In the end it was McCormick's marketing genius that would make his product the standard for mechanical threshing.

Despite the obvious advantages of the reaper, developing the business proved difficult. McCormick swiftly set about remedying the situation. He started by eliminating the competition in the minds of the consumer. He arranged a head-to-head showdown with his rival in 1843, in which the McCormick reaper cut down 17 acres in the time it took Obed Hussey to clear just two. Word soon travelled through the farming community about the disparity in performance between the two machines.

Next, McCormick developed a licensing system. Manufacturers close to market were granted a licence to produce the McCormick reaping machine. In some cases the agreement operated like a franchise, demarcating area in return for a franchise fee; in others it was simply a question of paying McCormick $20 for each reaper produced and sold.

> *He arranged a head-to-head showdown with his rival in 1843, in which the McCormick reaper cut down 17 acres in the time it took Obed Hussey to clear just two.*

To obviate the need to walk alongside his machine, McCormick designed a seat so the operator could sit above the reaper. This design, known as the 'old reliable', became the standard model.

In 1840, from his Walnut Grove base, McCormick sold two machines—they both broke down. The following year, he sold seven. In 1844, still in the Virginia Valley, production had risen to 75 machines, 25 manufactured under licence.

In 1847, McCormick moved to Chicago. The decision was motivated by the knowledge that, although he had manufactured 75 reapers in 1846, this was still a long way short of the demand. Devotion to his father, Robert, had kept McCormick in his hometown. When his father died in 1846, there were few reasons for him to remain in the backwoods of Walnut Grove. In Chicago, McCormick built a plant on the banks of the Chicago River. Over 7,500 square feet of factory space and river frontage meant completed machines could be loaded onto river transport. This allowed McCormick to expand production rapidly. In 1849, before completion of the factory, McCormick's company produced 1,500 reapers. By 1859, in new factory premises, production had rocketed to 4,119 machines a year.

By 1860, some 70% of the country's wheat harvest was gathered using McCormick's reaper. Before the reaper, it took a man 40 hours to harvest an acre of wheat. With the McCormick reaper, two people could harvest an acre of wheat in a day. In the decade leading up to 1859, US production of wheat boomed from 100 million bushels to 173 million. The agricultural revolution made McCormick a millionaire. It also made him a worldwide celebrity. The machine, first described by *The Times* as a 'contraption seemingly a cross between a wheelbarrow, a chariot, and a flying machine', won the main prize at the Grand Exhibition at Crystal Palace in 1851. This award was followed by prizes at the Hamburg Exposition, the Vienna Exposition and the Paris Exposition.

McCormick continued to manage his business well into his seventies. It was quite a feat, considering some of the severe setbacks the business suffered. Production was slack for the duration of the American Civil War, starting in 1861, during which time McCormick took the opportunity to promote his machine in Europe. By 1870 his factory was producing a staggering 10,000 machines year. Then in 1871 a devastating blow was dealt to his business when the great fire of Chicago destroyed $188 million worth of property at his manufacturing plant. The resilient McCormick built an even bigger factory and production complex that sprawled over a 160-acre site. It opened in 1873.

McCormick died in 1884, with the business safely in the hands of his enterprising son, Cyrus McCormick Jr. In the final years of his life McCormick successfully promoted his business abroad, taking the reaper to the both the Pacific and South America.

McCormick continued to manage his business well into his seventies. It was quite a feat, considering some of the severe setbacks the business suffered.

CONTEXT AND CONCLUSIONS

In 1831, the year that McCormick invented his mechanised reaping machine, 80% of all workers in the United States worked in farming. By the 1930s this figure was down to just 2%. That dramatic reduction, which freed up the workforce to better mankind in other ways than through the drudgery of manual agricultural work, is largely due to Cyrus Hall McCormick and his 'Virginia Reaper'. The effects of his achievements cannot be overstated. The commercial success of his machine accelerated the colonisation of America's West Coast, and allowed for the wholesale exploitation of the bread basket of the Midwest, which in turn allowed for a rapid expansion in the United States population. This growth, coupled with the release of workers from work on the land, was a significant factor in the growth of the United States as the biggest economy in the world.

Would this have happened without McCormick? Possibly, but McCormick was blessed with talents that many of his competitors lacked. His inventiveness extended beyond the creation of machines. He pioneered marketing innovations such as hire-purchase plans, commission sales, and money-back guarantees, that ensured every farmer who wanted a McCormick reaper could have one.

CLOSE BUT NO CIGAR
JOHN DEERE
Inventor and entrepreneur John Deere was a contemporary of Cyrus Hall McCormick. A blacksmith by trade, Deere invented the first self-polishing steel plough in the 1830s, just as McCormick was testing his reaping machine. In the end, McCormick's invention proved the more

significant of the two. By 1855 Deere was selling 13,000 ploughs a year. He went on to found Deere & Company in 1868, today a million-dollar company. He survived McCormick by two years, dying in 1886.

OBED HUSSEY
The 'almost-ran' of agricultural invention, Obed Hussey could justifiably lay claim to the invention of the reaping machine. A former whaler, Hussey patented his device in 1833, a year before McCormick. However his big mistake was to stay in Baltimore, Maryland, miles from his market. McCormick bit the bullet and moved from Virginia to Chicago in the Midwest. Hussey also lacked McCormick's flair for marketing and was unwilling to accommodate improvements to his design suggested by others.

THE BEST SOURCES OF HELP
Books:
Casson, Herbert. *Cyrus Hall McCormick: His Life and Work*. Chicago: AC McClure & Co, 1909.
Dobler, Lavinia. *Cyrus McCormick: Farm Boy*. Indianapolis, Indiana: The Bobbs-Merrill Co, 1961.
McCormick, Cyrus. *The Century of the Reaper—Cyrus Hall McCormick & Business*. Boston: Houghton Mifflin Co, 1931.

SCOTT McNEALY

1954	Born.
1972	Attends Harvard University.
1978	Admitted to Stanford Business School's MBA programme.
1982	Joins start-up company called Sun Microsystems.
1984	Three-year, $40-million deal to supply Sun-2 workstations. Made interim CEO in place of Vinod Khosla.
1985	Becomes permanent CEO.
1986	Company has its IPO.
1988	Revenues reach $1 billion.
1991	Network, the greater Swiss mountain dog, born.
1992	Revenues reach $3 billion.
1994	John Gosling and others develop Java.
2001	Revenues reach $17 billion.

> **SUMMARY**
>
> An amateur ice-hockey player and a 3-handicap golfer, Scott McNealy combines the charm and easy-going affability of a best buddy with the competitive drive required to be a successful athlete or business executive. Breezing through Harvard University and Stanford Business School, McNealy managed to combine his interests in beer and sport with the academic study necessary to obtain an economics degree and an MBA.
>
> A laid-back start in the manufacturing industry gave way to the job of CEO at Sun Microsystems in 1984, when his friend and cofounder Vinod Khosla was persuaded to step down. Since then life has been one long crusade against arch-foe Bill Gates and the Microsoft vision of a PC-dominated world. Enlisting the help of some unlikely allies along the way, including a 135-lb greater Swiss mountain dog and an animated character called Duke, McNealy continues to give his competitors a run for their money. With revenues of $17 billion and rising in 2001, the future looks bright both for him and for Sun.

LIFE AND CAREER

Scott McNealy was born on 13 November 1954, in Columbus, Indiana. His father was an executive for American Motors, and much of McNealy's early childhood was spent in towns scattered across the mid-west. The McNealy family finally rolled to a standstill in Bloomfield Hills, Michigan, where McNealy attended Cranbrook, a private preparatory school. Academic achievement and social popularity came easily to him. He devoted a great deal of his time to sports, yet still managed to get a perfect score of 800 in his SAT college maths test, earning him a place at Harvard University.

At the time McNealy's ambition was to become a doctor, but he ended up studying for a degree in economics. When he wasn't studying, he was immersing himself in the Harvard social scene. An excellent golfer (*Golf Digest* magazine ranked him number one among *Fortune* 500 CEOs in 1999), McNealy captained the university golf team. By an interesting quirk of fate, he was at Harvard at the same time as his long-time business adversary Bill Gates. McNealy, however, has no memory of their paths crossing.

Scott McNealy

When he left Harvard, McNealy embarked on a career in manufacturing, working at a tractor body-panel factory in Illinois. Life in the agricultural machinery business didn't appeal to him; he applied to Stanford University's Business School and, accepted at the third attempt, packed his bags and headed for California.

CONTRIBUTION

McNealy graduated with the Stanford MBA Class of 1980 and went to work for FMC Corporation, building military vehicles. In 1982 another Stanford alumnus, Vinod Khosla, contacted McNealy about a possible job. Khosla and graduate student Andy Bechtolsheim had combined forces to develop a workstation for computer networks. Bechtolsheim had been working on the Stanford University Network project, and so the two took the initials S.U.N. for the name of their start-up.

Khosla wanted someone with manufacturing expertise, and McNealy, by then working for hardware company Onyx, fitted the 'operations guy' bill. McNealy accepted the job of vice-president for manufacturing and operations at a celebratory meal in a McDonald's restaurant. The company enjoyed early success, winning a three-year, $40 million deal in 1984 to supply Sun-2 workstations to a company called Computervision.

This commercial success masked internal conflict over how the company should be run. Khosla, who had been the catalyst for starting Sun Microsystems, found the skills that had proved essential for getting the start-up off the ground were not necessarily those needed by a CEO to lead the company through the next phase of expansion and consolidation. The uneasiness over Khosla's stewardship of Sun placed McNealy in an awkward position. He had joined the company at the request of Khosla, who was a personal friend. Nevertheless the two other founders, Bechtolsheim and Bill Joy, wanted a change at the top. Together with McNealy they persuaded Khosla that he should step down. Eventually he left and went to work with venture capital firm, Kleiner Perkins Caulfield and Byers.

McNealy was installed as CEO in Khosla's place. It was an inspired appointment. His operational know-how and improbable combination of easy-going bonhomie and relentless drive kept the workforce engaged while pushing the company through a phase of rapid expansion. 'We wanted to make a Ferrari out of spare parts,' McNealy told the *New York Times*. 'We were either going to be incredibly successful or we were going to empty the pool out with a belly flop.' The company had its IPO in 1986. Sales continued to accelerate, from $1 billion in 1988 to over $3 billion in 1992.

McNealy realised early that one of the main obstacles to Sun's success would be the so-called 'Wintel alliance' (Windows operating system and Intel chips). He decided to meet this threat to the Sun UNIX platform head on. Shrewdly, he embarked on a campaign of antagonism directed at Microsoft's Bill Gates that attracted the attention of the media and created a buzz around Sun. McNealy took the position of network evangelist (a view diametrically opposed to Gates's), preaching that 'the network is the computer'. He even named his dog Network and gave it its own page on the Sun corporate website.

In 1994 McNealy was handed a secret weapon in his battle against the Microsoft hegemony when John Gosling's team of Sun programmers developed a new computer language. Provisionally named 'Oak', it was a cross-platform, write-once, run-anywhere language. Here, thought McNealy, was the big stick he could beat

Microsoft with. He put the full might of the company behind the new language, which, when 'Oak' failed to clear the lawyers, was renamed Java.

The story of how McNealy learnt about Gosling's project is indicative of his management methods. Sun may ostensibly have a hierarchical management structure, but McNealy was quick to grasp one indicator of the de facto organisational structure—the e-mail trail. Find out who is receiving the critical e-mails, he reasoned, and you know where the power is concentrated within the company. When McNealy kept coming across e-mails along the lines of 'Java group meeting', he reasoned that Java was something he ought to find out about.

He was right. With its strong branding and open standards, Java has become a universal language. NASA's 1997 Mars mission gave a real boost to the product by allowing interactive participation in the mission via the Internet. Java is seen as key to future domination of computing. The company's 'Sun One' vision sees an integrated set of Java-based hardware and software running on any platform, in contrast to proprietary systems like Microsoft Windows. By 2001, more than 2.5 million programmers were developing for Java and Sun had set up the Liberty Alliance of 34 leading companies who would allow secure Internet transactions based on Java. The company's success is also attributable in part to McNealy's excellence as a communicator. *Forbes ASAP* described him as one of the top ten speakers in the technology industry. *60 Minutes* dubbed him 'one of the most influential businessmen in America'—and he was quick to proselytise users to the benefits of Java. McNealy's enthusiasm for selling Sun systems extends to some high-profile networking. He famously challenged Jack Welch, General Electric's celebrated CEO, to a round of golf. McNealy lost, but so impressed Welch that he received a place on the GE board.

With McNealy in charge Sun has blazed a trail of innovation through the technology industry. In 2000 the company's annual revenues were over $12 billion. Still driven by McNealy's war cry of 'the network is the computer', the company continues to provide 'industrial-strength hardware, software, and services that power the Internet and allow companies worldwide to dot-com their businesses'.

CONTEXT AND CONCLUSIONS

Scott McNealy was thrust by chance into the driving seat of Sun Microsystems, the company he helped to found. Like his business contemporaries Bill Gates and Larry Ellison, McNealy has created a multi-billion-dollar company that is strongly associated with its founder and CEO. Think Sun Microsystems and you automatically think of Scott McNealy. McNealy has taken the competitive drive that makes him a good golfer and an even better executive and instilled it throughout the company. He has also proved himself a media-savvy leader. This is an essential quality in an age when the right words can propel a CEO to cult status, and the wrong ones can sink a company.

THE BEST SOURCES OF HELP
Book:
Southwick, Karen. *High Noon: The Inside Story of Scott McNealy and the Rise of Sun Microsystems*. New York: John Wiley, 1999.
Website:
Sun Microsystems UK: **www.sun.co.uk**

CHARLES MERRILL

1885	Born.
1907	Moves to New York to work for Patchogue-Plymouth Mills.
1911	Article 'Mr Average Investor' published in Leslie's Weekly.
1914	Founds Merrill, Lynch & Co with Edmund Lynch.
1928	Writes to clients advising them that 'now is a time to get out of debt'.
1940	Pierce & Co merges with Merrill Lynch.
1944	Suffers multiple heart attacks.
1947	Merrill Lynch largest retailer of stocks in United States.
1956	Dies.

SUMMARY

Co-founder of the first chain of stockbrokers, Charles Merrill brought stock ownership to the masses. In doing so he helped to shift capitalism from a relatively small base of rich investors to a much broader cross-section of US society, a process that has continued in recent years with the advent of online trading. Merrill came to stockbroking by chance. A broken romance led him to the hubbub of Wall Street when he left the textile company Patchogue-Plymouth Mills and joined the bond department of George H. Burr & Co.

As early as 1911 Merrill was contemplating the merits of wider share ownership. He articulated his radical ideas in the article 'Mr Average Investor'. He also became an expert on the financing of the relatively new concept of chain stores. It was a chain-store approach that he brought to stockbroking. With his friend Edmund Lynch, he founded Merrill, Lynch & Co in 1914. He then successfully steered the firm through the maelstrom of the 1929 Wall Street Crash. After the Second World War, with the expanded firm of Merrill Lynch, EA Pierce, and Cassatt, Merrill fulfilled his vision of bringing share ownership to the masses. By 1947 Merrill Lynch was the largest retailer of stocks in the United States, with $6,200,000 worth of sales and an advertising bill of some $400,000. Plagued by ill health, Merrill was forced to take a back seat, and died in 1956.

LIFE AND CAREER

The son of a shopkeeper and doctor, Charles Merrill was born in 1885 in the small village of Green Cove Springs, Jacksonville, Florida. His academic career was cut short when financial difficulties forced him to drop out of Amherst College without completing his degree. He later dropped out of law school. A stint as a semi-professional baseball player in Mississippi was followed by a reporting job on a West Palm Beach newspaper.

Through a girlfriend's father, Merrill obtained a job at the textile company Patchogue-Plymouth Mills and moved to New York. It was 1907, the year in which J.P. Morgan bailed out the US financial system. The financial crisis presented the young Merrill with an unexpected opportunity. He was dispatched to the National Copper Bank to obtain a loan that would save the company he worked for. It was a tall order, but the persuasive Merrill somehow managed to obtain a $300,000 loan from the bank president. Merrill thrived in the bustling environment of New York. When his budding romance with the boss's daughter ended, he extricated himself from an awkward situation by taking a job at the newly created bond department of George H. Burr & Co on Wall Street.

CONTRIBUTION

While Merrill was at Burr, two events occurred that were to shape his future professional life. The first was the realisation that it was possible to sell bonds and stock to the public, rather than just to powerful institutional investors. Merrill propounded his thoughts on this topic in his 1911 article 'Mr Average Investor', published in *Leslie's Weekly*. The second important event was Merrill's involvement in a financing deal for a chain of retail stores. At the time, chain stores were a new phenomenon. The economics involved made a significant impression on him.

In 1914 Merrill and his friend and colleague, Edmund Lynch, left Burr to form Merrill, Lynch & Co. In the first year of business Merrill won a contract to underwrite a $6 million chain-store financing deal. After a brief interlude due to the closing of the stock exchange at the outbreak of the First World War, the chain store was successfully brought to market in May 1915, earning him $300,000.

> *His academic career was cut short when financial difficulties forced him to drop out of Amherst College without completing his degree. He later dropped out of law school.*

Recognising that chain stores would become an essential feature of US post-war retailing, Merrill specialised in financing chain-store developments throughout the country. He retained a significant amount of stock in each deal. This not only made him a wealthy man but also gave the firm a decision-making role in the management of the companies it helped finance. Merrill used that power to great effect. At one point he even took control of a chain of grocery stores.

Remarkably, amid the rampant speculation of the 1920s, Merrill was one of the few who advocated caution. To his partner Lynch, he wrote, 'The financial skies are not clear. I do not like the outlook and I do not like the amount of money we owe.' When the financial storm came in 1929, Merrill Lynch was one of the few financial institutions to remain afloat. Clients who had taken Merrill's advice when he had written to them in 1928 advising them that 'now is a time to get out of debt', had much to thank him for. Anticipating a lengthy downturn, Merrill transferred his clients' accounts to another brokerage firm and devoted his time to managing a retail chain and looking after his own personal investments.

Merrill returned to Wall Street through the broking firm EA Pierce & Co, which merged with Merrill Lynch in January 1940. Through the newly created company of Merrill Lynch, EA Pierce, and Cassatt, Merrill brought stockbroking to the masses. It was the start of a financial revolution that introduced the chain-store approach to the elite world of stockbroking. Merrill ruthlessly drove down costs. With business conducted predominantly by phone, it was pointless having a large expensive building as the firm's headquarters, so he moved it to a cheaper, less prestigious location, 70 Pine Street. He also needed to whip up enthusiasm among his employees. To do this he recruited brokers from a wider base. The newcomers were unencumbered with traditional Wall Street ways. Merrill trained them in a specially established school for trainee brokers.

Charles Merrill

Having marshalled his forces, Merrill took his operation to the US public, building a chain of branch offices throughout the United States. The new brokers were paid salaries rather than working only for commission. This alleviated concerns on the public's part that the brokers would sell any stock, regardless of merit, merely to line their own pockets with commission. He backed up his campaign to broaden the appeal of stock buying by investing large amounts of money on advertising the firm's services. By 1947 Merrill Lynch was the largest retailer of stocks in the United States, with $6,200,000 worth of sales and an advertising spend of some $400,000. Its business was helped by the benign economic situation following the Second World War, as the United States began to reinforce its economic superpower status. During the cold war much was made of the power of the free market economy in the United States, and individuals were actively encouraged to buy stock in American companies through initiatives such as a Monthly Investment Plan scheme, introduced in 1954, which allowed the purchase of stock by instalments.

After suffering multiple heart attacks during 1944, Merrill was forced to enjoy the company's success from the sidelines at the behest of his doctors. He did, however, continue to run and organise the business by phone from a variety of destinations including Palm Beach and Barbados. Merrill died in 1956, by which time he had succeeded in broadening the base of stock ownership to include over two million ordinary Americans.

CONTEXT AND CONCLUSIONS

Charles Merrill took stockbroking out of the closeted world of Wall Street and onto the street. Influenced by his work financing deals for early chain-store development, he adopted the same model for selling shares. He strongly believed that the public would buy shares if they were readily available, an opinion he expressed in his 1911 article 'Mr Average Investor'. He predicted the Wall Street Crash in the 1920s and saved his clients' fortunes. Through the firm of Merrill Lynch, EA Pierce, and Cassatt, he then took share ownership to the masses. A chain of branches throughout the country, low transaction costs, an expensive advertising campaign, and the help of a government push to finance share purchasing among the US public, all helped make Merrill one of the leading stockbrokers in the United States.

CLOSE BUT NO CIGAR
WILLIAM ALBERT PAINE

Born in 1855 in Amesbury, Massachusetts, Paine worked as a bank clerk before founding his own stockbroking company, Paine, Webber, and Company in 1879 with partner Wallace Webber. The firm went on to acquire a host of other brokerages as it grew, and it is still in business today. It merged with UBS in 2000 and is now one of the biggest financial services firms in the world.

THE BEST SOURCES OF HELP
Book:
Perkins, Edwin J. *Wall Street to Main Street: Charles Merrill and Middle-Class Investors.* Cambridge: Cambridge University Press, 1999.
Website:
Merrill Lynch: **www.merrilllynch.com**

J.P. MORGAN

1837	Born.
1857	Joins Duncan, Sherman, and Co.
1862	Founds Dabrey, Morgan, and Co.
1871	Teams up with the firm of Drexel to form Drexel, Morgan, and Co.
1879	Puts together stock offering of $18 million for the New York Central Railroad.
1887	US government passes the Interstate Commerce Act.
1895	Helps avert US financial crisis.
1907	Bails out US government again.
1912	Appears before Pujo Committee.
1913	Dies.

SUMMARY

J.P. Morgan was one of the greatest financiers of his age. As a child he kept a close account of the receipt and expenditure of his allowance. As an adult he translated his attention to cash flow into a large fortune. He saw the American Civil War as an opportunity to make money, and in 1862 he founded his own company, Dabrey, Morgan, and Co. By 1871 he had teamed up with the firm of Drexel to form Drexel, Morgan, and Co. He swiftly established himself as one of the leading financiers in New York. Industrialists and governments regularly turned to him for advice, and he helped avert a US financial crisis in 1895. Morgan attempted to unify the railway bosses in opposition to the US government. A powerful influence in the formation of so-called industry 'trusts', his business empire was eventually cut down to size by US President Theodore Roosevelt.

LIFE AND CAREER

J.P. Morgan was born in Hartford, Connecticut, on 17 April 1837. In the year of his birth America was plunged into financial gloom. Morgan, however, was unaffected; his father was a rich commodity broker who managed to make the most of the financial downturn. While he was still a boy, his father moved the family to Boston where he became involved in the cotton trade.

Morgan took an early interest in business. Spurning childhood games, he spent much of his time poring over his accounts (a habit he carried with him throughout his life), detailing the receipt and expenditure of his allowance. He had a bookish nature—partly a result of his interest in business and money, and partly a result of a sickly constitution. Morgan was never a popular child at school. His aloof manner failed to impress his classmates, just as it would later alienate the US public. His habits, such as writing to Paris in fluent French to order a pair of $900 boots, only served to reinforce the impression of arrogance.

Morgan's education was in keeping with his privileged status. When his family moved to London, he was dispatched to a private school in Switzerland. He then

> *Morgan was never a popular child at school. His aloof manner failed to impress his classmates, just as it would later alienate the US public.*

studied at the University of Göttingen in Germany and so impressed his tutors that he was asked to stay on as an assistant to one of the professors. The ambitious Morgan declined, insisting that he had to start out in business.

CONTRIBUTION
Returning to America, in 1857 Morgan joined Duncan, Sherman, and Co, a firm with which his father had an association.

When the American Civil War broke out in 1861, Morgan treated it not as a calamity but as an opportunity. He avoided enlistment through the accepted practice among the wealthy of paying a substitute to take his place. (The going rate was $300.) In 1862 he left Duncan Sherman and founded his own company, Dabrey, Morgan, and Co. While the war raged, Morgan piled up the profits. By 1864 he had amassed over $50,000. The war ended, but Morgan continued to go from strength to strength. By 1871 he had teamed up with the firm of Drexel, based in Philadelphia, to form Drexel, Morgan, & Co, based on the corner of Wall Street and Broad Street in New York.

Morgan swiftly established a reputation as one of the leading financiers in America. His salary was more than $500,000, an astronomical amount at the time. It was during the 1870s that his association with the railways began. The financing of the railways required significant private capital, something that Morgan was only too happy to arrange.

His importance in the railway business grew to the extent that leading players would turn to him to resolve disputes and offer his opinion. In an industry where companies fought increasingly hostile battles to gain supremacy, Morgan found himself playing the role of mediator.

When the US government passed the Interstate Commerce Act in 1887, banning price-fixing collusion among railways, the railway companies naturally turned to Morgan again to organise a response. Obtaining a lasting consensus among the distrustful company bosses proved a task beyond even his talents. The misguided effort suggests a man whose ego was beginning to run out of control. Not only did he fail to unite the railways against the government, he succeeded in setting himself up as the head of a conspiracy and thus an obvious target for the US government, which was aiming to cut powerful business interests down to size.

Obtaining a lasting consensus among the distrustful company bosses proved a task beyond even his talents. The misguided effort suggests a man whose ego was beginning to run out of control.

By the 1890s Morgan had turned into a figure of hate among the US public. Yet, despite this perception, Morgan's greatest public service lay ahead of him. In 1893 the withdrawal of funds from the United States by British investors sparked a financial crisis. As banks failed and the stock market collapsed, the US government resorted to shoring up the financial system with its gold reserves. Statute prohibited the value of the reserves from falling below a prescribed level. The magic figure was

$100 million in gold. In January 1895 gold reserves collapsed to $58 million and the treasury secretary John Carlisle turned to Morgan to save the day. Morgan proposed a syndicate of investors who would sell gold coin to the US Treasury, paid for with newly issued bonds. It was a brilliant solution, as it provided not only an economic way out but also a politically expedient one. Morgan went further and guaranteed the scheme to the then president, Grover Cleveland. The Morgan syndicate intervention succeeded in stopping the financial slide and made Morgan a considerable profit, estimated at anywhere between $250,000 and $16 million.

This episode merely reinforced Morgan's already legendary financial prowess. He followed his rescue of the US financial system with a series of breathtaking deals such as the financing of United States Steel, the largest steel corporation in the world. From the 1900s onwards he devoted his attention to consolidating the railway companies through his concern the Northern Securities Corporation, and to building a shipping trust. Unfortunately for him, however, the incumbent president, Theodore Roosevelt, had decided that political advantage could be gained by cracking down on the so-called trusts. As the well-known figure of Morgan stood behind the Northern Securities Corporation, Roosevelt decided that it should be made an example of. This time Morgan had met his match. Apart from a brief respite in 1907, when a US president again turned to him for salvation during a financial crisis, Morgan's power waned.

By then in his 70s, Morgan devoted more time to his hobby of collecting art and to his private life. He died in Rome at the age of 76.

CONTEXT AND CONCLUSIONS

J.P. Morgan was a remarkable businessman. His success owed much to his self-belief and opportunism, and a little to his wealthy and well-connected father. He suffered ill health throughout his life, particularly the periodic embarrassment of a large red bulbous nose, a result of eczema, the appearance of which would inevitably send him into deep melancholia. Yet despite frequent periods of illness-induced rest and recuperation, Morgan managed to build a string of business interests in the fashionable industries of the day—railways, shipping, and electricity. He also, on more than one occasion, financed the US government out of a mess.

THE BEST SOURCES OF HELP
Books:
Wheeler, George. *Pierpont Morgan and Friends: The Anatomy of a Myth*. Englewood Cliffs, New Jersey: Prentice Hall, 1973.
Winkler, John. *Morgan the Magnificent: Life of J.P. Morgan*. New York: The Vanguard Press, 1932.
Website:
JPMorgan: **www.jpmorgan.com**

AKIO MORITA

1921	Born.
1946	Co-founds Tokyo Tshushin Kyogu.
1953	Travels to United States to license transistor technology.
1958	Company changes name to Sony.
1960	World's first all-transistor television.
1961	First Japanese company to list on New York Stock Exchange.
1963	Moves with his family to United States to set up Sony America.
1980	Sony produces Sony Walkman.
1982	Sony produces first CD players.
1993	Suffers stroke while playing tennis.
1999	Dies.

SUMMARY

Akio Morita passed up the opportunity to lead an easy and secure life at the helm of the family sake business. Instead he chose to pursue his love of electrical engineering and start his own business, with all the risks that entailed. Starting with a prototype for a humble rice cooker, Morita's small company TTK grew into the electronic products giant Sony. In a lifetime devoted to his company, Morita gave the world a stream of innovative technologies and gadgets, from the portable transistor radio to the Sony Playstation. He was also the man responsible for making music portable, introducing the word 'Walkman' into the global lexicon. In later life Morita refused to take a comfortable retirement, choosing to remain at the helm of Sony until he was forced to step down because of ill health.

LIFE AND CAREER

Akio Morita was born on 26 January 1921 in Nagoya, an industrial city in Japan. By Japanese standards, his family was affluent middle class. Morita was heir to the family rice-wine brewing business, although he showed little interest in his father's company. Instead he preferred to tinker with electronics equipment. He soon became a keen amateur electronics enthusiast, neglecting his studies to build electronic gadgets, including a radio and a record player.

Morita continued to pursue his interest in electronics at college by studying physics. He joined the Japanese army during the Second World War and rose to the rank of lieutenant.

After the war Morita passed up the easy career route of working in the family sake business. Instead, in 1946 he travelled to Tokyo, where he joined his future partner Masaru Ibuka. With a $530 loan, the two started a new company, Tokyo Tshushin Kyogu (TTK). It was housed in a bombed-out department store.

CONTRIBUTION

Morita eventually built one of the world's largest electronics companies, famed for its sophisticated miniaturised products. His first product prototype was a little less glamorous—a specialised rice cooker. But radio components and radio upgrades followed, and in the 1950s Morita produced his first major product, the tape recorder. It was the first in Japan.

Morita's biggest breakthrough was the transistor radio, despite the fact that the transistor was a US, not a Japanese, invention. Neither was the miniature radio that Morita produced using transistor technology the first of its kind. Morita had travelled to the United States in 1953 to license the technology from Bell Laboratories, but it was a joint venture between Texas Instruments and Regency Electronics that produced the world's first commercial transistor radio, the Regency TR-1, in October 1954.

TTK's first model was the TR-55, a set for which serious transistor radio collectors today would happily sell their grandmothers. Made in August 1955 in limited numbers, its production was restricted to Japan. TTK's first radio for export was the TR-63, produced in 1957.

Morita's small TR-63 was extremely successful for two main reasons. First, it was a truly innovative design, sold in a presentation box complete with a soft leather case, antistatic cloth, and earphone.

The second factor was Morita's dogged persistence. Taking the product direct to the distributors, he trekked around New York convincing electronic shop owners to stock the TTK radio. He even turned down one large order because the potential purchaser didn't want the TTK company name on the product. He returned to Japan with a full order book.

In 1958 Morita pushed through a change of name for the company. A keen proponent of globalisation, he was quick to realise that a name like Tokyo Tshushin Kyogu would prove an obstacle to capturing foreign markets. 'We wanted a new name that could be recognised anywhere in the world, one that could be pronounced the same in any language,' Morita said. He settled for Sony. This was a combination of the Latin word for sound, *sonus*, and the colloquial US term 'sonny'. Morita's strategy clearly worked. When US radio dealers were asked in a survey, 'Have you ever handled Japanese radios?' they answered no. Asked whether they had ever dealt with Sony radios, they returned an unequivocal yes.

> *Morita's biggest breakthrough was the transistor radio, despite the fact that the transistor was a US, not a Japanese, invention.*

Over the years TTK/Sony produced a steady stream of innovative electronic products: the pocket radio in 1957, the world's first all-transistor television in 1960, and in 1968 the first home videotape recorder.

In 1963 Morita moved to the United States with his family and set up the Sony Corporation of America. It was a bold move for a man from a country whose businessmen were traditionally isolationist and protectionist in outlook. Morita pushed Sony's products in the United States, positioning the brand as premium quality. Soon the company's products were available nationwide.

When Morita noticed that young people liked listening to music wherever they went, he proposed that the company develop a portable tape cassette player. Morita's colleagues were unconvinced there was a market for a tape player of any size that lacked a recording facility. Morita stuck to his guns and persuaded his colleagues, and the Walkman was born in 1980. In a characteristically idiosyncratic move, there was no market research to back Morita's hunch. 'The public does not know what is possible. We do,' he said.

Interestingly, 'Walkman' was not the product's universal name in the early days. Sony America thought the name poor English and changed it to 'Soundabout' for the US market. In Sweden it was known as 'Freestyle' and in the United Kingdom, 'Stowaway'. Morita wasn't keen on this approach. As soon as he received a bad set of sales figures he used it as an excuse to change the name to Walkman throughout the world. The word has since become part of the global lexicon.

Another Sony innovation was video technology. Sony's Betamax technology lost out to VHS in the video standards war, but the company was instrumental in making home video recording a mainstream technology.

As the company's profits grew, Morita relentlessly pursued his vision of globalisation. He used the expression 'think globally, act locally' to describe his philosophy of corporate values that transcended national boundaries. Management thinkers such as Theodore Levitt and later Kenichi Ohmae popularised the phrase, and it became part of the business vernacular.

Having built Sony into a multibillion-dollar company, Morita, by now a billionaire himself, refused to let up. Still brimming with energy, he spent time indulging in pastimes such as scuba diving, skiing, and tennis, all of which he started when he was over the age of 50. He pursued a relentless schedule until he suffered a stroke while playing tennis. Ill health forced him to resign as president of Sony in 1993, and he died in October 1999.

CONTEXT AND CONCLUSIONS

Akio Morita, along with entrepreneurs like Eiji Toyoda and Soichiro Honda, ranks as one of Japan's greatest business executives. Blessed with extraordinary drive, Morita was a risk-taker who would doggedly pursue his instincts. Time and again he followed his intuition, beginning with his original rejection of the safe option of working in the family business in favour of starting an electronics company with virtually no experience. The scale of his ambition was apparent in his decision to take his business to the United States at a time when Japan was not yet celebrated for its manufacturing techniques or the quality of its products.

It was Morita who helped put Japanese innovation on the world map by pushing through his globalisation agenda and, by backing his vision, he established Sony as a truly global company. He is responsible for making Japanese electronics a byword for innovative design and function.

THE BEST SOURCES OF HELP
Books:
Morita, Akio, with Edwin M. Reingold and Mitsuko Shimomura. *Made in Japan: Akio Morita and Sony*. New York: Dutton, 1989.
Nathan, John. *Sony: The Private Life*. Boston: Houghton Mifflin, 2001.
Website:
Sony UK: **www.sony.co.uk**

RUPERT MURDOCH

1931	Born.
1950	Attends Oxford University.
1952	Works in Fleet Street on the *Daily Express*. Returns to Australia.
1960	Buys the *Sydney Daily Mirror*.
1964	Founds the *Australian*.
1969	Buys the *News of the World* and the *Sun* in the United Kingdom.
1976	Buys the *New York Post*.
1981	Buys *The Times*.
1986	The 'battle of Wapping'.
1990	Saves business empire by restructuring debt.
1993	Buys into Star TV in Asia.
1997	Fox releases *Titanic*, biggest grossing film ever.
2002	Attempts to merge Sky TV with GM's Direct TV founder.
2002	Collapse of ITV Digital leaves Murdoch in control of 30% of UK media.
2002	Worldwide assets $42 billion, revenue $16 billion.

SUMMARY

Rupert Murdoch is one of the best known media barons of the modern age. After finishing his education at Oxford and a spell spent working on the *Daily Express* newspaper, Murdoch returned to his native Australia to take over from his father at the helm of the *Adelaide News*.

He moved on to expand his media empire through a spate of acquisitions across the globe. In the 1980s he branched into film and television, acquiring 20th Century Fox and Fox TV in the United States. In the United Kingdom he bought *The Times* and *The Sunday Times*, and emerged victorious from a bitter battle with the print unions. By the end of the 1980s the empire was mortgaged to the hilt, but after a major debt-rescheduling exercise, Murdoch marched on into the 1990s, acquiring Star TV in Asia.

LIFE AND CAREER

Now a US citizen, Keith Rupert Murdoch was born in Melbourne, Australia, on 11 March 1931. His early education took place at Geelong Grammar school in Geelong, Victoria. He was not an impressive student—he admits he was 'bone lazy' at school—other than in English, where his marks were above average. He also lacked sporting prowess. A restless child, he was more likely to be found cartwheeling across the outfield during play than scoring a century in the school cricket match. His lack of interest on the sports field led to him being disciplined on more than one occasion.

In 1950 he was sent to England to study economics at Worcester College, Oxford. While there, he stood unsuccessfully for president of the Labour Club—an interesting choice for a man whose political sympathies lay with the brand of right-wing ideology later embodied by Margaret Thatcher. His real education, however, took place on the *Daily Express* newspaper in Fleet Street, where he worked before returning home to Australia in 1952.

Back in Australia Murdoch, like the media baron William Randolph Hearst before him, was handed the opportunity to run a newspaper. On the death of his father, the Melbourne publisher Sir Keith Murdoch, he inherited the *Adelaide News*. It was the start of Murdoch's mercurial career as a news proprietor and media mogul.

CONTRIBUTION

To begin with the board was reluctant to hand over complete control of the newspaper to the young tyro. But Murdoch wasn't a man to take no for an answer, even at this early stage in his career. He steered the newspaper in an avowedly populist direction. Headlines like the sensationalist 'Queen eats a rat' boosted its circulation and gave it a new lease of life.

Murdoch's success with the *Adelaide News* spurred him on. He bought the *Daily Mirror* in Sydney and dabbled in television. His newspaper acquisitions were driven by opportunity rather than rationale at this point. 'We tended to take the sick newspapers, the ones that weren't worth much, that people thought were about to fold up,' he later observed. In 1964 he made his boldest move yet, founding the *Australian*, a national broadsheet. The *Australian* gave Murdoch political clout and influence and made him a national figure, though commercially it was less successful.

Murdoch moved on from these early triumphs to expand his media empire through a spate of acquisitions across the globe. In the United Kingdom in 1969, he galloped in as an improbable white knight to save the *News of the World*, a downmarket and populist paper, from falling into enemy hands. The enemy in this case was Robert Maxwell, the Czech-born entrepreneur and budding media mogul. The owners of the paper, the Carrs, were reluctant sellers and strongly opposed a sale to a 'foreigner'. However when no home-grown businessman would come to their aid, they turned to the Australian Rupert Murdoch. It was the deal that gave Murdoch a toehold in the United Kingdom.

Wapping was a defining moment not only in union history in the United Kingdom but in the world's perception of Murdoch.

Shortly afterwards in the same year he bought the tabloid newspaper the *Sun* for £500,000. In the United Kingdom the *Sun* is most closely associated with Murdoch's approach to selling newspapers. In 1976 he added the *New York Post* to his growing empire. He subsequently lost, then regained, control of the newspaper. All the newspapers he acquired received the Murdoch treatment, adopting a right-wing, populist tone.

In 1981 Murdoch made an acquisition that was to have a long-lasting impact on newspapers in the United Kingdom. Fighting off fierce competition, he bought *The Times* in London. A serious broadsheet, it seemed an unlikely target. Yet it was a clever purchase as it allowed him to reach a far broader cross-section of the British public. What followed was even more unexpected. Murdoch set himself on a collision course with the powerful UK print unions, challenging their inefficient working practices. He built a new printing plant at Wapping, away from Fleet Street, introduced computerisation, and cut out the unions. The unions decided to make Wapping their Waterloo, and for most of 1986 the plant was under virtual siege, becoming the site for a pitched battle between the progressive Murdoch troops and the traditionalist unions. The outcome was a victory for Murdoch and his no-nonsense approach to business.

Wapping was a defining moment not only in union history in the United Kingdom but in the world's perception of Murdoch. He emerged from the episode as a tough, ruthless proprietor who would go to almost any lengths to achieve his aims. The truth was a little more prosaic. If Murdoch hadn't challenged the unions, someone else would have done: Margaret Thatcher's Conservative government and the introduction of tough new anti-strike legislation had provided a political context that was bound to result in such a battle. And there could be no resisting the march of technological progress, even in the printing industry.

The rest of the 1980s saw Murdoch branch into film and television, acquiring Fox Studios in the United States in 1985, and seven Metromedia TV stations in 1986. By the end of the 1980s, however, Murdoch had overstretched himself, and a massive debt-rescheduling exercise was required in 1990. This successfully shored up his empire. Murdoch then marched on through the 1990s, one deal coming hard on the heels of another. Today his business empire is a truly global one: in all, he has over 750 businesses in over 50 countries. At the end of 2002 his holding company, News Corporation, was worth some $42 billion, with revenues of $16 billion. Companies in the News Corporation empire include HarperCollins Publishers, BSkyB, News International, the Los Angeles Dodgers, Fox TV, and Star TV.

Murdoch made his first move into Internet business in 1999 by taking a stake in WebMD, the company set up by Jim Clark as Healtheon. By 2002, News Corporation held 30% of UK media. BSkyB was given a boost by the demise of ITVDigital, a situation frustrating to the Office of Fair Trading, who had criticized the station just a year before for its dominant position. Murdoch attempted to build similar domination in the United States with an attempt to merge GM-owned Direct TV with his own Sky TV, but the merger was blocked by the Federal Communications Commission.

Murdoch continues to work long days at a fast pace and shows little sign of slowing down. There is endless speculation in the media about who will eventually succeed him, his children—Lachlan, James, and Elisabeth Murdoch—being the main candidates. His third wife, Wendy Deng, is another possible. For now, though, as demonstrated by his recent attempts to merge GM-owned Direct TV with his own Sky TV, megabillionaire Murdoch retains an iron grip on his empire.

CONTEXT AND CONCLUSIONS

Murdoch has more than his share of critics, many strident. He is accused of a range of sins from wielding too much power to 'dumbing down' his media vehicles. Perhaps the criticism is overdone. Murdoch has an innate sense of what the public wants, and he makes sure he provides it. He is an astute pragmatist and brilliant entrepreneur who has built the world's first global media empire through instinct, talent, and hard work.

THE BEST SOURCES OF HELP
Books:
Crainer, Stuart. *Business the Rupert Murdoch Way*. Oxford: Capstone, 1998.
Regan, Simon. *Rupert Murdoch: A Business Biography*. London: Angus & Robertson, 1976.

DAVID OGILVY

1911	Born.
1938	Travels to the United States.
1948	Starts new advertising agency, Hewitt, Ogilvy, Benson, & Mather.
1960	Challenges the advertising industry practice of charging 15% commission.
1963	Publishes book *Confessions of an Advertising Man*.
1965	Merges firm with Mather & Crowther to form Ogilvy & Mather.
1975	Steps down from position as creative head.
1999	Dies.

> **SUMMARY**
>
> It was fortunate for the world of advertising that David Ogilvy eventually found his way to its door. But he took a circuitous route. After working in Paris, he returned to England and pursued a career as an Aga cooker salesman. Next he dallied with advertising at the agency Mather & Crowther, enjoying the bright lights of London before upping sticks to head for America. A job as a pollster for Dr George Gallup was followed by a spell as a tobacco farmer with the Amish community in Pennsylvania. Finally in 1948, in his late thirties, Ogilvy started his own advertising agency. With a flair for copywriting, he was soon acknowledged by competitors and clients alike as one of the most brilliant advertising executives of his generation. He retired in 1975 after building Ogilvy & Mather into a business with annual billings of $800 million.

LIFE AND CAREER

The son of a stockbroker, David Ogilvy was born on 23 June 1911. He was dispatched to Fettes School, a prestigious private school near Edinburgh. What Ogilvy lacked in natural academic ability he made up for in application, securing a scholarship to study history at Christ Church, Oxford.

When he left Oxford, the young Ogilvy sought adventure abroad. In France he worked in the kitchens of the Hotel Majestic. When Ogilvy had tired of *la vie parisienne*, he returned to England to sell a new type of cooking stove, the Aga. As a salesman Ogilvy proved a great success, so much so that he was asked to write a manual for the Aga salesforce on how to sell the cooker. (Thirty years later, the editors of *Fortune* magazine announced that it was probably the best sales manual of all time.) Ogilvy sent his manuscript, 'The Theory and Practice of Selling the Aga Cooker', to his brother, who was working at the London-based advertising agency Mather & Crowther. His winning way with words earned him a place as a trainee at the agency.

CONTRIBUTION

Ogilvy enjoyed the London lifestyle, partying till dawn at every available opportunity. He combined his social life with hard work, showing a natural aptitude for his new vocation. Very early on he began to develop his own theories about advertising. 'Concrete figures must be substituted for atmospheric claims; clichés must give way to facts, and empty exhortations to alluring offers,' an enthusiastic Ogilvy wrote in a presentation to his colleagues in the early 1930s.

In 1938 he left his job and embarked on another adventure. This time it was the

United States that attracted his interest. He enjoyed himself so much that he decided to stay, moving to Princeton, New Jersey, where he worked with Dr George Gallup, the man behind the Gallup polls. The experience he gained working for Gallup was invaluable, if poorly paid, as it provided him with insights into US consumer preferences and the way they were formed.

During the Second World War Ogilvy worked for British intelligence in Washington. When the war ended, he decided to try his hand at tobacco farming, acquiring several acres of land in the heart of the Amish community in Lancaster County, Pennsylvania. Quite what possessed Ogilvy to pursue an agricultural career is unclear. What is certain is that he was most unsuited to it, and before long he was back in New York.

It is fair to say that, without the help of his brother, Francis, Ogilvy might never have become one of the great advertising figures of the 20th century. Casting around for a job, the 37-year-old enlisted the help of his brother to set up his own advertising agency in America. His brother not only rounded up $45,000 to help finance the new venture but also persuaded another British advertising agency, S.H. Benson, to invest a further $45,000 in return for a partnership. The newly created agency, Hewitt, Ogilvy, Benson, & Mather, opened for business in 1948. As an Englishman, Ogilvy struggled to win over US clients, although the addition of ex-J. Walter Thompson employee Anderson Hewitt helped. It was Hewitt who saved the day when the business threatened to run out of capital after only a few months. Fortunately, Hewitt's uncle was the chairman of JPMorgan and he lent the agency $100,000 with no security. And it was Hewitt who brought in the first major account, Sun Oil, worth some $3 million.

> *During the Second World War Ogilvy worked for British intelligence in Washington. When the war ended, he decided to try his hand at tobacco farming, acquiring several acres of land in the heart of the Amish community in Lancaster County, Pennsylvania.*

Despite the agency's diminutive size, it was clear from the beginning that Ogilvy's advertising intuition set the company apart from its competitors. His style was evident in an early campaign for shirt makers, Hathaway. Ads featured a man with an eye patch, known as the man from Hathaway, who supported the small shirt makers from Maine in their efforts to take on the giant shirt maker Arrow. Ogilvy used photographs, then still a rarity in advertising, featuring a male model complete with eye patch performing a variety of unusual tasks.

The Hathaway campaign made Ogilvy's reputation and was an early example of his approach to brand building and supporting brands through brand image. He followed the success of the Hathaway campaign with a campaign for Schweppes, the soft-drink manufacturer. Putting to good use the knowledge he gained with Gallup, Ogilvy assuaged US consumer sensibilities about class with Commander Edward Whitehead, the distinguished-looking gentleman who was boss of Schweppes at the time. Schweppes sales in the United States bubbled up by 500% over the following nine years.

Ogilvy's role at the agency was to be jack of all trades, master of most. The exception was administration, for which he had little time. To his credit he realised that this weakness was hampering the firm and employed Esty Stowell, a Benson & Bowles executive, as vice-president in 1957. Stowell took responsibility for managing the entire agency, with Ogilvy retaining control of the creative department only.

'At 60 miles an hour the loudest noise in this new Rolls-Royce comes from the electric clock.' This was Ogilvy's slogan for his Rolls-Royce campaign. It exemplified his approach of putting the product centre stage. 'Make your product the hero of the commercial,' he famously entreated. In 1960 he challenged one of the industry's prized but anachronistic practices, the 15% commission. As usual Ogilvy's stance was not merely ethical, but one guaranteed to attract publicity. It succeeded, bringing in new clients such as Shell who were only too happy to be rid of the 15% commission in exchange for a flat fee.

> *Ogilvy's role at the agency was to be jack of all trades, master of most. The exception was administration, for which he had little time.*

The 1960s was a big decade for Ogilvy. In 1963 he published his book *Confessions of an Advertising Man*, which sold well over half a million copies and cemented his position as an advertising guru. In 1965, the year after his brother's death, his firm merged with Mather & Crowther to form Ogilvy & Mather.

By 1975 Ogilvy & Mather was one of the top five advertising agencies in the world with around a thousand clients, offices in 29 countries, and billings of some $800 million. In the same year Ogilvy stepped down from his position as creative head to spend more time at his home in the south of France. In 1989, following a wave of mergers in the industry, Ogilvy's remaining share in the business was acquired by the WPP group.

CONTEXT AND CONCLUSIONS

David Ogilvy said the secret of success was simple: 'First, make a reputation for being a creative genius. Second, surround yourself with partners who are better than you are. Third, leave them to get on with it.' But the most important things that Ogilvy acquired in his time on Madison Avenue were the ability and creative flair needed to lead by example. 'The most important ingredient in any agency is the ability of the top man to lead his troops,' he said. He was a late starter in advertising at 39. Yet he still made it to the top of his profession—and made an indelible mark there too. Ogilvy died on 21 July 1999.

CLOSE BUT NO CIGAR
LORD SAATCHI

Charles Saatchi built not one but two successful advertising agencies. First there was Saatchi & Saatchi, the UK agency that helped win a general election with its 'Labour isn't working' posters for the Conservative party. Then, when Charles and brother Maurice got a little overambitious and were kicked out of their own company after an ill-conceived bid for the Midland Bank, they started up another agency. The new agency was M&C Saatchi. They took a few prestigious clients with them. Soon Maurice received a peerage, and M&C Saatchi overtook Saatchi & Saatchi in the billings rankings.

JAMES WALTER THOMPSON
J. Walter Thompson bought out William James Carlton, owner of advertising 'broker' Carlton & Smith, for $500 in 1877. The furniture cost $800. In 1887 the JWT Company became the first agency to write advertisements for their clients rather than just sell them advertising space. By 1909 JWT had opened in London. It went on to become one of the world's most successful agencies.

THE BEST SOURCES OF HELP
Books:
Ogilvy, David. *Confessions of an Advertising Man*. New York: Atheneum, 1963.
Ogilvy, David. *Blood, Brains and Beer*. New York: Atheneum, 1978.
Ogilvy, David. *Ogilvy on Advertising*. New York: Crown, 1983.
Website:
Ogilvy UK: **www.ogilvy.co.uk**

JORMA JAAKKO OLLILA

1950	Born.
1976	Studies at the University of Helsinki.
1978	Studies at the London School of Economics.
1981	Studies at the Helsinki University of Technology.
1985	Joins Nokia as vice president of international operations.
1986	Becomes CFO.
1988	CEO Kairamo commits suicide.
1990	Assumes control of mobile phone business.
1992	Becomes CEO of Nokia.
1994	Nokia listed on the New York Stock Exchange.
1999	Profits hit $4 billion.
1999	Nokia introduces world's first mobile phone with Internet access.
2000	Shares drop by 26%, wiping out $60 billion worth of market value in a single day.
	Nokia launches professional mobile radio with Internet access.
2001	Nokia launches first mobile phone with multimedia messaging.
2002	Nokia achieves first commercial 3G data calls.

> **SUMMARY**
>
> In Europe, high-tech corporate superstars are conspicuous by their absence. Names like Philips and Siemens just don't set the pulse racing. The exception to the rule is the Finnish company Nokia. It has created a buzz around its products unmatched by other European companies in recent years. Much of the credit goes to Jorma Ollila, who became CEO in 1992.
>
> Ollila took a 147-year-old company, comprised of an assortment of businesses from timber to rubber boots, and transformed it into a mobile phone colossus. In 1998, it passed the United States company Motorola as the world's number one mobile phone manufacturer. In less than eight years, Ollila had made Nokia the most valuable company in Europe.
>
> The product of an eclectic education including Atlantic College, the London School of Economics, and Helsinki University, Ollila came to power at Nokia at a difficult time. The suicide of the company's CEO, Kari Kairamo, followed by the collapse of the USSR and difficult trading conditions, had left Nokia in need of a makeover. After turning the mobile phone division around, Ollila became CEO in 1992. He shed all noncore, nontelecoms business and refocused on mobile phone manufacturing. Profits soared from zero in 1991 to $4 billion in 1999. By 2000 the company was being fêted by analysts, investors, and the media. The year 2001 brought more trying times, but Ollila continues to apply his unique style of management as Nokia tries to navigate a downturn in the telecoms market.

LIFE AND CAREER

Jorma Jaakko Ollila was born on 15 August 1950 in Seinjoki, Finland. His education was a little more unorthodox than most. Aged 17, he was recommended for a scholarship at Atlantic College by his school headmaster. Atlantic College, in Wales, is a unique educational establishment founded in 1962 by Kurt Hahn, a German national who evolved a distinctive educational philosophy. The rationale behind the college is to bring together individuals with leadership qualities who then go on to become political or commercial leaders throughout the world. Ollila was part of the school's first intake.

Ollila followed Atlantic College by earning a post-graduate degree in Political Science in 1976 at University of Helsinki, an MSc in 1978 at the London School of Economics, and an MSc in 1981 from the Helsinki University of Technology. With his academic career behind him, he joined Citibank where he worked on the Nokia account. In 1985, he joined the Finnish company as vice president of international operations. A year later, aged 35, he became chief financial officer.

CONTRIBUTION

The Nokia of today started life as three separate companies: the Finnish Cable Works, the Finnish Rubber Works, and the Nokia Forest Products Company. When the three merged in 1967, the new company took its name from the timber mill, which in turn took its name from the Nokia river in southern Finland.

The Scandinavian countries gained a head start in wireless telephony when they joined forces to develop technology first researched in Bell Laboratories in the United States. Despite the head start, Nokia almost managed to give the market away to Motorola in the 1970s. It was the beginning of a bleak period in the company's history. Nokia's CEO, Kari Kairamo, hedged his bets. The company took revenues from its more traditional businesses to fund its high-tech operations. Nokia bought a computer business from Ericsson, for example, and a German TV company, as well as making mobile phones. But Kairamo underestimated how big the mobile telephone business was going to be. Struggling to cope with the demand for mobile phones as well as to manage the other businesses it owned, Nokia lost market share to Motorola, which was well-equipped for mass production.

One problem after another beset Nokia. In 1988 Kairamo committed suicide, and in 1991 the USSR disintegrated, taking one of Nokia's principal markets with it. The company's largest shareholder even tried to sell its stake in Nokia to its rival Ericsson. Fortunately for Nokia, Ericsson wasn't interested. Into this difficult situation stepped Ollila in 1990, when he was put in charge of the mobile phone business. His first decision was a bold one: to keep the mobile phone unit rather than opt for the easy option of selling it. He set about raising morale and reorganising the unit.

By 1992, Ollila was CEO. He turned his attention to the rest of the company's divisions. He rationalised the company, ditching noncore activities like the paper, rubber, cable, computer, and TV businesses. Putting his telecoms strategy into action required cash, so Ollila turned to the United States for investment. Nokia was already listed on the European stock exchanges, but a United States listing was a prerequisite for raising the kind of money Ollila needed. In 1994 Nokia was listed on the New York Stock Exchange. In the period before tech stocks fell out of favour, Nokia's stock performance was nothing short of miraculous. Between 1994 and 1999, the share price rose over 2,000%.

Ollila had successfully dragged Nokia back from the precipice. One reason for the transformation was his focus on brand image.

Jorma Jaakko Ollila

Ollila had successfully dragged Nokia back from the precipice. One reason for the transformation was his focus on brand image. He abandoned the existing array of mobile phone brands produced by Nokia, concentrating on a product line emblazoned with the Nokia name. His strategy was 'telecom-oriented, global focus, value-added'—a slogan that came out of a brainstorming meeting. Competitors were obsessed with continually shrinking the size of the mobile phone. Ollila went further, hiring designers to make Nokia's mobile phone a fashion statement. He also brought in technicians to create revolutionary scrolling text displays and other refinements that made the phone as user-friendly as possible. At the same time Nokia hedged its bets, backing a range of technical standards from the European GSM to the Japanese PDS. The first digital offering by the company in 1993 was predicted to sell at least 400,000 units—it sold over 20 million. Profits soared from zero in 1991 to $4 billion in 1999.

Ollila cut out noncore business, and he also cut out internal bureaucracy. Out went hierarchical management structures; in came a flat organisational structure. Today things get done in the company through networks of individuals. It's an entrepreneurial, innovative environment within a large corporation. Then there is 'the Nokia Way'—a means of tapping into root feeling in the company. Brainstorming at a series of meetings throughout the company is synthesised into a vision statement by the top managers, and this is disseminated back through the organisation via a series of presentations. The Nokia Way keeps the employees plugged into the company.

As the new millennium approached, the future looked bright for Nokia. The company was the most valuable in Europe. It was tipped in *Red Herring* magazine's must-buy stocks for 2000. But Ollila hadn't bargained for a change in market sentiment that left telecoms stocks out in the cold. Investors, used to year after year of astonishing growth, ran for cover when Ollila warned of disappointing third-quarter results in 2000. Shares dropped by 26%, wiping out $60 billion worth of market value in a single day. Once the darlings of the stock market, suddenly telecoms companies were out of vogue. Worse, there was the threat of mobile Internet and other forms of mobile data transfer. 'It's a big paradigm shift,' said Ollila. 'We have the challenge of sailing in much more uncertain waters.'

The future of Nokia is clouded with uncertainty. As a handset manufacturer, Nokia faces a number of threats, not least that of commoditisation. Some 40 multinationals and more than a dozen companies in China have the ability to manufacture mobile phones. More manufacturers means more phones, resulting in lower prices, which mean lower profits. Ollila hopes the lure of the Nokia brand and its personalisation of phones will outweigh the attraction of low-cost, mass-market clones.

Then there is the threat of new technology making the mobile obsolete. Phone technology is due to move through GPRS to 3G broadband, promising the transmission of video and audio to a mobile. But technology isn't always what it's cracked up to be—witness the hype of WAP and its subsequent washout. Competing wireless technologies threaten the supremacy of mobile phones, as do voice-enabled PDAs and mobile computers. Nokia counters that these are mobile phones by another name, and adds that it plans to participate in a selection of alternative devices.

Despite that threat, Nokia has continued to innovate in its core business. In 1999, it introduced the first WAP Internet mobile phone and, in 2000, added the same capability to its professional mobile radio systems. In 2001, Nokia introduced the world's first multimedia messaging solution for mobile phones, giving users access to audio, video, images, photos, and text. And, in 2002, the company took its 3G capability a stage further by achieving the first commercial packet data call.

Network business offers some consolation for Ollila. A quarter of sales in 2000 came from this part of Nokia's operations, and the company is still well regarded. In INSEAD business school's 2001 report 'Competitive Fitness', a study of 67 multinationals, Nokia was ranked number one. But Ollila can't afford to rest on the company's reputation for long. Difficult challenges lie ahead. Only time will tell if Ollila is able to deal with them successfully.

CONTEXT AND CONCLUSIONS

Jorma Ollila specialises in achieving the impossible. Against the odds he took a cumbersome, unfocused company called Nokia and dragged it into the 21st century. He stripped out the unnecessary operations, ditched the paper, timber, rubber boots, and other distinctly low-tech business, and remodelled the company as a high-tech mobile telephone manufacturer. The transformation, accomplished by a mixture of clever brand development, radical organisational restructuring, and astute strategic thinking, made him one of the most talked-about managers in Europe and his company a stock market favourite. Ollila's job at Nokia is far from over. His reputation as a great businessman will rest partly on what happens over the next few years. He has made some big judgement calls, and only time will tell if he is right. But based on his record so far, regardless of Nokia's dip in fortunes, he remains one of the best CEOs in the world.

CLOSE BUT NO CIGAR
MARJORIE SCARDINO

Marjorie Scardino became chief executive of the international media group Pearson (owner of the *Financial Times*) in 1997. Before that she was chief executive of The Economist Group, in which Pearson has a 50% stake. In 1985, Scardino became managing director of the North American division of *The Economist*, where she increased circulation and profits. Before 1985, she was managing partner in a law firm in Savannah, Georgia and, with her husband, she was the publisher and founder of the Pulitzer Prize-winning newspaper the *Georgia Gazette*. Since taking over, Scardino has focused Pearson as a media company, selling a number of unrelated businesses such as Madame Tussaud's Waxworks, and purchasing various educational and publishing concerns. Scardino is the first woman to head a top-100 firm on the London Stock Exchange.

Despite a sparkling start, Pearson's recent results have disappointed, leaving Scardino searching for ways to leverage more value out of her media empire.

THE BEST SOURCES OF HELP
Books:
Merriden, Trevor. *Business the Nokia Way: Secrets of the World's Fastest Moving Company*. New York: John Wiley, 2000.

Steinbock, Dan. *The Nokia Revolution: The Story of an Extraordinary Company That Transformed an Industry*. New York: AMACOM, 2001.

PIERRE OMIDYAR

1967	Born.
1988	Graduates from Tufts University.
1991	Co-founds Ink Development Corporation in 1991.
1995	Starts eBay as homepage hosted by the local ISP.
1996	Ink Development, renamed eShop, sold to Microsoft.
1996	eBay profitable by February.
1997	Three million items sold. Recruits Meg Whitman as CEO.
1998	Completes 10 millionth auction in May. Over one million registered users. IPO in September.
2001	Over 29.7 million registered users. Net income totals $64.5 million to September.
2001	eBay stores launched. Named as second richest young American.
2002	Joint venture with Sotheby's.
2003	Business-to-business site launched.

SUMMARY

From an idea sparked by a casual conversation, Pierre Omidyar built one of the world's most successful Internet companies, eBay. Started in 1995, eBay is the online equivalent of Aladdin's cave, a treasure trove stuffed to the rafters with everything from Beanie Babies to grand masters. With millions of items up for auction and 600,000 new ones added every day, it is a collector's paradise. Profitable almost from the beginning, Omidyar's handling of his idea has been masterful. He started the business as a hobby but was astute enough to recognise the tremendous commercial possibilities. He got the right people in—including Jeff Skoll and Meg Whitman—to manage the company through rapid expansion, to IPO and beyond. But Omidyar was always on hand to make sure the business stayed true to his original vision. By 2001, eBay had nearly 30 million registered users and was still turning a handsome profit.

LIFE AND CAREER

Born in 1967, Pierre Omidyar moved to the United States from his native France at the age of six. The family settled in Maryland, where Omidyar's father took up a residency at the Johns Hopkins University Medical Centre. At school Omidyar played truant so he could spend more time on his hobby—computing. For six dollars an hour, he hired himself out to the school library writing computer programs to print out catalogue cards.

Omidyar studied computer science at Tufts University in Massachusetts. It was there he met his wife Pamela, who was studying for a biology degree. Pamela was to have a major influence on Omidyar's career in a way he could never have suspected. When he left university, Omidyar went into the computer industry, first as a software developer at Claris and then at General Magic Inc. His first attempt at starting his own company was Ink Development Corporation, set up with three friends. The company created software that allowed computers to interpret

For six dollars an hour, he hired himself out to the school library writing computer programs to print out catalogue cards.

Pierre Omidyar

instructions entered using a pen, rather than a keyboard. Later renamed eShop, the firm was sold to Microsoft in 1996 making Omidyar a wealthy man.

CONTRIBUTION

The question was what to do next? The idea for eBay emerged from a conversation with Pamela, then his fiancée, while Omidyar was still at General Magic. Pamela was a keen collector of Pez dispensers—sweet dispensers with a cartoon character head that tilts back. She hankered to meet other enthusiasts and swap dispensers. This gave Omidyar the idea for a website where collectors could meet to buy, sell and discuss their collections with fellow enthusiasts. The selling element would take the form of an online consumer-to-consumer auction. 'What I wanted to do was create a marketplace where everyone had access to the same information,' Omidyar later observed.

eBay started life as a humble homepage hosted by a local ISP (internet service provider) in 1995. A clue to its 'local' origins lies in the name eBay, which stands for 'electronic Bay Area' after the Bay Area of San Francisco. But what began as a small-scale hobby soon blossomed into a business. 'I didn't set out to create a huge business with eBay,' Omidyar noted in an interview with the *New York Times*. 'When it happened, I took advantage of it.' By 1996 he had given up his day job to look after eBay.

Online auctions were perfectly suited to the medium of the Internet. It soon became apparent to Omidyar that the commercial potential for his new business was huge. But his motivation in creating eBay was not primarily to become a billionaire. Rather, he says, it came from a genuine philosophical desire to use the Internet to create a more efficient market. 'I'd really given a lot of thought to the way efficient markets are supposed to work and how the financial markets work. What I realised is that individuals—ordinary people like you or me—usually can't participate in the most efficient markets because we don't get access to all the information the professionals do. The stock market is a great example of that. I wanted to create a place on the Web where—since everyone has access to the same medium—I could, in theory, create an efficient market.'

Others were persuaded by Omidyar's vision. Venture capital firm Benchmark Capital put in $6.7 million for 22% of the new company. By April 1999 the value of the stake had increased to $5.1 billion. And, unlike other dot-com businesses, eBay turned a profit as early as February 1996. From then on, it was just a question of marking the mileposts: three million items sold by the end of 1997; ranked number one e-commerce site on time spent by users in May 1998; completed its 10 millionth auction in May 1998; over one million registered users by August 1998. The IPO was in September 1998. From $18, the share price shot up to $53.50. eBay staff celebrated by dancing a conga. Omidyar was worth $274.1 million on paper.

Through luck or judgement, Omidyar had hit on one of the best business models on the Net. Revenue comes from the seller's fee, plus a commission on the realised price. Commissions may only amount to a few dollars, but with more than half a million new items added daily, it mounts up.

Omidyar was also astute enough to realise when his company had outgrown his ability to manage it single-handedly. He brought the right people in at the right time. Early on Jeff Skoll, a Stanford MBA and friend, was brought in as a partner.

And in 1997 he recruited former Disney marketing executive Meg Whitman from Hasbro to oversee the company's IPO.

By 2001 eBay was firmly established as one of the Internet's top brands, along with other virtual heavyweights such as Amazon.com and Yahoo! For the nine months ending 30 September 2001, revenues rose 78% to $529.4 million. Net income totalled $64.5 million, up from $24.4 million. There are over 29.7 million registered eBay users who buy and sell items in more than 4,500 categories. Millions of items are up for sale every day.

The company has remained one step ahead of the competition. It bought into traditional bricks-and-mortar auctioneers to add cachet, build brand and increase its user base. It has expanded aggressively into Europe, all but wiping out its competitors such as QXL. In 2001, the company established eBay Stores, a specialist site where groups of people selling similar goods could create the equivalent of an online store. In 2002, a joint venture with distinguished auction house Sotheby's took the company upmarket, capturing some of the premium auction business and richer clientele, by offering goods such as old master paintings. A year later, the company moved into the business sector by launching a business-to-business auction site.

Omidyar meanwhile is content to take a back seat. In 2001, he was named second richest young American. Like many wealthy businessmen before him, he has turned philanthropist. But he is approaching philanthropy with a new twist. In his self-declared drive to rid himself of 99% of his fortune during his lifetime, Omidyar has given birth to a new form of philanthropy—venture philanthropy. The theory is that he and his wife will seed a number of causes, favouring those that present a solid business plan and meet key criteria on points such as earnings streams. Then, in a scenario that mirrors the savage world of dot-com business, the nonprofits that perform poorly are dropped and the ones that prosper go on to become national organisations.

CONTEXT AND CONCLUSIONS

To date, eBay has been one of the most successful dot-com companies. Regardless of its eventual place in business history, Omidyar's achievements are significant. He was one of the first to show the business world that the promise of the Internet wasn't an illusion, that it does have the power to change markets. He has created the equivalent of the village market online. And it's a transparent market; the power of the specialist is eradicated in a click of the mouse. When it comes to collectables such as rare books and manuscripts, the specialist bookshop can no longer claim that its third edition of Adam Smith's *An Inquiry into the Nature and Causes of the Wealth of Nations with Additions (3 vols)* is worth $6,000. The would-be acquirer can now log onto eBay and discover it for sale for $1,500. Before eBay, the seller—who lives in the United States and the purchaser—who lives in Australia, would never have found each other. Omidyar has ripped the heart out of the vendor's local advantage, based on unequal knowledge and lack of choice. eBay offers the nearest thing to a perfect market that we are likely to see for some time.

CLOSE BUT NO CIGAR
JAY WALKER

Jay Walker founded Priceline, one of the most high-profile dot-com companies. Along with Omidyar and Amazon.com's Jeff Bezos, Walker became one of the most famous sons of the new economy. In 1998, Walker ran a $15 million radio blitz advertising campaign on Priceline.com Inc. The ads invited consumers to log on and name their price for airline tickets. Priceline soon became a household name. In its first year, the company generated revenues of $35 million. Its IPO in March 1999 valued the company at $13 billion.

Walker went on to try to extend his price distribution system beyond transport into hard goods such as groceries and petrol. When the dotcom crash came, a collapse in Priceline's stock market valuation forced it to scale back its ambitions.

THE BEST SOURCES OF HELP
Book:
Bunnell, David. *eBay Phenomenon*. New York: John Wiley, 2000.
Website:
eBay: **www.ebay.com**

DAVID PACKARD

1912	Born.
1934	Meets friend and future partner Bill Hewlett at Stanford University, Palo Alto.
1938	After a spell at General Electric, teams up with Bill Hewlett once more.
1939	Starts Hewlett-Packard in a garage in Palo Alto with just $538 of capital.
1942	HP turnover is $2 million.
1970	The company refuses to make wholesale redundancies when the US economy hits a recession.
1972	HP introduces the handheld scientific calculator, the model 35.
1980s	HP consistently in top five computer manufacturers.
1990s	Back-to-basics drive revitalises company fortunes.
1996	Dies.

SUMMARY

From a rented garage in Palo Alto, California, David Packard and Bill Hewlett founded one of Silicon Valley's most enduring IT companies, Hewlett-Packard. When Packard met Hewlett at Stanford University in the 1930s, Palo Alto was best known for its prunes. By the time he died, it had established itself as the epicentre of the most famous high-tech cluster in the world, and Hewlett-Packard had become one of the pillar companies of Silicon Valley.

Packard graduated from Stanford in 1934 and, after a spell at General Electric, teamed up with Hewlett to start a rent-an-inventor company in a garage in Palo Alto. First-year profits were $1,539. By 1942, turnover was $2 million. In the 1970s the company made a tactical switch to computing, and throughout the 1980s it was consistently among the top five IT companies. In the 1990s Packard revitalised it with a back-to-basics move.

LIFE AND CAREER

Born into a middle-class family on 7 September 1912, David Packard grew up in Pueblo, Colorado. At an early age he decided that he wanted to be an engineer. Unlike the millions of children whose ambitions to become an astronaut, firefighter, doctor, or nurse come to nothing, he was not be shaken from his goal.

Packard studied at Stanford University. It was there that he met his friend and partner-to-be, Bill Hewlett. When he graduated in 1934 America was still recovering from the Great Depression. Packard took one of the few jobs available to an electrical engineering student, working at General Electric. He also studied for a master's degree at the Massachusetts Institute of Technology. In 1938 Packard returned to Palo Alto and teamed up with Bill Hewlett. They decided to start their own company.

CONTRIBUTION

The company was founded in 1939 with just $538 of capital. The original location, a Palo Alto garage, was to become part of Silicon Valley folklore. It sent a message to all future entrepreneurs that great businesses could grow from small beginnings. A number of corporate giants were later to be hatched in the humble garage.

The original plan was for Packard to become a kind of rent-an-inventor. But his creativity soon ran riot, and he and Hewlett began developing their own gadgets together. The inventions were many and varied. Early designs included an electric-shock machine to help people lose weight and an optical device to trigger automatic urinal flushing. But the first invention that made money was a piece of equipment designed to help sound engineers make better recordings. By the end of the first year of business, Hewlett and Packard had amassed a profit of $1,539. The garage was replaced with more substantial premises in 1940. The company, by now named Hewlett-Packard, prospered during the Second World War, even though Hewlett joined the Signal Corps and left Packard to run the business. By 1942 turnover was up to $2 million. In the immediate post-war period, however, business dropped off alarmingly. Nevertheless, when Hewlett returned from the military, a number of talented staff were hired, and the business began to improve again.

In a division of duties, Packard assumed the managerial role, with Hewlett in charge of engineering and R&D. Although Packard had little theoretical knowledge of management—his only experience was growing the company—he proved a natural. He introduced a system of management that involved walking among the employees and maintaining a visible presence. This was in contrast to the idea, prevalent among companies at the time, that the management and the workforce were breeds apart and should have little to do with each other. That philosophy was perpetuated by corporate institutions such as the management dining-room, where the great and the good tucked into a three-course culinary extravaganza while the workers huddled around their workstations eating bologna sandwiches.

> *That philosophy was perpetuated by corporate institutions such as the management dining-room, where the great and the good tucked into a three-course culinary extravaganza while the workers huddled around their workstations eating bologna sandwiches.*

Packard, however, spurned the trappings of executive status. He maintained a policy of openness, making himself available to speak to employees. His accessibility and the practice of 'Management By Walking About' (MBWA for short) endeared him to the staff. Packard repaid their respect by empowering them in their daily work. 'We figured that people will accomplish more,' Packard said, 'if they are given an opportunity to use their talents and abilities in the way they work best.' While many managers have paid lip service to worker empowerment and enlightened management practice, these are often the first casualties in times of difficulty and economic downturn. Not in the case of Hewlett-Packard, however. In 1970, when the US economy slipped into recession, Packard did not make wholesale redundancies. Instead, he agreed a new working pattern with the staff. Employees worked nine days in every two weeks instead of ten. In addition, management and workforce alike took a 10% pay cut.

Within a year, the US economy was staging a recovery. Packard had avoided the unnecessary expense of redundancies followed by rehiring. Besides following forward-looking human resource policies, he took an innovative approach to organisational structure. 'I've often thought that after you get organised you ought to throw the chart away', he stated. It wasn't that Packard didn't believe in organisation, it was just that he believed in small agile units operating within the company. So, whenever a division grew cumbersome and unwieldy, Packard would break it up into small units.

In 1972 Hewlett-Packard introduced a handheld scientific calculator, the model 35, and during the 1970s and 1980s the company moved into the computer business.

Throughout the 1980s, HP was one of the top five computer manufacturers in the United States. In the 1990s, however, it struggled as competitors began to out-innovate it. Packard's solution was a return to basics, back to Management By Walking About. Although both Packard and Hewlett were approaching 80, they took action to reinvigorate the company. The HP hierarchy had grown unwieldy, they decided, so they took a scalpel to the organisation, cutting out unnecessary layers. The philosophy of small teams and less management was restored, as was Hewlett-Packard's competitiveness, and the company reclaimed its place among America's leading IT corporations.

David Packard died in 1996, knowing that his company was once more in shape to compete with the best. Today, HP's future looks less certain, but many of Packard's enlightened management principles remain etched in the company's culture.

> 'We figured that people will accomplish more,' Packard said, 'if they are given an opportunity to use their talents and abilities in the way they work best.'

CONTEXT AND CONCLUSIONS

From a small engineering company founded in a garage, Dave Packard, with the help of his friend and fellow student Bill Hewlett, built a multinational technology company with over 100,000 employees and annual revenues in excess of $40 billion.

Packard's key contribution to Hewlett-Packard and business, according to Bill Hewlett, his lifelong business partner and friend, was 'the HP Way', a set of values and management principles put together by Packard in 1957. In his book of the same name, he explains that one of the objectives of the company was 'to maintain an organisational environment that fosters individual motivation, initiative, and creativity, and a wide latitude of freedom in working towards established objectives and goals'. It is for this enlightened attitude to worker empowerment and the other forward-looking practices enshrined in *The HP Way* that Packard will probably be best remembered.

THE BEST SOURCES OF HELP
Book:
Packard, David. *The HP Way: How Bill Hewlett and I Built Our Company* New York: HarperBusiness, 1995.
Website:
Hewlett-Packard: **www.hp.com**

ARTHUR ROCK

1926	Born.
1948	Graduates from Syracuse University.
1951	Finishes MBA at Harvard Business School. Joins Hayden Stone.
1957	'Traitorous eight' leave Shockley labs.
1959	Fairchild Semiconductors formed.
1961	Founds the firm of Davis and Rock.
1968	Davis and Rock dissolved after a seven-year life. Backs Gordon Moore and Bob Noyce, who found Intel.
1970	Forms Arthur Rock & Associates; sets up on his own as Arthur Rock & Co.
1980	Invests in Apple Computing. Joins board of directors.
1993	Steps down from Apple board because of conflict of interests.
1994–1999	Director of Air Touch Communications.
1998	Appointed to board of governors of NASD.
2002	Named Business Leader of the Year.
2003	Donates $25 million to Harvard Business School.

> **SUMMARY**
>
> Arthur Rock is the man credited with coining the term 'venture capital'. Without the venture capital industry, there probably would have been no new economy or information revolution. Without Rock, there might not be a venture capital industry. Rock was the first venture capitalist (VC) operating on the West Coast of the United States. He organised the funding that got the computer revolution under way when he helped eight researchers break out from William Shockley's laboratories to found Fairchild Semiconductors. Then, he rounded up financing for some of the biggest companies in Silicon Valley, including Intel and Apple. It wasn't just money that Rock supplied. He also provided sage advice from his seat on the board of directors. He was still passing on the benefit of his considerable experience well into his seventies.

LIFE AND CAREER

The son of a sweet-shop owner, Arthur Rock was born in the United States in 1926. After graduating with an MBA from Harvard Business School in 1951, Rock went to work for Hayden Stone, a New York investment banking firm. Hayden Stone specialised in financing companies. At the time, the venture capital industry didn't exist in a formal sense: start-up capital tended to be provided by private family organisations, such as the one run by the Rockefellers.

Rock's lucky break came when he was shown a letter sent to one of the firm's brokers by the son of a client. The writer of the letter was Eugene Kleiner, a scientist at William Shockley's laboratory in California. Shockley was a brilliant but erratic research scientist who pioneered research on the transistor. Unfortunately his man-management skills were negligible and he was verging on the paranoid, making the atmosphere at the labs extremely unpleasant. Revolution was in the air. Key employees decided that they could no longer work with Shockley, but, before the team was split up, Kleiner wrote a speculative letter to Hayden Stone asking if anyone knew of a place where they could continue to work together. Intrigued, Rock persuaded one of Hayden Stone's partners to fly out to the West Coast with him and meet Kleiner and his associates.

CONTRIBUTION

Kleiner explained that the research team wanted to investigate the possibility of manufacturing transistors using silicon. If the process worked, it would revolutionise the computer industry. Rock was impressed with the young scientists and agreed that he would help Kleiner raise $1.5 million to set up a separate company. Rock contacted a long list of potential investors, but managed to raise nothing more than a few eyebrows. Luckily, at the last moment, he thought of Sherman Fairchild.

Sherman Fairchild was the largest stockholder in IBM; he had financed Tom Watson Sr when he founded the predecessor company to IBM. He was also an inventor. Fairchild thought Rock's proposal a good one and agreed to invest $1.5 million through Fairchild Camera and Instrument. Kleiner and his associates were given an option to buy all the stock for $3 million.

The new company was named Fairchild Semiconductors. It was the technology gene pool from which, eventually, the Silicon Valley high-tech phenomenon evolved. Rock's success with the Fairchild deal spurred him on to investigate other investment opportunities on the West Coast. He made friends with Tommy Davis. Davis was working for Kern County Land Company, advising the firm on using surplus cash to finance other companies. Davis left Kern County Land in 1961 to join up with Rock, and together they formed the investment partnership Rock & Davis.

Investment in Rock's first partnership fund came largely from private individuals on the East Coast who were his contacts. Institutional investors showed little enthusiasm. From an investment of roughly $3 million of the fund's capital, over $70 million was returned to the limited partners. Unlike some later VCs, Rock's approach was about much more than just investing money. He also sat on the boards of companies he invested in, working closely with them to increase their chances of success. In the case of Teledyne, one of the fund's first investments, Rock was on the board for 33 years. Another early investment was in Scientific Data Systems. The company was sold to Xerox in 1969 for some $990 million—in Rock's words, 'a humongous deal in those days.'

The world's largest producer of microprocessors started with a modest $5.5 million of private funding, raised on the strength of a business plan written on one and a half pages.

In 1970 Rock formed a new partnership, Arthur Rock & Associates. Fairchild Semiconductors was in a state of flux. Sherman Fairchild was dead and a new CEO, John Carter, was in charge of the Fairchild Group. Carter's ideas about business conflicted with the ideas of Bob Noyce and Gordon Moore, two of the key researchers at Fairchild. Disenchanted with life at Fairchild, Moore and Noyce approached Rock and explained that they wanted to start their own company to research and produce semiconductor memory. Rock raised $2.5 million from 25 investors to invest in the new company, including $300,000 of his own money. It took him two days. The new company was called Intel. The world's largest producer of microprocessors started with a modest $5.5 million of private funding, raised on the strength of a business plan written on one and a half pages. Rock remained on Intel's board for over 30 years.

The financing of two of the most important companies in the history of computing would have been enough to ensure Rock's place in the pantheon of venture capitalists, but Rock followed Intel with another seminal computing company, Apple Computers. Mike Markkula, ex-VP of Intel, tipped Rock off about a small fledgling computer company called Apple. Rock was not immediately persuaded and decided to pay a visit to the San José Homebrew Computer Show to see for himself. When he arrived he was unable to get anywhere near the Apple stand because of the assembled crowds, desperate to get a glimpse of the mock-up computer the two young entrepreneurs, Steve Jobs and Steve Wozniak, were demonstrating. But despite the obvious interest, Rock invested only $57,000. As usual he assumed his position on the board, a position he relinquished years later only because of a conflict of interest.

His contribution to technology business was recognized in 1998 when he was appointed to the board of governors of NASD, the technology investment governing body. In 2002, he was nominated Business Leader of the Year and, the following year, he set out to encourage others by donating $25 million to Harvard Business School to fund the Arthur Rock Center for Entrepreneurship.

A lot has changed in Rock's time as a venture capitalist. As Rock says, 'It's just a different world. It's an order of magnitude different. The pace of venture capital has changed. You don't get much time to look at the company. Sometimes you have to make up your mind that day.'

One of the questions Rock is asked most often is, 'What makes a good VC?' Is it luck, or perhaps a technology background? Rock says neither. According to him, being a good VC is about the ability to listen, about having a diverse range of interests and, above all, about being able to read people. It's a talent that takes years to develop, and Rock has it in spades. In his seventies, Rock works in the industry he helped to create. Based in San Francisco, he is a director on a number of boards, both profit- and nonprofitmaking. And he still recalls the words of his Harvard professor: 'If you're interested in building a business to make money, forget it. You won't. If you're interested in building a business to make a contribution to society, then let's talk.'

CONTEXT AND CONCLUSIONS

Arthur Rock is an important figure in post-war economic history. Rock lit the VC match that ignited the technology industry in Silicon Valley. Through his efforts, eight of the brightest researchers in their field were able to form Fairchild Semiconductors. Without him, the best research team in its field would have scattered across California, the United States, or even the world. Instead they worked together to give the world the silicon chip and then to found Intel, the powerhouse of

Rock lit the VC match that ignited the technology industry in Silicon Valley.

Arthur Rock

the personal computer revolution. Rock also helped shape the nature of the PC by investing in Apple Computers. The fact that Eugene Kleiner, one of the original 'Fairchildren', later went on to found the VC firm Kleiner Perkins means that Rock can also lay claim to having helped create the modern VC industry.

CLOSE BUT NO CIGAR
TOM PERKINS

After a stellar career with tech companies like Spectra-Physics and Hewlett-Packard, Tom Perkins founded the venture capital firm Kleiner Perkins in 1972. Perkins's partner in the firm was Eugene Kleiner, the man who brought Arthur Rock out to the West Coast. Kleiner Perkins and its later partnership incarnation (Kleiner Perkins Caulfield & Byers) was at the heart of the IT revolution on Sand Hill Road in Menlo Park. The firm pioneered the concept of incubators and hatched companies such as Genentech, Tandem Computers, America Online, and Amazon.

THE BEST SOURCES OF HELP
Website:
Intel UK: **www.intel.co.uk**

JOHN ROCKEFELLER

1839	Born.
1855	Starts work at Hewitt & Tuttle.
1869	Rockefeller, Andrews, & Flagler becomes the Standard Oil Company of Ohio.
1882	Standard Oil businesses brought under control of the Standard Oil Company.
1890	Nationwide distribution system reaches most towns in the United States.
1892	Trust dissolved by Ohio government. Reconstitutes as Standard Oil Trust (New Jersey).
1900	Standard Oil controls over three-quarters of the US petroleum industry.
1904	80% of US towns served by Standard Oil carts.
1911	Resigns as president. Standard Oil Trust dissolved.
1913	Establishes Rockefeller Foundation.
1937	Dies.

SUMMARY

In the course of his long life, US industrialist John Rockefeller (1839–1937), the son of a farmer, progressed from being an office boy earning $25 a month to being an oil tycoon worth over $900 million. Starting work aged 16, Rockefeller had his own firm within three years and by 1862 had moved into the oil business. After buying out most of the local competition, Rockefeller set his sights on building a national oil company with a national delivery network. He accomplished his vision with Standard Oil, which by 1879 controlled 90% of the oil refining in the United States. Rockefeller withdrew from active management of the company in 1897, remaining president until 1911, when the Standard Oil trust was finally dissolved by the US government. Rockefeller's final years were devoted to giving away the bulk of his huge fortune.

LIFE AND CAREER

John Rockefeller was born in 1839 in Richford, Tioga County, New York State, the eldest son and second of six children. His parents were farmers, and Rockefeller, along with his brothers and sisters, was expected to help out on the farm. Even at this tender age, the young Rockefeller displayed a keen business mind. He raised turkeys, sold them for a profit, and then lent the proceeds at 7%.

By the time Rockefeller was 14, his family had moved to Cleveland, Ohio. Here, in 1855, after a year at high school and a stint at Folsom Mercantile College, Rockefeller was offered employment as an office boy and assistant bookkeeper at the firm of Hewitt & Tuttle, produce commission merchants. No salary was agreed at the outset, and Rockefeller received no payment for 14 weeks, at which point he was handed $50 and put on $25 per month.

Rockefeller stayed at Hewitt & Tuttle for three years, leaving when the firm declined to meet his wage demands of $800 a year. Having spent the previous three

Even at this tender age, the young Rockefeller displayed a keen business mind. He raised turkeys, sold them for a profit, and then lent the proceeds at 7%.

years paying particular attention to how a business is run, Rockefeller decided to start his own.

CONTRIBUTION

With his partner, Morris Clark, and $1,000 borrowed from his father at 10%, Rockefeller started a produce business. He visited all the local farmers, charmed them, and left his card. The response was so good that, in its first year of business in 1859, the company's revenues were $500,000.

About this time oil was just beginning to make an impact in Ohio. Several refineries had been opened near Cleveland. Rockefeller, sensing the potential of the new fuel, wasted no time forming Andrews, Clark, and Co, oil refiners, in 1862. Later he sold his produce commission interests to Clark and bought out Clark's interest in Andrews, Clark, and Co, to form Rockefeller & Andrews.

By 1869 Rockefeller's firm had acquired a number of other similar small firms and was now called Rockefeller, Andrews, & Flagler. But the oil business generally was going through a tough time. With the proliferation of firms all trying to get in on the action, the price of oil became so severely depressed that many companies went bankrupt. Undeterred, Rockefeller chose to merge Rockefeller, Andrews, & Flagler into the Standard Oil Company of Ohio in 1869, with $1 million capital and himself as president.

He then proceeded to apply to Standard Oil's business the 'combination' strategy that J.P. Morgan had so successfully applied to the steel industry. The best way to ensure survival, he reasoned, was to spread the risk of operating in such a volatile and risky industry. The obvious way to achieve this was to buy up competitors, both locally and elsewhere in the United States. By 1872 Standard Oil had acquired all the refining firms in Cleveland. In 1882, after a prosperous decade, all the businesses belonging to Standard Oil were brought under the single umbrella of the Standard Oil Trust.

The dominance of the Standard Oil Trust soon gave rise to a barrage of criticism. In 1892 the Attorney General of Ohio won a suit to dissolve the Trust. During the court case, brought in 1890, Rockefeller was put under severe stress; he lost all his hair, including his eyebrows, and was reputed to have suffered a nervous breakdown. The effects of the court case on Standard Oil were less dramatic. The company simply reformed as the Standard Oil Company (New Jersey), because the laws of New Jersey permitted a parent company to own the stock of other companies. The Standard Oil Company (New Jersey) controlled three-quarters of the US petroleum business.

> *During his lifetime Rockefeller came in for much criticism, as well as some odd mythologising. It was claimed, for example, that he would eat only bread and milk.*

Rockefeller remained president of Standard Oil until 1911. That was the year in which the US Supreme Court finally ordered its dissolution, declaring the company to be in contravention of the country's antitrust laws. The 38 companies that made up the oil giant were split into separate entities.

During his lifetime Rockefeller came in for much criticism, as well as some odd mythologising. It was claimed, for example, that he would eat only bread and milk. Another persistent story was of his phenomenal capacity for hard work and long hours, something that Rockefeller denied all knowledge of. 'People persist in thinking that I was a tremendous worker, always at it, early and late, winter and summer,' he said. 'The real truth is that I was what would now be called a "slacker" after I reached my middle thirties...I never, from the time I first entered an office, let business engross all my time and attention.'

The latter years of Rockefeller's life were spent carrying out philanthropic work. He gave over $35 million to the University of Chicago, founded the Rockefeller Institute for Medical Research, the Rockefeller Foundation, and the Rockefeller Sanitary Commission, which eradicated hookworm in the southern areas of the United States. At its height Rockefeller's wealth was $900 million. When he died, aged 97, on 23 May 1937, at his home in Ormond Beach, he had given away all but $26,410,837.

CONTEXT AND CONCLUSIONS
John Rockefeller created the modern oil industry. The impact of Rockefeller's business on the United States may have been less immediate than that of Edison's electric light or Ford's Model T automobile, but without the cheap petrol that Standard Oil produced, it is unlikely that either the widescale electrification of the country or the mass marketing of the car would have happened when they did.

One of Rockefeller's greatest attributes was his understanding of the importance of hiring brilliant people. 'Men, not machinery or plant, make up an organisation,' was one of his sayings. He assembled a team of the brightest men in business and harnessed their collective abilities to drive Standard Oil's expansion. In later years he was vilified as the head of one of the hated 'trusts' dominating industry in the United States. It should be remembered, however, that, despite its controlling influence, the establishment of the Standard Oil Trust saw the oil industry through some difficult times, and ensured its strength in the United States for the following decades.

THE BEST SOURCES OF HELP
Book:
Chernow, Ron. *Titan: The Life of John D. Rockefeller, Sr.* London: Random House, 1998.

ANITA RODDICK

1942	Born.
1960	Attends Newton Park College of Education in Bath.
1962	Travels to Israel on a study scholarship.
1971	Opens bed and breakfast business in Littlehampton.
1976	The Body Shop opens in Brighton selling environmentally friendly cosmetics. Ian McGlinn's investment enables second shop to be opened.
1978	First informal franchises open. First franchise outside the United Kingdom opens in Brussels.
1984	The Body Shop goes public.
1988	The Body Shop opens in the United States.
1989	Roddick commissions environmental audit of all company's practices.
1998	Steps down as CEO.
2000	Sets up Anitaroddick.com to communicate environmental issues. Publication of *Business As Unusual*.
2001	Publication of *Take It Personally*.

> **SUMMARY**
>
> Anita Roddick, the British businesswoman and head of the cosmetics phenomenon The Body Shop, might never have started her business at all. It was an unusual combination of factors that led her to open her first shop in 1976. But The Body Shop concept—based on environmentally friendly cosmetics and begun as a cottage industry—soon outgrew her small shop in Brighton. If the company had expanded in the traditional manner, it might well have lost the small-business charm that made it so successful. Instead, Roddick expanded through franchises, a relatively new concept in the United Kingdom at the time, ensuring that the vibrancy and enthusiasm of the concept was maintained. By the year 2000 there were over 1,500 shops worldwide, and Roddick, who had stepped down as CEO two years earlier, was spending much of her time and energy championing ethical causes close to her heart.

LIFE AND CAREER

Born in Sussex in 1942, Roddick was the third of four children. Her parents ran a North American-style diner in the sleepy coastal town of Littlehampton. After secondary school, despite being offered a place at the prestigious Guildhall School of Music and Drama, Roddick attended the Newton Park College of Education in Bath.

After college Roddick flitted from one job to another. In Paris she worked for the *International Herald Tribune*; she taught in England; then she worked for the United Nations in Geneva. After the UN, Roddick followed what became known as the hippy trail to Africa, the Far East, and Australia, making her way around the globe. Her stay in South Africa was cut short when she was ejected for breaking the apartheid laws by attending a jazz club on 'non-whites' night. Her rebellious spirit may have earned her an early ticket out of Africa, but it was to stand her in good stead when she later launched The Body Shop.

Returning to Littlehampton, Roddick settled down, married, had children, and with her husband, Gordon, opened a hotel and then a restaurant. Running both businesses eventually became too demanding on family life. The restaurant was

Anita Roddick

sold, and Roddick's husband declared that he was planning an ambitious expedition of his own—intending to ride a horse from South America to New York.

CONTRIBUTION

Unable to curb her entrepreneurial instincts, Roddick looked for another enterprise on which to concentrate, one that would also earn some money in her husband's absence. After some thought she came up with the idea of a cosmetics business with a difference: the use of natural ingredients. Her husband helped arrange a bank loan using the hotel as collateral, and Roddick bought premises next to a funeral director's in the nearby town of Brighton.

On 27 March 1976, with her husband about to leave on his travels, Roddick opened for business, selling environmentally friendly cosmetics. The idea was not just to sell socially responsible products using natural ingredients, but to sell them in convenient small sizes that would tempt customers to try them out. Thus, many of The Body Shop's defining characteristics were decided upon at this early stage, though the decisions were often based on cost-effectiveness rather than any grand strategic plan. The walls were painted green, not in anticipation of the Green movement, but to hide the damp patches. Product packaging was minimal and recyclable, and Roddick wrote the labels out by hand.

> *After college Roddick flitted from one job to another. In Paris she worked for the International Herald Tribune; she taught in England; then she worked for the United Nations in Geneva.*

The Brighton shop prospered, and she was soon planning another in nearby Chichester. When the bank refused to finance her, she turned to a local businessman, Ian McGlinn, who agreed to put up £4,000 for a half share of the business. Roddick agreed. For McGlinn, it proved to be the investment opportunity of his life. By the time Roddick's husband returned in 1977, The Body Shop concept was unstoppable. Her friends and family ran the first few shops, but requests to set up branches elsewhere in the country were flooding in. To meet the demand for shops, Roddick and her husband began franchising the concept. Potential franchisees would finance the business and agree to buy their stock from Roddick, and, in return, would be licensed to use The Body Shop name. She interviewed many of the early franchisees herself. A high proportion of them were women, and she can justifiably claim to have helped change the traditional male-dominated image of entrepreneurs in the United Kingdom.

What she had started was not a conventional cosmetics business. Roddick had little time for the beauty industry, believing that it was in the business of selling unattainable dreams. The Body Shop was different. Roddick made no special claims for her products. In fact she didn't advertise, relying mainly on word of mouth to bring customers through the shop doors.

'Making products that work—that aren't part of the cosmetic industry's lies to women—is all-important,' Roddick has said. 'Making sure we minimise our impact in our manufacturing processes, clean up our waste, put back into the community...we go where businesses never want to because they don't think it is the role of business to get involved.'

Roddick espouses profits with principles. Through The Body Shop she has supported campaigns by Greenpeace, Friends of the Earth, and Amnesty International, among others. Messages on shopping bags and vehicles express The Body Shop's support for these causes.

In April 1984 the company became publicly listed. The share price shot up on the opening day, and Roddick, her husband, and Ian McGlinn all became paper millionaires overnight. From one small shop next to a funeral director's, The Body Shop network has expanded to over 1,800 shops worldwide, offering over 400 products. Roddick, now one of the richest women in England, has been showered with awards as a result of both her business endeavours and her social conscience. Besides the titles of London's Business Woman of the Year and Retailer of the Year, she has received the United Nations' 'Global 500' environmental award and the Order of the British Empire.

In 1994 Roddick brought in external management help to refocus the business. Unsurprisingly she found the shift from her hands-on role difficult to adjust to. In 1998 she stepped down as CEO, and remained as co-chair with her husband Gordon until 2002, when she adopted a new role as creative consultant to the company. The fact that she now spends less time with The Body Shop allows her more scope to champion the causes she so passionately believes in. One of her first actions was to set up AnitaRoddick.com, a website devoted to raising awareness of issues she cares about. She has also been busy writing books. *Business As Unusual* was published in 2000, followed a year later by *Take it Personally*, a book encouraging people to take action to change the world.

CONTEXT AND CONCLUSIONS

Displayed on the side of The Body Shop lorries is the following: 'If you think you are too small to have an impact, try going to bed with a mosquito.' The phrase is one of Roddick's favourite quotations—not surprisingly, considering her achievements. She has taken on the big cosmetic companies and captured a large share of the market with her ethically driven approach to business. She has built a global company from a one-woman cottage industry, changed the attitude towards businesswomen through her franchise operation, and, in addition, found time to make her voice heard championing the rights of minorities and unsung causes—often through her company.

THE BEST SOURCES OF HELP
Books:
Older, Jules. *Anita!: The Woman behind The Body Shop*. Watertown, Massachusetts: Charlesbridge Publishing, 1998.
Roddick, Anita. *Business As Unusual*. London: HarperCollins, 2000.
Roddick, Anita. *Take It Personally: How to Make Conscious Choices to Change the World*. London: HarperCollins, 2001.
Website:
The Body Shop: **www.thebodyshop.com/uk**

JULIUS ROSENWALD

1862	Born.
1885	Moves to Chicago.
1885–1895	Manufactures men's summer clothing as Rosenwald & Weil.
1895	Takes share of Sears, Roebuck as sleeping partner.
1896	Becomes vice-president of Sears.
1900–1906	Total sales increase from $11 million to over $50 million.
1908	Sears retires. Rosenwald becomes president.
1916	Over 40 million catalogues distributed.
1925	Opens first retail store. Becomes chairman. Personal holdings worth $150 million.
1932	Dies.

SUMMARY

Julius Rosenwald started in the retail business at the tender age of 21, with his own clothes store in New York. He then showed an excellent nose for an opportunity, first by ditching his retail business to manufacture men's summer clothing, and then abandoning manufacturing to join Sears, Roebuck as vice president. His big break was choosing Chicago as the base for his manufacturing business. There he met the entrepreneur R.W. Sears, who made his fortune with a mail-order business. Sears needed the right person to take his business into the 20th century—he chose Rosenwald. By the time Rosenwald died in 1932, the company had revitalised its mail-order business, expanded its product range, introduced innovative work practices, and opened hundreds of retail stores throughout the United States, leaving competitors like Montgomery Ward far behind.

LIFE AND CAREER

Julius Rosenwald was born in Springfield, Illinois in 1862. As a child he would sell goods door-to-door in his hometown. He pumped the bellows on the church organ, peddled pamphlets, and sold chromolithographs, the latest consumer craze. During the summer holidays, he worked in a fancy goods store.

At 16, Rosenwald left school to work for his uncle's wholesale clothing business in New York. By living frugally, he saved enough money so that at the age of 21 he could afford to buy a small retail clothing store on 4th Avenue.

One day Rosenwald was in idle conversation with the owner of a nearby business. The man, who manufactured summer clothing for men, revealed that he was struggling to keep pace with orders.

He pumped the bellows on the church organ, peddled pamphlets, and sold chromolithographs, the latest consumer craze.

Rosenwald turned the statement over and over in his mind until, in the middle of the night, he dramatically resolved to abandon his retail store. Chicago was the city that Rosenwald chose to start his new business. There, with partner Julius Weil, he formed Rosenwald & Weil, manufacturers and wholesalers of summer clothing.

Julius Rosenwald

CONTRIBUTION

One of Rosenwald's best customers was Richard Warren Sears of Sears, Roebuck and Company. Sears's one problem was that he needed more capital to expand. He asked if Rosenwald was interested in investing in the business. Rosenwald agreed, and took a quarter interest in Sears, Roebuck for $70,000.

To begin with, Rosenwald was a silent partner. However by 1896, Sears—who ran the company single-handed—asked Rosenwald to join him as vice-president. Over the next 30 years, Rosenwald transformed Sears, Roebuck into one of the largest retailers in the United States.

Rosenwald first turned his attention to the Sears, Roebuck catalogue. As Ingvar Kamprad of IKEA would find out over 50 years later, Rosenwald discovered that if mail-order companies were less than honest in the wording and illustration of their catalogues, it damaged the reputation of the entire industry. Even Sears, Roebuck was guilty of delivering products that didn't always correspond to the promises of the lavishly-worded and sumptuously-illustrated catalogue.

Rosenwald insisted on a fastidiously precise correlation between the advertisements in the catalogue and the goods supplied. First, he ensured that every illustration and description in the catalogue was carefully compared with the relevant article. He set up laboratories and employed scientists to examine merchandise received from suppliers. Any defective goods were immediately rejected and returned. To increase consumer confidence, he introduced a novel concept—a 'money back if not satisfied' guarantee, supported by an advertising campaign. In this way Rosenwald removed the burden of risk from the consumer and placed it squarely on the shoulders of Sears, Roebuck.

Once consumer confidence was secure, Rosenwald set about broadening the range of products offered in a mail-order catalogue. Soon everything from buttons to bungalows was sold by mail order. Other innovations were introduced. To secure quality supplies, Rosenwald constructed factories employing over 20,000 workers. Technological innovations such as the conveyor belt were introduced (it was said that Henry Ford 'borrowed' Rosenwald's idea for his assembly lines). The catalogue was expanded, and special editions were introduced for seasonal goods and special events. New goods like shoes and books were featured in the catalogue. Shoes, an unlikely candidate for mail order, earned revenues of $1 million a month. The sales of *Encyclopaedia Britannica* alone added an incredible $5 million in revenues to the annual balance sheet. Between 1900 and 1906, total sales increased from $11 million to over $50 million. By 1914 they had reached $100 million.

> *He spurned the trappings of status, preferring to be seen as one of the workers.*

Rosenwald was also making changes to the way the company's employees were treated. He spurned the trappings of status, preferring to be seen as one of the workers. Asked what it felt like to have so many people working for him he replied, 'I always think of them as just working with me.' When he was presented with an oriental rug to cover the floor of his executive office, it remained rolled up in the corner. Rosenwald decided that if linoleum was good enough for everybody else, it was good enough for him. 'I have played only a very small part in the building up of

Sears, Roebuck and Company,' he modestly told his admirers. To improve the lot of his workers, Rosenwald introduced recreation facilities, as well as an innovative 'employee savings and profit-sharing scheme'. True, his management style was a little paternalistic. He was overprotective of his female employees, for example— familiarity between men and women was forbidden at social functions, and the sexes were segregated in the cafeteria.

Eternally cost-conscious in business, Rosenwald encouraged his workers to be equally parsimonious. Employees who earned below $1,500 received a bonus on the anniversary of their joining the company. The bonus was a percentage of the annual salary, equal to the number of years an employee had worked for the company. Starting in the fifth year, it rose to 10% in the tenth year, and remained at 10% thereafter. His employees, Rosenwald suggested, should save the bonus.

On Sears' retirement in 1908, Rosenwald became president and, in 1925, chairman. In the 1920s he took the company in a new direction. The mail-order catalogue was still an essential element of the Sears, Roebuck retail strategy, but now Rosenwald expanded into retail stores. In 1925 Sears opened its first retail outlet in Chicago. By 1929 there were 324 stores with the name Sears, Roebuck above the doors.

In his final years, Rosenwald focused his attention on philanthropy. He established the Julius Rosenwald Fund, a charity for the economic, medical, and cultural advancement of African Americans, with an endowment of $30 million. He gave money to aid the Jews in the Middle East and to help German children after the First World War. He also endowed the University of Chicago and helped to establish the Museum of Science and Industry in Chicago. He died in 1932.

CONTEXT AND CONCLUSIONS

Julius Rosenwald took a promising business and turned it into a great one. Without his intervention, it is arguable whether Sears, Roebuck would have become the retailing giant it did. At the time Rosenwald joined, the reputation of the mail-order industry was under a cloud because of the less-than-scrupulous practices of many of the companies involved. Through a variety of innovations, Rosenwald breathed new life into a tired format. Greater choice, better quality, and a money-back guarantee were among the features that won the customers back. Internally, Rosenwald concentrated on ensuring a quality supply of merchandise and keeping the workforce happy. Finally, he moved to secure the future of the company by extending the brand and opening a chain of retail stores.

THE BEST SOURCES OF HELP
Books:
Harris, Leon. *Merchant Princes*. London: Harper & Row, 1979.
Sorenson, Lorin. *Sears, Roebuck and Co: 100th Anniversary 1886–1996*. St Helena, California: Silverado Publishing Co, 1985.
Werner, M.R. *Julius Rosenwald: The Life of a Practical Humanitarian*. New York: Harper & Brothers, 1939.

DAVID SARNOFF

1891	Born.
1916	Sarnoff states his vision for radio.
1919	Radio Corporation of America (RCA) incorporated.
1920	Cuts a deal with Armstrong to secure the latter's radio technology patents.
1921	RCA begins radio broadcasting.
1930	Aged 39, Sarnoff becomes president of RCA.
1933	Has new headquarters constructed for RCA. Armstrong invents FM.
1939	Introduces television to the United States just before the Second World War at the World's Fair.
1954	Introduces colour television.
1965	His son, Robert, becomes president of the company; Sarnoff becomes chairman.
1970	Dies.

> **SUMMARY**
>
> David Sarnoff (1891–1970) was a media pioneer. He was responsible for the introduction of radio and television in the United States as forms of mass media. Born in Russia, Sarnoff emigrated to the United States in 1900; by 1930 he was president of the Radio Corporation of America (RCA). He went on to develop FM radio on a commercial basis and bring colour television to the American people. Behind Sarnoff's public success story with RCA, however, lay the personal saga of his long-running relationship with the inventor Edwin Armstrong. Originally based on friendship, the relationship descended into animosity and ended with Armstrong's suicide in 1954. Sarnoff was succeeded at RCA by his son, Robert, in 1965. The remaining years of his life were spent bitterly watching his son modernise the company that he had spent his life building.

LIFE AND CAREER

David Sarnoff was born in Uzlian in Russia. His father, Abraham, was a Jewish painter who travelled to the United States in 1896, determined to earn enough money to bring the rest of his family across the Atlantic to join him. It took him four years.

When Sarnoff arrived in Manhattan on 2 July 1900, his father was renting a squalid flat on the lower East Side. In the four years since Abraham had arrived in the sprawling metropolis, he had been struggling to make a living. Not only was he reduced to doing menial work for little pay, but his health had deteriorated to the point where he was unable to provide for his family. At the tender age of nine, therefore, Sarnoff became the family breadwinner.

He started by selling Yiddish newspapers on street corners, earning a quarter for every 50 papers sold. To supplement his income he delivered another paper in the

Like several other great business leaders of his generation, Sarnoff started out on the path to success in the employ of a telegraph company—in this case, American Marconi Wireless Telegraph.

morning and sang at the local synagogue for a small fee. Despite the long hours—he rose at 4.00 a.m. for the morning round—Sarnoff still managed to find time to study at a local school, the Educational Alliance. Within a year he could read the English newspapers. At 14 he opened his own newspaper stand, employing his father and brothers.

Like several other great business leaders of his generation, Sarnoff started out on the path to success in the employ of a telegraph company—in this case, American Marconi Wireless Telegraph. At that time Marconi's US operation was a loss-making company, unlike its English parent. Sarnoff started at Marconi as an office boy, little realising that he would spend the next 60 years at the company and its successor, the Radio Corporation of America, rising to become president before the age of 40.

CONTRIBUTION

Cheekily, Sarnoff introduced himself in person to Marconi as the newest employee of the company. His impudence paid off, and he was promoted to junior wireless operator, and not long after to chief inspector.

It was as chief inspector that Sarnoff met the man who was to change his life. Edwin Armstrong was an inventor who had been working on an improved wireless receiver. At a demonstration of his invention in front of Sarnoff and three other Marconi engineers, Armstrong received radio signals from Clifden, Ireland, and a radio station in San Francisco. Sarnoff, immediately aware of the commercial potential of the machine, advised his bosses to explore the possibility of developing a similar device.

Unfortunately for Sarnoff, his superiors were not as impressed, preferring to stick with the existing point-to-point system that had served Marconi so well. In 1916 Sarnoff, with considerable foresight, wrote a memo to the board: 'I have in mind a plan of development which would make radio a household utility in the same sense as the piano or the phonograph.'

During the First World War the US Navy made significant technical advances in radio engineering. At the end of the war companies queued up to purchase the new technology. The US government was reluctant to hand over its know-how to a British company like Marconi, so a new company, Radio Corporation of America (RCA), was incorporated in 1919. The new company held the patents of GE and Marconi; its commercial manager and second-in-command was Sarnoff. Now in a better position to lobby for his vision of ubiquitous radio, Sarnoff sent a 28-page 'blueprint for success' to the chairman. Sarnoff got his way, and RCA began to churn out radio sets. The ensuing radio craze assured RCA's success, despite competition from companies like Westinghouse.

Armstrong, meanwhile, was continuing to develop radio technology. In 1920, hearing that Armstrong had come up with yet another breakthrough, Sarnoff cut out the middlemen and went straight to him to secure the technology patents. After some tough bargaining, he got the technology and Armstrong received enough stock in RCA to make him the leading shareholder—plus some cash. Armstrong also agreed to give RCA first refusal on future innovations.

The Wall Street Crash of 1929 and ensuing financial chaos hit RCA badly. This was despite the company's domination of its market, the increasing popularity of radio as a form of entertainment, and the creation of the National Broadcasting Company. In January 1930 after a boardroom shuffle, Sarnoff, aged 39, became president of RCA.

David Sarnoff

In December 1933 Armstrong surfaced once more with yet another invention: Frequency Modulation (FM). This time, however, Sarnoff was less interested; his focus was directed towards television rather than radio. He introduced television to the United States just before the outbreak of the Second World War at the 1939 World's Fair.

After the war a private conflict broke out between Armstrong and Sarnoff over FM. Eventually, after years of banging his head against the giant RCA, Armstrong was forced to agree a settlement in the courts. In 1954, embittered by the outcome, Armstrong jumped to his death from a 13th-storey window. Sarnoff's only comment on learning of the death of his one-time friend was, 'I didn't kill Armstrong.'

Sarnoff carried on business as usual. He introduced colour television in 1954. To avoid damaging litigation, he placed all RCA's colour television patents in the public domain and at the same time tripled spending on colour programming. Any manufacturer could produce a colour television set, but RCA had first-mover advantage in colour broadcasting.

Colour television was Sarnoff's last throw of the dice. The protracted litigation with Armstrong may have taken more of a toll on him than he realised at the time. In 1965 his son, Robert, was made president of the company and Sarnoff became chairman.

A change of name and logo for RCA, pushed through by his son, roused Sarnoff one last time, and he fought successfully to reinstate the old name. In reality it was a hollow victory. The RCA that Sarnoff had created metamorphosed into a conglomerate containing a disparate collection of companies, including Hertz car rentals and Random House Publishing. After a lengthy illness David Sarnoff died in December 1970.

CONTEXT AND CONCLUSIONS

Sarnoff was more than just a forerunner of modern media magnates such as Rupert Murdoch and Ted Turner. He pioneered the mass-market entertainment industry of radio and television. Edwin Armstrong played a large part in creating the technology of commercial radio, but it was Sarnoff who had the vision to recognise the commercial potential of Armstrong's scientific inventions when others did not. Moreover, Sarnoff had the sense to tie up the technology patents in the case of radio and, more remarkably, to place all RCA's colour television patents in the public domain. This last act alone is testimony to Sarnoff's genius and was a forerunner of the approach taken by Linus Torvalds when developing the computer operating system Linux.

THE BEST SOURCES OF HELP
Books:
Bilby, Kenneth M. *The General: David Sarnoff and the Rise of the Communications Industry*. London: Harper & Row, 1986.
Lyons, Eugene. *David Sarnoff: A Biography*. New York: Harper & Row, 1966.
Myers, Elisabeth P. *David Sarnoff: Radio and TV Boy*. Indianapolis, Indiana: Bobbs-Merrill Co, 1972.
Sobel, Robert. *RCA*. New York: Stein and Day, 1986.
Website:
RCA: **www.rca.com**

RICARDO SEMLER

1959	Born.
1975	Takes summer job in father's company.
1980	Takes over Semler and Co; fires 60% of top management.
1983	Starts out on acquisition trail.
1984	Forced by illness to reassess working methods.
1993	Publishes *Maverick*.
1998	Achieves 500% increase in profits.

> **SUMMARY**
>
> Ricardo Semler is the man behind a magnificent Brazilian experiment in management and corporate structure. After a flirtation with a career in law, he went to work for the family company, Semler and Co. If his father believed that Semler would carry on the family tradition, managing the company just as he had done, then he was very much mistaken. On his first day in the job, Semler fired 60% of the management. He carried on as he had started by radically overhauling the management structure, not once but several times, until eventually he was nominally in charge of a company in which the workers hired the management, fired the management, and set their own pay. They were also free to leave and start their own businesses using the company's resources. Remarkably, this topsy-turvy corporate culture produced astonishing results and made Semler's company one of the most-written-about businesses in the world.

LIFE AND CAREER

Ricardo Semler was born in Sao Paulo in 1959. Both his parents were Austrian. His father had arrived in Brazil via Argentina and the DuPont Company. His mother had fled to Brazil from communist China. By the time he was born, his father had built up a thriving engineering company, Semler and Co, and earmarked him as heir to the family business.

Semler had other ideas, however. He was a poor scholar, whose lack of interest rather than lack of intelligence led to a large collection of D grades. His parents also were frequent visitors to the school offices to discuss his misdemeanours. Yet Semler excelled in other ways. He had a natural authority and was popular with his peers. At high school he was class president, captain of the athletics team, and photography editor of the school yearbook. He also showed a flair for business while running a snack stand. The stand was intended to raise funds to send students on the class trip the following year. Semler treated the enterprise as a business instead, opening for longer hours, encouraging competition among suppliers, and charging a

He seemed more interested in rock and roll, and, in particular, mastering a few good riffs on his Gibson Les Paul electric guitar, than in working in the family business.

commercial price for his goods. The snack stand impresario raised so much money he was able to fly the entire class to a resort.

In spite of his promising flirtation with business, he was still a worry to his father. He seemed more interested in rock and roll, and, in particular, mastering a few good riffs on his Gibson Les Paul electric guitar, than in working in the family business. Nevertheless, after a spell in a summer job in the purchasing department of Semler and Co, and aware of the limitations of his musical abilities, he weighed up his options and decided that business was preferable to a career in music.

One barrier remained before Semler could take his place in his father's company. In Brazil men were obliged to serve in the military for at least one year at the age of 18. Although Semler tried to persuade his mother to overrule his father's keen approval of this practice, he soon found himself at the local recruiting office. Passing the medical and written examinations, Semler fell at the last hurdle when he expounded his views on the stupidity of joining the army to the officer in charge. Instead of national service he went to Sao Paulo State Law School, the finest university in Brazil. Once again he scraped by with substandard grades, although this time he had an excuse. He had to juggle his course with a job at Semler and Co.

CONTRIBUTION

From the moment he started work, there was tension between Semler and his father. His offices were next door to his father's, and his father would frequently open the partition that separated the offices and barge in during meetings. Their methods of conducting business were dramatically different. Semler was laid-back, happy to do work at home; he liked to put his feet up on the desk and generally had a relaxed approach to his work. His father, by contrast, was straight out of the old school, keeping a regimented schedule and presenting a formidable figure to employees and clients alike. He also was unwilling to cede authority to his son.

Frustrated, Semler looked for another job, and spotted an opportunity in a company that made ladders but had financial difficulties. He negotiated for nearly a year to buy the business, beating the owner's asking price down from $1 million to just $1. Then, just as he was about to leave to run his new company, his father relented, transferring a majority of seven-day shares into his son's name, thus effectively ceding control. He then went on a trip telling Semler, 'Whatever changes you want to make in the organisation, make them now.'

He took his father at his word. By 6.00 p.m. on his first day in charge, he had fired 60% of the top management.

Semler had his work cut out at the company, which he renamed Semco. A recession in Brazil had left it in poor shape, partly because it was heavily reliant on shipbuilding. Semler determined to diversify. He also pledged to strip away the stifling autocratic control exercised by his father.

What followed was one of the most remarkable transformations of a company anywhere in the world. In what became something akin to a socio-corporate experiment, Semler introduced a series of fundamental changes at every level of the company. In fact there were so many changes implemented that there is only room to mention some of the more radical initiatives.

As far as structure was concerned, Semler struggled to find the right organisational model. After trying a matrix structure (confusion of reporting lines) and autonomous business units (too much power-base building and dispute among fiefdoms), he settled on a lattice model in which small teams were responsible for all levels of the production process. Each group had control of its own budgets and, more controversially, its own targets. Although 30% of middle managers left between 1985 and 1987 as a result of the apparent stripping away of authority and the new way of working, unit costs went down and production soared.

Confronted by a severe recession in the early 1990s, Semco implemented severe cost-cutting measures, but did so in agreement with the workforce. Under the agreement, management took a 40% salary cut, all other wages were cut, too, but productivity bonuses went up, and the workers were given the right to approve all company expenditure. The responsible attitude shown by the workforce during this time encouraged Semler to push his experimentation with worker empowerment and participation even further.

The company was altered once more, as autonomous teams were based on product lines. Those teams had more power than ever before. They could recruit and fire employees at all levels including their bosses. All decisions were taken democratically. To foment change in the company, Semler also introduced the idea of the satellite organisation. Able employees who might otherwise leave the company would be provided with the necessary resources to take an idea away and turn it into a business. They answered only to themselves, but had all the resources of Semco at their disposal. In return for this freedom, Semco took payment in the form of profits or savings from their individual new ventures. Eventually, the satellite businesses comprised over two-thirds of the business conducted by the firm.

> *No secretaries, receptionists, or PAs worked at Semco; employees, including Semler, handled their own administrative chores and made their own coffee.*

These changes were just the tip of the iceberg. No secretaries, receptionists, or PAs worked at Semco; employees, including Semler, handled their own administrative chores and made their own coffee. Job titles were rendered virtually meaningless because of the workplace democracy that existed. All information in the company was freely available, including all salary information. Management salaries were capped. All noncore competencies were outsourced, although outsourcing was often to a satellite company. Employees set their own salaries. Employees decided whether to recruit a new worker and whether that worker should be a boss or not. Positions were bid for by workers every six months and accepted or rejected taking into account skills, salary requested, and other factors. Finally, managers were rated out of 100, and the results posted up. Consistently falling below 75 would eventually lead to a manager losing his position.

The measures introduced by Semler were astonishing, nothing less than a corporate revolution. Yet, as late as 1998, he thought the job was only 30% complete. Most important of all, his changes have been greatly beneficial to the company's bottom line—a key criterion as far as Semler himself is concerned. Between 1990 and 1996 sales grew from $35 million to $100 million. By 1998, against a background of recession and hyperinflation, Semco, under Semler's guidance, had grown sixfold, productivity had increased nearly sevenfold, and profits had risen fivefold. The company was so popular that it had built up a backlog of more than 2,000 job applications.

CONTEXT AND CONCLUSIONS
The name of Ricardo Semler is fairly well known within management circles but little known by the public at large. Had he been the CEO of a US *Fortune* 500 Company, he would undoubtedly be one of the most celebrated and famous managers of his generation. At his Brazilian company, Semco, he has carried out one of the most radical programmes of organisational change conducted in an international corporation. He hasn't just rewritten the handbook of management; he has ripped it to pieces and started over again. Most businesses would think it madness to allow the employees to hire and fire the bosses and set their own wages, but that is exactly what happens at Semco. Most amazingly, this revolution in worker empowerment has resulted in substantial increases in productivity and profits. Managers from all over the world now beat a path Semler's door for an insight into this amazing man's methods.

CLOSE BUT NO CIGAR
LARS KOLIND
Danish business revolutionary Kolind was CEO of the hearing aid company Oticon from 1988 to 1998. At Oticon he implemented a radical organisational shake-up. He called the new model he created the spaghetti organisation. It involves a boundaryless criss-crossing of reporting lines and competencies. It should have been chaos, but in fact it worked rather well, turning the ailing company around. When things got a little stale again, Kolind overhauled the organisational structure and working practices again. 'To keep a company alive,' says Kolind, 'one of the jobs of top management is to keep it disorganised.'

THE BEST SOURCES OF HELP
Books:
Semler, Ricardo. *Maverick!* London: Century, 1993.
Clutterbuck, David. *Doing It Different: Lessons for the Imaginative Manager*. London: Century, 1993.

STAN SHIH

1944	Born.
1971	Joins Unitron Industrial Corporation.
1972	Joins Qualitron Industrial Corporation.
1976	Founds Multitech (later Acer).
1981	MicroProfessor-I is the company's first branded product.
1985	Establishes AcerLand, Taiwan's first franchised computer retail chain.
1987	Creates 'Acer' name.
1988	Acer Inc. launches IPO.
1994	Introduces world's first dual-Pentium PC.
1999	Seventh in list of top ten PC manufacturers. Revenues $8.5 billion.
2000	Announces planned reorganisation of company.
	Invests $200 million in China.
	Repositions company as Internet enabler.
2002	Launches multimedia handheld computer.
	Launches service business.

SUMMARY

IT visionary and corporate philosopher, Stan Shih is the man who took the Taiwanese IT industry from parochial to global. Putting aside his desire to become an academic, he ended up teaching commercial realities to the family-run businesses of Taiwan. With a mixture of solid financial grounding, brand awareness, and quality control, he propelled a small electrical engineering company to international fame by concentrating on the microprocessor and the PC. In a world where there is a PC on every desk, there is an Acer component inside every PC. Its reliability and ubiquity have placed Acer firmly on the top ten list of PC manufacturers and made Shih a very wealthy man.

LIFE AND CAREER

Stan Shih was born on 18 December 1944. An only child, his father died when he was just three years old, leaving his mother struggling to bring him up alone. She ran a small grocery store and Shih helped out, learning the fundamentals of commerce at an early age. The business made a lasting impression on Shih. Many years later, he recalled that the stationery sold at a profit margin of 50% but only turned over every two or three weeks. The sale of duck eggs, while producing a smaller profit margin, was better business because it turned over every day. The importance of stock turnover was not wasted on him, even at such a young age.

Shih was an excellent scholar. He studied for an electrical engineering degree and then, in 1971, for a masters degree at the National Chiao-Tung University in Taiwan. His intention was to become an academic, but for some reason he changed his mind and decided to work in industry. It was not the usual career path for a Master's degree holder in Taiwan, but then Shih was not the stereotypical student. He had two job offers. One was from the international electronics giant Philips and the other from the Taiwanese family-run business Unitron. Because of his poor English, he chose Unitron. More important still was the fact that Unitron was the first company in Taiwan to have an R&D department.

CONTRIBUTION

Shih quickly made an impact at Unitron. He built a calculator—not the first to be designed at the company but the first to be commercialised. His achievement earned him a promotion to manager of the semi-conductor assembly line, in charge of 800 people. Then he was promoted to director, all in the space of a year. Although it was early in his career, Shih was beginning to formulate the management theories that would influence his management at Acer. 'First, it is important to maintain good relationships among peers and never to take sides with any clique. Conflicts can put you in a disadvantageous position,' he wrote in his autobiography *Me-too Is Not My Style*. 'Second, we must have a sense of responsibility.'

> *Shih quickly made an impact at Unitron. He built a calculator—not the first to be designed at the company but the first to be commercialised.*

Shih had been at Unitron for just over a year, when the boss's son Li asked him if he would like to help set up another company, Qualitron. Shih agreed and, together with Li, created a successful business manufacturing calculators. Four years at Qualitron with Li taught Shih the importance of marketing, a discipline neglected by most Taiwanese companies of the time. While at Qualitron, he developed the first hand-held calculator in Taiwan. He also received a painful lesson in the potential drawbacks of working for a family business. Qualitron was doing well; the Lin family's textile business was not (it was the time of the global oil crisis, and the textile industry was in difficulties). The Lin family decided to subsidise their ailing business with the profits from Qualitron. Shih was alarmed, but there was nothing he could do. Qualitron closed. Shih determined that any future businesses of his would be founded on stable financial management and would look after the interests of employees.

Together with colleagues from the Qualitron R&D department, in 1976 Shih founded Multitech, the company that would eventually become Acer. Shih's wife took on responsibility for the finances. The starting capital was US$25,000. Shih and his wife took a 50% share. The intention was always to focus on the microprocessor industry, although industrial design brought in some welcome initial revenue. When the two designers left, however, it crystallised Shih's approach. The remaining members convened a meeting and agreed on a number of defining principles: first, that decision making would be collective despite Shih's controlling interest; second, that the company would concentrate on R&D, brand name products, and international marketing. Shih took a 50% pay cut; his wife took a two-year pay freeze.

The company survived. Over the following few years, it established a name for itself as an innovative electronics company, not just in Taiwan but across the world. Within five years, Shih and his team had designed 40 applications based on microprocessors. Selling was difficult because the product was unfamiliar. For some reason, confused customers thought that Shih was in the low-tech garden machinery business. Salespeople called on Multitech trying to sell gardening books. Shih took the misunderstanding with good humour: he styled the company 'the gardeners of microprocessor machines' and published a monthly customer magazine entitled *Gardener's World*. The magazine was free. Its initial run was 2,000, but it eventually reached 20,000 copies a month, and was therefore quite costly. Nevertheless the publicity it received made it worth every dollar.

In the 1980s the company completed its transformation to a PC-focused corporation, and continued to cement its growing reputation worldwide with a number of firsts that extended into the 1990s. The company beat IBM to the post in 1986, producing a 32-bit based PC. Then, trading as Acer (following a 1988 IPO), the company created the world's first 386SX-33 chip set; led the way in developing recyclable cardboard packaging technology to replace polystyrene, and introduced the dual Pentium to the world in 1994.

As the 1990s drew to a close, it seemed as if Shih had achieved his aim of building a world-renowned IT brand. Microsoft and Intel conquered the PC world overtly by making their products synonymous with PCs. Stan Shih conquered the market more stealthily, but no less effectively, by supplying the components that make the guts of the PC. 'I am looking for Acer to be inside [every PC] just like Intel,' he said. 'Whether it's a CD-ROM, memory module or LCD panel, we'd like to see all computers, no matter what the brand name, have some Acer parts inside.' By 2000, Acer was ranked seventh in the world among PC manufacturers, with $8.5 billion of revenue and more than 120 separate businesses, employing 34,000 people around the world. It was the only non-Japanese Asian company in the top ten.

> *For some reason, confused customers thought that Shih was in the low-tech garden machinery business. Salespeople called on Multitech trying to sell gardening books.*

As Acer entered the new millennium, Shih started shaking up his company once again, just as he did 20 years previously when he refocused the business on the PC market. This time, the shift is away from PCs towards Internet services and software development. Part of the process involves splitting Acer into five independent units. He also repositioned the company as an 'Internet enabler'. To enhance the company's development and production capability, Acer invested $200 million in facilities in China. One of the first results of the company's new direction was the launch of the first multimedia handheld computer in 2002, followed closely by the introduction of a service business. It's a tough proposition, more difficult to accomplish with today's billion-dollar business than the small local Taiwanese company Shih transformed in the 1980s. But if anyone can manage it, it is Shih the eternal optimist—the man whose company culture rests on the principle that human nature is basically good. Shih has announced that he plans to retire in 2003.

CONTEXT AND CONCLUSIONS

Shih has done more than merely build a globally recognised IT company from a provincial Taiwanese business. He has inculcated a special kind of culture at Acer that reflects his belief in the goodness of human nature. The cynical may scoff, but

Shih's trust has been amply rewarded. He has fostered a culture where risk-taking is encouraged and costs incurred through employees' inexperience are written off as 'paying tuition'. The result is a 'tradition of integrity, open-mindedness, partnership, and ownership' that—combined with other elements such as a learning culture, innovation, and excellent customer service—has created a world-beating IT company.

CLOSE BUT NO CIGAR
KEN OLSEN
Olsen was once hailed by *Fortune* magazine as 'the most successful entrepreneur in the history of American business'. Founding Digital Equipment Corporation in 1959, he spent the next 35 years riding the IT rollercoaster at the helm of his company. The man who pioneered the minicomputer, Olsen was heavily influenced by the writings of Alfred Sloan and organised DEC along similar lines to General Motors under Sloan's control (small business units). Olsen left in 1992 to found Advanced Modular Solutions Inc. DEC was bought by Compaq in 1998.

THE BEST SOURCES OF HELP
Books:
Chen, Robert. *Made in Taiwan: The Story of Acer Computers*. Taipei: McGraw-Hill, 1997.
Shih, Stan. *Me-too Is Not My Style: Challenge Difficulties, Break Through Bottlenecks, Create Values*. Taiwan: Acer, 1997.

ALFRED SLOAN JR

1875	Born.
1899	Buys a controlling interest in Hyatt Roller Bearing Company.
1903	Hyatt makes profits of $60 million.
1916	Sloan becomes president of the United Motors Corporation.
1918	United Motors becomes part of General Motors.
1923	Sloan becomes president of General Motors.
1937	Steps down as president, but remains chairman and CEO.
1946	Steps down as CEO.
1956	Relinquishes position as chairman.
1966	Dies.

> **SUMMARY**
>
> Alfred Sloan Jr (1875–1966) was both a brilliant engineer and a forward-thinking manager. After transforming the fortunes of the Hyatt Roller Bearing Company, Sloan became president of the United Motors Corporation, which soon merged with General Motors. Sloan succeeded Pierre du Pont as president of General Motors in 1923.
>
> From this position Sloan created one of the most influential organisational designs of the 20th century. He restructured the company along divisional lines, with an executive committee sitting above the divisions. Sloan's design became the organisational blueprint for corporations for the next 50 years. Six years after Sloan took over the GM presidency, net sales were $1.5 billion and the stock price was up by 480%. During his tenure he consistently out-thought his main competitor, Ford, turning GM into the world's greatest automobile manufacturer.

LIFE AND CAREER

Alfred Pritchard Sloan Jr was born in New Haven, Connecticut, on 23 May 1875, the first of five children in a prosperous family. His father, an engineer by training, was an importer of coffee and tea, who later became a wholesale grocer.

At the age of ten Sloan moved with his family to Brooklyn, New York, where he studied at the Brooklyn Polytechnic Institute. Sloan wanted to go on to the Massachusetts Institute of Technology. Told he was too young, he persisted with his application and eventually took his place there to study electrical engineering. The youngest member of his class, he graduated in 1895 after just three years.

Having displayed a talent for engineering, Sloan went to work at the Hyatt Roller Bearing Company in Harrison, New Jersey. To his disappointment he was employed as a draftsman, salesman, tea boy, and general dogsbody. Sloan could see no future at the company, so he left to join a household refrigerator business. But he was not there long before he changed his mind and in 1899 returned to Hyatt. The firm was in financial difficulties and, with help from his father, Sloan bought a controlling interest.

The ambitious young man soon brought his influence to bear on his new company. Aged 24, Sloan became president of Hyatt and proposed that the company manufacture a new anti-friction bearing for automobiles. With this move to manufacturing products for the rapidly growing automobile market, Sloan forged a connection with the industry that would propel him to greatness.

Alfred Sloan Jr

CONTRIBUTION

Until Hyatt's production of the anti-friction bearing, the automobile industry had been using a well-greased axle. Immediately the Olds Motors Company, followed by Ford and the other automobile manufacturers, turned to Sloan and signed contracts for the new bearing. By 1903 Hyatt was making profits of $60 million.

As part of the drive to keep Hyatt's customers happy, Sloan organised a big party once a year. Known as 'frictionless feasts' in reference to the company's auto bearings, these events drew the great and the good from the automobile industry. Sloan would mingle with luminaries such as Henry Ford and the Dodge brothers as guests drank cocktails pumped from a 50-gallon container made to resemble a service-station oil drum.

> Sloan forged excellent contacts in the industry, particularly with Henry Leland, who became his mentor.

Sloan forged excellent contacts in the industry, particularly with Henry Leland, who became his mentor. Leland, one of the architects of manufacturing using interchangeable parts, had worked for Olds, Cadillac, and General Motors, and created the Lincoln car. Leland's watchword was quality—a mantra that rubbed off on Sloan.

Despite Sloan's apparent success at Hyatt (people would comment on the constant emergence of new buildings as they passed the plant on the Pennsylvania Railroad), he was still concerned about the company's future prospects. Its two largest customers were Ford and GM, and either of these giants, Sloan knew, could easily build a plant to manufacture bearings.

In 1916 Sloan sealed his own and Hyatt's future by securing a deal in which William Crapo Durant, who had just regained control of GM, took a financial interest in Hyatt. Hyatt merged with several other companies to become United Motors Corporation and Sloan became president of the new company. United Motors was in turn subsumed into GM in 1918, with Sloan becoming vice-president in charge of accessories and a member of GM's executive committee.

At GM Sloan worked closely with its founder, Durant. He admired Durant's tenacity while frequently disagreeing with his methods. By 1920 Sloan had risen to the position of vice-president. In the same year Durant was forced by his bankers to relinquish his position in the company and was succeeded as president by Pierre du Pont. In 1923 du Pont was succeeded by Sloan.

As company president Sloan set about reorganising GM. The organisational architecture he developed secured his place in business history. He structured the company into separate divisions. Under Durant's management GM cars had competed with each other in the market; Sloan ensured that each car and truck division had its own price and style categories. Each GM model was updated annually, offering greater choice to the consumer than Ford's mass-market Model T (famously available in any colour—'as long as it's black').

Soon companies under the GM umbrella, such as Buick, Cadillac, and Pontiac, were semi-autonomous, responsible for almost every aspect of their business. This mix of decentralisation and co-ordinated policy control left Sloan and the senior executives free to worry about GM corporate strategy, with the divisional managers running their divisions as they saw fit—providing, of course, they made a profit.

And make a profit they did. When Sloan took over GM's presidency, net sales were $698 million. Just six years later, net sales were $1.5 billion and the stock price was up by 480%. With Sloan's new organisational structure came a new type of employee, the professional manager. Sloan took management—until then conducted largely in an amateurish, entrepreneurial manner—and turned it into a serious professional discipline focusing on decision-making based on facts, particularly financial facts.

Sloan remained president of GM for 14 years, from 1923 until 1937, continuing as chairman until 1956. He ran the company quietly from behind the scenes, known by his workers as 'Silent Sloan' and preferring to trust in the ability of his managers. He also liked to get out of the office and visit his clients; he travelled the breadth of the country regularly.

Later in life Sloan made considerable philanthropic donations. He established the Alfred P. Sloan Foundation, to which he and his wife gave $305 million during his lifetime. Gifts from the foundation have benefited, among other institutions, the Sloan-Kettering Institute for Cancer Research in New York and Sloan's alma mater, MIT. Sloan died of a heart attack in 1966, aged 90.

As company president Sloan set about reorganising GM. The organisational architecture he developed secured his place in business history.

CONTEXT AND CONCLUSIONS

Alfred Sloan made his name by revolutionising the structure of the corporation and, in doing so, making General Motors the greatest automobile company in the world. Unlike his contemporaries Henry Ford and William Crapo Durant, Sloan was as comfortable with his management role as he was in the workshop. A prudent man who took measured risks, Sloan restructured GM along divisional lines and introduced rigorous financial controls. At the same time he created a new type of business executive—the professional manager. Sloan may justifiably be remembered for his contribution to the US automobile industry because of his work at General Motors. He should be remembered equally for his role in the evolution of management and corporate structure.

THE BEST SOURCES OF HELP
Book:
Sloan, Alfred P. Jr. *My Years with General Motors*. Reissue. New York: Doubleday, 1996.
Website:
General Motors: **www.gm.com**

MASAYOSHI SON

1957	Born.
1973	Travels to California to study English.
1981	Returns to Japan. Founds Softbank, using $80,000 from $1 million made by selling a patent to Sharp.
1992	570 employees, 15,000 dealer outlets, and revenues of $350 million a year.
1995	First major move in the US Internet market, buys shares in Yahoo!
1996	Investment pays off when Yahoo! goes public.
1999	Shifts attention to Japanese Internet stocks.
2000	Wealth falls by over $40 million. Softbank's value falls from $190 billion to $23 billion. Partnership with World Bank to fund Internet start-ups in developing countries. Buys Nippon Credit.
2001	Joins broadband alliance with Yahoo! and Sony.
2003	Announces sale of holdings in Yahoo! Japan.

> **SUMMARY**
>
> Through his company Softbank Corporation, Masayoshi Son took the Japanese keiretsu business model and applied it to Internet companies. It is too soon to know if the bold approach will work. But Son has already made a reputation in the business world that demands attention. Dubbed the 'Emperor of the Internet' by the media, his track record is proof that he is a talented, and highly persuasive, entrepreneur. A bright schoolboy, more interested in business than sports or other childish pastimes, Son demonstrated an early entrepreneurial flair. Arriving in California from Japan in 1973, he combined his studies at the University of California with inventing a personal organiser. Pocketing a tidy profit of $1 million from the sale of the patent, he developed a thriving video-games business before returning to Japan in 1981. His next company was the Softbank Corporation, which collected stakes in nascent dot-com companies like boys collect stamps. Shrugging off the effects of hepatitis, Son struck gold with his stake in Yahoo! In 1999 he shifted his attention to Japan, buying stakes in the lagging Japanese dot-com market. When the Internet revolution fizzled out, Son suffered but survived. A restructured Softbank, he argues, is well placed to take advantage of the post-recession e-commerce market.

LIFE AND CAREER

An ethnic Korean, Son was born on 11 August 1957, in Tosu, Japan. He was brought up on Kyushu, where his father ran a small business. Accepted at a prestigious school in Fukuoka, Son showed an early interest in business. While other children idolised musicians or sports stars, his hero was Den Fujita, the man who made McDonalds a success in Japan. He was star-struck enough to telephone Fujita's office and arrange to meet him in Tokyo. The meeting fired up Son's interest in the United States, and in 1973 he headed for California to study English.

In California Son soon mastered English and before long was studying at the University of California with economics as his major. His obsessional nature was already apparent. Some teenagers have pictures up on their bedroom walls: pop stars, sports personalities, pets, family, and friends. Son was different. Aged 19, he saw a picture in a magazine that captivated him. He didn't know it, but it was to change his life. He cut the picture out, covered it in a see-through plastic wrapper, and put it in his bag, carrying it wherever he went. He even slept with it. The picture that captured the imagination of this economics undergraduate was of a microchip.

CONTRIBUTION

While still at university, Son decided that the way to make money was to invent something. And the way to invent something, he decided, was to come up with a new idea everyday. One of these ideas was for a personal organiser. The electronics giant Sharp bought the patent to the organiser (which became the Sharp Wizard) for $1 million. Son's ambitions to earn a living by inventing had paid off sooner than he might have expected.

Son took the cash and moved on to his next venture: importing cheap video-game machines from Japan—Space Invaders. At the time, video games had yet to catch on in the United States. Once again Son predicted a consumer trend. Within six months he had imported 300 machines, making his company the top games vendor in the area. He then handed the business to a colleague and, fulfilling a promise to his mother, returned to Japan.

In 1981, using $80,000 of his own money and funds raised from the Japanese bank Dai-Ichi Kangyo, the 23-year-old Son started a software distribution company called Softbank. It was testimony to his powers of persuasion that, at such a young age and in an economic environment relatively hostile to young entrepreneurs, he managed to talk the Japanese banks into financing the business. The company soon ballooned into a huge computer services giant. After ten years Son had 570 employees, 15,000 dealer outlets, six divisions, five subsidiaries, five joint ventures—and revenues of $350 million a year.

While other children idolised musicians or sports stars, his hero was Den Fujita, the man who made McDonalds a success in Japan.

Son demonstrated his inventive thinking with the acquisition of Japanese citizenship. The authorities refused to grant citizenship under a Korean name. Son had his Japanese wife change her name legally to Son. He then pointed out to the authorities that Son was listed as a Japanese citizen's name, and he was permitted by the naturalisation service to keep it.

The early days at Softbank were difficult times for Son. Shortly after he founded the company, he became critically ill with hepatitis. The illness dogged him for many years, but once he had shaken off the initial effects he rediscovered his characteristic enthusiasm for business. It was 1994, and a new communications phenomenon was just taking off: the Internet. Just as Son had understood how the microchip would change the business world, he recognised that the Internet would have a profound impact on people's lives. At that time global e-commerce revenues were still well below $500 million.

Back in the United States again, Son backed his instinct with a portfolio of investments in nascent Internet companies such as buy.com, E*Trade, E-LOAN, and Webvan. These included a 30% stake in an Internet company called Yahoo!, for which he paid $100 million. By luck or judgment Son had hit the Internet jackpot. Yahoo!, the Internet index and portal, went public in 1996.

Ditching some of the companies Softbank had acquired in its pre-Internet existence, Son focused his activities on the Web. Ex-Cisco and Intel man Gary Rieschel was hired to run a new venture capital arm of Softbank, Softbank Technology. The limited partnership fund was run from San Jose, California. The firm raised $170 million from Japan for its first fund—$60 million came from Softbank.

Towards the end of 1999 Son shifted his attention to Japan. For Softbank's assault on the Japanese market, Son adopted a different approach from the one he had used in the United States. He created a vertical Internet giant by taking majority stakes in companies and building others from the ground up. With e-business in Japan lagging behind the United States, Son exploited the opportunity to claim a substantial slice of the Japanese Internet industry. The key to Son's plan was the acquisition of a majority stake in Yahoo! Japan. He hoped to steer virtual consumers through the Yahoo! portal to other businesses owned partly or wholly by Softbank, among them the Japanese incarnations of E*Trade, GeoCities, Broadcast.com, CarPoint, and E-shopping Toys.

Such a large investment in the Internet meant that Son's and Softbank's fortunes were closely tied up with those of NASDAQ. The turn of the millennium was the beginning of a roller-coaster ride for Softbank investors. Son's personal fortune also took a pounding. When the market plunged early in 2000, Son saw his own wealth fall by over $40 million. By the end of the year Softbank's value had fallen from $190 billion to $23 billion. But that did not deter him. During 2000 he bought Nippon Credit to give Softbank a vehicle for offering financial services on the Internet. In the same year, he established a partnership with the World Bank to fund Internet start-ups in more than 100 developing countries. Broadband was a major focus in 2001, with Cisco investing $200 million in Softbank to fund broadband wireless projects and an alliance with Sony and Yahoo! Japan to develop broadband in Japan. 2003 saw a break with the past as Softbank announced that it was divesting all of its holdings in Yahoo! Japan. The final verdict on Son's audacious empire-building ambitions has yet to be written. The dot-com bubble may have burst, but e-commerce is still growing and has a significant part to play in the world economy. Son's challenge is to restructure and steer Softbank through the recession. In 1997 Son was asked about a target he set himself of building a $10 billion company. Ever ambitious, Son replied: 'The number is not a goal, just a measure, only a milestone. I'm now developing a 300-year plan.' Clearly Son aims to be in business for a while yet.

CONTEXT AND CONCLUSIONS
Few people who saw the Internet in its infancy could have predicted how huge a phenomenon it would become. Masayoshi Son was one of the few. While others stood on the sidelines arguing for caution, Son, founder, president, and CEO of Softbank Corp, was putting his money where his vision was. A born trend spotter, he anticipated the growth of personal organisers and video games. His approach to the Internet was no different. What had changed was the size of his investments. Some of the companies he invested in, such as Webvan, no longer exist, but the successes such as Yahoo! have so far outweighed the failures. Softbank may yet, however, crash as a result of the dot-com implosion; Masayoshi Son's final place in business history remains to be seen.

CLOSE BUT NO CIGAR
DAVID WETHERELL

After a leveraged buy-out of CMG (College Marketing Group), Wetherell renamed the company CMG Information Services and took it public in 1994. He then built a diverse network of Internet companies, where synergies between group companies boosted profits. It worked fine until the dot-com meltdown, when lack of investor confidence brought the stock price crashing down and cash burn threatened to bring the company to its knees.

THE BEST SOURCES OF HELP
Website:
Softbank: **www.softbank.com**

LEVI STRAUSS

1829	Born.
1847	Sails to join half-brothers in the United States with sisters and mother.
1853	Becomes US citizen, and sails to San Francisco.
1866	Levi Strauss makes its headquarters at 14–16 Battery Street.
1872	Jacob Davis writes to Levi Strauss, tells him about riveting process.
1873	Levi Strauss and Jacob Davis awarded patent for rivets on men's trousers; they begin manufacturing of copper-riveted 'waist overalls'.
1890	Levi Strauss & Co incorporated. Number 501 used for identification.
1902	Dies.

> **SUMMARY**
>
> Born in Bavaria, Germany, Levi Strauss emigrated to the United States in 1847. He stopped long enough in New York to study his brother's dry-goods business and learn to speak English. Then he joined the crowds heading west to the California gold rush. Strauss didn't do any digging though. Opening a dry-goods wholesalers, he got his customers to dig into their pockets to buy his newfangled riveted 'waist overalls', the toughest trousers in the West. So popular was the new style of jeans that Strauss was known as the 'cowboys' tailor'. By the time of his death in 1902, jeans had made Strauss $6 million, a considerable amount more than most prospectors ever achieved.

LIFE AND CAREER

Levi Strauss was not born in Nimes, France (from which denim—'of Nimes'—derives its name) but in Buttenheim, Bavaria, on 26 February 1829, one of seven siblings. Strauss's father died of tuberculosis in 1845, and two years later the Strauss family were in New York. Two of Levi's brothers, Jonas and Louis, had already made the journey and set up J. Strauss Brothers & Co, a dry-goods business where Levi worked. (Levi was christened Loeb, but in the 1850 census he is listed as Levy.)

In 1853 Strauss, now a US citizen, headed for the West Coast to share in the prosperity generated by the California gold rush. He planned to make his fortune not from panning gold, but from selling provisions to the prospectors. He took the boat around the Cape of Good Hope. When he set out he carried cloth, silk, some luxury goods, and a roll of canvas, all donated by his brothers. When he arrived in San Francisco, he had sold them all bar the canvas.

CONTRIBUTION

When Strauss arrived in San Francisco, so the story goes, a dishevelled miner approached him demanding to know if he had any trousers to sell. The rough terrain of the mines wore hard on the miners' trousers; they were a valuable commodity. Strauss, spotting an opportunity, replied that although he hadn't brought any trousers to sell, he could make a pair from the leftover canvas. He did, the miner was happy, and so Strauss started in the trousers business. It's a nice story but, although often recounted, probably not true.

What is known is that, more mundanely, Strauss set up a San Francisco branch of the family dry-goods business, opening first at 90 Sacramento Street under the name 'Levi Strauss'. The waterfront location was convenient for receiving goods delivered by boat from his brothers' business in New York.

Through the 1850s and 1860s Strauss expanded his business and moved addresses several times, each time to larger premises, finally coming to rest at 14–16 Battery Street. During this period the company was renamed Levi Strauss & Co (1863). The premises at Battery Street were a grand affair, complete with a lift and gas chandeliers, still a relative rarity at that time. As the dry-goods business expanded, Strauss slowly became a recognised and respected figure. He played an active role in the city's Jewish community and belonged to San Francisco's first synagogue, the Temple Emanu-El.

Enter Alkali Ike, a rough, tough prospector who worked the Comstock Lode mines in Nevada. The Comstock Lode was one of the greatest single mineral strikes in history, containing predominately silver deposits rather than gold. The citizens of the West swarmed to mine in the Washoe region of Nevada, hoping to get rich, and mining towns sprang up everywhere. The new metropolis of Virginia City, with 20,000 inhabitants, became the second largest city in the West. There, among the teeming transient population digging out their claims, sweated Alkali Ike, a man who suffered from pocket trouble.

> *When the riveted 'waist overalls' first appeared on the market, Strauss was convinced that these new garments would be very successful. He was right. They became so popular through the Southwest that he was known as the 'cowboys' tailor'.*

Ike was sick of his pockets giving way under the weight of the valuable nuggets he carried in them. It was a common problem. 'Nothing looks more slouchy in a workman than to see his pockets ripped open and hanging down, and no other part of the clothing is so apt to be torn and ripped as the pockets,' commented the *Pacific Rural Press* of 28 June 1873. Ike complained bitterly to his local tailor, Jacob Davis, and insisted he find a solution. Davis, with a flash of inspiration, thought of riveting the material together with copper wire. A few weeks later Ike was back, this time not to complain but to thank his tailor for solving the problem.

Davis, who regularly bought material in bulk from Strauss in San Francisco, wrote to Strauss telling him of the popularity of this new design feature. Davis couldn't afford the patent fee of $68. He suggested that Strauss should help him safeguard his new discovery. Together they filed for a patent, which was granted on 20 May 1873. The day is now considered the birthday of the firm Levi Strauss & Co. The new Strauss jeans sold for 22 cents a pair.

When the riveted 'waist overalls' first appeared on the market, Strauss was convinced that these new garments would be very successful. He was right. They became so popular through the Southwest that he was known as the 'cowboys' tailor'. He brought Davis to San Francisco from Nevada to supervise the cutting and production. As demand increased, production was scaled up and factories on Fremont and Market Streets were opened. Encouraged by the popularity of the waist overalls and denim, Strauss expanded his product line to include blanket-lined trousers and coats. To maintain the quality of the product, Strauss purchased the Mission and Pacific Woollen Mills in 1875.

Levi Strauss & Co was incorporated in 1890, the same year that the number 501 was used to identify the denim waist overalls. Strauss by then had handed over the day-to-day running of his business to his nephews, Jacob, Sigmund, Louis, and Abraham. Much of Strauss's later life was dominated by philanthropic and other work in the community. He was a member of various organisations, including the San Francisco Board of Trade, the Hebrew Board of Relief, the San Francisco Gas and Electric Company, and the Liverpool, London and Globe Insurance Company. He died in 1902, leaving close to $6 million in his estate.

CONTEXT AND CONCLUSIONS

Levi Strauss was a clever man. Instead of risking anguish and heartbreak by joining the masses on the gold and silver strikes of the West, he found a more certain route to riches. Miners wore trousers; miners worked over rough terrain; miners' trousers wore out quickly; *ergo* miners needed stronger trousers. The problem was how to make them stronger. Luck was with Strauss when Davis offered him the solution. But luck had little to do with Strauss's thorough exploitation of the new clothing technology. Continually refining his 'waist overalls', he produced a clothing item that became a national icon—19th-century Levi jeans can be worth up to $100,000. Like Hershey bars and Coca-Cola, Levis are synonymous with American style and culture, and the word 'jeans' is synonymous with Levis.

> *Continually refining his 'waist overalls', he produced a clothing item that became a national icon—19th-century Levi jeans can be worth up to $100,000.*

CLOSE BUT NO CIGAR
JOHN BARBOUR

In many ways the British equivalent of Levi Strauss, John Barbour left his family farm in Galloway, southwest Scotland, for South Shields, at the age of 20. There, from 1870, he worked as a travelling draper. He started his own firm, J. Barbour and Sons, supplying oilskins and other waterproofs to the sailors, fishermen, rivermen, and dockers who worked in the unpredictable North Sea weather. Before long his business had become an international one, supplying countries across the world via his mail-order catalogue. He died in 1918. Today the Barbour jacket has taken on an iconic status in the United Kingdom.

THE BEST SOURCES OF HELP
Book:
Finlayson, Iain. *Denim. An American Legend.* London: Simon and Schuster, 1990.

EIJI TOYODA

1913	Born.
1933	Cousin starts automobile production.
1936	Toyoda joins the firm, which is renamed Toyota.
1950	Toyoda visits Ford River Rouge plant in Dearborn, Michigan.
1955	Crown model successful in Japan but not in United States.
1967	Becomes president of Toyota.
1968	Successfully launches Corolla in United States.
1975	Toyota replaces Volkswagen as number one imported car in United States.
1989	Launches luxury Lexus model.
1994	Resigns.

> **SUMMARY**
>
> If Eiji Toyoda hadn't joined his family business, the Toyota name might have been associated with the textile industry rather than with automobiles.
>
> Toyoda helped to grow a thriving automobile business from a loom manufacturing company. He joined the company in 1936 and was responsible for recruiting the best research engineers and organising production. Toyota's breakthrough came when Toyoda visited Ford's Rouge automobile plant in the 1950s. It was a revelation for him. He returned to Japan determined to combine the best of US manufacturing processes with his own innovative approach to production. The result was the Toyota Production System. Successful models—from the Corolla right through to the introduction of the Lexus—paved the way for the company's global success.

LIFE AND CAREER

It is no surprise that Eiji Toyoda grew up to be an industrialist. Born on 12 September 1913, Toyoda spent much of his childhood in and around his father's textile mill near Nagoya. From his earliest years he was surrounded by both business and heavy machinery.

The driving force behind the textile business was Toyoda's uncle, Rashomon Sakichi Toyoda. Sakichi was a carpenter by trade and an inventor by nature. In 1929 the British company Platt Brothers paid Sakichi £100,000 for the rights to a textile loom he had invented. Sakichi put the money to one side to invest in automobile production.

Given the nature of the family business, Eiji Toyoda's choice of an engineering degree was a natural one. He started his studies at Tokyo Imperial University in 1933. While Toyoda was taking his degree his cousin Kiichiro, Sakichi's eldest son,

> *The driving force behind the textile business was Toyoda's uncle, Rashomon Sakichi Toyoda. Sakichi was a carpenter by trade and an inventor by nature.*

was setting up an automobile plant at the Toyoda Automatic Loom Works. In 1936, his degree completed, Toyoda joined his cousin in the plant. In that year the company changed its name from Toyoda Automatic Loom Works to Toyota.

CONTRIBUTION

Toyoda's first assignment was to organise the company's research facility, hiring talented scientists and engineers to work on research and development. Next he worked on the shop floor in production planning.

At that time Toyota was producing a car designed to be built with parts from the US General Motors model Chevrolet. Toyota's first cars rolled off the production line in 1936. The timing was unfortunate: the advent of the Second World War and Japan's entry into the war in December 1941 meant that Toyota's production expertise had to be redirected towards the manufacture of trucks for the war effort.

After the war Eiji Toyoda made plans to set up a chinaware business. Kiichiro Toyoda was diversifying the company, expecting the occupying forces to place limitations on the automobile business. Instead, as Japan underwent a period of reconstruction, the Toyota car plant was called upon to build vehicles to help get the country moving again.

Despite the boost in production, trading conditions were still extremely tough; Toyota was driven to the brink of bankruptcy. The company was saved only by dramatic cuts in the workforce, which Toyoda had the painful task of enforcing. He also created a new company, Toyota Motor Sales, to help ease cash-flow problems and satisfy his bankers' concerns.

It wasn't until the 1950s that Toyota firmly established itself as a major car manufacturer. The breakthrough came when Toyoda visited Ford's immense River Rouge plant at Dearborn, Michigan. Toyota had by then been in the car business for 13 years and had produced just over 2,500 automobiles. The River Rouge plant turned out a staggering 8,000 vehicles a day. Impressed with the scale of US automobile production, Toyoda realised that if he could combine the best of US and Japanese production methods, Toyota could be a world-beater.

With the help of his production guru Taichi Ohno, Toyoda established the Toyota Production System (TPS), also known as 'lean production'. It was a revolutionary approach to manufacturing, comprising three main elements. The first is just-in-time production. There is no point in producing cars simply hoping that customers will buy them. Waste (Japanese *muda*) is bad; therefore production must be linked to the market's requirements. Second, responsibility for quality rests with everyone, and any quality defect needs to be rectified as soon as it is identified. The third element is the 'value stream': instead of seeing the company as a series of unrelated products and processes, it should be seen as a continuous and uniform whole—a stream that includes suppliers as well as customers.

Toyota's first full-scale production car, the Crown, proved a somewhat shaky start. Driven off the production line by Eiji Toyoda—dressed in a dinner jacket—on new year's day, 1955, the Crown was a success in Japan, but it failed to make any impression on the US market when it was introduced in 1957. Designed for Japanese roads, it was slow and prone to overheating—problems that made it ill-suited to US highways.

Persistence eventually paid off and by the 1960s Toyota cars were a hit, with the Corona and Corolla both selling well. The success of the Corolla in 1968 enabled the company to make a big leap forward, and by 1975 Toyota had replaced Volkswagen as the number one imported car in the United States. In 1984 the company entered a joint venture with General Motors to build Toyota vehicles in the United States. Along the way Toyota established an unrivalled reputation for build quality. But it was the Toyota Lexus that finally secured the company's reputation in the United States.

The Lexus was a personal triumph for Toyoda. In August 1983 he had convened a top-secret meeting inside the company, asking those present, 'Can we create a luxury car to challenge the very best?' The answer was a resounding yes.

In the luxury car market Toyota faced competition from a range of established brands, including Mercedes and BMW. Undaunted by the scale of the task, Toyota created a new brand, the Lexus, to create psychological distance from the other Toyota value-for-money models. Toyoda neutralised any concerns over the reliability and quality of the Lexus by insisting that the company should out-engineer Mercedes and BMW. The eventual result was the Lexus LS400. It took seven years, $2 billion, 1,400 engineers, 2,300 technicians, and 450 prototypes—and generated 200 patents. The Lexus was tested in Japan on miles of carefully built highways that exactly imitated roads in the United States, Germany, and the United Kingdom. Toyota even reproduced foreign road signs.

Toyota is now the dominant car manufacturer in Japan and the third biggest car maker in the world (behind General Motors and Ford). It now sells approaching 1.5 million cars in the United States every year. Toyoda stepped down as president in 1994.

CONTEXT AND CONCLUSIONS
Eiji Toyoda didn't found the Toyota Motor Corporation, but he did help make it a world-beater.

After an inauspicious attempt to crack the US market with the Crown, Toyoda was quick to admit that Toyota would need an extra competitive edge to compete with the likes of Ford and General Motors. It was no good trying to compete on price alone—instead Toyoda concentrated on efficiency and quality.

He employed the inventive Taichi Ohno to help develop a new production system that came to be known as the Toyota Production System. Through quality and reliability, Toyoda took on the great US automobile manufacturers and emerged victorious. And if imitation is the sincerest form of flattery, the modest Toyoda must be embarrassed by the number of US firms that have tried to adopt Toyota's production methods.

THE BEST SOURCES OF HELP
Books:
Braddon, Russell. *The Other 100 Years War: Japan's Bid for Supremacy 1941–2041*. London: Collins, 1983.
Toyoda, Eiji. *Toyota: Fifty Years in Motion*. Tokyo: Kodansha International, 1987.
Website:
Toyota GB: **www.toyota.co.uk**

TED TURNER

1938	Born.
1970	Acquires the UHF station, Channel 17.
1976	Channel 17 goes nationwide. Transmits across the United States via satellite. Buys the major-league baseball team, the Atlanta Braves.
1977	Wins America's Cup with his yacht *Courageous*.
1980	Cable News Network launched.
1986	Acquires MGM Entertainment Company.
1991	*Time* magazine's 'Man of the Year'.
1994	Turner Broadcasting Systems merges with New Line Cinema.
1996	Turner Broadcasting Systems merges with Time Warner.
2001	Time Warner merger with AOL approved. Loses control of Turner Broadcasting.
2002	AOL Time Warner posts $100 million loss.
2003	Turner Foundation loses value and declines current fund requests. Resigns chairmanship of AOL Time Warner.

> **SUMMARY**
>
> Robert Edward Turner III started in business in unfortunate circumstances after his father's suicide. Showing considerable resilience, he went on to improve on his father's business and, ultimately, to help create the biggest entertainment and media company in the world: AOL Time Warner. Turner became president and chief operating officer of the Turner Advertising Company in 1963 and set out on a trail of acquisitions and channel launches. A UHF station, professional sports teams, Headline News, TNT, The Cartoon Network, Turner Classic Movies, New Line Cinema; all these and many more came under Turner's control as he built his company—the Turner Broadcasting System—into a media giant. Turner is probably best known for the creation of the news station Cable News Network, CNN, in June 1980, and the part he played in the formation of AOL Time Warner in 2000/2001.

LIFE AND CAREER

Robert Edward (Ted) Turner III was born in Cincinnati, Ohio, in 1938. His chequered school career was notable for eccentric and unconventional behaviour rather than academic excellence. At McCallie, an exclusive school for boys in Chattanooga, Tennessee, he was an unruly pupil who showed a peculiar penchant for taxidermy and for catching squirrels in pillowcases. McCallie's method of punishing offenders was to issue demerits. Each demerit required the recipient to walk a quarter of a mile. Turner earned over 1,000 demerits in his first year, farther than any pupil could walk in the time available. The school was forced to reinvent its disciplinary methods especially for him.

At Brown University Turner continued to challenge authority. Eventually, having been caught with a woman in his room, he was asked to leave but not before he had made a name for himself on the university sailing team. Sailing was to remain an abiding passion and he later won the America's Cup in 1977 with his yacht *Courageous*.

After university Turner returned home to work in his father's advertising billboard business. His father made him manager of the firm's operation in Macon, Georgia. Turner married and settled down to a tough schedule, working 15 hours a day for six and a half days each week. Like his father, he was a natural salesman making fast progress in the business.

Turner's often difficult relationship with his father came to a shocking end in March 1963 when he was just 24. His father, under severe pressure at work, took a silver .38 revolver and shot himself in the head. In these terrible circumstances Turner became president and chief operating officer of the Turner Advertising Company.

CONTRIBUTION

Turner expanded the company into television with an audacious move to acquire the UHF station Channel 17 in 1970. At the time Channel 17 was the worst placed of the major television channels in Atlanta. Turner engineered a deal that involved taking Turner Advertising public, acquiring the assets of Channel 17, and forming a new company, Turner Communications. Determined to lift the station's fortunes, he changed the programming schedule and fed the viewers a diet of reruns—classic shows and black and white movies. It worked. Bemused critics could only watch as the viewing figures shot up and the advertising revenue flooded in. In 1976 the station went nationwide, transmitting to cable systems across the United States via satellite: it was the start of the 'superstation concept'.

> *CNN was a hit. It brought news, like the Reagan assassination attempt, to viewers as events unfurled. It revolutionised the news industry.*

Turner continued to diversify and expand, and not always into obvious areas. In 1976 he bought a major league baseball team, the Atlanta Braves, and in 1977 the Atlanta Hawks of the National Basketball Association. Once again he was ahead of the game. His instincts told him that televised sport would attract a big audience.

In 1980 Turner used the profits from Turner Broadcasting System to launch CNN (Cable News Network). The critics were scathing, predicting inevitable failure for the twenty-four-hour all-news network. But once again Turner proved that, despite his often dogmatic approach, when it came to business he knew best. 'I am the right man in the right place at the right time,' he said. 'Not me alone, but all the people who think the world can be brought together by telecommunications.'

CNN was a hit. It brought news, like the Reagan assassination attempt, to viewers as events unfurled. It revolutionised the news industry. CNN cemented its reputation with its coverage of the Gulf War when, for the first time, a TV audience could watch a war in real time, from the comfort of their armchairs.

Turner continued to collect television stations: Headline News (1982), CNN International (1985), TNT (1988), SportsSouth (1990), The Cartoon Network (1992), Turner Classic Movies (1994), CNNfn (1995), and CNN SI (1997) were all added to the network. Shortly after Castle Rock Entertainment joined Turner Broadcasting in 1993, Turner merged TBS with New Line Cinema.

Not everything Turner touched turned to gold. Keen to purchase a film studio, he made a bid for CBS. The hostile takeover bid failed. Another Turner idea, the 'Checkout Channel', providing in-store news and information, proved a disappointment. Turner also paid $1.6 billion for the MGM film library, a sum many commentators considered too generous.

In 1996 he completed the biggest deal of his career to date, when he merged TBS with Time Warner. Holding 10% of Time Warner, Turner had the largest single shareholding. It was an astute move, leaving him well positioned to profit from the development of a new communication phenomenon: the Internet. He assumed the role of vice-chair in the new organisation, taking responsibility for Time Warner's Cable Networks division, which included the assets of Turner Broadcasting System, Inc. (TBS Inc.), Home Box Office, Cinemax, and Time Warner's interests in Comedy Central and Court TV. He was also responsible for New Line Cinema and the company's professional sports teams.

In 2001 Turner was involved in one of the biggest mergers of the post-war period when AOL merged with Time Warner to create the largest entertainment conglomerate in the world. Time Warner's shareholders received 45% of the new company to AOL's 55%. Turner became vice-chair and senior adviser of AOL Time Warner.

It proved an ill-fated move. Almost immediately Turner found himself side-lined and he lost control of Turner Broadcasting, the company he had built. In a bad year, his marriage to Jane Fonda ended and he lost his World Wrestling Championship, along with its star Hulk Hogan, to long-time rival World Wrestling Federation. Worse was to follow in 2002 as AOL Time Warner posted a record loss of $100 billion. In 2003, he resigned his chairmanship. The loss also hit the Turner Foundation badly since much of its value derived from AOL Time Warner investments. In 1997, the foundation hit the headlines when it made a $1 billion donation to the UN for humanitarian projects. In sharp contrast, 2003 saw the foundation unable to meet any funding requests.

CONTEXT AND CONCLUSIONS

Turner's career is distinguished by relentless drive, an uncanny ability to predict consumer demand, and a supreme confidence in his own vision. Competitiveness and drive are evident in his sailing achievements, too. He could have made a good living as an international yachtsman. Probably the best illustration of Turner's qualities, though, is the founding of CNN. Critics derided the idea of a nonstop news network. Turner thought differently and pursued his vision doggedly. He was right, the critics were wrong, and CNN's coverage of the Gulf War has become part of media folklore. Turner may make an occasional bad call, but more often than not his instincts have proved successful. It is this quality of vision, and having the guts to execute it, that has made him one of the world's great media magnates.

THE BEST SOURCES OF HELP
Book:
Bibb, Porter. *It Ain't As Easy As It Looks: Ted Turner's Amazing Story*. New York: Crown Publishers, 1993.
Website:
CNN Europe: **www.europe.cnn.com**

THEODORE NEWTON VAIL

1845	Born.
1878	Joins Bell Telephone Co.
1882	Secures control of Western Electric Co.
1885	Incorporation of American Telephone & Telegraph Company.
1887	Resigns as president of AT&T, buys a 200-acre farm in Vermont.
1907	Recalled as president of AT&T.
1910	Buys control of Western Union Telegraph Company for $30 million.
1913	Forced by Justice Department to dispose of Western Union stock.
1919	Retires from AT&T.
1921	Dies.

> **SUMMARY**
>
> Most individuals would be happy with one successful career. The US serial entrepreneur Theodore Newton Vail (1845–1921) enjoyed several. First Vail worked for the US government reforming the postal delivery system. The next chapter of his working life was spent setting up and expanding the American Bell Telegraph Company. Vail exemplifies the truth that behind every successful great inventor is a business innovator capable of building an enterprise from scratch. Finally, after retiring to a tranquil life on his farm in Vermont, the 62-year-old Vail was persuaded to come out of retirement to save the American Telephone & Telegraph company.

LIFE AND CAREER

Theodore Newton Vail was born in 1845 in Carroll County, Ohio, where his father, who was from a Quaker family, and his Dutch mother had temporarily settled. Two years later the family returned to New Jersey. They remained there until 1866 when they moved to a farm in Iowa.

Unhappy with farming life and restless for adventure, the young Vail headed west, landing a job as an operator in a Union Pacific boxcar. Telegraphy was in the Vail genes. His uncle Alfred had helped finance F.S.B. Morse in the development of the telegraph.

Before long the restless Vail moved out of the boxcar and into the railway mail delivery service. It was here that his talents began to shine. The railway mail service was a shambles with no sorting system in the trains, no routing for letters other than to the major cities, and no systemised train connections. Vail set about sorting out the mess. He pored over railway timetables and train connections, calculating the quickest routes. The result was a railway mail guide for the efficient transport of mail in the region.

CONTRIBUTION

Eventually Vail's endeavours came to the attention of the US government, and he was summoned to Washington. If he could reform local mail deliveries, the government reasoned, then why not the entire country's? Vail set about the task and swiftly rose from assistant superintendent of the mail service to general superintendent. It was a difficult task, not least because he was up against the vested interests of the railway companies. Rescheduling the entire country's delivery service cut into the revenues of some of them. Vail, however, resisted their lobbying and carried the day.

It was his indomitable nature that brought him to the attention of Gardiner Hubbard, the father-in-law of Alexander Graham Bell, inventor of a contraption that had been exhibited at the Centennial Exposition in Philadelphia, much to the amusement of visitors. The invention was the telephone. When they proposed creating a commercial enterprise founded on the telephone, Bell and Hubbard were ridiculed. The Times called it 'the latest American humbug'. Hubbard needed a man with a forceful personality and uncompromising drive to build a viable company to exploit the telephone. Vail was that man. He had the vision to see how the telephone could revolutionise communications not only on a regional, but also on a national level.

In 1878 Vail accepted the position of general manager at the newly founded American Bell Telephone Company.

In 1878 Vail accepted the position of general manager at the newly founded American Bell Telephone Company. 'I gave up a $3,500 salary for no salary,' he remarked at the time. His salary at Bell was ostensibly $5,000, but he rarely collected it. Instead he devoted his entire energy and passion to rolling out the telephone nationwide. In 1882 he oversaw the purchase of the Western Electric Co of Chicago, one of the premier manufacturers of telephone equipment. In 1885 the group of companies Vail presided over was incorporated as AT&T (the American Telephone and Telegraph Company). Despite attempts from competitors Western Union to seduce him away from Bell, Vail stuck to his post. He stayed with Bell until it was sufficiently well established to secure enough capital to expand across the country, city by city. When in 1887 that moment arrived, he bought himself a 200-acre farm in Vermont.

Before retiring to his farm, the nomadic Vail toured South America, replaced the horse-drawn trams in Buenos Aires with electric ones, opened offices in London, spent time in France and Italy, and installed electric lighting and telephone systems in numerous other cities. Finally, his wanderlust apparently sated, he became a farmer. The farm was rapidly expanded to 6,000 acres as Vail set about farming with the same intensity that he applied to his earlier careers. No comfortable slippers and armchair for him.

Little did Vail realise that, though he was retired and past 60, some of his greatest achievements still lay ahead. In 1907 confidence in big business plummeted. Companies had overextended themselves. Banks withdrew credit, capital dried up, stocks withered, and new share issues failed. Amid the economic turmoil dark clouds were gathering over AT&T. Its competitors had muddied the company's waters to the extent that the Federal Government was being urged to bust the 'telephone trust'. So, cap in hand, the directors of AT&T arrived at Vail's Lyndon ranch in Vermont and pleaded with him to help save the company. He said yes.

Using the considerable business acumen that he had acquired over the years, Vail swiftly raised $21 million of new capital, followed by a quarter of a billion over the next six years. He attacked the critics of the 'telephone trust' head on by buying up competitors and consolidating telephone networks under the AT&T umbrella. At the same time he campaigned under the slogan 'One system, One policy, Universal

Service' to persuade the public that a single telephone service was the best way. And to placate the government, he acceded to regulatory supervision. It was a masterful performance. Vail saw off the financial crisis of October–November 1907 and AT&T emerged as the unquestioned dominant force in telephony. Vail also earned the loyalty of the workforce by increasing pension, sickness, and accident benefits.

A man of vision, Vail was still pursuing new ventures into his 70s. In 1910 he bought control of the Western Union Telegraph Company for $30 million. His intention was to bring people closer together with the 'tel-letter'—mail delivered over the wire at a nominal cost. Unfortunately for Vail, the Department of Justice stepped in to break up the telegraph–telephone combine and Vail was forced to sell Western Union and agree that AT&T would not buy any more independents, thus scuppering his plans for the tel-letter.

> *Little did Vail realise that, though he was retired and past 60, some of his greatest achievements still lay ahead.*

CONTEXT AND CONCLUSIONS

Vail was one of a generation of entrepreneurs who helped change the face of the United States and the world at the turn of the 20th century. It was the era of the electrical revolution. The pioneering spirit of men such as Vail sparked the transformation from the steam age to the electrical age. A serial entrepreneur, the crowning glory of his achievements survives to this day: AT&T is one of the oldest companies quoted on the New York Stock Exchange.

When asked how he managed to achieve so much in one lifetime Vail answered: 'By never being unwilling when young to do another man's work, and then, when older, by never doing anything somebody else could do better for me.'

THE BEST SOURCES OF HELP
Website:
AT&T: **www.att.com**

CORNELIUS VANDERBILT

1794	Born.
1810	Mother gives him $100 to clear and plant eight-acre field. He buys a boat with the proceeds.
1812	US war with England.
1817	Robert Fulton and Robert Livingston introduce steamboats.
1829	Uses savings to start a steamboat business.
1851	Forms the Accessory Transit Company.
1863	Has amassed a fortune of $40 million. Switches focus to railways.
1869	Merges the Hudson River Railroad with the New York Central system.
1877	Dies.

SUMMARY

Cornelius 'Commodore' Vanderbilt is one of America's greatest-ever businessmen. Applying the principles of economy, competition, and innovation, Vanderbilt expanded from a small-time ferry operator to a shipping and railway magnate. In his lifetime Vanderbilt amassed fabulous wealth—some $105 million. Yet he did so by genuinely improving the lot of people. Wherever Vanderbilt opened for business, the prices came down and the services improved. He risked arrest to crack state-subsidised monopolies by running competing services illegally. By eradicating state monopolies, Vanderbilt increased the incentive to invest in improving technology to provide a competitive advantage. It was a classic case of how capitalism and competition can deliver a better deal for the consumer, and benefit a nation's economy.

LIFE AND CAREER

Cornelius Vanderbilt was born on 27 May 1794 on Staten Island, New York. His father was a farmer who sold produce in the markets of New York, sailing across the harbour to get there.

Vanderbilt paid little attention to school, preferring the outdoor life. As a child he could barely read and write. He did, however, take a keen interest in business. In 1810, when he was 16, Vanderbilt's mother gave him $100 to clear and plant an eight-acre field. Instead of frittering the money away, the enterprising Vanderbilt used it to buy a small flat-bottom sailing boat. He then started a ferry business, taking passengers between Staten Island and New York. The business almost sank in the first few weeks when the boat hit an obstacle, but both boat and business survived.

The ferry business taught Vanderbilt some important commercial lessons. Known locally as 'Cornele, the boatman', he discovered that by taking any fare, no matter how rough the weather, he obtained a reputation for both reliability and a willingness to please the customer. This in turn brought him repeat business. He also learned the simple economics of low costs, high turnover, consistently undercutting his rivals, and filling his boat.

CONTRIBUTION

Like many other entrepreneurs, when war with England came in 1812 Vanderbilt saw the conflict as an opportunity to improve his business. As well as continuing to ply his normal routes, he was awarded an army contract and also made extra money ferrying food along the Hudson River to a blockaded New York. With the profits, he bought an interest in two more boats.

By the age of 24, Vanderbilt had saved $9,000, expanded his business to ply the coastal routes between Chesapeake Bay and New York, and developed a retail business selling provisions to ships in the harbour. In addition, he owned interests in a number of boats. Things were going well for Vanderbilt when, in 1817, the steamboats arrived. Entrepreneurs Robert Fulton and Robert Livingston had brought their new technology to New York and were granted a monopoly on all steamboat traffic for a period of 30 years.

Realising that sailboats were about to become obsolete, Vanderbilt sold up rather than persist with outdated technology. He went to work for a small steamboat operator, Thomas Gibbons, a wealthy lawyer and plantation owner, and learned how to sail the steamboat. As soon as he was able, he began ferrying passengers from New Jersey to Manhattan in direct contravention of the monopoly. He persuaded passengers to use the service by undercutting Fulton and Livingston's $4 ticket price, charging only $1. The loss was made up on food and drink prices.

In 1824, the United States Supreme Court declared the Fulton and Livingston monopoly illegal. Now Vanderbilt could operate openly. With the monopoly broken, things changed quickly in the steamboat business. Prices came down, competitors entered the market and boat technology improved. In a competitive environment where innovation was rewarded, Vanderbilt thrived. In 1829 he used his savings to start his own steamboat business. He put together a connected service—steamboat, stagecoach, steamboat—from New York to Philadelphia. And, in what became a classic Vanderbilt business strategy, he immediately slashed prices. The competition, fearing a price war, clubbed together to pay him to go away.

Vanderbilt had discovered a new way to make money. Keen to protect the market and unwilling to cut their profits to provide real value to the customer, the lazy established operators would rather pay Vanderbilt to stop operating. It was the same story in the Hudson River. Up against the Hudson River Steamboat Association, Vanderbilt cut fares savagely until he was carrying passengers for free and, as before, making the losses up on the food. It wasn't long before the Steamboat Association caved in. They gave Vanderbilt $100,000, as well as ten annual payments of $5,000, in return for him leaving the area.

Before long, Vanderbilt—now Commodore Vanderbilt—owned over 100 steamboats and was worth many millions of dollars. His next move was inspired by the discovery of gold in California in 1848. The ensuing gold rush created a demand for transport from East Coast to West. Initially clipper boats took passengers around Cape Horn—a journey that took 90 days. Next, an alternative route was organised that involved land travel across the Isthmus of Panama. It was at this point that the ever-innovative Vanderbilt entered the fray. Studying the maps he discovered a new route, which involved sailing inland along the San Juan River; on across Lake Nicaragua, and finally across the shortest 12-mile land gap to the Pacific Ocean.

> *In 1824, the United States Supreme Court declared the Fulton and Livingston monopoly illegal. Now Vanderbilt could operate openly.*

Cornelius Vanderbilt

Vanderbilt formed the Accessory Transit Company, struck a deal with the Nicaraguan government, constructed a port on the Pacific Coast and, in 1851, started sailing the new route. As usual his fares were cheaper—$400 compared to the competition's $600. And as usual, after some political wrangling and manoeuvring, the competition offered Vanderbilt $672,000 not to operate a route to California. His first foray into the transatlantic and shipping routes was no less successful. Used to competing with government subsidised business by now, Vanderbilt cut fares, built volume, and used the latest technology in shipping so that, when government subsidy was finally withdrawn from the competition, he was best-placed to take advantage.

By 1863 Vanderbilt, in his sixties, had amassed a fortune of $40 million. For most people this would have been enough. Not for him. Over the next 13 years, abandoning water for land, Vanderbilt switched from old technology—steamboats, to new technology—railways.

By 1869, Vanderbilt had taken control of the Hudson River Railroad and the New York Central system. He merged the two companies, gained control of railway lines from New York to Chicago, and created a consolidated railway system between the two cities. Towards the end of his career, Vanderbilt continued to apply the principles of competitiveness, low costs, and innovation to the business. He upgraded iron rails with steel imported from England, doubled tracks, and built the Grand Central Depot in New York, the largest railway terminal in the world.

By the time of his death on 4 January 1877, Vanderbilt commanded a railway empire that extended over 740 miles of track and included 486 locomotives and 9,000 freight cars. Every year thousands of passengers were transported courtesy of Vanderbilt. When he died, he left a fortune of $105 million in his will.

CONTEXT AND CONCLUSIONS

Cornelius Vanderbilt was simply the most brilliant businessman of his generation. He combined an innate understanding of the principles of economics with a consummate grasp of business strategy. Everything that Vanderbilt touched turned to gold. Only once was he ever thwarted. When he tried to corner the stock in the New York and Erie Railroad Company, notorious financiers Jay Gould and Jim Fisk merely kept on issuing new shares until finally Vanderbilt had to give up. But no one ever beat him fairly. Why? Because Vanderbilt understood that delivering a reasonable service, at a low cost, would always win out over a government-subsidised monopoly. Rather than fleece consumers by providing a substandard, outdated, expensive service, Vanderbilt gave his customers innovation and value for money. In doing so he helped drive economic growth on both the East and West Coast, and to fast-track technological innovation in transport. And, in the process, he became fabulously wealthy.

THE BEST SOURCES OF HELP
Books:
Metzman, Gustav. *Commodore Vanderbilt (1794–1877): Forefather of the New York Central*. New York: The Newcomen Society of England, 1946.
Smith, Arthur Howden. *Commodore Vanderbilt: An Epic of American Achievement*. New York: Robert McBride, 1927.

SAMUEL WALTON

1918	Born.
1945	Gets franchise for Ben Franklin store in Newport, Arkansas.
1953	Obtains pilot's licence.
1962	Opens first Wal-Mart discount store in Rogers, Arkansas.
1964	Second Wal-Mart store in the town of Harrison, Arkansas.
1970	Raises $5 million on the stock market through a public offering of Wal-Mart stock.
1970s	Builds 452 new stores.
1974	Retires for two years.
1980s	Builds 1,237 new stores.
1985	Wal-Mart stock makes him wealthiest man in America.
1987	1,000th store opens.
1991	Wal-Mart overtakes Sears to become biggest retailer in the United States.
1992	Dies.

> **SUMMARY**
>
> Samuel Moore Walton created a retail empire after the fashion of the great Frank Woolworth. A hard upbringing in the depression-ridden Midwest was followed by university and then commerce. Having sampled the retail business courtesy of JCPenney, Walton opened a Ben Franklin store with $25,000 borrowed from his father-in-law. When he lost the lease on his first store he simply opened another, and then another. Soon he had a small collection of retail outlets. To keep tight control of them, he would fly himself from one to the other. Walton opened the first Wal-Mart in 1962 and the second in 1964. By 1987 there were over 1,000. At the time of his death in 1992, Walton had made millions from his retail business, and so had many of his shareholders. One hundred shares bought in 1970 for a mere $1,650 were, by 1992, worth a staggering $2.6 million.

LIFE AND CAREER

Samuel Moore Walton was born in Oklahoma on 29 March 1918. His father was employed variously as a farm loan appraiser, a real estate salesman, and an insurance salesman. Walton and his family moved from small town to small town in Missouri as his father pursued work. When they finally settled in Columbia, Missouri in 1933, Walton helped bolster the family income by taking on several jobs.

His work commitments did not prevent Walton from attending school. He was bright enough and hard-working enough to gain a place at the University of Missouri at Columbia, where he studied for a business degree, graduating in 1940. After college he decided to take a position as a management trainee in Des Moines, Iowa, at the retail store JCPenney. It was here that he learned many of the management techniques that he was to apply later—these included fostering a sense of inclusion by calling his employees 'associates' and managing by walking about or, in Walton's case, by flying about.

Walton enlisted to fight in the Second World War. Unfit for full service because of a heart irregularity, he spent the war in the United States serving in the military police. He also married during the war, in 1943. It was a fortunate marriage. When Walton returned to civilian life at the end of the war, he decided to set up in business himself rather than return to JCPenney. He borrowed $20,000 from his father-in-law

Samuel Walton

and bought a Ben Franklin store in Newport, Arkansas. It was September 1945, Walton was 27, and he was in the retail business.

CONTRIBUTION

Walton proved tough competition for the nearby better-established businesses. One such was the Sterling Variety store, where Bud Hewitt, who would become a great friend of his, worked. In 1947, however, they were in competition, and when Hewitt had a run on rayon underwear for women (he was cleaned out of stock), Walton was determined to outdo him. Rather than place an order, Walton went to Little Rock and bought the distributor. At a stroke, he cut the competition out of the market and secured his own store's supply of lingerie.

In 1950, despite his success, Walton was unable to renew the lease on his Newport store and was forced to sell out. He didn't give up though, he merely moved to nearby Bentonville, where he bought another Ben Franklin store, calling it 'Walton's Five and Dime'. Before long he had added to his burgeoning retail empire by acquiring a number of other stores in the region. They were spread out over a wide area and potentially difficult to keep in touch with and manage satisfactorily. He solved the problem imaginatively: he gained his pilot's licence in 1953 and acquired a decrepit pre-war aeroplane, in which he simply flew from one store to the next.

> *Rather than place an order, Walton went to Little Rock and bought the distributor.*

Walton then cast his eye further afield. He began by visiting a couple of Ben Franklin 'self-service' stores in Minnesota. The idea of self-service was then a new one, and the fact that it enabled the owner to pass on cheaper prices to the customer appealed to him. Back in Bentonville he opened his own self-service store. One of Walton's greatest strengths was that he was always willing to embrace innovation, whether it was self-service or, as in the early 1960s, the discount store concept.

The first Wal-Mart opened in 1962. It owed a great deal to the Kmart store in Chicago, a shop that Walton had visited to observe its operations at first hand. It was tough going initially. It wasn't easy to stock a full range of goods, since suppliers were reluctant to be associated with mass merchandising. Walton spent much of his time over the next few years experimenting with different layouts and different mixes of stock to create the perfect discount store. All this time he continued to earn the bulk of his income from his chain of Ben Franklin stores. The second Wal-Mart opened in 1964 in Harrison, Arkansas. The first day was a disaster, primarily because of the inhospitable temperature of 115 degrees. The manure from the donkeys providing rides was trodden through the store. The watermelons outside popped in the heat. Local businessman David Glass uttered the legendary observation: 'It was the worst retail store I've ever seen.' Glass went on to become president of the Wal-Mart Corporation.

In 1970 Walton raised $5 million on the stock market through a public offering of Wal-Mart stock. The 1970 financing enabled Walton to construct six more stores as well as a distribution centre. In fact, from the 1970s onwards, the rate of construction of new Wal-Mart stores increased phenomenally; 452 were built during the 1970s and 1,237 in the 1980s.

As the Wal-Mart empire blossomed, Walton spent more and more time keeping his employees happy and up to scratch. He would still travel from store to store by plane and, where he found a store that didn't meet his high standards, he would close it on the spot and not reopen it until it was ready. He wrote a monthly column in the company newspaper, *Wal-Mart World*, he personally replied to letters from staff raising questions or suggesting ideas, and he insisted on attending the opening of new stores whenever possible. In 1983 he promised to dance down Wall Street in a grass skirt if the company posted profit targets. It did, and Wall Street was graced with the sight of Walton dancing the hula.

By 1987 Wal-Mart had opened its 1,000th store and was an early adopter of network technology linking all the stores through a satellite system, something that, sadly, obviated the need for Walton's airborne excursions, much to the relief of the shareholders. They profited greatly from his canny business sense. One hundred shares bought in 1970 for a mere $1,650 were, by the time of Walton's death in 1992, worth a staggering $2.6 million.

CONTEXT AND CONCLUSIONS

Frank Woolworth pioneered the concept of the five and dime store. He was also one of the first mass-market retailers with thousands of stores across the world. Sam Walton was a retailer out of the same mould, the Frank Woolworth of his generation, who steadily built up a network of mass-merchandise discount stores under the Wal-Mart name. Always keen to embrace innovation, he pioneered the self-service concept, was one of the first retailers to adopt network technology via satellite to link stores, and championed hypermarts. A stickler for high standards, he also was known to close down stores immediately if he felt they failed to come up to scratch. One of the greatest retailers of his generation, he died one of the richest men in the world, having built an empire of over 1,000 stores.

CLOSE BUT NO CIGAR

SEBASTIAN SPERING KRESGE

Kresge was a travelling tinware salesman who founded a chain of S.S. Kresge discount retail stores in 1912. All the goods were priced at less than a dime. First World War inflation pushed the price limit up to a dollar. Kresge opened his first Kmart store in 1962. He died in 1966, the same year company sales topped $1 billion.

RICHARD WARREN SEARS

Sears was station agent for the Minnesota and St Louis Railroad in North Redwood when he became the beneficiary of an unwanted consignment of watches. He sold them to other station agents and started the R.W. Sears Watch Company in 1886. This became Sears, Roebuck, & Co in 1893 with the addition of Alvah Roebuck, a watchmaker. Sears went on to build the biggest retail business in the United States through the use of the mail-order catalogue.

THE BEST SOURCES OF HELP
Website:
Wal-Mart: **www.walmart.com**

THOMAS WATSON SR

1874	Born.
1893	Sells musical instruments.
1898	Joins the National Cash Register Company.
1914	Joins Computing-Tabulating-Recording Co. Revenues $4 million.
1924	Company's name changed to International Business Machines Corp.
1944	IBM builds world's first large-scale computer.
1946	IBM revenues $115 million.
1952	IBM manufactures world's first commercially available computer, the 701.
1956	Dies.

SUMMARY

Thomas Watson Sr is reported to have made the unfortunately inaccurate prediction, 'I think that there may be a world market for possibly five computers.' But his misjudgement didn't prevent him from building the industrial and technological titan IBM. Watson graduated from hawking pianos to selling the cash register. He learned his trade under John Patterson, who taught him about commerce and social responsibility. When Watson was sacked by Patterson after an argument, he took with him progressive ideas about corporate culture and the working environment, and a small sign that said 'THINK!' At Computing-Tabulating-Recording Co, the company that eventually became IBM, he engineered a corporate transformation, pumping money into research and development, nurturing exciting new technologies, and galvanising the sales force.

LIFE AND CAREER

Thomas Watson Sr was born in Campbell, New York, on 17 February 1874. Son of an upstate New York farmer, Watson's upbringing was a traditional, rural 19th-century one. Life was shaped by a strong moral code. Dignity, respect for others, self-respect, conscientious work, optimism, and loyalty were values ingrained in Watson throughout his childhood. Unlike many of his peers, he carried the values throughout his public and private life.

His first real job was as a bookkeeper at Clarence Risley's Market in Painted Post, New York. Later, when he was 18, Watson drove a horse and buggy across northern New York State, hawking an unlikely combination of pianos and sewing machines to farmers. As farmers were often short of cash, he took all manner of goods in trade. Animals, farm equipment, and produce were all exchanged and then sold again by Watson. It was invaluable training. It taught him the value of goods and that if he kept his customers happy, more people would buy his goods on recommendation.

> *His first real job was as a bookkeeper at Clarence Risley's Market in Painted Post, New York.*

CONTRIBUTION

In 1898, Watson went to work for the National Cash Register Company, known universally as 'the cash'. NCR was run by John Patterson, an eccentric, charismatic businessman and a remarkable business pioneer, who introduced many enlightened liberal working practices. Watson joined as a salesman. His first few weeks were spent calling on various prospects, without success. His manager, after giving the dispirited Watson a talking to, promised to accompany him and show him how it should be done. He was true to his word; they travelled together, and Watson finally made a number of sales. The attitude of his manager made a great impression on Watson. Later at IBM, he made sure all managers were able to work with their staff and provide them with adequate training.

With his first few sales in the bag, Watson made swift progress. In 1899 he was promoted to manager of the company's Rochester branch and then to general sales manager—Patterson's right-hand man. While at NCR he came up with the slogan that would later become firmly associated with IBM—'THINK!' Not many people know that the motto was originally conceived, and used to good effect, to pep up a dispirited NCR sales force.

After a number of disagreements with Patterson, Watson was sacked from NCR. In 1914 he moved on to the Computing-Tabulating-Recording Company (CTR), an alliance of three small companies, as general manager. When he arrived, CTR was in poor shape. Worse still, as a newcomer brought into shake things up, Watson was resented by the staff, who naturally feared for their jobs. But Watson did not get rid of a single member of staff. Instead he determined to make the existing workforce better at their jobs. This was the foundation of IBM's famous policy of job security. This policy was even adhered to during the great depression. Despite one quarter of the United States' labour force being unemployed, IBM carried on expanding, producing excess inventory and stockpiling it, a gamble which ultimately paid off.

> *At IBM, Watson always went out of his way to keep his employees happy. In 1939, he took 10,000 people to IBM Day at the World's Fair, at the company's expense.*

At CTR, Watson also took a lead from Patterson's liberal working practices and theories. He didn't have the resources to build a modern, forward-looking factory like NCR's in Dayton, but he did do everything in his power to create an enthusiastic atmosphere at the company. This included staging concerts, picnics, and other entertainment, as well as giving rousing speeches. This close and almost paternalistic relationship with his employees led to the 'open door' policy, where Watson made himself available in person to see his employees whenever they wished and actively encouraged their visits. This policy was another key element of Watson's management strategy at IBM and only lapsed after his death, when the size of the company made it impracticable.

At IBM, Watson always went out of his way to keep his employees happy. In 1939, he took 10,000 people to IBM Day at the World's Fair, at the company's expense. The sales conferences became increasingly extravagant affairs. Waking delegates were greeted with newspapers recounting the previous day's events, and overseas visitors were provided with headphones through which they heard a translation of the proceedings. A visit by General Eisenhower in July 1948 was extended, after some persuasion by Watson, to allow Eisenhower to address workers at the IBM plant, who were all given time off work to attend.

Watson's obsession with excellent customer service is illustrated by an incident that occurred during the Second World War. On Good Friday in 1942, an official from the War Production Board telephoned Watson late in the afternoon. He placed an order for 150 machines and challenged Watson to deliver the equipment to Washington DC by the following Monday. Watson agreed. Saturday morning saw him, with his staff, phoning IBM offices across the country to organise the dispatch of 150 machines over the Easter holiday. To emphasise the effort he was making, he instructed his staff to let the War Production Board people know the minute each truck began its journey to Washington, no matter what time of day or night. Police and army officials were rounded up to escort trucks, which were driven through the night. A makeshift factory was also set up in Georgetown to deal with the reception and installation of the equipment. It was a remarkable effort, typical of Watson's attitude.

Between 1914 and 1946, IBM's profits grew 38 times, giving great weight to Watson's management strategy. And even though this growth was a magnificent achievement, it was nothing compared to what happened in the post-war period, as IBM grew its revenues from $115 million in 1946 to $1.7 billion by 1961, with employee numbers growing from 17,000 in the United States to 80,000 during the same period. One hundred shares bought in 1914 would have cost $2,740. By 1962, shortly after Watson's death, they were worth $5.45 million.

Much of this was due to the success of a new breed of computer. The Mach 1 was the world's first large-scale computer, built by IBM in collaboration with Dr Howard Aiken and presented to Harvard University in 1944. This was followed with the first commercially available IBM computer, the 701, in 1952.

Thomas Watson Sr died on 19 June 1956. A month earlier, he passed over his control in the company to his eldest son, Thomas Watson Jr.

CONTEXT AND CONCLUSIONS

Thomas Watson Sr achieved great things at IBM. He managed the growth of a small company with a promising technology into a billion-dollar company with a technology that changed the world. The history of computing is not just about the scientists and inventors. It is also about the men who manage creativity and innovation, and who help turn the fantastic dreams of scientists into commercial reality. Watson was one such man. He cajoled, he improved, he inspired. Many of his methods he owed to his inspirational mentor, John Patterson at NCR. Watson took Patterson's ideals forward into the 20th century and, in doing so, created one of America's most enduring companies.

THE BEST SOURCES OF HELP
Books:
Rodgers, William. *THINK. A Biography of the Watsons and IBM*. New York: Stein and Day, 1969.
Watson, Thomas Jr, with Peter Petre. *Father Son & Co. My Life at IBM and Beyond*. Rev ed. New York: Bantam, 2000.

JACK WELCH

1935	Born.
1960	Starts at General Electric.
1961	Almost quits General Electric.
1963	Put in charge of chemical development.
1968	Becomes General Electric's youngest ever general manager.
1981	Becomes CEO.
1986	Buys RCA.
1995	Introduces Six Sigma
2000	Postpones retirement to oversee Honeywell Bull deal. Receives $7 million book advance.
2001	Steps down as CEO.
2002	Public criticism of retirement settlement.

SUMMARY

One of the most renowned corporate leaders of the 20th century, Jack Welch maintained General Electric's reputation as a world-beater throughout his 20-year reign as CEO. Under Welch the company moved into new business areas and reached new heights.

Jack Welch, named in 1999 as *Fortune*'s 'manager of the century', started at General Electric as a trainee in 1960. At the age of 33 he became the youngest general manager in the company's history, and in 1981 became CEO. Over a 20-year period he oversaw revolution, reorganisation, Six Sigma, tough targets, and a blaze of corporate acquisitions. The results were a 600% increase in profits, 100 consecutive quarters of increased earnings, and a status as one of the most profitable companies in the world. Welch stepped down as CEO in September 2001.

LIFE AND CAREER

Jack Francis Welch Jr, one of most celebrated managers and leaders of the 20th century, was born on 19 November 1935 in Peabody, Massachusetts. He grew up in Salem, where his father worked as a railroad conductor. As a boy he suffered from a stutter that might have badly affected his confidence, had it not been for his mother's imaginative explanation. 'She told me [it was] just that my brain worked too fast,' Welch said.

At school he was a keen sportsman; he also was described by classmates as the 'most talkative and noisiest boy' they knew. After high school he set off for the University of Massachusetts, where he studied chemistry. Then came the University of Illinois, where he obtained a PhD in chemical engineering. From there he moved to Pittsfield, Massachusetts, to start his first real job at General Electric.

CONTRIBUTION

Welch's meteoric career at General Electric (GE) almost didn't happen. In 1961, sick of the cumbersome bureaucratic systems, Welch quit. Fortunately for GE, his boss at the time persuaded him to stay. In 1963 Welch was put in charge of chemical development, and in 1968, aged 33, he became GE's youngest general manager ever. By 1972 he had risen to the position of divisional vice-president and set his sights on rising even higher. On his employee evaluation form Welch was asked to state his long-term ambitions—to become CEO, he wrote. By 1979 he was vice-chairman and executive officer.

Along the way he built plastics into a formidable $2 billion business, turned around the medical diagnostics business, and began the development of GE Capital. In December 1980 Welch was announced as the new CEO and chairman of GE, at 45 the youngest chief the company had ever appointed and only the eighth CEO in 92 years.

At the time, GE was in reasonable shape. That year *Fortune* magazine voted it the best-managed company in America, and Reg Jones, the CEO who Welch had replaced, was ranked number one among CEOs. Yet GE's stock was performing poorly. Against the backdrop of a faltering world economy, the Japanese were posing a real threat to US manufacturers with new production systems such as 'lean manufacturing'.

During the 1980s, recognising that GE would have to change in order to compete successfully on the world stage, Welch declared that it was going to become the world's most valuable company. This meant getting rid of all unprofitable areas. The focus was shifted to service industries, creating over 1000 new businesses, and resulting in the disposal of 70 existing businesses.

> *On his employee evaluation form Welch was asked to state his long-term ambitions—to become CEO, he wrote. By 1979 he was vice-chairman and executive officer.*

But that was only a start. Next Welch turned his attention to the organisational structure. He pared down the organisation, devolving power to the individual business units in a massive push for decentralisation. An elaborate management hierarchy was tossed onto the scrapheap. 'Fight it. Hate it. Kick it. Break it,' railed Welch in an anti-bureaucracy exhortation to the troops.

Nearly 200,000 GE employees left the company and over $6 billion was saved. The media dubbed Welch 'Neutron Jack'. But by the end of the 1980s, having proved that he could tear the company apart, Welch moved on to stage two: rebuilding a company fit for the 21st century. To encourage innovation and the communication of ideas, he vowed to create what he called a 'boundaryless' organisation. 'Knock down the walls that separate us from each other on the inside and from our key constituents on the outside,' was the way he put it. In the pre-Welch era, employees with a good idea would squirrel it away. Now they would be willing to share their ideas and would be encouraged to do so, and the culture would make sure that they received the praise they deserved.

To make sure that all employees were pulling in the same direction, Welch used corporate values as a reference to guide behaviour. He famously carried a copy of them printed on a card.

In the mid-1990s, in a drive for quality, Welch adopted the concept of Six Sigma, developed by Motorola in 1985. A statistical term, Six Sigma refers to products with a 99.9998% perfection rate. Implementation relies on rigorous measurement and testing to deliver results. Welch made sure that the adoption of Six Sigma had 100% management backing, and attributed a 3% increase in profit margins between 1995 and 1999 to the roll-out of Six Sigma at GE.

A stack of figures attest to the success of Jack Welch's reign: between 31 March 1981 and November 1999, for example, the GE stock price rose from just over $4 to $133 (allowing for four stock splits), an increase of 3,200%. From 1980 onwards, the average total return on GE shares was about 27%, and the company has returned 100 consecutive quarters of increased earnings from continuing operations. To put the company's performance in context: if you had bought $10,000 worth of General Electric shares in March 1981 and reinvested the dividends, by the end of 1999 they would have been worth $640,000. Over the same period GE sales rose from $27.2 billion to $173.2 billion, while profits rose from $1.6 billion to $10.7 billion. By 1999 General Electric was the second most profitable company in the world.

The only slight tarnishing of Welch's lustre came in 2001. Due to retire, Welch postponed his departure for one last hurrah: a mega-deal with Honeywell Bull, snatched from under the noses of intended purchasers, United Technologies. Despite Welch's best efforts, however, this deal was scuppered by European Union regulators. In some ways it was an unfortunate end to a majestic career. Commenting on the affair, Welch was his characteristic self: 'GE was a great company before I took a swing at it. It's a great company after. It would have been better if we had gotten it. But as far as regrets for doing it? No way. I'd do the same thing again tomorrow.' He finally handed over the baton to his successor, Jeff Immelt, on 7 September 2001. His next job: to promote his autobiography, *Jack: Straight from the Gut*.

Retirement started with promise, a $7 million advance from his publishers, and an extremely generous retirement package, but personal matters changed public attitudes. In 2002, he admitted to an affair with an editor of the *Harvard Business Review* and, during the subsequent divorce proceedings, there was public outrage when the scale of his retirement package was revealed.

CONTEXT AND CONCLUSIONS

The failed Honeywell takeover and the personal revelations dominated press coverage of the end of Welch's rule at GE. The actions of the EU regulators briefly blotted out the achievements of an exceptional leader. But the three stages of development under Welch—destruction, creation, and quality—have reshaped GE and made Welch the CEO role model of his generation. Inevitably, he also has his critics. They point to the size of corporate pay packets, GE's ecological record, high levels of redundancy, and the lack of loyalty throughout the organisation. But there can be little disagreement that Welch has made a difference where it matters, from the investors' perspective at least. History will remember Welch as one of the most important corporate leaders of the 20th century.

CLOSE BUT NO CIGAR
JOHN MAROUS

Concentrating on investor value worked for Welch, but it didn't work for Marous. A Westinghouse Electrical Company executive, man and boy, Marous had been at the company for 40 years before he became CEO in 1988. The similarities between Welch and Marous are many: both excelled at sports, were tough negotiators, and were results-driven in the extreme. 'Don't just bring me bad news, bring me solutions,' was a Marous motto. Under his leadership, some of Westinghouse's core businesses were sold off and Westinghouse Credit was given a free rein to lend, lend, lend. In 1990, the year Marous stepped down, the stock price was at its highest ever. But from there it was all downhill. After his departure the once great company drowned in the sea of bad debts left by its subsidiary Westinghouse Credit.

THE BEST SOURCES OF HELP
Books:
Crainer, Stuart. *Business the Jack Welch Way*. Oxford: Capstone, 1999.
Slater, Jack. *New GE: How Jack Welch Revived an American Institution* Chicago: Irwin, 1993.
Tichy, Noel M., and Sherman Stratford. *Control Your Destiny or Someone Else Will: How Jack Welch Is Making General Electric the World's Most Competitive Corporation*. London: HarperCollins, 1995.
Welch, Jack, and John A. Byrne. *Jack: Straight from the Gut*. London: HarperCollins, 2001.
Website:
General Electric: **www.ge.com**

OPRAH WINFREY

1954	Born.
1963	Moves to live with mother.
1972	Wins Miss Black Tennessee pageant.
1976	Moves to Baltimore and lands job with WJZ-TV.
1984	Achieves first major television success with AM Chicago.
1985	Plays Sofia in film *The Color Purple*.
1986	Goes nationwide with *The Oprah Winfrey Show*.
1987	Wins first daytime Emmy for *The Oprah Winfrey Show*.
1994	Repositions her show as 'change your life television'.
1996	Establishes Book Club.
2000	Diversifies into publishing, brings out new magazine called *O*.
1998	Named second most admired woman in the United States. Lifetime achievement award at Emmys.
1999	Launches Oxygen cable TV network.
2003	First African-American woman billionaire.

> **SUMMARY**
>
> The child of separated parents, the victim of childhood sexual abuse, poverty, and juvenile delinquency, Oprah Winfrey (1954–) overcame a difficult start to become an American icon.
>
> Her career in broadcasting began as a teenager reading the news on the radio. By the age of 30 she had become the talk-show queen of the United States, hosting the nation's number one talk-show. In 1988 she became the third woman ever to own her own film studio, Harpo Productions. At a time when talk shows seemed to be descending into the gutter, she pulled them back out again with a move to 'change your life' television. Winfrey's future seems assured: she has secured her talk-show contract until 2004, she publishes a number of magazines and produces other television programmes, and she is becoming more involved with social issues in the United States.

LIFE AND CAREER

Oprah Winfrey had a tough start in life. Born to unmarried teenagers on 29 July 1954, she grew up in poverty on her grandmother's farm in Mississippi. The first Winfrey's father knew of her existence was when he received an instruction to send some clothes for her. Brought up initially by her grandmother, at four she moved to Milwaukee to live with her mother. After a brief but happy interlude with her father, Vernon Winfrey, she again ended up with her mother in Milwaukee in 1963. During her time there she was raped, at the age of nine.

Her mother attempted to send her to a home for juvenile delinquents, but she was unable to wait two weeks for a place to become available. Winfrey was despatched back to live with her father. Had it not been for him, Winfrey's life might easily have been a tale of loss and waste. Luckily for her, her father was a strict disciplinarian, and with his help Winfrey began to turn her life around.

At 16 she got her first lucky break. As the first black girl to win a national beauty contest, she was invited on a tour of a local radio station to pick up her prize. Her

Oprah Winfrey

talent was spotted there and she was asked to read the radio news after school. She had her next big break at 19, landing a job as a reporter on the Nashville radio station WVOL. At the same time she enrolled at Tennessee State University on a performing arts course.

When she was initially offered a TV job, she turned it down until her college tutor persuaded her to change her mind. Winfrey became a news anchor at WTVF-TV in Nashville, the first African American to do so. Her star quality was evident from the moment she was put in front of the camera. On television she was a natural. Her personality lit up the screen.

CONTRIBUTION

In 1976 Winfrey moved to Baltimore, Maryland, and landed herself a job with WJZ-TV as a news co-anchor. The management wasn't impressed, criticising her appearance and eventually demoting her to a morning spot. Luckily a station executive, Phil Baker, offered her an opportunity to co-host a chat show on the station. Reluctant at first, she accepted. It was a risk for the station to put a black woman on as host of its principal talk show. And it was a risk for Winfrey, who thought her future lay in news. The show was called *People Are Talking*, and viewers were soon talking about Winfrey. They liked her down-to-earth style, and her Nielsen ratings began to rise. In 1984 she moved to Chicago to host WLS-TV's morning talk show, *AM Chicago*, going head-to-head with Phil Donahue, America's top-rated talk-show host. Her show ranked number one within a month. Winfrey was just 30 years old.

> *When she was initially offered a TV job, she turned it down until her college tutor persuaded her to change her mind.*

Winfrey continued in her own inimitable style, being open and honest about her past and her emotions. It struck a chord with her audience. Viewers empathised with her. Her high profile began to pay dividends as she was asked to audition for the part of Sofia in Steven Spielberg's 1985 film adaptation of Alice Walker's novel, *The Color Purple*. When she received a call telling her Steven Spielberg wanted her in his office in California the next day, she was at a health farm on one of her frequent attempts to lose weight. She was warned that if she lost as much as a pound it might jeopardise her chances of getting the part—she later joked that she stopped off at a Dairy Queen on the way to California. She got the part and was nominated for an Oscar for Best Supporting Actress.

The timing couldn't have been better for Winfrey. She was about to launch her nationally syndicated chat show, *The Oprah Winfrey Show*. It was 1986 and, despite one viewer in Iowa ringing in to say he could get better ratings with a potato, Winfrey had hit the big time. Her style remained unaffected, and she soon racked up ten million viewers across the United States.

Astutely Winfrey took control of her own destiny in 1988 by forming Harpo Productions—her name spelled backwards—acquiring the rights to her show from Capital Cities/ABC. She also spent $20 m on a production facility in Chicago, a step on the way to becoming only the third woman to own a major studio (following in the footsteps of Mary Pickford and Lucille Ball).

Winfrey's professional life was blooming, but her personal life was plagued by her struggle with her weight. Her repeated and very public attempts to reduce her weight varied from exercise to a radical, four-month-long liquid diet. Eventually she managed to come to terms with herself and her weight, an achievement that helped her self-esteem and her bank-balance: her 1994 book *In the Kitchen with Rosie* (Rosie was her chef) became the fastest selling book in the country.

Winfrey's immense success spawned a host of imitators. Talk shows sprang up on every station, delving into the private lives of individuals, exposing the underbelly of human existence. Appealing to the lowest common denominator, such programmes can at times seem little more than a licence to televise sleaze. In 1994 Winfrey decided to distance herself from the excesses of the genre by repositioning herself in the marketplace. She vowed to concentrate on more uplifting and more highbrow issues, calling her concept 'change your life' TV. To her credit she has succeeded in both redefining herself and differentiating her show in the talk-show marketplace. The shift of emphasis has secured another series run through to 2004. The 'Oprah Factor' has also begun to move beyond television in recent years. The appearance of 'Oprah's Book Club' on US screens in 1996 had a dramatic effect on book sales in the United States, and any title recommended by Winfrey in the on-air book discussion group went on to massive success. The Book Club was revived in June 2003 after a 14-month hiatus, with John Steinbeck's *East of Eden* being the next book to feel the benefit.

In 1999, she launched the Oxygen cable TV network. 2000 saw her using her influence to encourage others. She made a series of $100,000 'Use your Life' awards to people who improve the lives of others. Her contribution to broadcasting has not gone unrewarded. In 1998, she was voted second most admired woman in the United States behind Hillary Clinton, followed by a lifetime achievement award at the 1998 Emmys. The material rewards were there too when, in 2003, she became the first African-American woman to become a billionaire.

CONTEXT AND CONCLUSIONS

Oprah Winfrey's story is one of triumph over adversity. It offers a message of hope to those from disadvantaged backgrounds. Overcoming a childhood marked by abuse and discrimination, Winfrey has become an American icon, a black woman who has conquered television and found a place in the hearts of the American public. She has succeeded by being herself and today Winfrey is one of the most influential people in the United States. Her widely publicised comments about not eating beef, for example, were followed by a 10% drop in beef futures, an event that resulted in an unsuccessful attempt by the beef industry to sue her for millions of dollars in damages. With no sign of Winfrey's star fading, who knows what she will turn her hand to next? A growing interest in social issues suggests that her career could take on a more political direction.

THE BEST SOURCES OF HELP
Book:
Mair, George. *Oprah Winfrey: The Real Story*. Rev. ed. Secaucus, New Jersey: Carol Publishing Group, 1998.
Website:
Oprah®.com: **www.oprah.com**

ROBERT WOODRUFF

1889	Born.
1919	Father's syndicate buys Coca-Cola Company.
1923	Becomes president of Coca-Cola.
1926	Creates Coca-Cola's Foreign Department.
1928	Coca-Cola supplies beverages for Amsterdam Olympics.
1930	Foreign Department becomes Coca-Cola Export Corporation.
1933	Automatic Coca-Cola dispensers introduced at Chicago World's Fair.
1939	Steps down as president.
1965	Officially retires.
1985	Dies.

> **SUMMARY**
>
> Robert Woodruff was the natural heir to the Coca-Cola empire. His father was behind the $25 million buy-out of the Candler family interests in Coca-Cola in 1919. Yet to begin with his familial advantage did Woodruff no good at all. When he sought a job outside the family's beverage interests, his father attempted to restrict his career at every turn. Woodruff succeeded on his own terms as a sales representative with the White Motor Company before bowing to the inevitable and joining Coca-Cola in 1923. For the next four decades until his official retirement in 1965, he ruled the company. He presided over a period of momentous growth that transformed Coca-Cola into a global corporation. By the time of his death in 1985 he had helped create one of the world's most valuable brands.

LIFE AND CAREER

Woodruff was born on 6 December 1889, in Columbus, Georgia. His father, Ernest Woodruff, was president of the Trust Company of Georgia, which was part of a syndicate that bought control of the Coca-Cola company. Ernest Woodruff became the company's president.

For the first stage of his education Woodruff was sent to the Georgia Military Academy. He proved a poor student. The school may have overlooked his disappointing grades, however, as the young Woodruff saved the academy from bankruptcy. Discovering that the Atlanta National Bank was about to foreclose on the school's mortgage, Woodruff paid a visit to the bank's vice-president, and through a combination of bluffing and name-dropping he persuaded him to hold off.

Woodruff's working life also got off to an inauspicious start. He was dismissed from a series of jobs for no obvious reason.

Woodruff completed his education at Emory College, where he paid other students to complete his homework. When asked later in life about his tips for a being a successful manager, he replied, 'If you can get someone to do something better than you can, it is always a good idea.' Despite delegating his college work, he still failed to complete his degree.

Woodruff's working life also got off to an inauspicious start. He was dismissed from a series of jobs for no obvious reason. In fact he was not responsible for his appalling employment record: his father was. Ernest Woodruff had arranged for his son to be sacked on each occasion to teach the young man that having a rich father was no guarantee of an easy life. Once, when Woodruff had a pay-rise held back, he discovered that his father was interfering in his career and swore that he would never work for him again.

Instead he went to work as a truck salesman at the White Motor Company, but was swiftly promoted through the company, becoming vice-president and then general manager.

CONTRIBUTION

While Woodruff was climbing the corporate ladder at the White Motor Company, his father had been putting together an investment group that in 1919 paid $25 million for the Candler family's interest in the Coca-Cola Company. As part of the deal 500,000 shares of Coca-Cola common stock were sold on the stock market for $40 a share. Asked by his father if he wished to participate in the syndicate, Woodruff agreed, picking up a large parcel of the company's stock at $5 a share.

In 1923, aged 33, Woodruff achieved a business reconciliation with his father by accepting the presidency of Coca-Cola. He must have wanted the position badly because he took a substantial pay cut and turned down an offer to be president of Standard Oil on a salary of $250,000. Woodruff later said that the reason he took the job was that it was the only way he could boost the value of his stock in the company.

Over the next six decades Woodruff oversaw the transformation of Coca-Cola from a promising US soft-drinks manufacturer into a global giant. His influence extended into every aspect of the company's operations and began with changing the company's marketing strategy. Only positive images were to be associated with the product; all negative connotations were banished, and Coca-Cola's medicinal roots were severed.

In production and distribution Woodruff set in motion a drive for quality. In 1928 soda fountains exceeded bottled sales, and Woodruff made sure the employees who serviced the fountains were highly trained and could pass their knowledge on to the storekeepers operating the fountains. A Fountain Training School was set up where sales representatives could learn how to mix Coca-Cola properly. Woodruff also introduced a standard procedure manual. At the same time, realising that the bottled drink was the future of the company, he introduced quality standards in the bottling plants. All employees were to wear uniforms, and hygiene and quality checks were introduced.

While all these changes were an essential part of Coca-Cola's success, Woodruff's most important contribution to the company was probably his move to open up international markets. As early as 1900 the Coca-Cola drink had been taken abroad by Asa Candler—the first international order was from England. Through the early 1900s the company built bottling plants in a number of countries from Cuba to the Philippines. But the expansion was disorganised, with no co-ordinated management of international product roll-out.

In 1926 Woodruff changed that by creating the Foreign Department, which four years later became a full-blown subsidiary, the Coca-Cola Export Corporation. Coca-Cola's march to global domination was inexorable under Woodruff. The company cleverly brokered a deal with the Olympics movement, with Coca-Cola being exported to Holland for sale at the 1928 Amsterdam Olympics. Woodruff secured Coca-Cola's beachheads abroad by investing in local economies, building bottling plants, and employing locals for the distribution. In this way the brand acquired goodwill in its export markets.

Although Woodruff resigned as president in 1939 he continued to play an active role in the company. As the Second World War approached he promised, 'We'll see that every man in uniform gets a bottle of Coca-Cola for five cents, wherever he is and whatever it costs our company.' The war helped proliferate Coca-Cola throughout the world.

In the post-war period Woodruff's efforts were increasingly concentrated on battling rival Pepsi-Cola. His influence at Coca-Cola persisted right up until and beyond his retirement in 1965. He remained a kingmaker, grooming potential CEOs, including Roberto Goizueta, from behind the scenes. He died on 7 March 1985, aged 95.

CONTEXT AND CONCLUSIONS

Robert Woodruff the private man was an enigma. He was not a cultured man: he didn't read, nor, unlike many other wealthy executives, was he interested in collecting art or antiques. He had a fear of being alone and would often call friends and colleagues to his home in the small hours to keep him company. Yet he was also an intensely private person who installed a private lift to his office.

Woodruff 'the Boss', however, was a different story. *The force behind one of the biggest corporate success stories of the last century, he was a restless, driven, controlling figurehead.* Unlike many entrepreneurs, Woodruff didn't invent the product his company sold. But he was responsible for aggressively marketing Coca-Cola to a thirsty world—and for taking a caramel-based fizzy drink and turning it into an American icon. Woodruff's personal creed was, 'There is no limit to what a man can do or where he can go if he doesn't mind who gets the credit'. Much of the credit for creating one of the world's most enduring products must go to him.

THE BEST SOURCES OF HELP
Book:
Pendergrast, Mark. *For God, Country, and Coca-Cola: The Definitive History of the Great American Soft Drink and the Company that Makes It*. 2nd ed. New York: Basic Books, 2000.
Website:
Coca-Cola: **www.cocacola.com**

FRANK WOOLWORTH

1852	Born.
1858	Family move to 108-acre farm near Great Bend, New York State.
1873	Woolworth goes to work at Augsbury & Moore's shop.
1878	The five-cent table causes a stir in US retailing.
1879	First Woolworth shop opens in Utica, New York State.
1895	28 shops and revenues of over $1 million.
1905	F.W. Woolworth & Co incorporated.
1913	Company moves into the tallest skyscraper of its time, in New York.
1918	In January the 1000th shop opens on Fifth Avenue, New York.
1919	Dies.

SUMMARY

Frank Winfield Woolworth (1852–1919) was a pioneer of the chain store. He came from a humble background, and became one of the richest men in America, despite many early setbacks in his career. Emerging from a small town in New York State, the farmer's boy rolled out his 'five and ten cents' concept first across America and then around the world. From a single shop in 1879 to a thousand in 1918, the growth of F.W. Woolworth & Co was phenomenal, changing the nature of retailing and bringing its founder riches and fame. Woolworths was the original price-driven retail chain. The secret of his success he put down to delegating well.

LIFE AND CAREER

Woolworth was born in Rodman, New York State, the eldest son of the family. In late 1858, when Woolworth was seven, the family moved to a 108-acre farm near Great Bend, New York State. In a town with a population of only 125, Woolworth's opportunities for education were limited: there was only a one-room schoolhouse, which he attended along with his brother. Much of Woolworth's time, in fact, was taken up helping his father with the family's eight-cow dairy herd rather than studying.

When he was 16 Woolworth attended commercial college for a brief period before offering his services first to the stationmaster's small shop, and then to Dan McNeil's general store in Great Bend as a clerk. On both occasions Woolworth worked for free. In return, Dan McNeil recommended Woolworth to William Moore, the owner of a leading dry-goods shop in Watertown, New York State. In 1873 Moore agreed to take Woolworth on.

At Augsbury & Moore Woolworth started at the bottom of the ladder. He swept floors, created window displays, delivered goods, and generally made himself useful.

At Augsbury & Moore Woolworth started at the bottom of the ladder. He swept floors, created window displays, delivered goods, and generally made himself useful.

Frank Woolworth

The hours were long—six days a week, 7.00 a.m. to 9.00 p.m.—and the pay offered little compensation. The owners initially wanted Woolworth to work for a year with no salary, but after some discussion Woolworth persuaded them to let him work for three months for nothing, rising to $3.50 for the following three months.

Two years later Woolworth moved on to another shop, Bushnall's Department Store, as a senior clerk. In 1876 he married Jennie Creighton, a Canadian, and purchased a four-acre farm. Unfortunately, the tough conditions and lack of support at work meant Woolworth suffered from fever and stress-related illness, which forced him to give up his position at Bushnall's and kept him at home for a year unable to work. As he was recovering, his old employer William Moore came knocking at his door requesting him to return to work at the now renamed Moore & Smith's. Woolworth accepted on a salary of $10 a week.

CONTRIBUTION

In 1878 Woolworth's daughter was born and his mother died. But it was also a year of radical change in the world of retailing. In shops in the Midwest a new tactic had made its debut: the five-cent table. Surplus merchandise was marked down to a nickel by retailers and displayed on a five-cent table. Customers snapped up the bargains and were then drawn into buying other goods at full price. Moore travelled to New York and came home with $100 worth of five-cent goods for Moore & Smith. Woolworth arranged the counter, and they were sold out in a day.

With goods supplied by Moore, Woolworth opened his own shop in Utica, New York State, selling only on the five-cent principle. 'The Great Five Cent Store' opened for business on a Saturday evening in February 1879 with $321 worth of five-cent goods. The first ever item sold was a fire shovel. However, the shop was a failure and soon closed. Undaunted, Woolworth opened another in June of the same year in Lancaster, Pennsylvania. Now he sold goods for five and ten cents. The Lancaster shop was a success. In November 1880 he opened a second shop in Scranton, Pennsylvania. This too was a success, and Woolworth never looked back.

In 1916 the F.W. Woolworth shops served over 700 million customers and had revenues of over $87 million.

Woolworth brought in family members to help expand his empire. By 1895 he had 28 shops, including that of his ex-boss William Moore, and revenues of over $1 million. The growth continued at breakneck speed. In 1900 there were 35 shops; by 1908, 189; and by 1911, 600. In January 1918 the thousandth shop opened on Fifth Avenue in New York.

Woolworth's one-man retail business had burgeoned into a global enterprise. In 1905, bowing to commercial pressures, he incorporated F.W. Woolworth & Co issuing 50,000 shares to executives and employees. Corporate offices were first located in the Stewart Building overlooking City Hall Park in New York. Then, in April 1913, the company moved into the Woolworth Building, the tallest skyscraper of its time. Woolworth's office was situated on the 24th floor. Thirty feet square, its design was based on Napoleon's famous Empire Room and contained the clock and other articles from the original room.

In 1916 the F.W. Woolworth shops served over 700 million customers and had revenues of over $87 million. Every town in the United States with a population of over 8,000 had a Woolworth's.

By the time Woolworth was installed in the Woolworth Building he was approaching the end of his career. With his health failing, he began taking periods of rest in Europe. His wife, Jennie, was suffering from premature senility. Woolworth's own health continued to decline steadily, partly due to a refusal to care for his teeth. On 4 April 1919 he fell desperately ill, dying four days later.

CONTEXT AND CONCLUSIONS

F.W. Woolworth & Co was the pioneer of price-driven retail. Laying down a tradition of value for money that was later followed by companies such as Wal-Mart, Woolworth was one of the first merchants to build a retail empire founded on chain stores and volume retailing.

Working for very little or no money, enduring long periods of ill-health, and with three out of his first five shops failing, no one would have blamed Woolworth for giving up his business dreams. Instead, his extraordinary persistence saw off all his five-and-ten-cents competitors and made him the most successful retailer of his time.

Woolworth's concept of a business based on bargain goods survived until the 1990s. In 1997, however, the Woolworth corporation announced that it was to close its last 400 F.W. Woolworth five-and-dime shops in the United States, finally retreating from the low-priced general merchandise business that had shaped its identity for 117 years.

What was Woolworth's secret? Delegation apparently: 'So long as I was obsessed with the idea that I must attend personally to everything, large-scale success was impossible. A man must select able lieutenants and/or associates and give them power and responsibility.'

THE BEST SOURCES OF HELP
Books:
Baker, Nina Brown. *Nickels and Dimes: The Story of F.W. Woolworth*. New York: Harcourt, Brace & World, 1954.

Nichols, John P. *Skyline Queen and the Merchant Prince: The Woolworth Story*. London: Trident Press, 1973.

Plunkett-Powell, Karen. *Remembering Woolworth's: A Nostalgic History of the World's Most Famous Five-and-Dime*. New York: St Martin's Press, 1999.

Winkler, John Kennedy. *Five and Ten: The Fabulous Life of F.W. Woolworth*. Freeport, New York: Books for Libraries Press, 1970.

INDEX

Acer computers 417–20
action-centred leadership 1–4
Adair, John 1–4
adaptive capabilities, organisations 171–4
administrative management 53–6
advertising
  Eastman 264–6
  Burnett 224–6
  Ogilvy 382–5
agrarian revolutionaries 363–6
air-conditioning 230–3
aircraft industry 216–19
airlines 312–14, 327–9
airmail 216, 218–19
Allen, Paul 281
Amazon.com 212–15
America OnLine (AOL) 234–6
American Express 288
American icons 453–5
American Museum 208
American Safety Razor Company 291–3
American Telephone & Telegraph (AT&T) 437–9
American Tobacco Company 257–9
An Inquiry into the Nature and Causes of the Wealth of Nations 175–8
Andreessen, Marc 244
Ansoff, Igor 5–8
anti-trust law 281
AOL Time Warner 234–6, 434–6
Apple Computers 319–22
Argyris, Chris 9–12, 171
arm wrestling executives 327
Armstrong, Edwin 410
The Art of Japanese Management 147–8
Astor, John Jacob 205–7
AT&T (American Telephone & Telegraph) 437–9
Australia 379–81
authority, Weber 199–202
automobiles
  Chrysler 241–3
  Durant 260–3
  Ford 278–80, 315–18
  Honda 309–11
  Iacocca 315–18
  Sloan Jr 421–3
  Toyoda 431–3

Bailey, James 208
balanced scorecards 101–4
Barnum, Phileas Taylor 208–11
Bartlett, Christopher 64–7
behaviour, Vroom 195–9
Belbin, R. Meredith 13–15
Bell Telegraph Company 437–9
Ben Franklin stores 443–5
Bennis, Warren 16–19
Bezos, Jeff 212–15
Blanchard, Kenneth 20–3
Bloomingdale 346
The Bodley Head 339–42
Body Shop 404–6
Boeing, William 216–19
Brazilian experiment 413–16
broadcasting *see* radio
browsers 281–4
'Buck' (James Buchanan Duke) 257–9
Buffett, Warren 220–3
Buick Motor Company 260, 262
bureaucracy, Weber 199–202
Burnett, Leo 224–6
business history 28–31
business magazines 353–6
business responsibility 61–3

Cable News Network (CNN) 434, 435
cameras 336–8
capitalism 440–2
career anchors 167
Carnegie, Andrew 227–9
Carnegie, Dale 24–7
Carrier, Willis Haviland 230–3
cars *see* automobiles
cartoons 254–6
Case, Steve 234–6
Center for Group Dynamics (USA) 109
centralisation 114
chain store finance 370–2
'chalk and talk' management education 163–6
Chambers, John 237–40
Chandler, Alfred 28–31
change
  discontinuous 80–3
  Handy 80–3
  Kanter 96–100
  Machiavelli 114–15
  management 96–100
  Toffler 191–4
The Change Masters 97–8
charts, Gantt 61
Chevrolet Motor Company 260, 261
Chicago Daily News 353
child labour 330, 332
China 179–82
chocolate bars 306–8
Chrysler Motors 241–3, 315–18
Chrysler, Walter 241–3
Cisco Systems 237–40
Clark, Jim 244–6
clothing manufacture 407–9
CNN (Cable News Network) 434, 435
Coca-Cola 294–6, 456–8
collectivism 88–91
competitive advantage
  capitalism alliance 440–2
  knowledge creation 131–4
  sustaining 135–8
competitive analysis 159–62
Competitive Strategy 155–8
competitive vitality 159–62
computers
  Acer 417–20
  Apple 319–22
  browsers 281–4
  Clark 244–6
  Dell 251–3
  graphics 244–6
  IBM 446–8
  Jobs 319–22
  McNealy 367–9
  Microsoft 281–4, 367
  operating systems 367–9
  Packard 394–6
  Rock 397–400
  Shih 417–20
confectionery industry 306–8
construction business 349–52
core capabilities 76–9, 131–4, 159–62
corporate culture 167–70
corporate leaders 449–52
corporate philosophy 417–20
Corporate Strategy 5
corporate structure experiment 413–16
cosmetics
  Lauder 343–5
  Roddick 404–6
Cotsakos, Christos 247–50
Covey, Stephen 32–6
'cowboys' tailor' 428–30
Crosby, Philip 37–40
cultural differences 88–91
customer service 205–7

Dabrey, Morgan, and Co 373–5
decentralisation 114
decision making 109–12

462

Index

defect reduction 139–42
Dell, Michael 251–3
Deming, W. Edwards 41–4
design, product quality 183–6
designer shops 346–8
Diller, Barry 270, 271
'dimensions' (Hofstede) 88–91
discontinuous change 80–3
Disney empire 254–6, 270–3
Disney, Walter 254–6
dot.com companies 212–15, 424–7
Drexel, Morgan, and Co 373–5
drills, oil industry 312–14
Drucker, Peter 45–52, 151
Duke, James Buchanan 257–9
Durant, William Crapo 260–3

E*Trade 247–50
e-commerce 212–15, 424–7
Eastman, George 264–6
eBay 390–3
economics 28–31, 45–52
Edison, Thomas Alva 267–9
Eisner, Michael 270–3
electrical engineering 357–9, 376–8
electronics 376–8
  see also computers
Ellison, Larry 274–7
emotional intelligence 72–5
employees 68–71, 143–6
empowerment 32–6
energy business 257, 258–9
entertainment 434–6
entrepreneurs
  Astor 205–7
  Buffett 220–3
  Durant 260–3
  Edison 267–9
  Ford 278–80
  Gillette 291–3
  Hershey 306–8
  Jobs 319–22
  Son 424–7
environmentally friendly products 404–6
Estée Lauder Inc 343–5
expectancy models 195–9
extravaganzas 208–11

Fairchild Semiconductors 397–400
fashion 346–8
Fayol, Henri 53–6
Fifth Discipline, The 171–4
film business
  Disney 254–6

Hearst 300–2
Hughes 312–14
Mayer 360–2
Murdoch 379–81
Winfrey 453–5
finance
  chain stores 370–2
  Kaplan 101–4
  Morgan 373–5
  Norton 101–4
  railways 374
Finland 386–9
flat-pack furniture 323–6
flight attendants 327–9
FM radio 410–12
Follett, Mary Parker 57–60
force field theory 109, 110–11
Ford, Henry 278–80
Ford II, Henry 315
Ford Motor Company 278–80, 315–18
Fortune magazine 251, 353–6, 449–52
Fox TV 379, 381
franchise networks 333–5
fur trade 205–7
furniture 323–6
futurology 16–19, 80–3, 191–4
F.W. Woolworth & Co 459–61

Gantt, Henry Laurence 61–3
Gates, Bill 281–4, 367
Geneen, Harold 285–7, 349, 351
General Electric 267–9, 449–52
General and Industrial Management 53
General Motors 260–3, 421–3
Gerstner, Lou 288–90
Ghoshal, Sumantra 64–7
Gilbreth, Frank and Lillian 68–71
Gillette, King Camp 291–3
global organisations 64–7
Goizueta, Roberto 294–6
Goleman, Daniel 72–5
group dynamics 109–12
Grove, Andy 297–9

Hamel, Gary 76–9
Handy, Charles 80–3
Harpo Productions 453–5
harvesting machines 363–6
healthcare 244
Hearst, William Randolph 300–2
Hefner, Hugh 303–5
Hershey, Milton Snavely 306–8
Herzberg, Frederick 84–7

Heth, Joice 208
Hewlett-Packard 394–6
hierarchy of needs 116
history 28–31
Hofstede, Geert 88–91
holistic approaches 32–6
Hollywood 254–6, 360–2
Honda effect 148
Honda, Soichiro 309–11
housing construction 349–52
How to Win Friends and Influence People 24
Hughes, Howard 312–14
human effectiveness 32–6
human relations 57–60, 61–3
Human Side of Enterprise 123–6
humanism 116–18
Hyatt Roller Bearing Company 421, 422
'hygiene-motivation' theory 84–7

Iacocca, Lee 315–18
IBM 288–90, 446–8
iconoclasts 127–30
IKEA shopping 323–6
In Search of Excellence 147
incentive wage plans 68–71
individual liberty 175–8
individualism 88–91
industrial organisation 57–60
industry pioneers 227–9, 401–3
innovation
  Carrier 230–3
  Edison 267–9
  Ford 278–80
  Gillette 291–3
  Hamel 76–9
  Kanter 96–100
  Land 336–8
  McCormick 363–6
  marketing 363–6
  Nonaka 131–4
  Ohmae 135–8
  Ohno 139–42
  Son 424–7
  Vail 437–9
  Vanderbilt 440–2
instalment plans 363
intangible assets 101–4
Intel microprocessors 297–9
intelligence quotient 72–5
international economics 28–31
Internet 237–40, 390–3
  see also computers
IT companies 394–6, 417–20
ITT telecommunications 285–7, 349, 351

463

Index

Japan
  automobiles 309–11, 431–3
  Deming 41
  electrical engineering 357–9
  Follett 57–60
  Honda 309–11
  management techniques 135, 147–9
  manufacture 139–42
  motorcycles 309–11
  quality management 92, 179–82
jeans, Levis 428–30
job issues 68–71, 84–7, 119–22
Jobs, Steve 319–22
Juran, Joseph 92–5
just-in-time delivery 139–42

kaban system 139, 142
Kairamo, Kari 386, 387
Kamprad, Ingvar 323–6
Kanter, Rosabeth Moss 96–100
Kaplan, Robert 101–4
Kelleher, Herb 327–9
Khosla, Vinod 367
KITA (Kick in The Ass) approach 84
Knight, Phil 330–2
knowledge creation 131–4
Kodak 264–6
Kroc, Ray 333–5

labour issues 177
'laissez faire' approach 176–7
Lancaster Caramel Company 306–8
Land, Edwin 336–8
Lane, Allen 339–42
large global organisations 64–7
Lauder, Estée 343–5
Lauren, Ralph 346–8
law of labour 177
lawyers 327–9
leadership
  Adair 1–4
  Bennis 16–19
  Covey 32–6
  Ellison 274
  Lewin 109–12
  McGregor 125
  Machiavelli 114
  styles 195–9
  Weber 199–202
Leadership and the One Minute Manager 22
learning organisation theory 171–4

Leo Burnett advertising agency 224–6
Levitt, Theodore 105–8
Levitt, William 349–52
Lewin, Kurt 109–12
Lexus 431, 433
liberty, Smith 175–8
Life magazine 353–6
light bulbs 267–9
low-cost housing 349–52
low-cost quality engineering 183–6
Luce, Henry Robinson 353–6
Lynch, Edmund 370

McCormick, Cyrus Hall 363–6
McDonald's burgers 333–5
McGregor, Douglas 123–6
Machiavelli, Niccolò 113–15
McKinsey consultancy 147, 288, 290
McNealy, Scott 367–9
macrofiscal issues 28–31
magazines
  Hearst 300–2
  Luce 353–6
  Winfrey 453–5
mail-order business 407–9
management
  see also quality management
  administration 53–6
  Argyris 9–12
  Blanchard 20–3
  Brazilian experiment 413–16
  consultancy 288, 290
  education 163–6
  Fayol 53–6
  Gilbreths 68–71
  Herzberg 84–7
  humanistic 116–18
  Japan 147–9
  knowledge 84–7
  Maslow 116–18
  new thinking 151–4
  people 24–7, 127–30
  Peters 151–4
  psychology 68–71
  quality 37–40, 92–5
  schools 61–3
  scientific 187–90
  strategic, Ansoff 5–8
  studies 45–52
  styles 123–6
  techniques 135
  theory 105–8
  thinking 119–22, 147–54
management gurus
  Argyris 9–12
  Drucker 45–52
  Porter 155–8

Taylor 187–90
manufacture
  clothing 407–9
  Japan 139–42
  paradigm shift 278–80
marketing
  benefits/shortfalls 105–8
  innovation 363–6
  Lauder 343–5
  Levitt 105–8
  'Marlboro Man' campaign 224–6
Maslow, Abraham 116–18, 124–5
mass media 410–12
mass production 278–80
mass-constructed housing 349–52
Matsushita, Konosuke 357–9
Mayer, Louis 360–2
Mayo, Elton 119–22
media
  Hearst 300–2
  Murdoch 379–81
  Sarnoff 410–12
  Turner 434–6
MEI (Matsushita Electric Industrial) 357–9
Men and Women of the Corporation 96–7
Merrill, Charles 370–2
MGM (Metro Goldwyn Mayer) 360–2
microprocessors 297–9, 417–20
Microsoft 274, 281–4, 367
military strategy 179–82
Mintzberg, Henry 127–30
mobile phones 386–9
model textile factory 143–6
money-back guarantees 363
Moore, Gordon 297
morality 177–8
Morgan, J.P. 373–5
Morita, Akio 376–8
motion studies 68–71
motivation
  Carnegie 24–7
  Herzberg 84–7
  Vroom 195–9
motor cars *see* automobiles
motorcycles, Honda 309–11
movies *see* films
Murdoch, Rupert 379–81

national culture 88–91
national economics 28–31
national identity cards 274
natural law 176–7
Net-centric powerhouse 274
Netscape 244–6
New Coke 294

464

Index

newspapers 300-2
Nike brand name 330-2
Nokia brand name 386-9
non-financial factors 101-4
Nonaka, Ikujiro 131-4
Norton, David 101-4
Noyce, Bob 297

Ogilvy, David 382-5
Ohmae, Kenichi 135-8
Ohno, Taiichi 139-42
oil business 401-3
oil drills 312-14
Ollila, Jorma Jaakko 386-9
Omidyar, Pierre 390-3
The One Minute Manager 20, 22
online business 244, 370-2
Oracle 274-7
organisations
 adaptive capabilities 171-4
 behaviour 195-9
 core competencies 76-9
 effectiveness 32-6
 Handy 80-3
 innovation 76-9
 issues 9-12
 knowledge creation 131-4
 Organizational Culture and Leadership 167-70
 'out of the box' thinking 135-8
Owen, Robert 143-6

Packard, David 394-6
paperback books 339-42
paradigm shift 278-80
Paramount 270, 273
Pascale, Richard 147-50
Patterson, John 446, 447
PCs *see* computers
Penguin books 339-42
people management 24-7, 127-30
people-centred management 123-6
personal organisers 424
Peters, Tom 151-4
philanthropists 440-2
philosophy
 corporate 417-20
 Machiavelli 113-15
 quality control 183-6
 Smith 175-8
photography 264-6, 336-8
planes, Boeing 216-19
Playboy magazine 303-5
Polaroid cameras/sunglasses 336-8
politics 208-11
Polo brand 346-8
portable music 376-8

Porter, Bill 247
Porter, Michael 155-8
postal deliveries 437-9
power concepts 88-91, 199-202
Powershift 193-4
Prahalad, C.K. 76, 159-62
problem sharing learning 163-6
problem solving models 195-9
property construction 349-52
property development 205-7, 216-19
psychology
 Vroom 195-9
 Lewin 109-12
 Schein 167
publishing
 Hefner 303-5
 Lane 339-42
 Luce 353-6

QualityIs Free 37
quality management
 control 183-6
 Crosby 37-40
 Deming 41-4
 Japan 92, 179-82
 Juran 92-5
 Ohno 139-42
 Sun Tzu 179-82

rabbits 303-5
raconteurs 208-11
radio
 Hearst 300-2
 Sarnoff 410-12
 Winfrey 453-5
Radio Corporation of America (RCA) 267-9, 410-12
railways 227-9, 374, 440-2
RCA (Radio Corporation of America) 267-9, 410-12
reaping machines 363-6
retail business
 Rosenwald 407-9
 Walton 443-5
 Woolworth 459-61
Revans, Reg 163-6
RJR Nabisco 288
Rock, Arthur 397-400
Rockefeller, John 401-3
Roddick, Anita 404-6
roller bearings 421, 422
Rosenwald, Julius 407-9

safety razors 291-3
Sarnoff, David 410-12
Schein, Edgar 167-70
Schon, Donald 171

scientific management 187-90
Sculley, John 319
Sears, Roebuck 407-9
self interest pursuit 175-8
self-service furniture 323-6
Semler, Ricardo 413-16
Senge, Peter 171-4
Seven Habits of Highly Effective People 32
7-S model (McKinsey) 147
sexual permissiveness 303-5
Sharp-Hughes Tool Company 312-14
Shih, Stan 417-20
shipping 440-2
shoes, sport 330-2
shopping 323-6
 see also retail business
showmen 208-11
singing flight attendants 327-9
Skoll, Jeff 390, 391-2
Sloan, Alfred Jr 421-3
Smith, Adam 175-8
social psychology 109-12
social responsibility 61-3
social well-being 45-52
sociology 199-202
Softbank Corporation 424-7
Son, Masayoshi 424-7
Sony 376-8
sport's shoes 330-2
Standard Oil 401-3
Star TV 379, 381
state monopolies 440-2
steel manufacture 227-9
stimulating desires 24-7
stock picking 220-3
stockbroking 370-2
strategic architecture 76-9
strategic intent 76-9, 159-62
strategy
 China 179-82
 Hamel 76-9
 Kaplan 101-4
 Machiavelli 113-15
 management 5-8
 military 179-82
 Norton 101-4
 Ohmae 135-8
 planning 5-8
 Porter 155-8
 Prahalad 159-62
 'stretch and leverage' 159-62
 Sun Tzu 179-82
Strauss, Levi 428-30
stress minimisation 68-71
stretch and leverage strategy 159-62
Sun Microsystems 367-9

465

Index

Sun Tzu 179–82
sunglasses 336–8

T-groups 16–19, 109, 111–12
Taguchi, Genichi 183–6
Taiwan 417–20
takeovers 114
talk shows 453–5
task-based management 116–18
Taylor, Frederick Winslow 187–90
team learning 172
team-role theory 13–15
teamworking 13–15
technology entrepreneurs 281–4, 319–22
technology start-ups 244–6
telecommunications 285–7
television
 Murdoch 379–81
 Sarnoff 410–12
 Winfrey 453–5
textiles 143–6
Theory X 123–4
Theory Y 123, 124
Theory Z 125
Third Wave 192–3
Time magazine 353–6
Time Warner 234–6
The Times 379, 380
tobacco business 257–9

Toffler, Alvin 191–4
Total Quality Management (TQM) 41, 92–5
Toyoda, Eiji 431–3
Toyota Production System 139–42, 431–3
TQM *see* Total Quality Management
training *see* T-groups
transformation 64–7
Turner, Ted 434–6
TWA airline 312–14
'two factor' theory 84–7

uncertainty avoidance 88–91
unfreeze–change–refreeze model 109, 111
United Motors Corporation 421–3
unorthodox businessmen 323–6

Vail, Theodore Newton 437–9
values survey module 88–91
Vanderbilt, Cornelius 440–2
venture capital 397–400
video-games business 424–7
videotapes 336, 338
Vroom, Victor 195–9

wage plans 68–71
Wal-Mart stores 443–5

Walkman portable music 376–8
Walton, Samuel 443–5
waste reduction 139–42
Watson, Thomas Sr 446–8
wealth creation 64–7
Wealth of Nations, The 175
Weber, Max 199–202
Welch, Jack 449–52
well-being, employees 143–6
When Giants Learn to Dance 98–9
Whitman, Meg 390, 391–2
Winfrey, Oprah 453–5
Woodruff, Robert 294, 456–8
Woolworth, Frank 459–61
work
 conditions 143–6
 hours 143–6
 modern society 80–3
 standards 68–71
 values 88–91
 worker exploitation 330, 332
Working with Emotional Intelligence 72
World Class: Thriving Locally in the Global Economy 99
Wozniak, Steve 319

Yetton, Philip 195, 197–8

466